W9-DDL-045

Social Services in the United States

Social Services in the United States

POLICIES AND PROGRAMS

Sheila B. Kamerman
and Alfred J. Kahn

TEMPLE UNIVERSITY PRESS Philadelphia

Research Collaborators

Dr. Brenda McGowan (Child Care and Children's Institutions)
Mrs. Aileen Hart (Child Abuse)
Dr. Carole Germain (Family Planning)
Dr. Harriet Blank (Service Delivery)

Temple University Press, Philadelphia 19122

Published 1976
Printed in the United States of America
International Standard Book Number: 0-87722-065-4 cloth;
0-87722-066-2 paper
Library of Congress Catalog Card Number: 75-35492

The research on which this volume is based was supported by the Department of Health, Education and Welfare, especially the Social and Rehabilitation Service grants under SRS 18-P-57394/2-01, and grants from the Office of Child Development under OS (DHEW) OCD-CB-386. A supplementary contract with the National Institute of Mental Health, PHS-ADM-42-74-86 (OPS), made possible the work in the middle-sized American city referred to in the illustrations. All this support is gratefully acknowledged, as is the cooperation of the following staff members: James Dolson, Dorothy Lally, Saul Rosoff, Frank Ferro, Thomas Plaut, Milton Levine.

Contents

Tables and Figures

Tables

Figures

Acronyms and Abbreviations

ACIR	Advisory Commission on Intergovernmental Relations
AFDC	Aid to Families with Dependent Children (public assistance, state and local administration)
AoA	Administration on Aging in OHD, DHEW
CB	U.S. Children's Bureau of DHEW
DHEW	U.S. Department of Health, Education, and Welfare
DOL	U.S. Department of Labor
DOT	U.S. Department of Transportation
DSS	Department of Social Services (local)
GAO	Government Accounting Office
HSA	Health Services Administration of DHEW
HUD	U.S. Department of Housing and Urban Development
LEAA	Law Enforcement Assistance Administration of the Department of Justice
NASW	National Association of Social Workers
NICH	National Institute of Child Health and Human Development, DHEW
NIH	National Institute of Health, DHEW
NIMH	National Institute of Mental Health, DHEW
OAA	Older Americans Act
OASDHI	The Social Security program incorporating old age, survivors, disability, hospital insurance
OCD	Office of Child Development, a subunit of the Office of Human Development, DHEW
OE	Office of Education of DHEW

OEO	Office of Economic Opportunity
OHD	Office of Human Development of DHEW
OMB	Office of Management and Budget
PHS	U.S. Public Health Service of HSA, DHEW
SITO	Services Integration Target Organizations (interagency)
SRS	Social and Rehabilitation Service of DHEW
SSA	Social Security Administration of DHEW
SSI	Supplementary Security Income (public assistance to aged, blind, disabled)
USDA	U.S. Department of Agriculture

Social Services in the United States

Context and Definition

Introduction

Throughout the industrial world a new social service system is emerging. Now increasingly identified as the general or personal social services,* it includes family and child welfare, social services for the young and the aged, social care for the handicapped, frail, and retarded, information and referral services, and community centers. No substitute for cash, medical care, housing, or education, they are needed even when these are available. They address unique needs and institutional circumstances and have their separate, identifiable, valued societal functions.

An important characteristic of these services is that they are not conceived as services for the poor alone. Moreover, the development seems to be taking place without regard to national ideology or political stance. Women, whether they live in Sweden, Germany, or the United States, are increasingly being drawn into the marketplace, out of commitment or from economic need, and their absence from the home creates a demand for day care services for their children. In like manner, the need for community care for the aged grows in each of these countries as more people live longer and as families are smaller and less able to care for aged parents.

*Throughout the volume, we use the terms "general" and "personal" social services indiscriminately.

The purview of social welfare has traditionally been limited to five fields: education, health, income maintenance, housing, and employment. All other social services have always been seen as just that—"other social services." The emergence of the personal social services in no way lessens the need for the other services; in fact, without these basic services in adequate supply, the possible sixth field—the personal social service system—cannot be effectively constructed. The new system does, however, require a shift in the average American's conception of social welfare. The traditional view, which might well be called the minimalist viewpoint, holds that the major thrust of social welfare should be limited to those in temporary trouble and that services should be withdrawn or redirected once these people are restored to health. In contrast, the philosophy underlying the personal social service system holds that a complex technological society is a difficult environment for many of us, and that good government works actively to make life easier for its citizens.

We cannot make progress until we have a clear picture of where we are, what is possible, what resources are necessary, and what advantages and disadvantages alternative strategies offer. Political science has not yet yielded us full understanding of the interplay among economic, cultural, governmental, political, geographic, historical, and other variables on the one hand and the country's social services on the other.[1] If such understanding existed, prediction would be easier than it is now and the surprises far fewer. The chapters that follow do not attempt to provide such an understanding. What they do attempt is a detailed program and policy description for a sampling of important personal social service areas, with emphasis on the dynamics of the system in which these services are developing. In the Appendix, we give the interested reader an overview of the demographic and governmental context and of the five service fields—income maintenance, health care, education, housing, and employment—already well established in this country, which supply the foundation for the emerging personal social service system. Here in Chapter 1, so as to assure the reader a comprehensive view, we survey those components of the personal social services not reported on in detail later in the book. The informed reader will notice the absence of sections on traditional child welfare (foster homes and adoption services), family welfare services (casework treatment), medical social work, and school social work. While we touch on these subjects peripherally in discussions of related fields, we have not given them detailed treatment because we determined from the beginning to "sample" in depth, not to undertake thin coverage.

We chose our topics from among the priority concerns of DHEW and Congress. In addition, however, we insisted that each topic we selected be able to contribute to an assessment of the potential for a personal social service system and its necessary characteristics. Consequently, each service area in the following chapters raises unique problems of definition, of boundaries, of responsibility, of access, which taken together suggest the complexity of the problems which a personal social service system must come to grips with. One of our major concerns is the need for developing a structure and organization for efficiently providing these services to society. Because of their very nature, and because of the ad hoc manner in which current programs developed, there are serious difficulties which must be overcome if the programs are to be integrated into a coherent system. In some European countries, there is a strong tendency to give the personal social services an independent structure, organization, and social mission to optimize their contribution; there are countervailing pressures and claims from other social service systems. Our work has disclosed similar needs for coherence and organization in this country. A detailed analysis of the problems has been reserved until Chapter 8, but the reader should keep such considerations in mind as he reviews the data and descriptions in Chapters 2–7.

To make the operational picture real and the processes specific, each chapter contains a section called "Programs in Action." We chose a single state—and, in particular, one of its middle-sized cities—and "moved in" with our research team for a period of program observations and visits. (The names of individual service programs and agencies in these sections are fictitious.) Throughout the text, we have included material about population, government, and social agency structures necessary for understanding the illustrations. Unless otherwise indicated, the budget and staffing data for individual service programs and agencies are for 1973–74. When we came to the issue of service delivery, we undertook systematic case reading and interviewing to develop a picture of issues and possibilities. The results appear in Chapter 7, as does a discussion of mental health–social service boundaries.

The several topics, then, offer a variety of vantage points, provide very considerable coverage, and serve to set the stage for the discussion in the final chapter of a personal social service system. Nonetheless, the book does not deal with everything. While specific fields are discussed in historical context, if briefly, we have made no attempt at a broad historical and philosophical perspective on American social policy generally, despite the great importance of the subject.[2] Nor do we take account, except in passing, of the economic, interest group, social class, professional, and political power struggles which provide the context in which these programs are launched and developed. It would be a naive analyst who would pretend that rationality will always—or often—prevail and that once the "answers" are found they will be adopted. The planning must take place and the services be administered in a world resistant to change. We have attempted to deal with fundamental programing and policy problems and issues; those who would advance an improved service program must be prepared to cope with basic political processes and interest groups.

There are also organizational questions which deserve further review, if elsewhere. Organizational sociology has much of value to say about the types of structures through which social services become most accessible to citizens in need of help. There is research and theory relevant to organizational hierarchy, administrative procedure, office scope, program size and location, all of which require serious attention as the social welfare field makes the transition from services concerned with satisfying donors to modern, effective resources responsible to a wide range of consumers.[3]

The objective, then, is improved social policy and the vehicle is better-planned and -administered social programs. The focus is the emerging system of personal social services. The larger domain is all of American social welfare. The future will be played out on a changing social scene in which organizational dynamics, interest groups, political forces, professional establishments, and consumers interact, affect one another, prevail or lose—and compromise. This volume offers students and citizens a road map and a basis for personal choice.

Personal or General Social Services

The main task of this volume is to clarify the activities, problems, and possibilities of a large number of discrete programs not clearly part of the five basic social program fields—income maintenance, health, education, housing, and employment. We shall explore the hypothesis that *some* of these activities are, could, or should become components of a sixth social program field, for which the names "personal" and "general" social services have been proposed.

As a backdrop for what follows, this section undertakes two assignments: to list and "cost" those other programs and benefits not covered under the five major fields which could be considered as possibly relevant to a coherent sixth field; and to provide orientation and detail for important programs not covered by the program and policy reports in the next several chapters, to orient readers new to the field and to ensure that the concluding chapter may be read in relation to the total domain. As will become apparent in the chapters which follow, definitions and boundaries are uncertain and data are not always easy to come by. On the other hand, for the individuals, groups, and communities involved the stakes are high; there is some evidence of growth and expansion; indeed the need for policy and programing clarity in this field—if field it is—is obvious.

The focus, then, is on those public- and private-sector benefits, goods, services, entitlements, and policies which are informed by other than market concerns and which are not included in the five earlier categories (income maintenance, health, housing, education, and employment). They are the services that are frequently lumped together under "other social welfare," a "leftover" category (see, for example, the expenditures table, Table A-2, in the Appendix). In an attempt to conceptualize these helping, access, and socialization-development services in another context, we estimated roughly —on the basis of Social Security Administration data—that they were expending through public and private channels about $10 billion annually in 1970, or about 1 percent of GNP, 85 percent of it public money.[4]

For present purposes we briefly describe these main service fields, their auspices and scale, giving most attention to programs not discussed in subsequent chapters.

Service Fields

Child Welfare Programs

The most readily described and defined system of personal social services offers substitute care and adoption for children whose homes or parents are no longer available or suitable. It also offers protective services in instances of abuse or neglect, and a variety of forms of residential treatment. Some aspects of the system are described in

Chapters 3 and 4. It also would, or should, serve children in their own homes through guidance, benefits, and intervention on the basis of a secondary prevention or treatment role as well. This latter activity has had limited development.

A public child welfare department or unit in a public social service or human resources agency in each state is statutorily responsible for these services and either operates them directly or participates in funding and standard-setting for local operations. Federal financial participation requires that one state agency offer child welfare services, generally, and social services for children on the AFDC load. Throughout the country the task is shared with large numbers of private child welfare agencies as well, many of them sectarian. Public welfare agencies often pay for some or all of the service in the voluntary agency through subsidy or a purchase-of-care contract.

The client meets these services through locally based public child welfare agencies decentralized for the county or the neighborhood (depending upon the density of population) and operated by state, county, or city government. Or he visits a local office of a private child welfare (or "family and child welfare") agency.

While, on paper, almost all AFDC cases have access to some social services in this sense, contacts are brief and superficial and many clients apparently define them as part of the eligibility investigation. Reporting systems are inaccurate and fragmented, but the following figures give a somewhat better, if incomplete, picture of the scope and scale of services: children in foster family homes, 250,000; children institutionalized as dependent, neglected, delinquent, disturbed (1972), 150,000; children processed by social agencies for adoption, (1970), approximately 65,000 (out of 175,000 adoptions); children in detention (secure) for brief or long periods before and during juvenile court disposition, turnover total unknown, but often "guessed" at 100,000; children seen in juvenile court social services as dependent, neglected, etc., 150,000–200,000. Of some 26,792 psychiatric inpatients under 18 and hundreds of thousands of psychiatric outpatients (1970), an unknown number receive social service help; as much may be said of some 95,000 in residential hospitals and schools for the mentally retarded and the handicapped. The child welfare labor force, using the term flexibly and including personnel having a variety of backgrounds and training, may total up to 100,000.

Federal leadership is provided by the Office of Child Development–U.S. Children's Bureau and the Social-Rehabilitation Service, all in DHEW. Voluntary sector leadership is provided by the Child

Welfare League of America. Basic federal funding in the past has been for child welfare services to the AFDC load and involves a formula under which most costs are divided 75–25 between federal and state governments. Foster care was a major claimant on these resources. Now, under Title XX of the Social Security Act, states determine the disposition of service resources (for the most part a 75:25 match). States may seek matching for public social services for adults and children up to their quotas in an overall federal ceiling of $2.5 billion—a ceiling imposed in 1973 for all social service cost matching under the service titles of the Social Security Act. States share costs differently with localities, depending on the state pattern and whether the state itself operates child welfare services.

Beyond this, states share what are called federal child welfare funds (Title IV-B of the Social Security Act) on a grant and "project" basis, to a fixed national total, and not limited to those eligible for public aid. Although congressional authorization is for $196 million, appropriations are far lower, totaling $47.5 billion in 1974.

Child Care and Related Programs

There is some debate as to whether programs for the day-time care of young children are to be seen as in the province of education or social service. In the United States, at least, those nursery schools supported by parent fees or on a cooperative basis are sometimes, perhaps most often, seen as education. All family day care homes or family day care groups, or group day care, as well as part- or all-day care in a compensatory program known as Head Start, are administratively and conceptually seen as social services—even though educators are in a major and often dominant staffing role. Detail is presented in Chapter 2.

The federal lead is taken by the Office of Child Development within DHEW. States have similar units or responsible agencies within their education and social welfare programs, for the most part, although other social sector departments also may have state administrative and funding responsibility. Operation is usually a function of local government or voluntary agencies, based on a mix of federal funding from several sources, state funds, local funds, fees, and a small amount of private philanthropy.

Social Services for the Aged

Counseling, community centers, food programs, information, and so forth have developed in the United States under a variety of auspices: voluntary social agencies, some of them sectarian, and many of them in recent years assisted by public funding; public welfare authorities in close association with means-tested public assistance programs for the aged (but now separated, following federalization of old age assistance and in administrative transition under Title XX); and public authorities committed to social services for the aged whatever their income status, but giving priority to the poor and to minorities, and funded on a "project" basis under the Older Americans Act. The subject is discussed in its entirety in Chapter 5.

Social Services for Families

There is no standard, uniform system for family services. Coverage is generally thin. In theory AFDC families have had counseling-guidance-casework-information-advocacy service as needed, through public welfare social workers. Coverage has always been token and much preoccupied with eligibility for financial aid. In recent years there has occurred, simultaneously, an effort to separate the eligibility question from the service delivery system on an administrative basis and to respecify just which services are to be required in all jurisdictions and which are to be permissive. Since federal reimbursements under the Social Security Act cover 90 percent of state costs for some services and 75 percent of state cost for most, these have been important questions, as is the question of whether reimbursement would cover only current recipients of public assistance, "potential" or "former" recipients as well, or even broader groups. The issue reached a stalemate for several years during a debate within the Congress and between the Congress and the administration. There was dispute as to whether general social services were important, and for whom, and about the extent to which policy and programing decisions should be made in Washington. There was little doubt that state and local delivery systems were generally very limited.

Most public welfare offices offer information and advice, employment-housing-health referrals, very limited patterns of concrete benefits, and other personal help. Services to the aged and children, in the sense sketched above, may be administratively found with these "family" services. Staffs are generally college graduates with no social work training, except what is offered on an in-service basis, or with very limited training.

Thus, although public welfare departments cover the country rather extensively, family social services per se are not widespread. Many cities, counties, and even states have discussed converting their public social services (or these services plus others) into relatively comprehensive coordinated networks, but there are as yet few model programs. Title XX allows the states great flexibility in designing social service programs. While there are specified goals and a requirement that a service address each of them, the goals are broad: self-sufficiency, protection, reduced institutionalization or appropriate institutionalization, self-support. While there is a priority for assistance recipients (half of the service) and a mandate to offer three services to SSI recipients, there is also flexibility allowing free service to those whose resources are below 80 percent of the state median income and (with fees) up to 115 percent of the median, permitting a virtually universal service. States are required to engage in visible, accountable planning and may, themselves, define and select service and determine service delivery structures. The Title XX initiatives may well restructure U.S. personal social services over the next several years.

Currently, intensive family social work is carried out in major cities and some smaller ones in the private nonsectarian and sectarian family service agencies affiliated with the Family Service Association of America. Over three hundred such agencies give psychological help of different degrees of intensity and some specific, concrete services to some 150,000 families each year. Most of the financing is from private contributions and fees; some is through public purchase of care. Most of the cases reach the family service agencies initially because of marital problems, parent-child problems, and problems of functioning in children.

Another national voluntary family agency, National Travelers' Aid, provides individual and family casework help, usually on a short-term basis, for problems growing out of people's being away from their home bases. Inevitably there is a major and ongoing need for such a service in an era of high physical mobility and personal travel.

An unknown number of American families or individuals also obtain help with personal or interpersonal problems in the "market" through the fee services of private practitioner psychiatrists, social workers, psychologists, counselors, psychotherapists, and practitioners of a variety of types of group therapy.

Other "personal" or family counseling, focused on individuals, couples, family groupings, or groups sharing similar problems or needs, is carried out by social workers and others of similar training in veteran programs (where, as we shall see, financial aid, medical service, and educational benefits are central), medical programs and hospitals, schools, unions, industry, community centers, camps. In these institutions, the social service function sometimes dominates and sometimes is an adjunct to implementing another primary mission (medical care, education). There are also a limited number of general social service programs located in local public housing authorities, getting their cases largely from among those groups of tenants who have difficulty in meeting rent payments or maintaining their apartments up to standard—or who in some way disrupt the housing community.

The antipoverty program created, from the mid-1960s to the early 1970s, some nine hundred neighborhood centers in which indigenous personnel and a small number of professionals concentrated on information and referral services and case and policy advocacy. The centers also incorporated other services having high priority for their neighborhoods: day care, neighborhood legal services, neighborhood youth employment programs, health services or referral, and the like. In general, few helped intensively with family or personal problems per se. Some still exist. Many have been phased out with the program from which they originated. A parallel program of neighborhood legal aid was recently given independent identity.

Varying by state, by locality, and even by court, juvenile and family courts may also offer intensive personal help and concrete service through intake divisions, probation departments, shelters and detention centers, day treatment, volunteer programs, and special projects. Some have decentralized and emphasized secondary prevention. There is no national picture available since programs are variously state-, county-, or city-run. In general, however, most of the programs are largely preoccupied with custody and control problems, with servicing the court with social histories to facilitate dispositions in family and child matters, and with locating and arranging access to placement resources.

Federal leadership for local family social services for assistance recipients and some others is assigned to the Social and Rehabilitation Service of DHEW. Hospital and school social work are in the domain of other DHEW units or of state agencies. Union-industry developments are relatively rare and are not centrally coordinated or encouraged. Several DHEW and Department of Justice units are concerned with juvenile and family courts. State participation and leadership is central to all these programs as well. Voluntary sector initiatives are in the domain of the Family Service Association of America, the National Council on Crime and Delinquency, accrediting bodies for schools and hospitals, and several professional associations, especially the National Association of Social Workers.

Homemakers, Home Help, Home Health Aides

These practical, supportive benefits take two major forms: "taking over" the family for brief emergency periods when a mother is incapacitated or away, to avoid family break-up while the father continues with his daily job; and undertaking household chores and errands for old people, from a few hours a week to a few hours a day, sometimes also providing routine and unspecialized medical chores, permitting isolated aged people who need some help to remain in community living arrangements.

Some 30,000 workers carry out this type of assignment in the United States on a nonprofit basis, often in close alliance with other social work services. They are variously employed by public welfare agencies (city, state) or voluntary agencies. Costs may be met by fees (on a sliding scale), federal-state-local sharing under the social service titles of the Social Security Act, voluntary philanthropy, Medicare or Medicaid, or private health insurance. For all this, as will be noted in our chapter on the aged, coverage is thin as compared with other industrialized countries. An additional service component of unknown scope and scale is offered by profit-making agencies.

Federal interest in these programs is centered in DHEW within the Administration on Aging, the Office of Child Development, and the Social-Rehabilitation Service. Voluntary sector efforts are coordinated by the National Council for Homemaker–Home Health Aide Services.

Related services such as house and home renovation, escort and shopping aids, and podiatry are relatively underdeveloped in the United States.

Veterans Programs

The programs for veterans, almost completely federal, present an annual bill to the treasury almost equal to that for health. They combine pensions and compensation for disability, direct health services and medical care, a small amount of general social service, and a program of educational and postservice readjustment benefits. Inevitably, historical series show fluctuation related to the times of discharge of large numbers of military men.

A large part of the bill ($6.6 of $12.9 billion in 1972–73) is accounted for by pensions and compensation, in a program of "exceptionalism" in which the right to grants is affirmed because of military service and risk. Both service-connected and non-service-connected disabilities are compensated and the boundaries are "flexible." A means-tested aid program has much more flexible practice than similar programs for nonveterans and covers almost 3 million recipients, nearly two-thirds of them widows and their children. Health and medical programs ($82.8 billion in 1972–73) are also flexible in interpreting eligibility but are mostly devoted to long-term care of the disabled, aged, and mentally ill. Educational benefits ($2.6 billion) cover training opportunity to make up lost time and transition for readjustment periods.[5] At certain times since World War II, the sum total of special educational benefits, unemployment compensation, housing aid, and business loans boosted the veteran ahead of the nonveteran, although it is alleged that the unpopularity of the Vietnam War resulted in unsatisfactory coverage, a situation modified recently by benefit increases.

Basic program administration and direct medical service is in the hands of a federal agency, the Veterans' Administration, which has regional offices and regional health and mental health facilities. What Gilbert Steiner calls an "intercessor group of veterans associations," some of them large and politically powerful, assure widespread information, advocacy, and general help in service access. This makes veteran programs more like the nonstigmatized, universal programs (social insurance) and less like stigmatized public assistance (AFDC) or mixed-message programs (public housing or food stamps). Veteran service and benefit take-up is therefore high.

Correctional and Penal Services

Some juvenile delinquency prevention activities are carried on by DHEW units; some court-related services for children in trouble or for families are carried out in state and local child welfare agencies or family service and mental health programs. Otherwise, the bulk of the expenditures in the field of correctional and penal services do not appear in our social sector expenditure table (Table A-2) in the Appendix.

Mention is made later of those juvenile court, probation, and family court activities which may be considered as general social services. Chapters 3 and 4 discuss juvenile courts as major components of the systems dealing with abuse and neglect and with the institutional care of children removed from their own homes. Here we take account briefly of the rest of the court-correctional-penal system, clearly part of social sector programing even if not included in Social Security Administration expenditure reports. The objectives are control, protection, punishment, rehabilitation, reform, and prevention.

Most direct activities with offenders are carried out in courts and facilities of state government, even though local government deals with minor matters (misdemeanors and offenses) in most states and major matters in some. Police work is the major exception; it is generally a responsibility of local government. The federal government deals with those who break federal laws or whose offenses are not limited to one state jurisdiction. In addition, units of the Department of Justice, particularly the Law Enforcement Assistance Administration (LEAA), try to strengthen local government and state capacity in law enforcement, correctional, and rehabilitation work with offenders and to encourage deinstitutionalization and "diversion" from the juvenile justice system. LEAA administers demonstration grants for this purpose, some of which involve programs and activities not unlike those previously of interest to various DHEW units, which have lost most of the delinquency mandate.

The probation field services this apparatus by manning intake services at doorways to some courts and exercising discretion about detention, by providing case assessments for the courts, by developing treatment plans, and by carrying out supervision and treatment. At various points in recent decades, sentiment has shifted from regarding probation as social work, a subdivision of general social service, to defining probation as a more eclectic field, with "peace officer" components. As much may be said for parole work (aftercare for those who have been in correctional institutions). It is generally agreed that custodial staffs in correctional institutions do not function in social service capacities, but some of the wardens, directors, and program staffs of such facilities try to or do. The professions of psychology, special education, rehabilitation, counseling are represented in these assignments, as is social work.

The following figures suggest scope and scale, if incompletely:

State and federal institutions for adult felons	
Prisoners received from courts (1971), transferred, returned as parole violators, etc.	308,376
Prisoners discharged (1971)	303,395
Prison population at year's end (1971)	197,838

Jails	
Population (largely misdemeanors) (1972)	141,600
Juvenile delinquency cases	
Excluding traffic (1972)	1,112,000
Rate per 1,000 population under 18	33.6
Total police arrests (1972)	6,707,000
Arrests for serious crimes	470,000
Estimated total expenditures for U.S. correctional programs and criminal justice system (1972)	$11,721,000,000

Community Centers, Settlements, Group Programs

There are a variety of community centers and programs, including settlement houses (some 350), Jewish Community Centers (450), YMCAs, YWCAs, Boys' Clubs, Boy Scout and Girl Scout houses, and the many storefront centers and coffee houses which came out of the antipoverty and Model Cities programs and continued under one or another auspice, as well as community centers in schools, churches, public housing. There are also special centers for the aging and for specific ethnic, racial, or religious groups. The programs generally stress socialization, development, recreation, education, self-help, cultural participation, physical exercise, and body care. Many are for the "normal" and adjusted, some for the deprived and the deviant. Many of the programs are themselves multipurpose, combining their core programs with education, manpower, cultural, day care, and therapeutic or counseling efforts. There are also similar programs for the handicapped, retarded, disturbed—and for subcategories within these groupings.

There is no way to estimate numbers of locations or participants. While several of the "clusters" have lead agencies on the national level (federations, national coordination bodies, etc.), there is no overall organization, field, discipline, or goal to which these efforts all hold allegiance. Except insofar as they serve specific groups of the handicapped, the ill, the deprived, or the deviant and are funded through Social Security Act service funds or on a project-demonstration basis from one of the National Health Institutes, from Department of Justice programs, from Office of Education efforts, or under the Older Americans Act, these tend to be locally funded efforts. Their main sources are United Way funds and some local public aid in some places, as well as endowments and fees.

Access Services

There is widespread agreement that access services are major responsibilities of the general social services: information, advice, referral, case advocacy, liaison. We review the U.S. situation—again, fragmentary coverage and no one pattern—in Chapter 7. Major funding comes through the social services provisions of the Social Security Act for reimbursing states and localities for social service efforts generally. Numerous other federal programs, ranging from the Older Americans Act to community mental health legislation, play a part in encouraging access services and funding them. Voluntary-sector categorical programs of all sorts, especially in the health field, have a role here too, as do remnants of and developments out of anti-poverty, Model Cities, and neighborhood legal service programs.

Special Programs for Refugees, Native Americans (Indians), Migrant Workers

Social service programs in the broad and narrow senses of the term, covering most of the categories discussed in this chapter and others but relatively small-scale when compared to the U.S. social service system as a whole, serve refugees, Indians, and migrant workers. Special detail will not be provided here.[6] The bulk of the effort is assigned to one or another unit within DHEW and to the Department of the Interior.

Components of Community Mental Health, Retardation Programs, Community Development

The boundaries of the general social services are unclear and shifting. As much can be said about community mental health and retardation, as well as about community development and area redevelopment efforts. Clearly some of the activities and programs listed under these efforts should be considered in relation to overall general social services programing, but some should not.

The community mental health field is especially interesting in this regard. For a considerable period beginning in the mid-1960s, it concentrated on "prevention" and early intervention and thus became involved in activities and programs parallel to those in many of the general social services, including broad-scale neighborhood self-help activity through community organization. This tendency has declined but not disappeared as community mental health has tended, of late, to concentrate somewhat more on psychiatric disorder. This latter aspect of the work, largely a subcategory of medicine, is encompassed by the health system (see the Appendix) despite a constant struggle to assure in- and out-patient psychiatric programs within general health provision and coverage for psychiatric care under various forms of insurance and other funding. To the extent that community mental health programs continue with a broad sense of mission and to the degree that psychiatric programs generally are guided by other than medical models of causation and intervention, their programs of direct service to individuals, families, and groups and their community organization activities are not distinguishable from (and perhaps should be seen as part of) general social services. When mental health programs are more specifically psychiatric-medical, the need for linkage with and some adjunctive staffing by general social service personnel remains and is recognized. This is especially true in day treatment centers, after-care programs, and programs to deal with psychiatric emergencies.

The antipoverty program of the 1960s generated a large community development effort which emphasized a function central to the general social services: participation. In local community action agencies which were organized and funded throughout the country, emphasis was placed upon local residents' helping to choose, plan, and implement local social services; upon local "community control" of antipoverty and other programs; upon social action related to the needs and interests of deprived populations; and upon staffing of new programs by local residents, "indigenous personnel" in paraprofessional roles, especially in access points and linkage services with welfare, education, housing, and job programs. Much the same pattern developed in a Model Cities program, stressing major urban renewal and social planning in a limited number of deprived areas. The concept later spread geographically, but resources and objectives became more diffuse.

The entire community development effort has been placed under DHEW, but kept separate and apart, and its character is unclear. It seems likely to be a component of the overall general social service initiative—while area redevelopment per se belongs to HUD and to certain Department of Commerce programs for areas in economic decline.

The Voluntary Sector

Our overall rough estimate is that, of the national expenditure for general social services, the public share of costs is supported by tax dollars up to between 85 and 90 percent of overall expenditures. The remainder is paid by private philanthropy, most of it raised in local community fund drives, contributed to church charities, or appropriated by foundations.

The largest part of the general social services delivery system is public (local public welfare offices, local child welfare offices, day treatment centers, foster homes, institutions, juvenile probation, medical social work, psychiatric clinics, etc.). However, a significant —if imprecisely delineated—component of public service (often the component requiring more skilled and specialized staff) is delivered through voluntary agencies on a purchase-of-care or subsidy basis.

In some fields the voluntary sector plays the major delivery role, probably using mostly voluntary funds (family services, settlements, centers, the aged). In some it shares significantly with the public (child welfare). It is of relatively minor significance in manpower and corrections, and has a mixed role in some other fields. Some voluntary programs are sectarian or ethnically specialized, but publicly funded programs are expected to be accessible to all.

The major national standard-setting and coordinating groups, giving leadership to voluntary-sector initiatives, are mentioned elsewhere in this chapter in context or described in the Appendix or in the chapters on specialized programs.

Manpower for the Personal Social Services

The social work profession is the core profession for the general social services, as is medicine for the medical system and education for the schools. However, many other professionals and other categories of workers are involved. Furthermore, because of staff shortages and uncertainty about social work, considerable staffing is found which ignores recommendations, standards, and nationwide practice. Finally, an emphasis in recent years upon the use of indigenous personnel and paraprofessionals has created uncertainty in many fields and there are great variations from place to place.

The National Association of Social Workers (NASW), the leading professional association in the field, has some 65,000 members. Until recently it required a social work professional degree at the M.S. level for admission. Now, social workers with certified B.A. concentrations are admitted but thus far constitute a very small part of the membership.

Most social workers in public child welfare, public welfare social service generally, and the institution field are not in NASW. (The leadership organizations are the Child Welfare League of America and the American Public Welfare Association.) Probation and correctional social workers are affiliated with and take leadership from the National Council on Crime and Delinquency. However, NASW affiliation tends to prevail among social workers in the voluntary family agencies, medical, psychiatric, and school social work fields, in large segments of child welfare, in community planning and coordination agencies at the local level, and in many administrative agencies in public welfare at the state and local levels.

As of the end of 1974 the U.S. social welfare labor force reached a total of 300,000 social workers and 70,000 aides.[7] Some one-third of these social workers were not college graduates. A rise to about 435,000 by 1985 was projected.

Ideology and Ethic

The United States developed in a physical environment which promoted an ethic of individualism and opportunity. Its economic history, too, encouraged such perspective: social mobility was a fact of life; constantly improved living standards were visible. The strong Puritan strain in American ideology reinforced such attitudes and, along with ideas that came from a French and British intellectual heritage and a particular political history, encouraged strong voluntarism in social welfare and a general distrust of government interventions as "clumsy," expensive, and having negative effects.

The bias has therefore been against social welfare developments, generally, if individual initiative or primary groups (family, neighbors, church, etc.) could meet a need. Where there was to be assistance, voluntary philanthropy was to be preferred. It could individualize, reform, and provide a needed outlet as well for the "good works" of donors. And assistance given where an individual was believed appropriately responsible for himself—so that the request represented moral failure—was best made inaccessible, unattractive, and even punitive. Thus British "poor law" found a natural habitat in the United States.

Attitudes, beliefs, and modes of practice become functionally autonomous. For this reason alone, many of these responses to individuals in need remain deeply imbedded in American culture.

Beyond this, some of the response may still correspond to and grow out of social realities: the limitations of big government as a program operator; opportunity for the "able," at least some of the time. Some of it may serve other ends: keeping costs down and controlling the deviant. Major changes have occurred, of course, some gradually with industrialization and urban concentration, some overnight with war, catastrophe, depression. The imperfections of the market and of the mobility channels have been recognized, the public stake in a minimal level of education and resources for living for all underscored, the necessity of provisions to assure more social justice increasingly accepted, the interdependence of populations noted. Clearly, too, voluntary effort could hardly achieve fairness, coverage, financing, efficiency, or even policy coherence on a large scale. Thus, governmental efforts, whatever the problems, have had to expand.

In any case, to use a phrase applied by others, the U.S. welfare state remains a "reluctant" one[8] and only partially developed. The following are components of the currently relevant ethic which will be seen in their mixed and conflicting influences in the chapters which follow:

Strong Support. Some social sector programs are recognized as essential to "normal" living for "normal" people in a complex, industrial society. These are programs which are believed beyond the ability of individuals to organize for themselves and of such great importance that the larger society cannot avoid initiatives. Prime illustrations are education (elementary, secondary, advanced), public health, mortgage guarantees for individually financed housing, retirement and survivor benefits under social security. Growth has been rapid and significant, especially during the 1960s and early 1970s.

Ambivalence. Some programs are recognized as appropriate for some groups with special problems and needs, because individual provision is often not practical and most people could have the need —but there are some mixed feelings in these fields and some of the attitudes are not generous. Prime illustrations are programs for the aged, Medicare, private family welfare, community centers and settlements, veterans' programs. SSI suggests a readiness to help dependent adults and the handicapped, even to the extent of guaranteeing funds, outside of a social insurance format.

Negative Feelings. Some programs are still approached with "poor law" attitudes. People who need help are believed at least partially responsible for their predicament, therefore inadequate, therefore to be controlled or treated punitively. As a result, programs for them are often poorly financed and staffed. Clearly in this category are the nonfederalized public assistance programs (AFDC and Home Relief), the antipoverty programs, correctional facilities, state mental hospitals. Most general social services for families, located in public assistance departments, have shared the stigma. We do not yet know if Title XX will change this. Child welfare partakes partially of these attitudes and partially of "ambivalence," varying with state and program auspice. Special housing programs for the poor (which often serve large numbers of minority applicants) are often here classifiable, as are food stamps.

Obviously these differential attitudes may tend to create social service "networks" based on social class and to work against coordination and integration growing out of program logic. They place large obstacles in the way of the personal social services, which often developed in close relationship with public assistance but which now address problems and meet needs relevant to many population elements—and which require financial support and broad public acceptance to play such a role. The attitudes and the administrative-organizational baggage they support may condition potential service users and staffs, legislators and voters. They are part of the explanation of the uneven, fragmented general social service development reflected in the chapters which follow.

Notes

1. For one interesting beginning, see Harold Wilensky, *The Welfare State and Equality* (paperback ed.; Berkley: University of California Press, 1975).

2. For some of this we call attention to John M. Romanyshyn, *Social Welfare: Charity to Justice* (New York: Random House, 1971); Harold L. Wilensky and Charles N. Lebeaux, *Industrial Society and Social Welfare* (paperback ed.; New York: Free Press, 1965); Alfred J. Kahn, "The Societal Context of Social Work Practice," *Social Work,* 10 (Oct. 1965); Robert Bremner, *From the Depths: The Discovery of Poverty in the United States* (New York: New York University Press, 1964); Peter Marris and Martin Rein, *The Dilemma of Social Reform* (New York: Atherton, 1971); *Encyclopedia of Social Work* (16th issue, 2 vols.; New

York: National Association of Social Workers, 1971), articles on "Social Welfare: History" and "Social Welfare: History of Basic Ideas," pp. 1446–76; Samuel Mencher, *Poor Law to Poverty Program* (Pittsburgh: University of Pittsburgh Press, 1967); Alfred J. Kahn, *Social Policy and Social Services* (New York: Random House, 1973).

3. The following suggest the scope of the field: Elihu Katz and Brenda Danet, ed., *Bureaucracy and the Public* (New York: Basic Books, 1973); Eugene Litwak and Henry J. Meyer, *School, Family and Neighborhood* (New York: Columbia University Press, 1974); Meyer N. Zald, ed., *Social Welfare Institutions* (New York: John Wiley, 1966); Amitai Etzioni, *Modern Organizations* (paperback ed.; Englewood Cliffs, N.J.: Prentice-Hall, 1964).

4. Kahn, *Social Policy and Social Services,* pp. 37–41. There are major problems of definition involved. Moreover, for several years, states charged a variety of services which would not meet any reasonable definition of social services. For a full account, see Martha Derthick, *Uncontrollable Spending for Social Services Grants* (Washington, D.C.: The Brookings Institution, 1975).

5. An analytic overview is offered in chapter 7 of Gilbert Steiner, *The State of Welfare* (Washington, D.C.: The Brookings Institution, 1971).

6. See Sar Levitan, *Programs in Aid of the Poor in the 70's* (Baltimore: Johns Hopkins University Press, 1973), or Subcommittee on Fiscal Policy of the Joint Economic Committee, *Studies in Public Welfare,* Paper No. 20: *Handbook of Public Income Transfer Programs, 1975* (Washington, D.C.: GPO, 1974).

7. Unpublished estimate, Philip Rones, Bureau of Labor Statistics, Washington, D.C.

8. Wilensky and Lebeaux, intro., p. xvii.

Child Care

Context and Definition

Child care differs from our other chapter topics in being mostly a social utility, a public social service available according to the user's status and not according to any problems he may have. As such, it raises a variety of questions as to how extensive provision should be, who should be served, what form programs should take, and under what auspices they should operate. Another basic question is what connection child care as a social utility should have to case services, to those services addressed to problems and pathology. An essential dilemma is one of location: Is day care a part of the educational system or of the personal social services? Should its goals be custodial, educational, developmental? For years, such questions have aroused considerable debate throughout the United States.

Although the debate goes on, U.S. "day care" policy is experiencing a period of relative quiescence. For over ten years, provision for the daytime care of infants and young children had been expanding, through a diversity of programs, governed by a variety of motives, and serving several different subcategories of the child population. During 1968–71, on the assumption that this expansion of facilities and funding would continue, extensive planning took place, arousing debate over administration, financing, program, control, standards. Then a presidential veto at the end of 1971 and the subsequent congressional turnabout led to a stalemate. As of mid-1975, the stalemate continued. There have been no major new commitments—especially in a period of inflation and recession. But there has been steady growth nonetheless, much research and writing, congressional hearings on legislative proposals, and a new clarity to the terms of the discussion. Major decisions which will shape further developments are yet to be made, but cannot be long deferred.

If able political figures, program leaders, and analysts arrive at different conclusions about what ought be done next about daytime arrangements for the care of young children, it may be because they start with different values and define the programs as having different parameters and different social goals. Some are concerned about taking care of the children of working mothers, or about increasing the options available to women. Others emphasize the need to assure children of deprived backgrounds a "head start" of socialization experience and cognitive development, so that they may be able to proceed at normal pace in the regular schools, or to enrich child development, generally, beyond what occurs in a family setting. Some want to change neighborhood and social institutions, in the "community development" sense. Others want to meet the special child care needs of families with problems, especially in instances of child neglect or handicap, or maternal illness and inadequacy.

If the debate reflects intense feeling, it is perhaps because some of the proposals involve an extremely large national investment, or because it is believed that the choices made may bring about fundamental shifts in the socialization of American children and, thus, in the role of the family.

And if it is difficult to marshall the facts, it is because the differing perspectives imply that different kinds of evidence are relevant to the decision-making. Moreover, the diversity of funding sources, administrative arrangements, and service patterns leaves no one in full command of all the essential information or in a position to see the full picture.

Child care programs expanded to new dimension and gained increased notice as a result of the creation of Head Start in 1965: a large program, mostly half-day initially, and designed to enhance overall social competency in poor (especially minority) children by offering health, nutritional, educational, and general social services, as well as encouraging parental and community participation. Conceived as part of the "antipoverty war," Head Start began as a summer program, became a year-round preschool program, and expanded rapidly. Its delivery system and hours were such that it offered more to the AFDC mother than to the working mother, yet it did add significantly to the numbers of children in care daily.

The other dynamic was the eightfold increase between 1940 and 1969 in the number of children under 16 with working mothers.[1] The increase continued into the 1970s, although the effects of the 1975 recession are as yet unreported. Thus, we might cite an absolute increase between 1970 and 1973 of 650,000 children who had working mothers (at a time when the total of all children in families in the United States fell by 1.5 million). All other issues aside, a reservoir of potential need of this kind often generates a programmatic response, or at least recognition that there is a question to be addressed.

Need

How, in fact, is the subject of "need" for child care arrangements discussed under such circumstances? We know that the criteria are debatable; that even if adequate resources were provided, the "take-up" is uncertain; that funding arrangements, the status of the labor market for women, and the specific location, types, quality of programs probably affect consumer response; that our picture of current provision is incomplete. We also know that overall social changes with reference to female roles and family values soon make any long-term estimates obsolete—and that program provision in itself provokes social change.

Data such as the following are often cited, even though estimations as to their relevance to "need" vary in accord with fundamental perspectives about family and child care. Of 64.3 million children under 18 in the United States in March 1973, 26.2 million had mothers in the labor force. Some 6 million of these children were under 6 years of age, constituting almost 30 percent of all children under 6. Mothers of children under 6 worked full and part time in large numbers (45 percent) and those whose children were 6–17 were even more heavily represented in the labor force (57 percent). The phenomenon is not confined to the mother of the poor or broken family. Half of all wives living in households with their husbands and with children between the ages of 6 and 17 worked during 1973. In March 1973, 29 percent of wives with children under 3 worked and 38.3 percent of those with children 3–5 did. The phenomenon characterizes both black and white wives, with a higher rate for the black mothers of very young children.*

*Throughout this chapter, 3–5 means from age 3 to a child's sixth birthday.

While the effects of the 1974–75 economic recession are as yet unknown, the prior picture was one of increasing labor-force participation by mothers, even married mothers living with their husbands: the percentage of married women in the labor force with children aged 6–17 rose from 26 to 51 percent between 1948 and 1974, and from 11 to 34 percent for married women with children under 6. Two-thirds of the mothers in these groups worked full time.

More and more children live in single-parent families than ever before, families in which the mother is usually the family head. Such mothers have higher labor-force participation rates than married women living with husbands: in 1974, 67 percent of them with children aged 6–17 worked (80 percent of these mothers worked full time), as did 54 percent with children under 6 (83 percent worked full time).

Data about mothers of children under 3 are also instructive. Of those married and living with husbands, 31 percent were in the labor force in 1974 as contrasted with 45 percent of the mothers in single-parent families.

A significant portion of those children whose mothers work are cared for by fathers, siblings, or other relatives or sitters in their own homes. Many others are cared for in the homes of relatives or nonrelatives, or in other ways, some of them allegedly questionable or even hazardous. Others—and although their numbers vary with the survey and the criteria employed, all agree they constitute a minority—are cared for in formal, licensed, private arrangements or public programs. In the 6–14 age group, many children are alone during the day with no formal adult care at all.

Estimates of "need" often go beyond children of working mothers and assume that there is some obligation to provide enriching or developmental child care experience for all children who are economically disadvantaged or have special handicapping conditions. High-need estimates often follow a pattern of analysis such as the following: Approximately 15 percent of all children are known to live in poverty families; 7.65 million of them are under 14. There are 2.2 million handicapped children under age 6. There are 3.3 million children under 6 who are members of linguistic or racial minorities or children of migrant workers, are maladjusted, or have special need for attention and help. Although there is undoubtedly much overlapping between these categories, it has been variously claimed on the basis of such facts, and adding in children of working mothers, that 24 to 38.3 million children, or 6 to 11.5 million under age 6, "require" some form of regular child care arrangements, at least on a part-time basis. Even those who advance such estimates would grant, however, that they report assumed or alleged need, not effective demand.

These totals seem exaggerated to many observers, who note that, overlapping apart, many of the families can and do make their own child care arrangements—or would not use facilities if they became available. Yet other observers consider these totals as completely inadequate: to them the mother's work is irrelevant. Child care arrangements should be available to assure true choice to all mothers of young children. In brief, the debates rage about "need" without agreement (and often without specification) as to whether the need is for (*a*) all-day child care for children of working mothers (or mothers who are to be freed for work); (*b*) preschool for all disadvantaged or handicapped children (i.e., part-day); (*c*) preschool for all children whose parents want them to have it (i.e., part-day); or (*d*) all-day child care for children in categories (*b*) and (*c*). Most observers are willing, as a base, to consider the children of working mothers who need care. Yet in a shifting labor market, and in the midst of major redefinition of female roles in many strata of the society, even data about current child care arrangements of working mothers are soon obsolete. The last comprehensive survey was made in the field in 1965. What is probably a fair approximation of the 1970 picture, however, is summarized in Tables 2-1 and 2-2. Approximately one-half of all preschool children, and over three-quarters of all school-aged children of working mothers, were cared for in their own homes by relatives or nonrelatives; another very sizable percentage were cared for in someone else's home, almost half in that of a relative. Some of the "cared for" children were actually in the "latch key" category. They were on their own. Only about 10 percent of all preschool children of working mothers were enrolled in organized day care centers, and an additional one-fifth in what is usually termed "family day care."* (The proportion of school-age children in these settings before and after school hours, while their mothers work, was even smaller.) Yet the interest and controversy about child care in the recent years and the investment

*A 1974 publication of OCD estimates that of 6 million preschool children of working mothers, 1.8 million are in family day care homes. See Office of Child Development, *Final Report on Family Home Day Care Systems Demonstration Project,* DHEW-OHD Publication No. 75-1074 (Washington, D.C.: Government Printing Office, 1974), p. i.

Table 2-1. Child Care Arrangements of Working Mothers, by Age of Children (1970)

Type of arrangement	Age of children: Under 6	Age of children: 6–14
Own home	49.9	78.7
By father	18.4	10.6
By other relative	18.9	20.6
By nonrelative	7.3	4.5
Mother worked during child's school hours	5.2	42.9
Someone else's home	34.5	12.6
By a relative	15.5	7.6
By a nonrelative	19.0	5.0
Day care center	10.5	0.6
No special care	5.0	8.3

Source: Charles L. Schultze et al., *Setting National Priorities: The 1973 Budget* (Washington, D.C.: The Brookings Institution, 1972), p. 261, citing the 1965 Seth Low and Pearl G. Spindler survey for U.S. Children's Bureau as well as Westinghouse Learning Corp. and Westat Research, Inc., *Day Care Survey—1970: Summary Report and Basic Analysis* (processed; Washington, D.C.: OEO, 1971). Rounded figures as published do not add to 100 percent precisely. Several other sources see the "someone else's home" totals as too high, noting "at work" care and after-school care by mother.

Table 2-2. Day Care Arrangements by Type (1970)

Type of arrangement	Age groups: 0–5	Age groups: 6–13	Arrangements reported by mother as unsatisfactory (% of total)
Total children	17,000,000	40,000,000	
Total with day care arrangements	4,000,000	9,000,000	7.6
Own home	2,000,000	4,000,000	6.2
By father	560,000	1,300,000	5.3
By other relative over 16	560,000	1,400,000	4.6
By other relative under 16	85,000	500,000	11.9
By nonrelative	600,000	620,000	7.6
Someone else's home	1,200,000	800,000	8.7
Group care center	220,000	50,000	8.2
By mother (while working)	580,000	1,100,000	4.9
By self ("latch key")	25,000–60,000	1,000,000	9.7

Source: Sheldon White et al., *Federal Programs for Young Children: Review and Recommendations* (DHEW O.S. Pub. No. 74-100, 4 vols., paperback ed.; Washington, D.C.: GPO, 1974), III, App. IIIA, 11, citing several sources. By 1973 the under-14 population total was 56 million.

in standard-setting have focused almost entirely on the care that is provided in the more formal arrangements—group day care and family day care homes. Or, in the context of antipoverty strategies, they have focused on compensatory preschool programs such as Head Start, for children whose mothers are not generally in full-time work or at work at all.

Preprimary programs (nursery school and kindergarten) have expanded rapidly in recent years and in 1974 accommodated 45.2 percent of the 3–5 year olds (78.6 percent of the 5s, 37.6 percent of the 4s, and 19.8 percent of the 3s); if we add those in elementary grades, the participation rate for 5 year olds rises to almost 90 percent. Yet they are seldom discussed as part of the picture.[2] The overlap of these preprimary statistics with data on day care is unspecified, since the census inquiry on which they are based asks about kindergarten and nursery, includes Head Start, but deliberately omits center day care and family day care as "custodial care" and "not an educational experience." (A new study will be more comprehensive and thus more useful; much other reported research is ambiguous on this point.) Of 4.7 million preprimary enrollees in 1974, 3 million children were in public facilities and 1.7 million in nonpublic; 76 percent had only part-day care, but 24 percent were cared for all day, an often ignored fact (33.2 percent of nursery school enrollees and 19 percent of those attending kindergarten).

It will be noted that none of these estimates provide systematic information about after-school arrangements for daytime care of children in the 6–14 age group. While the tables give some kinds of data about children of working mothers, we do not know exactly how many of the "latch key children" and others take part in community center, boys' club, scout, and settlement programs (usually volunteer), in public recreation programs (local and state), in recreational and other after-school programs in school buildings, in church and ethnic group programs, or in individual activities in church buildings, synagogues, and various types of centers.

Even the limited coverage for day care programs (but excluding preprimary classes and nursery schools) involves governmental expenditure of perhaps $1.7 billion. Only those day care places accommodating some one million children are currently licensed (805,321 children in licensed centers and 215,841 in licensed day care homes). Were there to be proposed expansion of licensed or standard-meeting facilities to accomodate all potential users under 6, the costs would rise several times over, the exact estimates varying with assumptions about eligibility, fees, and take-up from $4 billion to $20 billion, or even higher.

While female labor-force participation has risen, the geographic mobility of families and the decrease in the size of completed families mean that, whether or not kinship ties have actually weakened or kin networks are merely more extended geographically, young parents do have less access than they once may have had to child care help from grandparents, aunts, older siblings. The decreased availability of domestic labor as women rise in labor-market status both decreases at-home child care arrangements and makes formal programs more costly. Decreased agricultural labor by women also cuts at-home care. At the very same time, women's rights advocates have taken the position that in any case government is responsible for offering child care as a right, or as a precondition of the liberation of women—and that the costs of a large, universal program must be carried.

At the other side of the estimation picture is the practice of looking at the public welfare rolls, which exploded in the 1960s, and assuming that child care needs may be computed by totaling the numbers of AFDC mothers who have the education, or capacity, or job skills, to be trainable or employable and have preschool-age children. A 1973 AFDC survey[3]—despite considerable inaccuracy and ambiguity, and no provision for recording seasonal variations—showed that of 3 million families receiving AFDC, 22.4 percent had a caretaker away on a recurrent basis, with vendor payments being made for care of children in 18.6 percent of these cases. Of the care arranged, most was in the home. In a substantial number of instances arrangements were unknown—for children of both preschool and school-age groups. Group care arrangements could be identified for 15,239 children under 3 years old, 38,338 aged 3–5, 15,286 aged 6–11, and 2,220 aged 12–14. Of course, a family may have several children, so these data are not additive.

Children 12–14 were most likely to care for themselves while their mothers were away. "Need" here may be defined as the gap between recurrent absence and available care—but data on both sides of the equation are soft and there is no estimate of the adequacy of the arrangements for which payments is made. Indeed some arrangements are so informal that their actual availability has been questioned. Some AFDC mothers arranged child care through training or work programs—but current arrangements involving other than AFDC personnel were not reported.

Of course this way of estimating need is rejected by those who argue that mothers of young children should be granted financial aid to permit their remaining at home to care for young children. Their argument may be buttressed by child development evidence—the needs of young children—or economic analysis—these mothers have low earning power.

The debate thus ranges from policy to need, from program forms to financing, from facility control to location. It encompasses questions of group or family care, child care as preschool or child care as daytime care, professional or paraprofessional staff, child care as residual resource or formal child care as need and right. Before turning to detail, we offer a brief historical overview.

History

The "true" history of child care begins with the recognition that a child's biological mother is seldom the sole caretaker. If she has become so in modern times, that is the new thing, not the child's experience with several caretakers to whom he is connected with various degrees of intimacy and emotion. But if caring was or is shared by many members of a large household or is informal, it is not defined as day care or nursery—even if to the child the emotional, interpersonal, and cognitive experiences may be counterparts of those later offered in formal, licensed facilities. Thus the start of the "official" history of day care is usually dated for the United States in the 1820s or 1830s. The *day nurseries* (we would call them day care centers) established early in the nineteenth century were the first form of organized child care in the United States. They were created under voluntary auspices to care for the children of working mothers. Expanded subsequently in response to pressures created by the rapid industrialization and massive immigration which took place during the latter part of the century, they were custodial in nature, focusing primarily on the basic care and supervision of children. The first such day nursery was established in Boston in 1838 by a Mrs. Joseph Hale to care for children of seamen's wives and widows. The idea spread rapidly after the Civil War, and in 1898 the National Federation of Day Nurseries, representing approximately 175 agencies, was established.[4] Most day care until about 1920 was, then, for the relatively poor children of working mothers.

The other form of child care which has a long historical tradition in the United States is the *nursery school*. (Today it is a nursery school, a play school, or a public kindergarten, prekindergarten, or preprimary class.) Based on Froebel's ideas about the importance of free play and social cooperation as the foundation of learning, the nursery school movement had roots back in the mid-nineteenth century, but became quantitatively significant in the 1920s. This movement developed within a middle- and upper-class context and was primarily educational in focus. It also received impetus from the parent cooperative movement and university-based experimental programs.[5]

Although the federal government established a limited number of day nurseries for the children of working mothers following the Civil War, the first major governmental effort and expenditure in the child care field was the establishment of nursery schools during the Depression (1933), under the Work Project Administration (WPA).[6] The primary objective of this program was to provide employment to teachers and related school personnel. However, the nursery schools developed an educational emphasis under the influence of the wider nursery school movement. They were most frequently located in school buildings. By 1937, there were approximately 40,000 children enrolled in 1,900 nursery schools.

The pendulum swung back to the children of working mothers in the 1940s. The need for additional manpower during World War II caused a dramatic increase in the number of working women. As a result of agitation by various citizen groups, the federal government began to recognize its responsibility to the children of these women; in 1942, the Lanham Act was passed. This legislation provided funding for the establishment of day care facilities in war-impacted areas. (The centers could be considered "public works.") Between 1942 and 1946, the federal government spent over $50 million for some 3,000 centers located in forty-seven states. In addition to creating a large network of public child care facilities, the Lanham Act stimulated some innovative program developments and awakened the public to the concept of child care centers as a potential resource.[7]

After the war ended, most of the centers established under the Lanham Act were closed. Although many women continued to work, public ideology supported the idea that mothers belonged at home, and there apparently was widespread suspicion of governmental intervention in family life and allegedly little public support for a continuation of publicly funded child care facilities. In California, however, because of continued demand for women workers, the state legislature in 1946 authorized the establishment of a statewide program of child care under the auspices of the State Department of Education. The system continues. In New York City a somewhat different situation developed, because the area had not been eligible for funds under the Lanham Act. In 1942, the New York State legislature had passed the Mumford Act, providing for state aid to municipalities for day care centers. A Mayor's Committee on the Wartime Care of Children was established to administer day care funds, to be supplied one-third by the state, one-third by the city, and one-third through parent fees or community contributions. When state funds were terminated at the end of the war, this committee was able to serve as a nucleus for the citizen effort to ensure that the local public welfare department take over the administration of day care programs. As a result, there has been continued public support of day care programs in New York City since the end of the war, in the context of the public welfare program but with eligibility focused more broadly than in typical public welfare social services.

Little public support developed in the rest of the country for child care until the mid-1960s, except for a limited number of programs under the child welfare provisions (now Title IV-B) of the Social Security Act administered by the U.S. Children's Bureau as a social service to families with special problems or needs. Other than this, child care was assumed to be provided in the home, and organized programs were maintained only under voluntary auspices.

The two major traditions which were continued during this period were the nursery school programs, with an educational focus for middle-class children, and the day nurseries, which had served primarily a custodial function for the children of families who were presumed to be unable to or somewhat incapable of caring for their own children.[8] Surprisingly many who assess the facts for the current child care debate seem to ignore the coverage of nursery schools and public preprimary and kindergarten programs.

During the late 1960s and early 1970s, the number of public child care programs increased rapidly. This expansion both reflected and contributed to a resurgence of national interest in early child development. It was made possible in part because various types of federal legislation provided indirect and direct funding for child care programs, but also because state and local educational authorities were responding to the demand for kindergarten and prekindergarten classes, mostly locally funded. Although some of the programs established during this period had a strong educational emphasis, others provided what was essentially custodial care for children of working mothers. While attendance of children aged 3–5 in private nursery schools and public preprimary programs has exploded (from 3.187

million in 1964 to 4.234 million in 1973) and accounts for most of the care given to the 3–5 age group, it has not received much public discussion or attention.

According to a report from the Education Commission of the States, by 1974 some fourteen states and one territory had mandated school districts to offer *kindergarten* programs (and one state had provision effective 1976). Thirty-four additional states had permissive legislation. Only Mississippi and Idaho had neither provision. Some forty-six states provided kindergarten some form of state financial aid by 1974, using the standard and reliable state foundation formula. By contrast, only eleven states provided some support to their localities for *prekindergarten* programs (California, Georgia, Maine, Massachusetts, Missouri, Pennsylvania, South Carolina, Tennessee, Vermont, Washington, and West Virginia).[9]

While this is not "coverage," it is substantial. Yet despite the extensive growth in these preschool programs, there has been more public note taken of the efforts initiated by social welfare programs, which are focused primarily on children of the poor—especially of Head Start, designed to enhance social competence and programed so as to provide compensatory education, developmental experience, and broad services, or of other daytime care programs with a larger custodial emphasis established to encourage welfare recipients to find employment or to accept training.

To summarize briefly: child care programs in the United States have developed on a three-track system of preschool education, especially used for middle-class children; daytime care (programmatically rich or minimally custodial) for children of working mothers; or both preschool and day care programs for children with special handicaps or needs or whose families are considered to have special problems. During the past decade, new efforts have been made to provide preschool experience for children of the poor through daytime care programs which provide comprehensive service and cognitive stimulation. However, the myth that practically all mothers stay at home to care for their children has persisted, so that initially many of the new programs have provided only part-time care. Full-day public programs tend to be limited to children of relatively low-wage working mothers or the poor (even though the more affluent may purchase such care in one of several forms).

Child care in the United States has been considered ideologically as primarily a responsibility of the family and the voluntary sector; more recent governmental initiatives in this area have grown out of social goals, economic causes, or labor-supply needs but are not so visible as to contradict the ethic. The programs funded by the U.S. Children's Bureau have had child welfare, narrowly defined, as a primary objective—targeting on families who are considered somehow inadequate or in need of exceptional assistance. The past decade has witnessed increased public interest in early childhood programs as perhaps even universally needed. Public responsibility for child care continues to be debated vigorously.

Terms

There is a wide range of terminology in the child care field, and many of the same terms are used differently by various American spokesmen and authors in different contexts. Therefore, now that we have laid out the background, it seems advisable to clarify the way certain of the major terms will be used in the remainder of this discussion.

Child care refers to all arrangements for the part- or all-day care of children, either in or outside their own homes, when parents are unable to fulfill or choose to delegate this function. Child care programs may have varied auspices: education, social welfare, health. They may be public, nonprofit voluntary, or proprietary.

Organized child care refers to those child care arrangements which are provided in a formal, regulated manner and have public sanction, as distinct from those which are provided on the basis of an informal agreement between the child's caretaker and his family.

Comprehensive child care, also termed *developmental care*, refers to any public or privately sponsored child care program intended "to be sufficiently flexible and comprehensive to meet each child's physical, intellectual, emotional, and social needs, to be appropriate to his developmental stage, and involve and support the child's parent or care-taker."[10]

Preschool program refers to any organized program for children below the compulsory school-age of 6. There are three major types of preschool programs. *Nursery school* generally refers to a part-day program under voluntary or proprietary auspices which has an educational focus but may be rich in overall developmental stimulation. *Kindergarten* refers to a part-day (generally free) program which has an educational objective and serves children one year below compulsory school age; it is a public program, sometimes also called *preprimary* or *prekindergarten* if it covers children in the 3–5 year range. *Day care* refers to a program, usually full-day, which provides adult care and supervision for children outside their own homes. Such programs may have an educational focus, but the primary objective is child care. Day care may be provided in a group setting, which is called a *day care center*, or in a family setting, which is called a *family day care home*.

School-age children technically refers to all children of compulsory school age, which in this country is usually six to sixteen. As used in the child care literature, however, this term most frequently refers to children aged 6–14, since older children are able to care for themselves; therefore, in this report the term will be used to refer to children aged 6–14.

Head Start is a preschool program which began as part of the antipoverty program as a special, comprehensive program, a nursery school with many other components such as health, nutrition, social work. Some children now attend all day and some part day, so Head Start may resemble either a comprehensive day care arrangement or a nursery school.

Framework for Provision

American child care policy and practice are at a crossroads. To anatomize the current fragmentation of programs and the complexities facing those who would assemble sanction, organizations, personnel, and resources so as to change things for the better, we must consider: the legislative base of current public efforts and official policy, what is known about supply and demand, current eligibility and use, the diversity of governmental and nongovernmental auspices for operations, the problem of costs and payment, and the arrangements for planning and coordination. The next three major sections deal with these topics.

Legislation

It has been estimated that there are two hundred federal programs for children.[11] Since all these programs derive from enabling legislation of some kind, it would be impossible to describe in a modest report all the relevant legislation in the child care field. For example, limited funds for various aspects of child care have been authorized under such laws as the Child Nutrition Act of 1966, the Juvenile Delinquency Prevention and Control Act of 1968, the Higher Education Act of 1965, the Demonstration Cities and Metropolitan Development Act of 1966, the U.S. Housing Act of 1937, the Appalachian Regional Development Act of 1965, and the Small Business Act of 1953. This section will summarize, instead, only the major federal legislation related to child care. By far the most significant federal funding behind recent program growth is under the service provisions of the Social Security Act, the Head Start titles of the Economic Opportunity Act, and the Elementary and Secondary Education Act.

Social Security Act

Although the Social Security Act of 1935 authorized grants-in-aid for child welfare services including day care (usually on a project or demonstration basis) and the 1962 amendments to the Act raised reimbursement for services to 75 percent and authorized limited federal matching funds to states for the development of licensed day care facilities for children of welfare recipients, the 1967 amendments significantly altered and enlarged the authorization to pay for service outside the welfare departments. The impact is still visible. Therefore, this section will begin with a description of the significant day care provisions of the Social Security Act following the 1967 legislation—Title IV-A, Section 402(a) (Aid to Families with Dependent Children)—with a brief look at Title XX, effective October 1975, which could change social services substantially. State planning is only beginning as we write. The best current picture—and perhaps the continuing picture—is offered by the ongoing IV-A situation. It should also be noted that some uncounted child care funds are included in public assistance (AFDC) cash budgets, provided to pay for care, but there is no precise knowledge of totals or of use.

Title IV-A and Title XX. Title IV-A was intended to encourage state departments of public welfare to develop day care services for children of past, present, and potential welfare recipients. The legislation authorized the U.S. Department of Health, Education, and Welfare (DHEW) to reimburse state expenditures on a 75:25 matching basis. DHEW approval of the state plan for administration of AFDC funds was required to establish state eligibility. Regulations under 1967 amendments created a program in which the local matching funds could be derived from state or local governmental units, or could be donated by individuals, businesses, or charitable organizations. (Until 1973, rules were quite flexible; now voluntary funds must be true contributions, not token grants to generate federal dollars at 3 to 1.) Services could be provided directly by the state department of public welfare or contracted out to other governmental agencies or voluntary organizations. Eligibility, as defined in the state plan, could be determined on either an individual or a neighborhood basis (that is, in a poor neighborhood, all are deemed eligible). Day care facilities were required to meet the standards for state licensing, and the funds could not be used for construction or major renovation. Although the legislation was originally open-ended (Washington would match whatever a state would spend), in 1972 Congress passed legislation setting a $2.5 billion ceiling on funding for social services under the Act and providing a formula for allocation of funds among states on the basis of population. (This ceiling was carried into Title XX.) While this created alarm it did not for the first two years actually curtail programs. In the meantime, almost one-fourth of the Title IV-A social service funds were allocated to day care during 1974, for example, serving over one-half million children at a federal cost of $883 per child ($464 million). If one adds federal, state, and local funds (here the last comprehensive data are for 1972) child care commanded 15.6 percent of IV-A plus "child welfare service" expenditures.

Title XX, which superseded the social services part of IV-A in late 1975, is a block grant for social services, allowing considerable choice to the states. It is not known whether the day care allocations will increase or decrease. The social services budget ceiling remains at $2.5 billion, but free service may be available to those below 80 percent of the state's median income (or the national median, if lower); service on the basis of graduated fees may be offered to those with incomes ranging from 80 percent to 115 percent of the median. In short, eligibility is far more universal than under IV-A, but budget constraints remain. Half of all service must be reserved for relief recipients. The effects on day care are as yet uncertain.

Title IV-B. Title IV-B, Section 422(a) (Child Welfare Services), authorizes grants-in-aid and variable matching funds to state departments of public welfare (or other designated state agencies) for child welfare services, including day care, but the day care component is small. Federal funding is dependent upon DHEW approval of the state plan for the administration of child welfare services. The state plan must include provisions for cooperative arrangements between the public welfare agency and the state departments of education and health; a state advisory committee on day care; and plans to enhance parental involvement and improve the health and development of the children served. Eligibility for day care services must be established on the basis of individual need or problem. Day care facilities must meet state standards for licensing, and these funds cannot be used for construction or major renovation. Each state is allocated $70,000 and the remainder of the funding is apportioned by a formula specified in the Act. Once an important factor, when day care was a public service only for families with problems, this title is now targeted on a small fraction of need and is a small program ($1.8 million in federal funds in 1974 or a total of $24.4 million federal, state, and local funds in 1972—most of it from state treasuries).

Title IV-C. Title IV-C (Work Incentive Program) was intended to encourage states to develop job training and placement services for adult welfare recipients. Administration of the program was delegated to the U.S. Department of Labor by DHEW. Federal matching funds are provided to states on a 90:10 basis. The Talmadge amendments of 1972 require all AFDC recipients who are not responsible for children under six or otherwise incapacitated to register for work or work training. States are required to provide day care services for children of trainees. Welfare agencies may provide services directly or through purchase from voluntary agencies, or they may reimburse individuals for the cost of child care services. This effort, too, is relatively modest, involving about $47 million, some 197,000 children (78,000 of them under age 6) and mostly in-home care and family care in 1975. This was a very substantial increase over fiscal 1974.

Economic Opportunity Act

Title II-A. Title II-A, Section 222(a) (Head Start), of the Economic Opportunity Act (1964) is intended to provide a social and emotional growth experience and compensatory education for children from low-income families, as well as increasing parental involvement with children and providing necessary health, nutrition, and social services to them and to their families. The program is currently administered by the Office of Child Development of DHEW. Federal funds are provided through OCD regional offices to local community action programs on an 80:20 matching basis. The community action programs may provide services directly or through purchase from nonprofit organizations. State authority is limited to approval of the application. The legislation permits assignment of 10 percent of these spots to children from other than the poorest families—to achieve some social and racial-ethnic mix. Ten percent of the children served must be handicapped. A significant portion of all child care coverage comes through Head Start, much of it half-day, since it was designed as a compensatory program, not to meet the needs of working mothers. However, all-day care has increased. Of some 350,000 children in Head Start in 1973, about 120,000 attended full time at a federal cost of $123.2 million out of a total Head Start expenditure of $400 million. Per capita costs in 1974 were $1,034.

Concentrated Employment Act

Title I-B. Title I-B, Section 123 (AB), Concentrated Employment Act, is intended to provide and coordinate manpower programs for residents of areas with high rates of underemployment. Responsibility for administering the program has been delegated to the Manpower Administration of the Department of Labor. Day care is provided, along with a range of services intended to ensure the employability of participants in the program. Federal reimbursement funds of up to 90 percent are provided to a single sponsor, which may be a community action program, a state employment agency, or local government. Again, total coverage is small. For this purpose, federal expenditures were $10 million in 1974. Other work-related programs out of the Department of Labor expended $6.3 million in federal funds for child care.

Elementary and Secondary Education Act

Titles I and III. Title I of the Elementary and Secondary Education Act (1965) provides federal funding for programs to meet the needs of educationally disadvantaged children, including preschoolers from low-income families. Eligibility is established on the basis of the number of low-income families in local attendance areas. Title III provides funding for the development of model programs, including early education. The state plan for education must be approved by the Office of Education of DHEW. Funds are allocated to state departments of education on the basis of an apportionment formula specified in the legislation. Local educational agencies submit proposals to the state agencies, which also receive federal funds for the administration of the program. This is a significant program, expending $48.9 million in fiscal 1974.

Manpower Development and Training Act

Title II. Title II of the Manpower Development and Training Act (1962), as amended, authorizes several programs administered by the Office of Employment Development Programs in the Manpower Administration of the Department of Labor. The New Careers Program provides funds to state departments of employment and vocational education for career training in occupations for which there is local need, in education, health, and public safety. Child care services are provided free to participants. Job Opportunities in the Business Sectors (JOBS) provides training and employment in private industry for the hard-core unemployed. Child care is provided along with a range of services for participants in the program. Also, funds may be used for training in day care occupations. The On the Job Training Program (OJT) provides federal funding to nonprofit and profit organizations for work training in those fields in which changes in technology or job requirements require upgrading of skills. Federal reimbursement may cover up to 90 percent of the costs of training in child care occupations. Totals are small.

Tax Reduction Act

Child care tax deductions began on a very modest basis in 1954, were slightly liberalized in 1964, liberalized substantially in 1971 and again in 1975. The 1975 amendments permit parents (single parents or couples with incomes up to $35,000) to deduct up to $200 a month for one child, $300 for two children, and $400 for three or more children for out-of-home care of children. The maximum total deduction for in-home care of one or more children is $400. For those with incomes over $35,000 the deduction is reduced by fifty cents for each dollar of income over $35,000 (and is zero at the $44,600 level). The provision has the effect of creating an incentive for in-home care where there are one or two children. It is of value only to those who itemize deductions on tax returns (the more affluent) and is worth more to those with higher marginal tax rates. The cost of this program was $224 million in federal tax revenue for 1973, before the ceiling went from the then $18,000 to the present $35,000. The full effects of the change will be unknown until years of experience accumulate.[12]

Policy

There is no clear, identifiable national policy toward child care in the United States. Different branches and levels of government frequently announce different objectives and have established programs reflecting varying—and sometimes conflicting—policies. All the "motives" we listed at the beginning of this chapter can be traced in one governmental program or another.

In a statement requesting authority to provide child care services for children of welfare recipients as part of a new public assistance plan, the then President Nixon commented:

> The child care I propose is more than custodial. This administration is committed to a new emphasis on child development in the first five years of life. The day care that would be part of this plan would be of a quality that will help in the development of the child and provide for his health and safety, and would break the poverty cycle for this new generation.[13]

The statement reflects a policy of providing comprehensive child care on a selective, means-tested basis to children of welfare recipients for the purpose of providing current care and stimulation and preventing future financial dependency.

Less than three years later, in his message vetoing the Economic Opportunity Amendments of 1971, which made provision for comprehensive child development services for all children, the President commented as follows: "For the Federal Government to plunge headlong financially into supporting child development would commit the vast moral authority of the National Government to the side of communal approaches to child rearing over against the family-centered approach."[14] Since the President then continued, despite the statement, to support the provision of day care services for children of welfare recipients so that their parents might be trained or find work, his administration's implicit policy toward child care would seem to have been that child care services must be provided to those who are financially dependent for the purpose of making them self-sufficient; in all other cases, responsibility for child care should be left to the parents—and not carried by government.

Regulations proposed by the Department of Health, Education, and Welfare to govern social services early in 1973 reflected a similar policy but were frozen in a debate between the White House and the Congress. In testifying before the Senate Committee on Finance about the proposed regulations, Secretary Caspar W. Weinberger of the Department of Health, Education, and Welfare commented that the social service provisions of the Social Security Act "were intended to be of principal benefit to welfare recipients, not to some more general segment of the public."[15] He later said that two underlying factors influenced the proposed regulations:

First, services available to persons receiving benefits through the Aid to Families with Dependent Children (AFDC) program should be directed towards increasing the employment of heads of families.

Second, services should be targeted on those persons receiving public assistance or with incomes which placed them in a position that was likely to lead them to dependence on public assistance.[16]

In July 1975, speaking for the Ford Administration at hearings on legislation for a new, comprehensive family and child service bill advocated by some of the groups and legislators who had backed the vetoed 1971 measure, Secretary Weinberger added the following statements of position:

We strongly disagree with the idea behind this bill that we must build a wholly new delivery system for child care services which would bypass, even ignore altogether, the existing array of publicly funded services now directly and indirectly benefitting our children.

And we also seriously question the wisdom of the government diverting so much more of the national treasury to the kinds of services encompassed in this proposal.

We are strongly opposed to the idea, inherent in this proposal, that the Federal government should provide mass developmental day care for pre-school children all over the Nation.

Extragovernmental bodies established by the federal government formulated their own somewhat different objectives for child care. For example, in 1970 the Office of Child Development, in cooperation with the Office of Economic Opportunity, convened a workshop of nongovernmental child development experts to put together a statement which could serve as a basis for the formulation of public policy toward children. Their statement in part is as follows:

The U.S. Government has a public responsibility to provide day care service to any family desiring such services. When families reach beyond their own kinship resources for assistance with the care and rearing of their children they need a wide variety of arrangements for supplemental care. We advocate as national public policy the creation of programs to strengthen all kinds of supplemental day care arrangements that families strive to make. . . .

The primary objective of day care is to *meet the needs of children for experiences which will foster their developments as human beings*. The purpose is not just to free parents for other activity or to serve manpower requirements. Since so many of the influences that are critical for a child's development involve his parents, the primary focus of any effective day care program must be *the individual child and his family*.[17]

Although the director of the Office of Child Development did not endorse this statement as an official position, he said that it would serve as an important source of guidance for future planning.

The Report of the Forum on Developmental Child Care Services of the 1970 White House Conference on Children reflects a similar position. One of the resolutions passed by the forum delegates is as follows:

> Society has the ultimate responsibility for the well-being and optimum development of all children. The implementation of this responsibility requires that child development services such as day care, Head Start, and after-school programs be available in all the variety of forms to meet the needs of all children whose parents or guardians request, or whose circumstances require, such services. In further implementation of this concept, we propose that all child development services be completely separated from public assistance programs. They must not be developed to lessen public assistance roles [sic] but rather as a basic right.[18]

Congressional intent with regard to child care programs is uncertain. Some members of Congress oppose any public provision of child care services on the basis that such programs would tend to undermine stability of the family. Others propose a policy similar to that enunciated by the Nixon Administration. For example, in his statement opening the hearings on child care before the Senate Committee on Finance in 1971, Senator Russell B. Long focused directly on the need to provide child care services to the poor and financially dependent: "A key element of any welfare reform must be the provision of child care services to all welfare mothers who wish to work. In addition, we must go beyond this and insure that low-income mothers whose initiative has enabled them to stay off welfare also have access to good child care."[19]

In 1971 Senator Long hardly spoke for a majority of his colleagues. The Economic Opportunity Amendments of 1971, passed by both houses with large majorities and vetoed by President Nixon in December 1971, were the highwater mark of congressional enthusiasm for day care. The two major child development bills which passed Congress that year, one sponsored by Senator Walter Mondale in the Senate and one sponsored by Representatives John Brademas and Ogden R. Reid in the House, were resolved by a House-Senate Conference Committee and attached to the Economic Opportunity Amendments. This legislation provided comprehensive child care services for children of working mothers. Priority was given to children from low-income families but all children were eligible to participate, with fees based on a sliding scale. The bill emphasized parental participation and "community control," providing direct federal-local funding. (The bypassing of state government may have been as large a factor in the failure to override a veto as any other.)

At present, some leading members of the Congress are committed to universal, comprehensive, governmentally funded day care. Others, like Senator Long, have formulated and achieved enactment of policies mandating work-training for welfare recipients and assuring day care to facilitate it (WIN, Talmadge Amendments). Their tax policies favor middle- and upper-income people in relation to day care deductions and actually facilitate in-home care, avoiding any incentive to use the socially less costly group arrangements. The past three years have witnessed a congressional stalemate on new initiatives in day care, and the 94th has yet to express itself, despite hearings.

Senator Walter Mondale, a leading advocate, sees the need of a child care bill which will, more adequately than present provisions, meet the needs of working mothers, single-parent families, and deprived children generally. He joins child care provision with a variety of other measures which he believes would

> assure that parents will have the opportunity to choose among the greatest possible variety of child and family services—including prenatal care, nutrition assistance, part-day programs like Head Start, after-school or full-day developmental day care for children of working mothers, in-the-home tutoring, early medical screening and treatment to detect and remedy handicapping conditions, and classes for parents and prospective parents.[20]

The Congress has not yet fully absorbed and reacted to a new note struck in the policy debate late in 1974 by the leading teachers union. Long indifferent to day care, elementary teachers have noted the demographic curve and responded to declining elementary school population and empty school rooms by moving to support preprimary programs and to place them under educational (not social welfare or antipoverty or health) auspices. Backing new comprehensive legislation, the union urges technically qualified personnel, an education base, and nonprofit auspices, as we shall see later.

The major positions continue to be expressed in new congressional proposals and to be implemented in some pieces of previously enacted legislation. Contradictions are not yet resolved and the major future thrust is not yet clear: day care as available developmental provision for all children; day care to allow women to work with minimum disruption to families and with adequate child protection; day care as a component of public welfare policy, especially for single-parent families; day care as preprimary education for all 3–5 year olds whose parents choose it.

Supply: Services and Resources

U.S. child care programs are of three kinds: in-home (own-home) care, family day care, and group care in schools or centers. Each of these types may be provided on either an informal or an organized basis and may be under private (nonprofit or proprietary) or public auspices. Privately operated programs may be largely or completely publicly funded or may be supported by private fees or contributions —or by a "mix" of sources. For example, in-home care may be provided by a friend or relative, a paid housekeeper or sitter, or a homemaker employed by a voluntary or public agency. Family day care may be provided by a friend, an unlicensed person who cares for children in her home for profit, or a family day care mother licensed and employed by a voluntary or public agency. Group care centers are administered by a variety of public, voluntary, and proprietary organizations, and some are organized as parent cooperatives. They usually are based in education or in social service agencies or are licensed and inspected by them or by health departments.

Organized child care facilities are often also categorized according to the type of services provided: *custodial* services are those which offer food, shelter, and adult supervision; *educational* services provide shelter, adult supervision, and some sort of formally conceived educational program, and may provide food; *developmental* programs provide the same services as educational ones, and in addition may offer nutrition, health care, mental health, and social work services, parent participation activity, counseling, and social and creative activities.[21]

Although these latter categories are widely used and will be employed here, it must be noted that they lack precision and—to some users—carry a message of evaluation which may not be very exact. Thus, although technically *custodial* services are those which do meet the objectives of most or many parents who turn to the child care system (safe care, food, a pleasant, stimulating growth environment for the child while the mother works), in the atmosphere of the 1960s "custodial" became "merely custodial" and was equated with impersonal "warehousing" of children, insensitive supervision, and developmental "dangers." There are no data to show how much child care is wholesome custody, how much is stimulating, and how much is dangerous or harmful. The key thing about custodial care is its claim to serve the mother and family, rather than the child. As conceived by experts, it tends to be closer to organized baby-sitting than to education or to comprehensive developmental service. The child's physical well-being is to be protected. (However, a recent U.S. Office of Education report referred to all services as custodial if they lacked education auspices, whatever else the program content.)

Similarly, most parents who send their children to kindergartens, other preprimary programs, nursery schools, and Head Start centers obviously expect some educational content. The kindergartens, other preprimary classes, and nursery schools are clearly to be classified as education. Head Start's earliest rationales stressed (albeit as a component of social competence) "cognitive development," an environment to stimulate intellectual development so that poor children, especially minority children in poverty, would overcome their developmental deficits—ascribed to deprived home environments—and be closer to the normal pace upon entering elementary school. Despite all this, *educational* emphasis is criticized in some quarters as misplaced emphasis or as ignoring a child's fundamental social and emotional needs. Reacting to evaluations of Head Start as oriented largely to cognitive growth, OCD personnel call for balanced socioemotional development as well ("social competence"). While there is a debate as to what in theory is a good balance, it seems that in some Head Start programs, despite the image, cognitively stimulating experiences may sometimes be in short supply, and OCD is implementing stricter evaluation procedures. The problem becomes one of evaluation: How may socioemotional development be measured as well, since efforts to gauge I.Q. gains (the most available measurement of cognitive gain) do not represent fair assessments even of educational programs?

The watchword in child care over the past five years has been *developmental*. Leading advocates call for nutrition, health, social work, educational, and socialization services. They argue that only a contribution to a child's optimum development justifies organizing programs and recruiting children. They acknowledge that developmental programs are costly and that many parents choose convenience and familiarity over range and scope. A new OCD manual equates developmental care with "quality."[22] Head Start regulations authorized in 1975 insist upon balanced programing.

Since the terms are loosely normative, it is not clear just how much of what makes a program "developmental." Nor are we able to gauge whether the objectives of those who have created the concept of "comprehensive, developmental" services even exist in the minds of those who direct most of the programs: achieving coordination among generally fragmented elements which impinge upon a child's growth and socialization so as to assure comprehensiveness and balance.

There is no validated, representative research which establishes the relative long-term consequences for different children of participating in programs categorized in these several ways. Research thus far reported deals with children's responses to specific programs and environments which are not necessarily characteristic of their types. Nor do we know whether the variance between types is any larger than the within-type variance. In short, given all the variables involved, the quality of available experience may depend upon the specific program in which a child participates, not its general category.

The supply picture is incomplete both because data are hard to collect and because the domain is differently defined by social welfare personnel and educators. The census has used the education definitions. At present, therefore, there are no hard data about the number of various types of child care services and facilities available, and estimates vary. The most complete overall survey of child care facilities to date is the one conducted for the Office of Economic Opportunity in 1970.[23] On the basis of their sample, it was estimated that in 1970 there were 17,500 day care centers serving approximately 575,000 children and 475,000 family day care homes serving approximately 844,000 children. Since the study was limited to facilities providing full-day care, kindergartens, many nursery schools, and Head Start centers were omitted; actual numbers in care were somewhat higher.

More recently, the U.S. Department of Health, Education, and Welfare estimated that in March 1972 there were 20,319 licensed or approved day care centers with a capacity of 805,361 children, and 60,967 licensed or approved family day care homes with a capacity of 215,841. (Nursery schools, kindergartens, and other preprimary classes were not included.)[24] This means that organized, licensed day care facilities in the social services sense provided for slightly over one million children (1,021,202). To this one might add the Head Start total of about 380,000 (almost one-third of it all-day care) for a grand total of about 1.4 million. (As noted below one should add preprimary space, much of it part time, for 4.7 million 3–5 year olds to this total, noting that some Head Start facilities are included in the count so that the best estimate of formal, licensed resources, full and part day, is 5.7 million places.)

It is estimated that whereas approximately 90 percent of all day care centers are licensed, fewer than 10 percent of all family day care homes are licensed. Therefore, if there were some 61,000 licensed family day care homes in 1972, it is likely that the total number of family homes is well over one-half million and that their capacity is over 2 million children. By adjusting the figures for day care centers in a similar manner, it can be further estimated that slightly more than 3 million children have formal, organized coverage of very mixed quality. These totals (1 million licensed "slots" or overall provision for 3 million) may be compared to a base of 6 million children under 6 of working mothers, or 20 million under 6 including those whose mothers do not work. Or one may include only children of working mothers and add some or all the "disadvantaged" or "handicapped" estimated earlier in this chapter, yielding need estimates covering a wide range. Or one may refer to the uncared for children, or those in unlicensed care—or those on waiting lists. Or one may include an estimate of how many of the 4.7 million preprimary students aged 3–5 have their day care needs thus met and count the others. About one-fourth of nursery and kindergarten care is full day and Head Start, after all, is often full day, too—and under educational auspices quite often. Perhaps the coverage rate is best described as 39 percent (7.7 million out of 20 million), if we count unlicensed care, or 29 percent (5.7 out of 20 million) if we count only licensed care.

In short, there is no real consensus regarding the adequacy of current provision for child care. The reason this is so difficult to determine is that little is known about the real quality of unregulated arrangements and of proprietary care and of what the take-up would be if various types of child care services were available on a universal basis. Nor are there data about overlapping among the above categories or which mothers work part time. There are those who emphasize that the country now has only a little over one million licensed slots to care for those of the approximately 21 million children of working mothers who may require some form of part-day or full-day child care and that not all the space is thus assigned. Others suggest that prekindergarten and kindergarten coverage is often adequate or that most parents are content with the child care arrangements they currently use and that one should not ignore unlicensed places and uncounted after-school arrangements. Therefore, they say the nation need only be concerned with the approximately one million "latch key" children who are left on their own with no one to care for them.

Most advocates of expansion assume efficient use of available spaces, equating rated capacity with usage; but this is hardly the case in a very decentralized system with diverse funding and administrative agencies. Thus a confidential report for an eastern metropolitan area notes that the policy is to enroll 10 percent above capacity to take account of average daily absence and not underutilize expensive staff—assigned at a 1:5 ratio for the youngest pupils. However, only 57.5 percent of all centers had complied with the overenrollment mandate when audited. Twenty percent in fact had not even enrolled up to rated capacities. The entire system was enrolled at 105.4 percent of capacity and even this statistic was achieved only by artificial inflation of summer participation. In this instance the city was losing considerable federal reimbursement (based on actual participation, not rated capacity) and imposing an unnecessary burden on local taxpayers. The city was simultaneously seeking funds for new centers in response to local pressure groups and failing to understand its underutilization record.

There is much underutilized center and family day care space reported nationally. There are also waiting lists.[25]

Typical of expansion proposals frequently cited at public hearings is that of the Developmental Child Care Forum of the 1970 White House Conference on Children, which recommended that a network of comprehensive child care services be established on the basis of 500,000 new slots annually so that a total of 5.6 million children, or approximately 10 percent of the 57 million children "potentially" requiring developmental day care services, would be accommodated by 1980.

On the basis of their national study of day care needs and services, the National Council of Jewish Women urged the establishment of day care services for an additional 400,000 children a year over a five-year period, suggesting that an additional 2 million slots for children under 6 would eventually be essential to meet minimum needs.[26]

In a conservative projection, not quite so short range, Dr. Mary Keyserling highlights the needs of one million children of working mothers in unlicensed day care homes, another million receiving what she believes is unsatisfactory care in the home of relatives, 2.5 million aged 4–6 whose mothers do not work but who spend their days in very deprived environments, and several million aged 6–14 whose mothers work and who have inadequate after-school care.

Current projections of need at the Office of Child Development are based on the assumption that 85–90 percent of working mothers would choose to utilize publicly supported child care services and that, of these, 80 percent would prefer home-based care to center-based care. The resulting totals tend to be more modest than those cited above.

More determined proponents who ignore the preprimary system and count only social welfare day care resources assess the total of 3 million "slots" (licensed and unlicensed) against the "needs" of working mothers and the totals of poor and handicapped or deprived children and, then, call for a massive expansion.

No proponents or opponents have firm evidence on the subject of effective demand. Clearly, quality, accessibility, and cost affect preferences and utilization patterns. Nurseries and kindergartens are expanding rapidly for the 3–5 year olds without much public debate, and they are full.

In sum, the consensus appears to be that some child care expansion is needed in the U.S. The estimates of immediate need vary tremendously since hardly any of the proposals encompass both traditional day care and the nursery school–kindergarten systems, even though significant proportions of the latter offer all-day service and large numbers of day care enrollees attend only part-day. The demand is uncertain but apparently somewhat elastic. Nor is the backing for expansion universal. Some doubt the actual estimates of demand. Others oppose creating resources which might encourage mothers to leave very young children in the care of others.

Facility Distribution

One factor about which most analysts seem to agree is that day care facilities are not distributed evenly throughout the country. Whatever the expansion pattern, something will need to be done about geographic equity. For example, respondents in some specific geographic areas surveyed by the National Council of Jewish Women stated that day care facilities should be expanded anywhere between 300 and 700 percent and cited what they considered to be current unmet need.[27] For lack of adequate need data or criteria, it is not possible fully to assess the spotty information about geographic, income, or educational backgrounds of users.

The total number of licensed or approved day care centers and family day care homes, classified by state, auspices, and capacity is reported by the National Center for Social Statistics for March 1972.[28] Clearly, there was and is great variation among the states in regard to child care facilities. As of March 1972, half of all the licensed or approved day care center capacity was in seven states. As might be expected, the largest states have the greatest resources. California, for example, which has a state-supported day care center program, has the largest number of both day care centers and family day care homes. New York, which is second, weights family day care homes relative to day care centers more heavily than does California. Texas and Massachusetts, both of which have large numbers of children in day care centers, have relatively small numbers of family day care homes and these are all under independent auspices. Also, although the smaller states tend to have fewer child care facilities, a few have relatively large numbers of programs, and some of the larger states have surprisingly few facilities.

There do not seem to be any strong regional patterns, although the western states tend to have the largest number of facilities under public auspices, whereas the southern states appear to have the fewest publicly supported programs. Generally, large urban areas have a higher proportion of organized child care facilities than rural areas.

These figures, of course, only take account of licensed or approved facilities. There is no way to estimate accurately the number of unlicensed facilities, much less their distribution. This is especially true in regard to family day care homes, less than 10 percent of which—as we noted—are licensed. There is one respected estimate that 1–2 million children are cared for in this way.[29]

Head Start programs served under 380,000 children in 1974. Mississippi (20,000) leads in full-day Head Start, followed by Texas (9,000), Florida (8,300), New York (5,000), Alabama (4,800), Georgia (4,500), and many smaller programs, totaling 120,000. Clearly, factors other than the absolute poverty total operate.

Preprimary enrollment other than Head Start consists of nursery schools, kindergarten, and the prekindergartens in some school systems. Except for Head Start, take-up is biased toward income groups above the poverty line and favors children of better-educated parents.[30] Table 2-3 describes the regional variability in the proportion of eligible population served in preschool education programs in

Table 2-3. Proportion of Eligible Population Served by Preprimary Programs, by Age and Region (1973)

Age	Northeast (%)	Northcentral (%)	South (%)	West (%)
3 year olds	13.9	10.9	15.5	18.4
4 year olds	35.4	30.2	35.4	36.4
5 year olds	74.0	84.5	68.0	81.1

Source: *Current Population Reports,* Series 9-20, No. 268: *Nursery School and Kindergarten Enrollment: October, 1973* (Washington, D.C.: GPO, 1974).

1973. It is not known whether other types of facilities are similarly distributed. There are no hard data regarding the number and distribution of in-home arrangements for child care whether by geography, income, or education.

Expenditures

Current federal expenditures for child care and early childhood programs generally total some $1.3 to $1.4 billion by the latest approximations (see Table 2-4). The newly revised tax deductions will increase this. To this we might add state and local matching of some $350 million for child care[31] and direct state expenditures for prekindergarten programs in 1973 of $22.7 million. These totals omit local prekindergarten expenditure and after-school programs for children in the 6–14 age group: community centers, recreation, after-school activities in school buildings, and so on. And there are no data available regarding expenditures for child care in the voluntary sector. In a full accounting of societal investments, a price could also be placed on "free care" by relatives and neighbors and even upon care by the mother. In short, the total U.S. child care cost is not precisely known.

Eligibility

To summarize, almost all public child care programs in the United States which are social-welfare based are means-tested so that eligibility currently is restricted to low-income families; but day care does

Table 2-4. Federal Child Care Expenditures and Obligations (fiscal 1974–75, in millions of dollars)

Program	1974	1975
Department of Agriculture (food service)	43.3	59.0
Appalachian Regional Commission		
(Child Development Program)	12.3	12.3
Department of Health, Education, and Welfare		
Title IV-A AFDC		
Employment related	325.0	341.3
Nonemployment related	139.3	146.3
Title IV-A AFDC Special Meals	not available	not available
Title IV-A Income Disregard	85.0	89.3
Title IV-A Work Incentive	45.0	47.3
Title IV-B Child Welfare	1.8	1.8
Head Start	392.1	430.0
Office of Education	48.9	51.3
Department of Housing and Urban Development		
(Model Cities)	14.2	6.7
Department of Interior (largely Indian progam)	10.2	11.3
Department of Labor		
Concentrated Employment	10.0	10.0
Other	6.3	7.6
Office of Economic Opportunity	2.5	2.4
Small Business Administration	3.8	not available
Child care tax deductions	208.6	208.6
Total	1348.2	1425.2

Source: Committee on Finance, U.S. Senate, *Child Care: Data and Materials, October, 1974* (Washington, D.C.: GPO, 1974).

serve both AFDC and working low-income populations. Public preprimary programs are not means-tested.

In 1974, over 10.2 million American children below age 18 lived under an officially defined poverty line (15 percent of all children). Of the children on AFDC in 1973, 16.6 percent (1,284,477) were under 3, 17.6 percent were 3–5 (1,356,669), and 45.5 percent (2,513,620) were 6–13. Programs funded under the various titles of the Social Security Act and under Head Start funding are specifically aimed at these children. Thus programs under Title IV-A of the Social Security Act have been restricted to current, former, and potential recipients of AFDC and new regulations under Title XX include a means test and guarantee half the service to the poor, although the eligibility level for free service will be considerably above the public assistance line—and partial subsidies will cover some among the working "near-poor"—to 115 percent of median income, if the state so chooses. Head Start is limited to families living below the official poverty line, but 10 percent of the openings may be used for children from near-poverty families; families who receive day care subsidy through the WIN and AFDC income disregard programs must be AFDC recipients; and programs funded through Title I of the Elementary and Secondary Education Act must be targeted on low-income neighborhoods and populations. Other categorical programs funded through such agencies as Model Cities, Bureau of Indian Affairs, and the Manpower Administration also are aimed at low-income families. The major exception to limitations of federally funded social welfare programs to the poverty group may be some day care projects and demonstrations under Title IV-B (Child Welfare) of the Social Security Act—where the emphasis may be upon handicap, maladjustment, or family problems. Here users also may be from the lower middle class and working class rather than the poverty and public assistance populations—but one would expect concentration in categories of the low-income working poor. As much may be said of nonpoverty "consumers" of benefits under Title I of the Elementary and Secondary Education Act. Public kindergarten and preprimary class funds, not at all limited to the poor, are local and state funds, not federal. As already noted, preprimary program take-up is generally higher among the better educated and nonpoor.

Proprietary and voluntary child care programs are generally available to children from all families who can afford the fees. All families are, of course, eligible to take advantage of the income tax deduction for child care. However, tax deductions benefit only those families whose incomes are high enough to warrant their itemizing deductions and to involve a significant marginal tax rate. The benefit structure is such that it is most useful to families whose income is in the middle and upper range.[32]

Rivlin has commented with some justification that "a two-class system has evolved in day care, with a small proportion of the poor getting more comprehensive and costly care in subsidized day care centers than is available for the nonpoor in unsubsidized centers."[33] To which we might add that it is a three-class system if one also considers the quality in-home or nursery school care which the middle-class afford generally without subsidy but sometimes by virtue of significant tax benefits.

Four major population groups receive little or no governmental child care help and need it: (1) working parents of preschool children whose incomes are above the given state's public day care eligibility level (whether under Title IV-A or the new Title XX), but who cannot afford proprietary nursery or day care service and whose needs are not met by public free kindergarten or preprimary classes; (2) nonworking parents who elect to use child care resources but do not live in jurisdictions in which their children are eligible for public day care or in which there are no available preprimary or kindergarten programs—and who cannot afford proprietary care; (3) working parents whose preschool children have access to part-day Head Start or preprimary or kindergarten programs, but whose hours require all-day coverage—or whose school-age children need before- or after-school help for which there is no free or subsidized or tax-deductible coverage available; (4) families eligible for day care, Head Start, and similar programs under Title XX, Title IV-B, and related federal legislation, but who live in states and localities which lack the fiscal capacity to match federal funds and/or the administrative capability to mount programs—or which choose not to develop such programs. In short, the deprived are the poor whose political jurisdictions refuse to offer service or the people-in-the-middle who are ineligible for means-tested programs, unable to find affordable resources in the marketplace, and not fortunate enough to live in jurisdictions which offer universal programs (like public education, where eligibility is unrelated to income).

Utilization

Actual utilization patterns reflect these eligibility rules, parental preference, and the local or neighborhood availability of specific resources. However, while age, social group, and regional differences have been cited, it is not fully known just which factors determine rates of "take-up," especially the relative importance of parental preference and resource availability.

There clearly is a relationship between take-up in different child care programs and the race and income levels of the children. For example, there is a somewhat higher enrollment of minority children than white children at ages 3 and 4 in preprimary programs; however, at age 5 this reverses and there is a higher enrollment of eligible white children than minority children. Similarly, there is a higher percentage of minority children enrolled in full-day programs, but a higher percentage of eligible white children enrolled in part-day programs. Hence, there would seem to be a two-track system in which younger minority children are more likely to be enrolled in full-day programs, usually day care centers, whereas older white children are more likely to be enrolled in part-day programs, usually nursery schools or kindergarten programs.[34] Blacks are more likely to attend public nursery programs while whites more often attend private programs.[35] Head Start has relatively heavy minority enrollment, an inevitable result of the heavy poverty concentration in minority populations.

There is also a relationship between enrollment patterns and socioeconomic status. Generally, the percentage of eligible children aged 3–5 enrolled in preprimary education programs tends to increase with the income of the families. For example, in 1969, 23.4 percent of children aged 3–5 whose family incomes were below $3,000 were enrolled, whereas 41.1 percent of children whose family incomes were over $7,500 were enrolled in preschool education programs.[36] There are similar trends in relation to parental education and occupational status. This finding would again tend to support the concept of a two-track system.

Much less is known about take-up in other types of child care programs; and there is little consensus as to what parental preferences would be if adequate resources were available and there were no eligibility restrictions. For example, in opinion surveys parents often state that they would utilize good center-based programs for child care if these were available on a low-cost, convenient basis. On the other hand, parents usually state that they are satisfied with the child care arrangements they are currently using. Sometimes there has been a low rate of take-up in day care centers even after these have been established following parental preference surveys. For example, in Gary, Indiana, in an income maintenance experiment, only six out of fifty families in the sample who were eligible for free center-based care for their preschool children chose to take advantage of it.

It is generally thought on the basis of observation and expert testimony, that the factors influencing parental choice of child care options are: low cost, convenience in terms of specific street or neighborhood location, hours of operation, and the opportunity for an individualized relationship with the child care providers. The latter is a parent's easiest index of quality.

In a longitudinal labor-force study of women in the 30–44 age cohort, Jusenius and Shortlidge reported that one in ten used a day care center or home, but three times as many were willing to use such a service, if free service were made available. Significant numbers of nonworking women reported that they would work if they had access to free child care.[37]

Quality

Apart from the periodic and incomplete surveys (see Table 2-2) little is known about how most parents not caring for their own children really feel about their arrangements. They generally do not complain. However, whether or not parents are worried about programs, experts and advocacy groups are not satisfied: for example, in the survey conducted by the National Council of Jewish Women (NCJW) only about a quarter of the centers visited were found to be providing what might be defined—by modest standards—as developmental care. Although the NCJW study did not employ a random sample, effort was made to survey a cross-section of day care facilities, and members visited 431 centers and 166 family day care homes in seventy-seven locations throughout the country. Therefore, their findings provided at least one indicator of the quality of existing child care services. Their conclusions are not encouraging. On the whole, they found that Head Start centers provided the most creditable programs, and nonprofit centers generally provided better care than proprietary centers. Approximately 10 percent of the nonprofit centers and only one percent of the proprietary centers were considered superior in their ratings by visiting teams, whereas only 10 percent of the nonprofit centers and 50 percent of the proprietary centers were considered poor. The primary differences between the proprietary and nonprofit centers seemed to be the staff-child ratio and the qualifications of the staff. Both these factors are, of course, related to costs; and the costs of services in the nonprofit centers were considerably higher than those in the proprietary centers. About half the nonprofit centers, however, were considered fair, meaning that they provided what the NCJW surveyors defined as only custodial care; and although these centers were established to meet the needs of working mothers, very few made any effort to accommodate their schedules to the needs of women who must work early, late, or weekends. Findings on family day care homes were similar. For example, although 9 percent of the homes visited were considered superior, half were merely custodial in nature, and 11 percent were considered poor.[38] Of course, no one rates the bulk of care—in-home care by relatives and others.

A 1974 DHEW audit, *The Review of Child Care Services Provided under Title IV, Social Security Act,* reports on a review in nine states of a sample of day care centers, family day care homes, and in-home care arrangements which are funded federally. Of 552 centers and private homes, 425 did not meet health and safety requirements; one-third (especially centers) did not meet child-staff ratio requirements. On the other hand, there is evidence assembled during a 1975 public controversy on day care staffing that the bulk of federally funded programs are relatively close to staffing requirements. As much cannot be said of other programs. (The type of criteria employed in assessing standards is discussed later in this chapter.)

Thus, if need estimates are to relate to quantitative gaps and the qualitative failings, question may be raised as to whether the nation is meeting President Nixon's stated objective of providing high-quality developmental day care in the first five years of life for children from low-income families. On the other hand, there are many excellent child care programs, and effort is being made to improve the quality of care in many centers. In 1972, the Ford Foundation funded a Columbia University–organized visit by thirteen British experts to observe American programs for preschool children from low-income families. Although they noted great variation in the quality and content of care provided, the visitors were impressed with many aspects of the early childhood programs they visited. They were especially enthusiastic about the staffing standards, the relationships among professional, paraprofessional, and volunteer staff, the diversity of programs, and the degree of community control and parental involvement. They also noted, however, the disparity between nonprofit and proprietary centers and raised questions about the universal practice of age-grouping, the low proportion of handicapped children enrolled, the inadequate emphasis on preventive services, and the lack of continuity within and among programs. What is most significant, however, is that this group identified and commented on the gap between the multiplicity and ambitiousness of American objectives for child care and the adequacy of current provision.[39]

Government Agencies

Although much of the funding is federal (except for public pre-primary programs, proprietary nursery care, and the informal, unlicensed day care), child care activities are carried out through units of state or local government or by voluntary bodies, often with public funds channeled through state and local government or occasionally directly through Washington. Since most federal legislation offers options for states in relation to administrative arrangements and services, and since states and local governments in turn are organized in diverse ways and relate to different voluntary agency patterns, the resulting administrative and operational arrangements defy simple description. If the term "system" implies uniformity and coherence, there is no general child care system in the United States.

The listing in Table 2-4 suggests the diversity of federal outlets. Table 2-5, while outdated in some details, serves to illustrate the range of state agencies and eligible service operators involved in the diverse federally supported child care programs.

The Office of Child Development (OCD), established in 1971, operates Head Start and is the lead agency for DHEW and for the federal government in standard-setting, coordination, licensing, demonstration, research, and innovation, but it has a limited legislative mandate and is thus constrained. At the state level, responsibility for child care programs is also frequently shared among several agencies. Although a few states have assigned responsibility to a single agency such as a State Department of Education, Health, or Public Welfare, many states allocate responsibility among several agencies. One article describing child care programs at the state level lists at least eighteen different types of state agencies—with various titles—which have been assigned this responsibility. These agencies range from Departments of Health, Education, Social Services, and Rehabilitation to Departments of Labor, Commerce, Housing, Community Affairs, and Institutions and Agencies. There is similar variation in the types of agencies assigned responsibility at the local level. Coordination among administrative agencies, to the extent that it occurs, is effected by different types of mechanisms at the state and local levels. For example, several states have established Offices of Child Development to perform this function. A number utilize 4-C (Community-Coordinated Child Care) programs (see below); and others rely entirely on informal mechanisms. States are currently reorganizing, as they respond to the new planning and administrative options of Title XX of the Social Security Act, and this will, in turn, influence local administration.

For traditional center and family day care, state social services or child welfare units are most often the responsible licensing or lead agency. California's education-based program is of some interest, however, given the current educator bid for "prime sponsorship." California transferred child care responsibility to its education department in 1946 to meet continuing need for care of children of working mothers. Recently it reduced the optional kindergarten age to 4 as school enrollments fell.

Thus, in Los Angeles, there is now a local program of Children's Centers, open since 1943, operated by the school district at eighty-two locations (in specially-designed buildings) and serving 8,000 children, some of preschool age and some of school age. Centers are open from 6 A.M. to 6 P.M., five days each week, year round. There are long waiting lists for the program. The facilities are on or near school sites. Financing of operations is from all available federal sources, state funds, and parent fees (adjusted to income and family size).

In addition to the full-day Children's Center programs the Los Angeles school district operates three-hour part-day preschool programs (using the Center space that is employed after school for the school-age children), for groups of fifteen. Six hundred children participate. The education district also carries out prekindergarten programs under the Elementary and Secondary Education Act. These two programs are for deprived children and the handicapped. The district administers Follow-Through and parent education efforts too.

Voluntary Agencies

A large number of voluntary organizations have taken an active role in the child care field. Some of these organizations administer child care programs directly, whereas others direct their activities toward research, standard-setting, monitoring, and lobbying. In recent years interest has been high; most of the major national social welfare organizations, educational associations, women's organizations, children's agencies, and church groups have devoted some portion of their programs to child care concerns. While any full listing would contain scores of names recognizable on the national scene, there would be consensus that the lead agencies in this field in standard-setting, advocacy, innovation, education, research, training (at various times) are the Child Welfare League of America, the Day Care and Child Development Council of America, the National Association for the Education of Young Children, the Black Child Develop-

Table 2-5. Major Sources of Federal Funding for Day Care

Program	Federal share (%)	Administrative agency: Federal	State	Local	Eligible operators*
Social Security Act					
AFDC	75	DHEW (SRS)	Welfare Department	Welfare Department	1–8, 13–15
WIN	75	DHEW (SRS)	Welfare Department	Welfare Department	1–8
Child Welfare Services	33⅓–66⅔	DHEW (SRS)	Welfare Department	Welfare Department	1–20
Economic Opportunity Act					
Head Start†	80	OCD	Prime sponsor	CAA or single-purpose agency	1–5
Parent and Child Centers	80	OCD	Prime sponsor	CAA or single-purpose agency	3–5, 10, 12
Migrant and Seasonal Farm Workers	100	OEO	Prime sponsor	CAA or single-purpose agency	5, 11, 14
Manpower Development and Training Act					
Concentrated Employment Program (CEP)	100	Prime sponsor (CAA)	Public and private nonprofit agencies		3, 5, 14
New Careers (Training of day care workers, programs)	90 (in kind)	Manpower Administration	Regional or state employment service		5, 7, 13, 14
Operation Mainstream	90	Manpower Administration	Regional or state employment service	Private or public nonprofit agencies	5, 15
Neighborhood Youth Corps (NYC)	90	Manpower Administration, Bureau of Work-Training	Regional or state employment service	Public agencies	19
JOBS	90	Manpower Administration	State employment service	Industrial groups	6
On-the-Job Training Program (OJT)	90	Manpower Administration	Regional employment service		13, 14, 15
Demonstration Cities and Metropolitan Development Act of 1966					

Model Cities	80	HUD		City Demonstration Agency (CDA)	19
Neighborhood Facilities Program	80	HUD		City Demonstration Agency (CDA)	19
Elementary and Secondary Education Act of 1965					
Title I	100	USOE	Education agency	Education agency	9, 10, 19
Migrant Program	100	USOE	Prime sponsor	Education agency	5, 9, 10, 11, 12
Follow Through	80	USOE	Prime sponsor	Education agency	3, 5, 10
National School Lunch Act					
National School Lunch Program	75	Department of Agriculture	Education agency	Education agency	9, 11
Special Food Service for Children	75	Department of Agriculture	Education agency	Education agency	9–11, 14–15
Child Nutrition Act of 1966					
School Breakfast Program	100	Department of Agriculture	Education agency	Education agency	9, 10
Special Milk Program	100	Department of Agriculture	Education agency	Education agency	9–11
Nonfood Assistance Program	100	Department of Agriculture	Education agency	Education agency	9–11
Auxiliary and Misc. Support					
Small Business Act (1953)	90	Small Business Administration			
Department of the Interior		Bureau of Indian Affairs			
Education Professions Development Act	90	USOE	Colleges and universities		
Health Programs		NIH			
Research Programs		OEO, OCD, SRS, DOL			
Tax Benefits		IRS			

Source: Stevanne Auerbach, "Federally Sponsored Child Care," in Pamela Roby, ed., *Child Care—Who Cares?: Foreign and Domestic Infant and Early Childhood Development Policies* (New York: Basic Books, 1973), table 11-2, pp. 176–77.

*Eligible operators include: (1) state welfare agencies; (2) local welfare agencies; (3) community action agencies; (4) neighborhood organizations; (5) private, nonprofit organizations; (6) independent operators; (7) private employers; (8) direct assistance to individuals; (9) state education agencies; (10) local education agencies; (11) private, nonprofit schools; (12) colleges and universities; (13) labor unions; (14) public, nonprofit organizations; (15) private, profit organizations; (16) state employment services; (17) state health agencies; (18) local health agencies; (19) general purpose agencies; (20) governor's offices.

†The Head Start listing needs correction. States are not, in fact, "prime sponsors" and are not "eligible operators," nor are local welfare agencies. A few local human services departments which include the local welfare programs, are.

ment Institute, and the Children's Defense Fund (Washington Research Project).

Although, as we noted, federal monies have provided the major source of funding for nonprofit day care centers, a large portion of these centers are administered and operated under voluntary auspices. For example, in 1970, 5,600 or 82.4 percent of the 6,800 licensed nonprofit centers in the country were under voluntary auspices.[40] Churches appear to be the largest single group of operators for these nonprofit centers. On the basis of the sample in the Westinghouse Study, it was estimated that 44 percent of all nonprofit centers were operated by churches and that 21 percent (the second largest group) were operated by voluntary community agencies. A similar distribution was discovered among the centers visited in a study conducted under the auspices of the National Council of Jewish Women.[41]

A limited number of child care programs are also conducted under a variety of other nonprofit auspices. For example, unions such as the Amalgamated Clothing Workers of America have established day care programs in several states. Approximately 50–100 industry-based programs, a small total by any standard, have been established by firms in states such as Massachusetts, North Carolina, Kentucky, and Tennessee. The most notable experiment in industry-based day care was conducted under the joint auspices of the U.S. Children's Bureau and the KLH Research and Development Corporation in Cambridge, Massachusetts. A number of hospitals have also attempted to develop child care programs for children of employees. For example, in 1968, approximately 114 hospitals operated such programs, a number which constituted over half of all employee-supported child care.[42] Also, various types of women's organizations, such as the National Council of Negro Women, the National Council of Jewish Women, and the Young Women's Christian Association, have sponsored child care programs.[43] A more recent development has been the establishment of various types of child care programs under university auspices.[44]

Despite the rapid increase in publicly supported child care facilities, a major portion of the child care facilities in the United States are proprietary (profit making). The capacity of proprietary centers more than quadrupled in the decade between 1960 and 1970.[45] Proprietary interests continue to be a major force in the child care field, having at least the capacity of public and voluntary nonprofit centers combined. Most family day care is also proprietary.

Although most of the centers under proprietary auspices are small private ventures, a relatively recent development has been the establishment of franchised centers. The franchise system provides a local operator with a prepackaged curriculum, staffing pattern, budget, advertising, training, and management assistance. The operator usually pays the franchiser an initial fee and a percentage of operating costs. Although the franchise concept developed rapidly and has been a remarkably successful component of American industry generally during the past twenty years, very few child care franchise operations have been successful despite a flurry of excitement and expectation early in the 1970s. It is alleged that because staff costs are such a major component of child care costs, centers are usually able to operate at a profit only by sacrificing quality of care. Evaluative data are limited, however. A few of the franchise companies such as American Child-Care Centers are reliably reported as offering quality care on a profit-making basis.[46] There is no current evidence of any widespread interest in franchises.

Planning and Coordination

There has been active concern over the past decade about who is to be responsible for coordination. To the more than two hundred federal programs related to the needs of young children are added an untold number of children's programs under state, local, voluntary, and proprietary auspices. Clients, agencies, citizens at large, governmental officials see this system as difficult to negotiate.

Congressional recognition was first given to this problem in the 1967 Amendments to the Economic Opportunity Act. The Secretary of DHEW and the Director of the Office of Economic Opportunity were called upon "to take all necessary steps to coordinate programs under their jurisdiction which provide day care so as to attain, if possible, a common set of program standards and regulations and mechanisms for coordination at the State and local level."[47]

A Federal Panel on Early Childhood was subsequently established in April 1968, including representatives from the Office of Economic Opportunity, DHEW, Labor, Agriculture, Housing and Urban Development, Defense, Interior, and the Bureau of the Budget. In order to carry out this legislative mandate, the Panel initiated the Community Coordinated Child Care Program (4-C). The purpose of this program was to encourage state and local communities to develop administrative mechanisms which would enhance the opportunity for joint planning, program coordination, and resource-sharing in the child care field. The Federal Panel took several initiatives in order to encourage the implementation of the 4-C Program. For example, it established a Standing Committee on 4-C, allocated responsibility to DHEW for developing operating guidelines and assigning staff to the Federal Regional 4-C Committees, created twenty-four pilot projects throughout the country, and contracted with the Day Care and Child Development Council of America to provide technical assistance to the pilot projects. Subsequently a central 4-C office was established within the Office of Child Development (OCD), and OCD personnel were assigned specific responsibility for the program. Also, in 1970 OCD gave a contract to the Appalachian Regional Commission to supervise, conduct, and administer 4-C demonstration programs. By 1971, there were 278 active 4-C committees located throughout the country. These committees engaged in a variety of activities including information and referral, fund-raising, resource mobilization, staff training, development of new services, surveys, planning, and program coordination. Many had a strong grass-roots community-action flavor. Some coordinated a diverse group of day care advocates or sponsors; some gave central service. A few "decategorized" funds.* However, there has never been any clear consensus about what these committees were or are intended to do, and the nature and extent of their activities varied widely. Their power was limited —as were their resources.

In 1972 the National Research Council–National Academy of Sciences completed an assessment of the 4-C Program, and concluded that although the 4-C concept had great potential and 4-C committees in some communities had been very effective, "it is clear that a strong, nationwide movement has not been built. The idea has not taken hold at all in the large majority of the country's communities and, in many where they do exist, 4-C committees or councils are far from effective."[48] This panel attributed the failure of the 4-C Program primarily to the lack of federal legislative mandate and to the inadequate administrative mandate, staff, and funding allocated to the program. Since the time the report was issued, little has been done to enhance the 4-C effort at the federal level. Federal support and encouragement has faded. Hence, although 4-C committees still

*In this sense "decategorization" refers to creation of one integrated program by drawing upon diverse categorical funding sources.

exist in a great number of states and local communities, they are not serving the major coordinating function it was hoped they could fulfill.

A number of states have also attempted to initiate various types of coordinating mechanisms. For example, by 1974 sixteen states had established some form of an office of child development to coordinate and/or administer early childhood programs, and similar offices were planned in three other states. In addition, fifteen states have developed an advisory system for achieving coordination among administrative agencies.[49]

Other types of coordinating devices have also been attempted at the local level. For example, the Agency for Child Development was established in New York City within a Human Resources Administration in 1971 to serve as the administering and regulatory agency for Head Start, day care centers, and family day care programs and to play a variety of planning roles as well.

Because of the different guidelines put forth by the various federal funding agencies, however, the separate child care programs may all be administered separately in various jurisdictions or service locations; where they are administratively joined, operations may flow through separate program units. As a result, one operating agency may have as many as four separate programs (Head Start, group day care, family day care, and nursery school) serving what is essentially the same target population. Few localities have even considered the possibility of unifying preprimary and day care programs. The categorical funding and lack of legislatively based coordination among federal agencies sponsoring child care programs severely limit the degree of coordination which can be achieved at the state or local levels.

A Struggle for Control

In the past day care was recognized as a program in the general social services domain (public and private social welfare), while nursery schools and kindergartens clearly represented private or public education. In both instances, despite the difference in administrative auspice, the direct work with children was carried out or guided by early childhood educators. Family day care was and is social work–led. Head Start, a cross between the two main systems, has had mixed staffing but the high ratio of paraprofessionals obscured the issue of professional allegiance for a while. Administratively, Head Start is aligned with OCD, not the Office of Education, even though some Head Start programs are based in school systems. The new Child Development Associates, a career group for child care service sponsored by OCD, clearly are identified with early childhood education. The prekindergarten programs in the public schools, especially those sponsored under the Elementary and Secondary Education Act, are organized as educational enterprises on federal, state, and local levels.

As already noted, these programs are actually implemented through a diversity of administrative patterns and auspices. However, most day care and Head Start proponents have tended to see educational auspices as inappropriate for the major day care thrust. First, they believe that family and group day care should be integrated, and the former has a large social service component. Second, this type of child care calls for an amalgam of education, child development, social service, health, and parent participation efforts. It has been widely believed that teachers and educational bureaucracies cannot plan and implement the necessary pluralistic, flexible, developing system whose philosophy should be more open than that of most formal school systems.

These views began to be reconsidered when recent demographic trends became visible: given birth rate declines in recent years, fewer children are entering elementary school. There were 4,257,850 live births in the U.S. in 1960; that dropped to 3,760,358 in 1965, and the estimated 1972 total was 3,256,000. There were 59 million children enrolled in U.S. schools in September 1973 and 58.6 million in September 1974. The elementary school enrollment dropped by 730,000, according to a release in November 1974 from the National Center for Educational Statistics. Projecting future school enrollment for those children already born, educators note the inevitable drop by 2.3 million as elementary and secondary rosters fall from 49.8 million to 47.5 million between 1973 and 1980. Whatever the imprecision of the forecasts, there is agreement that empty classrooms and underutilized teachers at the elementary level are not an uncommon phenomenon already and the situation will persist for some years at least.

Some large cities are planning to close down relatively good school buildings and to consolidate. The job "market" for newly prepared elementary teachers is everywhere tight and low seniority teachers on staffs have expressed worry in some jurisdictions. Following an alternative tack several years ago, California became the first state to react to these demographic realities as it lowered optional prekindergarten to age 4. Teachers' organizations, long silent about day care, have begun to take note. Albert Shanker, President of the United Federation of Teachers, stated in a widely circulated column (November 8, 1974):

Sentiment continues to grow for a major federal effort to provide child care and early childhood education. The demand for such a program stems from many considerations, two of which are most important: first, that the early childhood years are the period in which the intellectual development of children can most effectively be aided, and second, that early childhood services are urgently needed by mothers who cannot afford to pay for private services but deserve what well-to-do women now enjoy—the freedom to pursue a career. . . .

As we move toward a comprehensive early childhood program, it is important that some of the shortcomings of earlier legislation be avoided. Programs such as Head Start and the Job Corps suffered greatly as a result of political compromises in which many different public, private, profit and non-profit agencies won government contracts for the needed services. The same helter-skelter pattern is already evident in the grants for projects to aid the handicapped, with sponsors as diverse as the University of Colorado, the Salvation Army of Honoulu, La Raza (a militant Chicano organization) and the Mister Rogers Neighborhood Television Program.

Shanker went on to quote Edwin W. Martin, Acting Deputy Commissioner of the U.S. Bureau for the Education of the Handicapped:

1) Public policy makers should "bite the bullet" and begin the process of making a specific decision about where the responsibility for early childhood education services should be lodged. . . . 2) Public policy must be based on the assumption of equal access for all children, and so a public system must be developed based on this "zero reject" concept. Private agencies can offer alternatives for those who can afford them, or serve as subcontractors for the public agency. 3) A single public agency should be charged with the primary responsibility. 4) That agency should be the public education agency.

When in June 1975 there was a joint session of responsible Senate and House Subcommittees to hear testimony on a proposed bill which would enact an updated version of the 1971 vetoed legislation, there was for the first time a large turnout of teacher union, education association, and other education interest-groups. Shanker became more specific: Apart from reminding the legislators of the "importance of the early years to the total intellectual and social development of children," he saw the possibility of meeting simultaneously the needs of working parents, single parents, professionals who work with children, and "the total development of the child." He called for a new policy: "public schools as the presumed prime sponsor for child development programs." Moreover: "Child development programs should be available to all children whose parents desire to utilize this service. It should not be restricted on the basis of means tests, sliding income scales, or other criteria that prevent the majority of our citizens from utilizing a highly desirable and crucial public service." "Profit-making entrepreneurs" would be eliminated. Other prime sponsors could be considered where schools were not interested.

Shanker and other educational leaders who followed him noted that sponsorship does not need to mean a monopoly of operations. Shortly thereafter, on July 13, 1975, the *New York Times* was to report from Honolulu that the American Federation of Teachers and the National Education Association, two million strong, had endorsed "expansion of schooling" for children from 3 to 5 "to help teachers in a shrinking job market and also as a solid educational measure . . . and as fulfilling the growing needs of families for day-care services."

As recently as 1973 there was confusion and objection to any discussion of day care and prekindergarten as part of one program cluster, one societal response to a group of needs and objectives. The terms of the U.S. debate have begun to change—largely because of the new position of this major interest group.

Discussion of Shanker's proposals is now widespread. Many who fear educational auspices as too formal and rigid are impressed with the logic of using available space and personnel. Others would prefer to begin with a view of programs: How should they be organized? What does this require?

Program Models

It is possible in a formal sense to identify four basic models for child care provision in the United States: in-home care; family day care; group or center care and its preprimary variations; after-school community center or recreation programs. However, there is much variation within each model, and some child care programs attempt to combine elements of each.

In-Home Care. The simplest model—and the one which has the longest history and is employed most frequently—is in-home care, perhaps most clearly described as own-home care. Under this model, children whose parents are unable to care for them or prefer other arrangements are provided for in their own homes. Care is supplied by a housekeeper, relative, friend, paid "sitter," or social agency staff member. In the Westinghouse Sample, 49.9 percent of the children under 6 and 78.7 percent of the school-age children were cared for in their own homes.[50] That this care is usually arranged on an informal, unpaid basis can be assumed from the fact that only 7.3 percent and 4.5 percent of these children, respectively, were cared for by someone other than a relative. The Jusenius-Shortlidge study (1971 data) reported that 61 percent of the children under 6 and 75 percent of those over 6 in the white group were cared for at home, while the percentages for blacks were 76 and 64. Care by nonrelatives accounted for very small numbers of the older children and 18–16 percent of the younger age group.[51]

This type of care thus is usually inexpensive, flexible, individualized, and provides care for the child in familiar surroundings by a person who is well known to him. Because of its informality, however, in-home care often has major disadvantages: it may be unreliable and "merely" custodial rather than educational or developmental in nature. The group care proponents argue that in-home care usually lacks both skilled personnel and the advantages of a group socializing experience. When they can afford it, parents seem to prefer in-home care for the very young and, later, nursery school.

Homemaker Service. Homemaker service is in-home care provided on a more formalized basis, usually under the auspices of a voluntary or public social agency. The service is rendered by a trained homemaker who performs light household chores and cares for children in their own homes on a scheduled, time-limited basis, usually because a parent is hospitalized or otherwise incapacitated. Homemaker service is seldom available on a permanent basis, but rather is designed to serve the temporary function either of helping families to cope with an emergency situation in which the mother is unable to fulfill her usual caretaking role or of teaching an inadequate mother how to fulfill her parental role more adequately. The market equivalent for the more affluent is the housekeeper—a declining labor force category, as salaries rise and women seek other occupations.

Family Day Care. A second major type of child care in the United States is the family day care home. Under this very popular model, which apparently often meets parental preferences for proximity, flexibility, and informality, one or more children are cared for in the homes of other families. Care may be provided for a part or full day and the provider is paid a fee per child. Such care is frequently private and informal: the parent and provider make their own arrangements regarding fees, hours, meals. Family day care is also provided through voluntary and public social agencies which are expected to evaluate the homes prior to use, conduct training programs, set regulations, make periodic inspections, provide ongoing consultation and support service, and handle the arrangements between parents and providers. Formally licensed and regulated family day care (perhaps 10 percent of all family day care) is usually limited to six children between 3 and 14, no more than five under 5, and no more than two under 2, including the provider family's own children.

There are two basic variations of this model. One is the family day care home which serves only as many children as can be integrated into the provider family's own physical setting and pattern of living. The other type of day care home is a special *group day care* home, which provides for six to twelve children in a family-like setting. Such a program is usually under agency auspices, requires more than one caretaker, and is considered most suitable for part-day care of school-age children.

The advantages of the family day care home model are that it provides relatively individualized care in a family-like setting on a somewhat flexible but regular basis. Group care advocates argue that it is usually not as educational or developmental in focus as formal center-based care (usually involving several groups and more varied personnel and resources) and that it is difficult to monitor so as to assure child safety and protection in the broadest sense. Proponents note that at its best it has the same advantages as socialization and development in one's own family. It can offer more group interaction than in-home care. Since it provides for mixed-age groupings, it is especially suitable for sibling groups. Where backed up, as it sometimes is, with central services and consultants and interaction with day care centers, it can be an enriched program. It usually is not. Currently OCD and several foundations are funding experiments in improved central servicing or consultation to family day care homes of both types. One three-year OCD demonstration showed high payoffs for modest costs.

Center or School Care. The third basic model of child care is the day care center, serving groups of twelve or more children and taking one of several forms. Center care is most frequently provided to children aged 3–5, but some day care centers also serve infants and school-age children. This model is used primarily for children of working mothers, but is also employed occasionally for children from families with special needs as, for example, those in which the mother is disabled or unable for other reasons to provide adequate care. Day care centers are conducted under independent, voluntary, or public auspices. Although there is usually a fee for service, some centers are operated as parent cooperatives or partial cooperatives in which the fee is larger if labor is not contributed. The objectives of various day care centers range from the basically custodial to the educational and elaborately developmental. Thus there is great variation in regard to the types of programs provided, the numbers of children served in each center, staff-child ratios, and physical facilities. Children are generally cared for on a full-day basis (five or more hours) in subgroups organized according to age, but surprisingly large numbers are present only part of the day in some centers.

Centers set their hours in accord with the work and travel patterns of parents, and they are often open eight to twelve hours a day. Variations on the traditional all-day, daytime, five-day-a-week center are the occasional night and overnight group day care centers and six-day facilities. Centers usually provide year-round coverage on their own or in collaboration with other centers, to meet the needs of working families. By contrast, nursery schools, kindergartens, and prekindergartens (see below) are limited to half-days, usually 3–4 hours, 5 days a week, during the school year. Most Head Start centers (2/3) are half-day but may be year-round except for a vacation month. There are also numerous public, voluntary nonprofit, and proprietary all-day summer day camps.

There are also group day care facilities staffed to undertake remedial and therapeutic work with special groups of children and to cope with handicaps and disabilities. There are also some drop-in centers without set registration, mostly nonprofit, which take a child occasionally if the mother has errands or appointments.

There are several other types of programs, employing some variation of this basic center-care model. Operation *Head Start,* for example, was organized in 1965 as a summer antipoverty program for preschool children from low-income families. Although it soon expanded to a full-year program, it provides only half-day care for about two-thirds of its registration; it was not designed to meet the needs of working mothers, even though one-third of the children now attend all day because the home situation seems to require it.

Rapid expansion, facility shortages, complexities arising from decentralized administration and control of local antipoverty community-action agencies (the sponsors of most Head Start programs originally) made standard-setting and program leadership difficult. Nonetheless, much progress was made and it was possible to tap creativity and initiative deriving from parent participation, some community control, and the hiring of indigenous personnel and paraprofessionals. The leadership agency, now OCD in DHEW, moved slowly in formulating program guides and requirements as experience accumulated. The Head Start goal is now unambiguously described in new regulations as child development and "social competence"—with an emphasis on socioemotional growth, cognitive development, health, and nutrition service—and not on care of children so as to permit other activities (work or training) by mothers.* Although all Head Start programs are expected to provide education, health, nutrition, and social work services to children and their families, to provide employment for community residents, and to encourage a high degree of parental and community participation, programs are run under local leadership and inevitably vary a great deal. Some offer little more than basic group custody. Others are inventive and outstanding. About 30 percent of Head Start programs are based in school systems.

An important program under Head Start, the Home Start Demonstration Program, was launched in 1972. Targeted at children in the 3–5 age category who do not make use of Head Start, this is not a child care program at all. It is, instead, an in-home parent education effort implementing Head Start's social competence objectives, and it derives from encouraging experimental research. All the services associated with Head Start are included (health care, nutrition, social service) but a project worker visits the home and the mother becomes the program intermediary. Educational play materials are em-

*New, high Head Start program performance standards for grantee and delegate agencies were published in the Federal Register, Vol. XL, No. 126, Part II (June 30, 1975). They were effective July 1, 1975. The implementation procedure, involves a detailed manual which includes "guidance" for each performance standard, a requirement for a multidisciplinary detailed site visit and review to each program every third year by the regional DHEW staff, a more routine review every year, and a self-assessment procedure involving completion of a detailed self-assessment instrument prepared by OCD.

ployed to buttress the parents as educators of their own preschool children. The programs make heavy use of indigenous personnel. Some sixteen projects were serving 2,500 children in this demonstration effort in 1973.[52]

Aware of the diversity of community needs and parental preferences and eager to uncover new and effective measures, Head Start leadership continues to encourage experimentation and innovation. The directives and guidelines spell out a policy under which "Head Start programs will be permitted and encouraged to consider several program models in addition to the standard Head Start model and select the program option best suited to the needs of the children served and the capabilities and resources of the program staff." Apart from the standard model, program options include: variations in center attendance (number of days per week), double sessions, home-based programs, locally designed variations.

The Office of Education also administers several programs of the center-based type under Title I of the Elementary and Secondary Education Act. All these programs are intended for children from low-income families. For example, there is a program of preschool education conducted in elementary schools; a Follow Through program which provides educational enrichment services to maintain the progress made by children in Head Start centers; and an extended school-day program which offers recreational and cultural activities before and after school for children in poverty areas where there is a high rate of maternal employment.

Another prevalent form of center-based care is the *nursery school* or *play school* or *prekindergarten* or *preprimary class*. Like day care centers, nursery schools are conducted under a variety of auspices. However, they usually provide only half-day care and—when private and proprietary—usually serve children from middle- and higher-income families. But the picture is mixed. In 1974, 33.2 percent of the children aged 3–5 in nursery schools and 19 percent of those in kindergarten attended a full day.[53] The major objective of all nursery school programs is presumed to be socialization and education, and all activities are expected to contribute toward this end. However, nursery schools are also frequently used by families as a means of providing a respite from child care for the mother—or as day care.

Although many formal public and private social agencies may provide more than one of these basic models of care, the facilities are frequently administered as separate entities and there is little attempt to merge or coordinate them in a total child care system.

Instead, it is left to the families to discover the child care "package" which best meets their needs. For example, because of funding patterns and their resulting administrative requirements, a large settlement house in New York City currently operates three entirely separate child care programs—a day care center, a Head Start program, and a nursery school. In addition, the day care center administers an after-school program and a family day care home program, each of which must meet its own distinct guidelines, standards, personnel requirements, and serve its distinctive eligible parent-child populations.

In a few cities or counties, however, effort has been made to combine elements from these various models and programs in one system.[54] The theory is that whatever the sponsoring department, legislation, or financing, the money should be "decategorized" and the services developed into a system of differentiated elements which will meet different child-family needs.

There are also a series of initiatives involving buttressing of informal child care and integrating it with formal programs. For example, a project in Portland, Oregon, has attempted to study the "natural system" of child care within the neighborhood and to introduce programs which would enhance these informal arrangements rather than attempt to establish a completely separate formal child care program. At Yale University, a new program has been established, The Edith B. Jackson Child Care Program, in which family day care homes are organized around a child care center in natural housing units so that the children are able to spend part of the day in family care and part in group care, and the day care providers are able to exchange resources and build a system of mutual support and education. The Day Care Consultation Center at Bank Street College of Education is presently experimenting with the development of total family-focused child care systems in five selected sites. Emphasis is placed on cooperatives and building upon other informally initiated arrangements. OCD is initiating and supporting experiments which mix part-day center care with part-day family day care. The various latter initiatives all represent efforts to combine some of the positive aspects of each of the various models of child care and to introduce greater choice and flexibility into the child care field and to explore approaches which might be less costly.

After-school centers, etc. After-school programs hardly constitute a true "model" and we have not assembled systematic data. It is best seen as a function discharged in one of many ways. In general after-school programs for children 6 to 14 do not differentiate those whose mothers work from other participants. They run two to three hours or more and involve: a building with facilities where the participant chooses and coordinates his own facility or activity (swimming pool, gymnasium, hobby rooms, clubs, dance classes, etc.); a club or organization which supplies leadership and/or facilities (campfire girls, scouts, boys' club, church meeting group, etc.); or a school building offering access to gym, swimming pool, library, study center, and perhaps special activities and remedial help.

Parent Participation

Head Start, as it developed in the mid-1960s, featured new forms of parent participation, indeed parent "control." This emphasis was both a recognition of the contribution of parent participation to program enrichment and success in many places and a response to political pressures of the more activist among day care advocates in the 1970s. The point requires brief elaboration.

Parents always had active roles in cooperative day care or nursery arrangements, or in programs established through parent initiative in middle-class areas. In such environments parents saw themselves as policy-makers, employers, and autonomous consumers. At the very least, parents were expected to cooperate by "sitting in" until a child accepted the transition from home to center routine, and they would, from time to time, get a report on the child's progress and suggestions from the teacher or center director. In the day care centers which grew out of the child welfare system, prior to the 1960s, day care was seen as solving a parent or child problem. Therefore, appropriate participation was defined by the case situation. The parent was seen as patient or client, not as a potential board member. It was and is not easy for working parents to get to meetings. Family day care was often a business arrangement between the parent as contractor and the family day care mother as proprietary provider. Or, in a social agency program, the arrangement was part of a "case" plan.

It was inevitable that Head Start would be different. The developmental psychologists and others who conceptualized the programs derived from their theoretical backgrounds and research the notion that children would achieve greater gains if the efforts could be buttressed by parallel work with parents. In this sense parent participation meant educational meetings at which the program was interpreted, efforts to engage the parents in activities with their children so that the child's new experiences would be supported and encouraged and his home environment changed, and inclusion of parents in programs as volunteers and as paid staff paraprofessionals so that children might have "models" out of their own backgrounds.

But Head Start grew in the midst of a larger antipoverty community development effort which featured "maximum feasible participation" of area residents. The latter slogan, too, had many meanings: activities for and with deprived people; policy and program advice from "consumers"; jobs for local people in social service programs meant to benefit them; program control in the hands of local consumers; a power base for minority group populations. In this context Head Start was the most popular program, the most acceptable to the nonpoverty constituencies, one of the best sources of jobs for indigenous personnel. In a few places Head Start also became *the* vehicle for militant community development and, then, political activity. In many places, the concept of parent participation evolved into the practice of including parents on staff and policy and planning boards.

At the 1970 White House Conference on Children, as at all similar forums in the late 1960s, there was widespread agreement that activities involving parents as well as children were essential to the success of programs for the deprived, such as Head Start. It was agreed, too, that unless program policy and leadership was in the hands of community people like those with whom the children lived daily, programs would fall short of their "social competence" goals. Many participants urged that parents of current enrollees have one-third to one-half of all voting places on child care center boards. Many favored selection of center directors by such boards. Some wanted the boards to hire and fire teachers as well, but others noted that this would truncate the roles of directors.

In any case, in the 1970s the call for expansion of developmental day care was frequently accompanied by advocacy of broad-based parental participation and full control of these programs. Many of those who rejected extreme positions (arguing that the community stake in programs and policy is broader than the interests of the parents—the comparatively few active parents—of current enrollees) nonetheless believed that programs with some significant degree of community and parent involvement would be more positively experienced.

The spillover effect relating both to community control and community action has been substantial. As White and his colleagues comment, parent advisory programs and parent control have been built into Office of Education programs such as Follow Through and antipoverty components of the Elementary and Secondary Education Act.[55]

The research evidence that parent participation produces more lasting effects on children is convincing. New Head Start guidelines mandate four major kinds of parent participation in local programs and elaborate how such participation may be implemented:

1. Participation in the process of making decisions about the nature and operations of the program.
2. Participation in the classroom as paid employees, volunteers or observers.
3. Activities for the parents which they have helped to develop.
4. Working with their children in cooperation with the staff of the center.

A 1972 assessment by a team of British observers is of interest. (Jule Sugarman, formerly national director of Head Start, was at the time administrator of New York City's Human Resources Administration.)

It would be wrong to be too starry-eyed about the extent to which community control and parental involvement have been put into effective practice. Clearly there are difficulties, of which American commentators are aware. . . . Parental involvement goes in cycles. The parents begin by taking no part. They then try to take over the running of the centre or programme, reducing the professionals to impotence. After this they become frightened and bring the professionals back. This is followed by a loss of interest and apathy, during which the professionals resume full control. Sugarman feels that in the long-established day care centres parental involvement is at present relatively small. However, other American commentators have a more optimistic view of the extent and permanence of successful schemes of this kind. And certainly, in spite of all the limitations, the various kinds of parental involvement in day care and early childhood education have got further in the USA than in the UK. In particular there are more examples of parents in the classroom, of teachers and aides in parents' homes, and of parents being involved in decision-making about the programmes that are being run. . . . Such involvement may go a long way towards building up the self-image of parents, and children's images of them, by demonstrating their capacity to play a part.[56]

In addition to local participation, parent and/or community participation is generally mandated for the statewide planning and advisory committees in child care. Their influence varies among the states. Part of the latent agenda in a current conflict about future designation of prime local and statewide sponsors for child care programs relates to the nature and scale of consumer-parent influence, particularly the roles of minority and non-middle-class parents and community activists.

In sum, there is consensus about the desirability of a parent role at all levels in child care and there is widespread implementation. But there also is debate as to how to balance participation as management-control, on the one hand, and as sharing the child's learning, at the other extreme. The task, after all, is also to permit those working with the children optimum opportunity to make their contribution. Recent directives tend to hedge, and different jurisdictions reflect different resolutions. Parents previously closed out from influence on the institutions around then, and now politically active, may have more concern about trusting those who are assigned program responsibility than do others. They want to hire and closely supervise center directors and teachers—and to go over curriculum in detail. Most middle-class suburban parents remove themselves once they feel satisfied that they are dealing with qualified professionals; their influence is held in reserve, for use as needed. In any case thinking and practice are in transition.

Criteria of Quality

There were no comprehensive federal day care regulations before 1968. The Federal Interagency Panel on Early Childhood issued a set of day care requirements in 1968 which are still operative and, with some revisions, remain effective under the new services Title XX, in the Social Security Act. Tougher implementation would create funding ineligibility for many current programs and would impose considerable costs. A Senate Finance Committee compilation in October 1974 noted, with reference to the 1968 standards, that "it is generally acknowledged that they are rarely monitored."[57] Nonetheless, it is also the consensus that center care standards are higher than those for family day care and are better enforced. As noted, OCD has prepared, circulated, and begun to monitor and enforce new, stricter Head Start regulations. States have their own requirements for staffing, physical facilities, and program components, and some of them do regulate and monitor more rigorously than others. It is acknowledged that the federal government role in licensing should be advisory but that regulations tied to funding can have great influence.[58]

Of course, all child care requirements here referred to are limited to day care and related social welfare funded programs and to other federal efforts specified, such as Head Start. Proprietary nurseries and state-funded efforts based in the educational system are responsive only to state requirements (which may be more or less rigorous than those which originate in Washington).

Federal Interagency Day Care Requirements, as modified by June 1975 regulations, are a prerequisite for federal financial participation in state/local day care programs under Title XX of the Social Security Act. They prescribe specific regulations regarding the grouping of children, licensing, location and suitability of facilities, educational services, social services, health and nutrition services, training of staff, parent involvement, and administration, coordination, and evaluation. As modified in June 1975, educational services under the requirements are only "recommended." The staffing standards for children under age 3 in day care centers and group day care homes require a ratio of 1:1 for children under 6 weeks of age, 1:4 for children aged 6 weeks through 36 months, 1:5 for 3 year olds, and 1:7 for 4 and 5 year olds. States may, at their option, require fewer children per adult. Required staffing ratios for school-age children in day care centers are at least one adult to fifteen children aged 6–10 and at least one adult to twenty children aged 10–14. Because these requirements were difficult for many states, an administrative, legislative, and court battle about staffing standards developed in the fall of 1975, leading to postponement, modification, and funding of plans to upgrade staffs.

The Child Welfare League of America issued a set of standards for day care service in 1960, which were revised in 1969. The League and Interagency documents provide the major criteria by which child care programs can be evaluated. More recently a coordinating body, the National Council of Organizations for Children and Youth, drafted a model code. There is, in fact, a good deal of overlap and similarity among these several documents.

The Child Welfare League's standards, for example, suggest that the essential components of a day care service are facilities that are safe and suitable for their purpose; qualified staff; participation of parents; a planned program which ensures individualized care, protection of the child's security, and educational and developmental experiences; health evaluation and supervision; social work service;

and administrative planning and coordination. OCD's Head Start guidelines call for even more enrichment and parent participation.[59]

The general criteria against which programs are measured can be summarized briefly as follows. All programs are expected to meet state and local licensing requirements. Staff-child ratios should be related to age and kept as low as necessary to ensure individualized attention. In regard to physical facilities, it is suggested that programs be located in areas which are convenient, accessible, and close to other community resources. In addition to safety and sanitation, it is suggested that facilities have space and equipment for rest, play, privacy, and a range of indoor and outdoor program activities, and room for a child who becomes ill.

It is recommended that all child care services provide age-appropriate educational opportunities under trained personnel, family-focused social service programs, health screening and preventive maintenance, and adequate and nutritious meals. In addition, child care facilities are expected to provide opportunities for staff training and full parental involvement. Finally, agencies are expected to follow accepted administrative and personnel practices, to coordinate their programs with other community agencies, and to engage in periodic ongoing evaluation.

It is generally agreed that there is a trade-off between federal and state regulation enforcement and licensing rigor, on the one hand, and program expansion—or even survival—on the other. Inevitably fire and safety standards have first attention and many program components are examined "flexibly." Federal and state funds continue to subsidize much low-standard care.

Staffing

There are many child care staffing patterns. This is inevitable in a field with many types of programs, financed out of several legislative mandates, either unregulated or under the jurisdictions of diverse governmental units—local, state, federal—and "claimed" by several professions, semiprofessions, and occupational groups. The differences in concepts and programs among kindergartens and nursery schools, day care centers, Head Start centers, and the several types of after-school programs create different staffing requirements. The rapid expansion, diffusion of authority, and limited resources often result in a staffing arrangement based on "getting by" rather than achieving an optimum program environment. The debate about goals (child care to meet parent needs or optimum child development, quality service or maximum quantitative expansion, etc.) fosters honest differences about optimum staffing.

Nursery schools and kindergartens are generally administered within educational systems and staffed and led by personnel with credentials recognized in the field of education. In high-standard states the rules are rigorous; elsewhere there is little expectation as to staff credentials or experience. Day-care centers, to the extent that they are not very small and are in jurisdictions which mandate standards, often assign their program leadership to personnel with educational credentials as well. For these several purposes the credential may be an elementary school training certificate, a kindergarten certificate, or special qualification in what is known as the field of "early childhood education." No easy generalizations can be made about Head Start, family day care, or after-school programs for school-age children. Moreover, each of the program models described may draw upon social workers, nurses, nutritionists, recreation personnel, "mature, experienced adults" with no particular specialized training, and college graduates or indigenous personnel, whether or not specially trained as paraprofessionals.

Although totals for staff members in some of these child care programs are reported from time to time, no recent estimates are available. An informed guess would be that no fewer than 300,000 persons staff currently licensed programs.

By way of detail, it may be noted:[60] Thirty-one states accept an elementary teaching certificate for kindergarten and prekindergarten teaching jobs, but usually insist on supplementary credentials in early childhood education as well. Forty-eight have certification requirements for kindergarten teachers and administrators, but only six have such requirements for paraprofessionals. Twenty-five have certificate requirements for prekindergarten teachers and administrators, but only six have such requirements for paraprofessionals. With a few special exceptions the State Board of Education is the certifying agency for all these. Thirteen states require certification for day care personnel. All but two states have postsecondary education programs in early childhood education (college, junior college, or community college). The largest concentrations are Massachusetts (100 programs), New York (24), and Virginia (16). All the above is understandable in view of the historical tradition, the program emphases, and the fact that the state departments of education are the sole administrative agency for kindergarten programs in thirty-seven states and for prekindergarten programs in six states.

Day care centers have a strong social work tradition as well. However, the field of early childhood education is more often seen as providing preparation for directors and administrators and for the child care staff. According to Chambers, "the academic and experiential requirements for day care are minimal in most states. No state has special training requirements for personnel in either 'in home' or Family Day Care homes, and approximately a third have none for those in group Day Care centers."[61] Many states have no requirements at all for the aides who are in daily contact with the children but some have recently revised requirements to specify either high school graduation or that the applicant be working toward a high school equivalency diploma.

In general, where standards are set, social workers and elementary school teachers have found themselves often closed out of day care director or group leadership jobs for lack of early childhood education certificates or degrees. On the other hand, as federal funds become increasingly important the Federal Interagency Day Care Requirements could prevail, specifying that the overall program director might have experience and an advanced degree in one of several fields (early childhood education, social work, psychology, etc.); the director of education have an early childhood education degree and relevant experience; the director of social work have a social work degree and relevant experience; the teachers have degrees in early childhood education, nursery or kindergarten teaching, and relevant experience; the nutritionists have appropriate B.A. training and the career development director have one of several degrees; the teacher aides have appropriate informal experience and personality.

Since promulgation of these standards, there has been widespread expansion of paraprofessional and professional training and staffing for Head Start, day care, and preschool programs within school systems. A large OCD effort has been promoting expansion of a new child care career line. Using the term Child Development Associate, the Head Start experimental effort, led by a federally funded Child Development Associate Consortium, is defining competencies for center work with 3–5 year olds, developing model training techniques and curriculum materials; developing, adopting, implementing, and promoting credentialing systems; and adapting all of this to state operations and launching large-scale recruitment, training, and implementation. The fiscal 1974 budget is $1.2 million for thirteen projects and the consortium itself. Several hundred associates have already been certified. There is some interest, too, in applying the associate approach to family day care as well.

While this effort continues, there are efforts, too, to upgrade staffing requirements, increase certification levels, and perhaps to assign qualified elementary teachers to day care.

Costs per Service Unit

Cost estimates for the various models of child care vary greatly. There is much inconsistency among jurisdictions in the extent and manner in which cost estimates do or do not include capital costs, start-up costs, central administration, services which originate in other agencies. Thus, when DHEW projected new 1972 social service regulations, subsequently discarded, center child care was estimated as "costing out" for operations alone at an average annual per-child expenditure of $1,782 for children aged 3–4½ and $1,438 for children aged 4½–6. The costs for family day care for these age groups, respectively, were $1,455 and $1,044.[62] However, by 1973 many actual operations were more expensive.

Slightly higher estimates were made earlier, in the late 1960s, in a study carried out by the Children's Bureau and the Day Care and Child Development Council of America. These 1967 estimates are based on the annual operating costs per child of different models and levels of care. While the specific costs are made obsolete by inflation, the ratios may hold interest. For day care centers (for children mostly aged 3–5) the maintenance of minimum standards cost $1,245, acceptable care cost $1,862, and desirable care cost $2,320. For family day care (for children mostly under 3), the costs were $1,423 (minimum), $2,032 (acceptable), and $2,373 (desirable). For before- and after-school and summer care (for children over 6), costs were $310 (minimum), $653 (acceptable), and $653 (desirable). It should, of course, be noted that these center and family day care totals are based on full-time care (10–12 hours a week, 52 weeks a year). They cover cost of rent or the equivalent and do not include capital or "start up" costs. Care provided on a less than full-day, full-year basis would be proportionally less. The range in costs is almost directly attributable to changes in the staff-child ratio, as staff costs make up approximately 70–80 percent of the cost of running any child care program.

In 1970 Abt Associates reported to the Office of Economic Opportunity that in quality child care centers the annual cost per child would vary as follows, depending upon the size of the facility: with an average daily attendance of 25, annual per-child cost would be $2,349; for 50 children, $2,223; and for 75 children, $2,189. Great geographic variations are reported, reflecting salary differences, costs of space, and the levels of staffings that are locally enforced.

A 1970 Inner City Fund study for OCD priced new proposed higher standards, especially the setting of more favorable staff-child ratios. Under these estimates, again obsolete because of inflation, but interesting for the ratios, "medium level" costs for center care would have been $2,868 for infants, $2,551 for toddlers, $1,811 for preschoolers, and $1,134 per child at after-school centers. Space requirements, enrollment rates, the types of meals and snacks served, and the overall regional price levels create considerable variations in cost estimates.[63] The same source priced the mean cost of family home care for a full day for an infant (0–18 months) at $2,625 and for a toddler (19–35 months) at $2,122, not allowing for any overhead or capital costs.[64] Parents now pay much less and get less, it is believed.

Clearly, while family day care is cheaper than center care if relatively low-quality, it becomes as expensive or more expensive when there are central services, supervision and consultation, careful screening, and adequate salaries.

Another way to get at costs is to examine actual expenditures. Thus, in 1974 average annual costs per child of care provided under the AFDC social service program and including both federal and state outlays was $1,177 (a special 1973 analysis showed a range of between $240 and $3,000). For 1973, national average per-child federal Head Start costs were $1,041, ranging from $69 to $2,222. Parents were apparently paying $1,000 per year in centers and $700–1,100 in homes in 1973, when not eligible for free or subsidized service. Of course, different services were delivered for the different sums, for different daily and annual periods,[65] but there are no qualitative assessments in which costs are clearly tied to effects.

We have not attempted similar estimates of private nursery or public kindergarten costs. The former are not widely reported, even though specific surveys suggest that they are not above public costs in many cases. The latter are difficult to disaggregate from elementary school averages generally.

Even before the late 1974 price increases there were high-cost areas reporting annual day care center costs in the $3,500–$5,000 per year category. Programs visited in 1973 in a middle-sized northeastern city charged $35–$45 weekly (see below) and were pressed financially. In New York City, a high-salary, high-cost area, Keyserling reported weekly per-capita budget costs, assuming capacity attendance as follows, noting that costs are not correlated with quality. (In general, older centers ranked highest in quality, and interim centers lowest.) Her findings are summarized in Table 2-6.

Table 2-6. Average Weekly Per Capita Child Care Budgeted Costs, on a Capacity Basis, According to Impressions of Care and Type of Center

	Per capita cost ($)			
Type of center	Excellent care	Good care	Fair care	Poor care
Older	71.29	71.15	77.77	
New	70.70	73.39	76.42	84.58
Interim		76.29	83.39	83.87

Source: Mary Dublin Keyserling, *New York City Child Care Programs: Challenges Ahead* (New York: The Day Care Council of New York, 1974). The figures do not include part-day and infant care centers, central overhead costs, services provided by other city agencies, funds raised by parents of boards or supplied by foundations, or capital and start-up costs.

There are no recent "cost to consumer" surveys in this field. The Spindler and Low 1965 estimates, published in 1968, are clearly obsolete.[66] Working-class parents employing proprietary centers or unlicensed family day care are spending far less than the price of quality center care which is regulated, licensed—and bureaucratized. This is also apparently the case even for most parents utilizing private nursery schools. New fee scales are being issued for public day care in the various states in connection with new regulations for services under Title XX of the Social Security Act. Low-income people will enjoy some measure of public subsidy, while those at the poverty or public-assistance level will receive completely or almost completely subsidized care. Kindergarten and preprimary care remains universal and free.

In the debate about day care to permit (or compel?) AFDC mothers to work, the following comparative items are of interest, the data having been chosen in relation to cost estimates already cited. AFDC average monthly payment, in mid-1973, per recipient was $53.98 nationally, $14.48 in Mississippi, $81.32 in New York, $65.73 in California, $21.36 in Alabama, and $62.46 in North Dakota. In 1972 women earned the following average (median) annual salaries: professional, technical, etc., $5,903; clerical etc., $6,054; sales, $4,445; operative, $5,004; domestic, $2,295; service, $4,483. The median salary for women in 1973 was $117 per week. In May 1973 female heads of household averaged $124 weekly and the average rose to $134 in May 1974. Wives of heads averaged $117 and $126 in 1973 and 1974 respectively. Household workers averaged $39 in 1973 and $50 in 1974.

Child care is more expensive than child support at the AFDC level for mothers who remain at home to care for their children. It has been shown to be a poor investment from the point of view of societal economic costs, at least, as a way to get unskilled and poorly educated women into the labor market.[67] One must make a quite different argument about societal benefits or value to the child in order to justify the budget for large-scale, high-quality provision.

Research and Evaluation

Increased congressional and White House interest in evaluation and growing concern in the social and behavioral sciences with policy in recent decades have produced relatively large research budgets, large numbers of individual studies, several major and nationally discussed evaluations, several comprehensive research reviews—and a recent recognition that there is a long road to be traveled from appropriations in Congress to firmly grounded policy and programing conclusions.

Theoretical and research literature is plentiful. A recent publication on day care, for example, lists some eight hundred items. In 1970, the Interagency Panel on Early Childhood Research and Development was established to coordinate research efforts on the federal level. This panel has published annual reports describing research plans and programs of the various agencies, describing primary foci of programs, and making recommendations regarding priority needs in research. The panel reported[68] that in fiscal year

1974 there were 2,307 early childhood research programs sponsored by seventeen federal agencies. Approximately $239.1 million was expended. Some 53.7 percent of the projects and 72.3 percent of the funding were for studies and demonstrations classifiable under "education." OCD funded 40 percent of the projects and spent 3.4 percent of the total expended ($8.1 million). An analysis of several years of reports from the Interagency Panel shows that education, cognitive development, and overall effects of early childhood programs rank very high as research priorities, but recent years have seen much growth in the research investment focused on the child more broadly and on the family. Summarizing 1974, Hertz and Harrell state:

> An examination of the next largest category of research [after education] —growth and development—shows that physical development, cognitive development and socioemotional development are included in the general focus of about the same percentage of studies (22.3%, 22.8%, and 22.2% respectively). As a primary focus, however, physical development is included in about three times as many studies, and cognitive development about twice as many studies, as is socioemotional development.[69]

The various federal funding mechanisms generate considerable service reporting as required for reimbursement. Little of it, however, provides feedback of great help for planning and evaluation purposes. We have already seen the extent to which definitional, jurisdiction, and administrative differences and the lack of overall coordinative sanction result in a paucity of data that can be aggregated and used for such purposes.

The more formal research push, especially out of Head Start, has been for what federal personnel have called "summative" evaluations: large-scale estimates by such outside contract groups as the Westinghouse Corporation to determine whether programs achieve their primary objectives. Lesser energy has gone into the generally more persistent "formative" evaluations, usually from "within" the field or agency. These latter evaluations may assess input, process, or small-project effects.

To some observers, the summative evaluation process seemed to distort Head Start. Called upon to measure results and to do so rapidly, the researchers used available tools. Of all the components of "social competence," cognitive capacity, as measured by sustained gains in I.Q. scores, was most accessible. As a consequence, early evidence of cognitive gain was stressed by researchers and greeted enthusiastically by funders. These findings led to some tendency to redefine the program—or oversimplify it—as remedying cognitive deficits. Programmers gave great emphasis to this component. Then, later, came disillusionment: I.Q. gains tended to "wash out" when the children were several years into the "normal" school systems. Evidence of health-problem location and referral, nutritional improvement, social service attention, social and emotional development was "soft," often unquantifiable, and unconvincing. For the past two years OCD has sought to undo the probable damage to the program by encouraging evaluations of broader scope and by more carefully interpreting child care objectives. In addition, the agency is stressing development of standard measures of socioemotional growth. Other current research thrusts feature clarification of parental child care preferences, an overview of actual care arrangements at present, and efforts to determine the impact on children of different staffing ratios and different levels of staff professionalism, both of which represent large cost elements in programing.

Whatever the substantive problems which remain and the research tasks not yet faced, few arenas of social policy can match the recent efforts made to assemble knowledge relevant to policy planning and to programing in child care.

By now, the basic research in child development, health care, early education, preschool projects, day care, family intervention, and similar fields, financed because of interest in child care or in the antipoverty program generally, has produced a library of results. While many of the projects are on "micro" scale, even the major expensive projects constitute a long list. For present purposes, therefore, we must limit the overview to research summaries and assessments, which, also, are by now voluminous and considerable. Even a brief review cannot ignore four major works: a review by Bronfenbrenner prepared for a committee of the National Research Council–National Academy of Sciences, a collection edited by Grotberg, a four-volume encyclopedic effort by Sheldon White and his colleagues at the Huron Institute, and a review by Fern and Clarke-Stewart under the sponsorship of the Foundation for Child Development. One specific project, a Head Start study by Zigler and Abelson, will also be mentioned.[70]

Two things become clear at once: first, the great gap between the rhetoric of the public debate and firm knowledge in this field; second, the limited solid data available about the diversity of programs and their differential impacts on the complexity of environmental circumstances, parent-child situations, and differentially held goals. Let us summarize, perhaps too briefly, thus risking some misreading, and interpret the results rigorously: We do not know that children are harmed in the various types of improvised child care settings and in the many kinds of informal arrangements which professionals deplore. This does not mean that there are no bad effects. On the other hand, despite the dedication of advocates and considerable positive anecdotal testimony, there is little firm evidence to support the claim that the preferred early childhood programs have long-range beneficial effects on child development unless built upon by follow-up efforts and reinforced in supportive work with families. The initially positive impact on cognitive development of certain early childhood programs, as measured by I.Q. scores and reported in a number of studies, appears to level off after a few years if nothing else happens. Usually, nothing else does. Follow-through programs seem to consolidate gains. Developmental day care programs have good records in health referral, case-finding, nutrition, parent education—on the face of it—but there is little research as yet to establish long-term effects. But all of this is said tentatively in the knowledge that most of the reported studies are limited or somewhat flawed. No results have been followed long enough. Researchers have over-stressed cognitive gains, given the limited educational inputs and the more comprehensive goals. On the other hand, there has been little emphasis in the past on standardizing measures of socioemotional development and increased social competence. (These latter matters are now an OCD/CB research priority.)

Some elaboration may be helpful.

In an unpublished preliminary paper reviewing the implications of child development research for public policy, Bronfenbrenner suggests that there are two principles which can be derived from recent research:

> The psychological development of the child is enhanced through his involvement in progressively more complex, enduring patterns of reciprocal contingent interaction with persons with whom he has established a mutual and enduring emotional attachment. . . . The extent to which such a reciprocal system can be developed and maintained depends on the degree to which other encompassing and accompanying social structures provide the place, time, example, and reinforcement to the system and its participants.[71]

Bronfenbrenner suggests that child development programs will have little effect unless they influence not only the child but also the significant persons and institutions in his environment. Therefore, child care programs should be designed to enhance the development of families, to maximize the integrity of the communities in which families live, and to encourage social integration and cohesion. His interests extend to home–child–workplace relationships, child care in relation to other social institutions, and similar issues.

Perhaps the most complete analysis of research findings in the child development field was carried out by Sheldon White and his associates at the Huron Institute for the Office of the Assistant Secretary for Planning and Evaluation, DHEW. Their four-volume report, entitled *Federal Programs for Young Children: Review and Recommendations*, summarizes existing data about disadvantaged children, from birth to nine years old, and analyzes the results of evaluation studies of federal programs designed to assist this group of children. The project was undertaken in order to make recommendations for federal program planning.

Like Bronfenbrenner, this study concludes that there is no single variable that predicts adult characteristics and that manipulation of any one variable—for instance, cognitive capacity—is likely to have minimal effects. It seems clear that child development is a function of many interacting variables and must be examined as such. Furthermore, to be successful, efforts to help the child may have to be directed toward social institutions or to the interface between the child and his environment rather than to the child himself.[72] The study reviews evaluation studies related to five types of intervention on behalf of disadvantaged children: early education, preschool, early day care, family intervention, and health care. Summarized briefly, their conclusions are as follows:

Early Elementary Education Projects. "The characteristics of compensatory education projects in the early primary grades which are common to those projects which produce significant achievement gains are: (1) clearly stated academic objectives; (2) small group individualized instruction; (3) parent involvement; (4) teacher training in the methods of the project, together with careful planning; (5) directly relevant and intensive instruction; and possibly (6) high expectations and a positive atmosphere."[73]

Preschool Projects. "There is an immediate increase in I.Q. scores for children in most preschool projects. . . . The effects of most preschool projects on I.Q. scores do not persist beyond the second or third grade. . . . Children in preschools which focus on specific academic skills show an immediate improvement in performance on achievement tests. In some cases the achievement gains persist longer than the I.Q. increases, but typically they decline in a manner parallel to that of I.Q. scores. . . . The amount of improvement varies with the explicitness of objectives, the soundness of instructional methods, the time invested in attaining the objectives, and the similarity between the instruction and the performance required by the tests. . . . Data on non-cognitive effects of preschools are extremely limited and are typically based on instruments of unassessed reliability and validity. Some data do suggest an increase in desirable social behavior."[74] In the latter regard Abelson, Zigler and DeBlasi show gains if day care is reinforced with a Follow Through program. While the economically disadvantaged children studied do not then attain the levels of the more advantaged, they sustain gains by grade 3 in I.Q., achievement, and sociomotivational measures as compared with non–Follow Through children.[75]

Day Care Projects. The review was limited to effects on children aged 0–3. "The most reasonable conclusion about existing data for early day care would seem to be that the data are limited, preliminary, and inconclusive. . . . No reports of measurable harm were found and only a few highly specialized and costly models were reported to have produced measurable effects. It appears that day care programs implemented within the limits of the federal and state regulations appear to be neutral in their effect on human development insofar as their effects can be evaluated by existing techniques."[76]

Family Intervention Projects. The review examined effects of four types of family intervention projects: parent education, parent training, family social casework, and parent therapy. Since the measures of benefit were all somewhat limited, it is difficult to generalize from the findings reported. However, it appears that parent training for cognitive stimulation of their children does produce some gain in I.Q. or achievement test scores and that these gains remain for at least a year. Family casework seems most effective when concentrated on instrumental areas of family functioning such as child rearing and health care and when supplemented by adequate income support and an adequate level of social services in the community. Parent education appears to have more limited value but might provide some benefit for certain groups of mothers if accompanied by day care and babysitting services. Parent therapy in the psychoanalytic tradition has produced no measurable results and is generally offered to middle-class rather than disadvantaged families. Behavior modification appears to be a more promising approach.[77]

Health Care Programs. Health care programs have not been monitored or evaluated sufficiently to permit generalization. Therefore, description of the effects of federal child health programs is conjectural and inferential. There is spotty coverage and poor integration of services in the programs which do exist; yet certain programs, such as early diagnosis and treatment of handicaps and chronic conditions would seem to have potentially great impact if expanded and targeted appropriately.[78]

The major recommendation of the report is that future emphasis should be placed on individualizing services and working with the family rather than around it. More specifically, the White report suggests preschool programs such as Head Start should be diversified to include a more comprehensive range of child development services, including health screening and programs for children with special needs; also, the focus should be broadened to include home-based and parent training programs. All these proposals are consistent with current OCD program thrusts for Head Start. In regard to day care programs, the report suggests that there is need to develop systems of day care services, including center care, in-home care, family home care, and homemaker service. The preoccupation with group care as the ideal model is not supported. (Here, too, OCD is in agreement and has already made the necessary moves.) In addition, it is recommended that programs for early educational and health screening be developed and that appropriate services be made available to deal with the problems identified. Finally, it is suggested that efforts be made to develop housing designs which would promote informal child care arrangements among neighbors.[79]

Policy derivations from recent major reviews would appear to be mutually consistent. Effort should be made to develop a broad range of child care programs, including in-home, family home care, and center-based care. Since there is no evidence that one model of care is more beneficial than another for all children and under all circumstances, parental preference should be the determining factor in selecting a particular model of care. Programs intended to enhance child development should be family-focused and comprehensive in nature (health, nutrition, social service, mental health, parent participation); efforts directed at enhancing parent-child interaction are likely to be more effective than those which focus on the child alone. Child care programs should be linked with all aspects of the community, and research efforts should be expanded to consider the total range of informal and formal child care arrangements which develop spontaneously in neighborhoods and their possible implications for child development. Parent care per se is so valuable that social policies which offer a mother (or, increasingly, a father) a financially viable "stay at home" option, which allows her to "borrow" or "save up" leave and vacation time from work so as to have extended periods with her infants and young children (if she wishes), and which make part-time work satisfying and possible, may be as important to child development as program models and organized child care styles.

Programs in Action

The picture will become clearer if we look at a representative middle-sized city in the northeastern United States. In 1974, nobody would have cited it as a model for child care programs. Nor was it a failing city. An overview of the day care situation in this community during that year will therefore help to illustrate what has already been presented. We will follow the illustration with brief looks at two other programs.

Services, Programs, and Benefits

Site of a leading university and of major medical, psychiatric, and retardation training and research, our illustrative city has the advantage of above-average professional stimulation and leadership. Inhabited by a well-educated and informed population and political leadership, it does not miss grant-in-aid or other funding opportunities at the national or state levels. Nonetheless its child care programs are not extraordinary. Several individual programs or aspects of programs may be above average, but the effort as a whole serves to characterize the general national effort.

We meet here at once the split between education and social services. Discussions of day care usually do not include a large prekindergarten program under the Department of Education unless special effort is made to define it as relevant. State Department of Social Service "day care center" regulations include as day care those facilities known as well by such other names as "day nursery, nursery school, child play school, child development center, early childhood center and the like" if the facility serves seven or more children and is not a "kindergarten or nursery school operated by a school or academy" and chartered by the State Education Department or operated by a local education authority as an integral part of its school system. (Also excluded from the day care characterization are services for the "mentally disabled," certified by the relevant state department.)

In short, the day care–education distinction is administrative, not programmatic. The relevant directory from the Community Information Service covers group day care centers, nursery schools, prekindergarten programs, and family day care homes. The relationship of all these services to one another as part of a child care system which should be presented as such is acknowledged, generally, despite the dual system of state and local administration.

The major local child care services include sixteen group day care centers, thirty-seven nursery schools, three Head Start programs (one all day and two part day), two special nursery school facilities for retarded children, three special university day care facilities, about two hundred family day care homes, and one prekindergarten program. Coverage is better understood from the following: group day care centers serve 600 children; Head Start serves 45 children all day and 135 children part day; the Board of Education prekindergarten program serves 50 children all day and 450 children part day; family day care serves 600–800 children (estimates as of June 1974). There are no data on nursery schools. The total child population (1970) under 5 is 16,463.

The day care centers (apart from the two specialized university demonstration research projects, which are nationally known) are all voluntarily run and funded primarily through social services funding (Title IV-A, Social Security Act). Of these centers, serving some six hundred children, three are associated with the Community Child and Family Service (a voluntary nonsectarian agency), two are affiliated with the Salvation Army, and two with Catholic Charities. The remainder are independent; the main sponsors of these are Protestant churches. Many of the centers are housed in churches.

One of the centers serves the staff of the medical center, one serves the university staff, and one—under Catholic Charities—reserves space for children of employees of the health department.

There are little systematic data about the private nursery schools and the children they serve, all but six of which are half-day. Licensing is by the State Education Department and costs are met by parental fees. The population is assumed to be middle-class and better-paid working class.

The school district's prekindergarten program is designed for three- and four-year-old children from culturally deprived backgrounds, under the terms of state educational legislation and Title I of the Elementary and Secondary Education Act.

Eligibility and Coverage

Although there was a period early in the 1970s when federal funding under Title IV-A was "open ended" and day care served many low-income working families with income above poverty or public-assistance levels, subsequent efforts to impose tighter means tests, a social service ceiling which slowed expansion, the expectation of more stringent federal limitations, all led to tougher state fee scales and had the effect of making the day care facilities, group and family, more than ever a program for very poor families (public assistance or very low wage). The nursery schools serve the middle-class population. The eligible working poor not on welfare probably are served by a vast "grey market" of unlicensed, unregulated family day care and private arrangements—where relatives and friends do not meet the need. To some extent they still enjoy partial public day care subsidy.

The registrations listed above total up to some two thousand children in all-day or part-day care. If the private nurseries double this, city coverage is not very far from national norms.

There is no accurate way to connect these totals to "need" until there is some choice among the diverse concepts of the role of day care. We noted, however, at the time of our review, that significant numbers of the day care centers had unused space. They all reported parents who wanted care but who were ineligible because they were above the public-assistance-pegged eligibility levels (that is, were not in poverty or close to it) yet could not themselves pay the weekly fees ranging from $35 to $45 per child per week as specified by the public welfare authorities and paid by them for eligible users. Regulations effective in October 1975 could ease the situation.

A few centers had waiting lists. Two centers which could be defined as traditional in terms of current day care "thinking" were in demand. Several innovative programs were significantly underutilized yet could not fill up because of fee rules. A few centers ignored the rules and charged parents who were above the specified income levels a more modest fee than the weekly costs specified by authorities. Most were in constant financial crisis because of the problem; fees were computed on the assumption of capacity enrollment. Reimbursement always followed billing for service already rendered. There were no guarantees. Centers ran "hand to mouth" and incentives for expansion were few. Staff turnover was inevitably high.

The prekindergarten program, under federal rules, serves a population in poverty but it develops its own yardstick and tends to supplement income criteria with factors relating to home deprivation and problems. This is a more stable program since staff are public employees, the program is permanent, and salaries are part of the education budget. Administrative personnel estimate (but cannot document) that they meet 20 percent of need.

We noted that group day care and family day care, as all-day programs (usually 7:30 A.M. to 5:30 P.M.), can and do meet the needs of families where mothers work. The nursery school, prekindergarten, and half-day Head Start hours are not attuned to the needs of most working mothers, except for those in part-time employment or with unusual schedules. Two of the Head Start centers are open all day. There is no coverage in public group care for most working mothers on night or late-night shifts for full seven-to-eight hour days.

There is very little coverage here for school-age children by afterschool programs of any kind. A small number of such children are served in family day care. A community task force has developed proposals and budgets and one of the agencies is prepared to launch a program, but the lack of start-up funds and a reimbursement guarantee is an obstacle. Here, too, billing must follow the fact of service unless the state welfare department offers funding as a "demonstration."

Costs

For the most part, at the time of our visit, the all-day programs were being reimbursed at $45 a week by the county department (this would be $2,340 per child for a 52-week year), leaving out all central administrative, coordination, training, and start-up costs. Some centers were at a $35 level. Part-day programs charged less and were less costly. However, prekindergarten programs, which had higher salaries and more supplementary specialist staffing, were budgeted at $450,000 for three hundred children. This is not inexpensive for a program which does not offer all-day, all-year coverage.

For a six-hour day, family day care rates were about one half the center rates ($22.50 per week). After-school family day care, in turn, charged half this.

The centers reimbursed $35–$45 were often spending $45–$60 per week and trying to raise money from private philanthropic sources. Funding is often in crisis. Most of the proprietary nursery schools pay lower salaries; some meet lower physical standards. (They are not subject to the Department of Social Services regulations.) Thus, the most popular charged $30–$32 weekly.

Objectives

From what we have already stated, it is clear that several objectives prevail. For most of the parents, center leaders, and public authorities, family day care and the day care centers serve the needs of working mothers, mothers seeking work, or mothers being trained or encouraged to take training under several types of manpower and public-assistance legislation. The county social services intake personnel, responsible for certification of eligibility, operate under criteria built around financial need. "Case" reasons include abuse-neglect and related family problems, situations in which day care is part of a family-centered treatment or service plan (and in which child welfare funding is also possible).

Thus the public day care does not build its rationale on increasing parental options or child development. The nursery schools, by contrast, reflect the interest of middle-class parents in enriched experiences for their children and more flexible parental routines. Head Start is focused on the child—enriching the daily experiences of children whose home environments are deprived—and on utilizing the child's participation as leverage for engaging the parents in experiences which will enrich their lives (and thus the child's environment). Home Start reflects this latter perspective in complete form: the parent is the medium for enriching the child's development.

Access

The city has no widely accepted and publicized access point. Most parents seeking center day care service go to centers and are referred to "intake," at the county welfare department, to determine eligibility for public payment. Welfare department personnel encourage parents who need the service to seek it out and arrange appointments with the specialized personnel who review eligibility. Similar procedures are followed for family day care. Welfare and employment personnel make referrals in instances where the service need grows out of welfare eligibility requirements or is related to a work or training referral.

Parents who wish to use nursery schools develop their own contacts and information. They have access to the widely distributed directory from the Community Information Service, as do the parents eligible for free service.

Parents may apply for prekindergarten admission for their children in the facilities of the school system. However, some effort is also made to "reach out" to those unable themselves to initiate application for their children. Program personnel employ public-assistance and free-school-meal eligibility lists to identify neighborhoods with a high percentage of potential enrollees, and home visits are made by the teachers or aides in whose groups the recruits would be placed. There is a similar type of outreach in connection with part-day Head Start and with Home Start, but there are many self-referrals in Head Start, too.

It is not known how many children in need of service are deprived of it because parents do not know about or cannot establish their right to it; there is some evidence of deprivation because family day care homes are not located in the areas in which there are children in need and because transportation is poor to such homes and to centers. (Major efforts have been made to improve bus service generally; the City-wide Child Care Council has developed special transportation projects for the day care group.) The group for whom access is a large problem is the working poor, those above the public welfare eligibility level under federal and state regulations and unable to pay to the centers fees equal to what the centers are reimbursed for public charge cases. (This situation could be relieved, depending upon the state's response to Title XX.) There is also some evidence that the part-day prekindergarten programs in the public schools could expand and be well utilized if funds were available. There is no estimate of the need for and potential take-up of school-based prekindergarten programs for 3 and 4 year olds whose parents are not in the poverty or special-need categories.

Coverage in group programs is largely for 3–5 year olds. It is not known whether the licensed and the unregulated family day care meets the need for service for those under three. Of the centers, only one, sponsored by Catholic Charities, serves children 2 years old. Given the experience elsewhere, one might assume shortages in this category, but there is professional controversy as to whether such programs are wise policy.

Administration and Coordination

The main administrative agencies are the county welfare department and the city school district. The former refers situations of special need, certifies and recertifies client eligibility, and processes agency applications for licensing–certification or project grants under the several titles of the Social Security Act or special state legislation. (This city was one of the few jurisdictions in its state successfully to negotiate funds for a new day care center building under state legislation.) The school district recruits and processes applications for and actually administers the prekindergarten programs. Its state counterpart administers the relevant licensing for private nursery schools.

When public child care first expanded in the late 1960s, the city developed two coordination groups for child care, one in its Model Cities (poverty) area and one elsewhere. By 1974, these activities had been consolidated in a City-wide Child Care Council, which was essentially the lead agency in the Model Cities–Poverty area but which broadened its scope in cooperation with the United Way and sought to become the planning, central services, and coordination agency for day care for the entire county.

The City-wide Child Care Council began with the task of upgrading inner-city day care, focusing first on inadequate physical facilities and, then, concentrating on an ambitious and impressive training effort. Its overall mission covers funding, training, development of physical facilities, new program initiatives and parent involvement. As a result of its work with the university, courses have been made available and incentives created to upgrade staff. The university's Community Education Division has helped train staff working with children who have special needs. The Council committees have developed and submitted a series of broad-ranging proposals, some of them subsequently funded and implemented, some pending and some rejected, related to transportation for day care, after-school programs, a "drop in" day care center, funding arrangements. The Council successfully organizes day care facilities for social action and for presentations at appropriate public hearings from time to time.

The need for a broader coordination mandate has been widely acknowledged in the city. Central services and training resources might upgrade programs and facilitate economies of scale. Furthermore, since funding remains categorical, some planning and meshing is essential. Moreover, it has been asked, since the Council and Head Start emphasis on parent participation is consistent with the themes of the White House Conference on Children, federal day care standards, and the findings of child development research, why not organize for such participation in county planning? Late in 1973 the Council proposed creation of a county-wide structure, much like a 4-C organization. The plan received strong backing from its constituency of thirty-six centers serving some 1,200 children. Shortly thereafter a subcommittee of the county legislature commissioned a consultant report which developed similar proposals. An assembly of agencies would constitute a governing council; operating control would be assigned a board of one-third service consumers, one-third staff, and one-third community groups. The new organization has not yet taken complete shape, but it is under serious and favorable consideration, apparently blocked by a fight for control. Proprietary groups, too, will be included on a voluntary basis if the problems are overcome. Central services, fund "decategorization," program initiatives, and some planning will be even more possible if the new organization actually is implemented as discussed.

The Programs

The basic official philosophy in this city's day care is "open classroom" in the modern, progressive educational–child development sense, but the group programs actually carried out ranged from traditional, formal, and educational to unorthodox, experimental, expressive. The range is found among all the auspices: nursery schools, prekindergarten, center day care in the Model Cities area, other center day care, experimental programs. Family day care is largely good physical care; but it, too, shows range. There are university experimental research programs, special programs for a few categories among the handicapped, and a better-than-ordinary capacity to integrate handicapped children into "regular" programs. Age grouping is common, but there are also undifferentiated groups (mixed, 3–5). It is usual for groups to have "home rooms," but some centers differentiate rooms by objective and type of play: "large muscle" exercise, arts and crafts, quiet reading, withdrawal for a tired or ill child, etc. Outdoor play space is required and programs adhere to state regulations for safety, sanitation, space per child, staff qualifications, and ratios. Center direction and group leadership are generally assigned personnel trained in the educational speciality known as "early child development." The aides, especially in Head Start, have varied backgrounds. Many lack formal education beyond elementary school but are regarded as having attractive personal qualities plus the advantages of being from backgrounds familiar to the children. Others have college degrees—undergraduate, graduate, and professional.

Most of the day care centers and most Head Start units have been connected with a public Family Health Center, launched under the antipoverty effort some years ago to serve deprived people. But funding arrangements are such that the Center cannot offer much service to day care units as such (even though there is some training, screening, emergency work, consultation). The children and the parents remain financially eligible for the Center and use it as individuals. This illustrates one of many linkage lapses in the public social sector.

Most of the centers do their own cooking. Some share food services among themselves. Plans for broader cooperation and economy are under consideration. Some of the centers have nutritionists. Most have a person with knowledge of nutrition. A few have social work personnel in direct service roles with parents and children.

Prekindergarten. Inspired by Head Start and focused entirely on 3–4 year olds in deprived areas, the prekindergarten program under the school system is largely conducted in churches or schools with declining enrollment. "Classes" are assigned eighteen children but daily average attendance is fourteen or fifteen. Each class has one assigned teacher and one paraprofessional, so the adult to child ratio is 1:7. The program also has a group of specialist consultants as well: a social worker, a parent education coordinator, a psychologist, a speech pathologist, a nurse, a part-time pediatrican. Children are examined physically and defects followed up.

Each of the centers holds a weekly parent meeting at which subjects range from family planning to child development. Many parents seem to need basic socializing experiences. The social worker, who leads some of the discussions, offers the parents a "brokerage" service vis-à-vis social services generally, especially the public welfare department. Parents serve as volunteers, attend parent meetings, and elect advisory council representatives (two per center). Some parents are given small salaries for part-time aide work in centers and receive special training.

The program has child development–educational goals for the children and tries to strengthen the parents in their roles. So important is the work with families that a number of the centers serve children only four days to free teacher and aide time for home visits and other work with parents—and for "outreach" recruitment. For this reason and because of the hours, 8:30 A.M. to 3:30 P.M., school vacations, and other curtailment, these centers cannot substitute for day care, for working mothers. They parallel Head Start in many ways but are based in the educational system.

Change. The local antipoverty unit (CHANGE) is the administrative agency for the local Head Start programs, which include a Home Start program for 100 children in two rural areas, part-day Head Start for 135 children in three centers, and the all-day program for 45. All-day Head Start is funded by Title IV-A. The other programs receive their funds through the Office of Child Development, a continuation of the original OEO funding.

About a year before our visit, a shift to a largely part-day from full-day Head Start activity had been made following a consumer survey of preferences and needs. The survey also supported a shift for most of the program to a nine-month year and suggested the need for the rural program.

All but 10 percent of those served are below the poverty line; the others are in the very low income category just above the line. Of the children included, 15 percent are handicapped. Large numbers are from single-parent families. While the concentration is upon children 3–5, all younger ages are included in the Home Start effort.

The program formulates as its goal enhancing the capacity of parents to perform their parental roles more adequately. This is clearly the central objective. Whether through Head Start or Home Start, parents are encouraged to do more with and for their children and to draw increasingly upon available community resources and services. Health, social work, nutrition, and educational components are included in the program per se, and (with an eye to one-parent families) certain "socializing" activities as well.

For the Home Start program there are two administrators and six full-time and three part-time staff members. Their training is in education or social work, except for local personnel with "community" experience. A full caseload is thirteen children (6–10 families). Each family is visited at least once a week—for "education" and "linkage" to community resources.

Each of the centers employs four professionals (again, from education or social work) plus aides. Part-day centers are open three days a week; all-day centers are open four days. Again, these are family caseloads and there is a heavy emphasis on the visiting and liaison functions.

One assumes that so large a staffing investment in family-related activity is justified only as an effort to assure "take off" to the most deprived—and on the basis of experience that this is required. While there is anecdotal "evidence," there is no firm research validation as yet. According to staff much of the time goes into getting to know the mother and meeting her needs for emotional support and for resources available through other institutions.

There is interest, which has not gone beyond discussion, in a family day care and center care "mix" for families and children.

Family Day Care Home. Geographic matching is important in family day care. There is a shortage in the central city. Much of the central city housing will not meet licensing criteria. Payment rates are too low to attract most AFDC mothers, the major potential work force.

Most of the family day care homes serve infants or school-age children before and after school. Turnover is high, usually because of frequent shifts in jobs and circumstances of the mothers using the homes. A caseworker with a "load" of thirty homes told us that complaints come far more often from the day care mothers about the childrens' parents than they do from the mothers about the care arrangements. The voluntary agency sponsoring the program was concentrating on more training for the day care mothers, nonetheless.

A visit was made to an "outstanding" home. It is located in a working-class neighborhood, on a tree-lined street, one of a group of two-family houses. The family day care mother, an AFDC recipient, has three children of her own, aged 9 to 12. She is an excellent budgeter and home manager. She was caring for two siblings, aged 16 months and 28 months, whose mother, a bookkeeper at a nearby hotel, dropped them off at 6:45 A.M. and picked them up at 3:30 P.M. The family day care mother said that because they arrive so early she often lets them take a nap immediately. When they wake from the nap she gives them some breakfast and then they are left to do pretty much what they want to. She said that they often "sort of follow" her through her daily activities, playing quietly with each other. If they seem to be bored she will read them a story or engage them in playing with some toy. She feeds them a full hot meal at noontime, after which they take another nap. After their nap they again play freely in the house until their mother picks them up to go home. She found the children "amazingly easy to care for" and wished only that she could have more children.

We were struck by the children's passivity and wondered whether this home failed to offer adequate stimulation—or whether these were simply relatively passive and dull children. We got the impression that the family day care mother treated the children kindly and attended to their needs; however, there was generally a lack of involvement and enthusiasm in the whole relationship between the woman and the children. Certainly they were not behaving normally for their ages.

There was nothing really "wrong" with this home or with the arrangements. The children were in safe care and the house was well able to provide for their physical needs; they were probably receiving as good, if not better, care than many children receive in their own homes. However, unlike family day care in some places, the home did not offer a positive opportunity for child development. There was not the training, consultant backing, or equipment favored by some family day care advocates.* If anything, one could apply here the argument of center care proponents about the advantages of having several staff members present and exposing the children to group stimulation. Nonetheless, to the extent that feedback data are available, the mother-consumers are satisfied and compare family day care very favorably with babysitting.

A Day Care Center. The Shady Hill Day Care Center is located in the administration building of a downtown church, a rather imposing stone structure at a major intersection in the business district. The day care center occupies the second floor and uses the kitchen and dining room facilities, as well as the gymnasium in the basement, for some of its activities. Because of the small size of the city the center is within a fifteen-minute drive from the suburbs and a short walk from the major housing area for low-income families. It is, in short, very accessible.

At the time of our visit, the center served thirty children aged 3–5. So as to increase enrollment, the license had just been changed to cover 2 year olds. The children were primarily black from lower-income families, almost all living in subsidized housing; 75–90 percent came from one-parent families.

The center was five years old, an independent, private, nonprofit organization. The minister of the church had seen the need for day care facilities and recognized that public funding had become avail-

*See page 122.

able. He also saw sponsorship as a way of making the church more visible in the community. Although the church does provide back-up facilities and permits the center some freedom of movement and extra space that would not be available in a separate building, the church provides no direct funding. Shady Hill has an independent board of directors, with decision-making power, composed of seven members, two of whom are parents of children in the center and two of whom are representatives from the church.

The center's professional staff of seven includes the director, four full-time teachers, and two volunteer teachers who work for the church. In addition there are two aides who assist in the afternoon, a Neighborhood Youth Corps student who works in the afternoon, a cook, and a housekeeper. The staff are all relatively young and informal, including the director, a small woman who looks like a college student. However, she holds a Master's degree in Early Childhood Education, spoke very knowledgeably about the field, and had a clear sense about the way in which she wants this day care center to function. There are three male staff members and three blacks. The majority are white women.

The director described the primary objectives of the center as providing an opportunity for women to work or to fulfill their own interests and as offering a positive, open environment for the children. Since many of the children are what would be generally termed "culturally disadvantaged," she hoped that the experiences in the center might eliminate some later problems in school. However, the primary concern is to strengthen the family unit by enhancing parent-child interaction and promoting the socioemotional development of the children. The staff are concerned about language and educational skills, but emphasize cognitive development far less than socialization.

There seemed to be a happy, relaxed atmosphere in the center. Efforts are made to promote easy staff and child interaction as well as parent-child and parent-staff interaction. The orientation given to the parents is considered very important. Staff want to encourage an ongoing relationship with the center. Because of their location in the downtown area they frequently are able to invite the mothers to have lunch in the center with their children and with staff. In addition, the director often talks to mothers when they come in to pick up or drop off their children and attempts to relate to them and their children together.

Children are not assigned to groups by age. Shady Hill has a flexible arrangement whereby the children move around from one room to another, according to their interests, and participate in a graduated age group. In addition the teachers move around so that there is a good deal of interaction among various staff members and children.

There are three rooms for the children. One, which they call "the large-muscle room," has a jungle gym, mats, and plenty of space for physical activity and exercises. There is a large crafts room, which is used primarily for painting and other types of "messy" crafts. Then there is a third large room, one section of which is essentially a quiet room and the other section of which is another crafts room. In the quiet section there is a big couch, comfortable for sitting and reading, a science area in which there are some gerbils and science games children can become involved in, and a small playhouse. In the crafts section of the room there are two tables with drawing and coloring books and various types of small craft activities.

The staff are responsible for planning activities in the various rooms and assign themselves to the activities, "signing in" for them for specified periods of time. The children are free to move from one activity to another depending on their interests. None of the staff members have worked under the more traditional pattern in which children are assigned permanently to one room by age group, so that it was difficult for them to compare the effectiveness. This system requires close cooperation. Under the more common arrangement, which is much easier administratively, each teacher simply is responsible for her own room. However, staff thought this pattern gives the children much greater opportunity for different relationships and experiences and that it is certainly worth the extra trouble. It is "workable" only for small groups—in this instance a total of thirty-five. They doubted that 2 year olds could fit in.

Our impression was of a high level of interest since there are shifts and changes in the activities going on every day for the children. The very fact that the staff members move about and in a sense have to "attract" children to their areas means that they put more into the activities that they plan. They, too, experience stimulation and change.

The center opens at 7:30 A.M. and the children generally arrive sometime between 7:30 and 8:30. This time is left quite unscheduled: the children who arrive early generally stay in the one room. It is time for "visiting." The children entertain themselves and try out different toys and activities. At 8:30 the staff assign themselves to one of the various rooms and there is an hour of essentially planned activity. At 9:30 the children have the mid-morning snack. The period from 10:00 A.M. until 11:30 A.M. is used for large group activities. For example, two days a week the children go swimming. (All the children cannot go at once but every child swims at least two days a week.) The cook takes a group of children with her each day down to the kitchen and involves them in the planning of lunch. Other groups may go on small trips or have a planned game in the recreation room down in the basement, go outside to play in the park, watch a movie, and so on. At times this period is simply used for planned activities, too, but generally it is a time in which something special happens.

Lunch is served at 11:45 A.M. The staff have their lunch with the children in the dining room; it is eaten "family style" in that the children sit at tables for six or eight with a staff member and are served by the teacher. They are encouraged to enjoy the meal, to carry on conversation, and to participate as though they were in a home setting. Following lunch, they nap from 1:30 P.M. to 3:00 P.M. One of the staff members remains on duty, while the rest use the time to prepare their activities for the following day. From 3:00 to 5:30, the program is much the same as in the morning, but somewhat less structured. At about 4:30 P.M. the children begin leaving, and the center closes at 5:30.

On a late afternoon visit we found a rather calm, easy atmosphere in the center. The children did not seem as tired as one would have expected. A number were playing in the front room, making clay models with teachers at two small crafts tables, and a group of about four or five boys were with a male teacher in the science area. They had gone into that area to play with something, but as we entered they seemed to be engaging in some roughhousing. There were a couple of children playing on the jungle gym and another small group was painting. As parents began to arrive to pick up children, there was easy exchange between staff and parents. Because some hearings were scheduled on new state regulations for day care the next day, the director asked several parents if they planned to attend the hearings, seeming to want to involve them in community activities. There were a number of announcements and posters up for various types of social action programs, as well as announcements for free health testing and educational opportunities available in the community.

The director said that the major problem in running the center was the relationship with the Department of Social Services. She said they had had trouble keeping the enrollment up since the tight new fee regulations announced a year before. The center was paid a reimbursement rate of $45 a week by public welfare authorities and is not permitted to charge any families not on public assistance less than this. Therefore they cannot fill their empty spaces with children whose parents might be able to pay $25 or $30 a week. The slots go empty if they do not have children for whom the county welfare department is paying the fee. In addition, problems are created for them because they are forced to collect the fees or portions of the fees from the parents. If a family does not pay a fee, the center is without the money. The only recourse is to drop the family—and this can be quite destructive.

Another Center. The ABC Center is located in the administration building of a suburban church, near a major highway at a meeting point between the city and the suburb. Consequently, the center draws from the families in the city, suburbs, and rural areas. Established in 1971, ABC is administered by the board of directors of the church as a department within the church. The center does not have a separate budget and the minister makes the major decisions although there is a board of directors or a board of elders for the church. Although this arrangement is rather cumbersome, it offers the center some financial backing.

The center building is located on a large open field and has a large, well-equipped playground outside. The indoor rooms are off one corridor in a low, modern structure, leading to the main administration building. A chair at the corridor end serves effectively as a symbolic barrier.

The center is licensed for fifty children from 18 months to 5 years. It also enrolls a few 6 year olds who have been in the program before. The average enrollment is forty-two, but this number goes down to the low thirties in the summer, when many parents are able to stay home from work. The center has approximately 50 percent of its children on a private basis, and the other 50 percent are paid for by the Department of Social Services. The weekly fee was $40. We visited this center because it was favorably described by several local day care leaders.

A number of the "private" children are drawn from the university community and there is a good socioeconomic and racial mix of children. Center hours are 7:30 A.M. to 5:30 P.M., but most of the children are present from 8:30 to 4:30. A child must come four days weekly. Most remain only one year.

In addition to the director, a young man in his late twenties holding an M.S. in Early Childhood Education, there are six full-time teachers, two teachers who come in on a substitute basis, one work-study student, a cook, and a volunteer family counselor whose child is enrolled. The effective staff to child ratio is 1:7 (given average absence rates) although the center enrolls on a 1:9 basis.

Salaries are low and staff turnover, like child turnover, is high. Most staff members remain only one year—yet experience demonstrates that a staff "team" cannot be created in less than nine months.

The ABC Center is not unlike Shady Hill in basic philosophy—but may have gone further with it. Each staff member is assigned to a modern room and to one group of children. There are four major rooms: a "large-muscle" room, two crafts rooms, one of which is reserved for the younger children, and a classroom in which science and various types of work projects are carried on. In addition the hall is used as an extra room, and one teacher is assigned as a "floater." The teacher responsible for a specific room makes the rules, sets up the room physically each day, starts the various projects, and gets whatever equipment is necessary. In addition each teacher is assigned to a small group of children. This means he is responsible for speaking for these children at staff meetings, noting any special needs or behavioral changes. In addition the teacher meets with his small group of children at 11:30 A.M. each day for a very brief group meeting in order to discuss whatever might be on the children's minds that day. However, the teachers are encouraged to rotate or swap assignments, so long as their own assignments are covered. Here, too, teachers have to "perform" and attract the children or else they will be sitting in rooms. They do seem to be encouraged to be creative and to respond to the children.

The primary stated objective of the center is to provide a structured environment in which children can be free to develop to their fullest potentials. The director said that he thinks day care centers should provide alternatives to public schools, a place where children can develop positive self-images and have broad socializing experiences. The center supplements family life and is a particular relief for one-parent families. Children with two parents are said to find the group experience broadening and enriching.

To illustrate the center's philosophy of "freedom within structure" we note that the mid-morning snacks are available on what they call an "invitational" basis. This means that the children are told when the snacks are ready; but since the center has a limited number of chairs, if the child does not go right away, he may have to wait to be served—as in a restaurant. Somewhat similarly, children are free to move from one room to another and from one activity to another. However, if a teacher is in the middle of an activity with a group of children, he may close the door, indicating that the children are not to come in until the group has completed what it has been working on, without disruption. Staff hope to encourage children to learn to make decisions and to take some responsibility for those that they make. They are free to choose but then they must live with the consequences.

Perhaps because it is not rooted in any community, or perhaps because the heavy university constituency is accustomed to turning things over to professional experts, the center achieves far less parental involvement than Shady Hill. Parents are talked with as they drop children off and pick them up. They may remain to observe. They receive a newsletter. They do not complain about the fact that the church board carries overall responsibility without involvement of their representatives.

A Cooperative. In the cooperative we visited, a public department "cooperates" with a private sectarian agency to offer service to the department's staff. The department supplies five full-time staff members. Sixty-eight children, aged 2 months to 6 years, are cared for—one-third from the department, one-third paid for by the Department of Social Services, and one-third fee-paying. The institution in which the center is located provides laundry and maintenance services. This, in addition to the contributed staff time from the Department of Health, helps to keep costs down ($33 a week at the time of our visit). Whether because of low cost, program quality, auspice, or convenience, this center, unlike some, has a waiting list, even for 3–5 year olds.

The center is organized around age groups. There are eight infants approximately two months to a year old. These are cared for by two staff members. The seven "walking infants," who are approximately a year to 20 months old, are staffed by one licensed teacher and one aide. In another room there are fifteen toddlers, who are approximately 20 months to 3 years old. There are three teachers for this group. For the nineteen preschool children aged 3–4, there are four staff members, including one teacher and three aides; and for the twenty children of kindergarten age (4–5), there are four staff members.

Although the center's facilities are spacious, they are located in the rather depressing basement area of a well-located but obsolete children's institution. The walls of the infant room are all lined with cribs. The children are obviously well cared for; staff in each of the two rooms were holding children, playing with them, and giving them individual attention when we visited. As is often the case in infant nurseries everywhere, children reached out to us for attention. They were obviously known and dealt with individually. Apparently, parents are happy to get their children into the center with its nurse coverage and seem to prefer it to care in a private home or with a babysitter. The director is an experienced, knowledgeable person from the child development field. The program offers good family-centered care at a minimal cost and is organized primarily to meet the child care needs of working parents. While it might raise questions for students of child development theory in search of optimal environments, there was no evidence of any child suffering in the setting. It provides good physical care, and a serious attempt at social interchange with children and ongoing contacts with parents.

A Proprietary, Mixed Setting. The Joan Adler School is a privately owned institution which includes a nursery school, a kindergarten program, and an elementary program for children through the third grade. The school is forty years old, and was founded by the mother of the current director, who operates it with her husband, the business manager. Originally started as a part-day nursery program, during World War II it was expanded to a full-day program because of the number of women who had gone to work in war-related industries. After the war, they discovered there was still need for a full-day program. The school has gradually expanded to include older children, at the request of parents who wanted their children to continue where they were. Some appreciated the fact that the facility opens at 7:30 A.M. and does not close until 5:30—unlike nursery schools.

The school was experiencing charter and license problems when we visited, since it combines an educational program with a day care center and is therefore subject to two state authorities. There were currently fifty-five children in the nursery program, aged 2 to 5, and forty children in the elementary school program. Although the academic program runs on a regular school-day and school-year basis, the school also offers an after-school program and a summer program. The students are drawn from a wide population range. They are all attending on a private basis, but there is a good ethnic mix and a number of graduate students and people at the university use the facility as well as local residents and others in the community at large. Although tuition is charged by semester, it worked out to be $38 a week, plus a $60 equipment fee each year. The school does occasionally make arrangements to take children for reduced fee, asking for some service from the parents in return. Here, too, there is concern about the children who are caught in the category between eligibility for public welfare funding and ability to pay for a full-day program at full fee levels.

The school is located in two large old houses in a residential area. They are extremely big, comfortable facilities, with wide staircases and halls, a large veranda surrounding the house, in a wooded area. The nursery school and kindergarten are conducted in these buildings, while the elementary school is held in the facilities of a church across the street. The physical facilities and equipment are in some respects more limited than those in some of the other centers. On the other hand, there is a spacious, easy feeling to the surroundings, and equipment is adequate. There are a good many old clothes for children to dress up in, and heavy wooden blocks that have been around for years but which are still just as good as new.

The entire school has a sort of "old fashioned feeling" to it and is conducted on the traditional nursery school model. The children are organized by age groups. There are ten 2 year olds, with two teachers; fifteen 3 year olds, with three teachers; twenty-five to twenty-eight 4 year olds, with four teachers; and twenty-five kindergarten students, with three teachers. In addition, the elementary school is run on an "open classroom" basis, with four teachers for the forty children. There are two cooks and two part-time music teachers. The school attempts to bring in parents to provide some special programs.

Discipline and routines are firm and traditional. To move from one activity to another, for example, the children lined up very quietly and all moved together, on our visiting day. They all wore name tags, everything was carefully labeled, and the program ran according to a very tightly organized schedule.

All the teachers have at least two years' experience in junior college in nursery education, and several of them are college graduates and have state certification in early childhood education. The director prefers teachers with a background in nursery education. She said that they have had much more in-service training than those who have just taken academic work, and are much readier to handle a classroom.

To an observer, this is a solid, adequate program. Certainly the children are well cared for and are receiving a standard nursery school program. Several professionals in the community reported that their children are extremely enthusiastic about their days at the school.

Local Currents

Our city reflects the mixed motives and goals in child care. Is it education, personal social service, labor policy? If it is one thing, what is the hierarchy of objectives? If it is several things, should it or should it not be several systems? Whose needs are at center stage: Parents' or children's? Or perhaps the concerns of the wider society about the dependency of the welfare poor or the deprivation of children whose homes offer too little?

The matter of start-up costs, of fees for parents above the public welfare day care means-test level, and priority claims on day care spaces will need consideration in the context of some resolution of these issues. As a starting point it will be necessary to determine just how much society wants children in day care: Which children? Group or family care? If the child is at the center, research about effects of alternatives on children will matter. If the objectives are in the domain of labor market and welfare policy and women's rights, other data will be relevant.

This city, in the meantime, typifies the situation—a pluralistic, decentralized, categorical system, varied in quality and philosophy, not adequately serving the very young and the school-age children of working mothers (if that is the goal) and running the risk of pricing out of the market the working-class users above welfare eligibility scales.

The new county-supported planning and coordination could meet an obvious need. It would be a useful center of cooperation, initiative, training, central services, planning—but it could not solve all the problems arising from national level categorization and goal conflicts. Head Start, WIN, Concentrated Employment, the Elementary and Secondary Education Act, Titles XX and IV-B, have their own rules about eligibility, priority, program. Their differing target populations create procedural and organizational differences, too. A local coordinating body such as the one proposed could do useful things but would hardly be in a position to decategorize and to create a coherent delivery system and program unless there is corresponding initiative nationally as well. Of this, more in the final section.

Two New York Programs

New York City and Nassau County round out the picture with two additional programs: a Head Start program involving considerable parental participation and a central service approach to the strengthening of family day care.

First, by way of context, we reproduce a table from New York City's Agency for Child Development (Table 2-7). The table summarizes coverage for public social welfare–related child care, leaving out most voluntary programs (except "purchases of service") and those which are based in the education system. The bulk of the public care is group care. Table 2-8 shows the federal, state, local cost allocations for these programs (approximately 50:25:25).

Parent-Controlled Child Care

New York City doubled its day care capacity during the late 1960s. Community groups interested in organizing their own child care programs were responsible for much of the expansion. Many of these programs were opened in store fronts with limited facilities and resources by groups of parents in need of care for their own children. The centers often began as cooperatives with parents and volunteers serving as staff. As the centers received public funds, the volunteers were replaced by professional staff. In some instances, parents were hired to fill teaching and administrative positions, completing academic requirements while on the job. Parents, however, maintained control of the board.

The Bartlett Street Day Care Center typifies the emergence of a parent-controlled child care center. It is located in the vicinity of a major urban university, in a community that is shifting rapidly from middle to low income. A group of parents worked for more than a year just to locate an appropriate space they could use rent-free in the community. The center opened with twelve full-time children aged 11 months to 5 years, in a rent-free facility provided by the university. The center was staffed by parents with the assistance of other community volunteers. Since the participants were all low-income families, the fees charged were minimal. The parents organized training sessions, evolved an educational policy and philosophy for the running of the center, and organized the community in support of the program. The group obtained donations of equipment and furniture, and were creative in locating free supplies and resources. After much effort, they were successful in obtaining public

Table 2-7. New York City Day Care Enrollment (Jan. 31, 1975)

Program	Centers or homes	Children
Group day care	413	36,999
Purchase of service*	18	565
Total in centers		37,564
Family day care cluster program	659	2,633
Family day care career program	900	3,903
Purchase of service*	591	1,529
Total in homes		8,065
Head Start	118	6,127
Total		51,756

*Dec. 1974.

funding, to allow the center to expand to thirty-five children and to hire staff. Even with funding, the parent-community board continued to play a major role in the day-to-day and policy operations.

The relationship between the board and the staff differed in significant detail from that of a typical day care center. First, several of the parents were hired as staff members of the center, thus mixing their roles as board and staff members. Second, many of the parents spent extensive time in the Center and felt that they each should have a direct say in the day-to-day programing that affected their children, though this feeling gradually dissipated as more and more professional staff were hired and procedures were regularized. Third, the parents were responsible for assuring that the funding of the Center continued and that major sums of money were raised to cover the costs of renovations. Fourth, the parents were active in their community and in the day care movement, involving themselves and the children in political demonstrations and other organizing activities.

In addition, since the Center was not affiliated with a private social service agency, the board had responsibility for working with staff in making appropriate links with other community agencies, to provide medical and dental care for the children, social services for families, and other necessary referrals. Such activities placed significant strain on mothers of the Center, all of whom were working full time and many of whom were single parents.

As the Center matured, the relationships between the board and the staff shifted. At the time of our visit, the director of the Center indicated that he relies heavily on the support of the board but that he finds it necessary to take responsibility for more and more of the Center's activities. Previously, for example, the board had almost

Table 2-8. Estimated New York City Funding Sources for Group and Family Day Care (1974–75)

	Formula	% of costs	Total amount (mill. of $)	City (mill. of $)	State (mill. of $)	Federal (mill. of $)
Title IV-A	75–12½–12½	60	87.3	10.9	10.9	65.5
WIN	90–5–5	3	4.4	.2	.2	4.0
Income maintenance	50–25–25	7	10.2	2.6	2.6	5.0
City and state general revenue	50–50	30	43.6	21.8	21.8	—
Total		100	145.5	35.5	35.5	74.5
(Percentage)			(100)	(24.4)	(24.4)	(52.2)

total say in the hiring of staff. Now the director has major responsibility, simply seeking final approval from the board. Funding is assured for thirty-five preschool children ages 2–5 and twenty afterschool children ages 6–9. Several major program items are basically determined by the public funding agency—money is allocated according to a predetermined per-child cost, and staffing patterns and staff requirements are set by the licensing and funding agency, as is classroom size and the approved ages for accepting children. Even with these rigid limitations, the board continues to play an active and aggressive role in determining program goals and philosophy of the Center. Board membership is limited to parents and a few active community supporters. Several of the original founders continue to support the Center as board members.

Although parent control of child care is not the major political issue it once was, the concept of parent involvement in policy-making is firmly established as an integral part of child care centers in New York City.

Family Day Care Resource Center

Home-based child care, sometimes referred to as family day care, has existed over the years. Often a mother with young children would decide to take care of neighbor's children as well. Recently professionals in the child care field became interested in how to coordinate or organize these services to provide additional resources and supportive services to the provider of care and to the children. The profession is still learning about how to reach many of these family day care providers. In a tightly structured program a private or public agency is responsible for selection and training of the providers, licensing of the provider's home, and for selection and placement of the families who will use the care. In these programs the providers are paid by the agency and any fees from the parents are paid to the agency. In order to utilize the programs, families must meet established income eligibility requirements. In a more loosely structured program, resources are made available to the providers in the community, often through a neighborhood resource center. Some providers will serve families referred from public agencies; others will make private arrangements. The day care provider in these instances is more of a private entrepreneur providing a service to the community. In both, the defined need for service does not differ greatly, and both share common goals—the support and strengthening of home-based child care arrangements.

The Drop In program is an excellent example of how a resource center can be utilized in the community. The Drop In program serves a small, low-income suburb of New York City with a high percentage of working mothers. The community has few group care facilities and is typical of other communities of similar size. The program was organized through the auspices of a public agency with support of the local department of social services to meet the following objectives: to determine the effectiveness of informal continuing education through workshops and short courses in strengthening the care-giver's role in working with children; to test the effectiveness of serving as a broker between the users and providers of care; and to explore the possible role of coordination and linking of agencies responsible for comprehensive child care in the community.

The storefront resource center, open daily, is the focal point for program operations. It is accessible and visible to provider mothers, parents, and community agencies. The facility is small, consisting of three rooms with a children's playroom, a meeting room, storage facilities for equipment loaned to day care mothers, and office space for the staff. A number of services are available to the provider mother. Providers are encouraged to "drop in" to exchange information and ideas with the staff and with other mothers and to give the children in their home an opportunity to interact with other children and adults. Children use the playroom facilities, which are organized like those in a typical day care center. The center also has books and other play equipment to lend as well as special equipment for infants. Providers are encouraged to build their own play equipment. Examples of easy-to-construct equipment are available in the center.

The center serves as a clearing house of information on services, events, and activities in the community, including health, nutrition, libraries, parks, museums, farms, fire, police. In addition, there are a series of educational activities which include weekly meetings and discussions with providers, distribution of a monthly newsletter throughout the community, and a certificate training course of licensed family day care providers. The providers are anxious to upgrade their skills and to receive appropriate credit where possible. The training is focused around specific program needs of the providers and includes developmental issues, social interactions, play activities, and community resources.

Parents in need of child care are invited as well to visit the center to learn about child care services available in the community. The staff assists parents to better clarify their particular child care needs.

Where appropriate, parents are given the names of several day care providers. They are encouraged to stay in contact with the center and to provide feedback to the resource center.

Despite a limited budget ($60,000 in 1974) and small staff (three full-time), the program has had an impact in strengthening community awareness and support of family day care and in providing a network of support services for the provider. Providers visit the center regularly and have been active participants in the workshops. They have also established a family day care organization to represent their interests with regard to licensing and legislation. In the future, the staff intends to emphasize work with parents in need of child care.

Several variations of the Drop In model are being tried in other communities. In order to succeed, they require financial support from public and private agencies in the community and a willingness on the part of these agencies to share resources.

Trends and Issues

There Are Many Other Parties to the Debate

Perhaps the most vocal critics of arrangements for child care in the United States are associated with the women's liberation movement. Their concerns are expressed on several different levels. The basic demand is for free, twenty-four-hour care available at parental option for all children. Underlying this demand is the conviction that women will not have full economic and social status in society until they are free of the responsibility for child care and can compete economically with men. In this context, child care is viewed as a responsibility of the total society rather than of the individual family or parent. Moreover, the day care center as a concept is thought to provide a sort of ideal environment in which children can be raised free of the sexual stereotypes and limitations imposed by life in a nuclear family and in which they can develop in a spirit of cooperation, communal identity, and self-determination. There are, of course, many variations on this theme, but in the feminist programs, which are usually established as cooperatives, day care is as much an ideological as a pragmatic approach to child care.[80]

Another perspective on child care is offered by various minority groups, most of which tend to emphasize the need for community control of day care facilities. For example, the Black Child Development Institute has three major premises underlying its child care proposals: first, because of the need to enhance children's psychological well-being as well as their physical and cognitive development, program content should strengthen the black child's sense of racial identity and pride; second, because the American educational system has failed to prepare minority children for full participation in society, decision-making power with regard to educational policy should rest with the local community, which can be trusted to give priority to the interests of black children; and third, because economic and social growth of community institutions is necessary for individual and collective progress, child development programs should be used as catalysts for total community development.[81] Representatives of this viewpoint see real advantages to child care in group settings. They urge staffing which assures ethnic identity of children and group leaders and which offers attractive adult models.

Beginning with individual child development and family enhancement as the goal, other analysts criticize the "over-reliance" on group care in planning. Emlen, for example, has recently attempted to highlight the benefits of and degree of parental preference for family day care services. He suggests that the need is not to create new child care facilities, but rather to improve the use of existing resources. This could be accomplished by developing adequate information and referral services, allowing parents to follow more flexible work schedules, and correcting some of the basic socioeconomic conditions such as unsafe housing, poor nutrition, and inadequate income, which contribute to poor child care.[82] Those who debate Emlen are either skeptical about the possibility of upgrading family day care, or hold that to do so is prohibitively expensive. Some proponents of women's liberation also oppose family day care as reinforcing the stereotype of the woman as child-minder, whereas group programs can use men as staff members.

The Day Care Consultation Service of the Bank Street College of Education has also questioned over-reliance on educational programs in center-based facilities, and has called for a family-centered approach to child care. Here the initiatives are inspired by child development research as well as cost considerations. With the financial aid of both the Carnegie Corporation and the Ford Foundation, they are carrying out a child care systems project which attempts to help people develop alternative models of child care and to create comprehensive child care networks. Although the models and programs developed will vary in different communities, all will be family-centered approaches which emphasize the utilization of all types of informal and formal child care resources, the building on neighborhood initiatives and cooperation, the provision of adequate information and referral services to families in need of child care, and the sharing of information and resources among child care providers.

Other assessments of child care needs are provided by social policy analysts. Many assume that day care policy must be made in relation to the "mother at work" issue. In the analysis of the proposed federal budget for fiscal 1975 by the Brookings Institution, for example, it is suggested that child care may be one of the essential goods and services, like housing and medical care, which the federal government should help people purchase through a system of transfer payments. The basic argument for public subsidy of child care is presented as follows:

> It is important to both mothers and children and to society as a whole that children be well cared for while mothers work; many mothers, especially those with low incomes, cannot afford to pay for the quality of care that society thinks children ought to have; therefore, the government should take steps to see that adequate care is available, especially to low-income families who need it most and can least afford it.[83]

The authors go on to analyze the relative advantages of increased grants to public and voluntary institutions for child care programs versus a system of vouchers to help families purchase child care in the private market. A voucher system maximizes parental option and minimizes cost; however, opponents of this plan fear that it perpetuates the use of informal child care arrangements, which are frequently low-standard and difficult to monitor. Therefore, it is suggested that the best policy may be a mixture in which the voucher system is supported by an adequate information system, training programs for child care providers, and public efforts to ensure the provision of high-quality center-based care for the families which choose to purchase this service.[84]

A somewhat different approach is recommended by Dr. Harold Watts of the University of Wisconsin in an unpublished working paper for the Advisory Committee on Child Development of the

National Research Council. Watts notes committee agreement that the family is primarily responsible for the rearing of young children, and that—given the apparent conclusions from behavioral research—the best way to enhance child development is to provide a system of family support, a basic component of which is a guaranteed minimum income. Although day care services would ideally be available to all on a free and optional basis, a major income redistribution program to strengthen families would preclude simultaneous major expenditures on day care for all. Furthermore, if a choice must be made between basic income security and heavy public subsidy for child care, Watts would definitely prefer income redistribution for all low-income families over a selective subsidy limited to those low-income families who choose or are forced to use extra-familial child care resources.

If an adequate system for providing a guaranteed minimum income to all families were instituted, parents could choose (under the Watts proposal) whether to care for their children at home or to purchase outside child care, the costs of which would be deductible from earnings. This position can be argued on the basis that it promotes equity, economic efficiency, and parental self-determination. On the other hand, it does little to ensure that an adequate supply of acceptable child care facilities will be made available. Therefore, in addition to guaranteed income and tax deductions for child care expenses, Watts also recommends the development of a system of local inspection and regulation of child care facilities and the establishment of District Child Care Authorities, which would take responsibility for conducting an annual census of child care needs and resources, providing information, referral, and brokerage services, receiving and adjudicating parental complaints, and planning the development of needed new services.[85]

Kagan, analyzing the problem from the child development research perspective, reminds us that the crucial variable may not be the physical facility "but rather the psychological atmosphere." He emphasizes variables such as "how the child is handled," what values are taught, the educational program. He reminds us: "The child can be happy or sad, frightened or secure, trusting or angry in a neighbor's apartment, a commune, or a newly built day care center." From his knowledge of individual and group differences, Kagan calls for a "pluralistic" day care strategy: one kind of program cannot be best for all children.

Since parents have a stake in the values and skills taught to their children, they should be involved in the implementation and strategies of care in day care centers. Since there is no perfect set of traits for a child to possess, the task of deciding what his ideal psychological goals will be is an ethical rather than a scientific process. There is some information, however, that psychologists can provide.[86]

And, we might add, some constraints and demands which the larger society will set.

Finally, we note the child care researchers. They come back to what is known about child rearing, maternal deprivation, and separation and ask whether the mixed research picture should not make one uneasy about promoting expanded care arrangements for infants under 2½ years of age. It is one thing if mothers of very young children either need to work or choose to do so, they say. It is another to encourage or coerce such practice as public policy.

How can Americans absorb these viewpoints? From what vantage point can policy be made and programing attempted?

While many views are expressed, it is clear that, in fact, the major private child care investments have been made by middle-class people who have purchased nursery school or private at-home enriching growth experiences for their children, by working mothers who have paid for the most readily available family or group care they could afford, and by better-paid working women whose private arrangements are aided by tax relief. In contrast, public child care investment of the past decade through social welfare programs has been motivated by labor market and public assistance objectives (to provide care for children of low-income working mothers and to free AFDC mothers for work or training, whether at their own or public policy initiative) and a desire to help poor children, especially minority children, with a "head start" in learning and personal development.

A parallel, considerable investment in expanded kindergarten and public preprimary classes has grown out of a commitment to deprived children, on the one hand, and a general public demand to offer socialization and development experiences, mostly part-day, to all children, on the other. The strength of the latter motive is uncertain; but teachers and their representatives have recently come to the fore with a strong campaign for optional preschool from age 3. Among those who generally support this view it is noted, however, that at least six states have no public kindergartens for even 5 year olds* and that few places offer all-day kindergartens. They would start with these latter gaps and then move down to the 4 and 5 year olds.

Obviously Head Start has not and could not have eradicated poverty, even though we may eventually know more precisely something about which champions of Head Start already hold firm convictions based on their impressions and observations: that it has boosted significant numbers of children out of a cycle in which they were trapped (or—probably more accurately—that it was a significant component in a social strategy begun in the 1960s which contributed to such an effect because of what it offered to parents and to children). For those with access to it, day care clearly achieves its primary goal of caring for children while mothers work or in instances of child or family problems and special needs. Here the issues are the scale of required expansion and the degree of program upgrading which is necessary. Little is specifically known about the impact on children of the many types of day care and nursery school programs available. OCD is currently sponsoring needed research to determine child-staff ratio and staff-qualification level effects on outcome, since these are major components of the very high day care cost levels which have developed. What is already known is that rising costs make it necessary to ask whether day care access must be validated as well in economic terms: Should its development be curtailed except where the mother's resultant productivity more than returns the investment in the program?

In this sense, the development of day care under several Social Security Act titles as a way to compel AFDC mothers to accept work or training seems to be questionable policy in a cost-benefit sense. Child care is expensive and the mothers involved are mostly unskilled and poorly educated. Moreover, severe equity problems occur if there is subsidy for AFDC mothers while working women at low-income levels pay their own way and get little help from tax deductions, under present legal provisions.

There are other current rationales for child care expansion, especially those stressing options and choices for women, the benefits of early group exposure for young children, the equality of the sexes (and the importance, in the view of some, that women work). At

*By mid-1975 it was reported that of the six (Vermont, North Dakota, New Hampshire, Mississippi, Idaho, Alabama) several were actively considering kindergarten legislation. Some 11,500 of 16,300 U.S. school systems had some kindergarten coverage by 1975.

the moment, these positions are not moving legislators. Indeed, even the more central arguments do not lead to new programs, as the White House and the Congress absorb the lessons of the past, sponsor incremental growth and research-demonstrations, and fully assess the current troublesome labor-market picture. Especially potent in the analysis, as we noted, are the recognition that quality care under existing models has become extremely expensive and the evidence that child care programs do not produce readily verifiable and substantial growth results in young children, even though they are probably helpful. Sustained and significant effects probably depend upon ongoing service in health, income, housing, and nutrition and upon family-community programing as well. This, too, is costly and in many ways complicated. Also, work requirements and attendant day care clearly do not cut welfare rolls significantly and parental preferences among the nonpoor do not necessarily run to the center-care programs sponsored by public policy (although the picture is complex).

All of this has produced the opportunity for the consideration and debate mentioned at the very beginning of this chapter. And the debate does continue even though little has occurred legislatively during the 1973–75 period.

Guidelines for Discussion

There is no question of turning off the further development of child care programs: too many women work, too many children are inadequately cared for, too many poor and deprived or handicapped children need experiences and resources which their parents cannot provide—and there is a worldwide trend in industrial countries to offer at least half-day preschool experiences to 3–5 year olds at parental option.[87] Where the latter programs are inexpensive or free, parents use them. Thus there will and must be some expansion of programs for all-day and part-day care of children in the United States and it will not be stopped by evidence that alternative models of family life and child rearing are attractive and wholesome. Social change does rearrange familial and societal responsibilities in child care.

This much said, many issues remain open, but the overview does suggest some policy and program guidelines.

1. For one thing, *it is necessary to reaffirm the welfare of children as a criterion.* Forcing mothers of infants under 2½ to work, or

subsidizing care so that they may, answers labor force or welfare questions, perhaps; but it would be good to revive questions about child development effects and costs. If mothers exercise options, that is their decision; if they are coerced or subsidized, that is another matter. The empirical basis for policy is cloudy and the philosophical basis is garbled. When programs are geared to other purposes, not to "child welfare," this should be faced. And the search for firm data about what programs do or can do to and for children remains of highest priority. In any case, whatever the research and prevalent ideologies, parents have the right to reject preschool care for their children, or to seek it out—and programs should be organized for maximum protection and enrichment. Nor is it just to offer options to parents who can afford them and to refuse options to the poor.

2. *Our planning in this field needs decategorization, as do operations.* Social welfare advocates and personnel talk about day care as though there were no kindergarten classes and nursery schools. Educators do not even count day care in their preprimary coverage reports. Yet all available data point to the fact that kindergarten and other preprimary classes and nursery schools do serve to offer all-day care to a significant minority of users and that working parents often find that part-day care under these facilities actually meets their coverage needs. On the other hand, group or family day care is often half-day or utilized only part of the day. Moreover, the variability within each program category (day care, preschool) is as great as the variation between them. Thus, school-based programs may be developmental, in the day care sense, and day care programs may make a significant preschool educational contribution. The issues are: What are the guidelines and their enforcement? What is the staffing? What is the program philosophy and goal?

In this sense the child care resource in the United States today is not only the licensed and approved day care total of 1.2 million places or the unlicensed additional coverage of approximately 1.8 million. It is also the 4.2 million nursery and kindergarten places for 3–5 year olds and the uncounted before- and after-school coverage for school-age children. Expansion over the past decade and tendencies in European industrial countries point to ever larger coverage in this latter category, coverage not to be ignored as all-day care, funded out of social welfare systems, is projected.

Planning should, therefore, look at the total resource and the potentials in each program category in relation to the diversity of needs. Moreover, the access machinery in a given community obviously should be organized to allow a given parent the broadest picture of what is possible as he or she undertakes planning for a child. Patterns of administration or funding reflect federal and state legislative history and the American tendency to develop administration by accretion of categories. This need not distort ways of meeting needs for particular consumer-users.

Nor does decategorization mean sameness. If there is a large reservoir of child care programs they can and should specialize to meet diverse needs and preferences. Of this, more below.

To summarize: Whatever the ultimate administrative home(s) for child care (perhaps the options should be exercised at the state level), national planning calls for decategorization. The diversity of funding sources, eligibility bases, administrative rules, have precluded wise deployment of services and have placed unnecessary burdens on the user-consumer. In one or two administrative units at the local level, it should be possible to regulate, license, purchase care, or offer service to all pre-elementary children, whatever their economic levels, and whether they pay all or no costs, whose parents exercise the option—and to the level of coverage offered by the community. The causes of population integration, program enrichment, program diversity, parental options, and administrative efficiency could all be advanced by such policy—the decategorization of delivery systems and the integration of access provision.

3. While comprehensive, developmentally oriented child care programs are extremely advantageous for deprived children, probably for all children, *child care programs should not be assigned the full costs of all supplementary services, nor are they necessarily the appropriate service delivery outlet for all service to families with young children.* When very deprived children participate in day care programs, particularly programs which meet Head Start or similar guidelines, they are assured good food, health screening, mental health surveillance, and some effort to bring their parents out into the community. Some of these functions are not appropriate charges on child care, however, since they really correct for deficiencies in other systems. Nor can most child care for most U.S. children be expected to meet all such needs, given the diversity of auspice, size, location, and length of day. What is more, comprehensive center care, where these programs are generally delivered, touches very few children and it cannot be otherwise for a long time. There is inequity in depriving the others, and no evidence that the need is greater among those in the centers, as compared to family day care, or as

compared to the larger numbers in own-home care or whose parents do not use child care arrangements at all. In a sense, then, some of the components of so-called "developmental" child care are only a temporary substitute and could be a diversion from the problem of addressing health and nutrition coverage as public policy issues. Larger issues of policy and organization should and will settle the mode of service delivery for such services. Given the pluralistic child care pattern in the United States it is unlikely that child care programs can be the institutional base for all these services in many places, even though some "outposting" of services within child care might prove desirable—and despite the special case for comprehensive services in deprived areas.

4. *It may be useful to distinguish a basic coverage child care program to meet average, ordinary circumstances, available at parental option* and community capacity to supply (a public social utility), *from child care as a case service,* meeting special family problems or the needs of handicapped or extremely deprived groups. Both should be planned and operationally coordinated as one system with permeable boundaries.

Public kindergartens and preprimary classes, most of them half-day, serving the 3–5 year olds, could be the core of the utility, as they are becoming worldwide. They would be universal and voluntary, and administered by personnel geared to balanced child development, whatever the administrative arrangements in state and locality. Day care (group and family) and its Head Start variations would be the core of the case service but could continue to be used as a utility.

For children under 3, public policy can and should remain neutral; it should not coerce mothers to place children in care, create incentives to do so—or make care unavailable for those who do make the deliberate choice. The child development research evidence is mixed, the experts are concerned, yet there are worldwide social changes which make it inevitable that significant numbers of infants will come into care. Many are in care already, much of it unregulated and unprotected. There is enough experience that infant day care and family day care need not be harmful, and can perhaps be a successful growth experience. The Federal Interagency Day Care Requirements are a good point of departure. Social welfare administration auspices and close coordination with health departments seem essential.

5. If the concern is truly with children whose mothers are away from home in order to work, it would be wise to *stop talking about*

day care as a public assistance measure. The strongest day care case is for service reflecting parental preference and their market behavior: working women do place their children in convenient care, usually the best care they can afford out of what is available. Public policy could increase the availability of quality care nearby for those who would exercise the option.

This is not "public assistance." Indeed the evidence is very substantial that it is excessively costly to subsidize most AFDC mothers with child care on the assumption that they will become self-supporting.[88] Day care to meet the needs of children of working parents is a basic public social utility and should be available at the user's option, at a cost that represents a neutral public policy as to whether mothers of young children do or do not work, or without cost if the society is willing to offer socializing and developmental experience to all children, or those in the 3–5 age group.

Social Security Act amendments (Title XX) open wide discretion for the states in reorganizing their social service programs. Day care could become a universal social service, organized and financed to meet state objectives for families and children and liberated from its inappropriate public-assistance coercive role. Placed under the spotlight of state social service budgeting, day care could be given the level of priority citizens feel it merits as a universal measure.

Preschool programs, usually covering the 3–5 age range, are an expanding utility too. Elementary education, universal and compulsory, is an established state responsibility, with limited federal help since the mid-1960s. Only fourteen states now mandate that kindergartens be made locally available for 5 and 6 year olds, although all but two do offer state aid to kindergartens if localities decide to establish them, and eleven states also provide some form of aid (limited pilot programs, usually for the handicapped) to prekindergartens. As a preliminary to federal backing of a day care utility, states might be expected to carry kindergarten for children a year below compulsory elementary age as a universally available service, at local option.

6. *Day care could continue as a "case service" in relation to specified family or community need.* Given the basic day care public social utility, available at parental option, financed so that families neither gain nor lose by placing children, certain situations would remain. There are family problems (abuse, neglect, parental incapacity, child handicap) out of which a specific case need arises for part-day or all-day care of a child. There are deprived communities and groups in which programs like Head Start will be needed to help

open opportunities and launch development. It is not difficult to sustain day care as a case service and to finance it in special ways if the objectives and criteria are put down. The policy and organizational problem in the United States comes from translating case service principles into guide lines for the utility.

7. Available evidence on effects does not make a case for center care as against family day care, the latter apparently preferred by parents of very young children. Besides, many parents clearly prefer care in their own or relatives' homes. However, family day care is in need of major upgrading and regulation. It needs more central servicing. Once this occurs, family day care may become prohibitively expensive. On the other hand, we have yet to learn whether some of the accepted staffing ratios or requirements for center care are actually related to results. While all these matters are being explored, as is the consumer preference question (and they are on the OCD research agenda), *a pluralistic, empirical, experimental stance on program forms and staffing standards is needed.*

8. *A pluralistic stance is also merited in relation to administrative arrangements and service delivery auspices.* There is reason to explore separating the infant care systems (up to age 3?) from the preprimary programs (from 2½ until kindergarten?). Perhaps retrained elementary teachers, utilizing classroom space now becoming freed in elementary schools, could serve the latter, as the teacher union contends. The issue would be whether present educational bureaucracies could nurture open and diverse child development programing with much parent involvement. Younger children might be served by systems under general social service and health leadership —or a special child development authority.

This is not a proposal but a recognition that the separation has occurred in some countries and that political and resource realities require that the claims of educators be faced. Of course, retraining of reassigned elementary teachers and special administrative protections, as well as sound guidelines, would be needed if such programs were to develop in the schools.

9. Stripped of functions which belong to health or income maintenance, *child care remains an interdisciplinary activity.* Social work personnel are needed for case finding, referral, and assistance with child adjustment and parent-child problems in all programs. They will have more extensive work in the day care programs meeting the needs of populations with special problems, and in settings serving infants. The daily program activities, in turn, require the guidance of

those skilled in early childhood education. Nutrition and health services, if only part time, are also essential. Whether the early childhood education specialists can protect their unique specialty in a traditional education department will need to be determined. Whether the needed social work personnel should be assigned administratively to the staffs of day care and Head Start centers, prekindergarten programs in the school system, and family day care central resource offices, or should, rather, be outposted by integrated community-wide personal social service departments, will be determined by the eventual local pattern of service delivery and is a marginal issue for the child care system.

We shall conclude with a final thought from Steinfels, who attempts to look at day care policy in the perspective of changes in the American family.[89] The movement of women into the labor market on new levels and on a new scale, changes in family roles, the push toward equality, proposals to reorganize work, increased family planning, all create new diversity in families, a wide variability in preferences, evidence that there is no one way, no one pattern, no single norm. There remain major regional, class, and group differences in preferences—and there is not likely to be one optimal way for children to be reared. All this speaks for pluralism, choice, alternatives—and for a diversity of child care administrative and programing patterns as well. Not easy for policy makers—but probably better for children.

Notes

1. Jerome Kagan, "About the Book," in Greta G. Fein and Alison Clarke-Stewart, *Day Care in Context* (New York: John Wiley and Sons, 1973), p. xvii.

2. *Current Population Reports*, Series 9-20, No. 268: *Nursery School and Kindergarten Enrollment: October 1973* (Washington, D.C.: GPO, 1974). As updated by U.S. Office of Education personnel.

3. This survey is from the National Center for Social Statistics, DHEW, 1974.

4. Virginia Kerr, "One Step Forward—Two Steps Back: Child Care's Long American History," in Pamela Roby, *Child Care—Who Cares?* (New York: Basic Books, 1973), p. 158.

5. Irving Lazar and Mae E. Rosenberg, "Day Care in America," in Edith H. Grotberg, ed., *Day Care: Resources for Decision* (Washington, D.C.: OEO, 1971), pp. 66–67.

6. Kerr, "One Step Forward," p. 16, and Anna Mayer and Alfred J. Kahn, *Day Care as a Social Instrument: A Policy Paper* (New York: Columbia University School of Social Work, 1965), pp. 24–25.

7. Kerr, "One Step Forward," pp. 162–64.

8. Mayer and Kahn, *Day Care as a Social Instrument.*

9. See Education Commission of the States, Report No. 65: *Early Childhood Programs: A State Survey, 1974–75* (Denver, Col.: The Commission, 1975).

10. Grotberg, *Day Care*, p. 73.

11. Ronald Parker and Jane Knitzer, *Day Care and Preschool Services: Trends and Issues* (Atlanta, Ga.: Avatar, 1972), p. 16.

12. Philip J. Harmelink and Nancy E. Schurtz, "Child Care Expenses: Current Status and Alternatives," *Taxes*, 53, No. 8 (Aug. 1975), 479–84.

13. President Richard M. Nixon, "Family Assistance Plan," Aug. 11, 1969, cited in Grotberg, *Day Care*, p. vi.

14. "Veto Message—Economic Opportunity Amendments of 1971," Message from the President of the United States, S. Doc. 92-48, 92 Cong. 1 sess. (1971), pp. 4, 5. Cited in Charles L. Schultze et al., *Setting National Priorities: The 1973 Budget* (Washington, D.C.: The Brookings Institution, 1972), p. 288.

15. Hearings, Committee on Finance, U.S. Senate, *Social Service Regulations* (Washington, D.C.: GPO, 1973), I, 7.

16. *Ibid.*, p. 9.

17. Committee of the Day Care Workshop, *A Statement of Principles* (DHEW–OCD Pub. No. 72-10; Washington, D.C.: GPO, 1971), pp. 1–2. Emphasis supplied.

18. *White House Conference on Children, Report to the President* (Washington, D.C.: GPO, 1971), pp. 286–87.

19. Committee on Finance, U.S. Senate, 92nd Congress, *Child Care*, Hearings on S. 2003, Child Care Provisions of the H.R.I., and Title VI of Printed Amendment 3/8 to H.R.1, Washington, D.C., Sept. 22, 23, and 24, 1971.

20. Senator Walter F. Mondale, Opening Statement at Joint Senate-House Hearings on "Child and Family Services Act of 1975," July 15, 1975.

21. Westinghouse Learning Corporation and Westat Research, Inc., *Day Care Survey—1970: Summary Report and Basic Analysis* (processed; Washington, D.C.: OEO, 1971), pp. 12–20.

22. Donald J. Cohen, *Serving Preschool Children* (DHEW–OCD Pub. No. 74-1057; Washington, D.C.: GPO, 1974), p. 1.

23. Westinghouse, *Day Care Survey.*

24. The most recent statistical compilation, which warns of incompleteness and inaccuracy, is Committee on Finance, U.S. Senate, *Child*

Care: Data and Materials, October, 1974 (Washington, D.C.: GPO, 1974).

25. For example, Mary Keyserling, *Windows on Day Care* (New York: National Council of Jewish Women, 1972), and Vivian Lewis, "Day Care: Needs, Costs, Benefits, Alternatives," in Subcommittee on Fiscal Policy, Joint Economic Committee, *Studies in Public Welfare*, Paper No. 7: *Issues in the Coordination of Public Welfare Programs* (Washington, D.C.: GPO, 1973), pp. 110–19.

26. Keyserling, *Windows on Day Care*, pp. 222–23.

27. *Ibid.*, p. 18.

28. *Child Care: Data and Materials*, pp. 60–63.

29. Arthur E. Emlen, *Slogan, Slots, and Slander: The Myth of Day Care Need* (processed; Portland, Ore.: Field Study of the Family Day Care System, 1971).

30. *Current Population Reports*, Series 9-20, No. 268. As updated by personnel, U.S. Office of Education.

31. Estimates are reported in *Child Care: Data and Materials.*

32. Lewis, "Day Care," and Michael Krashinsky, "Day Care and Welfare" in *Studies in Public Welfare*, Paper No. 7, pp. 102–220.

33. Rivlin in Schultze, *Setting National Priorities*, p. 262.

34. Parker and Knitzer, *Day Care and Preschool Services*, pp. 11–12.

35. *Current Population Reports*, Series 9-20, No. 268.

36. *Ibid.* and Parker and Knitzer, *Day Care and Preschool Services*, pp. 11–12.

37. Carol L. Jusenius and Richard L. Shortlidge, Jr., *Dual Careers: A Longitudinal Study of Labor Market Experience of Women* (Columbus, Ohio: Center for Human Resource Research, Ohio State University, 1975), III, 57, 92.

38. Keyserling, *Windows on Day Care,* pp. 1–6. In a later New York City study, costly programs were not necessarily superior. In fact, poorly rated programs for which licensing and staffing standards were deferred were as costly as the best-standard programs. See Mary Dublin Keyserling, *New York City Child Care Programs: Challenges Ahead* (New York: Day Care Council of New York, 1974). Cited, page 89.

39. Tessa Blackstone, *Education and Day Care for Young Children in Need: The American Experience* (London: Centre for Studies in Social Policy, 1973).

40. Keyserling, *Windows on Day Care*, p. 72.

41. *Ibid.*, p. 74.

42. Susan Stein, "The Company Cares for Children," in Roby, *Child Care*, p. 245.

43. Grotberg, *Day Care*, pp. 75–76.

44. Adele Simmons and Antonia H. Chayes, "University Day Care," in Roby, *Child Care*, pp. 228–44.

45. Keyserling, *Windows on Day Care*, p. 72.

46. Stein, "The Company Cares," pp. 256–57.

47. Economic Opportunity Act, Section 522(d). Cited in National Research Council–National Academy of Sciences, *Report of the Panel on the Assessment of the Community Coordinated Child Care Program* (processed; Washington, D.C., 1971), p. 1.

48. National Research Council, *Report,* p. 33.

49. Sally V. Allen, "Early Childhood Programs in the States," in Roby, *Child Care*, p. 193, updated.

50. Westinghouse, *Day Care Survey.*

51. Jusenius and Shortlidge, *Dual Careers*, p. 40.

52. For details, *The Home Start Demonstration Program: An Overview* (DHEW–OCD Pub. No. 74-1069; Washington, D.C.: GPO, 1974). Also Ruth Ann O'Keefe, "Home Start: Partnership with Parents," *Children Today*, Jan.-Feb., 1973, pp. 12–16.

53. Data from U.S. Office of Education.

54. Exemplar "systems" are described in Cohen, *Serving Preschool Children.*

55. Sheldon H. White et al., *Federal Programs for Young Children: Review and Recommendations* (DHEW O.S. Pub. No. 74-100; Washington, D.C.: GPO, 1974), summary, IV, 6.

56. Blackstone, *Education and Day Care*, pp. 40–41.

57. See report of DHEW nine-state audit in 1974 as summarized on page 61 above for statistics of noncompliance.

58. State licensing requirements and current DHEW guides are summarized on pp. 104–47 of *Child Care: Data and Materials.* In passing Title XX in late 1974 the Congress instructed the Secretary of DHEW to issue certain modifications. See page 76 above concerning Head Start regulations.

59. Child Welfare League of America, *Standards for Day Care Service* (New York: The League, 1970). New Head Start regulation enforcement is described on p. 76.

60. This inevitably somewhat outdated but useful summary from Allen, "Early Childhood Programs," pp. 191–227, and includes some updating from Education Commission, *Early Childhood Programs.*

61. Guinevere S. Chambers, "Staff Selection and Training," in Grotberg, *Day Care*, p. 398.

62. Cost analyses are summarized in Roby, *Child Care*, and Schultze, *Setting National Priorities.*

63. *Child Care: Data and Materials.*

64. Lewis, "Day Care," p. 105.

65. *Ibid.* Nor are capital costs at all consistently considered in any of the reports.

66. Seth Low and Pearl G. Spindler, *Child Care Arrangements of Working Mothers in the United States* (Washington, D.C.: U.S. Children's Bureau and U.S. Women's Bureau, 1968).

67. Lewis, "Day Care," p. 143.

68. Thomas W. Hertz and Adele U. Harrell, *Toward Interagency Coordination: Fourth Annual Report* (Washington, D.C.: Social Research Group, George Washington University, 1974).

69. *Ibid.*, p. 44.

70. Urie Bronfenbrenner, *Is Early Intervention Effective? A Report on Longitudinal Evaluations of Preschool Programs*, Vol. II (DHEW–OHD Pub. No. 74-25, paperback ed.; Washington, D.C.: GPO, 1974). Also Sally Ryan, ed., *Longitudinal Evaluations*, Vol. I.

Edith H. Grotberg, ed., *Day Care: Resources for Decision* (paperback ed.; Washington, D.C.: OEO, 1971).

Sheldon H. White et al., *Federal Programs for Young Children: Review and Recommendations* (DHEW O.S. Pub. No. 74-100, 4 vols., paperback ed.; Washington, D.C.: GPO, 1974).

Greta G. Fein and Alison Clarke-Stewart, *Day Care in Context* (New York: John Wiley, 1973). Also see Frances Degen Horowitz and Lucile York Paden, "The Effectiveness of Environmental Intervention Programs," in Bettye M. Caldwell and Henry N. Ricciuti, *Review of Child Development Research*, Vol. III: *Child Development and Social Policy* (Chicago: University of Chicago Press, 1973), pp. 331–402.

Willa D. Abelson, Edward Zigler, and Cheryl L. DeBlasi, "Effects of a Four-Year Follow Through Program on Economically Disadvantaged Children," *Journal of Educational Psychology*, 66, No. 5 (1974), 756–71.

71. Urie Bronfenbrenner, "Developmental Research," unpub., 1973.

72. White, *Federal Programs*, IV, 6–14. White's bibliographies, research summaries, charts, tables make this a major source for scholars and policy-makers.

73. *Ibid.*, IV, 22.

74. *Ibid.*, IV, 23–24.

75. Abelson et al., "Effects of a Program."

76. White, IV, 25.

77. *Ibid.*, IV, 25–27.

78. *Ibid.*, IV, 27–28.

79. *Ibid.*, IV, 29–31.

80. Elizabeth Hagan, "Child Care and Women's Liberation," in Roby, *Child Care*, pp. 284–98.

81. Roby, *Child Care*, pp. 71–85.

82. Emlen, *Slogan, Slots, and Slander.*

83. Edward R. Fried et al., *Setting National Priorities: The 1974 Budget* (Washington, D.C.: The Brookings Institution, 1973).

84. *Ibid.*, pp. 160–69.

85. Harold Watts, unpub. working paper on child care policy.

86. Kagan, "About the Book," p. xviii.

87. Sheila B. Kamerman, *Child Care in Nine Countries* (Washington, D.C.: DHEW-OHD/OCD, 1975).

88. Lewis, "Day Care," and Krashinsky, "Day Care and Welfare"; also Hamelink and Schurtz, "Child Care Expenses."

89. Margaret O'Brien Steinfels, *Who's Minding the Chidren?* (New York: Simon and Schuster, Touchstone Books, 1973).

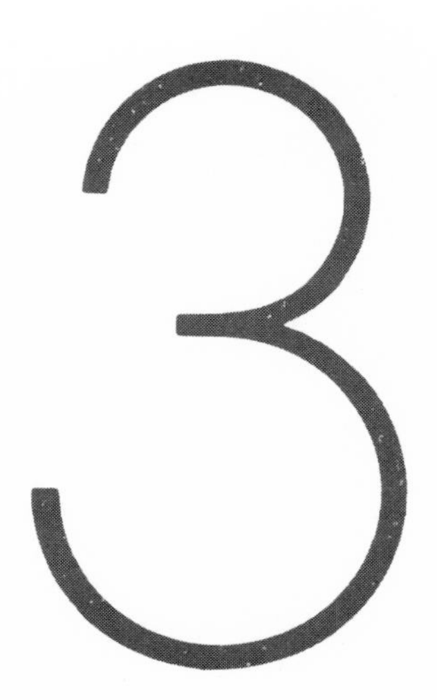

Child Abuse and Neglect

Context and Definition

Unlike child care, services for the abused or neglected child are clearly in the category of a case service. They are only for children and families diagnosed as needing such help. Here the issue is not one of boundaries, goals, or coverage. This topic highlights problems of fragmented and uncoordinated services in different systems, provided through different disciplines. It raises such basic questions as: What are the consequences of delineating a special subcategory of case service within an already existing categorical program (child welfare)? How can accountability and responsibility for continuity of care be assured? Who should take such responsibility?

Passage of the Child Abuse Prevention and Treatment Act (1974) highlighted nationwide alarm about one particular group of children and the concern that child abuse could be far more prevalent than previously recognized. Representing a new and substantial federal initiative, the Act provided, among other things, for the establishment of a national center to deal with child abuse and neglect. Its passage culminated a little more than a decade of research, experiment, and legislative activity.

The process began with the specific identification and labeling of a medical syndrome describing the most severe form of the abuse-neglect problem—the battered child syndrome. The concern it aroused gave birth to increased interest, activities, research—and frustration—on the part of pediatricians, psychiatrists, social workers, and lawyers to define, delineate, identify, diagnose, treat, prevent, and predict incidents of child abuse and to the passage of legislation in all fifty states requiring that incidents of child abuse be reported. These developments—and the burgeoning of public interest generally—were spurred on by myriads of newspaper articles recounting specific cases of child abuse; the major efforts of several voluntary child welfare organizations to publicize the existence and dimensions of the problem; growing interest on the part of physicians, especially pediatricians, in a problem now defined as falling within their purview; expanding activities in the field of civil rights, now moving toward concern with protecting the rights of children; and articles and statements highlighting a frequent correlation between early childhood experience of abuse and adult violence.

Although child welfare is traditionally the concern of social work, federal intervention in the problem of child abuse is clearly the consequence of emerging interest—and growing efforts—on the part of the medical profession, and to a somewhat lesser extent the legal profession, at publicizing the problem and the difficulties in eradicating it. Public concern has been stimulated by all these efforts as well as by the involvement of the media (television, newspapers, magazines) in publicizing the horrors of specific cases. The needs of the abused child represent, nationally, a bipartisan issue for which broad-based congressional support could be easily elicited. Funding and staffing of the newly established National Center is generating increased activities in the child welfare field generally. The availability of funds for research and demonstration programs is stimulating initiation and development of other efforts around the country aimed at reducing abuse and neglect cases.

Clearly, attention to the needs of abused or neglected children is an idea whose time has come. In what follows, certain basic questions will be addressed regarding the nature of the problem, the current state of knowledge regarding abuse and neglect, the range of national provision directed toward its solution, and the major issues involved. Specifically, these questions will include seven major topics:

What do we mean by "child abuse and neglect"? How are they defined? Are abuse and neglect one problem or two? How extensive is (or are) the problem(s)?

Since it is certainly not a new problem but rather one newly recognized or newly labeled, how was abuse/neglect perceived earlier? How was it dealt with? What is the relationship between the current approach and that taken earlier?

What is the nature and extent of existing national provision—federal and state, public and voluntary? What legislation relates to the problem and to the provision of relevant interventions and services? Which are the major concerned governmental and nongovernmental agencies?

What kinds of programs have been developed to deal with the problem? How extensive are they? Whom do they serve? Who staffs them?

What is the nature of relevant research? What is known and what knowledge is being sought?

How is one community attempting to deal with the problem? Is it doing something different now from before, and if so what? Why has it changed its approach?

What are the major issues currently identified by experts in the field? What, if any, are the other issues which our explorations have uncovered?

The Problems of Definition

There is no clear, consistent, and agreed upon definition of "child abuse and neglect." It is sometimes defined as one broad problem category, encompassing several subcategories of problems (physical abuse, sexual abuse, emotional deprivation); sometimes as one narrowly defined problem (the battered child); sometimes as two separate and distinct problems (abuse and neglect). Some definitions are oriented toward the behavior of the perpetrators (parents) and some toward the consequences of such behavior (the child's symptoms). Some include actual behavior (or consequences of this behavior) only; others include the potential for abusive behavior as part of the problem. Some definitions are operational-descriptive; others are concerned with the dynamics and etiology of the phenomenon. Conceptual definitions are far easier to develop than actual operational definitions in this field. Yet it is clear that how the problem is defined—in particular how it is defined operationally—determines our perspective on the size and gravity of the problem(s), on policy, program, and the whole range of efforts involved in solving it (them).

The major federal legislation of 1974 was entitled The Child Abuse Prevention and Treatment Act. This legislation defined abuse and neglect as a single entity, encompassing

physical or mental injury, sexual abuse, negligent treatment or maltreatment of a child under the age of 18 by a person who is responsible for the child's welfare under circumstances which indicate that the child's health or welfare is harmed or threatened thereby, as determined in accordance with regulations prescribed by the Secretary.[1]

Another approach to viewing abuse and neglect as one entity is encompassed in Fontana's concept of child "maltreatment."

Any treatment by which a child's potential development is retarded or completely suppressed, by mental, emotional or physical suffering, is *maltreatment* whether it is negative (as in deprivation of emotional or material needs) or positive (as in verbal abuse or battering).[2]

A variation of this definition is that of C. Henry Kempe. Here we see a beginning distinction between physical abuse and other forms of abuse and neglect.

The most severe form of child abuse is seen in the battered child syndrome. The syndrome lies at one extreme of a spectrum of insufficient care and protection. The term, the battered child syndrome, is used by us to characterize a clinical condition in young children who have received significant physical abuse, generally from a parent or a foster parent. Different, and less lethal forms of child abuse include those in which injuries are repeated but not serious, instances of "failure to thrive" due to insufficient love or nutrition, cases of sexual abuse, emotional and social deprivation, and, finally, that most difficult of situations where there is an absence of love, of nurturing affection on the part of the parents, but at a level which is not sufficient to result in demonstrable physical or marked emotional retardation.[3]

The Child Welfare League of America, a major national organization concerned with the welfare of children, specifically states that child abuse and child neglect are not two separate child welfare problems: "We recognize the physical abuse of children as being the above surface tip of a huge iceberg known as child neglect. . . . Physical abuse is the most severe manifestation of neglect."[4] It seems implicit here that, if not a separate problem, abuse in some sense can be distinguished as a phenomenon from the overall category of neglect.

Still another definition does distinguish abuse from neglect, defining child abuse as "*intentional, non-accidental use of physical force, or intentional, non-accidental acts of omission*, on the part of a parent or other caretaker in interaction with a child in his care, aimed at hurting, injuring, or destroying that child."[5] As Gil himself acknowledges, even if the definition is sound conceptually it clearly cannot be operationalized, since the crux of the definition is whether or not the behavior is intentional or nonaccidental, something often impossible to determine. In addition, he points out that public concern is tied only to individual cases of abuse, and rarely to the overall problems of children in society generally, problems which he defines as "societal abuse" of children.

Attempts have also been made to distinguish abuse from neglect on the basis of the adequacy of child care and the consequence to the child. The range of symptomology, according to one such continuum, includes the following:

> Children that are physically *neglected* with regard to food, shelter, and clothing;
>
> Children that are morally *neglected*—subject to influences which have corrupted or which pose present danger of corrupting them;
>
> Children that are emotionally *neglected* by failure to provide the nurturing qualities which are necessary for the development of a sound personality;
>
> Children that are medically *neglected* by parental ignoring of their need for diagnosis or treatment of a medical condition;
>
> Children that are educationally *neglected* by parental failure to provide the education required by state law;
>
> Children that are victims of *community neglect*, through acts of commission or acts of omission;
>
> Children that are *physically abused* when they are on the receiving end of acts of commission;
>
> Children that are *sexually abused*.[6]

The dynamics and etiology of abusive or neglectful behavior is another locus for discrepancies among definitions. Two types of causative factors are frequently cited in the literature: one psychiatric; the other cultural.

The most sophisticated psychiatric studies are being conducted at the University of Colorado. For clinical and research purposes, a "battered" child "is any child who receives non-accidental, physical injury as a result of acts (or omissions) on the part of his parents or guardians."[7] This definition is based on the premise that parents who abuse their children, regardless of their socioeconomic status, exhibit common internal stresses and behavior patterns. Characteristic symptoms include a rigid, unrealistic expectation of a child's ability to gratify the parent's needs, extreme sensitivity to criticism, and fragile and mistrustful interpersonal relationships.

Another causative factor frequently attributed to abusive behavior is cultural predisposition. Gil, for example, notes that poorer parents often have been exposed to violence as an acceptable expression of hostility.[8] Such an explanation of abusive behavior is based on the premise that chronic, situational stress due to living in poverty can be an impetus for physical violence. This assumption is disputed by other analysts.[9]

Other studies that distinguish abuse from neglect on the basis of etiology and consequence do so by defining abuse as a single, specific act of commission and neglect as chronic omission.[10] Frequently, physical abuse is attributed to psychological stress and neglect to social stress, or poverty.

Finally, the definitions utilized in state statutes encompass a range similar to that already described.[11] Despite variations, all include three basic characteristics: (1) The behavior violates a norm or standard of parental conduct—for instance, of the parents' obligation to the child. This includes the child's right to have his basic needs met, not violated. The substance of such needs is defined by cultural norms. (2) The infliction is deliberate—that is, a nonaccidental injury. (3) The abuse or neglect is severe enough to warrant intervention of some type, whether that intervention be medical, social, legal, or a combination.

In summary, medical practitioners tend towards a definition of child abuse which focuses on the consequences of the behavior for children and singles out specific physical symptoms as seen in child patients (e.g., battered child syndrome, failure to thrive syndrome, sudden infant death syndrome). Mental health workers tend to include emotional and psychological damage. Lawyers search for a definition that describes specific behavior of the perpetrators and insist on operational, not just conceptual, definitions. Social workers generally support the most comprehensive definitions—including physical, sexual, and psychological abuse, emotional deprivation, inadequate care because of parental incapacities or lack of resources (income, housing, nutrition, medical care), societal abuse—be it deliberate or not deliberate, intentional or unintentional, individual or societal.

We should note that current federal legislation reflects a "mixed" position in that it includes abuse and neglect as one entity, focuses on the consequences for the child as well as the behavior of parent or guardian, does not deal with the problem of "intent" or define "maltreatment" more specifically, and limits its concern to those individuals or persons specifically responsible for the child's welfare.*

The Incidence of Abuse and Neglect

The severe shortage of reliable statistics concerning the incidence and extent of child abuse and neglect reflects the inadequate state of research and data collection in the field. Clearly, how the problem is defined determines what incidents an investigator counts in attempting to discover the extensiveness of the problem nationally. As long as there is no consensus as to whether or not abuse and neglect are one, two, or a cluster of related entities, accurate statistics cannot be kept. Even then, until there are consistent reporting laws, consistently implemented, and mechanisms or devices for accurately identifying and reporting existing cases, such figures cannot be reliable.

Until the early 1970s, when the Department of Health, Education, and Welfare (DHEW) began funding a variety of research projects, almost no relevant information was available or even sought. To date, the few statistics that have been compiled have no common basis for interpretation or analysis. Although by now all states have mandatory reporting laws (see below), inconsistencies among them (e.g., definition of problem, age of child) and variations from state to state in the nature of the reporting system contribute to existing inaccuracies and inadequacies in the data. Furthermore, existing statistics, whether gathered from state registry systems, from hospitals, or from voluntary agencies, reflect a built-in bias toward reporting cases from lower-class families, although existing research indicates no variations in actual incidence correlated with socioeconomic class. Existing statistical analysis of the scale of the problem reflects only those cases brought to the attention of public authorities; and private physicians are a notoriously poor source for reporting incidents of abuse, preferring not to expose such incidents among their private clients.

For the most part, extant statistics are based on one of four sources: statewide registries that mandate the reporting of abuse and

*The term "person responsible for the child's welfare" includes staff of residential centers and other institutions caring for children, as well as parents and/or guardians. Staff in nonresidential centers (e.g., schools) are not included.

neglect cases; DHEW figures based on the level of funding allocated to states under Titles IV-A and IV-B and Title V of the Social Security Act for abuse and neglect programs (see below); figures collected by various voluntary institutions such as hospitals, child protective agencies, and study centers such as the American Humane Association; and findings from limited research. In his testimony before the Senate Subcommittee, Vincent de Francis, the director of the American Humane Association (Children's Division), noted that "there is little factual knowledge about the size of the child abuse problem in this country. We have 'guesstimates,' but there is no current study to determine the true incidence."

A completely accurate assessment of the incidence of child abuse and neglect is almost impossible. Among other reasons, there is no way of accounting for cases unknown to agencies, professionals, authorities. Testimony before the Senate Subcommittee on Children and Youth of the Committee on Labor and Public Welfare indicated that estimates range from 60,000 cases annually nationwide to 20,000 cases annually in New York City alone, and Gil suggests a range between 2.5 and 4 million.[12] (The 60,000 figure is the one that appears most frequently in the literature. The Gil figure, generally assumed to represent an exaggeration of actual incidence, is based on a survey that asked, among other questions, if the respondent knew anyone who had abused a child; the question as posed assumed no overlap in such reports.) One article reporting more recent efforts at analysis offered the following data: reported incidents of abuse and neglect, 600,000; substantiated incidents of abuse and neglect, 360,000; abuse only, 167,500.[13] In the same article, another national estimate of confirmed child abuse is reported as 41,104.[14] Other estimates include 30–40,000 physically abused children; 100,000 sexually abused; 200,000 emotionally and psychologically damaged; and 500,000 neglected (a figure seeming to encompass all the above but not clearly specified).[15]

Such an enormous range, and such disparity in estimates, is clearly indicative of the inadequacy and unreliability of current statistics. Regardless of what definition, reporting system, or basis for estimate of incidence is employed, all experts—even those who initially claim that there is no distinction between the two—seem to agree that the incidence of neglect is about three to four times as great as the incidence of abuse.

An Historical Overview

Obviously, the problem of child abuse and neglect did not suddenly emerge in the middle of the twentieth century. Throughout history, some children have been mistreated by their parents or guardians. It has even been noted that "child abuse may be a regression to a character which comes close to being natural to the human condition."[16] Whether by infanticide, mutilation, harsh discipline, or exploitation, abuse and neglect of children—beginning with the biblical accounts of Moses, Abraham and Isaac, and of the "slaughter of the Innocents" from which Jesus was saved—have often been recognized, if not encouraged, by the cultural fabric of society. Note the wording of a popular nursery rhyme, for instance:

> There was an old woman who lived in a shoe,
> She had so many children she didn't know what to do
> She gave them some broth without any bread
> And spanked them all soundly and sent them to bed.

Whether child maltreatment has occurred in order to appease a god or to exploit children for economic profit, to maintain discipline or to control population (infanticide), the burden of parental responsibility for the cruel treatment of children has historically been transferred to a higher institution, thus leaving the individual perpetrator blameless. The United States, in this regard, inherited a relevant stream of English common law stipulating that fathers had a legal right to the custody of their children—including the right to inflict arbitrary or severe discipline.

Efforts at reform—increased government intervention in family life—began during the first half of the nineteenth century. This reform had two bases, one legal and one social. The legal underpinning of reform was based on the concept of parens patriae, the right of the state to intervene as the guardian of a minor deprived of parental care. The social thrust of such reform was to prevent neglected or abandoned children from becoming criminals or a societal burden.

The establishment of the country's first child protective societies began in 1874, in New York. In consonance with other reform efforts of the times, the early thrust of these societies was to remove children from homes in which they were abused. The protective interventions initiated by these child welfare agencies culminated in a series of laws designed to prevent the maltreatment of children and to punish the perpetrator. Their major thrust was to remove children from unsavory environments such as mixed poorhouses and almshouses, prisons, and even homes in which they suffered abuse. They also contributed to the subsequent establishment of special juvenile and family courts to handle delinquency and such interpersonal problems as child abuse or neglect.

While most protective agencies continued in the "enforcement" and court tradition, others joined what became the movement to create an administratively separate child welfare system, sometimes tied to and at other times independent of the public assistance ("welfare") authorities. Child welfare stressed "child saving" initially, but after World War II emphasized skillful, expert, professionally guided foster home and institutional care programs and adoptive services. Its literature stressed prevention, but it was largely a child placement service.

Child welfare services began initially as voluntary agency services but soon gained a measure of federal support under the original Social Security Act (now Title IV-B). Nationally, the responsibility for services is shared by voluntary sectarian and nonsectarian groups and public authorities at all governmental levels. Increasingly, voluntary agencies have received public funds to pay for child placement and other services. In some states, public services are relatively developed; in others, the service is largely voluntary. By now, however, the public treasury bears the bulk of the costs.

As child welfare has spread and become professionalized, society's responsibility toward the abused or neglected child has been carried out by social agencies; child protective services have generally been thought of as a specialized form of child welfare.

In some states, child welfare agencies—public and private—have often been given responsibility for receiving reports of abuse and neglect cases and channeling them to the appropriate legal authorities. Furthermore, in states where reporting to legal authorities is not mandatory, agencies have frequently had the additional responsibility of invoking the authority of the court when the assigned family would not otherwise accept the possibility of treatment offered by the agency. However, the overall goal of the protective services approach of recent decades has been ameliorative and rehabilitative, not persecutory or punitive. The intent is to keep the family intact when possible; to provide supportive or substantive care when indicated.

To summarize: The first child protective agency in the United States was the New York State Society for the Prevention of Cruelty to Children (SPCC), created in 1874, following a notorious child abuse case. From the late nineteenth century until passage of the Social Security Act in 1935, child protective services were provided by voluntary agencies—the various Societies for the Prevention of Cruelty to Children, Juvenile Protective Associations, Children's Protective Associations, many of these affiliated nationally with the Children's Division of the American Humane Association (see below for a more extensive description). Since passage of the Social Security Act, child protective services have become the responsibility of state public child welfare programs, but voluntary child welfare and child protective agencies are often their instruments. As in all social services, there are two approaches to service provision: state supervision or monitoring, and state direct operation of services. Since 1962, amendments to this act have stressed even further the obligation of the states to implement such provision.

Most authorities now seem to agree that existing child protective services have not been adequate in their response to the overall problem of abuse and neglect, and that current federal initiatives reflect dissatisfaction with existing child welfare services, generally, and a search for a new and more effective approach to protecting children. However, the reasons offered for this failure vary. One group (social workers, some DHEW administrators) states that the failure of protective services is a consequence of inadequate resources (money, staff, training), inadequately implemented state reporting laws, and inefficient and ineffective case-finding mechanisms and devices. They point out that regardless of substantially higher congressional authorizations for child welfare services, actual federal appropriations have remained at about $46,000,000 annually since 1968 ($50,000,000 for fiscal 1975), and programs funded under Title IV-A (now Title XX, with a potentially more flexible eligibility rule) have limited families served to those falling within certain means-tested criteria.

A second group, primarily pediatricians and other physicians, acknowledge the validity of the problem, but insist that as long as social workers persist in viewing child protective services as their own purview, effective intervention cannot be implemented. They stress the importance of multidiscipline intervention and the need for widespread community education and publicity to facilitate case finding.

Lawyers, in particular juvenile court judges, have criticized existing public protective services further, for the fragmentation of provision as well as the fragmentation of responsibility for ensuring provision. According to one well-known authority, "At times it was possible to identify as many as eight to ten medical, legal, judicial or social 'intake' workers with no one person accepting the responsibility for the care of the child or his family."[17] Further criticisms include: conflicting dispositions where several children are involved in a neglectful situation; the failure of any single agency to assume major responsibility for working with the family toward its stabilization; the failure of any individual agency to accept responsibility for intensive work with the natural parents toward return of a child once the child has been removed; lack of interest in ensuring how and when a child can return home, or whether a home is safe, if and when the child is returned.

Finally, a last general criticism relates to the need for further decentralization, developing local service centers to provide the needed services at the neighborhood level.

Regardless of their rationale, current efforts at dealing with the problem of abuse and neglect are generally ascribed to dissatisfaction with existing child protective services, in particular, and child welfare services generally, whether these inadequacies are defined as a consequence of one, some or all of the following: inadequate legislation, too little money, too few staff, poorly trained staff, inadequacy of unidisciplinary interventions, interdisciplinary conflicts, lack of commitment (staff, administrators, funders, community), fragmentation and unresponsiveness of services, inaccessibility and unavailability of services, lack of accountability and failure to assure responsibility for continuity of care, lack of knowledge. How current approaches are attempting to deal with the problem of abuse and neglect, and the differences between the earlier traditional programs and emerging and newer approaches, will be discussed later.

Framework for Provision

Federal Legislation

The Child Abuse Prevention and Treatment Act (1974) authorized an $85-million, four-year measure establishing a national center to deal with child abuse and neglect. Under the aegis of DHEW, Office of Child Development (OCD), U.S. Children's Bureau (CB), the agency will authorize grants and contracts for research purposes and demonstration projects dealing with child abuse, neglect, prevention, and treatment programs. In brief the legislation authorized an outlay of $15 million for the fiscal year ending June 30, 1974, $20 million for 1975, and $25 million for each of the following two fiscal years. (The actual appropriations, inevitably, were much smaller.)

The mission of the National Center on Child Abuse and Neglect includes the following five functions: to compile, analyze, and publish an annual summary of recent and current research on abuse and neglect; to develop and maintain an information clearinghouse on all programs, including private programs, showing promise of success for the prevention, identification, and treatment of child abuse and neglect; to compile and publish training materials for personnel who are engaged or intend to engage in the prevention, identification, and treatment of child abuse and neglect; to provide technical assistance (directly or through grant or contract) to public and nonprofit private agencies and organizations to assist them in planning, improving, developing, and carrying out programs and activities relating to the prevention, identification, and treatment of child abuse and neglect; to conduct research into the causes of child abuse and neglect and into its prevention, identification, and treatment. The demonstration programs and projects are to encompass various facets of the prevention, identification, and treatment of child abuse and neglect. Project grants may be used for purposes which include developing and establishing training programs for personnel in the fields of medicine, law, education, social work, and other relevant fields; for establishing and maintaining centers serving specific geographic areas, providing a broad range of services relating to child abuse and neglect; for furnishing consultation to teams of personnel who are working in this field; for developing innovative projects including self help, treatment of drug-related child abuse, and other programs.

For their part, the states have to meet ten specific criteria to qualify for assistance through state grants.[18] They must have in effect a child abuse and neglect law that includes provisions for *immunity for those reporting* instances of abuse and neglect from prosecution. They must provide for the *reporting of known and suspected cases* of abuse and neglect. They must have provisions for the immediate *investigation of reports* and for the *protection* of the health and welfare of the abused or neglected child or any other child in the care of the same adults. They must have administrative *procedures* (such as trained personnel) and necessary *facilities* so as to deal effectively with such cases (to receive reports, to verify reports, to decide upon treatment or service needs, to provide services, to use courts when needed). They must provide *confidentiality* for records to protect the rights of all concerned. They must provide for *cooperation from law enforcement officials*. They must provide for the *representation of the child* in all litigation. They must maintain a *level of state expenditure* that does not reduce below the levels provided during fiscal year 1973. They must provide for the *dissemination of information* to the public with respect to the abuse-neglect problems and facilities. And they must ensure recognition and *support of parental organizations* combatting child abuse and neglect to the extent feasible.

The bill provides for an advisory board to be composed of representatives from various federal agencies that have responsibilities for programs and activities related to abuse and neglect. These include OCD, OE, NIE, NIMH, NICH, SRS, and HSA. This advisory board is to have various responsibilities: to assist the Secretary of DHEW in coordinating all programs and activities related to abuse and neglect administered or assisted under the Act; to help in the development of federal standards for abuse and neglect prevention and treatment programs; to prepare and submit a report on programs assisted.

In brief, the legislation is to provide a National Center on Child Abuse and Neglect with the power to institute demonstration programs and projects designed to prevent, identify, and treat child abuse and neglect; to train personnel to deal with child abuse; to furnish technical assistance for the initiation of innovative projects, including support of parent self-help organizations, which show promise of contributing to prevention or treatment in this field. It is to provide demonstration, planning, and catalyst buttressing for existing legislative programing in the field of child abuse and neglect.

Apart from the Social Security Act of 1935, which launched federal grants to the states on a modest scale, major federal participation became possible as a consequence of amendments to this legislation, in 1962. Reimbursement for social services was raised from 50 percent to 75 percent of state costs. These amendments also refined the definitions of public child welfare to include services that prevent or treat problems of child abuse, neglect, or exploitation.

The specific parts of this act which provided for protective services are Title IV, Parts A and B, entitled "Grants to States for Aid and

Services to Needy Families for Children and for Child Welfare Services (AFDC). Part A mandated state provision of protective services to children of present, former, and potential recipients of this category of public assistance. Part B authorized support for specified child welfare services (including foster care, day care, institutional care, as well as protective services) for children and parents needing services regardless of income. The only criterion for receipt of services, which included a broad range of counseling and legal services to abused children and their parents, was established need for preventive or interventive service. Title XX took over the Title IV-A role in October 1975. Some additional protective services are provided under Title V, the Maternal and Child Health Services.

Current criticism of the existing system of child protective services as implemented under this legislation has been summarized above.

Federal Expenditures

Between fiscal years 1971 and 1974, the DHEW estimated that $224,362,000 of Title IV-A funds were spent on protective services, including immediate intervention and support and other related activities on behalf of abused and neglected children. In addition, $655,000 was slated to be spent on research and demonstration programs related to the problems of abuse and neglect.[19] These figures pertain particularly to Titles IV-A and IV-B. Similarly, DHEW estimated that during fiscal years 1971–74, $2,543,000 of Title IV-B (child welfare) funds was spent on abuse-related programs. An additional $76,132 was spent under Title V. In fact, however, this testimony revealed that these were estimates: there is no way to discern the specific amounts allocated by the federal government to abuse and neglect programs during these years since they are part and parcel of services to AFDC families and general child welfare.

Estimates of federal allocations to abuse and neglect programs made outside of DHEW are considerably lower. The Child Welfare League of America, for instance, estimates that, out of the $46 million allocated for Title IV-B, $2.6 million was spent on protective services; and of this amount, 90 percent was spent on foster care.

State Legislation

Although the Social Security Act is the major federal legislation supporting child welfare and protective services at the state level, and providing most funds for these services, it is the state governments that must initiate, administer, and operate or delegate these programs. Thus the nature of these programs is contingent on state legislation as well. Many state reporting laws have been passed—or revised—within the past decade; several reflect efforts at going beyond traditional child welfare, incorporating growing concern with the problem of abuse and neglect, and newer approaches to facilitating case identification.

All states now have legislation that is specifically directed toward the problem of child abuse. There are five general dimensions on which the statutes can be contrasted: the purpose of the statute; the legal definition of the problem; reporting procedures; provision for immunity for the reporter; and emphasis on a central registry for the reporting of cases.

The purposes of child abuse legislation vary from state to state. In some states, the intent of the law is to protect the child from being abused by his parents. In others, the major legislative objective is to rehabilitate the family unit, providing necessary services to the family as a whole. In still another group of states, the major purpose of the law is to punish abusive parents. As of 1973, some 65 percent of the states incorporated statements of protective and/or rehabilitative purpose in their reporting laws.[20]

Legislation varies greatly from state to state in terms of the specificity with which child abuse and neglect are defined. Some statutes indicate injury of a precise nature (e.g., physical or emotional abuse, by deliberate commission or negligent omission); some stipulate only that an injury must be inflicted by other than accidental means. Colorado, Idaho, and Wyoming, for instance, define abuse in specific symptomatic terms, while Alaska stipulates only "the infliction by other than accidental means of physical harm upon the body of a child." Most laws consider physical abuse only, although two states include sexual and emotional abuse as part of their definition.

Similarly, age limits for reportable children vary from state to state. A total of twenty-six states have an upper age limit of eighteen; five states stop at age seventeen; and eight states use sixteen as the upper limit for reportable children. Oregon and the Virgin Islands provide for the protection of abused children who are under age fifteen only. And California's upper age limit is twelve years. Nine states do not stipulate an upper age limit and refer in their statutes to "children" or "minors."

Reporting procedures also vary from statute to statute. Written reports as a follow-up to oral reports are required in thirty-one states. Three states call for a written report initially; and four other states allow for written follow-up to oral reports at the discretion of the agency receiving the initial oral report. One state demands a written report from a physician, but not from other sources. In recent years, there has been a general tendency away from mandatory written reports altogether. They have been perceived as superfluous to the instituting of child protective services.

Most states agree upon what is reportable: The reporter must have just cause to suspect that a child's injuries were inflicted by other than accidental means.

All states and territories deem the medical professional as primarily responsible for reporting incidents of abuse. However, many states also oblige other professionals such as social workers, school personnel, or clergy to report suspected cases. Five states do not place mandatory onus to report on any one professional group; rather they charge any person with cause to suspect child abuse with the legal responsibility to report his belief. Twenty-two states specify professional groups as reporters, but "place statutory duty to report on any other person who encounters" a possible case of abuse.

In most states, reports of suspected child abuse include identifying data, information about the nature of the injuries, and additional relevant information. Some twenty-three states call for the reporting of incidents to a single community agency, most notably to a department of welfare or law enforcement agency; twenty-one states offer a choice of two agencies; and seven require that reports go to two agencies. Twenty-nine others include a penalty clause for not reporting cases (e.g., liability for damages; commitment of a class A misdemeanor).

In all fifty states the primary agency receiving the report is responsible for follow through and attention to a case. Forty-four states specify a mandate to the agency receiving the report.

Immunity against criminal or civil action for having filed a report is found in all fifty states. Such protection applies most commonly to the medical profession. In only a few cases does immunity extend to those who are not mandated to report—"those who report in good faith." Forty-four states forbid "privileged communication" between a physician and his patient and thirty-two between man and wife in cases of suspected child abuse. However, all but three states maintain the privileged communication between attorney and client.

With regard to protective custody, eight states authorize select professional groups to hold a child against parental wishes in deleterious circumstances. Six statutes go further, specifying conditions under which a child can be removed from his home. In New York and Kentucky, certain officials are granted immediate custody if a child is in danger at home. In South Carolina and Tennessee, court intervention is required before a child can be removed from his home. And in Ohio and Nevada, welfare departments must be consulted before such action can be taken. Rights of entry are granted certain officials in four states. Provisions for guardians are generally found in juvenile court statutes.

Central registries are now required by thirty-three states, and thirteen others maintain registries although they are not mandated. While the principal function of central registries is to amass pertinent data about the phenomenon, they are also utilized to identify individuals who have been reported on more than a single occasion.

National Policies

National policy is directed toward increasing public awareness of the problem of child abuse and neglect, obtaining more accurate information about its incidence, increasing knowledge about the problem generally (etiology, prediction, prevention, treatment), expanding the development of interventive programs and techniques and improving their effectiveness.

In addition, underlying all the above, are certain other policies which DHEW officials have specified as being directly relevant to the problem. The major policy objective is "to strengthen the family as a child nurturing unit . . . , to intensify efforts to provide parents, parent surrogates, or child care givers with the necessary support to nurture children in their care," in order to reduce the potentiality of abuse and neglect of children.[21] A final objective is to provide treatment to the child abuser so that a child may remain with his family. These policies are implemented through federal grants for research and relevant demonstration programs, through federal dissemination efforts, and through federal aid to states and localities in carrying out their responsibiilties for the protection of children.

Government Agencies

The major federal governmental agency concerned with the problem of child abuse and neglect is DHEW. Within DHEW, the OCD/CB had been named the lead agency in coordinating federal initiatives in funding research and demonstration programs, commissioning state of the field reports, and surveying existing programs.[22] Participating in the interagency effort led by OCD, part of the Office of Human Development, are the NIH/NIMH/NICH, HSA, SRS, and OE. The major agencies involved are OCD and SRS. (A more extensive discussion of their activities will be included in that part of the chapter describing research endeavors.)

At the state and local levels, all state public welfare departments which want federal social service funds under the Social Security Act are mandated to provide child welfare services. These services include foster family services, adoptions, day care, and other services as well as protective services (including administration of special abuse reporting mechanisms, identification and treatment of abused children). Most programs are operated at the county level by local authorities or by the state—or by voluntary agencies which are publicly subsidized or reimbursed. In addition, juvenile courts are called upon to authorize removal of children from the home when this is deemed necessary.

Government agencies have assumed a catalytic role in the field. Particularly, the federal government has sponsored a variety of demonstration programs and research efforts. The basic research being conducted and the state of the field and program evaluation efforts subsidized by DHEW augment its leadership role.

Nongovernmental Agencies

The voluntary sector has maintained its own leadership caveat. Two long-standing voluntary agencies, the American Humane Association (Children's Division) and the Child Welfare League of America, assume leadership and coordinative functions with regard to their affiliates throughout the country. In addition, they act as advocates nationally, and offer technical assistance and extensive research facilities and disseminate relevant information and educational material. The teaching and consultation functions they assume emanate from their active leadership in research endeavors.

Programs based in professional, university, and medical center settings also offer leadership to the field. They lend professional perspective to the development of case reporting and intervention methods mandated by state legislation. They assume research and teaching roles with regard to the planning, coordinating, and monitoring of identification (case finding) and treatment programs. They distribute substantive information about the phenomenon and supply consultative assistance to communities or agencies interested in program development. Finally, the voluntary agencies involved in the field act as advocates for abused children and their families, as well as for the institutions concerned with delivering services to them; that is, they try to plan, coordinate, and monitor existing programs of intervention and they monitor the quality of existing services and dramatize gaps in quality and quantity. They also call for institutional reform in behalf of the abused and neglected child.

The following are descriptions of three of the major nongovernmental organizations concerned with the problem of abuse and neglect:

Child Welfare League of America. Established in 1920, the Child Welfare League of America is the national voluntary accrediting and standard-setting organization for child welfare agencies in the United States. It is a privately supported organization devoting its efforts completely to the improvement of care and services for children. There are 370 child welfare agencies affiliated with the League, representing voluntary agencies of all religious groups as well as nonsectarian public and private nonprofit agencies (e.g., state and city departments of welfare; Jewish Child Care Association). It is funded by dues from member organizations, project and research grants from the federal government and private foundations, and individual philanthropy. Leadership is provided by an executive director and staff and policy is determined by a board composed of representatives from the lay and professional community in both the United States and Canada.

The League program is multifaceted, including encouraging and giving technical aid for direct service provision (e.g., day care centers, residential treatment centers, homemakers, foster care, adoption), providing leadership in the child welfare field, lobbying for legislative action on relevant issues, and disseminating relevant information to the public. Its prime functions include setting standards for child welfare services, providing consultation services to local agencies and communities, conducting research, issuing child welfare publications, sponsoring regional conferences, and maintaining liaison with federal agencies and congressional committees which have an interest in child welfare issues.

With regard to the specific problem of child abuse and neglect, the League "does not view child neglect and child abuse as separate from child welfare problems [but rather sees] the physical abuse of children as being the above-surface tip of a huge iceberg known as child neglect."[23] It stresses the need for child protective services generally, rather than emphasizing the problem of abuse and neglect; and it urges concern with prevention before the fact, rather than treatment only after an abusive incident has occurred. It distinguishes its own perspective on the problem from what it terms the "medical view."

In 1960 the League published the first *Standards for Child Protective Services,* providing guidelines to social agencies and the general public regarding practice and procedures in protective services (e.g., the roles of the court and the community; the nature and range of services required—day care, foster care, health, legal, homemaker, counseling; the role of social work; the need for a multidisciplinary approach). These standards were revised in 1973 to reflect the current thinking of lawyers, doctors, nurses, law enforcement officers, public administrators, and child welfare workers.

The American Humane Association. The American Humane Association (Children's Division) (A.H.A.), with national headquarters in Denver, Colorado, is a voluntary nonprofit organization founded in 1877, having as its major objective "the prevention of cruelty, especially to children." A.H.A. activities on behalf of neglected and abused children date from its very inception. Early social action efforts on behalf of children included: the promotion of child labor laws; creation of shelters for children separated from their homes and families and detention facilities to keep children out of jails; support of special courts for children; and promotion of child protective services under the aegis of local humane societies or "Societies for the Prevention of Cruelty to Children." Since the early 1900s it has been these latter organizations that composed the major part of the membership of the national A.H.A., and constituted the only agencies specifically operating to prevent neglect, abuse, and cruel treatment of children. During the 1930s, many of these agencies were either terminated or combined with other agencies due to lack of financial support. Although various humane societies and protective societies still exist throughout the nation, most of what had originally been uniquely their function—preventing abuse and neglect of children—has been taken over by public agencies.

The A.H.A. is the national association for state, local, public, and voluntary child protective agencies. These agencies include probation services and juvenile courts, welfare planning councils, educational services, and health services, as well as interested citizens. A.H.A.'s specific objectives are to inform on the nature, extent, and dimensions of problems of child neglect, abuse, and exploitation; to promote understanding about causative factors contributing to these conditions; to advise on ways to identify children in need of protection and on services for meeting their needs; and to assist in organizing new child protective programs in keeping with the optimum social work standards and to improve existing programs. To achieve these goals the A.H.A. is engaged in a multifaceted program which includes research and surveys dealing with the problems of abuse-neglect and with services, as well as laws relating to these problems. It also publishes reports, monographs, and training manuals and offers consultation to states and communities. It carries out training activities of several kinds.

The A.H.A. has published a total of over sixty books, pamphlets, and leaflets dealing with various facets of the problems of neglected and abused children. These written materials deal with a variety of topics. Some are surveys of existing child protective services. Others deal with child abuse legislation. Some detail the problems of victims, while others deal with characteristics of abusers. Legal material deals with the rights of parents versus those of children, and with the jurisdiction of juvenile and family courts. Written newsletters and publications of national symposiums on child abuse are also available.

The A.H.A. has defined child protective services as a specialized area of child welfare services generally. As such it is concerned with "preventing neglect, abuse, and exploitation of children by 'reaching out' with social services to stabilize family life. It seeks to preserve the family unit by strengthening parental capacity for good child care. While the Association is child centered, its special focus is on the family whose unresolved problems have produced visible signs of neglect or abuse; on the home situation that presents actual or potential hazards to the physical or emotional well-being of children."[24]

The A.H.A. defines abuse as the most visible part of the whole problem of child neglect. It stresses the role of child protective services in eliminating the problem and identifies current inadequacies and failures of the service as the result of inadequate funding and staffing resources, and the failure of existing case-finding, identification, and reporting systems. It defines the social services–based protective services as being the major responsible agencies for intervening in this problem locally, but requiring input and support from the medical and legal professions with regard to case finding, reporting, and immediate intervention when needed.

Its current initiatives and ongoing monitoring activities are derived from the following conclusions: Although all of the fifty states have legal frameworks and ongoing programs for child protection, no community has a program adequate in size to meet the needs of the abused and neglected child and his family. Further congressional action is needed so that child protective services may be mandated in every state plan for social services; this implies the allocation of sufficient funds earmarked particularly to fund child protective services in each state. Much increased participation by the federal government in providing training for personnel is indicated. Federal support for research is imperative. Sufficient stimulation of case finding is lacking at present. Federal support for gathering relevant data about the general problems of child abuse and neglect is called for.

In July 1973, the American Humane Association was funded by a grant from OCD/CB to establish a National Clearinghouse on Child Neglect and Abuse. The purpose of this center is to collect, analyze, and disseminate information concerning the problem and the incidence of child maltreatment. The Clearinghouse will make available on a nationwide basis data about case identification and reporting systems, and about the quality of legislative provisions for child protection. The information will be deployed to upgrade this entire field through innovation, planning, legislative initiative, increase of services.

The American Academy of Pediatrics. The American Academy of Pediatrics is a professional organization for certified pediatricians in the United States. In addition to the many functions performed by any professional group for its specialized membership, it studies and disseminates information about various problems that affect children medically.

In 1966, its Committee on Infant and Preschool Child issued a statement about the problem of the battered child. This publication offered a historical perspective and definition of the problem, as well as recommendations for the identification and protection of the abused child.

In 1972, the Committee reviewed its 1966 statement and reaffirmed its recommendations that the physician adopt an active role in the identification, investigation, and treatment of child abuse cases. It called for stronger investigation and evaluation units within protective service agencies, for central clearinghouses of information about individual cases, and immunity for the physicians who reported suspected cases to public authorities.

In recognizing the inadequate quality of existing information, the Committee recommended the development of techniques for identifying potential abusers, crisis management programs, diagnosis and treatment programs, day care services, and increased hospital involvement with child abuse cases.[25]

In consonance with its recommendations, the Committee has supported the testimony of its members before the U.S. Congress.[26] It has developed a self-instructional program of educational materials designed to disseminate relevant information about program development in the abuse and neglect area. Also, it has developed liaison with various nationwide programs for consultative purposes, including Head Start, the American Public Health Association, and the juvenile courts. In addition, the Committee conducted a descriptive study of nine health-based programs in the field of child abuse and neglect, under the sponsorship of the Health Resources Administration.

The network of services for abused and neglected children is a complex meshing of the public and private sectors. Much of the voluntary sector programing—in particular the direct service programs—is subsidized by funding authorized by Social Security legislation; and most of the research and demonstration programs, even though under voluntary auspices, are also funded by public resources. This provides both obligation and opportunity for public leadership—or, if that is not sought, coordinative efforts.

Program Models

There is no real primary prevention for so vaguely delineated a phenomenon as abuse and neglect except good social policy for children[27] and good provision for socialization of children and families in interaction with their communities.[28] Therefore, what the following program models really deal with are case finding and identification, case reporting, investigation, diagnosis, treatment, and follow-up.

Programs may be conducted under either public or voluntary (private, nonprofit) auspices. Regardless of auspice, the major models fall into two categories although some programs include a combination of both: 1) *case finding* or locating, *reporting,* identifying, and *investigating* cases as critical for intervention in the problem of abuse and/or neglect; 2) *variations in treatment modalities (including diagnosis, treatment, and follow-up)*. All concerned understand that both of these functions—all the tasks, in fact—are essential for a comprehensive system of coverage, but no one program can do everything. What follows does not even begin to be complete. We describe the programs merely to illustrate alternative approaches and variations in implementing functions.

Case-Finding and Reporting Programs

These programs have as their primary function at least one of the following: location and identification of abuse and neglect cases; reporting of cases and clarification of prior status (previous validated reports of abuse or neglect); receipt of reports; investigation and validation of reports; information, advice, referral for emergency services for such cases. Programs in this category may be established with one of these functions or more in different combinations. One problem is that the efficacy of these programs is partly contingent on widespread public education regarding the problem. Another, and far more important, is the lack of clarity regarding the combination of functions and their appropriate implementation.

As discussed earlier, all states have legislation requiring the reporting of child abuse cases to public authorities; thus, all have some basic mechanism for case finding. However, the effectiveness of the mechanism varies with the strength of the law and the means with which it has been implemented. For whom is reporting mandatory? Only physicians or all professionals working with children? To what extent are reporters protected against legal action as a result of reporting an incident? What occurs once a report is made? To what extent has the public at large been made aware of the problem and the appropriate mechanisms and channels for reporting?

One model for the identification and reporting of cases is the centralized *state registry*. At present, forty-six states have registries. Supported and staffed under state auspices, the registry is a clearinghouse for information about individuals known to have been involved in an incident of child abuse. The reports are made by professionals or laymen, and once validated, information is made available to a variety of relevant institutions such as hospitals. Such information is available only to individuals and institutions specified under the law. Providing it to unauthorized persons is punishable under law. The state registry provides a liaison to community agencies for the treatment, follow-up, and feedback of child abuse cases.

Registries also exist at the local level, in certain counties and cities (e.g., New York).

Another reporting and case identification mechanism is the *hotline.* Hotlines are continuously staffed telephone lines accessible to an abusive parent or to anyone wanting to report a case of abuse. Some hotlines are professionally staffed and include provision for arranging referrals to treatment agencies; some are conducted directly under the aegis of a treatment agency or institution; some are informal hotlines conducted by and for groups of parents who are—or are at risk of becoming—abusers.

Regardless of auspices, the focus of a hotline is to counsel abusive parents on an emergency basis, as well as to contribute to more effective home management and psychiatric rehabilitation when possible. It is a nonpunitive, semi-authoritative approach based on the concept that the best interests of the child are supreme. To be effective, adequate telephone outlets must be available and sufficient staff to answer the telephones (constantly busy lines will inhibit callers and reduce effectiveness); staff must be skilled in information gathering and interviewing, and committed. Furthermore, qualitatively and quantitatively adequate therapeutic and interventive services must be available.

Various types of institutions, including hospitals, departments of welfare, and voluntary social agencies also provide for the reporting and identification of child abuse cases. Cases are reported to a central place within the institution and information about known cases is shared with appropriate community resources.

It is important to note, however, that none of the above measures do anything more than provide vehicles for bringing the abused child to the official attention of society. No benefit to the child (or to society) results unless proper follow-up procedures are instituted. In this context, we stress the fact that neither reporting systems, registries, nor hotlines can be effective unless interventions and services can be provided immediately, as needed.

Diagnosis, Treatment, and Follow-Up Programs

Diagnosis, treatment, and follow-up programs stress the use of various therapeutic interventions. Their primary function may be either to develop effective interventive techniques and service delivery mechanisms or to expand knowledge (etiology, prediction, secondary prevention, program evaluation) through research. Most of these interventive efforts include some coordinative and integrative function, both among different disciplines and among different agencies.

The major goal of all forms of therapeutic intervention is to protect the child by identifying, intervening, and/or preventing abuse—or re-abuse—wherever possible. Secondary goals include preserving the family unit whenever possible and increasing the parents' self-esteem and their capacity to handle crises.

Models of therapeutic intervention vary according to auspice, staff, and degrees and type of involvement with the child and his family. Some treatment programs are carried out in institutions, such as hospitals, courts, or departments of social service; one or more categories of relevant professionals may be involved. Other programs are staffed by laymen, and implemented in the community. And some are self-help programs in which abusive—or potentially abusive—parents help themselves and each other.

Therapeutic intervention models are based upon a concept of what constitutes an abusive pattern; a parent that has the potential for abuse; a child who is particularly vulnerable to abuse; and some form of crisis.[29] One criterion for distinguishing models relates to the varying degrees of therapeutic involvement with the abused child and his family. Thus, a "zero" degree of involvement is a total lack of intervention. The child remains at home, and abuse continues. At the "one" level of involvement, the child remains at home and a therapist (lay or professional) makes a home visit once a month, to recommend that the parent be a "good parent." The next degree of involvement (the "two" level) assumes that the child has been separated from the family by a court mandate. (In reality, separation is not a viable therapeutic solution on any long-term basis.) The "third" level is a stronger degree of involvement and assumes that the home can be made safe by early intervention. It assumes that the parent is willing to become involved in long-term therapy, and that a professional, capable therapist is available on a long-term basis. In reality, it is this third level of involvement—that is, the one based on the assumption that early initiation in therapy (broadly defined) can make a home safe for a child and his family—that is realistic and desirable.

Another criterion for categorizing program models relates to the target of intervention: the parent, child, or family unit. Thus, intervention may involve punishing the parent (court action and penalties imposed on the parent), a "once-a-month" telling the parent to be "good," or self-help and mutual assistance from within a group of "abusive" parents. It may involve removing the child from the home, on an emergency, temporary, or long-term basis. Or intervention may involve a combination of temporary removal (brief foster care, day care), self-help, and several other interventions (homemakers, counseling) in order to support the family unit. (This latter approach could also be included under "level three" above.)

One model of intervention that focuses solely upon the child's needs is practiced under the auspices of a public or voluntary social agency and/or the court, and is crisis-oriented. Depending upon an agency's assessment of the family's suitability, a child may be removed from his home on a temporary, long-term, or permanent basis, with arrangements made for the child's psychiatric and social needs to be met by agency-provided services. Foster care, adoption, or institutional care is arranged as indicated.

An illustration of such a community-based model is a new and improved version of a public child protective service, now redesigned and restructured as a comprehensive emergency service (CES) for children in crisis. This model stresses the development of a system of coordinated services involving both public and voluntary agencies and consists of the following basic components: twenty-four hour emergency intake service, emergency caretakers, emergency homemakers, emergency foster family homes, emergency shelters for families, emergency care for adolescents, and outreach and follow-up service. The CES is premised on the assumption that continuity of service is a key factor in implementing such a program. By providing a 24-hour, 7-day-a-week emergency intake service (which anyone can call on), and with a case worker maintaining responsibility for seeing that services are provided, it is possible to assure an integrated and coherent approach to what frequently is fragmented provision elsewhere. In effect, this model provides for accountability and case integration,* by guaranteeing immediate response and intervention and by assuming primary responsibility for the provision of multiple and multidisciplinary services, as needed by the child or his parents. It is the responsibility of the CES coordinator to ensure the cooperation of other agencies and other relevant service systems (e.g., health, education, judicial). Regular conferences for coordination and clearly

*See Chapter 7 for a discussion of the role and function of case integration, and for further discussion of the concept of accountability.

and precisely written contractual agreements between agencies are essential to the functioning of such a system. The prototype for this model is the Metropolitan Nashville–Davidson County's Emergency Services System. This project was funded as a demonstration project by DHEW, OCD/CB.

Another child-oriented crisis-treatment model is practiced in a hospital setting. When a child is admitted for medical treatment as a result of having been abused or neglected, a consultation team participates in the management (diagnosis, evaluation, treatment, referral) of his case. The team generally includes pediatricians, social workers, psychiatrists, and case coordinators–integrators—or liaison workers—who function in relation to community agencies.

The function of the team is to encourage the meshing of the services of different departments, professionals, and agencies around a case to ensure the delivery of adequate services to the child and his family. The consultative team meets regularly to discuss treatment and disposition plans for individual cases. Members of the team participate in treatment, case management, disposition, and follow-up.

Often supplementing this approach are several other forms of intervention, described below. On occasion, these may also be employed as individual interventions, although most experts recommend that they be used in a cluster. For example, the lay therapist model focuses primarily upon the needs of the parents. Usually supervised and supported under the aegis of a hospital or social agency, the lay therapist intervenes after a professional assessment and recommendation has been made. This intervention consists of regular home visits and continuous availability calculated to resemble an intense, nonprofessional friendship. On occasion, two "therapists" may alternate in providing a supportive relationship—and being available—to the parent. The primary goal of the therapy is to prevent crises and incidents of child abuse by offering the parent empathetic, uncritical support. Intermediary goals include helping the parent recognize when a crisis is about to occur, and helping him to establish healthy and realistic relationships with his children, spouse, and acquaintances.[30] A variation on this is the use of "parent aides" and/or specially trained homemakers to intervene in child care, provide role models for parents with impaired or inadequate parenting knowledge and capacity, and, equally important, provide emotional support and surrogate parenting for the parents themselves.

Another parent-focused model of intervention is known as the "crisis nursery." Housed in churches, foundling homes, or other family-centered institutions, they are residential facilities for child abusers and, in some cases, for their children. Crisis nurseries are available as a respite place or on an emergency basis to parents who are afraid they are about to abuse their children. Staffed by professionals and paraprofessionals, the crisis nursery offers counseling and educational guidance in child rearing. Crisis nurseries may be operated as a residential or day care center and may or may not admit children as well as parents.

Related to this model are therapeutic day care programs—programs which provide a brief respite for parents, offer good care for children, and provide opportunities for socializing experiences for the parents. This approach is often employed as an additional or supplementary form of intervention, when parents are also involved with a "lay therapist" program or self-help program (see below).

A very different therapeutic model than those described above is one based on a concept of self-help. Parents Anonymous may be the best-known example of this model, although other similar organizations exist called Mothers Anonymous and Families Anonymous. This is a crisis intervention focused on the prevention and treatment of destructive or abusive behavior by parents. Its goal is to perpetuate an organized program for parents who fear they might abuse a child—or are actively engaged in any form of physical or emotional abuse toward a child—and to help rehabilitate parents who are engaged in such physical or emotional abuse.

In some ways akin to Alcoholics Anonymous, Parents Anonymous functions by means of weekly group therapy meetings which may be attended, but are not led, by professionals. (One reason that professionals may be excluded from leading or officially participating in these groups relates to the unanticipated consequence of mandatory reporting laws when confronted by new interventive techniques.) Between meetings, members have access to each other twenty-four hours a day should a crisis arise, or should they feel the need for support.

Administratively, these groups establish a liaison with community agencies that allows for appropriate referrals and consultative services but does not violate the confidentiality and self-help concept of the program. All Parents Anonymous groups are loosely affiliated. Guidance in program development is provided by the charter organization located in California. The group is privately financed as a charitable, nonprofit, tax-deductible agency.

The following are illustrations of some of the models described above: the first is a case-finding and identification program generally described as the best statewide program of its type in the country; the next three are varying approaches to therapeutic intervention, all employing a multidiscipline and multiprogram approach. We note that at present there are no data available to indicate the number of such programs in the country today, nor, obviously, the number of cases so treated annually. Neither are there any firm data to indicate the effectiveness of such programs.

Illustrative Program Models

Hotline and Registry

Florida's statewide program for investigation and intervention into the problem of abuse and neglect is an example of a legally mandated, coordinated reporting and feedback mechanism.[31] This system functions under the aegis of the state public welfare department, and is aimed at implementing case finding, rapid investigation, and follow-up as part of the statewide protective service system.

Florida's child abuse legislation was revised in 1971 to call for mandatory reports of suspected cases from physicians, social workers, nurses, teachers, and other employees of private or public children's organizations. It mandates a central registry, the provision of records to be shared with juvenile courts, and immunity and waiver of privileged communications in relevant judicial hearings.

Florida's program is composed primarily of a public-media campaign designed and developed by an advertising firm and a 7-day-a-week, 24-hour-a-day hotline service, using inward and outward WATS lines for the receipt and dispersal of child abuse reports from all parts of the state. The media campaign consists of spot commercials on radio, television, and billboards as well as newspaper articles designed to alert and educate the citizenry about child abuse and neglect as well as to instruct them about how to report suspected cases. Television and radio stations are offered a variety of materials from which to choose an appropriate format. Different public service announcements and different length "commercials" are used for different types of programs.

The campaign is based upon a coordinated, twofold theme: "who would hurt a little child?" and "lift a finger to save a child." This theme is expanded through articles explaining the problem and the rationale for the hotline and through releasing the phone number for the hotline. The wording of information released on the radio, on television, and on billboards is similar; the public reads about the problem in the newspaper, sees a billboard, is reminded of the hotline telephone number, and hears about the program on the radio. All media refer to the same headline and use the same language.

In addition to the major media, ancillary media material is also utilized. Bulletin board posters and telephone stickers are distributed in appropriate institutions and buildings throughout the state.

Some of the time and space not provided for by state subsidy has been supplied by the media and by billboard companies. Also, federal legislation requiring that radio and television grant public service time has been exploited on behalf of the child abuse program. Television has proved to be the most efficacious medium in encouraging the reporting of child abuse cases. Billboards and radio commercials have also been successful. By and large, newspapers have been reluctant to print public service messages.

In addition to its public media campaign, Florida's program offers a 24-hour hotline reporting and protective services unit which is designed to accept and investigate reported cases within a 24-hour time period. Toll-free calls are accepted at any time. The social worker who answers the call compiles as much information as possible, then alerts the health and rehabilitation unit in the county from which the call was made. From there, both social and legal intervention are supposed to be initiated within a 24-hour time period. Each case is recorded and followed to its final disposition by the staff of the central registry to which it was originally reported.

Between 1971 and 1974 (over a 29-month period) the number of cases reported per year increased from 17 in 1971 to more than 25,000. (The state's population is approximately 7.7 million, with 2.3 million children under age 18.) The state now receives about 2,500 reports a month, of which two-thirds are investigated; and of these, about 60 percent are found valid or substantiated.

Florida's coordinated approach to the problem of case finding is the most successful statewide effort in the country. It has resulted in a substantial increase, both in the numbers of cases reported and investigated and in the number of statistics available. Unfortunately, despite the increase in public education about the problem and in the number of cases reported, the level of state funding for case (report) investigation and follow-up has proved limited. Because of the shortage of staff, the state investigates only two-thirds of those cases reported to the central registry, and even among those, many investigations are delayed for long periods of time (five or six months). Some reports indicate that because state resources are stretched so thin, less serious cases may not be receiving the sort of attention that might serve to prevent their becoming more severe. Finally, the rate of recidivism or repeated reporting is not currently being investigated.

We note these problems in order to underscore an issue of major importance: Regardless of how outstanding a case-finding system may be, adequate resources and provision for follow-up and intervention and treatment are essential in order for the overall program to be fully implemented. This problem of inadequate follow-up is not unique in Florida, as we will see in subsequent material on New York State.

Trauma X

Trauma X is a hospital-based interdisciplinary and interagency consultation unit.[32] Its purpose is twofold: to provide diagnostic, interventive, and follow-up services to child abuse victims; and to serve as a clearinghouse of information about individual cases and about the problem and development of services for abused children in general. Its base is one particular community—the neighborhood served by the hospital. Its major limitation is that its responsibility for cases ends soon after discharge and referral to community services.

The program functions under the aegis of the Department of Medicine and Psychiatry at Children's Hospital, which is located in the center of Boston, Massachusetts. It is responsible for its policy decisions to an advisory board composed of the chairman of the above department as well as the director of social service and an associate administrator of Children's Hospital.

Trauma X participants include medical, social work, and nursing staff from the hospital, as well as a case coordinator, whose function it is to arrange meetings and coordinate the administrative details of the unit. Three community agencies also provide personnel for the team. These agencies include the Division of Family and Children's Services unit of the Department of Public Welfare and two voluntary protective services agencies. Legal counsel for the team is provided by Harvard Medical School through Children's Hospital and the Laboratory of Community Psychiatry as well as by the juvenile courts.

In addition to the ordinary funding sources of participating agencies, the program is funded by the OCD as part of a Family Development Study grant and by the Office of Judicial Administration in Boston.

Trauma X was initiated in response to the inadequacy of preexisting services. Until its inception, cases had been reported to the Department of Public Welfare; however, the protective services they were capable of providing were severely limited by inadequate funding and staffing. Founding Trauma X was an attempt to devise a systematic method for case finding, education, intervention, and follow-up.

The program team meets weekly to provide information about individual in-patients. Hospital staff are involved as relevant and appropriate. Pertinent information is collected and provided by community referral resources and by the hospital social worker involved in the case. Records are maintained to ensure effective delivery of service as well as to increase the data base about the incidence of the problem. These records include identifying information about individuals and families, the history of interventive efforts on their behalf, and plans for future intervention, discharge, and follow-up.

The in-hospital staff members of the program are composed of a group of medical and social work consultants. They are responsible for intake and coordination with the management team responsible for an individual case. Decisions for an individual case are made by a clinical management team. Trauma X functions as a consultative unit to the clinical management team. Referrals to the program are initiated by a physician and referred to a "designated consultant," who follows the case until the patient is discharged from the hospital. A case is discussed at a Trauma X meeting only when the data are complete or when there is a lack of consensus among professionals or agencies about case-management.

Cases referred to Trauma X are followed by a hospital management team and the designated consultant until the patient is discharged from the hospital. At that time the case's data coordinator files a record of demographic data, discharge plans, and recommendations. Each case is followed up at specified intervals, the length of which is based upon perceived risk to the child. Referrals are then made to appropriate agencies.

Between 1972 and 1973, 72 cases were hospitalized and followed by the Trauma X consultation unit. Of these, 61 were referred from within the hospital, 33 of these by physicians. Seven cases were referred by private individuals. Symptomatology included 28 fractures, 14 bruises, 12 cases of "failure to thrive," and 7 burns. Between

1970 and 1972 the rate of re-injury was reduced from 8 percent to 1.7 percent of the cases served by the unit.

Temporary Shelter

The Temporary Shelter was established as the result of a New York City Task Force recommendation that comprehensive service programs be instituted for abusive parents and their children.[33] The program was originally funded as a demonstration program by DHEW, and sponsored on a permanent basis by the City and the State of New York, and by the New York Foundling Home. Most of the funding comes from the City's Department of Social Service; some comes from the Department of Mental Health and Mental Retardation. The total annual operating budget is approximately $300,000.

The Temporary Shelter is located in one wing of the New York Foundling Hospital. Under the auspices of the Sisters of Charity, this hospital has been in existence for 104 years. Its primary goal has been the prevention and amelioration of problems besetting abused, neglected, and dependent children and their families. In connection with various medical centers throughout Manhattan, it offers comprehensive medical and social services to such families.

The facilities of the Temporary Shelter are modern, spotless, and beautifully appointed. They include two conference rooms; a large nursery, brightly decorated and filled with stimulating toys; a modern and well-equipped kitchen and community dining room. Ten large bedrooms accommodate a mother and child comfortably. A meeting room is used for various classes including consumer education, arts and crafts, and exercises.

The Temporary Shelter program is a multidiscipline team program, the major goal of which is to rehabilitate indigent abusive and neglectful mothers. The therapeutic and educational program is geared toward strengthening the patient's ability to mother. It provides crisis intervention for mothers and protective intervention for children primarily on a residential or in-patient basis; an expanded out-patient program has been started, which includes community outreach services and a 24-hour hotline manned by the in-patient staff.

The forty mothers who have been in-patients at the temporary shelter have been referred by the Bureau of Child Welfare, the courts, or city hospitals. Participation in the program is voluntary. However, in a few cases, residential treatment has been strongly recommended as the only alternative to having the child removed from home. To be accepted into the program, the mothers must be on welfare, between 16 and 30 years old, and have no more than two children. Larger families are treated on an out-patient basis. All participants live in the greater metropolitan area.

Of those mothers who have been treated to date, 50 percent have been black, 15 percent Spanish, and 35 percent white. The average age has been 22, the age range has been 17–28. One mother completed high school. The I.Q.'s have ranged from 59 to 114. All but two were single parents.

At any given time, eight patients live at the Temporary Shelter for a stay of from three to six months. The two extra rooms are saved for crises and short-term emergency admissions. Following an intake interview with a psychiatrist, psychologist, and social worker, an individualized treatment plan is formulated. For all residents, the program consists of individual and group therapy, intensive and frequent contact with the professional and paraprofessional staff, and educational classes. The classes include lectures on consumer information, nutrition, grooming, and child care and infant stimulation. In addition to attending therapy sessions and classes, the residents take turns planning and preparing meals. While they are living in the Temporary Shelter, the mothers are encouraged to go out frequently, and to entertain visitors. Most visitors tend to be the patients' mothers and boyfriends.

As progress is noted, the mothers are encouraged to gradually resume their lives in the community. With assistance from the staff as needed, they seek new apartments if necessary, enroll their children in day care programs, enroll themselves in job training or high-school equivalency programs, and begin to leave the shelter for a few days at a time. Once the mother has returned to the community, she continues to be followed closely by the staff. Social service assistants make home visits two or three times a week, and the patient returns to the hospital for therapy at least twice a week. After one year, referrals are made to other community agencies as needed.

The staff includes twenty professionals and paraprofessionals, who participate on a full- or part-time basis. The professional staff includes a psychiatrist, a psychologist, a sociologist, and social workers. The paraprofessional staff includes group mothers and social service assistants. The role of the group mothers is to function as mother surrogates and as role models for the residents while they are living at the shelter. The group mothers teach the patients how to dress, feed, and care for their babies, how to groom themselves. The task of the social service assistant is to act as an advocate for the patient as she begins to resume her life outside the shelter. The social service assistant may help the patient find an apartment and become known to the social service agencies she may need, and is available on a 24-hour basis in case any emergency arises.

The social service assistants and group mothers have been chosen not on the basis of educational qualifications, but because of their understanding of the role of a mother, because of their attitudes toward the problems of mothering, and for their ability to "mother" the patients. All are mothers themselves. Selected by the personnel department of the New York Foundling Home in tandem with the staff of the Temporary Shelter, these paraprofessionals undergo in-service training and intensive supervision.

The atmosphere of the in-patient service is permeated by constant activity, enthusiasm on the part of both staff and patients alike, and warmth and sensitivity. The staff is obviously close-knit. The mothers seem to respond to the friendly, informal, and nonauthoritarian atmosphere. For instance, they do not hesitate to express their opinions about daily plans, about one another's problems, and so on, both during formal group meetings and informally. The dedication of the staff is clearly appreciated by the mothers. Long after they have been released from the shelter, the mothers return to visit, and feel free to contact the staff when they need help. Contact has been maintained with every past resident.

The staff claims total success in that no past resident has subsequently abused her child. In fact, 65 percent of the mothers have been fortified enough to be able to keep their children at home. Thirty-three percent have been able to place their children voluntarily. In only two cases has the staff found it necessary to take a mother to court in order that the child be removed from the home.

National Center

The National Center for Prevention and Treatment of Child Abuse is located in Denver, Colorado.[34] Supported by private sources, it was founded in 1972 as an outgrowth of the work of the Child Protection Team of the Department of Pediatrics of the University of Colorado Medical Center. The Center's two primary goals are to provide ongoing services to abused children and their families and to disseminate appropriate knowledge and skills to professionals in the field. The staff includes pediatricians, social workers, psychiatrists, psychologists, nurses, attorneys, and lay therapists. It also includes researchers, a coordinator, and secretaries. The Center is equipped with a library, videotape and audiovisual aids, and other educational materials.

Referrals come to the Center from the University of Colorado Medical Center, as well as from welfare departments, school physicians, schools, and social agencies throughout the state. Psychiatric and social service evaluations precede a case disposition conference held weekly.

Various treatment modalities are employed. They include a lay therapist program in which paraprofessionals develop a supportive relationship, primarily with the parents. Each lay therapist works with two families at a time and participates in weekly supervisory meetings under psychiatric and social work supervision.

A second treatment modality used at the Center is a "families anonymous" approach. This self-help approach consists of weekly discussion groups attended, but not directed, by a professional staff member. A 24-hour answering service is staffed by and available to group members during crises.

The Center's crisis nursery provides emergency care for parents and children on a short-term basis. The purpose of this service is to provide immediate services on an emergency basis. "Parenting" skills are developed and taught to the mother. Supplementing this, or as an alternate, is the use of quality day care programs to provide good short-term care for children, offer parents respite from child caring, and provide socializing opportunities for parents.

The training program is extensive. While the program of instruction focuses on the phenomenon of child abuse and alternative treatment modalities, it includes didactic material on the development of multidisciplinary child abuse programs. Various modalities of self-instruction are employed. An extensive library includes audiovisual materials as well as more traditional teaching materials. In addition to monthly didactic meetings, the Center offers short- and long-term training for professional and lay groups. It also supplies consultants and speakers to social agencies throughout the country and has been a major influence nationally. A periodic newsletter circulates information about current trends and programs.

Research and Evaluation

Formal research and evaluation is in its incipient stages. Because there is no consensus in the field—either about the nature of the phenomenon or about the effectiveness of alternative methods of intervention—no provision for reporting, evaluating, or providing feedback has been agreed upon.

Despite a myriad of hypotheses,[35] little information is available about the etiology and dynamics of the abuse-neglect problem. It is not known how often children of abusers become abusers as adults, or what the relationship is between abusive behavior and neglect or such other psychosocial problems as alcoholism, drug abuse, or delinquency. Nor is there any knowledge regarding prediction or likelihood of abusive behavior.

In addition, little documentation is available about the demographic parameters of the phenomenon. Identification of abusers varies with the nature of the laws governing the reporting of abuse cases to authorities; therefore, there is no way of knowing exactly how many cases there are. Without knowing the number of existing cases, there is no way to assess the ratio of extant cases to that of cases known to social agencies or legal authorities.

There are no data regarding effective strategies for intervention with abusive parents. Needless to say, no valid technique for program evaluation in the field exists. Controlled field studies, even classification of existing programs according to predetermined criteria of effectiveness, have yet to be undertaken.

Those studies that have been undertaken are indicative of the chaotic and underdeveloped nature of what is definitively known. Research supported and/or initiated by DHEW indicates the incipient nature of existing research; major current efforts by OCD and SRS include the commissioning of state-of-the-art papers, surveys of existing program resources and facilities, exploratory studies regarding new approaches to intervention and to training personnel, new approaches to case finding, and the development of a national clearinghouse for information about abuse and neglect programs around the country.

In 1973, four DHEW offices (OCD, SRS, OE, OS) represented on the Intradepartmental Committee on Child Abuse and Neglect funded research projects in the above areas, costing $4 million. These include an effort at revising the 1962 Model Child Abuse and Neglect Reporting law, a survey of existing child abuse programs, development of an improved reporting form, and support for over one hundred self-help groups for parents. The funds have also financed eleven county and local demonstration projects to assist victims of child abuse and their families. Funded partly by OCD and SRS, many of the demonstration programs are designed to coordinate existing services, to demonstrate effective ways to operate county-wide prevention and treatment programs. These projects will be evaluated under a separate grant that will focus on organization of programs, staff training, cost analysis, and the combinations of services that are most effective with different population groups. In addition, the grants support another group of twelve demonstration centers responsible for comprehensive service programs to abused and neglected children, including investigation, assessment, treatment, referral, public education, hot lines, supportive services and coordination with other agencies, and eleven regional resource projects to promote more effective use of community resources and provide technical assistance to state and local programs to help them initiate or improve services.

Another $2 million in grants was awarded (in July 1974) to fifteen research projects focused primarily on identifying causes of child abuse and neglect; and an additional $2.8 million for the expansion of the regional service projects described above and for the development of innovative programs to serve isolated population groups such as Indians, the military, and rural and immigrant families.

The major research priorities continue to be the causes of child abuse, the relationship of the use of drugs and alcohol to abuse and neglect, the long-range effects of abuse on children, treatments having lasting effects, factors causing parents to stop abusive behavior, and measures of the effectiveness of child abuse services.

NIMH is supporting similar types of research, as well as a study that will explore the role of the juvenile courts in cases of child abuse and the legal barriers which present obstacles to the use of diagnostic, preventive, and rehabilitative treatment modalities.

Outside government, research is concerned with problems of identification, etiology, effective intervention, prevention. Thus far, little is known regarding effective predictive or preventive strategies, or effective strategies for intervention with abusing parents.

In general, lack of knowledge and lack of consensus make any existing findings questionable. The need for research is considerable. Few studies address the problem of neglected children generally. Most current efforts, both federally funded and other, are concentrated on the problem of child abuse, in particular physical abuse. Yet even here the need for rigorous research is enormous. Most existing research is descriptive and/or inductive. Completed studies exhibit "soft" findings that have relevance only within the context of the researcher's definition of the problem. Many studies are based on very small samples of uncertain representativeness. Findings are not really generalizable; yet conclusions are drawn as if, in fact, they were. Much more extensive information is needed—not only about the etiology, function, dynamics, and incidence of the problem, but about the effectiveness of alternative methods of intervention. Until such knowledge is available, program development will continue to be severely handicapped. Finally, because of these enormous gaps in basic knowledge, effective program implementation will continue to be limited, handicapped as it is by inadequate knowledge regarding interventive strategies as well as by inadequate information regarding adequate and appropriate staffing and administration and by difficulties in ensuring accountability.

Programs in Action

Let us look in some detail at one community's efforts to deal with the problem. The local picture is illustrative of what is currently going on nationally in the field, and reflects the same confusion about definition and boundaries of the problem, the inadequacy of existing knowledge, and the emergence of new initiatives in working with physically abused children. Here, too, one sees the highlighting of a particular aspect of the problem—physical abuse of the young child—and the duality, sometimes even dichotomy, in approaches between traditional child welfare and protective service, on the one hand, and newer programs employing comprehensive and multidisciplinary interventions, on the other. Finally, and perhaps most important, this community provides some revealing material and insight into why the traditional approach was and is ineffective and why the newer approaches seem better.

Before examining the community efforts, we should place the programs in context. This northeastern state, unlike some others, has no state-operated child welfare programs other than some institutions. However, it does participate in the funding of certain county- and city-operated child welfare services, and in the costs to local governments of purchasing such services from voluntary agencies. It mandates that each county provide child protective services as specified by the federal government (DHEW). In addition, like all other states, it has passed specific legislation on the problem of child abuse. In fact, a new Child Protective Services Act was passed in 1973, and is designed to facilitate case finding and identification of both abused and maltreated children. A "maltreated" child is defined as any child under the age of 18 who has been declared neglected by the court (e.g., "whose physical, mental or emotional condition has been impaired, or is in imminent danger of becoming impaired as a result of the failure of his parent or other person legally responsible for his care to exercise a minimum degree of care" in supplying adequate food, shelter, education, or medical, dental, optometrical, or surgical care) or who has had serious physical injury inflicted on him by other than accidental means. The law mandates reporting of incidents of physical abuse, sexual abuse, and maltreatment, by a wide range of professionals and officials having contact with children. Among those persons required to report such incidents are all medical personnel (physicians, residents, interns, nurses), other hospital personnel, mental health workers, police, school teachers, social workers, child care workers (e.g., day care workers). In addition to those required to report, any other person suspecting such incidents may report to the appropriate place or person. All those who report are assured of immunity against legal action; and the law provides for penalties for failure to report by those mandated to do so. Finally, there is a statewide reporting system and registry, established specifically to receive reports and maintain a registry of validated cases of abuse and maltreatment, to eliminate or validate such reports, and to refer for service those needing or requesting help.

The first year that the State's Child Abuse and Maltreatment Central Register was in operation, it received an enormous number of reports (about 35,000, involving more than 70,000 children). As a result, state officials have been faced with the need for greatly expanded follow-up services. Thus far no county has provided the necessary staff development and training programs to offer the quantity and quality of staff necessary to meet this need. Other features of the statewide program that require strengthening include the ongoing public information and community education program.

Programs, Benefits, and Services

The county itself has a locally based reporting system which provides initial screening for cases, before reporting them to the state office and registry. For the most part, however, the problem of neglected and abused children is dealt with by the Protective Service Division of the Child Welfare Services of the County Department of Social Services (DSS). Problems are categorized as physical abuse; sexual abuse; school-identified problems; neglect. Approximately one hundred referrals are received monthly, and after exploration and study, about two-thirds of these are considered as valid problems requiring some form of intervention. Existing interventive approaches include removing a child from his family and placing him in an institution or group home for dependent and neglected children or in foster family care. In addition to these traditional interventions, Protective Services refers physically abused children under the age of 5 to a recently established program called the County Child Abuse Coordinating Program.

A number of other agencies also work with the problem. The Neighborhood Health Center, a city-based family health center initially established as an OEO-funded neighborhood health center and subsequently supported by DHEW, is involved in identifying and treating both abused and neglected children seen in its clinic; the Medical Center and Memorial Hospital fulfill a similar function, but primarily for the physically abused child. The Child Abuse Coordinating Program is a case integration and case accountability program that illustrates a new and innovative approach to intervention. Modeled after the program developed by Kempe and Helfer at the University of Colorado Medical School, it represents an excellent operating example of the newest program initiatives described earlier. (An extensive case study from this program as well as a general description is included at the end of this section.) Finally, a Parents Anonymous program is in the process of being organized.

Access

Unlike most other services, those relating to abuse and neglect are rarely sought out voluntarily by people needing help. Instead, services tend to be imposed through outside legal and/or community authority, sanction, and pressure. However, to facilitate identification of those needing service and help, the state law mandates reporting, and a central state reporting office and registry exists to implement this law. In addition, a local county reporting office provides emergency interventions, exploration, and screening. Staff at the local hospitals and Neighborhood Health Center also identify cases and refer to DSS, as do staff in the local school.

Service Auspices and Sponsorship

The major source of protective services for the county is the public child welfare service. As in several other fields of service, however, there is substantial intermingling between public and voluntary sectors, with most actual service provided by the voluntary agencies, although usually purchased by the public department. Hospitals and clinics providing relevant services are under both public and voluntary auspices. Homemaker and day care services, frequently used as components of treatment programs, are also predominantly under voluntary auspices. Finally, the most innovative program—the one dealing only with the problem of child abuse—is under quasi-public auspices, and is funded jointly by public (county) and voluntary (United Way) agencies.

Physical Facilities

The administrative office of the county child welfare service is in an enormous loftlike room with many desks, numerous staff, and little privacy. Facilities for dependent and neglected children exist, but are few in number. The special Child Abuse Coordinating program was housed initially within the Family and Children's Service agency. However, since this is a case integration program, referring and linking needed services but providing no direct service itself, it is only the facilities of the direct services which are really relevant to users. Since such services include hospitals, clinics, mental health programs, public welfare departments, courts, day care programs, and so on, the accessibility, comfort, and attractiveness of the facilities inevitably vary.

Staff

The staffing situation clearly is one of the major inadequacies of the public protective services. Although approximately twenty-five people compose the staff of Protective Services, it is only at the administrative and supervisory level (five people, an overall administrator and heads of four units) that MSWs are employed. Most case workers are B.A. level. Civil Service rating and pay are low. As soon as staff obtain experience and are able to get higher-paying jobs (e.g., in probation or mental health clinics, with state level salaries; or in private agencies), they leave. Positions are often vacant for extended periods of time. Thus, limited training and experience and high turnover tend to leave this service inadequately staffed as regards both quality and quantity.

The Neighborhood Health Center, a major source of case finding as well as treatment, is heavily dependent on its excellent staff of pediatricians and nurses. It has only one social worker, because the Center's funding precludes a larger social work staff.

The Child Abuse Coordinating Program is directed by a highly experienced social worker who had worked previously for County Child Welfare Service, Protective Services, and Probation. This program stresses the use of a multidiscipline team (pediatrician, nurse, probation worker, lawyer, social worker) in diagnosing cases, assessing and developing alternative treatment plans, deciding on and implementing a recommended plan, and maintaining continuity of care. The function of the program coordinator is to act as case integrator, coordinating the team members as well as meshing and linking the various services needed by child and family, once a treatment plan has been developed.

User-Participant Roles

Although user-participant roles have not yet been developed in the existing programs, the projected establishment of a Parents Anonymous program would represent the incorporation of such an approach, since this is essentially a self-help program predicated on the assumption that abusing parents—those parents needing the service most—are often most able to help themselves and each other. It is worth noting here that the comprehensive interventive repertoire suggested by Kempe and Helfer includes the use of such self-help groups as part of an overall treatment program.

Administrative Structure and Linkages

Except for the coordinating program, all the programs follow traditional hierarchical patterns of administrative staff, supervisory staff, and line staff. The major structural distinction between these and the coordinating program is that the latter illustrates a horizontal structure—a team, or professional peer group—rather than the conventional vertical pattern. In this program one person acts in a coordinating and integrating role: initiating and responding to multidiscipline team efforts stimulated by the identification of an eligible child (physically abused, aged four or less) in a participating hospital; being called by the person referring the case (physician, nurse); calling a team conference of the relevant professionals (treating physician, nurse, DSS worker); and subsequently implementing the recommended plan for intervention and treatment.

Needless to say, it is the horizontal linkages among agencies, implemented and maintained by this worker, that are essential to this program's effective functioning. And, according to other experts in the community, it is the absence of any similar integration of services—the lack of accountability of any one agency assuming responsibility for ensuring continuity of care—that is so characteristic of other existing and more traditional programs, and results in such fragmentation of provision.

Research

No research studies are currently in process in this community with regard to any aspect of the problem, or with regard to any aspect of relevant program development.

Child Abuse Coordinating Program: Description and Case History

The Child Abuse Coordinating Program illustrates one of the new diagnostic and treatment programs described earlier in the chapter. It stresses case integration and accountability as well as an interdisciplinary approach to intervention. It involves the close working together of public and private agencies to serve families at risk.

Established in 1972, the program had helped close to two hundred physically abused children aged 4 and under and their families by the end of 1974. And during this period, there had not been a single instance of recidivism—that is, no child who had been included in the program had been reported as subsequently abused, and in only two cases were siblings abused after the program's involvement with the family. One reason for this is that once taken on, no case is considered closed unless a family moves out of the county. Although as family problems are resolved and the family situation appears stabilized frequency of contact may diminish, some contact is maintained on a continuing basis even if only every few months. Furthermore, parents are encouraged to contact a staff person, often a parent aide who may still be helping the family a few hours a week, if an unforeseen crisis or emergency arises. Where there has been a strong and continuing relationship that has survived a difficult period, experience has shown that parents will turn to team members for help. The attitude on the part of the project staff is that in incidents of child abuse the parents tend to be young; there will often be additional children; the family will generally have problems, emergencies and crises; and, therefore, the family will be vulnerable and "at risk." In this context, the important thing is to minimize the possibility of social isolation. Where there is someone to talk to in times of trouble—someone who can help and who is recognized as being able to provide help—child abuse is less likely to occur.

The program is quasi-public in nature and has been sponsored by a combination of three different agencies since its inception. Since 1974, it has been administered autonomously under the auspices of the County Department of Social Services, and physically based at Catholic Charities (that is, the director and staff have offices there). Its funding is predominantly public. As of late 1974, staff included a director or overall coordinator, two community service resource coordinators, who function similarly to the project director in integrating services as needed around the individual cases, an administrative assistant, and two supporting office staff. In addition to its basic program function of case integration and service coordination, the program stresses the training of parent-aides, or homemakers, who may be assigned to families to help the mother, demonstrate more appropriate parenting roles, and provide a role model for a mother who may have never had a "good mother" of her own.

One problem faced by this program has been the difficulty in providing the needed panoply of services for children in families just above public assistance and Medicaid eligibility levels (a problem exacerbated by state and county differences and only just relieved by specific funding out of the county's share of revenue sharing funds). Passage of Title XX of the Social Security Act permits a universal (non-means-tested) approach to the provision of services needed for child protection, and it is anticipated, therefore, that the problem will be eliminated if the state exercises this option.

It is interesting to note that despite public funding and the major role of public services in child protection and child welfare, this community has made particular efforts to maintain an independent auspice for its special child abuse program outside of public child welfare. The rationale is that this is a way to assure quality staff, maintain leverage, assure a range of service resources, and minimize constraints that accompany large bureaucratic operations.

In order to provide some sense of how this program works, we present an abbreviated case history of an abused child treated in the program. Although the facts are accurate, the names, dates, and other descriptive data have been changed to avoid any breach of confidentiality. The case is presented here merely to illustrate the approach followed by this particular program, not in any way to indicate that this approach is more effective than other alternative approaches.

Christopher, the 6-month-old son of a white, Catholic couple aged 23 and 21, was brought to the Emergency Room of a local hospital by his parents. He was severely bruised on his head and body. An initial medical examination and X-ray revealed a fractured skull and right arm as well as older, partially healed bruises all over his body. In addition, the baby was suffering from a severe diaper rash. His parents, Mr. and Mrs. Jones, claimed that he had fallen from his high chair when his mother turned her back to get some milk for him. The physician on duty noted that it was impossible for the injuries to have occurred as the result of such a fall. For injuries such as these, the fall would have had to be greater—the baby would have to have been thrown or hurled against the floor, for example.

In a hospital, clinic, health station, or similar setting, any instance of severe physical injury to a child that does not correlate with the reason given for it immediately raises the question of child abuse; and the doctor in this case was aware of this. Similarly, nurses and staff in the waiting rooms attached to hospital emergency rooms are also trained to watch for certain clues: How do the parents relate to the child they bring for emergency treatment? Are they frightened, concerned about the baby's condition? Anxious to know what the doctor has to say? Or do they bring the baby in and "dump" him, so to speak, on whomever will take him? Are they disinterested and unconcerned—or perhaps concerned only about other personal problems?

In this case the parents' behavior immediately stimulated the nurse's suspicions and later helped confirm those of the examining physician. Neither parent showed any affection for the baby or revealed any concern about his crying. Instead, Mrs. Jones complained irritatedly about how he always cried, wouldn't eat, and had been a problem since he was born. Christopher was the youngest of three boys; the others, aged 5 and 4, were "very active and always into things."

The physician agreed that the baby's condition seemed to indicate abuse, but decided to complete additional tests and take more X-rays to confirm his diagnosis. The decision was to hold a hospital team conference the following morning to make a final determination. In the meanwhile the parents were informed that the child's condition would require hospitalization. The nursing staff commented subsequently that the parents seemed relieved to leave the baby behind and didn't even ask to see him again before leaving. They were told to return the following morning to be given information on the baby's condition and to talk with the doctor.

Within twenty-four hours a conference had been held that included the emergency room physician, a second physician, more experienced in dealing with abuse cases, the floor nurse, and the hospital social worker. The discussion was relatively brief since the diagnosis seemed clear cut. Talk focused more on what should be done: informing the parents of the finding and explaining what would happen next; contacting the county child protective service; treating the baby; beginning plans for a comprehensive family treatment program.

As usual in these cases, immediately after the conference the hospital social worker met separately and privately with the parents and told them directly and matter of factly what the finding was and that a referral would have to be made to the county protective service. Quietly and nonpunitively, without anger or disgust yet in a way that left no doubt as to the gravity of the situation and what was to occur, the social worker told the parents that the hospital diagnostic team had examined the baby carefully and that all agreed that the baby had not been injured in the manner claimed; that the baby would have to stay in the hospital for a while until he was better; that the law required that the protective service be notified; and that a special meeting would be held subsequently of people who would try to make some plans to help them—the parents—as well as the family generally.

The worker gave the Joneses some sense of what the process would be and the pace at which things would—or might—occur, and then spent some time talking to them about what had been happening lately at home. Were there any special problems lately? A brief history had been obtained from the mother by the nurse in the emergency room. Additional information came out in this interview. It appeared that the father drank heavily and became violent when drunk, beating her and the older boys. The family was on welfare and the father had been unemployed for six months, since the baby was born, and had only worked intermittently for several months previously. Throughout the interview Mr. Jones was quiet and withdrawn, clearly angry about the report to the protective service. The social worker tried unsuccessfully to discuss this with him. After the interview, the social worker called the intake worker at Protective Services and made a formal referral of the case. She then called the child abuse coordinator and arranged for an evaluation and planning conference the next day.

The next day (and always within forty-eight hours after a report is made to the protective service) a conference was held at the hospital. Attending it were the physician who was treating Christopher, the floor nurse, the hospital social worker, a public health nurse, the protective service worker, and the child abuse coordinator. At this meeting, the discussion focused on such things as:

What is the problem? The team discussed the abuse of the child; the lack of warmth, affection, or any positive interaction between mother and child; the tension in the marital relationship; the financial problems in the family; the mother's feeling of being overwhelmed, and isolated and homebound with two active preschoolers and one infant; the general disorganization in the house and the mother's own very limited capacities.

What will Protective Services do legally about the case? An abuse petition would be filed by Protective Services and the parents would be requested to place Christopher in foster care until the case went to court. The other children would be included in the petition but left in their own home for the present.

What should the treatment plan be? In this context, the team agreed to a plan whereby the baby would be placed temporarily in foster care, a parent aide would be assigned to the family for twenty hours a week to provide a role model for the mother in household management and child care, encouraging her, among other things to get some immediate medical care for the older boys, both of whom had severe coughs. The child protective worker arranged for day care for the boys also, and it was agreed that some effort would be made to get the parents into marital counseling.

Once the plan was proposed, the protective worker took it back to her supervisor. When it was approved, she referred the case to the legal division of DSS, where a stipulated order was prepared and placed before the court for approval. In effect, this is like a contract whereby the child abuse coordinator assumes responsibility for the various services and agencies who have agreed to provide certain services to the family; it is also stipulated that the whole case and plan will be reviewed again in three months, and a report brought before the court at that time.

This whole process generally takes between one and four weeks. In the Joneses' case, it took three weeks, and by that time Christopher had been discharged from the hospital and placed in foster care. Although the parents refused to have marital counseling, it was clear that the parent aide assigned to them was welcomed as a great help. Six weeks later the older boys were placed in a half-day day care program, and soon after that the mother joined a day care mothers group where the mothers met twice a week to discuss some of the problems and frustrations of marriage and child rearing.

The team continued to meet weekly until the plan was completely in place, and then biweekly. The protective service worker visited the house weekly at a time when Mr. Jones was home, to observe his behavior with the family. Christopher was returned to his parents after four months. (Babies are usually returned to their families after three to six months.) The team continued to meet biweekly and then monthly throughout the rest of that year. Mr. Jones continued to have a drinking problem, but there was no evidence of physical violence—just some shouting and noise. The parent aide continued to help, although the number of hours was reduced to ten a week after the first year. Mrs. Jones maintained participation in the mothers' group, but not regularly. On two occasions she called the parent aide when feeling particularly upset, but one of the objectives of the program is to reduce mothers' social isolation, and to structure contacts with representatives of the program, so this behavior is considered not only appropriate but desirable.

Even after a year and a half, selected team members continued to meet every three months to confer about the current status of the Jones family. The case would not be closed as long as the family remained within the jurisdiction of the program.

Trends and Issues

The development of national policies and programs for abused and neglected children has been haphazard. Program development has been limited by inadequate knowledge of the phenomenon, lack of clarity regarding its parameters, confusion and conflict as to which profession should have responsibility for intervention, and a scarcity of resources, both financial and staff. Knowledge regarding effective intervention is negligible.

The situation is similar at the state level, although certain other aspects exacerbate it. Although all fifty states have developed statutes requiring the reporting of cases to public authorities, the definition of the phenomenon, provisions for mandatory reporting and immunity for reporters, the nature and adequacy of interventions and treatment services, and the implementation of existing statutes vary from state to state. No state maintains an adequate registry of cases and only four states have exchange registries with other states. Since legal provisions and requirements for case reporting are inconsistent, little communication exists among states, or even among social, legal, and medical institutions wthin a state. If fragmentation of services, quantitative and qualitative inadequacy of services, turf conflicts among different professional disciplines, and general ignorance regarding effectiveness of interventions persist, problems in identifying existing cases can only worsen an already horrendous situation.

Clearly, underlying any analysis of these inadequacies is the need to define the phenomenon itself and to clarify its parameters. We note here that although current federal legislation seems to indicate that abuse and neglect are one entity, some duality is implied by separating administrative responsibility and focus within DHEW. For example, SRS-CSA is responsible for neglect and commissioned a state-of-the-field paper, *State of the Knowledge of Child Neglect*, while a similar paper on child abuse was commissioned by OCD. The resulting papers reveal (among other things) the difficulty in separating the entities as well as the limited knowledge about either. Definitions which are premised on the distinction between deliberate, intentional, nonaccidental behavior, on the one hand, and unintentional, accidental behavior, on the other, may be simple to conceptualize but are almost impossible to operationalize, in particular at the margins, or the grey area, where most such behavior occurs. Although we are not interested in adding another definition to the plethora of existing ones, we are concerned with identifying a perspective that can lead to viable policy and programing options. Therefore, since the nature of motivation is often unclear, definitions that stress differentiation in motivation may impede needed intervention. Our real concern is with the consequences for the child, be the damage physical, emotional, mental. Our conclusion is that the phenomenon represents one entity (perhaps maltreatment best describes it), but that there are variations within it encompassing a continuum of severity of consequences for the child. We would stress concern for the overall welfare of children generally, but we also recognize that priorities for intervention must be identified. Although it is essential that societal concern and provision address the problem of children who are maltreated in any fashion, sanction for such intervention is clearest where the danger is (or may be) greatest—for the child who is physically abused. We would describe physical abuse as the most visible, perhaps the most severe, aspect of the whole phenomenon—the "tip of the iceberg."

Clearly, primary prevention must be directed toward the whole phenomenon and address the entire spectrum of variables which may impinge on the welfare of children. Intervention here would include overall social policy, or family policy, that recognizes that social stress (e.g., poverty, bad housing, parental ill health or unemployment, physical or social isolation, or stigma) has as severe consequences for children as psychological stress.

However, if one acknowledges the existence of an acute problem, one could argue, as is being done today in the United States, for a categorical program directed specifically at reducing the incidence of physical abuse. In highlighting this acute problem, and in searching for a "solution" to it, we must immediately recognize that traditional approaches have been inadequate, either because they have been inadequately implemented (too few resources, service fragmentation, interprofessional conflicts) or because they have been ineffective even when implemented, because the state of knowledge has been inadequate and there are no known effective strategies. The current search for new approaches to case identification, treatment, and prevention can be equated with open criticism of existing child welfare services. Similarly, the absence of effective intervention for treatment and prevention of recidivism demonstrates the inadequacy of existing knowledge and research.

Once the phenomenon itself is defined and clarified—and parameters set—research must focus on developing effective strategies for intervention and prevention as well as knowledge of the nature of the phenomenon. Until such time as knowledge and understanding are adequate, programing for this acute problem should stress more effective implementation of existing programs (state laws, reporting systems, hotlines), support of those interventions that currently seem most successful, and initiation, testing, and comparison of innovative approaches (e.g., what device is most effective in ensuring case integration?). What seems critical here is the issue of where major responsibility for program development and implementation should be placed (in which discipline, and whose professional role it should be); how accountability for each case can be assured; and how the range of programs can be incorporated or integrated into any treatment plan. Although traditionally child welfare programs—protective services—have a valid complaint regarding the inadequacy of funding and the lack of trained staff, existing evidence seems to indicate that increasing the resources available to these programs still would not eliminate the major problems of service fragmentation, lack of accountability, and interdisciplinary conflicts. As the Executive Director of one court-related Association for Prevention of Cruelty to Children stated, "It is difficult to try to work with all the agencies and groups that have taken a part in some cases that come to us. There is confusion, lack of mutual sharing, some feeling that we ought not to come into a case previously handled by a service agency."

Those few programs that seem to demonstrate effectiveness do so when assessed on the basis of one criterion: a low rate of recidivism. All such programs employ a wide range of interventions, representing several disciplines (medicine, nursing, law, social work, psychology, early childhood education) and committed lay efforts. Although little is known yet that assures "cure" to the abusing parent, it seems clear that only multiple intervention approaches, applied simultaneously or sequentially, result in reduced recidivism; and that these approaches require integration and sustained effort. The fulcrum of these programs is a generalist case integrator whose major function is to implement the recommendations of a multidisciplinary team to mesh and coordinate the different services needed by parent and child (medical care, homemaker, day care, counseling, parent groups).

Through reviewing the literature on these programs, visiting and interviewing staff, we have reached certain conclusions. First, no one discipline can provide a comprehensive service program in this field; rather, several disciplines provide essential services. Second, there is an essential linkage and integrative function which can be implemented by a social worker and appears to be an appropriate role for the personal social services. It is this role which seems to assure the integration of services around a particular case/child/family even when several services and multiple arrangements are needed; and it is this role which also assures service commitment, continuity of care, and concern over as long a period of time as some attention seems desirable. (A critical question not yet dealt with is, At what point in time does service end?)

In the context of the above, we note that the direct per-capita dollar costs of these programs are extremely high. Yet when compared with the costs of long-term institutionalization or foster care, they may be cost effective. (Training schools and other institutions cost $15,000 per child per year; foster care costs $3,600 per child per year in direct payments and may be ten times as much if one includes overhead.) Finally, we point out that unless national social policy is directed toward supporting the welfare of children generally, we will continue to see the results of societal neglect and maltreatment of children and the consequences for each succeeding generation of children. Even if demonstrably effective, policy and program that focus only on the physically abused child, and not on the larger concern, imply that only if and when a parent physically abuses a child is he entitled to the resources which might have prevented abuse if they were available earlier.

Notes

1. *Congressional Record*, U.S. House of Representatives, Dec. 31, 1973.
2. Vincent Fontana, *The Maltreated Child* (New York: Macmillan, 1973).
3. C. Henry Kempe, M.D., *Child Abuse (The Battered Child Syndrome), Position Paper for Hearings of the Subcommittee on Children and Youth of the Committee on Labor and Public Welfare*, U.S. Senate, March 31, 1973, Denver, Col.
4. Statement of William G. Lunsford, Director of Washington Office, Child Welfare League of America, before the Select Committee on Education, U.S. House of Representatives, Oct. 5, 1973.

5. David Gil, "Violence against Children," in *Hearings of the Subcommittee on Children and Youth of the Committee on Labor and Public Welfare*, U.S. Senate, March–April 1973.

6. American Humane Association, *National Symposium on Child Abuse* (brochure), p. 7.

7. C. Henry Kempe and Ray E. Helfer, eds., *Helping the Battered Child and His Family* (Philadelphia: Lippincott, 1972), p. xi. See also Helfer and Kempe, eds., *The Battered Child* (Chicago and London: University of Chicago Press, 1974).

8. David Gil, *Violence against Children* (Cambridge, Mass.: Harvard University Press, 1970), esp. ch. 5.

9. For example, Howard E. Erlanger, *An Empirical Test of the Subculture of Violence Thesis* (Institute for Research on Poverty, Discussion Papers; Madison, Wis.: University of Wisconsin–Madison, 1973).

10. See, for example, Leontine Young, *Wednesday's Children* (New York: McGraw-Hill, 1964); Alfred Kadushin, *Child Welfare Services* (2d ed.; New York: Macmillan, 1974); Vincent de Francis, in American Humane Association, *National Symposium on Child Abuse*, p. 7.

11. See differences among state statutes as analyzed in de Francis, *Child Abuse Legislation in the 1970s* (rev. ed.; Denver, Col.: American Humane Association, Children's Division, 1973).

12. Gil, *Violence against Children.*

13. Saad Z. Nagi, "Child Abuse and Neglect Programs—A National Overview," *Children Today*, May–June 1975, pp. 13–17.

14. Cohn and Sussman estimate, reported in *ibid.*, p. 16.

15. See de Francis, in *Hearings of the Subcommittee on Children and Youth of the Committee on Labor and Public Welfare*, p. 293.

16. Mason P. Thomas, Jr., "Child Abuse and Neglect: Historical Overview, Legal Matrix and Social Perspectives," *North Carolina Law Review*, 50 (March 1972), 293.

17. Justine Wise Polier, "The Family Court in an Urban Setting," in Kempe and Helfer, *Helping the Battered Child.*

18. DHEW, OCD, "Child Abuse and Neglect Prevention and Treatment Program, Rules and Regulations," *Federal Register*, Dec. 19, 1974, pp. 43940–41.

19. Steven Kurzman, Testimony before the Subcommittee on Children and Youth, Committee on Labor and Public Welfare, U.S. Senate, March 27, 1973, p. 5.

20. De Francis, *Child Abuse Legislation in the 1970s*, p. 7; see also, Monrad G. Paulsen, "Child Abuse Reporting Laws: The Shape of the Legislation," *Columbia Law Review*, Vol. 12 (1967), and "The Law and Abused Children," in Helfer and Kempe, *The Battered Child*, pp. 153–78; Barbara Daly, "Wilful Child Abuse and State Reporting Statutes," *University of Miami Law Review*, 1969, pp. 283, 318, 343.

21. Kurzman Testimony, U.S. Senate, p. 88.

22. See special issue on "Combatting Child Abuse and Neglect," *Children Today*, May–June 1975, for an overview of OCD strategy.

23. Lunsford statement, House of Representatives Hearings, p. 141.

24. American Humane Association, *Speaking Out for Child Protection* (pamphlet), pp. 8–9.

25. Newsletter supplement, Feb. 1, 1972, "Committee Statement," Commission on Infant and Preschool Child, American Academy of Pediatricians.

26. Dr. John Allen and Dr. Henry Kempe, in *Hearings before the Subcommittee on Children and Youth of the Committee on Labor and Public Welfare*, pp. 167–225; 157, 1666.

27. See Gil, *Violence against Children.*

28. See Urie Bronfenbrenner, "The Origins of Alienation," *Scientific American*, Vol. 231, No. 2 (Aug. 1974); Bronfenbrenner, *Is Early Intervention Effective? A Report on Longitudinal Evaluations of Preschool Programs*, Vol. II, DHEW–OCD Pub. No. 74-25 (Washington, D.C.: GPO, 1974).

29. The following illustration is derived from Kempe and Helfer, *Helping the Battered Child.*

30. For further discussion of this approach, see *ibid.*, ch. 3, "Innovative Treatment Approaches."

31. The description is derived from various materials and reports made available to us by OCD.

32. This description is derived from Children's Hospital Medical Center, First Annual Report: *Family Development Study*, submitted to OCD, Aug. 1973, as well as several telephone interviews.

33. This description is based on personal observation as well as the site visit report of the Special Task Force of the Committee on Infant and Preschool Children of the American Academy of Pediatrics, April 1974; see also *The New York Times*, Sept. 12, 1974.

34. This description is derived from material distributed by the Center as well as from Kempe and Helfer, *Helping the Battered Child.*

35. See, for example, Gil, *Children of Violence* (Cambridge: Harvard University Press, 1968), and Kempe and Helfer, *Helping the Battered Child.*

4 Children's Institutions and Alternative Programs

Context and Definition

Like abuse and neglect, the programs dealt with in this chapter are again case services, but this time with a residential base. Children's institutions and alternative programs raise issues both of policy and of program. There is debate as to auspice: Should all of this be considered part of child welfare (a subcategory in the personal social services)? Or is juvenile justice the key system? Or can there be a viable division of roles? And because of its residential nature, the subject gives us an opportunity to assess the campaign for deinstitutionalization, its programing viability and its implications for boundaries between fields.

Residential institutional care, especially for children, has been under attack in the United States in recent years. In some sense, this is strange, since it is generally acknowledged that the personal social services and programs for the retarded and emotionally disturbed require some provision for substitute care ("away from own family"), as well as community- and home-based helping measures. And among the substitute care facilities—it is assumed almost everywhere —there probably must be both foster home and adoption services and several types of group residential arrangements. Indeed, whether in the United States or elsewhere in the world, substitute care arrangements have tended to develop earlier and more extensively than community- and home-based social services. Foster home care ranges from the traditional-informal to the highly professionalized-structured; group residential facilities may vary from the normal, "family-like" environment to the carefully shaped and controlled therapeutic milieu.

Despite its long history and almost universal practice, the use of residential institutions as "warehousing" and banishment has been attacked, and a crusade for "deinstitutionalization" has been under way in the United States. It is therefore important in a personal social services overview to report on children's institutions and the alternatives, to explore the use and nonuse of group facilities as components of the personal social services, and to identify the options. To keep the analysis and presentation within manageable dimensions, we have deliberately and artificially omitted institutional care of the mentally retarded, mentally ill, and physically handicapped, while discussing facilities for the unruly and neglected. This discussion of programs both for a very stigmatized category (delinquents) and for a far less stigmatized group (neglected children) coincides with an attempt in practice to avoid labels and circumstances and to focus on children's needs. The difficulties in treating all children through one system, as reported from the field, as well as the conceptual complexities, suggest—as we will see—that some fundamental questions are being ignored.

Group care of children has a long history; and the debate about the most appropriate form of substitute care for children is almost as long. The Old Testament and the Talmud both refer to the practice of providing foster care for dependent children, and the early Christian church initiated the custom of paying widows for the boarding of children. The first institutions for such children were established at the end of the second century. These two models of care—foster homes and institutions—and their several variations continue even today to be the primary methods by which society provides for dependent children.

The American colonies adopted the English system of indenture by which children were bound out to master craftsmen, and the larger communities established almshouses to provide for children and other needy persons whose labor was not in demand or who were too young to work. The first major change in what we now call child welfare services in this country took place during the nineteenth century as a consequence of the Industrial Revolution and the massive immigration taking place at that time. First, there was considerable growth of orphanages and institutions for dependent children (and a few for delinquents) established under the auspices of various religious groups and, later, public authorities as a means of providing for their members and protecting the religious heritage of the children. Second, foster home placements became much more common by the middle of the century. Charles Loring Brace, of the Children's Aid Society of New York, initiated the practice of placing vagrant children from New York in rural homes to the west and northwest of the city—and his work was copied by a large number of similar Children's Aid Societies.

Foster Home versus Institution

These two developments precipitated what Wolins and Piliavin have termed a "century of debate" over the relative merits of foster home versus institutional care.[1] The debate was frequently vitriolic and the positions taken were based as much on religious differences and organizational self-interest as on any real knowledge about actual costs and benefits. Finally, toward the end of the nineteenth century, Charles Birtwell of the Boston Children's Aid Society suggested that each case should be treated as unique and that the placement alternative should suit the needs of the individual child.[2] Since that approach was not only reasonable but in accord with professional experience, it serves from time to time to still the debate slightly. But child welfare practitioners continue to differ over which placement alternatives are best for which types of children, and each new article or study published on the subject continues to precipitate a new round of arguments. Positions derive most often from personal professional experience—from tunnel vision—rather than from knowledge based on research. As Meisels and Loeb commented in a major criticism of foster care published in 1956: "There is concern with the results of the programs, and there is recognition of problems. [But] the methods which are suggested [for mitigating these problems] . . . are based not so much on systematic exploration of the facts in the situation, as on [workers'] acceptance of axioms, convictions, opinions, speculation, and inferences."[3]

In 1964, when Wolins and Piliavin published their analysis, they could describe a relatively high degree of consensus among child welfare professionals regarding the suitability of different types of care for different types of children. There seemed to be general agreement that "the institution setting is best utilized for adolescents, highly disturbed and potentially violent children, children who are extremely uncomfortable in close relationships, youngsters whose parents cannot tolerate the 'competition' of foster parents, and physically handicapped youth. All other children, and in any case all children under 6 years of age, are generally regarded as properly cared for only in foster family homes." The authors suggested, however, that these assumptions were supported by very little systematic empirical evidence and predicted that the future might well see a resurgence of the debate as practitioners' convictions began to shift and additional research studies were carried out.

As predicted, another round in the debate is now under way, precipitated this time by developments in the field of mental retardation. In 1971 the President's Committee on Mental Retardation announced as a major objective the "deinstitutionalization" of one-third of the mentally retarded currently confined in state schools and initiated a program designed to achieve this goal. This concept of "deinstitutionalization" was quickly adopted by leaders in the mental health and juvenile justice fields and gradually began to influence child welfare. As a result, there has been renewed interest in the deinstitutionalization of dependent, neglected, and delinquent children and a revival of the "institution versus foster home" controversy. The most dramatic example was provided in Massachusetts, where the Commissioner of the Department of Youth Services closed all the state institutions for delinquent youth in 1972, substituting contracts with voluntary agencies offering group care, some county-based therapeutic institutions, and a range of community treatment alternatives.[4] A number of other states, while acting more slowly and displaying reluctance to close all institutions, moved steadily in the same direction. And at the federal level, the Secretary of DHEW described the development of alternatives to institutionalization as a major policy objective. Implicit in all these moves toward deinstitutionalization, of course, was an attack on institutional care even though, in fact, the influential Massachusetts initiative repudiated only the public training schools for delinquents, which were considered custodial and authoritarian, despite some general and vocational education and some individual and group therapeutic programs.

A shift toward a more balanced view had become apparent by 1975. Title XX of the Social Security Act, for example, states that federal service funds are to be spent:

> For the purpose of encouraging each State, as far as practicable under the conditions in that State, to furnish services directed at the goal of—

(4) preventing or reducing inappropriate institutional care by providing for community-based care, home-based care, or other forms of less intensive care, or

(5) securing referral or admission for institutional care when other forms of care are not appropriate, or providing services to individuals in institutions.

During 1975, before various forums, spokesmen for the Office of Child Development, the President's Committee on Mental Retardation, and the New York State Division for Youth affirmed the need for a range of treatment alternatives, including good institutional care. Several years earlier, participants at a conference convened at the University of Chicago to discuss the implications of a major national survey of residential child care facilities had concluded that what is required is a continuum of care, including services away from the community, in the community but away from home, and in the home.[5] In 1974, Wolins presented some of the recent literature and basic research on group care in order to encourage fuller exploration of the potential benefits of this form of service.[6] Hence, the debate would seem to have come full circle.

The emphasis on deinstitutionalization, however, has encouraged the development of a wider range of child care provisions and has highlighted the importance of in-home services. It has solidified the consensus against large, isolated, congregate facilities. Therefore, although the basic controversy over institution versus foster care persists today, the debate perhaps has been enlarged to include consideration of a fuller range of treatment alternatives, and effort is being made to conceptualize a continuum of care. Jeff Koshel of the Urban Institute, Washington, D.C., for example, has proposed the foster care continuum for dependent and neglected children presented in Figure 4-1.

The rationale of the continuum is consistent with common sense. As the remaining sections of the chapter will make clear, remarkably few systematic data are available to support the various extremist positions on child care. In fact, most policies and practice decisions are still based primarily on value judgments and assumptions. And until more conclusive data are available regarding all aspects of child care, it seems likely that the question of what forms of care have what effects on what types of children under what circumstances will continue to be a major issue. The inevitable consequence will be fluctuating policies and irrational programing.

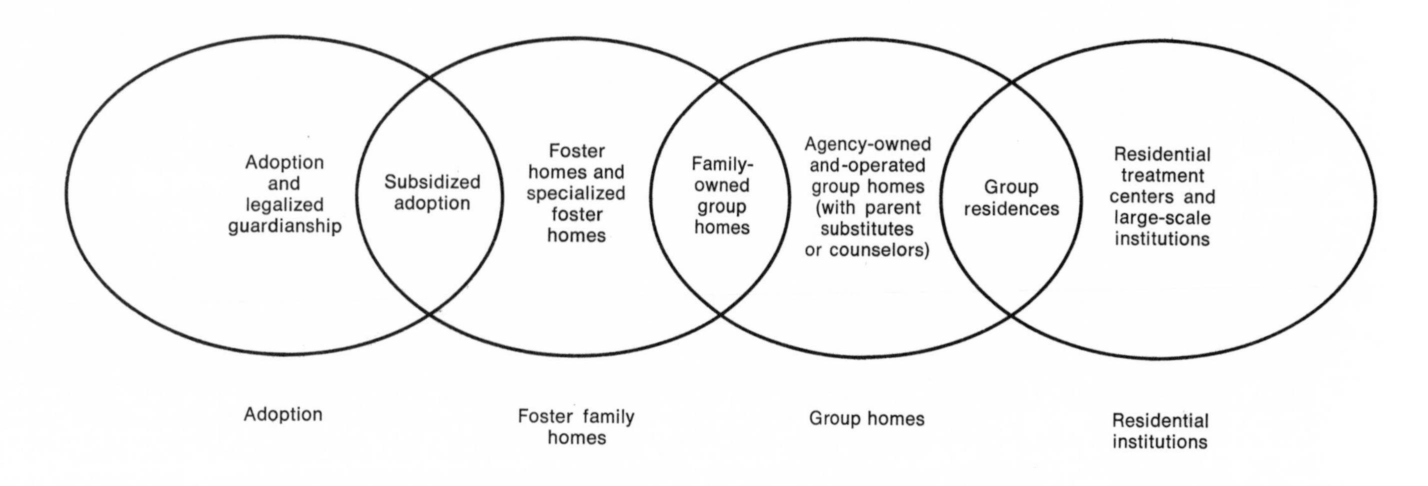

Figure 4-1. **Foster Care Continuum for Dependent and Neglected Children.**

From Jeff Koshel, "Deinstitutionalization—Dependent and Neglected Children," Working Paper 963-7A (Washington, D.C.: The Urban Institute, 1973).

Child Welfare and the Juvenile Court

Another issue which dominates discussion in the child care field relates to the boundaries among those service systems which impinge on our target population. In this area, too, there are remarkably few systematic data available and the controversy is an old one, best described in an historical context.

Besides the expansion of children's institutions under religious auspices and the establishment of the Children's Aid Society's program, a third major influence on the development of U.S. child care services during the nineteenth century was the establishment of the juvenile court. The first Juvenile Court Act was passed in Illinois in 1899; and by 1917, all but three states had passed juvenile court legislation. Whatever the intention of the leaders of the juvenile court movement, it is clear that this movement significantly affected the way children's services are delivered in this country.[7] During the nineteenth century the distinction between dependent or neglected children and delinquent children had little meaning. Serious juvenile offenders were handled in adult criminal courts; and the chief efforts of reformers in the juvenile field were directed toward providing services to children who were thought in danger of becoming adult criminals—paupers, vagrants, the "disorderly." Since their primary objective was preventing delinquency, the reformers made little distinction between neglected and deviant children. For example, referring to those under 14 years of age, the noted English penal reformer Mary Carpenter stated: "All may be classed together under this age, for there is no distinction between pauper, vagrant, and criminal children, which would require a different system of treatment."[8]

The primary thrust of the juvenile court movement was to remove children from the jurisdiction of the criminal courts so that children could be treated individually and those in need could be helped rather than punished for their misdeeds or misfortunes. One of the probably unanticipated consequences of the juvenile court movement, however, was the development of labels to distinguish the various groups of children coming before the court ("dependent and neglected," "stubborn child," or "person in need of supervision," and "juvenile delinquent") and the proliferation of agencies designed to serve the needs of these various groups. Moreover, during the early twentieth century, the juvenile courts were influenced by psychoanalytic thinking, which emphasized individual psychodynamics as the primary determinant of behavior and called for a relationship between diagnosis and treatment. Therefore a whole spate of treatment-oriented agencies and services developed to serve the needs of the juvenile court.

Paralleling this expansion of programs and services in the juvenile justice system has been an increase in the number and function of traditional child welfare agencies, both voluntary and public. As the juvenile justice and child welfare systems expanded, the attempt was made to distinguish which children were served by which system. Traditionally, juvenile justice agencies have taken responsibility primarily for children who were thought to require care and treatment because of their own behavior; the child welfare agencies have taken responsibility for those who were thought to require care because of parental neglect or family problems. This, at least, is one view. An alternative interpretation is that the court and facilities related to it have been employed whenever it was believed that community norms needed to be strongly affirmed and that more powerful sanctions were necessary, whatever the problem. Not that the picture was entirely clear in either case; until recent decades, since child welfare services were nonexistent or in short supply in many counties, the court was the only available institution. To complicate the picture further, federal policy brought more dependent and neglected children into the courts in 1967, when, for the first time, the federal government agreed to share in the costs of foster care for dependent and neglected children—but only those who were court-placed and whose families were in financial need.

A further complication developed in the 1960s when a subcategory of cases now variously known as PINS ("Persons in Need of Supervision") or CHINS ("Children in Need of Supervision") was added to the delinquency and neglect categories. These are cases where parental neglect is difficult to sustain in the courtroom, where the conduct offends community norms, but where the act is not legally a crime if committed by an adult—for example, truancy, sexual misconduct, refusal to obey parents. Rights proponents felt that juvenile courts were damaging such children by processing and disposing of them as delinquents. (Another interpretation states that the categories were invented to bring more children into the court.)

At the present time, there is a good deal of controversy about what the boundaries between the child welfare and juvenile justice systems should be, or if they should exist at all. As we indicated, there is much overlap between the two systems. The local bureaucratic pattern, class, ethnic background, and race, geography, and chance often determine which system is involved. While the juvenile court has been given jurisdiction over all children coming into care on an involuntary basis, a number of child welfare agencies within the voluntary and public sectors have developed treatment programs for children who display behavioral problems. As indicated, localities have a financial incentive to go to court, where federal cost-sharing is possible. Also, knowledge of family dynamics has increased to the point that few professionals are willing to make a clear distinction between individual and family problems; all recognize the interchangeability of some of the children among the categories.

Many commentators have expressed concern about the consequences of this separation between the child welfare and juvenile justice systems. Because the treatment services in the child welfare system are more frequently under voluntary auspices in some jurisdictions, or are more benign, they sometimes have tended to serve a select group of children and families, primarily white and middle or working class, who are considered motivated and able to benefit from treatment. This means that in such jurisdictions low-income, minority youngsters are more likely to be served by the public facilities and institutions in the juvenile justice system than are children of other backgrounds.

Exposés of poor living conditions, incompetent and inadequate staff, and poor administration of state training schools and detention facilities have raised questions as to whether the current pattern of service delivery cannot be characterized as both discriminatory and punitive. Moreover, it is hypothesized that the very process of labeling certain children as delinquent or in need of supervision, combined with the practice of confining all these children together, may result in an increase of deviant behavior because of the effects of stigma, self-fulfilling prophecy, and peer group influence ("secondary deviance"). Why not, then, it is argued, divert all but the hard-core criminal types from "juvenile justice"?

We shall not review the development in the 1960s of a delinquency theory grounded in what became known as "labeling theory." The general notion is that many young people participate in nonviolent antisocial behavior and deviance, but that only some (the selection relating to class, race, ethnicity) are processed and labeled as delinquents. Moreover, participation in rehabilitative programs exposes them to experiences that can create "secondary deviance." Facilities find their reputations and labels defined by the most stigmatized category of children they serve. From this point of view, much of the solution to delinquency is to avoid labeling a given child, to minimize the use of stigmatizing labels generally, and to divert as many young people as possible from the delinquency system. If used benignly, however, labels do offer differential classification for treatment; and the public insists on labels even if the professionals avoid them.[9]

Given these considerations, there is currently a good deal of debate in the child care field about the relative costs and benefits of our present system of service delivery. It is probably safe to say that no one is satisfied with the existing arrangements. While the current effort to divert youngsters from the juvenile justice system parallels in many ways the effort made by earlier reformers to create "juvenile justice" so as to divert youngsters from the criminal justice system, there is little consensus as to the right course of action for the future. Some would argue that the whole "child saving" movement has been a failure and that the wisest solution would be to remove from the jurisdiction of the court all children except those who have committed serious offenses which would be considered criminal if committed by an adult; moreover, those youngsters who must come before the court (and the age of responsibility would be high) should be accorded the full legal rights and procedural protections guaranteed to adults and their age should be a consideration only in regard to sentencing or disposition. This in any case has been the direction of recent Supreme Court decisions. The protective and parenting posture of the court should be defined as unreal—in this view—and not used to subvert legal protections. All other than hard-core law breakers—that is, all other children requiring care and protection—should be handled in nonjudicial settings, probably under the jurisdiction of state departments of social services. Many other countries have followed such policies and some states have. Pennsylvania, for example, recognizes only two categories of children: delinquents (those who have committed "criminal offenses") and deprived (all others in need of care).

Others still argue that it is appropriate for the juvenile courts to have jurisdiction over all children requiring care and protection and that the court should take responsibility for such children. However, the current labels distinguishing various categories of children should be eliminated. Instead, the court should simply take responsibility for fact-finding in order to determine whether or not a child is in need of treatment or service no matter what the cause; if so, the child should simply be remanded to a central children's service agency which would take responsibility for treatment planning and execution. In other words, the reason a child comes into care should have no bearing on the type or duration of care provided; these decisions should all be based on treatment considerations. Logically, this view would remove the juvenile court from the correctional system.

Still others argue that although services might be more efficiently organized, the main problem is the lack of adequate services and resources in both systems. Therefore, to debate the boundaries of the various service systems is to tackle a false issue. Instead, primary effort should be directed toward enhancing the service capacities of all relevant public service agencies. Those holding this view would engage the court as the most powerful instrument for achieving this end.

It is obvious that there are no easy answers to the boundary question and that trade-offs are involved, no matter which option is selected. There also are, of course, a number of alternative positions expressed about these issues.* What is again most striking, however, is the almost total lack of definitive research or even systematic data to support the many positions—and the extent to which public debate often fails to address the issues.

There are, of course, subsidiary issues in the child care field regarding program models, treatment methods, staffing patterns, funding and accountability mechanisms, and the like. These will be discussed where relevant in the main section of the chapter, even though choices made must eventually grow out of more basic decisions. For the moment, we note that deinstitutionalization and its outcome must be determined in part by the resolution of the juvenile justice questions as well.

A further introductory comment: Despite increasing federal interest and involvement and the influence of higher court decisions, services in these categories are in the province of state and local government in the United States—especially of local government. Added to the reporting difficulties inherent in the boundary issue, this fact means that definitions, structures, procedures, are so diverse as to make the accumulated data inaccurate and—since data collection is subject to voluntary cooperation—very incomplete. Thus any picture

*And because it is outside the purview of this report, we have not discussed the many problems in service delivery to physically handicapped, mentally retarded, and mentally ill children; however, in relation to this population, many questions are also being raised regarding the appropriate boundaries between the health, mental health, and child care fields.

which can be drawn is partial and of uncertain validity. Dr. Robert Vinter, for example, asserts that fewer than one-fifth of all states have good information about children in care. Few would challenge him.[10]

Parameters

To discuss the subject of children's institutions and alternatives is to face the complex problem of relevant domains. In effect, defining the parameters of the problem is in itself policy-making.

For example: We have introduced the "institution versus foster home" debate. The discussion of deinstitutionalization tends to focus on community-based group residences and residential treatment centers versus large, isolated congregate-care institutions. Given the objectives of this overall exploration of general-personal social services, we shall attempt a similar focus. But it would be just as logical to deal in detail with problems and trends in foster home care, a subject we shall forgo because of the considerable available research and writing in that field.

Again: We have introduced both "child welfare" and "juvenile justice" components of the problem, yet we need to acknowledge that institutionalization, deinstitutionalization, and alternatives have different meanings in those two "sytems," which have varied boundaries depending on jurisdictions. Current juvenile justice reforms would "divert" youth from or "minimize penetration" into the police-court–correctional facility network—presumably therefore, drawing more heavily upon child welfare services, or so-called youth bureaus, which would offer to "unruly" youngsters the equivalent of child welfare help without labeling them. In any case the alternatives for court-related youth, particularly the allegedly delinquent and the PINS-CHINS, are the nonauthoritative social services broadly defined—even foster homes and institutions other than training schools.

For the dependent-neglected children, who may, too, get to court for temporary care, substitute care, or termination of parental rights, a different system, or at least partially different system, usually operates. There is a lesser or different stigma (varying with whether one is dealing with what is seen as parental "misfortune," "pathology," or "misconduct") and the alternatives are "save the family," "arrange temporary separation," "give the child a new family or *living* environment." With community protection presumably not at issue, the foster home–institution debate can be carried out with reference to the question of what is better for the child's own development. We have summarized that history from the Wolins-Piliavin overview.

But logic takes one further. Since the 1909 White House Conference on Children, there has developed a field of child welfare known as "services to children in their own homes." Much talked about but poorly financed, conceptualized, or developed, this is regarded as a field of secondary prevention (early case-finding and intervention) and community-based treatment. A full exploration of alternatives to institutionalization, especially of the dependent, neglected group, should involve a survey of home-based child welfare services.

This, however, is hardly the whole story. In child welfare, a comprehensive analysis of alternatives would involve broader aspects of family policy: income maintenance for families and children, employment opportunities for parents, child care arrangements, housing subsidies, and so on. Obviously, to deal with all such subjects in the context of arrangements for children who must leave home becomes meaningless. These topics are as relevant to mental health, education, and health programing as well. At the level of strengthening the family and community—of basic preventive-perfective social welfare policy development—the target cannot be said to be any specific pathology. Whatever the political rhetoric, the prevention of mental illness, delinquency, family instability, personal maladjustment, school problems, and so forth depends upon an undifferentiated cluster of policies and programs. Primary prevention is not symptom-specific or problem-specific. At any given moment, then, the social service planner in a given field focuses on specific interventions for those children or families whose disorders or problems are already apparent, channeled, and socially defined. As the discussion of prevention reaches the shared level of policy or abstraction, it should not be couched in terms specific to one system.

These considerations—and the motives which initially inspired this exploration—bring us back to narrower parameters. This chapter deals with children who need substitute living and care arrangements, brief or long term, for reasons socially classified as abuse/neglect/dependency or delinquency/person-in-need-of-supervision. Bypassing foster home care, we will examine the varieties of group living arrangements being employed as alternatives to the large, congregate institutions for the dependent-neglected and the training schools for the delinquent and predelinquent.* We shall also give attention to

*Very imprecise categories, as we shall note.

community alternatives employed to avoid or shorten placement of those children and youths who have been committed or would have been had alternatives not been available.* We shall proceed initially on the premise that the two streams of intervention known as "juvenile justice" and "child welfare" can and should be discussed together. One of the issues considered at the end will be whether this is a viable perspective.

Thus, whatever the logical imperatives, this chapter will say very little about foster home care, nothing about family policy and primary prevention, very little about youth bureaus, probation, and various types of secondary prevention, and virtually nothing about some of the broader aspects of adult mental health and family counseling.

Definition of Terms

Children. In the most general sense, "children" refers to all persons who have not yet reached the age of majority, or the age at which they are free to exercise the full civil and personal rights of adults. Although 21 has traditionally been considered the age of full majority and defined as such in the statutes of most states, there have been many exceptions and the drift downward to 18 has been widespread. For example, the criminal statutes of many states permit children to be dealt with as adults at the age of 15, 16, or 17. Secondary school is usually completed at about 18. Federal legislation bearing on social services generally defines children as persons under the age of 18 or 19; and the Bureau of the Census has historically classified as children all persons under the age of 18. Therefore, for the sake of simplicity, unless otherwise specified, in this chapter the term "children" will refer to all persons under the age of 18.†

Dependent and Neglected Children. This term also is used in many different ways in different contexts. A typical definition of dependent and neglected children suggests that they are children "who suffer from inadequate parental supervision, insufficient food, shelter, or clothing, severe physical abuse or neglect by parents or dissolution

*It will be necessary to ask if this can be known.

†When last reported the maximum age for original juvenile court jurisdiction was 17 in 33 states, 16 in 12 states, and 15 or under in the others. See Mark M. Levin and Rosemary C. Sarri, *Juvenile Delinquency: A Comparative Analysis of Legal Codes in the United States* (Ann Arbor, Mich.: National Assessment of the Juvenile Corrections, 1974), p. 13.

of the family or home."[11] The difficulty of providing a precise definition of "dependent and neglected" arises from the fact that, as Kadushin points out, children so described do not present any personal identifiable characteristics such as mental retardation or physical handicap but rather are categorized because of some pathology in their social situation.[12] For our purposes, the definition of dependent and neglected children offered above will be employed; it is important, however, for the reader to remember that these children do not constitute a target population of identifiable *personal* characteristics but rather are children who have been classified under this label so that they may be provided specific services designed to ameliorate or compensate for deficiencies in their *social* situations. There may be similar children not identified or so designated. The term is seldom applied to children in their teens.

Delinquent Children. This term is used to describe children who have engaged in one of two types of behavior: activities proscribed in state criminal laws and local ordinances which would be criminal offenses if committed by an adult; activities such as truancy, running away, and refusal to submit to parental control which are "status" offenses in that they are proscribed for juveniles but are not criminal offenses if committed by an adult. Despite long failure to differentiate these subcategories, the term *juvenile delinquent* now is often but not always used only to describe a child who has committed the first type of offense. A child who commits the second type of offense may be termed a "person in need of supervision" (PINS), "child in need of supervision" (CHINS), or "stubborn child," or may be identified by a variety of other labels depending on the particular state in which he resides. For the sake of clarity in this report, the term *delinquent* will be used here only to describe a child who has committed an act which would be a criminal offense if committed by an adult, and who has been adjudged as such by a court; the term *status offender* will be used to describe a child who has committed any other offense proscribed under the juvenile statutes and who has been adjudged as such by the court.*

Group Care. "Group care" refers to institutional arrangements for the care of children away from their own homes in settings other

*According to Sarri, Vinter, and Kish some 26 states now distinguish delinquency from status offense, as part of a "decriminalization" process. See Rosemary C. Sarri, Robert D. Vinter, and Rhea Kish, *Juvenile Injustice: Failure of a Nation* (Ann Arbor, Mich.: National Assessment of Juvenile Corrections, 1974; processed).

than traditional adoptive and foster family homes. There are four major types of group care: *agency-operated boarding homes, group homes, group residences, and large institutions.* The capacity permitted each varies by state and locality. One common pattern would allow, respectively, maximum capacities of 6, 7–12, 13–25, 26 and over. (In 1971 there were eleven U.S. training schools and one detention center each with a designated capacity over 500.)

Diversion. A term which became popular in the late 1960s, diversion describes "the process whereby problems otherwise dealt with in a context of delinquency and official action will be defined and handled by other means."[13] Since one cannot "divert" a youth until he is first identified as delinquent—it is hard to tell to what extent his problems are being handled outside a "context of . . . official action" —the concept has an unclear meaning and uncertain referents, as will become apparent. In practice diversion means an effort to implement a philosophy which states: "minimization of penetration . . . within the juvenile justice system from court to another official or semi-official program" is a good policy;[14] young people should not be introduced to the system at all if it can be avoided.

Deinstitutionalization. The term "deinstitutionalization" became popular early in the 1970s to describe efforts to move residents of large, closed, congregate institutions into smaller, community-based facilities which more closely approximate home living situations or provide for therapeutic interventions.

Youth Bureaus. This term was introduced as part of the "diversion" philosophy to describe a local service which deals informally with what might have become official delinquency cases, accepting referrals from police and other authorities and carrying out "individually tailored work with troublemaking youth." Counseling, concrete services, referrals, job placement, education, recreation, and the like may be included. A national study disclosed no standardization of concept, administration, staffing, or auspices for youth bureaus.[15]

Target Population

The 1970 census reported that there were almost 70 million children under the age of 18 in the United States (Table 4-1).* Approximately 67 million (96.5 percent) of these children reside in homes

*By 1973 the total was only a little over 65 million, but what follows could be reported only on a 1970 census base.

Table 4-1. Family Status of Children under 18 by Age and Race (1970)

Family status	Under 18 (all races)		Number under 6 (all races)	Number 6–13 (all races)	Under 18 (white)		Under 18 (black)	
	Number	Percent			Number	Percent	Number	Percent
All children	69,522,812	100.0	20,930,883	32,866,919	59,124,604	100.0	9,463,108	100.0
Living with both parents	57,743,949	83.1	17,724,157	27,370,062	51,565,759	87.2	5,441,037	57.5
Living with father only	1,339,184	1.9	314,480	647,071	1,039,862	1.8	277,488	2.9
Living with mother only	7,979,085	11.5	2,263,625	3,791,705	5,011,925	8.5	2,853,290	30.2
Living with neither parent	2,460,594	3.5	628,621	1,037,541	1,507,058	2.5	891,293	9.4
In families	1,619,115	2.3	458,706	705,716	888,435	1.5	695,347	7.3
Nonrelative of head of household	434,423	0.6	126,632	182,494	319,294	0.5	98,107	1.0
In group quarters	407,056	0.6	43,283	149,331	299,329	0.5	97,839	1.0
Inmate of institutions	247,234	0.4	13,834	97,687	187,101	0.3	55,235	0.6
Secondary individuals*	159,822	0.2	29,449	51,644	112,222	0.2	42,604	0.5

Source: *1970 Census of Population, Subject Reports: Persons by Family Characteristics* (January 1973), table 1.

*A "secondary individual" is a lodger or resident employee living in a household or a resident of group quarters who is not an inmate of an institution.

where at least one of their own parents is head of the household; approximately 1.6 million (2.3 percent) are related in some other way to the head of the household (grandchild, sibling, niece or nephew, etc.). Consequently, fewer than one million (1.2 percent) of the total child population are not living in the homes of parents or relatives. Of this group, some 407,056 are in group quarters (dormitories and rooming houses), leaving the institutional group of 247,234 as the outside limits of the target population for group care facilities. The picture available is a one-moment "snapshot" and does not cover turnover in the course of a year. There is no way to place a meaningful statistic on the large number of youths for whom one targets "alternatives" or offers "diversion." As indicated above, we shall focus on group care of the traditional congregate type and its community-based alternatives.

Over half of the children not in their own homes or with relatives do reside in individual households, presumably in either formal or informal foster home arrangements. Hence, we will focus primarily on the 247,234 children reported to be living in institutions. However, because children who are retarded, physically handicapped, and/or mentally ill constitute a large portion of these children and have also been excluded from consideration in this discussion, the children with whom we are concerned are very considerably less than one-quarter of one percent of the total population under 18, probably between 100,000 and 125,000 at a given moment; the total given annual turnover could be two or three times as large.* A very sizable proportion of total child welfare and juvenile justice resources (financial, manpower, research) has, however, been devoted to this population subcategory. (The total institutionalization rate is about half of one percent—225,000–250,000 children in all types of institutions (see Table 4-2).

As we noted earlier, dependent and delinquent children in group care facilities have not traditionally been viewed as a distinct or unitary group. Therefore, most of the data on these children must be obtained from studies of the facilities in which they are placed. Because of inevitable limitations and emphases built into studies which concentrate on specific service programs and facilities rather than specific target populations, and because of the difficulty of com-

*On the assumption that several facilities not so classified are actually devoted to these categories, our estimate is somewhat larger than the totals shown in the tables which follow.

bining data gathered from several independent sources, the statistics we report will necessarily be incomplete and somewhat biased. They seldom are more than one-time cross sections.

Some estimates of the age and racial characteristics of our target population can be derived from Table 4-1. It will be noted that children under 6 constitute only 25.9 percent (628,621) of the total group of children not living with parents, although they comprise 30.1 percent of the total child population. But they constitute 29 percent of the population living with nonrelatives. On the other hand adolescents aged 13–18 comprise 28 percent (125,297) of the children not living with relatives and 55 percent (135,717) of those living in institutions, although they are only 22.6 percent of the child population.

The proportion of children out of their own homes also shows marked variation by race. For example, although blacks constitute only 13.6 percent of the total youth population, they account for 36 percent of children living apart from their families and 22 percent of those living in institutions. These differences become even more pronounced for adolescent blacks. Of whites under age 18, 2.5 percent live with neither parent whereas for blacks the rate is 9.4 percent.

The Census Bureau publication *Persons in Institutions and Other Group Quarters* provides some additional data about our target population (see Table 4-2). It will be noted that not only does this population have a large proportion of adolescents and minority group youngsters, but also that approximately two-thirds are boys. And as will be seen, it is this group of black adolescent males who have attracted the most attention in the group care literature.

As discussed earlier, our focus is on dependent and delinquent children in group care. However, these children often move through several different types of settings; and there is some evidence to suggest that the reason youngsters are assigned to specific types of facilities may be more related to their age and race than to their personal characteristics or legal status. Therefore, it is important to examine the total range of institutions in which they may reside.

As Table 4-2 demonstrates, facilities for the retarded account for almost one-third (29.3 percent) of the total of children living in institutions; and training schools and homes for the dependent and neglected each account for approximately one-fifth. However, there are marked differences by age, race, and sex. For example, approximately half of all black children who are institutionalized are in correctional facilities (prisons, jails, training schools, and detention centers) whereas only about one-third of whites are in these facilities. Similarly, children of Spanish origin are overrepresented in homes

Table 4-2. Persons under 19 in Institutions by Sex, Race, and Age (1970)

Facility	Total*	Sex		Race			Age			
		Male	Female	White	Black	Spanish-speaking	Under 5	5–9	10–14	15–19
All institutions										
Number	238,090	155,370	82,720	179,837	53,228	13,300	9,017	34,482	92,576	162,504
Percent	100.0	100.0	100.0	100.0	100.0	100.0	100.0	100.0	100.0	100.0
Facilities for retarded										
Number	69,752	42,348	27,404	58,559	10,079	1,953	3,593	14,615	29,934	34,287
Percent	29.3	27.3	33.1	32.6	18.9	14.6	39.8	42.4	32.3	21.1
Training schools										
Number	51,932	39,836	12,096	31,348	18,740	3,968	162	844	15,563	42,767
Percent	21.8	25.6	14.6	17.4	35.2	29.7	1.8	2.4	16.8	26.3
Homes for dependent-neglected										
Number	43,867	26,556	17,311	36,311	6,641	4,020	2,102	9,112	22,124	11,921
Percent	18.4	17.1	20.9	20.2	12.5	30.1	23.3	26.4	23.9	7.3
Psychiatric facilities										
Number	26,792	17,255	9,537	21,423	5,101	824	401	3,198	10,523	20,978
Percent	11.3	11.1	11.5	11.9	9.6	6.2	4.4	9.3	11.4	12.9
Prisons, jails										
Number	10,180	9,411	769	4,883	5,018	465	113	143	1,044	34,919
Percent	4.3	6.0	0.9	2.8	9.4	3.5	1.3	0.4	1.2	21.5
Detention homes										
Number	9,709	6,176	3,533	6,359	3,173	673	207	274	3,642	5,937
Percent	4.1	3.9	4.3	3.5	5.9	5.0	2.3	0.8	3.9	3.7

Schools for physically handicapped										
Number	16,489	9,183	7,306	13,974	2,259	520	518	4,512	7,186	6,052
Percent	6.9	5.9	8.8	7.8	4.2	3.9	5.7	13.1	7.8	3.7
Homes for unwed mothers										
Number	2,351	329	1,922	1,774	524	163	843	—	214	2,172
Percent	0.9	0.2	2.3	0.9	0.9	1.2	19.3	—	0.2	1.3
Hospitals (TB & chronic diseases)										
Number	4,650	2,743	1,907	3,198	1,371	588	689	1,300	1,553	1,936
Percent	2.0	1.7	2.3	1.7	2.5	4.1	7.4	3.7	1.7	1.2
Homes for aged										
Number	2,368	1,433	935	1,990	322	170	389	485	793	1,535
Percent	0.9	0.9	1.1	1.1	0.6	1.3	4.3	1.4	0.9	0.9

Source: *1970 Census of Population, Subject Reports: Persons in Institutions and Other Group Quarters* (1973), various tables.
*"Total" column shows children under 18 only.

for the dependent and neglected, and there is a high proportion of whites in facilities for the retarded.

It should also be noted that there has been a shift over time in the distribution of children among different types of institutions (see Table 4-3). Although institutions for the retarded, dependent, and

Table 4-3. Children in Institutions by Type of Institution (1960 and 1970)

Type of institution	1960	1970	Change
Mentally handicapped	73,879	83,304	+ 9,425
Dependent-neglected	70,725	56,368	−14,357
Delinquents	45,229	61,697	+16,468
Prisons	19,474	9,099	−10,070
Mental Hospitals	19,169	36,158	+16,989
Deaf	10,978	8,589	− 2,389
Blind	6,138	5,684	− 454
TB	4,329	1,017	− 3,312
Other physical	4,472	4,283	− 189
Unwed	2,685	3,576	+ 941
Aged and dependent	2,265	3,335	+ 1,070
Chronically ill	1,616	5,020	+ 3,404
Local jails	13,133	12,846	− 287
Detention	9,866	10,680	+ 773
Total	283,008	301,615	+18,615

Source: *1970 Census of Population, Subject Reports: Persons in Institutions and Other Group Quarters* (Washington, D.C.: Bureau of the Census, U.S. Dept. of Commerce, 1973), tables 3–11; and *America's Children and Youth in Institutions* (Washington, D.C.: CB, DHEW, 1965). Table prepared by Don Rademacher, Children's Defense Fund, Austin, Texas.

neglected also accounted for the largest proportion of children in institutions in 1960, their rank order changed between 1960 and 1970 because of a 12.8 percent increase in population in facilities for the retarded, a 20.3 percent decrease in homes for the dependent and neglected, and a 36.4 percent increase in facilities for delinquents. Moreover, there was an 88.6 percent increase in the population of psychiatric facilities and a 24.3 percent decrease in the population of hospitals and facilities for the physically handicapped during this period. Although there have no doubt been changes in some of the population characteristics during this period (for example the decline in TB hospitals was to be expected), these marked shifts suggest that dramatic changes may have taken place in the referral and admission procedures for various types of facilities. This suggests that the boundaries between dependent, delinquent, and emotionally disturbed children remain arbitrary.

Framework for Provision

Who offers what to these children? What are the key statutes? Is there a policy? What are the major group-care resources?

As already noted, policies and developments at the federal level have had relatively little impact on provisions for the group care of children in the past. This is a matter left primarily to the discretion of states and localities. Since the passage of the Social Security Act in 1935, the development and administration of state provision for the care of dependent and neglected children have traditionally been the responsibility of state departments of social welfare (alternatively called departments of social service, public welfare, child welfare, child guardianship, child and family services); the actual responsibility for the provision of care has frequently been left to local or county departments of welfare, depending on the degree to which the system involves state operations and/or supervision. And responsibility for the development and administration of juvenile justice services has been left almost entirely to local initiative, with some elements of state administration or supervision. States, however, have tended to operate "training schools" for delinquent youth.

Note has recently been taken of a trend toward the development of juvenile justice programs at the state level—and some states also have recently transferred responsibility for the provision of child welfare services to state-level agencies. Both these trends probably reflect the states' desire to take advantage of federal funding opportunities which require state-level planning and/or administration; and in this way, the federal policy is having some local impact. However, there are still major differences among the various states in the way group care programs are organized, funded, and administered. The picture is very incomplete, but the National Assessment of Juvenile Corrections, in its preliminary report, has noted contradictory trends among the states, different system boundaries, and a general lack of accurate data which allow interstate comparisons. Where state data are assembled, the local picture is vague.[16]

Legislation

Although federal aid in its present form began in 1935 (see Chapter 1), child care legislation is largely a state matter. There are, however, several pieces of recent federal legislation which have had an impact on group care programs for delinquent children. The first is

Public Law 92–381, known as the *Juvenile Delinquency Prevention Act*, which was passed by Congress on August 14, 1972. This act authorizes an appropriation of $75 million, under which the Secretary of DHEW is authorized to make grants to public or nonprofit agencies outside the traditional juvenile justice system to establish and operate coordinated, community-based preventive services to youths who are in danger of becoming delinquent. Such service may include individual, group, and family counseling, diagnostic services, education, vocational training, social and recreational activities, health services, emergency shelters, halfway houses, foster homes, and community-based treatment facilities. Under the provisions of this act, $100,000 is reserved for each state, the remainder of the funds to be allocated on the basis of the relative cost-effectiveness of proposed programs; youth unemployment and school dropout rates; extent of comprehensive community planning; provision for parent participation; and degree of coordination with other existing and proposed state and community programs for youth.

In September of 1974, in a major policy shift, the Congress affirmed its approval of earlier work by the Law Enforcement Assistance Administration (LEAA) in the Department of Justice, created initially as part of a 1968 "law and order" thrust in a Crime Control and Safe Streets Act of 1968. This new legislation, the *Juvenile Justice and Delinquency Prevention Act of 1974* (P.L. 93–415), reversed a pattern of forty or sixty-two years' duration (depending on one's earlier readings), during which the U.S. Children's Bureau and other units in DHEW were the lead agencies. The act assigned to this new unit in the Department of Justice major responsibility for overall leadership of the federal effort "relating to prevention, diversion, training, treatment, rehabilitation, evaluation, research and improvement of the juvenile justice system in the United States." LEAA had already shown its interest in more accurate reporting of law violations, in youth diversion from the criminal justice system, in rigorous research on effects of programs, and in the rights of young offenders. In its new role, it will create a National Institute for Juvenile Justice and Delinquency Prevention to coordinate data collection, carry out training, set up an information bank and clearinghouse, and sponsor research-demonstration-evaluation functions.

LEAA will administer a state-aid program of modest proportions (fiscal 1975 budget, $2.5 million)* to encourage states and local

*No special appropriation but assigned from LEAA budget. The authorization for federal assistance for state and local juvenile delinquency prevention

governments "in developing, maintaining, and expanding programs and services designed to prevent juvenile delinquency, to divert juveniles from the juvenile justice system, *and to provide community-based alternatives to juvenile detention and correctional facilities*" (emphasis supplied). Funds voted will be divided among the states as block grants on a child-population basis. To be eligible a state will be required to submit a plan and create a planning capability under terms of the 1968 act, create an advisory and local-consultative process, meet 10 percent of costs ("cash or kind"), and pass two-thirds of the grants on to localities except where the state government is the major operating entity in this field.

While all of this is new, LEAA intends to use its resources and influence to improve the juvenile justice system and to encourage new modes of prevention, diversion, community-based service, and protection of rights. Although it lacks the long history of identification with the problem which DHEW has, and will thus inevitably repeat some history, LEAA has a new mandate, increased funds, and—for the moment—high credibility. (DHEW was authorized to continue its own youth development demonstration program through fiscal 1975.)

One might add, as an aside, that as often happens in the correctional system in the United States this is one more instance in which a correctional agency (Department of Justice) creates a program which in its very nature implies a negative evaluation of its core activities, holding that offenders—or juveniles—are safe only if kept away from the system. Two leading criminologists cite this as a "damning commentary" on the juvenile justice system.[17]

Titles IV-A and IV-B of the Social Security Act, discussed in Chapters 1 and 3, are also relevant to service provision. The latter title has funded a variety of special experiments in prevention and treatment (as have special grants to local and state governments, institutions, and individuals from the National Institute for Mental Health). Coverage here inevitably is uneven, limited as to place and duration. Since it was extended to cover foster care, Title IV-A has provided federal funding on a significant scale for delinquents, PINS-CHINS, and neglected children. Title XX, effective in late 1975, may also provide some service funds related to institutional and community residential care of delinquent, neglected, dependent, or

---

programs under formula grants over a three-year period is for $350 million. Grants may also be made to public and private agencies for "special emphasis" prevention and treatment programs.

out-of-control children, if states so decide. Such services meet the Title XX goals summarized in our chapter introduction.

Policy

There is no explicit national policy toward group care of children but the preferences of the ethic have been clear. Sentiment about the importance of the nuclear family is strong and, historically, there has been great opposition to any state intervention in the parent-child relationship. Where government is to intervene, local government is preferred. If states administer training schools or institutions for the dependent and neglected, it is because most localities have too little need for such facilities to require their own (and perhaps because of a nineteenth-century implicit "pact" in which states would remove certain "undesirables" if localities did the rest). If states recently have mandated case finding and reporting in abuse and neglect (see Chapter 3), this is a new thrust reflecting, as does the new youth diversion and deinstitutionalization approach, a concern with rights and new insight into previous abuses and neglect by public authorities. Moreover, the activity mandated is usually reserved to the local government.

Despite national commitment to the nuclear family, however, child welfare funding and administration have usually been more responsive to the need for substitute (foster home or institutional) care than to the possibility of using resources to keep families intact and children in regular family environments. Despite arguments of economy, more generous support of families is supposed to undermine other important motives and to create undesirable incentives.

However, underlying all the laws related to child welfare (and despite governmental unwillingness to fund it generously) is the assumption that children are best cared for in their own homes and that they have a right to family life and parental care. The original Aid to Dependent Children provisions, enacted as Title IV-A of the Social Security Act, were designed to provide financial assistance to families so that they would be able to care for their children in their own homes. Title IV-B of the Act, enacted at the same time, was designed to encourage the development of public social services for the care and protection of dependent and neglected children. This law recognizes that some children cannot be cared for in their own homes and establishes the concept of public responsibility for dependent children. Hence—despite the ambivalence about voting money for preventive and developmental purposes—official policy would seem to endorse the view that children are best cared for in their own homes, but that when parents are unable or unwilling to provide adequate care, the state has a responsibility to provide for the welfare of the child.

Given the intertwining of responsibility in this field among several levels of government, between two service systems, and between public and voluntary agencies, it can be said that there is no legislated, single explicit policy. In effect, however, an implicit policy is widespread, and it is now relatively explicit and almost universal: foster home care is preferred to group care, community residential care to care in isolated institutions, treatment facilities to custodial group care, small residences to large. But costs, manpower, available plant, and an overlay of alternative ideologies and motives serve to inhibit implementation and to protect most of what has long existed —even where not consistent with these preferences.

Another policy supported explicitly by the Youth Development and Delinquency Prevention Administration of DHEW and the more recent LEAA legislation is the concept that insofar as possible juvenile offenders should be diverted from the juvenile justice system (or should not be allowed to penetrate it too deeply) and should be treated in community-based facilities. Although all the states have special laws governing juvenile offenders, giving explicit recognition to the concept that children have special needs and should be treated differently from adult offenders, there is currently strong emphasis on the importance of keeping youngsters out of the criminal justice system entirely. This reflects the increasing tendency for juvenile courts to be defined as part of such system in fact, even if that is not formally the case. For those children who must come before the court, there is increasing official recognition of the need to provide children the same procedural guarantees provided to alleged adult offenders. This policy is indicated most clearly in the famous *In re Gault* (387 U.S. 1, 1963) and *In re Winship* (397 U.S. 358, 1970) decisions of the U.S. Supreme Court which established a number of procedural guarantees for children and insisted on proof "beyond a reasonable doubt."

In summary, official policy supports the right of the child to live in his own home whenever possible; it is assumed that the state has a right to intervene only if the parents are unable to provide adequate care or if the child violates adult laws or norms governing child behavior, and that in any case of potential state intervention in family life for alleged delinquency, children should be protected by basic procedural guarantees. In instances of antisocial behavior, the preferred first response is diversion from the juvenile correctional system. If the state does intervene to take children from home, implicit policy would seem to support the concept that children are best cared for in family settings in the local community and that public intervention is best kept at a minimum. Therefore, group care of children is viewed as a residual service which should be considered only when the family and established nonresidential community services have failed. If group care is needed, the policy increasingly favors locally based community residences, not large, congregate, custodial institutions far from the home community.

This is what national policy wants. We now turn to an overview of what actually exists. What types of group care have been "invented"? On what scale do facilities exist? Who is served? What are the "alternatives"?

Program Models

Residential Care

There are several possible ways to classify group care facilities for children: size, length of stay, target population, auspices, and function. Since licensing requirements, state regulations, and statistical data are usually presented in relation to the size of the facility, it seems most useful to organize our data on this basis. There are four basic models of group care, in this sense, although there are a number of variations within each model. Some of these variations will be described more fully in the section illustrating developments in New York State.

Agency-Operated Boarding Homes. These facilities employ the traditional foster home model. Six or fewer children who may or may not be related and may span a wide age range are cared for in a normal family setting in which the wife cares for the children full time and the husband is usually employed outside the home during the day. What distinguishes agency-operated boarding homes from foster homes is that in the former the houseparents are usually employed on a regular basis by the sponsoring agency, and they reside in a home either owned or rented by the agency. The basic function of the home is to provide substitute care and an opportunity for normal family living for children who cannot remain in their own homes. The children attend neighborhood schools or go to work. The role of the caretakers is essentially parental rather than therapeutic, although these facilities are often used for children who could not be placed in regular foster homes because of factors such as physical handicap, emotional or behavioral problems, age, or size of sibling group. Because the home is administered by the sponsoring agency, the agency usually retains closer contact with and more control over the facility than is possible in a typical foster home. In one variation, the husband and wife both stay home, or the husband is a student and works part time. As we will see in one illustration, the role of the foster parents may be deliberately therapeutic.

Group Homes. These facilities provide care for from seven to twelve children aged 6 or over in a home setting. The facilities usually serve unrelated children within a narrow age group who have common needs or present specific behavioral or placement difficulties. Some group homes employ a family model in which the caretaker's role is seen as essentially parental; others employ a therapeutic or educative model in which the caretakers are expected to serve specific remedial functions. Staffing patterns vary. Some have a primary set of houseparents who are relieved on their days off by substitute parents or child care workers. Others have a regular child care staff of approximately five to eight adults who rotate shifts during the week. (The staffing pattern usually reflects the function of the group home.) The home is usually located in an apartment or house owned or rented by the agency, and the agency frequently provides some assistance with maintenance and housekeeping. Like agency-operated boarding homes, group homes are often used for children who would not be accepted in regular foster homes. For example, a number of group homes have recently been established as halfway houses for children discharged from large institutions in order to provide a traditional placement before the child returns home. Others are used as long-term placements for retarded children or older adolescents. Some are used for youngsters who would otherwise be placed in residential treatment centers. The basic attempt is usually to provide placement in a community-based facility which approximates insofar as possible a normal family setting. Children attend local schools and training facilities or work. Group homes expanded rapidly in the early 1970s.

Group Residences. These facilities serve between thirteen and twenty-five youngsters, usually in a local community setting, but sometimes more isolated. Like group homes, they usually attempt to maximize the residents' involvement in established community institutions and activities. For example, depending on age the youngsters may attend public schools, participate in neighborhood recreational activities, and seek employment in the community. On the other hand, because of their size, group residences are ordinarily subject to state regulations for large institutions regarding staff to child ratios, staff requirements, living space, safety and sanitation requirements. In New York State, for example, the Board of Social Welfare stipulates that there must be one child care worker for every twelve youngsters during the day and one worker for every thirty youngsters during sleeping hours. Actually, staffing patterns are likely to be more complex than this. In the New York State Division for Youth, for example, group residences are supposed to be staffed by a director, two counselors, three full-time child care workers, one part-time worker, a secretary, and a maintenance man. Although efforts are made to maximize community involvement and to approximate a normal living environment, the very size of group residences precludes the possibility of a family model of care. The staff are considered child care workers rather than houseparents; they work regular shifts; and although the residents are expected to help with housekeeping, the traditional domestic chores such as shopping, cooking, maintenance, and record-keeping are usually performed by specialized auxiliary personnel.

Like other types of group facilities, group residences may attempt to provide a therapeutic experience for their residents or may simply be designed to provide as normal a living situation as possible for children who cannot be cared for in their own homes. Group residences ordinarily serve a specific age and problem group and are perhaps most frequently used for older adolescents who are able to function on a semi-independent basis.

Because of the size of group residences, they must be housed in facilities designed for group living. This factor, of course, often mediates against the community acceptance and integration they were designed to promote.

Camps, ranches, and similar outdoor small facilities are isolated group residences, most often for boys, which stress outdoor work and play and strenuous routines. Sometimes they are large enough to belong in the next category, "institutions."

Institutions. The only distinguishing characteristic of children's institutions is their size: they provide care for at least twenty-six but may serve up to five hundred at one time. Beyond that, they vary tremendously in regard to their primary characteristics. They may serve a very narrow age or population group or may be designed to serve all children between birth and 18. They may have a very high staff to child ratio, or a very low one. For example, some facilities such as the Children's Center in New York City have approximately three staff members for every child in care, whereas others may have one adult for each ten or twelve children. Institutions may provide a full range of medical, psychiatric, psychological, social work, vocational, and recreational services or they may provide little more than basic educational services. In the 1966 census of children's institutions, for example, it was found that although only 23 percent of the facilities had more than seventy-five children in care, 65 percent of the children being cared for lived in such institutions; moreover, approximately 12 percent of the children lived in the twenty-five largest institutions, each of which had more than five hundred children in care. It was also determined that the largest institutions tended to have the widest range of services and programs, but that the smaller institutions had better staff to child ratios.

Most children's institutions have a formal organizational structure in which there is a clear hierarchy, a high degree of specialization, and specific role delineation. The children are usually housed by age group in dormitory or cottage living arrangements and supervised by child care staff who do not have professional training and are expected to provide basic nurture, guidance, and discipline. While occasionally in the midst of heavily settled areas, the institutions are quite often situated in rather isolated locations and attempt to provide for the total life needs of their residents. For example, children most frequently attend school on campus, receive specialized medical and counseling services within the institution, and participate in the recreational activities provided by the facility.

Like the other types of group facilities described, children's institutions may attempt to provide a therapeutic experience or may simply serve as a substitute living arrangement.

As suggested previously, there are a number of other dimensions besides size along which a typology of group care facilities could be organized. One approach suggested by Craig McEwen and his associates at the Center for Criminal Justice at Harvard University is that of program strategy. They delineate three major approaches: *rehabilitative*, in which the primary effort is directed toward changing the individual youth; *reintegrative*, in which the primary effort is directed toward changing the relationship between the child and the community; and *custodial*, in which the major concern is simply that of providing basic care and supervision.[18] It is obvious that this analysis cuts across the more traditional breakdown by size since boarding homes, group homes, group residences, and institutions could all adopt any one of these strategies. There is no way to estimate the actual distribution of available facilities along these dimensions, particularly because of the gap between institutions' aspirations and rhetoric on the one hand and their ability to realize these intentions on the other.

Another classification scheme employed frequently distinguishes group facilities by target population and function. For dependent and neglected children, residential arrangements would be as follows:

Size	*Temporary care*	*Long-term care*
Agency-operated boarding homes	Shelter boarding homes	Foster homes
Group homes	Halfway houses	Group homes
Group residences	Halfway houses, reception centers	Group residences
Institutions	Shelters	Schools, residential treatment centers

For delinquent and predelinquent children, the following typology would be used:

Size	*Temporary care*	*Long-term care*
Agency-operated boarding homes	Nonsecure detention homes	Foster homes
Group homes	Halfway houses, nonsecure detention homes	Group homes
Group residences	Halfway houses	Group residences
Institutions	Secure detention centers*	Training schools, camps*

Under this scheme, the short-term care provided children who are admitted to the child welfare system on an emergency or temporary basis ranging from a few days to three months and sometimes longer is termed shelter care. There are three major types of shelter care,

*Perhaps, if "institution" is defined as "over 25 children," these categories also should appear under group residences.

all of which are intended to provide an opportunity for evaluation of the long-term needs of the child: *shelter homes,* which are foster homes or agency-operated boarding homes; *reception centers,* which are group residences providing a full range of diagnostic and evaluation services; and *shelters,* which are usually large children's institutions providing a full range of temporary services in an open setting. The temporary care provided to allegedly delinquent children from the time they are arrested until a final disposition is made is termed *detention.* There are two major types of detention: *nonsecure detention,* which provides temporary care on an open basis in foster homes, agency-operated boarding homes, and group homes; and *secure detention,* which provides temporary care in a large locked facility in which all services and activities are provided on the premises.

The other type of temporary facility which is employed in both the child welfare and juvenile justice systems is the *halfway house.* These facilities, which may be described technically as group homes or group residences depending on their size, are customarily used for youngsters during an interim period of approximately six months between their discharge from a long-term congregate care facility and their return home or to the community.

The typology above also includes three types of specialized long-term care institutions. *Residential treatment centers* are facilities designed to provide a full range of therapeutic services for emotionally disturbed children in the child welfare system. *Training schools* are large, closed facilities designed to provide care and protection for children adjudged as delinquent; although they were originally used for all such children, their use is now generally confined to older adolescents who are considered likely to endanger themselves or the community. They most closely resemble adult prisons and can best be described as a cross between a prison and a children's institution. *Camps* are moderately large facilities which provide care, education, and work training and experience for adolescent male delinquents in an outdoor, semi-open setting.

The following slightly different classification system has been employed by the National Assessment of Juvenile Corrections (University of Michigan) and has been beyond the capacity of some states to apply: *institutions* (public, private); *camps, ranches* (state, local, or private); *community-based residential programs* (state, local, or private with state funds, local or private without state funds); *foster homes; temporary care* (detention, shelter); *reception and diagnostic centers; day treatment programs.*

Alternatives

Our topic demands an overview of *institutions* and *alternatives,* yet thus far we have presented a typology of residential arrangements. What of alternative arrangements other than the residential? Are there models?

Here, then, is the conceptual dilemma alluded to in the introduction to this chapter: if deinstitutionalization means anything it means alternatives for those who would otherwise be institutionalized. Apart from the occasional special effort, as in Massachusetts or Illinois, where deliberate campaigns have been waged to close down facilities and do something else with their inmates, it is difficult to identify just what is relevant. What are alternatives to institutions: better schools, child guidance services, summer work programs for youth, improved foster home care, recreation programs—or what? In fact, what that is constructive for youth is not relevant?

To keep this part of the overview manageable, therefore, we must face the fact that there are no typologies and statistics for arrangements other than residential and that, as we indicated in the introduction, such a typology would be suspect anyway, since it must encompass much of social policy and provision, not delinquency-specific or neglect-specific service alone. As soon as a program is specifically geared to delinquency, for example, it is no longer full "diversion." Alternatives to institutions for abuse-neglect-delinquency thus would cover all of child welfare and family enhancement. We therefore restrict ourselves to brief references to a few obvious alternative models: probation, youth bureaus, and other diversion programs.

Youth Bureaus. The "diversion" literature stresses the importance of youth bureaus, and the notion is identifiable conceptually as a local service which deals by informal means with what might otherwise be official delinquency. However, the *National Study of Youth Bureaus* disclosed no standardization of concept, administration, staffing, or auspice. The concept is still developing, and no one can judge whether a viable pattern will emerge. The idea would appear to be that each neighborhood would have what we would call a youth social service center. The center would automatically accept court, probation, police, parole, and school referrals with no questions asked. It would offer counseling, access to concrete services and benefits (employment, health, education, housing), and some measure of case advocacy, focusing on youths who are troublesome or in trouble, but not ignoring self-referrals. As a place (whether under public or private auspices) to which one goes voluntarily, it might be able to avoid stigma and labeling.

The survey indicates that 170 such programs could be located in 1972. However, it is unlikely that any widespread coverage program, standardization, or even systematic testing will appear in the near future, given the range of philosophies, staffing, goals, resources. The key dilemma arises from the difficulty of attempting to create a facility for the troublesome which is not to coerce or stigmatize, yet will command generous resources and cooperation—while reassuring a community that it is not endangered by "diversion."

Probation Subsidy. Probation is not an innovation. It is a court service which investigates alleged or adjudicated cases of abuse, neglect, PINS, delinquency, so as to propose dispositional plans to the court. Where possible, the probation unit also carries out "treatment"—long-term supervision, guidance, counseling, and service delivery—in a context of community protection and dealing with children and/or parents, varying with the category.

Probation has over the years also carried out a diversion activity which is now more precisely characterized as "minimization of penetration." By staffing court intake and exploring whether formal court process is necessary or useful, probation personnel arrange something called "informal probation" (the service without the court order), or arrange referrals for other forms of help, or discharge with a warning. In some courts, like New York City's this latter activity, a form of "diversion," is traditionally called "adjustment."

In a more specific sense, probation is diversion only when probation treatment is offered as a direct and immediate substitute for commitment to a correctional facility. California's probation subsidy program meets this definition.[19] Developed during a period when California correctional research showed the superiority and economy of community-based treatment and the reasonableness and safety of a goal involving a 25 percent commitment decrease (youth and adult), the program sought a way to create incentives for those making the case decisions. The program which evolved offered counties specific subsidies to upgrade probation services on the basis of commitment rates lower than base rates (for the 1959–63 period or the 1962–63 period, whichever was higher). (An outsider notes inequities in relating commitments to a population total, ignoring demographic shifts, but one should not be too critical of a proven effort.) The rate of reimbursement relates to the size of the decrease, the amount to the total number of commitments involved. The subsidy money is to be used for intensive probation work, small caseloads, and all the supports needed to assure both community protection and effective help. This interesting form of "performance subsidy" is reported upon enthusiastically[20] and is said to save substantial money, because the generous subsidies are below commitment costs, and to be effective, because probation officers have time to help. Nonetheless, an outsider cannot help but be confused by the fact that in California a person may be placed in a county jail as a condition of probation. This happens to half of all California probationers, and the period of incarceration may vary from three to twelve months. One ends, therefore, with a mixed picture of probation subsidies as "diversion."

Facilities

If the new thrust means substituting localized, small, community-based group residences for large, isolated, congregate institutions, state operated, the current space shortages would be such that most of the country could hardly accommodate half of the placed or committed delinquency and PINS cases, according to the Michigan National Assessment of Juvenile Corrections. Still, the trend in recent years has been toward phasing out large congregate facilities and toward the establishment of more small coed residences and more open facilities, as well as greater attention to rights. This does not necessarily assure a lower rate of placement or commitment but is nonetheless considered an improvement, especially for the delinquent-PINS group traditionally confined to the large facilities which Ohlin and his collaborators have described as follows:

> A key organizing principle of traditional training schools is punishment. There are efforts at vocational and general education in the training schools, but the institutions are basically custodial and authoritarian. Resocialization efforts are commonly reduced to instruments for creating conformity, deference to adult authority, and obedience to rules. Regimented marching formations, shaved heads and close haircuts, omnipresent officials, and punitive disciplinary measures have been the authoritative marks of the training school.[21]

Inevitably, according to the former director of New York State's Division for Youth, most institutionalized delinquents and PINS get worse.[22]

What, in fact, is the picture now? Have the diversion and diversification movements had real impact?[23] What type of care is now provided?

There are no hard data regarding the exact number of dependent or neglected and delinquent children in specific subcategories of group care facilities. Fragmented responsibility, inconsistent state legal codes, and differing boundaries between juvenile justice and child welfare systems in different states and even in different localities within states make this inevitable. A decision to count as "have received services" all AFDC children on whose behalf states request reimbursement creates confusion and inaccuracies. To illustrate the problem we may quote an assessment from the National Assessment of Juvenile Corrections: "The federal government *requests* the states to request their juvenile courts to cooperate in compiling statistical cards on each case. There are some *entire states* that do not participate. In almost every other state *many* counties do not *participate.*"[24]

Detention data are completely unsystematic. There is more leverage in obtaining child welfare statistics because of federal participation in funding, but that funding is relatively recent and the reporting systems are minimal and not fully standardized. Data under service titles of the Social Security Act (services to AFDC cases) are very limited. Most of the statistics are generated by reimbursement requests, and the services for which reimbursement is obtained are not generally standardized or audited—nor is the reporting more than a matter of counting check marks. New reporting of Social Security Act services from late 1975 may enrich the picture, but there have been no comprehensive national child welfare data for five years. Census reports use definitions and typologies which often do not provide the detail essential for program assessment.

The most complete, but increasingly outdated, census of children's residential institutions was conducted in 1966 by Pappenfort and Kilpatrick at the University of Chicago. This survey's count of various types of residential institutions and the number of children in these institutions is presented in Table 4–4. Group home facilities were excluded from the survey. However, this census provides the only detailed data available regarding facilities for dependent or neglected *and* delinquent children, their staffing and programs.

A DHEW estimate of the number of children served by public and voluntary child welfare agencies in March 1971 indicates that there were 64,303 children in 1,459 child welfare institutions and

Table 4-4. Children in Residential Institutions, by Type of Institution (1966)

Type of institution	Number of children	Number of institutions
Dependent and neglected	60,459	955
Delinquent	55,000	414
Emotionally disturbed	13,876	307
Psychiatric in-patient unit	8,028	145
Maternity home	5,835	201
Temporary shelter	1,832	54
Detention facility	10,875	242
Total	155,905	2,318

Source: Donnell M. Pappenfort and Dee Morgan Kilpatrick, *A Census of Children's Residential Institutions in the United States, Puerto Rico, and the Virgin Islands: 1966,* Vol. I: *Seven Types of Institutions* (Chicago: University of Chicago, Social Service Monographs, 1970), tables 1 and 3, pp. 2, 41.

Specifically excluded were 701 facilities for the mentally retarded and 373 for the physically handicapped, leaving 2,689 of the 3,763 children's institutions originally identified. A total of 2,542 were surveyed, as 147 did not fit definition; of these, 58 refused to participate but an additional 12 were identified, making a total of 2,554. Findings are based on information from 2,318. Excluded are 53 better classified as group homes, 93 under the Bureau of Indian Affairs, and 32 infant units of maternity homes.

Children's institutions were defined as facilities administratively more complex than foster family or group homes and administratively at least as distinct as a physically separate children's section of a larger institution within which children under 21 were living apart from their parents. Excluded were acute or short-term medical facilities, summer camps, and purely educational boarding schools.

4,532 in 849 group home facilities.[25] (At about the same time, we note for comparison, some 260,430 were in foster homes). This estimate would, of course, cover only those children considered dependent or neglected. Special surveys of juvenile detention and correctional facilities reveal that there were 57,239 children in juvenile facilities in 1971 and 45,694—or 16.5 percent fewer children—in these facilities in 1973. Table 4-5 summarizes the findings of these surveys carried out by the Bureau of the Census under the guidance of DHEW and LEAA. This table is interesting for several reasons. First, we note that although the total number of facilities increased by 72 (9.9 percent), the total population in these facilities decreased by 11,545 (16.5 percent). This suggests that the average number of children per facility is decreasing sharply (79.2 in 1971 compared to 57.5 in 1973). It should also be noted that although the total number of facilities increased, this was due almost entirely to the increase in group homes and halfway houses; there was actually a decrease in the number of training schools and camps. Similarly, the

Table 4-5. Number of Public Detention and Correctional Facilities and Number of Juveniles, by Type of Facility
(June 30, 1971, and June 30, 1973)

Type of facility	Number of facilities 1971	Number of facilities 1973	Number of juveniles 1971	Number of juveniles 1973
Total facilities	722	794	57,239	45,694
Detention centers	303	319	11,748	10,782
Shelters	18	19	363	190
Reception or diagnostic centers	17	17	2,486	1,734
Training schools	192	187	35,931	26,427
Ranches, forestry camps, and farms	114	103	5,666	4,959
Halfway houses, group homes	78	149	1,045	1,304

Source: LEAA, *Children in Custody: A Report on the Juvenile Detention and Correctional Facility Census of 1971* (Washington, D.C.: GPO, 1974), p. 1; LEAA, *Children in Custody: Advance Report on the Juvenile Detention and Correctional Facility Census of 1972–73* (proceesed; 1975), pp. 6–9.

population decrease was due almost entirely to the decrease in training school population.

These data definitely suggest that modest deinstitutionalization is, in fact, taking place within the juvenile justice system. Unfortunately because comparable data are not available for the child welfare, mental health, and adult correctional systems, we cannot say with certainty whether children who might formerly have been committed to juvenile facilities are actually being maintained in the community or are simply being placed in other types of residential facilities. For example, child welfare agencies in states such as New York and Massachusetts are now being asked to care for many of the status offenders who were previously handled through the juvenile justice system. Moreover, it is feared that increasing numbers of juvenile offenders are now being waived to the criminal courts and confined in adult correctional facilities or in local jails. Only four states use community care as much as institutions. State-run institutions hold 28,001 offenders, while community programs serve 5,663.[26]

The 1973 LEAA study shows marked state and regional variations in deinstitutionalization. For example, although there has been a decline in the population of juvenile facilities in DHEW Region 1 (New England), there has been only a 13 percent decline in Region 4 (Southeast) and only a 6–8 percent decline in Regions 9 and 10 (West). As might be expected, juvenile facilities in Massachusetts experienced a dramatic population decrease between 1971 and 1973 (−70 percent), but sharp declines can also be noted in other states such as Alaska (−43.6 percent), Connecticut (−40.8 percent), and Delaware (−40.0 percent), where the effort to empty juvenile facilities has not received such widespread publicity. On the other hand, some states have undergone only a small decline during this period—for instance, California (−5.3 percent)—and the population in juvenile facilities in a few states actually increased between 1971 and 1973—for instance, Oklahoma (+24.4 percent), Mississippi (+19.8 percent), Oregon (+6.5 percent).

Regional variations such as these result from the absence of federal leadership and the lack of national policy in regard to services for this population. Moreover, these variations support the view that some states are increasingly relying on out-of-state placements as a means of reducing the population in their juvenile facilities and highlight the need for uniform data collection on a national level.

The National Assessment of Juvenile Corrections, working toward more accurate data, offers the following interim overall preliminary estimates, which may be regarded as objective and informed and do not estimate "repeats" of a given person in any year: 2 million annual juvenile court cases (not children); 60,000 admissions to state public institutional programs annually (not including detention); an unknown number of admissions to local and private institutional programs for delinquents, PINS, CHINS; 100,000–500,000 juveniles jailed annually (to age 19); 500,000 juveniles held in detention at some point (again involving many repeaters over a year; about 12,000 was the one-day count).

It is urgent to note that these data do not cover the "child welfare" population.

Since our focus here is on interim care (detention and shelter) and ongoing care (institutions, training schools, camps, community group homes), for both the dependent and neglected group on the one hand, the delinquent group on the other, and the PINS-CHINS in between, it is necessary that we define the domain covered in this present exploration of policies and programs as leaving out the jails, in which many children are inappropriately detained, and also leaving out the specialized facilities for the mentally ill, retarded, handicapped, and emotionally disturbed, as well as maternity homes. We do not know how many separate children are resident in these facilities one or more days in a given year. Returning to Tables 4-1 and 4-2 we do note a one-time assignment of some 250,000 children to institutions by the census—for both the categories we have included and for excluded categories, such as the retarded, the psychiatrically ill, and the handicapped. For our two categories, then, we may estimate that about 100,000–125,000 children are in care at any moment, about 0.2 percent of the cohort if all children are counted and over 0.3 percent if children under 6 are dropped. The annual "turnover" figure which would be most valuable is not available; it would require a special research effort.

Characteristics

Classifications for child care facilities in general have already been listed. As already noted, there is no universally employed typology of group care facilities. Nonetheless, in one of our two major subcategories, the juvenile justice field, these facilities have traditionally been classified as detention centers, shelters, reception or diagnostic centers, training schools, ranches, forestry camps and farms, and halfway houses and group homes. This is the classification used in most recent survey of juvenile facilities, *Children in Custody;* the distribution of these facilities and the number of children in care in 1971 and 1973 is reported in Table 4-5.

Returning to the less current but most thorough survey of children's residential facilities under child welfare auspices, conducted in 1966, we find institutions classified as facilities for dependent and neglected children, predelinquents, and the emotionally disturbed, psychiatric in-patient units, maternity homes, temporary shelters, and detention facilities.

Neither of these surveys made any effort to classify facilities along any single dimension. The juvenile justice survey employed the criteria of function and the child welfare survey employed criteria both of target population and function. Neither approach tells very much about facility characteristics or quality. However, there are three variables on which we can report at least some comparable data: auspices, size, and treatment services. The facilities included in the juvenile justice survey are all under public auspices; 367 (46 percent) of these are operated by state agencies and the remainder, 427 (54 percent), are under local auspices. However, the distribution between state and local auspices varies according to size of facility and location. For example, the majority of facilities in the East and South are under state auspices, whereas a majority of the facilities in the Midwest and West are under local control. It should also be noted that shelters and detention centers are primarily under local auspices, whereas long-term facilities such as training schools and newer types of programs such as halfway houses and group homes are more frequently under state auspices.

The auspices of facilities for dependent and neglected children are somewhat different. The 1966 census and subsequent DHEW-SRS reports show almost five times as many children in voluntary as in public facilities—and about 6.5 times more facilities in the voluntary sector (since they are smaller).

Table 4-6. Size of Children's Residential Institutions (1966) and Juvenile Correctional Facilities (1971)

1966		1971	
Size	Percent	Size	Percent
1–25	36.0	1–24	33.0
26–50	27.6	25–49	19.0
51–100	20.5	50–99	20.0
101–250	10.8	100–299	21.0
251–500	3.9	300–499	5.0
Over 500	1.2	Over 500	2.0

Source: Donnell M. Pappenfort and Dee Morgan Kilpatrick, *A Census of Children's Residential Institutions in the United States, Puerto Rico, and the Virgin Islands: 1966,* Vol. I: *Seven Types of Institutions* (Chicago: University of Chicago, Social Service Monographs, 1970), tables 1 and 3, pp. 2, 41; LEAA, *Children in Custody: Report on the Juvenile Detention and Correctional Facility Census of 1971* (Washington, D.C.: GPO, 1974), p. 1. *N* (1966) = 2,311; *N* (1971) = 722.

The size of the facilities included in the 1966 and 1971 surveys is reported in Table 4-6 above. It will be noted that there is a striking similarity in the size range of facilities for dependent and delinquent children. Approximately one-third of the facilities reported in both of these surveys have twenty-five children or less and therefore would not even fall within the definition of an institution. Similarly, fewer than one-third of these facilities have more than one hundred children in residence and only a very small proportion report a capacity enrollment of more than three hundred. Hence it would appear that the days of very large, congregate care facilities are passing. However, the few very large institutions which still exist account for a disproportionate number of the total population in residential care.

As reported earlier, data regarding the services provided in child care facilities are scarce. For example, the 1966 census reports that 52.6 percent of the children in residential care were receiving regular treatment by psychiatrists, social workers, or other professionals.[27]

There were marked differences regarding the proportion of children receiving regular treatment according to the type of facility in which they were confined. For example, approximately two-thirds of the children in pre-delinquent programs and psychiatric in-patient units received regular treatment, and over four-fifths of those in maternity homes and facilities for the emotionally disturbed received such treatment. On the other hand, only about one-third of the children in facilities for dependent and neglected children and only about one-fifth of those in temporary shelters and detention facilities received regular treatment. Of course, gross measures such as these tell one little about the quality or frequency of the treatment provided.

The percentage of juvenile facilities with educational, counseling, and job placement services is reported in Table 4-7. It is interesting to note that that individual counseling is the service offered in 94 percent of the facilities and group counseling in 77 percent, whereas both academic and vocational programs are offered in only 55 percent of the facilities. Certainly, this highlights the strong treatment orientation which has tended to characterize residential programs for juveniles regardless of the specific type of facility. However, in this survey, as in the 1966 census of residential institutions discussed above, detention centers and shelters apparently offered the lowest levels of services.

Criteria for Quality

Basic regulations regarding residential child care facilities are customarily established by the state department of social services or board of social welfare. These regulations cover such matters as physical facilities, food, health care, staffing requirements, and program components. Federal agencies such as the Children's Bureau and the Youth Development and Delinquency Prevention Administration issue publications describing the criteria for quality programs, and national voluntary associations such as the Child Welfare League of America establish standards for various types of child care programs. Licensing requirements are intended to ensure a minimum acceptable level of care. Programs of higher quality are generally distinguished by comfortable physical facilities designed to serve program objectives; low child to staff ratio; experienced and well-trained staff; a relaxed, open atmosphere; and a full range of educational, health, counseling, and recreational services. Depending on the evaluator's theoretical orientation, special emphasis may be given to the degree of community involvement, parent participation, opportuni-

Table 4-7. Number and Percentage of Juvenile Facilities with Educational, Counseling, and Job Placement Services by Type of Facility (fiscal year 1971)

Type of facility	Total no.	Educational services (%)				Counseling services (%)				
		None	Academic only	Voca-tional only	Both academic and vocational	None	Individual counseling	Group counsel-ing	Counseling with juve-nile and his family	Job placement programs
All types	722	9	36	6	55	4	94	77	57	100
Detention centers	303	19	54		27	9	88	57	50	
Shelters	18	11	28	6	56	17	83	50	56	
Diagnostic or reception centers	17		65		35		100	94	59	
Training schools	192		12		88		99	92	64	46
Ranches, forestry camps, farms	114	2	35	2	61		100	96	64	16
Halfway houses, group homes	78	5	17		78		96	97	58	37

Source: LEAA, *Children in Custody: A Report on the Juvenile Detention and Correctional Facility Census of 1971* (Washington, D.C.: GPO, 1974), p. 15

ties for peer group counseling, specification of improved behavior toward which the program is geared.

Costs

Daily and annual costs of service in the various service models vary greatly depending on geographic location, auspices, and quality of program. Comparisons among jurisdictions are difficult because of the several approaches to capital costs, the different dates of the available reports, and the fact that facilities with the same "name" ("residential treatment center," or "group home") actually represent very different service packages. Furthermore, the alternatives (probation, child guidance service, etc.) represent different costs in different jurisdictions because of wage scales and the degree of professionalization. So the significance of cost levels, too, will vary from place to place.

The average per capita operating expenses for juvenile correctional facilities increased from $6,989 in 1971 to $9,582 in 1973.[28] This sharp increase reflects inflationary total operating expenditures as well as a sharp decrease in total population. There are marked variations by state, however. For example, the per capita operating expenditure for 1973 was $19,368 in Maine but only $3,798 in Mississippi; yet these are both relatively poor states with small populations in their juvenile facilities. Similarly, New York and California, two relatively affluent states with large juvenile residential populations, reported very different per capita operating expenditures in 1973 (New York, $17,410, compared to California, $9,255).

It is generally assumed that the cost of care in foster homes and small group facilities is considerably less than that in large institutions and that long-term institutions are less expensive than short-term or temporary facilities. This assumption is generally borne out by cost data. In New York City, for example, average daily rates paid to voluntary agencies in 1973 were as follows: foster home, $11.00; agency-operated boarding home, $19.18; group home and group residence, $28.66; and institution, $29.70.[29] And the cost of care in a city-operated temporary care facility is now estimated at well over $100 a day, although the maximum reimbursement for institutions under voluntary auspices is still only $32.50 a day.

We may clarify matters somewhat by looking at a single example which compares costs of group and institutional care in one New York voluntary agency. Here, annual cost of care in the group home program is over $2,000 less than that in the institution. There are, however, hidden costs to the community in group home (as in foster home) programs since the costs of public education, sanitation services, community recreation, and the like are not computed in the annual cost of care, although these expenses are in some way charged to tax monies. Thus, cost data should be looked at carefully: Is it total cost or cost to the operating agency? One would assume that if true costs were computed, the large institution, which enjoys economies of scale, could be cheaper—unless its bureaucratization reaches pathological extremes.

The expense budget of the voluntary agency operating both a group home program and an institution for male adolescent PINS, illustrates the cost differentials between the two kinds of care. For 1972, the agency reported a total operating budget (including administrative and educational costs) of $350,000 for four group homes serving a total population of 29 boys. Another $3,141,746 covers an institutional complex of eleven cottages serving approximately 220 boys.* The annual cost per child in the group homes was thus $12,069, versus $14,281 per child in the institution.

In this agency's group home program there are higher per capita costs per child for several items, namely children's allowances, utilities, household supplies, equipment, and staff salaries. Staff costs are higher because the ratio of staff to children is higher—three adults for eight boys in the group home as contrasted to four child care workers for twenty boys in the institutional cottage. City-based youngsters need larger allowances for such expenses as transit fares. And there is less bulk purchasing in small group homes. But these higher costs are more than offset by the savings in maintenance and recreation. In group homes, funds can be directly used for personal services for the children; in institutions, the physical plants consume a large part of the budgets for their upkeep.[30]

Selection for Group Care

Since provisions for dependent, neglected and delinquent children vary considerably from state to state, it is only possible to describe —to the extent we know it—the national "output" of the existing procedures (who gets into group care) and, then, to specify pro-

*This figure represents the average number of boys in care for an entire year, but fluctuations do occur. Figures were provided by the agency.

cedure and results for a particular state (New York) and city (New York).

It will be recalled that we have already summarized data suggesting that more minority children than whites end up in institutions, especially in latency age groups and early adolescence, and more boys than girls. The systematic national assessment by Vinter, Sarri, and their associates notes preliminarily that urban areas provide the bulk of the placements and that—at least for institutions in the "juvenile justice" network—half of the youth are from minority groups. The mean age is 15.6.[31]

On the basis of several studies of requests for foster care, Kadushin concludes that the population which can be identified as at high risk of needing substitute care "is most likely to include children who are *not* physically, mentally or emotionally handicapped but who *are* living in families . . . characterized by three inter-correlated factors. One is a structural factor—the family is likely to be a single parent family; the second is an economic factor—the family is likely to have a very small income; and the third is race."[32] Ohlin has reached a similar conclusion regarding the children most likely to be confined in institutions for predelinquent or delinquent children. He points out that only a small percentage of youngsters who violate the law are actually apprehended or officially labeled as delinquents. As we mentioned earlier, there is frequently a very fine line between the child who misbehaves and does not come to attention at all, the one who is diagnosed as emotionally disturbed, and the child who misbehaves and is defined as a child in need of supervision. In general it has been found that "the operating criteria at each major point of decision in a juvenile justice system—arrest, charge, court intake, adjudication and sentencing, and release—are biased in the direction of generating a residential population in juvenile correctional institutions drawn largely from poor and disorganized families who are residents of urban slum communities and recent racial and ethnic minority group migrants to urban centers."[33]

The level of emotional disturbance or disordered behavior displayed by the children confined in group care facilities included in the census of 1966 is presented in *A Census of Children's Institutions*.[34] Nearly half of the children in facilities for dependent and neglected children were considered to display no particular emotional disturbance or behavior problems, as opposed to only 13 percent of those in institutions for the predelinquent or delinquent. This finding would tend to confirm the conclusions of Kadushin and Ohlin cited earlier that a relatively high percentage of dependent and neglected children are apt to come into care because of family problems rather than problems related to their own behavior. In fact, many of the personality problems displayed by the children in these institutions may have been precipitated by their placement rather than by any pre-existing condition. Moreover, there is only a relatively modest difference between the amount and degree of emotional disturbance displayed by children in institutions for the emotionally disturbed and those in institutions for the predelinquent. This, too, supports Ohlin's conclusion that the selection of a particular type of institution for a child who displays behavior problems may be related as much to his race and class as to the type of disturbance he displays.

Research and Evaluation

Localism, pluralism, and decentralization have characterized both the child welfare and the juvenile justice programs in the United States; and such circumstances do not make for comprehensive and uniform reporting. On the one hand, there is the split between public programs and the operations of sectarian and nonsectarian private agencies. Then, within each field there is often administrative separation between institutions and community-based services. Few states have unified or coordinated services completely, even as some have tended in recent years toward somewhat more comprehensive child welfare and juvenile justice programs, often stimulated by federal funding and related planning requirements. No state has united or fully integrated child welfare with juvenile justice at the state level.

The federal government has intepreted its leverage as limited, whether with reference to basic state and local organizational structures or planning requirements: its grants for training, research, and experimentation, its child welfare program grants, and its matching social service funds are not defined as sanctioning strong overall guidance for a coverage system despite issuance of service regulations and some guidelines and standards in relation to specific laws. The states experience federal initiatives as leaving them large degrees of freedom, and localities have similar experience vis à vis many states. Indeed, philosophic and program rationale is moving even further in this direction at the very moment that funding in most service fields mandates increased planning. Age jurisdictions, laws, and policies vary among the states, creating further complications for those who would assemble experience. Furthermore, as we have seen, there are major debates about philosophy and operations at all levels, as well as conceptual ambiguities ("diversion," "minimized penetration," "prevention"), which continue to inhibit systematic programing and integration.

The result, as we have already seen, is that there are no national uniform data collection systems. The program and system evaluation projects tend to be discrete, sporadic, local. A census of institutions and residential care arrangements is a one-time thing, quickly outdated, and does not cover all types of programs. A detention or state institution survey gets only partial responses and inconsistent interpretations of the local domain. Census bureau data are useful but do not answer all questions. Child welfare service reports are based on state justifications for reimbursement; they are neither complete nor a source of an accurate picture of services. And so on.

Thus, uniform data collection and monitoring is yet to be achieved in the field, despite very large investments in reporting and administration. On the other hand, there has been very extensive child care and juvenile justice research, also based on large-scale expenditure and considerable scholarly and professional interest.

Three major review sources are readily available: Alfred Kadushin assessed child welfare research between 1964–69 in *Research in the Social Services;* Ann Shyne reviewed research on child-caring institutions in *Child Caring;* Martin Wolins edited a major volume of research on group care entitled *Successful Group Care,* which contains a good deal of his own writing and particularly examines group care in a cross-cultural perspective. Several child development research reviews assemble basic research findings on such fundamental processes and phenomena as separation, deprivation, group experience, delinquency, behavior modification, environmental intervention.[35]

As Shyne has pointed out, research in group settings creates several methodological problems. One problem which has become more acute as the concept of institutions has changed is that if the total institutional experience is viewed as the intervention method, then it becomes very difficult to specify, measure, and isolate specific input variables. In short, if the entire experience is viewed as a treatment intervention, it is almost impossible to take all the relevant factors into account or to control for certain factors in comparing institutions. The other major problem in institutional research is that of specifying desirable outcome criteria and determining at what point in time these should be measured: Is the key question adjustment while in residence, at the time immediately after discharge, or at some point in the future?

There have been several studies of the factors influencing the decision to place a child in an institution or foster home and the type of institution selected. Studies by Wolins and Pilavin, Maas and Engler, and the Child Welfare League of America all show tremendous regional variation in the use of institutional placements, indicating that these decisions may be influenced more by availability of resources and historical and cultural patterns than by any compelling theory regarding the types of placements best suited for various types of children. An experimental study by Scott Briar of caseworker judgments regarding foster placements found that parental preference and placement pattern in the workers' agencies were the primary factors influencing the workers' judgments—not variables relating to child needs. Unfortunately, there is still little convincing evidence regarding the type of care most suitable for particular types of children, so ideology and chance continue to be major factors in placement decisions.

Following the publication of Bowlby's work in the 1950s on the destructive effects of maternal deprivation, a number of studies were conducted to examine this phenomenon more precisely. Recent studies by Yarrow, Henicke and Westheimer, and Decarie all support the contention that maternal deprivation is stressful and that institutional placement presents a risk for development. However, Thomas, Chess, and Birch have shown that the effects of maternal deprivation vary depending on constitutional factors in the child. Moreover, several recent studies indicate that the effects of deprivation may be reversible if the child's subsequent experiences are positive. For example, Province and Lipton compared seventy-five infants in family homes and institutional settings; although they noted that the institutionalized children displayed behavioral disturbances, those later placed in foster homes improved markedly. Similarly, Heston and his associates studied two groups of adults, one of which had been institutionalized in early childhood for an average of three years but was later placed in family settings. They found no difference in I.Q. scores and personality adjustment between the members of this group and those who had never been institutionalized. In his overview Wolins notes the frequency with which negative conclusions about institutional care derive from studies in which "good" families are contrasted with "inadequate" institutions. While showing, cross-culturally, "the possibility of good asylums," he does not ignore "persistent difficulties that tend to plague them," particularly the "closed" institutions.[36]

There have been a number of efforts to develop a classification scheme of children's characteristics which could be used as a base for selecting appropriate interventions and/or placements. However, most of these schemes have been developed for use in specific programs and have not had general applicability. The California Youth Authority uses an Interpersonal Maturity Level Classification developed by Marguerite Warren and associates in which it is hypothesized that particular types of delinquency are associated with different levels of interpersonal maturity (I-levels) and that treatment choice should be related to the I-level of the delinquent. The New York State Division for Youth has also experimented with this scheme. However, thus far, despite considerable research interest and some validation, projects involving differential treatment have not been too encouraging and the system has not had widespread use outside California. Quay and his coworkers have derived classifications statistically and others find research validation for the system. Again, the critical gap is between use of classification systems and established treatment success. Shyne suggests that one of the limitations of classification schemes is that they focus entirely on the child and do not take into account the life situation which has such a significant impact on treatment. To which we might add that if labeled deviance is a person-situation confluence, relating to time and place, it is questionable whether person-oriented classification alone can guide intervention planning and enhance its success substantially.

There have also been many studies of child care facilities (communication patterns, staff roles, etc.). Ohlin and Lawrence first focused attention in 1959 on the influence of inmate subculture on the change objectives of institutions. Polsky's participant observation in a cottage of delinquent boys highlighted the importance of this observation in that he found great difference between the goals of the peer group and those of the institution and a tendency on the part of child care workers to support the delinquent subculture in order to maintain peace in the institution. In a later study of staff roles he found that child care workers spent approximately half their time exercising a supervisory or monitoring function, 28 percent of their time providing support and nurture, 9 percent on guidance activities, and 5 percent on harmonizing relationships between residents and staff.

More recently, Ohlin and his associates at the Harvard Center for Criminal Justice have examined subcultures in different types of programs serving youth assigned or referred from the Massachusetts Department of Youth Services. They found distinctive differences between the subcultures in programs which have a rehabilitative emphasis and those which have a reintegrative focus. The rehabilitative programs, especially those described as therapeutic communities, attempt to influence and control the subculture by isolating youth from outside influences and building an in-group subculture very different from the delinquent subculture. In contrast, reintegrative programs tend to accept the delinquent subculture as a reality and work toward teaching youth to cope with negative influences and to develop constructive relationships in the community. The degree to which staff are able to have an impact on peer subculture appears to be dependent on the size of the facility and the degree of staff hierarchy and differentiation.

The issue which is of perhaps greatest interest to researchers and policy-makers is that of outcome. As suggested earlier, however, there are a number of problems associated with standardizing, specifying, and measuring input and output variables, and many outcome studies tend consequently to be descriptive. There are, however, several notable exceptions.

Allerhand and his associates carried out a carefully designed study of fifty boys who had been, for at least six months, at Bellefaire, a superior residential treatment center. The most striking aspect of the findings was that although all boys made at least some progress while in residence, adjustment at discharge was not predictive of adaptation a year or two after discharge. The presence of constructive or destructive factors in the boys' environments after discharge had a critical influence on later adjustment. This, of course, suggests —in Kadushin's terms—that residential treatment may be better suited to preparing youth for adequate adjustment in the institution rather than in the community. Project Re-Ed developed at Peabody College in Nashville has attempted to deal with this problem by limiting the length of stay and directing all efforts toward normalizing youths' experiences insofar as possible and intervening in the youths' ecological systems in whatever way necessary to achieve a more satisfactory balance between the needs of the residents and other significant needs in their families and communities. As a result, the youth's reentry to the community is eased and constructive experiences in the community are supported by project staff. To date, this project is reporting very satisfying results at low cost.

One model of treatment for delinquents which has been widely followed and adopted is that developed by Elias at Highfields, a public institution in New Jersey. This model, which develops the peer group as the primary rehabilitative instrument, is employed in small facilities (such as the New York State group homes) in which the residents generally attend school or work away from the institution and attend guided group interaction sessions daily to discuss the problems of the members and of the group. The approach is postulated on the theory that youth will change only if their behavior is acceptable to their peers and that change is achieved most effectively if the entire group is the target of change and change occurs through a process of interaction with others. A formal evaluation of the program indicated a 17 percent rate of recidivism within a year of discharge as compared to a 49 percent rate among comparable boys treated in a state reformatory. There have, however, been some methodological questions raised about the research.

Early findings on the "deinstitutionalization" approach adopted by the Department of Youth Services in Massachusetts indicate a lower rate of recidivism within six months of discharge among youths treated in community-based facilities as compared to those confined in traditional training schools. For example, a study of recidivism among boys at the state training school in 1962 showed a 49 percent rate within the first six months whereas the population in community-based facilities in 1972–73 showed a recidivism rate of only 24 percent within the first six months. Unfortunately, however, children from the Boston area were not included in the latter study, so the recidivism rate may be higher when these urban youths are included. Also, preliminary data on girls are not so encouraging in that female recidivism rates increased somewhat during 1972–73 and the 1973–74 sample showed a 30 percent rate of recidivism. Moreover, the study does not look at overall costs and the consequences of decreased use of state-sponsored institutions, the tendency to keep more deviant youth in the community, the need to provide custody in other ways, such as sending youth to other states for secure custody, and so on. Indeed, there is some national evidence from Vinter, Sarri, and their colleagues that, because there are no real alternatives and communities are determined to be protected, the closing down of large state institutions sends many more youngsters to oppressive local jails.

As mentioned earlier, the California Youth Authority has carried out major research efforts since 1959, and results have generally supported the move toward developing community alternatives to institutionalization.[37] Classification generally follows the "I-level" scheme and parole revocation is the failure criterion. Warren concludes overall that some subtypes profit more from institutionalization and others from community programs.

Because we have used New York State here to illustrate group care provisions in the United States, we might note that since 1968 its Division for Youth has carried out a series of studies designed to develop means of predicting and understanding program outcomes. In general the studies have not approached the California work in national impact. Perhaps the most interesting was a multivariate analysis of characteristics related to postdischarge arrest, commitment, and failure to graduate. The study found that the characteristics most related to postdischarge arrest tended to be indicators of previous rule violations by the youth and of his family's economic need. Also, failure to graduate from the programs tended to be associated with higher rates of subsequent arrest and commitment. Postdischarge commitment following arrest, however, tended to be related to length of previous incarceration and school status. These findings led the researcher to suggest that forms of behavior and reactions to particular types of behavior tend to be repetitive. Therefore, previous delinquent behavior and official sanction against this behavior may be predictive of later difficulties. A somewhat surprising finding of the study was that the type of program was not related to postdischarge arrest or commitments, although it was related to failure to graduate. There were, however, significant differences among individual programs in regard to postdischarge arrest and nongraduation. This, of course, suggests that differences among individual programs may be more significant than differences among types of programs, at least as program types are now conceptualized.[38]

It is difficult to summarize the research findings on child care because so many of the studies reported are discrete, exploratory efforts, often related to foster home and adoption practice problems or adult-child matching procedures. It seems clear, however, that group care can have some positive effects, and that the results of early deprivation are reversible. On the other hand, it may be that institutions do a better job of helping dependent and neglected youngsters to achieve a satisfactory adjustment with the institution than of preparing them for re-entry into the community. The influence of the peer group is great, especially among adolescents, and facilities which attempt to mold the resident subculture and use this as an instrument of change may be more effective in the long run than those which ignore or oppose it. Although there are hardly grounds for definite conclusions, it also appears that small community-based facilities which focus attention on the relationship between the youth and his environment are more in tune with humanistic values and may be more effective in "normalization" than large, closed facilities. Clearly, some programs which treat the youth entirely in the community have beneficial results and serve to raise questions about any decision to place youth in a residential program unless there is absolutely no alternative. But there often is no alternative and, as Wolins notes, group residential care can be constructive and has been.

Programs in Action

We have generally characterized the system, or nonsystem. The issues are now laid out. Clearly we are going in several directions at once. For the families and children involved there is neither fairness nor assurance of wise and effective help. For the community, there is questionable protection and poor investment.

At this point we could turn to the question of how the issues might be ordered and the policy-program debate focused. The reader who wishes thus to be engaged may turn at once to page 301. But readers not intimately acquainted with these services may want a more detailed picture of a system in action. For this purpose we go over the same ground we covered nationally, but for New York State alone.* Then we present a series of profiles of residential

*New York is not representative, but no state is. The overview does, however, generate the issues that must be faced everywhere in this field. The illustrations will introduce readers to the several types of facilities.

facilities, so that the reader may visualize them in real life. This is a long presentation because it requires understanding of structures and procedures for both child welfare and juvenile justice. It is a complex presentation because data are incomplete and jurisdictions overlapping. It is a tentative presentation—because the choices and directions are muddled.

We begin with several relevant definitions. *A dependent and neglected child* is defined in New York State law as a child under the age of 18

> whose physical, mental or emotional condition has been impaired or is in imminent danger of becoming impaired as a result of the failure of his parent or other person legally responsible for his care to exercise a minimum degree of care (*a*) in supplying the child with adequate food, clothing, shelter or education, medical, or surgical care, though financially able to do so or offered financial or other reasonable means to do so; or (*b*) in providing the child with proper supervision or guardianship, by unreasonably inflicting or allowing to be inflicted harm or substantial risk thereof, including the infliction of excessive corporal punishment; or by using a drug or drugs; or by using alcohol and beverages to the extent that he loses self-control of his actions; or by any other acts of a similarly serious nature requiring the aid of the court; or who has been abandoned by his parents or other person legally responsible for his care.[39]

A *permanently neglected child* is any child under 18

> who has been placed in the care of an authorized agency, either in an institution or in a foster home, and whose parent or custodian has failed for a period of more than one year following the placement or commitment of such child in the care of an authorized agency substantially and continuously or repeatedly to maintain contact with and plan for the future of the child, although physically and financially able to do so, notwithstanding the agency's diligent efforts to encourage and strengthen the parental relationship when such efforts will not be detrimental to the moral and temporal welfare of the child. In the event that the parent defaults after due notice of a proceeding to determine such neglect, such physical and financial ability of such parent may be presumed by the court.[40]

Delinquent children are now distinguished from *persons in need of supervision* (PINS):

> The "juvenile delinquent" means a person over 7 and less than 16 years of age who does any act, which, if done by an adult, would constitute a crime.

"Person in need of supervision" means a male less than 16 years of age and a female less than 18 years of age who is habitually truant, or who is incorrigible, ungovernable or habitually disobedient and beyond the lawful control of parent or other lawful authority.[41]

Dependent and neglected children may come into care voluntarily or be committed by a court. Delinquent children and PINS come into care on the basis of court commitment. However, some children are placed in juvenile facilities on what is described as a "voluntary" basis, although the "voluntarism" may only be technical; for a youth on probation the real alternative is commitment. Complete parental or youth "initiative" in seeking placement without any authoritative pressure is rare in the juvenile justice system and is even infrequent in the case of dependent and neglected children. The frequency increases with retarded and psychiatrically disturbed children and youth.

Although procedures vary slightly in different areas, non-court placements are usually initiated by a referral to the child welfare agency from a variety of sources. In a study of the requests for foster care in seven metropolitan areas conducted by the Child Welfare League of America, it was found that parents accounted for 46 percent of the total requests, the court or police for 17 percent, other agencies for 22 percent, relatives and friends for 7 percent, and such sources as schools, physicians, and clergy for 6 percent. Only 2 percent of the youngsters were self-referred.[42]

Once the child is referred for placement, a caseworker from the child welfare agency usually conducts a study commonly referred to as an "intake" in order to determine if placement is necessary and what type of placement is indicated. It is assumed that the caseworker will attempt to provide whatever resources are necessary to maintain the child in his own home if this is possible. If the decision is made that placement is necessary, selection of the particular type of care is made on the basis of the child's needs, the family's needs and preferences, and available resources and traditions. Whenever possible, children usually remain at home until the intake process is completed and an appropriate placement resource has been selected. The intake process might be as short as a few days or as long as several months. If it is necessary for a child to enter placement immediately, either because of some personal risk to the child or some emergency in the family situation, he may be placed immediately in a temporary shelter or in an emergency foster home. If the parents or legal guardians agree to the placement, it is usually only necessary for them to sign a foster placement agreement, giving temporary custody of the child to the child welfare agency and granting permission for medical services and the like.

Many states require that children who are placed voluntarily be channeled through the courts in any case. There are two reasons for this. First, many child welfare agencies feel that once a child comes into care they need the control over him and the protection provided by a court commitment. Secondly, as noted earlier, federal social service funds are available to pay for a considerable share of the costs of placement for children eligible for Aid to Families with Dependent Children, if they are placed by the courts. Therefore, there is financial incentive for public welfare agencies to secure court commitments of the dependent and neglected children in care.

If the parents do not place a child voluntarily, then it is, of course, necessary to obtain a court commitment. This procedure is usually carried out in two stages. First, a child may be placed temporarily because of what is seen as imminent danger to his health or welfare, and in such situations a petition may be filed requesting the court to give permission for emergency placement. If such permission is granted, or if the child is already in care and the agency wishes to obtain long-term custody, then a petition is usually filed requesting that the child be declared dependent and neglected or permanently neglected as defined in the statutes cited above. If the child is bound over to the public agency on the basis of a court commitment, the agency is usually required to file intermittent reports on the child, reporting on his status in care and plans for his future.

The placement process for children defined as delinquent is quite different. In New York State, for example, the procedures are as follows:

A child who is alleged to be a PINS or a delinquent is first seen at Probation Intake, where a decision is made as to whether or not a particular situation requires court intervention. It is reported that approximately half of all cases seen at Probation Intake are adjusted and not referred to the court.

If a case is referred to court, a petition is drawn and the case is inially heard by a judge sitting in an intake part. He determines if the court has jurisdiction, whether the child should be paroled or detained pending a fact-finding hearing and, unless therein is admission by the child, refers the case to another judge sitting in an "all purpose" part for a hearing. A child who is detained pending a fact-finding hearing is entitled to such a hearing within 72 hours. Children who are detained are sent either to secure detention (locked institutions) or to non-secure detention (foster homes and group homes). [The police are permitted to make direct referral to detention care during the hours that the court is not in session.]

The children are represented by counsel at all stages of the court proceedings and the allegations must be proved beyond a reasonable doubt. In addition, it must be found that a PINS child is in need of supervision or treatment if a disposition of probation or placement is to be ordered. In a delinquency case a child must be found to be in need of supervision, treatment or confinement. Two types of hearings are held: fact-finding and dispositional. Each type of hearing may require a number of court appearances before a fact-finding or disposition is made. The court may proceed immediately to the dispositional hearing after finding has been entered. In practice, however, there are generally adjournments to allow time for probation investigation and, frequently, psychiatric and psychological evaluations.

The court has a number of alternatives that can be ordered for each type of petition after a fact-finding has been made. For both PINS and delinquency cases the court may:

1. Dismiss the case: of a PINS child found not to require either supervision or treatment; of a delinquent child found not to require supervision, treatment or confinement.
2. Suspend judgement for up to one year.
3. Place the child on probation (for delinquents up to two years, for PINS up to one year, with permissible one year extension for both).
4. Place the child for up to 18 months (*a*) in his own home or that of another suitable person or relative, (*b*) with the Commissioner of Social Services, (*c*) with an authorized agency, or (*d*) with the Division for Youth. One year extensions of placement can be authorized up to the child's 18th birthday.

The court may commit a 15 or 16-year-old, found to have committed a serious delinquent act before his 16th birthday, to specified correctional facilities. A serious delinquent act would be a Class A or B felony such as homicide, rape, armed robbery, etc. PINS children may be discharged without a warning. Finally the court may, at its discretion or at the re--quest of the child or his counsel, order the substitution of a PINS petition for a delinquency petition. [It should also be noted that the child may be referred to the Division for Youth for placement as a condition of probation so that no court adjudication is made but the child is placed in group care.][43]

New York's Statistical Overview

In New York State on December 31, 1971, there were 49,099 children in foster care in facilities under the supervision of the State Board of Social Welfare. In addition there were 5,092 adjudicated delinquents in training schools under the supervision of the State Division for Youth.* This total of 54,191 reflects a relatively high placement rate when looked at against countrywide norms. Figure 4-2 presents a breakdown of these figures according to the status of the child and type of facility. As demonstrated in Figure 4-3, although the population in foster care increased steadily during the 1960s, the number in institutions remained relatively constant during the period, and there was a decline in the total number of children in foster care in the early 1970s. The decline continued in both categories, child care under social services and juvenile justice, into the mid-1970s.

Total expenditures for foster care of dependent and neglected children in New York were $212,873,000 in 1971. Of this, 46.8 percent were paid by state funds, 44.2 percent by local funds, and 9.0 percent by private funds.[44] The JD-PINS costs are paid in so many pieces as to defy summation. The state expends approximately $242 million for foster care of 54,000 children or approximately $4,500 for each child in care. As the cost data reported earlier indicate, however, the costs per child of group care are considerably higher than this overall average. An average cost per child for training schools was given as $20,000 in 1975; the two secure facilities were averaging out at annual totals of $30,000.

Unlike other social services the *cost* of group care of children is paid almost entirely by public funds. Delinquent children who are adjudicated by the court are of course paid for out of public funds. In addition, although the attempt is made to charge parents on a sliding-fee basis for the cost of care for dependent and neglected children, almost all these children are also paid for by public funds. For example, in New York State in 1971 only 3.2 percent of all dependent and neglected children in care were paid for on a private basis. There are no data available regarding the actual portion of costs covered by private charges.

In addition to the many voluntary agencies involved in the delivery of group care services, a number of public agencies in New York State have responsibilities in this area. The primary agencies involved in the group care of children are the New York State Department of Social Services, the State Board of Social Welfare, the New York State Division for Youth, the Division of Probation, and

*Accurate data are difficult to come by. *Children in Custody,* May 1975, has a New York total of 2,682 for 1971 and 1,922 for 1973. Other New York reports are closer to this figure too. The higher figure probably includes parolees.

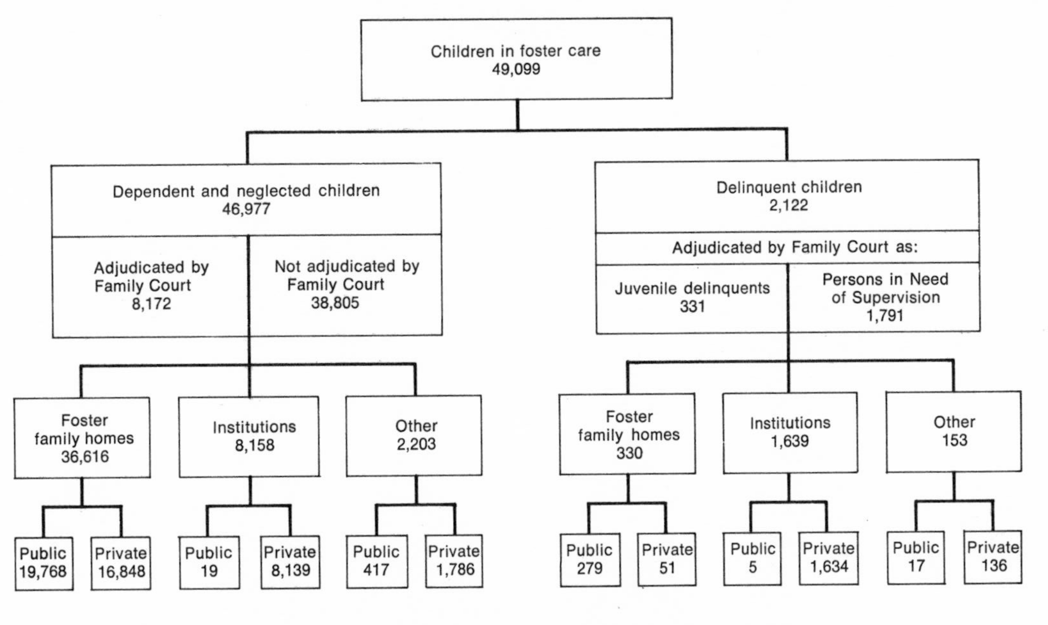

Figure 4-2. **Children in Foster Care under the Supervision of the New York State Board of Social Welfare and the New York State Department of Social Services** (Dec. 31, 1971). From New York State Department of Social Services, "Foster Care of Children in New York State" (Program Analysis Report No. 54; Albany, 1974), p. 14. At the end of 1971 there were, in addition to those enumerated above, 5,092 delinquent children in the New York State training school system supervised by the New York State Division for Youth. Also excluded are children cared for by institutions and agencies providing temporary or special services such as schools for the blind or deaf, convalescent homes, and temporary shelters.

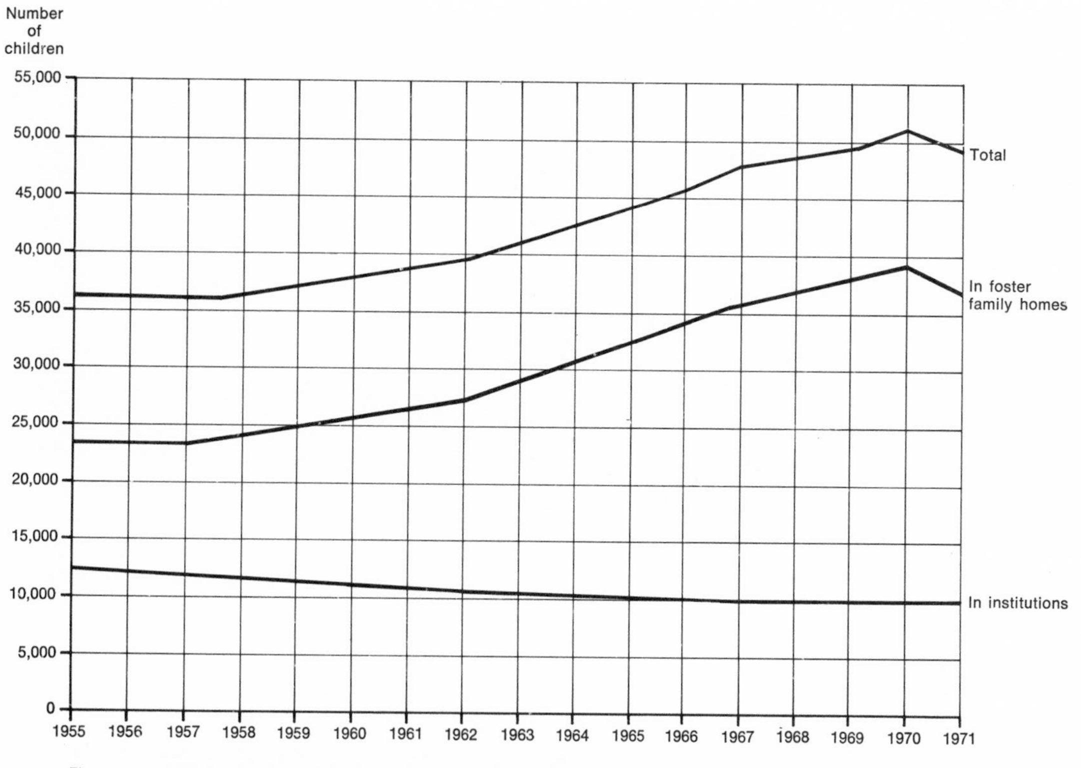

Figure 4-3. **Children in Foster Care by Type of Care, New York State** (1955–71). From New York State Department of Social Services, "Foster Care of Children in New York State" (Program Analysis Report No. 54; Albany, 1974), p. 16.

the Family Court. The complexity of the existing pattern for service delivery was given recognition by Governor Nelson Rockefeller when he established an Interdepartmental Commission on Services to Children and Youth which includes the heads of eleven state agencies.[45]

The following excerpt describes the formal roles of the various agencies involved in the care of dependent and neglected children.

The Public Sector. Local, State and Federal agencies play differing roles in the administration of foster care services. The fifty-eight county departments of social services in New York State have primary responsibility for the provision of services. Caseworkers in the county agency work directly with the children, parents and others who are involved. The procedures for arranging placement vary among agencies since under State law each has a considerable amount of administrative autonomy. At the State level both the Department of Social Services and the Board of Social Welfare have administrative responsibilities related to foster care. The Board of Social Welfare visits, inspects and supervises agencies and institutions caring for dependent and neglected children. Under State law, no person with the exception of certain relatives or a legal guardian may provide board for children in New York State without a certificate or license. These are issued only to persons who maintain homes that meet basic requirements for safeguarding the health and welfare of children. The requirements are set by rules of the State Board of Social Welfare.

The State Department of Social Services is authorized and required by law to prepare and implement plans for child welfare services, including foster care, with the view of providing those services which will best promote the welfare of children and their families. The main functions of the Department are to set standards under which public funds are paid and within this context to see that appropriate plans are made for children who are paid for as public charges. The Department is responsible for assuring that when public funds are expended appropriate goals are set, a specific plan is made, steps to carry it out are conceived and executed, and appropriate follow-up activities are conducted. It is also the State Department's responsibility to allocate and disburse to counties, or other local subdivisions of the State, moneys available for payment of part of the cost of foster care and related welfare services.

The role of the Federal government in the administration of foster care is primarily one of financial reimbursement to the State for children placed in care as a result of a judicial determination that continuation of care in the child's own home would be contrary to the welfare of such child. Federal financial reimbursement may be obtained by the State for certain foster care services, and for children who are receiving Aid to Families with Dependent Children (AFDC) or would have received

AFDC if an application for it had been made. The State's desire to increase Federal financial participation has recently resulted in the enactment of legislation which makes it mandatory for local social services districts to comply with eligibility requirements for Federal reimbursement. It is expected that this will substantially increase the Federal share of expenditures for foster care. The Federal Government's impact on the administration of foster care is brought to bear therefore in relation to the eligibility requirements it sets for Federal financial participation.

The Private Sector. Private agencies, usually referred to as voluntary agencies, play a significant part in the provision of foster care services in some areas of the State. Traditionally, voluntary agencies in New York City have been extensively involved in providing a variety of foster care services. There are currently over seventy agencies in New York City from which the public social services department purchases foster care services. These services are principally related to the placement of a child in the residential care of a voluntary agency boarding home or institution. More than 88 percent of all children in foster care in New York City are in the direct care of voluntary agencies, even though over 90 percent of the children placed are supported by public funds. . . . Based on their strong commitment to serving foster care needs and the large number of children which they care for, voluntary agencies maintain considerable influence in matters regarding foster care in New York City.

Another source of private sector influence on the administration of foster care is the large number of associations and organizations which have an interest in some aspect of foster care. The Child Welfare League of America, the National Action for Foster Children Committee and other professional associations concerned with family and child welfare all play a role. Through their publications, conferences, research, and other activities these groups often influence the development of policy and procedures related to foster care.[46]

In addition to the agencies discussed above, which have responsibility for dependent and neglected and certain delinquent children, there are several agencies which assume responsibility for children who are placed through the courts. The Family Court has jurisdiction over all juvenile offenders and in all matters related to child custody and protection. When a child is first brought to court, the first responsibility of the judge is determining whether or not the court has appropriate jurisdiction over this matter. If so, the case is usually turned over to another judge, who first holds a fact-finding hearing in which all allegations must be proved beyond a reasonable doubt. If a finding is made, the court then holds a dispositional hearing, at which time the judge makes a final disposition of the case. The Office of Probation has two major responsibilities in regard to the care of children. When a child is first referred to the Family Court, the Intake Office makes an initial investigation in order to determine if court intervention is necessary or justified. Then, when a finding is made by the court, the Probation Office conducts a thorough investigation and makes a recommendation to the court regarding disposition. Figure 4-4 represents the process of entry into foster care in New York City.

The other state agency having major responsibility in regard to group care of children is the Division for Youth (DFY). This agency was originally established as an experimental department in the Executive Office of the Governor to carry out a variety of prevention activities and to provide treatment alternatives for youthful offenders aged 15–17. In 1971, however, DFY was given responsibility for running the state training schools and handling all adjudicated delinquents and status offenders who are sentenced to them by the Family Court, a function previously assigned to the state social service department. The court now may assign youngsters directly to DFY for a period from eighteen months to two years, and the Division must assume responsibility for their care. In addition, the Division accepts a number of voluntary referrals, who may request service independently or as an alternative to probation. Youngsters placed by the court (for up to eighteen months) may be admitted directly to one of the Division's "Title III" facilities (training schools) although after subsequent evaluation they may be transferred to one of the "Title II" facilities (voluntary, especially camps, urban homes, etc.). ("Title II" and "Title III" refer to the relevant statutes, which have become classifications in New York.) Because of a court ruling in July 1973, PINS children may not be placed with delinquents, so DFY must maintain two parallel systems. Youngsters admitted on a voluntary basis are studied in one of the DFY intake offices located in regional centers throughout the state; the intake worker then makes a recommendation to the director of placement, who refers the youngster to an appropriate facility. Court referrals are similarly channeled. The director of the local facility has the option of accepting or rejecting each referral to assure a "fit." (Table 4-8 shows New York State dispositions involving the placement and commitment of juvenile delinquents and PINS in 1973–74.)

The distinction between Title II and Title III facilities has more than historical interest. Indeed, it typifies public ambivalence and

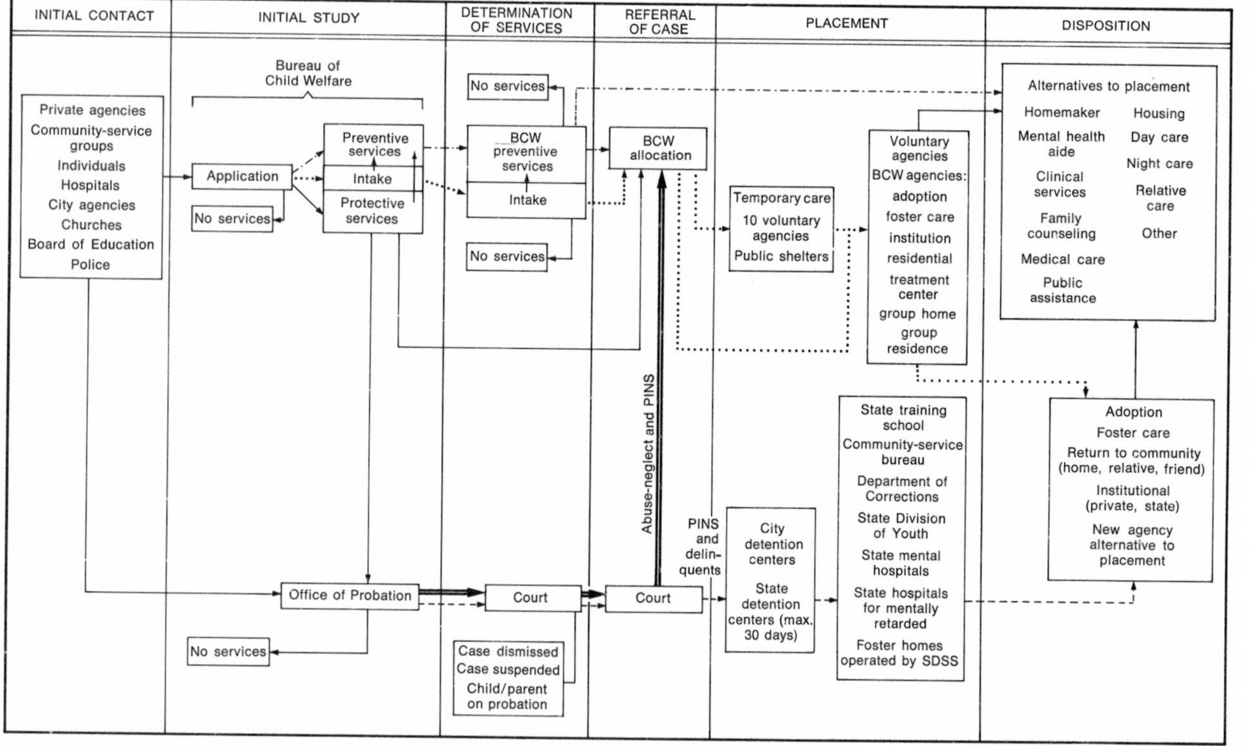

Figure 4-4. **New York City Child Care System Flow.** From David Young, "Referral and Placement in Child Care: The New York City Purchase-of-Service System," Public Policy, XXII, No. 3 (summer 1974), 296–97.

illustrates the complexity of "diversion." The Division for Youth was originally justified as a vehicle to encourage innovation and experimentation outside of the social service department bureaucracy. Its original version (the New York State Youth Commission) covered recreation, youth social services, local youth boards, research—and an important grant-in-aid program for localities. These are still major activities, but we are not concerned with them here, except insofar as they serve as "alternatives" to placement. The youth facilities—camps, Start (see below), youth homes, halfway houses, etc.—began as alternatives to traditional facilities in the corrections department; 15–17 year olds were assigned "voluntarily" or as a condition of probation. The state invested heavily in changing the individual commitment pattern in this way, beginning in the late 1950s.

Table 4-8. New York City Juvenile Delinquency and PINS Proceedings Leading to Placements or Commitments (July 1, 1973–June 30, 1974)

Placement	Boys		Girls	
	Delinquency	PINS	Delinquency	PINS
	13,191	4,309	1,545	3,962
Private institutions	265	284	15	247
Private agency	24	37	2	42
Public welfare department or offices	186	201	15	229
Division for youth	444	131	28	78
Own home or relative	26	20	2	18
Foster home (non relative)	18	14		10
Training school (placement or commitment)	202	55	18	41
Department of Corrections	10			
Other	4			1

Source: *Twentieth Annual Report,* State of New York, Administrative Board of the Judicial Conference, 1975, tables 64, 65, 69, 70.

In 1971, when it was decided to give the Youth Division responsibility for training schools, long the province of the social service department, the law continued the distinction between the two systems (Titles II and III). (There is also an age inconsistency: the DFY serves youth to age 18 but the New York State Family Court's delinquency jurisdiction extends only to 16.) More important, the law continued to distinguish the facilities as two systems. The one involves "volunteering" or referral and acceptance via intake and screening; the other is a commitment (even if called "placement") by court assignment to a training school—usually as a last resort and only if space in a voluntary institution is not available. But the courts also insist on the PINS versus delinquency distinction for placement facilities. Thus the "diversion" continuum is as follows: (1) referral to a voluntary community service; (2) a voluntary agency's community-based or institutional facility; (3) a Youth Division facility or residence (Title II before III); (4) a state training school or residence for PINS. The hierarchy of stigma and labeling reflects the continuum and is reinforced by the very active efforts of law guardians and private counsel to make it illegal to commit PINS to training schools, and to avoid training schools for delinquents at all costs.

Despite the DFY's obvious opportunity to take the large system of facilities which it now administers, to give each a unique character and specialization (its announced objectives), and to design one integrated system in which need and facility are matched, DFY perpetuates existing definitions and distinctions, and the training schools are universally described as undifferentiated, lacking resources, and ineffective. The more ambitious step of creating a differentiated system on an even more elaborate and sophisticated level by including the private residential resources for which the city largely pays has not even been entertained. The consequence is even greater pressure for diversion—to keep youth from the training schools—almost made ineffectual by policy and collusion.

Before the DFY appeared on the scene, the training schools had attempted to become diversified within their own system, at least. However, it was their failures or at least community and governmental dissatisfaction which led to the 1971 changes.

There are over 200 agencies in New York State serving children and youth: 130 of these serve dependent children; 128, neglected children; 61, persons in need of supervision (PINS); and 41, delinquents. The totals overlap. Many of the agencies serve more than one type of youngster, and the majority maintain some type of group care program.

There are no precise figures available regarding the number of group care facilities in the state. The system is developing quite rapidly. However, at this writing, the Division for Youth maintains the following residential facilities at fifty locations throughout the state: 934 spaces in Title II and 820 in Title III facilities in seven training schools and annexes, somewhat differentiated and none with high security (there are eight facilities in the system with over 100 youngsters); five residential centers, somewhat more flexible, two of which accept volunteers and probationers; five camps, away from metropolitan areas, for volunteers and probationers, each with room for 60 fifteen to seventeen years olds, two designed for drug users; four Start (Short-Term Adolescent Resident Training) programs, each for approximately 20 youths, who have occupational assignments at neighboring state or municipal facilities and participate in intensive counseling; three youth development centers in New York City to deal with adolescent drug users, each having both a residential and a mini-residential treatment program; two halfway houses, with a capacity of seven beds, for youth in transition from residential facilities; and eighteen group homes and residences, including an apartment complex in the Bronx, offering urban living, adult guidance, a variety of treatments, and small homelike settings, for 15–17 year olds (but planning for the 11–14 age group is under way). Capital costs are $9,500 per bed in a home and $40,000 in an institution; operating costs are $7,400 in the former and $15,000 in the latter (1973–74).

In December 1973 the Division for Youth was responsible for 5,541 youths who had been placed in Type III facilities (delinquents and PINS) of whom 778 were in residence and the balance were in after-care (which could be intensive or a superficial control, varying with location and other factors). Some 1,112 youths had been in and out of Title II facilities (volunteers or on probation) during the year, 622 on a given day. The anti-training school campaign was being felt. These totals reflected a considerable decline from the earlier population levels, particularly from training schools (Title III).

The New York City Department of Social Services, through its Bureau of Institutiions and Facilities/Special Services for Children, maintains three shelters, one reception center, a secure detention facility, two group homes for nonsecure detention, five long-term group homes, two group residences, and one school. These facilities cared for 3,853 children, or 13.6 percent of the 28,265 children in care in December 1973. The other children were cared for in facilities under over eighty voluntary agencies, most of them organized on a sectarian basis, from which the city purchased care on a daily basis. Of the total number of children in care in December 1973, 7,321 or 25.9 percent were in institutions and 1,860 or 6.6 percent were in group homes and residences. Table 4-9 presents the breakdown of these figures by age, race, and agency auspices—and does not include those placed through state training schools or other Youth

Table 4-9. New York City Children in Care (Dec. 31, 1973)

Children and agencies	In institutions (%)	In group homes and residences (%)	In boarding homes and agency-operated boarding homes (%)	Total
Children, by ethnic group				
White	27.7	7.1	65.2	100.0
Negro and other	22.2	5.6	72.2	100.0
Puerto Rican	31.9	8.3	59.8	100.0
Children, by age				
Under 2	4.1	.0	95.9	100.0
2–5	6.8	.1	93.1	100.0
6–11	26.2	3.9	69.9	100.0
12 and over	37.7	12.9	49.4	100.0
Agencies				
Catholic	29.8	7.2	63.0	100.0
Protestant	25.8	7.7	66.5	100.0
Jewish	49.2	12.2	38.6	100.0
Unaffiliated	9.7	2.8	87.5	100.0
Public	11.3	2.3	86.4	100.0

Source: Department of Social Services, New York City.

Division facilities. What is perhaps more interesting is the shift in distribution of children in foster care between 1974 and 1975 as revealed in Table 4-10. During this brief period, there was a marked increase in the percentage of children in group homes and agency-operated boarding homes and a sizable decrease in the number of children in public institutions. This suggests an effort on the part of the foster care system to develop alternatives to the traditional institutions.

A more recent New York City study, again not covering cases in training schools and "voluntary" State Youth Division facilities —the more seriously delinquent, the more difficult acting-out cases, or those whom the voluntary agencies do not accommodate for other reasons—presents a trend picture for the foster care channeled through the public social service department and estimated by probation officers and hospital psychiatric units.[47] While the picture is somewhat atypical in that New York City relies heavily on publicly subsidized voluntary agencies, it tells a good deal about those who need substitute care, the range of facilities required, and the frequent mismatch between child and available resource. It thus serves our overall purposes.

First, the report documents the growth in foster care in New York over the previous twenty-five years and the very heavy placement rates for Hispanic and black children, as compared with non-Hispanic whites. Then, there is evidence of a marked increase of children over 12 as a factor in the under-care population, from 30 percent of the total in 1960 to 42 percent in 1974. (The number of children under 3 went from 12.8 to 9.9 percent and children 3–6 from 18 to 12.9 percent.) Third, in Table 4-11 we see the location in December 1974 of the 29,726 children placed or awaiting placement. The report notes that, of these children, 78.2 percent were included for parent-related problems (30.6 percent because of "parental unwillingness to care for child, including desertion" and 31.0 percent because of "emotional or behavioral problems of child-caring person") and only 14.5 percent for child-related problems (the other reasons being unknown). The largest component of the latter group of problems (10.1 percent) involved "emotional or behavioral problems of child." Only 0.5 percent in the group were adjudicated delinquent and 1.4 percent adjudicated PINS. In short, the system basically serves the traditional "child welfare" mission (placement for parent-related reasons, mostly) and not the juvenile justice mission (placement for child-related reasons). Indeed the

Table 4-10. Children in Foster Care in New York State (March 31, 1974, and March 31, 1975)

Children	Voluntary agencies			Public agencies		
	1974	1975	% change	1974	1975	% change
Total in care	29,582	30,180	+ 2	19,628	18,808	− 4
In institutions	8,965	8,920	− .5	20	13	−35
In group homes	1,575	1,970	+25	61	72	+18
In agency-operated group homes	468	514	+10	37	43	+16
In family boarding homes	14,624	14,275	− 2	17,918	17,172	− 4
In adoptive homes	1,020	1,113	+ 9	904	797	−12
In subsidized adoptive homes	296	432	+46	129	120	− 7
In free homes	19	8	−58	48	51	+ 6
In wage, work, or self-supporting homes	9	16	+78	15	4	−73
Elsewhere	2,606	2,932	+12	496	536	+ 8

Source: Statistics published by New York State Department of Social Services in *Social Statistics*, XXXVI (April 1974) and XXXVII (April 1975).

latter group was separated out, even though the study was commissioned by the State Social Welfare Board. We will return to the matter in the final section, as we have noted it throughout, since it introduces one of the major issues in planning for institutions and alternatives.

Table 4-11. Percentage Distribution of New York City Children in Foster Care or Awaiting Placement, by Type of Placement and Ethnic Group (Dec. 1974)

Placement	Total	White (non-Hispanic)	Black and other	Hispanic
Temporary foster homes	3.6	4.7	3.4	3.2
Temporary group care*	1.3	1.2	1.3	1.3
Foster homes†	45.3	42.1	49.1	39.7
Group living‡	7.0	8.3	6.2	7.7
General institutions	13.3	8.7	11.4	21.2
Residential treatment centers, type A	3.0	8.7	1.9	0.6
Residential treatment centers, type B	0.9	2.4	0.4	0.6
Institutions for the retarded	0.9	3.9	0.1	
Foster homes, prospective adoptive	15.4	11.8	17.0	15.1
At home on suspended payment	4.8	3.5	4.5	6.4
Awaiting placement	3.0	4.3	2.6	2.9
Other	1.5	0.4	2.1	1.3
Total percent	100.0	100.0	100.0	100.0
Total number	29,726	6,045	16,279	7,402

Source: Blanche Bernstein, Donald A. Snider, and William Meezan, *A Preliminary Report: Foster Care Needs and Alternatives to Placement* (New York: Center for New York City Affairs for the State Board of Social Welfare, 1975).

*Includes temporary group homes, temporary group residences, diagnostic centers, and temporary institutions.

†Includes agency-operated boarding homes.

‡Includes group homes and group residences.

The Bernstein-Snider-Meezan survey also serves to dramatize the problem of poor child-facility match, whether because of system-process reasons or lack of resources. Thus, expert case readers, employing carefully developed criteria, rated cases as appropriately placed or not, as of the initial placement and currently. The percentages of those inappropriately placed were respectively 55.3 and 42.8. (The miscategorized groups were, especially, 9–18 years of age, Protestant, black, and Hispanic.) Table 4-12 identifies the specific need as compared to the placements. The report offers detail on deficits and surpluses, going beyond what is relevant to our current purposes. Special note is taken of the deficit in residential

Table 4-12. Percentage Distribution of New York City Children in Placement by Whether the Type of Placement Is Appropriate by Age, Religion, and Ethnic Group (Dec. 1974)

Characteristic of child	Appropriate	Inappropriate	Unclear	Total no.
Age	55.7	42.8	1.5	29,726
Total under 3	72.0	28.0		2,213
3–6	62.4	37.6		3,927
6–9	61.9	37.6	0.5	4,617
9–12	54.1	43.8	2.1	5,593
12–15	48.1	50.4	1.5	6,379
15–18	46.2	50.8	3.0	5,617
Over 18	69.0	27.6	3.4	1,380
Religion				
Total	55.7	42.8	1.5	29,726
Catholic	58.5	40.7	0.8	14,209
Jewish	77.0	19.7	3.3	1,451
Protestant	51.1	47.3	1.6	13,233
Other	42.8	48.6	8.6	833
Ethnic group				
Total	55.7	42.8	1.5	29,726
White (non-Hispanic)	69.3	29.5	1.2	6,045
Black and other	51.9	46.1	2.0	16,279
Hispanic	52.7	46.6	0.7	6,045

Source: Blanche Bernstein, Donald A. Snider, and William Meezan, *A Preliminary Report: Foster Care Needs and Alternatives to Placement* (New York: Center for New York City Affairs for the State Board of Social Welfare, 1975), p. 14.

treatment centers, a gap which becomes even larger when age projections over a decade are added to the picture.

Two other types of problems were repeated in an upstate city and New York City at the time of our review. One was the feeling on the part of those responsible for neglected children, PINS, and delinquent children that the child welfare and juvenile justice systems were expected to care for severely disturbed and retarded youngsters whose needs did not meet the eligibility and service categories of programs under the State Department of Mental Hygiene. Two recent studies have documented this.[48] Each system has boundaries but there is an intervening chasm. Conflicts are constant and horrible case stories of consequence are heard constantly. The second problem was that the funding and reimbursement systems do not assure coordination and planning. In an upstate New York city, in the summer of 1974, it was realized that urban residential facilities for children and youth were overexpanded: Catholic Charities, the State Youth Division, the YMCA, the Salvation Army, the Department of

Mental Hygiene, and others had responded to the new thinking independently and somewhat competitively.

Examples of Programs

The following public and voluntary programs located in an upstate New York city, in New York City, and in the New York City metropolitan area illustrate some of the major program models and their variations.

A Traditional Child Care Institution

St. Michael's is a large children's institution under Catholic auspices located in a center-city area. The facility is a large, seven-story building similar in appearance to the urban public schools built during the early part of the century.

The institution, which has a capacity of 120, provides care for boys aged 8–17, although those who go on to college are permitted to stay until they complete their education. The current population is primarily adolescent, about 50 percent black, 50 percent white and Puerto Rican. Most of the youngsters in care are dependent or neglected, but PINS referrals are accepted on occasion.

Historically, St. Michael's was the last residence for youth who grew up in Catholic child welfare institutions in this locality. Preschoolers who came into care were placed in one institution, transferred to another one for their grammar school years, and eventually graduated to St. Michael's for their high school years. In recent years this pattern has begun to change as the population in care has shifted and greater emphasis has been placed on the need to offer a range of services and living arrangements in order to provide for sibling groups and to give more individualized care for children. Consequently, St. Michael's now no longer automatically receives the graduates of other Catholic institutions; it has a large proportion of youngsters referred for temporary care, and has developed its own foster home and group home programs.

The primary orientation of the facility, however, continues to be that of providing care for boys who have no home in order to teach them self-sufficiency and to prepare them for entry into adult life. Each of the youths is assigned to a social worker and there is a mental health unit on the premises which is licensed by the state department of mental hygiene. Yet the administration continues to view education as the primary means of self-development and upward mobility. As a result, little attention is given to work with natural families or to use of the group as a therapeutic or socialization device. Each boy is encouraged to achieve at a maximum level in school—the social work staff tend to concentrate on school adjustment problems in their counseling sessions and "good marks" are required for promotion to more desirable dormitory rooms.

The agency is organized on a functional basis. There are two assistant administrators for the institution—one is the business manager and the other oversees the child care, mental health, and social service units. Each of these units has a director who has line authority over the staff in his department. There has been no effort to organize on a team basis. With the exception of the nurses and a couple of social workers, the staff is entirely male. The social work staff tend to be white and middle-class, and approximately half have graduate degrees. The child care staff has a larger proportion of minority group members and has a mixed age range.

The boys are assigned to one of seven living units, each of which occupies a separate hall and has six semiprivate rooms and one dormitory for new residents. Most of the living units have a living room with a television and space for study and quiet recreation as well as a bedroom for the night child care workers. There is a central dining room as well as a gym and a large outdoor playing field.

With the exception of a small school on the grounds for about fifteen youngsters with special needs, the boys attend public schools throughout the city. Because the city's public schools now operate on split sessions, the residents attend school at different hours and function quite independently during the day. Their different schedules make it almost impossible for the facility to run organized programs during the school week. On weekends the boys often go on field trips or to the camp where they spend summer vacations. Consequently the impression, especially during the week, is that the residents are often hanging around with little to do.

In many ways the institution appears to be an historical anachronism. The youths are provided food, shelter, education, and some recreational opportunities as they move toward adulthood, but few of the recent trends such as coeducation, group socialization experiences, and counseling oriented toward family and community reintegration have hit this facility. Instead the facility is reminiscent of the Catholic boarding schools of another era in which education, sports, and clean living were considered sufficient and little attention was given to the social or affective needs of the students. Yet many youngsters continue to grow up in institutions such as St. Michael's —and "fads" such as deinstitutionalization and communitization have little influence on the type of care they receive.

A Training School

New York operates a number of large, expensive training schools. The official specifications for one of them is as follows:

Youth Served: JD boys. 7–16 inclusive.

Area Served: [The southeastern region of the state, including eleven counties and the state's largest city.]

Rated Capacity: 160–180.

Plant Facilities:

Residential Units: single-story brick. Sleeping accommodations for up to 22–23 boys; 11 individual rooms; 11–12 in a dormitory situation. Centralized cooking. Dining in the unit.

Educational: Separate school building, vocational building, auditorium-gym complex and physical education building which includes a gym, health room, canteen–multi-purpose room, and Olympic-sized swimming pool.

Services Provided:

Psychiatric: full-time psychiatric services (actually five part-time psychiatrists for one day each). Every resident given an initial diagnostic evaluation. Selected residents given regular psychiatric treatment on an individual basis. Each psychiatrist also conducts a weekly group session for up to six selected residents.

Psychological: full-time psychologist. Initial psychological evaluations and referrals from other staff. Both diagnostic and treatment services. Also conducts group counseling sessions.

Social Work–Counseling: One program services director and eight cottage coordinators. There are eight residential units at Lansing. Each has a cottage coordinator who serves as unit administrator and program director. All social workers serve as unit coordinators. Group sessions based on the guided group interaction approach are conducted in each unit at least four times weekly. Group work is the primary treatment method supported by individual counseling. Program continues to be built by addition of more leadership staff.

Child Care Staff: Houseparents (male and female couple) are assigned to each unit. On duty from 3 P.M. to 11 P.M. Male child care staff on two other shifts for 24-hour supervision and care.

Education Program: Full day school including vocational courses. Emphasis on remediation in the basic skills such as reading and arithmetic. Full library and physical education program are provided. Vocational instruction of an exploratory nature.

Academic courses offered: Reading, language arts, mathematics, social studies, science and spelling.

Vocational courses offered: barbering, electricity, carpentry, printing and general shop.

Also work training in: Kitchen, hospital, staff buildings, maintenance, tailor shop, storeroom, bakery, staff dining room, paint shop, garage, plumbing, infirmary, electrical, masonry-plastering, carpentry.

Now, a volunteer report, also from early in the winter of 1975. We do not know which report has greater validity, but the "non-expert" observations by concerned citizens do add to the picture.

A Visitor's Observations:

Seven hundred beautiful acres on a scenic hilltop, all covered with snow on the day of our visit, is the setting of Lansing School for Boys. A really terrific snowman stands outside one of the buildings, but he is the closest approximation of a person visible out of doors on a perfect winter day.

In the administration building, we are greeted warmly by the director (Superintendent) of Lansing, and a coordinator for the Division for Youth, which operates Lansing as one of its five training schools in the state. The former is a quiet, gentle, warm man with a sense of humor to temper his inevitable cynicism. He has been at Lansing only 2½ months. Later we are joined by the Principal of the school at Lansing, and a Supervisor for both Lansing and a nearby school.

The capacity of Lansing is given as 180; the present population is 157 boys, aged 14 to 16, all of whom are juvenile delinquents sent here by the Family Court. Of the 157, 112 are black, 32 are white, and 13 are Puerto Rican. Younger boys are siphoned off to other places (Title II facilities can admit both JDs and PINS). The average length of stay is ten months. About 80 percent of the boys come from New York City, some from Nassau/Suffolk and some from counties surrounding Lansing. A few have been transferred here from the Industry Training School. One major problem at Lansing (there are many) is the large number of runaways—there were 96 in December 1974. In the two week period prior to our visit, one group of four boys had run away five times. Nearly all the runaways are found by the staff or local police, but on the day we were there, 74 boys were unaccounted for—runaways or nonreturns from home visits—some of these dating back to 1972. (Discharge is permitted without knowing what happened.)

The first thirty days of a boy's stay are devoted largely to a diagnostic process. Medical, dental, and academic examinations are given, the boy's basic needs identified, and short and long term goals established for the Lansing period and after-care. Eighty-seven percent of the present population read below sixth grade level. Treatment needs are not determined on the basis of the crimes committed, but there are practical exceptions to this thesis. Boys found responsible for especially serious crimes are labeled "sensitive cases" by the DFY, and thus arbitrarily have certain restrictions placed on them, such as no permission for home visits for at least six months. While there are no mandatory sentences for JDs, there must be some adjustment to the community response to the crime, so in practice serious offenders are apt to remain at Lansing longer than others regardless of how well they are doing. The administration is quite open with the boys on this point. The boys do not know how long they will be staying at Lansing—a source of considerable frustration for them and of ambivalence on the part of the staff.

The boys are housed in cottage units of about 20, with round-the-clock staff in three shifts, consisting of 1 coordinator, 1 assistant coordinator, 2 teachers, and 7 child-care workers. There is a critical lack of clerical support, thus wasting much valuable time of the professional staff in taking kids to and from courts and hospitals, typing up reports, etc. Each team meets once a week. Staff turnover is low, due to the decent salary scale, relatively isolated location and economic situation in the area, civil service benefits and tenure. There are crucial staff problems related to the occupational hazards—many work 16-hour shifts repeatedly, and become "burned out," emotionally and physically exhausted, cynical, tunnel-visioned. The strain is particularly evident with the child-care workers who are responsible for the constant supervision of these very difficult boys and have the lowest pay and the least academic preparation.

In addition to the Administration, the staff is composed of 16 teachers, 18 social workers (8 of whom are coordinators), 1 psychologist (there is a vacancy for an additional psychologist), 3 RNs, 2 MDs, 3 psychiatrists, and 80 child-care workers. There are 18 maintenance workers, but they cannot keep up with the need for immediate repairs such as broken windows and damaged walls caused by behavior eruptions. The physical plant has deteriorated grossly in the last 1½ years according to the Superintendent, who views this as one of his most serious problems; but we saw only minimal evidence of this, and certainly found other inadequacies more compelling.

The three psychiatrists on the staff are part time. Group therapy is used in the cottages except for those who cannot function in the group and must be isolated for therapy with a social worker. The Superintendent sees a need for more psychiatric time to be used with the staff in order to develop more consistent programs, better facilities for coping with the boys' problems. However, it is very difficult to get the entire staff together because of the three shifts. The director feels that individual psychiatric treatment on a once-a-week basis for the boys is a waste of time and money. Individual crises are now dealt with on a relationship basis, but there should be systemic means of coping. Kids have been allowed to act out far too much and too long before someone intervened. One approach to developing such systems, which he hopes to implement, is to involve each staff team in the intake and diagnostic procedures, the coordination with the medical and education departments, the liaison with outside agencies(courts and others), and the on-going therapeutic programs.

Every boy attends the on-campus school. Each cottage group is escorted to and from the school building by the child-care workers who remain in the classrooms during the academic session of one hour and twenty minutes. Classes are small, 7–10 boys in each. Most of the emphasis is on remediation in reading and mathematics. In addition, science, English, and social studies are taught. The average reading improvement here is a 3-month jump in testing score for each month in the program. The teachers are all certified. Classrooms are self-contained; there is no departmentalization. There is no fine arts program at this time, nor are there any cultural supplements, although the principal would like to have them. There is a nice library with a circulation rate of 4–5 books per month per boy. Because so much attention is given to the needs of the majority of students, the ones who are badly shortchanged are those who are up to grade level (less than 15 percent) or close to completing high school. The facilities for them are woefully inadequate, sometimes makeshift, when a teacher will voluntarily coach a boy in French by staying a few pages ahead of him in a borrowed text. There is at least a two-grade spread in any classroom, but with the constantly changing population, this tends to widen.

In addition to the academic program, each boy is also enrolled in one of five vocational workshops (wood, electric, mechanical drawing, printing, etc.) for a period equivalent to the academic one, one hour and twenty minutes a day. The workshops are in a separate building and are very well equipped, but when we visited them we saw only two boys in one workshop, although the vocational director and several of his staff were present. We were given some lame-sounding excuses for why there were no students there.

The third assigned part of each boy's day is one hour and twenty minutes of physical education. The most outstanding building on the campus is the new, magnificent gymnasium, which also houses an Olympic-size swimming pool and a large, beautifully furnished room where boys may meet with their visitors, and a canteen (now closed because it was broken into so often). There were about a dozen boys practicing basketball in the gym while we were there, with several others sitting on the sidelines reading or doing nothing. There is only one recreation person on the staff; he is there 40 hours a week and volunteers some extra time to coach the basketball team for games with other schools. By law, the pool must be manned by a qualified life-guard, and so it is almost never used. Four or five full-time staff members for recreation could be used. Basketball is virtually the only sport, although there is ample space on the 700 acres for nearly every sport imaginable. One of the boys told me there wasn't a single football at Lansing! Except for the members of the basketball team, it seemed that there was no sports or physical education for the boys. And in all those rolling fields of snow, I saw no snowballs being thrown, no boys playing outdoors.

The Superintendent determines who may go home for a visit and for how long, except for the sensitive cases noted above. First visits cannot exceed seven days. A bus from the school runs to and from New York for week-end visits and for the longer stays permitted some boys at Christmas and other school vacation periods. The Superintendent believes the whole question of home visits needs reexamination as to timing (often done too early when not in the child's best interest) and what the boys are going home to. Some visits are very damaging to boys, as evidenced by extreme acting out before or after visits. After-care field service (part of DFY) checks on the boys during their home visits. When boys are finally released from Lansing, some go to their homes, others to foster homes or special programs in the city. The wholly inadequate resources for following up on boys who leave currently set the recidivism rate at less than 50 percent but the training school does not take much credit for this low figure, attributing it instead to legal protections for children built into the state law, age limitations on JDs, etc. Nearly all the boys here have had 3–5 incidents of trouble before being sent to a training school; many have been in other types of institutions earlier. There was some interesting musing on the part of the Superintendent about what the criteria are for a rehabilitated boy, a useful life, and a satisfactory adaptation to society. He does exert strong pressure on the boys to continue in school even after they are 16, because jobs just don't exist, and the only alternative is trouble, which they realize.

Some boys are involved in a work program at Lansing, doing small jobs on the campus or assisting the staff on certain projects. There is not nearly enough productive work for them to do. The director would like to institute a system of paying the boys reasonably well for chores and then charging them for clothing and other items, in order to develop a sense of responsibility about handling money. Also, more privileges for the boys are needed, ironically because removal of privileges is a chief form of punishment. DFY provides copies of a handbook on children's rights detailing what rights children have that cannot be taken away from them as a punitive device or at the whim of a social worker, and what responsibilities they have to the institution. An Ombudsman is at Lansing several days each week, paid by DFY, to investigate legal or on-campus injustices boys feel they have suffered. A chaplain is available, too. The group influence on behavior can be used effectively in positive ways, but not in disciplinary situations (e.g., stealing) because the group cannot be trusted to act reasonably under stress conditions. The social areas—how to deal with a peer group, how to handle rejection, frustrations, failure, internal and external pressures—are viewed as critically important by the staff and used as the major factors in determining when a boy is ready to return to his home.

Lansing relations with the surrounding community are poor, because of the constant problem of runaways, stolen cars, etc. There are some volunteers from the area—JCs [from the Junior Chamber of Commerce], a reading specialist, a church group. The director does not appear to have any ideas on improving this situation in the foreseeable future, but he will deal with individual incidents as they occur.

We divided up for lunch in the cottages, where we were encouraged to converse freely with the boys and the staff. Lunch was a substantial dish of pasta and tomato sauce, salad, bread, pudding and milk. The cottage I visited had a very large room which served for dining space, recreation (pool tables, television, games, etc.), and sitting around area. It was clean, fairly cheerful in decor, but only sparsely equipped with enough to keep twenty energetic boys occupied for long periods of time. The boys I spoke with expressed muted dissatisfaction with Lansing (not enough sports, too little to do) but seemed to relate well to the cottage staff. They also seemed to suffer some misinformation, such as the "fact" that Lansing receives $10,000 for each boy and they're entitled to use every cent of it in clothing, bandages, etc. One member of our group ate lunch with a spoon in a cottage which had had all its knives and forks confiscated the previous evening after an outbreak of fighting with those implements.

Lansing's annual budget is $2½ million, provided by New York State, plus an additional $100,000 in Federal Education funds. The new Superintendent's immediate goal is to do the best he can with what he has available. He seems to feel that his staff is capable and dedicated beyond the necessary requirements, but he is aware of the many lacks in the program. He stressed the importance of after-care to give the boys continuing support in the academic and social skills to enable them to cope with their lives in the non-controlled atmosphere of the post-Lansing community. What happens with the right to refuse treatment when strongly indicated? The Superintendent went on to describe how training schools must seek to find a middle ground between the polarized feelings of society about JDs (kids do no wrong vs. lock the bastards up and throw away the key). I believe that this strong and sensitive man will only improve conditions at Lansing.

A Voluntary "Residential Treatment" Institution

The Centerton Residential School (CRS) is a residential treatment center sponsored by the Voluntary Child Care Association of New York, and is located on a 156-acre campus. There are approximately twenty cottages on the grounds, each housing eight to twelve boys and girls between the ages of 7 and 14. The general population is composed of "emotionally disturbed children of normal or potentially normal intelligence who need care in a total therapeutic environment. Children must be able to live in an open setting." The total population numbers approximately 140 boys and 40 girls, although the total number of children served during 1973–74 was 262. The additional 80 children were treated in the Diagnostic Center, which is separate from the regular cottage community.

In addition to the living cottages, there is a large, modern school, administered by the local school district. The school is open all year and staffed by specially trained teachers and recreation counselors. An outdoor swimming pool, tennis, and basketball courts, as well as an indoor gymnasium, are part of the school's recreation program, as are two other programs: a day treatment program and a cottage day program for younger children. Class size during the school year is limited to ten children. Special tutoring programs and evening study hours in the cottages are part of the curriculum. High-school-aged children who are able to cope with academic courses attend the local high school. Others whose interests and abilities indicate vocational training receive off-campus instruction from the county board of educational services. During July and August, the school operated a day camp and remedial education program. Opportunities for the CRS children for play and special interests are provided in sports, club, and hobby groups, arts and crafts, social activities, and outings, which are sponsored by both the school and the CRS staff.

The day treatment program for approximately eighteen children aged 7–14 from the Centerton area operates within the school program. This program provides "education, recreation, and treatment for children who might otherwise be hospitalized." The day care program accommodates thirty preschool children and emphasizes "education for children of different economic, racial and social backgrounds, as well as for those with special needs."

CRS was founded some fifty years ago with an educational focus, but has shifted to a more therapeutically oriented program, while still maintaining its educational emphasis. The impact of psychological knowledge is seen in the lowered classroom sizes, the structured setting that is provided in the group living context, and in the type of child who is accepted for placement. There has evolved what the leadership defines as an integration of both educational and psychological approaches to childhood disturbances, and a total treatment approach in which neither is dominant, and each complements the other.

Cottages are, for the most part, similarly built and appointed, containing a large living room, small kitchen, and coat room on the first floor, and from four to six bedrooms on the second floor. Depending on the child's age, bedrooms are either triple, double, or single rooms, the older children occupying either single or double rooms.

No meals are served in the cottages. A large dining hall, in close proximity to the cottages, is used exclusively for meals, which are brought to tables by cart. Residents eat together at assigned tables, each resident being responsible for the serving and clearing away of dishes. Although staff members are present, their roles are minimal and not directly related to dining room protocol, except to assure that food is dispensed on time and adequately. Residents are encouraged to make their preferences known concerning favorite menus and foods.

The cottages are arranged around a circular drive, and give the impression of being well spaced, with each seen as a separate unit in relation to other cottages. Children are allowed to ride bicycles on the grounds and proficiency in this activity, as well as other activities, is encouraged through competitions, which are held periodically throughout the year, depending on the season.

A modern, well-appointed building houses the school, which is built close to the dining hall, and in keeping with the rustic setting. There are carpeted halls, cheerful colors, and well-equipped classrooms with modern furnishings. There is a TV studio, where taped shows are made by the students, as well as arts and crafts rooms, a woodshop, and student-teacher lounges, which are accessible at times other than class time; each lounge has a kitchen for snacks. A library with several librarians is available to students both during and after school hours.

The Diagnostic Center was opened in August 1973 as a "much needed service to children referred by New York City's Family Court and the Bureau of Child Welfare." The Center provides short-term placement and intensive diagnostic evaluation for boys, usually ranging in age from 10 to 14 years, although younger and older boys have been accommodated. Following a determination of the psychiatric, social, and educational strengths and weaknesses of the child, the Center submits a comprehensive report and recommendations for future disposition to the referring agency. When long-term placement is indicated, "strenuous efforts are made to secure placement in appropriate facilities," which may include CRS. During 1973–74, 88 children were in residence at the Center. The majority of these children were found to require long-term placement. Of these eighty-eight children, eighty-eight percent were successfully placed.

Stays at the Center are for thirty-day periods, during which time the boys are tested and observed by a staff of teachers, social workers, psychiatrists, psychologists, and recreation specialists. The perspective gained in observing children in a residential setting is said to make for better understanding and interpretation of their needs and to facilitate their eventual placement.

Referrals to the Center are made directly. An increasing demand for the service has come from Family Court probation officers, who need a more precise picture of a child who may require placement. Other departments of the VCCA also refer as needed.

The Center is located in a large building somewhat distant from the other residential cottages, on the CRS grounds. Meals and sleeping are in the Center building, which contains recreation rooms, a library, arts and crafts areas, and offices. For the most part, Center children are not allowed onto the CRS grounds at will, and are contained within a periphery of the Center which contains a ball field, basketball court, and general grounds.

All children at CRS, regardless of the particular part of the program to which they may belong, are treated for minor ailments at the main infirmary building. There are nurses on duty at all times, and doctors are on call at hours other than their on-duty times. Children may be treated at the infirmary as in-patients, usually for flu and the like, while more serious illnesses are treated at local hospitals. All children are required to have physical examinations before acceptance into any CRS program, regardless of the program's focus. General supervision of medical staff is through the VCCA medical department in New York City.

All employees of CRS are accountable to the VCCA of New York. The team employed for treatment includes a social worker, who is the primary therapist, a psychologist, and a psychiatrist. The social worker is the prime coordinating person between these specialized services and the cottage house parents, who are responsible for the day-to-day activities of daily living with the children. House parents are usually couples who live in the cottage and are on duty for 24-hour periods of time, with appropriate time off. Weekly team meetings are held with all staff for purposes of discussion and coordination and to note progress and problems with the children. The CRS director is accountable for all staff.

Approximately 85 percent of monies received at CRS are from public funds, and the remaining 15 percent are received from endowments, scholarships, donations, VCCA funds, the Federation of Philanthropies, and the Greater New York Fund. Reimbursement from public social service funds to CRS for fiscal 1973 amounted to $36.90 per day per child, with an added $4.61 per day per child for Medicaid coverage. The daily cost per child to VCCA was $47.15, for which a deficit accrues of $5.64.

All intake, except for the Diagnostic Center, is through a cooperative service operated by several sectarian agencies in one welfare federation. This intake service is a single headquarters "where families may apply for the placement of children and adolescents in foster care or residential treatment facilities." The stated objectives are "to assure the widest range of planning for children and adolescents of the faith requiring placement, and to serve youngsters of other faiths as vacancies permit; to make optimal use of the facilities of the cooperating agencies, and expedite appropriate transfers within those facilities; and to determine unmet childcare and youth needs in the community."

Referrals to CRS are made by parents, the courts, and other social agencies, either by telephone, by letter, or in person. Children from the sponsoring sectarian group are offered top priority; public social service and other social agency referrals follow in that order. Cases are screened initially by a senior and/or a supervising staff member, who is a trained social worker. An evaluation is made of the factual material submitted, and a determination is made as to the appropriateness for treatment facilities of the cooperating agencies. The case is then assigned to a staff social worker, who sets up a series of appointments for the child and his parents to be seen at the CRS offices for purposes of compiling a psychosocial history, which includes a psychiatric, psychological, and medical examination. The social worker determines the child's need for placement based on the information obtained through these interviews. The psychosocial data include a present and past history of the functioning of the child, his parents, siblings, and other important family members. Home visits are rarely made by intake workers.

Psychological tests given usually include projective tests, an I.Q. measurement, if unobtainable from the child's school, and a psychiatric evaluation, if not completed earlier. Psychiatric examinations require the presence of both child and one or both parents. The examining psychologist and psychiatrist each receives a copy of the psychosocial history before seeing the child.

If the social worker, psychologist, and psychiatrist agree on the need for placement, the intake social worker forwards to an appropriate treatment center copies of the diagnostic material, which in turn is reviewed by a social worker and/or assistant director of the facility. In all instances, the child and his parents are interviewed by treatment facility staff, who recommend acceptance or rejection for placement.

Generally, for placement at CRS a child must meet minimal criteria: his I.Q. must be 80 or above; projective tests and psychiatric examinations must indicate nonpsychotic behavior which is amenable to treatment in CRS's open setting. The child's parents must be motivated to participate actively in the child's treatment, either by regular visits to CRS, home visits, interviews with the treating social worker at CRS, or a combination of all of these. Although parental psychopathology may interfere with treatment, this in itself does not exclude a child's consideration for placement. However, in practice, either the child's specific pathology or his parent's are strong determinants for acceptance or rejection. Reactive maladjustments of the child to either school or home environment are considered inappropriate. School behavior which is seen to be noncorrectable through remediation or adjustment reactions which are socially and emotionally based and cause learning blocks are evaluated as marginal and could be a basis for rejection.

Financial arrangements to cover the costs of placement are based on the $47.15 cost per day. A cost of $17,213.00 per child per year, exclusive of educational costs, is quoted, toward which parents are expected to contribute according to their means. The Bureau of Child Welfare receives from CRS a notification of acceptance or rejection of placement, and determines payment in the light of the parents' financial status.

Children unable to return home after a period of residence may be placed in other facilities of VCCA. The post-placement service at VCCA sees the child after his leaving to help support the transition.

We could not locate data on treatment results of children placed at CRS. Neither were data available from the post-placement service as to how many CRS children were placed further after leaving the school.

Implicit in the criteria for placement at CRS is the child's functioning, as well as the motivation of his parents. Work with parents is a stated purpose of the school, yet it is not apparent that any extensive home visiting program is carried out, either at the intake level or at CRS.

It is not clear whether the Department of Social Services on city or state levels has procedures for assessing program effectiveness. Much of their role seems to be focused on the payment aspects of placement and not on accountability for quality and effectiveness of treatment.

Data regarding the type of contacts CRS has with parents in the community is unclear, except as it relates to the child's treatment at the school. One stated function of the intake service is to assess unmet community needs, and whether CRS communicates with intake on this aspect of needs is unclear. Visiting at CRS is connected to the child's treatment and adjustment to the school. The intake service rarely, if at all, makes home visits when assessing the need for placement. It is unclear whether the intake unit would or should be the primary agency to assess these community needs.

The intake process appears to assume that an application for placement involves implicit validation of need for placement, and that alternatives to placement have been tried and have failed. Symptomatic and reactive maladaptive behavior at school or at home appears to be a valid reason for placement consideration, despite formal policy. It does not seem to be a function of the intake policy as such to explore alternatives to placement, or to prevent placement, if possible, despite special projects with such objectives.

A State "Residential Treatment" Center

The term "residential treatment" covers many things. The facility described briefly below (and perhaps unfairly) is coed and by now reserved for PINS aged 13–16, most on transfer because they did not do well in other facilities. Its capacity is sixty. Facilities and programs are officially described as follows:

Plant Facilities:

Modern, single story brick multi-winged building housing administrative offices, academic school and individual rooms for residents. Four wings, 15 residents to each wing. Also includes gymnasium, recreation wing, central and dining room.

Services Provided:

Psychiatric Services: Two part-time psychiatrists for one full day per week. Diagnostic on every new admission, and consultation with staff.

Psychological: One part-time psychologist. One full day per week. Psychological testing of every new admission and testing prior to release. Some specialized individual counseling upon referral from staff.

Social Work–Counseling: Each wing supervised by a social worker. They emphasize individual and group counseling. Behavior Modification and individual treatment used as part of rehabilitation.

Education: Full day academic program (8:30 A.M. to 3:30 P.M.) for all residents. Fully accredited by the State Education Department. Principal plus five (5) licensed teachers. Class size maximum of 10 but average 6 to 8. Math, science, social studies, English, typing, home economics, health education, physical education. Vocational training in cosmetology, child care, nursing arts and supermarket cashier. Residents who complete training in child care and nursing arts receive the opportunity to work off campus in a nursing home and day care center in the nearby town.

Health Services: Three full-time nurses and a part-time doctor and dentist—one morning per week plus on call. Complete physical for every new resident upon admission. Infirmary with two beds in building. Local hospital used in emergencies. Unusual problems are referred to the Albany Medical Center.

Recreation: Full-time recreation worker and part-time staff. Full program of recreational activities for all youngsters.

Visitations: Two Sundays scheduled per month. Other weekend visits upon special requests. Monday-Friday, 10:00 a.m. to 4:00 p.m. Visiting also allowed.

Home Visits: None regularly scheduled; all visits based upon treatment needs of each individual resident.

Now, the view of several lay visitors (1975) who are sophisticated and informed:

Visitors' Observations:

After driving for more than two hours from New York City, we arrived at the Center, located out in the midst of open fields in farm country. The modern U-shaped building surrounds an interior court which is enclosed on the fourth side by a high wall. We entered through a locked gate, walked across the courtyard and into the main office area. We then never emerged from the building again during our entire stay.

Everything is in that one locked building: dormitories, school, health facilities, kitchen, dining room, gym, and even a chapel. We were greeted by the new assistant director. She immediately turned us over to two girls and a boy who were assigned to guide the five of us around, so we broke up into small groups with one or two to each guide. We had complete freedom to talk with our guides and with any staff members we met along the way.

The Center draws from all over New York State, and is designed to house 56 boys and girls divided into four wings of fourteen each. At present there are three girls' wings (two PINS and one JD) and one boys' wing (PINS). The girls were aged 13–16, while the boys' wing had a wider age span (11–16) which seemed to be causing some problems. All the boys and girls have been transferred here from some other training school. They are assigned here for a maximum of eighteen months, with a year's extension possible, but most stay for about a year.

This Center has gone through a number of changes in the last year or two, making it very difficult to maintain any coherent program. Since the ruling that PINS and JD's must be separated, the Center has successively housed only PINS girls, only JD girls, and PINS boys. When the boys were added a year ago, they were promised male staff, shop supplies, etc. to adapt their program for the boys. One year later, they have just gotten a male social worker to head up the boys' wing and there is still no sign of any shop supplies.

When we asked the fifteen-year-old girl who was showing us around how she felt about life at Centerton, she replied vehemently: "Anyone would hate being locked up like an animal." And she proudly told of the many times she had gone AWOL. Indeed, by the end of the day, even we, as visitors, were feeling intensely claustrophobic.

A number of aspects of the Center struck us as intolerable. Not only was there very little psychiatric help, job training, or constructive recreation, but the confinement and boredom of life seemed to us positively dehumanizing. The rooms were small, single cubicles on either side of a long hallway in each wing. The windows in the rooms could not be opened, and the only lighting fixture was a ceiling light controlled by a switch outside the door.

Visitors are allowed two Sundays a month and Monday–Friday from 10 A.M. to 4 P.M. They must provide their own transportation. Home visits are not even considered until a youngster has been at Centerton for at least five months.

The boredom of life must be overwhelming. From the time they are all awakened at 6 A.M. until they go to to bed at night, there are hours and hours with nothing to do but watch TV and play cards. Between 6 and 8 A.M. they must shower one at a time and pick up their rooms. They are not allowed out of the wing until 8 o'clock, when the childcare worker takes them all to breakfast in a group. Seats are assigned for all meals, usually *not* with friends, said our guide. The morning is taken up with school, which seemed terribly dull and unimaginative. There seems to be little attempt to gear the school program to the individual needs and interests of the students, even though we saw no more than four students in any one class. The girl who was showing us around said she was a good student, but didn't go to school here because it was so boring. The principal seemed to have very little knowledge of any programs or treatment going on elsewhere in the building.

The afternoon homemaking program for the girls also appeared very uninspiring to say the least. There was no job training of any sort, no shop, art, dance, drama, or music. They did have a gym, used mainly for basketball and some gymnastics. When our visiting group complained that the kids were being kept inside on such a beautiful day, four girls were finally allowed out in the locked courtyard to build a snowman; but no one could find more than two pairs of mittens, so the girls had to pass them around.

Each wing is supervised by a social worker and a childcare worker, but their functions appeared to be mainly custodial. Some individual counseling apparently does take place, but most of the "behavior modification" is pursued through daily group meetings. Psychological treatment is minimal since the psychiatric staff is exceedingly limited; one psychologist one day a week and one psychiatrist one day a week. There is an infirmary with three (?) full-time nurses. A doctor and a dentist each come one morning a week.

At present the Center seems to be a place where wayward kids are locked up, but not trained or treated. However, the new director seems intent on improving the situation.

His first goal is to get staff to concentrate more on dealing with bad behavior in a constructive way instead of just controlling it by putting a child in the "cooling-off room." He also recognized the need for more constructive programming in such areas as job training and arts and crafts. He hopes to make more use of volunteers from the local community. Another high priority item is reducing from five months to three the waiting period for consideration of a first home visit. He hopes to obtain much more intensive psychiatric help for all his kids by instituting an intensive care wing at Centerton.

We were all most impressed by the new director and his ambitions. It will be interesting to see in a year or two if there really are any basic changes. For the present system surely can't be doing anyone any good, not the youngsters nor the communities to which they will return.

Community Group Homes and Residences

SGE is a large voluntary child welfare agency in New York City. Several years ago, under a special contract, the agency agreed to provide long-term care for fifty adolescent girls identified as hard to place. However, unlike practice in the programs of other voluntary agencies with the city, this contract stipulates that the Department of Social Services subunit can determine which girls enter the program. The city in turn gives priority to girls who are residing in large public child care facilities and who have been considered hard to place because of emotional disturbance, acting-out behavior, and similar problems. Although SGE has agreed not to refuse any youngster referred by Special Services, it works closely with the liaison person from the city, who knows the composition of the facilities and understands their limitations. In addition the SGE staff retain the right to select the facility within its program that is best suited for a particular youngster. SGE is able to make this agreement to accept any child referred because of the close working relationship with the referral person and the fact that they maintain three facilities, which represent alternative resources.

The first of the three programs operated under this contract is a group home called Project Self. This home, which is located in an old renovated building in a section of the Bronx, is near the shopping area and has access to transportation to all the other areas of the city. Project Self is designed to provide temporary care of one to six months in a highly structured setting for girls who are considered seriously disturbed and unable to function in most community settings. The basic focus of the program is to help girls discover positive things about themselves which they would like to develop. They are encouraged to develop a better understanding of themselves, to identify talents and skills, and to discover their vocational interests and abilities. At the heart of the program is the hope that the girls will be able to function more independently in a long-term setting. The program utilizes a very highly structured behavior modification approach in which girls are given "points" for doing chores, participating in home life, and so on. Each movement of the girls is controlled by the number of points she has earned.

The home is structured into three residence floors: freshman, junior, senior. When the girl is on the freshman floor, her freedoms are quite limited, but as she displays some capacity to regulate her behavior, she is gradually moved to the junior and then to the senior floor, where she has minimal supervision and additional privileges. At this point she is considered ready to begin to move out, either to return to her family or to another program within the SGE set-up.

The second program operated by SGE under this contract is called Project Living. This residence is located in a luxury co-op in Brooklyn in which the agency owns two apartments, each consisting of three bedrooms with a bath and a half, dining area, kitchen, and living room. This program provides for twelve teenage girls on a long-term basis. While the girl is in the home the emphasis is on learning new vocational and educational skills, developing a new attitude toward life, and adopting a meaningful lifestyle.

The third program is entitled Project Freedom. This is located in a YWCA residence in Queens. It is designed for girls from 16 to 21 who are ready for semi-independent long-term living arrangements.

This program has specific vocational or educational goals. The girls are enrolled in school either full or part time and are considered capable of handling responsibility. Each girl has her own bedroom, has flexible rules governing her daily living, and is expected to make most of her own decisions.

One of the unusual aspects of the SGE programs is the extensive amount of preparation given to each girl before she enters the program. Each girl has at least two interviews and meets with the girls in the home before moving in. In addition, she is given a very explicit contract to sign which describes her rights and responsibilities in the program and the rights and responsibilities of the SGE staff. The house rules are discussed and each girl is encouraged to raise objections so that when she enters the home there is a very explicit contract with which the staff can work in order to discuss the girl's behavior in the home and help her move in the direction to which she agreed prior to entering the home.

Each program is staffed by child care counselors on rotating shifts, and each has an educational and vocational counselor and a social worker. The staff to resident ratio is about 2:1 in Project Self and decreases gradually as the girls move on to the other programs in which they are able to assume more responsibility for themselves. The daily costs, of course, decrease proportionately as the staff to resident ratio is reduced. The girls receive individual and group counseling in all the programs, but much of the treatment is provided through a behavior modification approach which specifies certain kinds of behavior and punishes noncompliance with regard to the rules of the home. The girls are all expected to be enrolled in some sort of educational and/or vocational program and to contribute as far as possible to the care of the home and to taking care of their own needs. They have group meetings once a week and are expected to eat dinner together each night. The activities in each of the programs vary slightly because of the composition of the groups. For example, Project Self provides many activities within the home, whereas in Project Freedom the girls are expected to select recreational activities in the "Y" and to behave in a more flexible and self-responsible manner. In each of the homes visited there was a happy, informal, but disciplined atmosphere and a sense of commitment to the program on the part of the girls as well as the staff.

At the time of our visit, the program had only been in operation for a few months so it is impossible to evaluate it. However, both the staff of SGE and of DSS were pleased with the results. The girls seemed equally enthusiastic. The major problem was that of staff, especially in Project Self, which has the most disturbed girls, because there has been high staff turnover and the administration has not yet been able to identify the types of people who can best work in an intense and trying setting such as this. On the other hand, some of the girls in this program had already moved on successfully to more independent living arrangements; and since these are girls for whom the traditional child welfare system had no answers, it seems clear that the staff is doing something right. The very tightly controlled behavior modification approach is disturbing to some people in the field; yet it has seemed to work in terms of helping the girls to learn controls and to begin to develop a sense of their own potentials and responsibilities.

A State "Residential Treatment" Center

The Victoria Start Center is a Title II facility operated by the Division for Youth. Start is an acronym for "Short Term Adolescent Residential Treatment." The Start Center provides care for up to twenty-five girls aged 15–18 for a period of four to six months. Although the center can take juvenile delinquents or PINS, during our one visit the girls in residence had all come into care on a voluntary basis because of difficulties they were having at home, in school, or in their communities. The center is located in a one-story building which from the outside appears to be a cross between an army barracks and a ranch house. It is in a suburban, almost rural, area of Staten Island almost directly across from the Victoria State School, an institution for the mentally retarded. Located on the same ground is a trailer which is a transitional home for girls who are leaving the Start Center before they move out completely on their own. Many aspects of the Start program are strikingly similar to the SGE program. Essentially it is designed as a short-term program intended to help girls to develop a sense of their own identity and to learn responsibility, accountability, and the ability to make decisions governing their own lives. Although the program uses a behavior modification approach of sorts, and has the girls move through four levels quite similar to the freshman-junior-senior program of the SGE operation, there is heavy reliance on peer counseling and interaction as therapeutic strategies.

The girls are divided into three basic levels: the first level is the one the girls enter when they first come into the program and are still getting oriented. At that time they work doing the housework for the Start Center during the mornings and attend informal classes at the center in the afternoons. The girls at levels two and three can work in the community doing volunteer work in local nursery schools, Head Start programs, and so on. The classes at the center are intended to prepare them to take the general education diploma examination. Five nights a week (for two-and-a-half to three hours) the girls attend group sessions led by experienced therapists. There are two basic groups, again divided by level, but the girls take turns attending each other's group sessions. The group therapy is focused on peer interaction, current behavior and feelings. Although the setting is open, there is a closed quality permeating the atmosphere, somewhat reminiscent of places like Odyssey House and Encounter, in which almost total emphasis is on what has happened to the girls in the center; and contacts with outsiders are kept to the minimum, although as girls move from the first level they gradually increase their contacts with family and friends.

The center accepts referrals from community agencies and DFY as well as self-referrals. Any girl wishing to move into the center must come to what is called a "peer take," where she meets with the entire group and expresses her reasons for wanting to enroll in the Start Center and the problems which she hopes to solve while she is in residence. The other girls have to assess her motivation and take responsibility for the decision to accept a new girl into the center. They take their responsibility quite seriously; they recognize the rejection any girl may feel and what desperation impels a girl to come and ask twenty-five people for admission. The staff do some preliminary screening in terms of refusing to accept any girl who is severely drug dependent, psychotic, or having a character disorder. The girls they serve have severe family problems, have been involved in some drug use and sexual acting-out, but manifest some degree of health and motivation to change. At the time we visited the girls were primarily white, although there were a few blacks in residence, and they were primarily from working-class families, many of whom came from communities on Long Island. The center has a residence-staff ratio of 3:1. They have 8.5 staff members, including a director, therapists, a cook, a maintenance man, and child care workers. The annual cost per girl is $9,500. Families are expected to contribute as far as they are able; however, most of the girls are paid for by a combination of county and state funds. The county is charged $28.00 a day, and they receive 50 percent reimbursement from the state. The girls who move into the trailer are expected to have jobs and to pay their own costs for food, electricity, and the like, although the trailer itself is maintained by the center.

The staff and the girls expressed enthusiasm about the program; they evidently had a very high success rate, which they all attributed to the director. The assistant director, who was about to take over as director, said that the major problem they faced was an inadequate budget. For example, $235,000 a year is needed to maintain the facility; however, with inflation they are finding it extremely difficult to make ends meet and they have severe problems with regard to transportation, arranging recreational programs for the girls, and so on.

There are some inevitable tensions between the administration of the facility and the Division for Youth central staff in terms of the population served. The center refuses to take girls unless they feel they can "make it" in the program, while DFY is under pressure to keep the population at 100 percent capacity at all times. The staff feels that this is not a program for severely disturbed girls and that to take girls who were not motivated or could not make it in the program would be destructive for the individual as well as for the group as a whole. The atmosphere was a happy and relaxed one; the girls very comfortably accepted us at lunch time and talked freely about their experiences in the program. The program is being copied in other parts of the county.

A Private Agency Group Home

Addison Street Home is one of several group homes developed by Catholic Social Services after it closed down a large, traditional, congregate institution for children ages 7–16 in the "dependent and neglected" category. Several motives came together: questions in the field as to whether children belong in large institutions, a deteriorating physical plant occupying a valuable piece of property, an agency updating its program.

The decision to develop a group home for adolescent girls grew out of the institution's experience with girls "on their own" at 16 with no place to go. The home serves five girls, ages 13–17, in the "dependent and neglected" category. Although the girls manifest varying degrees of behavioral difficulty, the range is probably no greater than that of other youngsters in the neighborhood. This residence is not conceived of as a treatment center or facility; it is, rather, a home for girls who do not have families available to care for them. This home was established three years ago, in the central city. However, the location did not seem sound. Girls became involved in acting-out problems, especially drugs, and the staff felt strongly that much of this was due to the environment to which they were exposed. While the director had originally felt strongly that any group homes established should be close to the environment from which their clients came, he concluded that staff were fighting social forces greater than they could handle. He finally came to the conclusion that they either had to give up or attempt to move the home to the suburbs. Therefore, by summer, they obtained their present residence. They were able to obtain needed zoning variances because of a variety of favorable circumstances—a relatively new experience for the agency which had had difficulty on this issue with other homes.

The house is located on a side residential street. It looks like every other house on the street, all evidently built as part of a development of small ranch houses, probably twenty to thirty years ago. The houses are in fairly close proximity to each other, but all are well kept and the neighborhood itself looks like any typical working-class–middle-class suburban community. The house itself has a living room, dining area, kitchen, and bedroom for the house parents on the first floor, and three bedrooms on the second floor, as well as a playroom in the basement. None of the rooms are especially large, but they are very adequate, and the house is attractively furnished, looking much like any home one might visit.

The houseparents are a young couple, in their late twenties, who have had two years' previous experience as houseparents in group homes and had previously worked at two institutions as child care workers. They are in the home five days a week, and are replaced by a woman who covers the two days that they are off, and who assumes what they see primarily as a caretaking role. In other words, there is no attempt to define the substitute as a "parent" to the youngsters in the house. The agency social worker spends one day a week in the home. She meets with the houseparents weekly for consultation. In addition, every other week she stays in the home from approximately 2:00 to 8:30 P.M. in order to be available on an individual and/or group basis to the residents. A consulting psychiatrist worked regularly with the girls and the staff when they were first getting established in the house. The current psychiatric consultant is available as needed, but her services are used infrequently.

The girls receive medical and dental services in the community from a family physician and dentist.

The girls all attend the local public schools. Three of them are in junior high and two in high school. They also all have case workers at the Department of Social Services who are responsible for making any final decisions regarding their placement and for maintaining contact with their families. The social worker assigned to the home spends a good deal of time serving as a link between the girls and these Department social workers. There are semiannual conferences regarding each girl, as part of a complete case review. Since most of the girls are really quite separate from their families, the split accountability does not present any serious problems. For example, two of the girls are orphans, and others have minimal contact. On the other hand, this arrangement is said to be much more difficult for the younger children in the institution who frequently are in contact with families with whom the social workers in the institution do not have regular contact.

The home's primary objective is to help the girls reach independence and be able to move out on their own. This view sometimes conflicts with the belief that an expensive home should feature short-term treatment and high turnover. However, staff feel that these girls can never be expected to return to their families. Therefore, it is essential that the agency make a commitment to provide a home for them until they are able to go out on their own. They do provide counseling and treatment as needed but do not see this as a treatment center. The emphasis is on operating a program which will help the youngsters to attain their natural potential for growth and fulfillment.

When asked to describe what went on during the usual day or week, staff said that they find the girls very non-program oriented; the girls generally resist participation in group activities. They do eat dinner together every night, but otherwise they are very much on their own. In the morning they get up, get their own breakfasts, and leave for school as quickly as possible, so there is little communal activity at that time. When they return from school, each takes off to do whatever she wishes. The only real rule is that they must ask permission and say where they're going, what for, and roughly when they plan to return. Girls who have been having trouble in school may be requested to stay in to do homework in the afternoon, but otherwise this is left to the girls' discretion. Generally, the younger ones stay in the house or go over to visit friends' houses, and the older ones spend the afternoons with their boy friends.

The group have dinner together, but are free to invite guests or to go out if they are invited out. All have been assigned chores and help with the regular housework. For example, one will do the dishes, another will do the laundry every night. The housemother does do all the cooking, although she encourages the girls to work with her, and if they choose to prepare a meal they are free to do so. After dinner, the girls again are free to visit with friends, talk, do homework, or watch television. On weekends they are free to do what they choose, and may go into the city, or plan activities with their friends. They are given $3.00 a week as allowance, and are given extra money for specific activities. They also receive a clothing allowance and are encouraged to take responsibility for themselves in this area.

The houseparents maintain a rather relaxed atmosphere. Yet they have very specific behavioral objectives for each girl and are quite deliberate in the way they treat girls and respond to them in relation to these objectives. When they started, the housefather identified the primary problem as the amount of lying that went on. Therefore, he made that the subject of concentration and had no hesitation about checking up to make sure that the girls were doing what they said they would. If he found out that a girl was lying, he doubled whatever the punishment would normally be (which is usually some form of confinement to the house for a limited period of time). He made clear to the girls that there was no way they could begin to work on any problems until they faced their situations. This was why he felt lying was the most serious problem of all: they needed to be honest if they were going to begin to work on anything. Within six months the problem had almost disappeared. The other major problem was drinking. At first the houseparents focused on what happened when somebody got seriously drunk. Then they began to talk about problems of drinking even in moderation. By now the girls are hesitant even about a sip of beer.

The houseparents try to reinforce and encourage appropriate behavior and to discourage inappropriate behavior by confining the girls for a limited period of time and then forgetting about the incident altogether after that. They do engage in a great deal of informal conversation with the girls and with their friends. Often they feel that they are as much of a resource to the neighborhood youngsters as they are to their own girls. A great deal of informal counseling goes on primarily about current situations: problems with boy friends, high school mores, feuds with friends, feuds among the girls. The houseparents define themselves in a parental or foster parent role. However, they realize that the girls do not completely see them in this light and are in a somewhat ambiguous relationship with them. They do not pretend to give formal treatment or counseling, but do consider the informal contacts and discussions important, and in a sense are working on very deliberate plans of intervention for each girl. A visitor is impressed with the way the houseparents seem to function and their capacity to understand and relate to the various youngsters. The staff are pleased about the fact that the home now is located in the suburban area. They say that the girls are all doing much better academically and socially. Their behavior is more appropriate. They have had amazingly few difficulties in the community. In the beginning, there were complaints because of the type of friends the girls were bringing around (boys with leather jackets and motorcycles); however, the complaints have dropped off as the friends have changed. The girls rarely have caused trouble. However, if there is any noise or difficulty the neighbors are quicker to call them than anyone else on the street. The houseparents attempt to respond to this appropriately, however, and they feel that they have gradually earned some real acceptance in the community.

A Youth Camp

In the 1950s, forestry camps were the most exciting alternatives to large correctional facilities. Several midwestern states and California pioneered. Simple facilities, hard work, an atmosphere creating intimacy, wholesome role models would all combine for constructive results. The excitement is now gone since most of the committed and placed youths come from urban ghettos. The camp atmosphere is strange and frightening to many, not attractive. Because it is different from the environments to which most of them will return, the camp is no longer very popular. It still remains part of the DFY repertoire, and is believed excellent for a carefully selected small subgroup of those in trouble or for volunteers. The boys take part in outdoor activities but do not have real forestry work.

The camp system may be illustrated by the Samuel Barkins Camp, located on 8,000 acres of forest land in upstate New York. (Several camps are in far more remote areas.) The facilities include a comfortable dormitory building, dining hall, and kitchen, and an administration-education complex. The grounds are spacious. The outdoor recreation program is comprehensive and year-round. The residents are between the ages of 15 and 17. The average youth remains for ten months in a program of peer pressure through group counseling. The boys have three hours of remedial academic work daily, some of it with volunteers. Classes are small.

Trends and Issues

We have written about agencies and facilities, laws and policies. This is inevitable, given our purpose. Yet, before discussing how improvement and clarity might be achieved, it is useful to recall that fragmented programs also may mean fragmented families, that unfocused interventions create disoriented clients. The New York case illustration which follows could be duplicated in other big cities. It may be read as a specification of human costs—or of economic price—depending upon the reader's predilection.[49]

Susan K.—Eleven Years of Shuttling

In September 1963, when she was not quite 4 years old, Susan and one of her sisters were placed for one week at Children's Center while their mother, a chronic alcoholic, was hospitalized. Four months later, they were placed in a short-term foster home, then later in 1964, along with two more sisters, placed in a long-term foster home. Susan was described as a difficult child from the very onset of her stay in foster care. Her school also complained about her behavior, and in April 1967 a "psychological" was done. Psychiatric treatment was recommended but not provided. A year later, under threats of suspension by the school, psychotherapy and medication were begun, and Susan was said to improve considerably. But during the summer her case was closed, and Susan's behavior deteriorated. Susan was permanently suspended in November 1969 and placed on home instruction.

In April 1972 she was admitted to Jacobi Hospital psychiatric center following several incidents of running away coupled with aggressive behavior. Her foster mother was no longer willing to keep her and no other residential placement was found. No therapy had been resumed either. In May 1973, Susan was admitted to Elmhurst Children's Center on a court order and despite her age and 400 mgs. of Thorazine a day had to be transferred to an adult ward because of her aggressive behavior. She was subsequently placed at Harlem Confrontation. Two months later, however, she was admitted to Bellevue Hospital's psychiatric ward after threatening some fellow residents with a knife and then threatening to jump out a window. She remained in Bellevue for ten days, was moved to Juvenile Center (detention), but was brought back to Bellevue after running away.

For the second time, Bellevue found her in serious need of help and recommended a highly structured environment. She was discharged in November and returned to the Commissioner of Social Services. The same day a PINS petition was filed and she was seen by the court diagnostic team. She was now disturbed enough to be labeled a catatonic schizophrenic and was sent a third time to Bellevue. The following day Bellevue returned her to the court saying again that Susan was found nonacceptable by Manhattan Children's Treatment Center yet needed a highly structured environment, while adding that any further deterioration in her condition would necessitate her being admitted to a state hospital.

In December 1973, Susan was placed in Highpoint Hospital, but she complained about being the only black there and asked to leave. She was returned to Spofford (detention) and then moved to a private psychiatric hospital, Falkirk. She stayed at Falkirk until July 1974, when she was returned to Children's Center, but then, because of more aggressive behavior, she was transferred once again to Bellevue. Bellevue now contemplated placing her at either a training school or an out-of-city children's agency, but because of newspaper attention questioning that type of placement, she was sent to Rockland State Hospital instead. Presumably, she is still there.

A detailed cost analysis was prepared to document the costs of Susan's care for one year. That analysis follows.

Facility	*Days*	*Costs*	*Subtotals*
Juvenile Court	12/4/72–12/21/72	17 days @ $90/day	$1,530.00
With relative	12/21/72–1/19/73		
JC	1/19/73–1/29/73	10 days @ $90/day	900.00
With relative	1/29/73–2/22/73		
JC	2/22/73–3/22/73	10 days @ $90/day	900.00
Commissioner of Social Services (e.g., Callagy Hall Annex)	3/22/73–5/24/73	63 days @ $62/day	3,906.00
Elmhurst	5/24/73–6/14/73	21 days @ $100/day (approximately)	2,100.00
JC	6/14/73–6/27/73	13 days @ $90/day	1,170.00
JC	6/28/73–7/5/73	7 days @ $90/day	630.00
CSS	7/5/73–7/20/73	15 days @ $62/day	930.00
Bell.	7/20/73–8/16/73 (approximately)	27 days @ $122.50/day	3,307.00
CSS	8/16/73–9/13/73 (approximately)	28 days @ $71/day	1,988.00
Bell.	9/13/73–10/19/73 (approximately)	36 days @ $122.50/day	4,410.00
CSS	10/19/73–11/12/73	24 days @ $71/day	1,704.00
JC	11/12/73–11/13/73	1 day @ $90/day	90.00
Bell.	11/13/73–11/28/73	15 days @ $122.50/day	1,837.00
JC	11/28/73–12/4/73	6 days @ $90/day	540.00
Total		302 days @ $83.15/day	$25,943.00

Thinking About Alternatives

Basic data on alternatives to institutions are fragmentary and non-additive. The research results are not definitive. Indeed, the experimental efforts and the research designs are far from comprehensive. Therefore, as we have seen, much of the history of the field is a story of faddism or response to broader societal developments. Deinstitutionalization grew out of evidence of failure of large institutions and concern with children's rights, as well as a humanistic impulse, and was not the product of clear evidence of better effects from community-based residences. "Diversion" had similar genesis, even though no one knew quite what it meant or where it would lead, let alone what it might accomplish.

The field has not yet had the kind of systematic data collection, research, scientific analysis, and value debate which can generate rational policy and coherent administration. (The federal government has not even as yet taken the elementary step of introducing a few basic questions about substitute care into the current population survey.) Nor has the field faced whether a coherent perspective is a real possibility, given fragmentation of responsibility among federal, state, and local governments—between public and voluntary sectors—and among several service systems: child welfare, juvenile justice, mental health, education, health, employment, and so on.

Nonetheless, analysis and value debate may become necessary, as the social and money costs of policy sprawl and non-system become ever more visible. We would emphasize the following for such future exploration:

Child or Family Life-Space. It is one thing to respond to physical or emotional illness with individual therapy, or to lack of competence with education. It is another to intervene in a dynamic family situation or family neighborhood interaction when responding to the symptomatic behavior of one member. Intervention strategies fluctuate and compete between these goals. The research does not suggest at what age, or under what circumstances, or in which places one should respond to neglect, unruly behavior, delinquency, by treating a *person* (and thus using typologies of the sort developed in California), and when by intervening into the *family* or *community* situation. The slogan of "community treatment above all" may be dysfunctional. Some youths may be better off far away from home for a considerable time. Restoration of the "normal" family structure may or may not be a constructive goal. There is no reason to believe that the choice must always be community any more than it once always was institutionalization. Only as the research gives further cues as to reasonable intervention objectives and effective strategies will helpful typologies emerge and appropriate education goals be set. In the meantime, clarity is properly demanded for the policy debate at a given time and place.

Labels and Intervention as Defining Deviance. While this societal process cannot be eliminated (societies inevitably create norms and define some major departures negatively), it does call for analysis and self-conscious choice. There are those who would close all conventional institutions and mental hospitals as a way of cutting down criminality and mental illness; but we doubt that our communities and their citizens would be willing to bear the burdens of troublesome and destructive conduct, albeit unlabeled.

Current reformers do not note it, but their posture leads back to the anti-labeling intent of the original juvenile court. (Look at the child's needs, not his legal category or his offense.) But because juvenile courts dealt with some cases that aroused hostility or a sense of frustration, negative attitudes developed toward delinquents. Because large institutions with a mix of deviant children could achieve little and perhaps taught the wrong things, their inmates were further stigmatized. Then, in response, the society decided to minimize the damage. Some children would be called PINS or CHINS, not delinquents. Juvenile delinquency would be transferred from child welfare generally, to a child welfare specialty—then but a unit of the criminal justice system. The latter, in turn, recognizing the disadvantage of the labels would encourage "diversion" or "minimal penetration," and would encourage service under other auspices, on the premise that a court would not itself do anyone any good. But no one was or is fooled: delinquents know that they thus become leftovers from a sorting-and-sifting system in which the majority escape; those who work with delinquents regard most of them as hopeless and not worth the try; and the public reacts accordingly and renews the process, thus only deepening the stigma.

In an elaborate scientific, comprehensive overview of labeling, Hobbs and his collaborators documented in detail how the labeling process and labels themselves create and reinforce deviance and hurt children; and how labels are boundary-makers for the professions and serve many functions extraneous to constructive intervention on behalf of children, families, or communities.[50] However, they also noted that classification is absolutely essential for research, planning, administration, advocacy, and effective individualized service. If the constructive possibilities are to be maximized it would be necessary and wise to classify and categorize in ways which reflect intervention needs and service requirements, not by behavior symptoms. In short, we would comment, the rejected juvenile court premise would be restored. We would join the worldwide tendency to raise the age of criminal responsibility, define all children below this age (the non-criminal) as needing help, care, and supervision, and create a strong child welfare system to implement such help—under one name or another.

Within the child welfare system, knowledge, preferences, and facilities, which could vary by community and ethnic-social-religious group, would find a balance among substitute family care, small-group residences, large institutions. (Not unequal resource distribution, but allocation by preferences is here implied, since the field cannot always select the "best" technically, preference being an important element.)

None of this quite solves the problem because there are children for whom child welfare controls are inadequate, and there are those of the delinquency jurisdiction age—whether it is under 16, 17, or 18—who are not successfully treated or controlled in a "diversion" or "community care" or "open institution" regime and who attack the community again and again if they are institutionalized for very brief periods and returned automatically to their former environments.

It must be understood that an attempt to make distinctions among children along these lines, growing out of what is known about workable intervention strategies, is quite different from what is revealed by our national and state overviews. Too often, today, child welfare and juvenile justice deal with the same children: the channeling depends upon chance, color, income, religion, sex, residence. Yet the way in which one is channeled has grave consequences. This is a strong argument for federal and state planning initiative and court alertness: fairness and equity demand it and the problem is beyond the locality. But it also argues for developing a sound decision rule for how the "juvenile justice" system is to be used if it is to be retained.

For all this suggests that there is no escaping a public policy which creates one category of intervention and service designated for those who are not successfully diverted, reintegrated, "normalized." Courts exist because communities wish or need to impose strict sanctions in some situations. Research and experience must be assimilated to tell us (a) which of these adjudicated delinquents can be "normalized" by our responding to individual and family needs, wiping out the label, and offering service outside the juvenile justice system and (b) which interventions must be attempted under the umbrella of court and correctional system authority (what is in some places called the "juvenile justice" system—as contrasted with child welfare).

The research does not show it to be hopeless. One could even argue deductively, in terms of sociological and psychological theory, that reality-testing is a pathway toward change. In any case, what is left after all the "diversion" and channeling into psychiatry, education, health, employment, rehabilitation, and family or child welfare will be a significant system. Once nobody is wearing blinders, it should be possible to use research and experience to construct for "juvenile justice" a network of community-based treatments and services (under an administrative umbrella called "probation"?) and a network of diverse residential arrangements ("corrections"?) which would range from education to vocational training to several different therapies to merely providing protected "living" while the resident uses community resources.

Each program would have its *modal* commitment period, and its *annual* times for admission and discharge relating to program logic. By what alternative logic is it assumed that youngsters with weak egos, personal problems, and poor experience in school should be able to jump into a continuing program as one jumps onto a carousel in an amusement park—and manage quickly to phase into a complex educational-vocational endeavor? Or what logic assumes that teachers or supervisors can define and achieve specific goals for youngsters in an environment in which people are constantly jumping off and on the moving vehicle—and not staying very long? These problems cannot be overcome unless it is assumed that youngsters who are placed or committed, after all the screening and filtering, should be expected to enter at a strategic time of year and to stay long enough to achieve something, even if there must be some months of waiting in a decent, humane interim secure environment (detention).

Still others, symbols of the limitations of knowledge and the fallibility of our social institutions, may need to be committed for long periods because we do not know how to change them and society has a right to protection—as do they. This is a difficult and unpleasant area. We do not like to admit our failures, become angry at those who symbolize them, and forget that none of this nullifies either constitutional guarantees or the community's right to protection.

In short, the length of commitment and degree of security could vary by the need for community protection and the length of time reasonably associated with a service goal (completion of a training course, participation in a specific treatment). All this would in some way be constrained by offense. The system would also acknowledge its high failure rate and the need to confine some people relatively long, if only for community protection.

In summary, there will need to be two networks: juvenile justice and the other. Each should be a full network. The diversion philosophy should not relieve the former of the need to become effective, to have form and content, and to retain the many children and youths for whom it has legitimate responsibility, even though its caseload should be far smaller than that in child welfare.

Risk-taking and the Sharing of Burdens. Distant, remote institutions were invented for good reason: to "extrude" offenders and unpleasant deviants. To refuse to commit, or to place in group residences in urban neighborhoods, is to reject banishment. Many community members refuse to pay the price of having dangerous, strange, unpleasant, different children and youths on their streets and in their schools. There has often been neighborhood opposition to creating urban group homes, especially for adolescents. Often the humane policies involving community care are imposed by the affluent on the less powerful. Since such policy does involve risks and social costs, should they not be paid more uniformly or debated more openly? "Community care" must mean in everybody's community; "diversion" means into one's own local facilities. A community's willingness to accept this defines the constraints it places on the reform.

"Rights" versus Services. There is increasing affirmation of the "right" to services or treatment, and courts are now being called upon to release institutional inmates who have not had help. The development is generally constructive, although what is done cannot go beyond the state of the art, and courts cannot become wise administrators and budget-makers for all social services.

Courts make their optimum contribution by serving as regulators: guarding basic rights and monitoring performance of public agencies. Service agencies must be expected to retain and implement diagnostic and treatment responsibilities. The court role might be further modified were administrative agencies more creative in the development of mechanisms for ensuring accountability and redressing grievances.

The subject has other aspects not normally introduced into the discussion, largely because it is not popular to note that the path to reform is complex and involves value trade-offs which may be distasteful. The policy debate should, however, explore the possible conflict between expanded emphasis on rights and the full maturing of a system of diagnostically oriented helping services. The rights approach demands a specific offense, due process, a very specific label (which, once appended after very substantial resistance and adversarial court procedure, must carry a strong stigma), and very specific restrictions on length of commitments related to the offense. The diagnostic strategy calls for flexible approaches of open-ended duration, allowing treatment dynamics to determine the length of therapy or control; institutions are created around intervention strategies, not court categories.

We have suggested a mixed approach: a therapeutic strategy, except where the "justice" network is to serve; then, a careful protection of rights and an acceptance of the consequences for the character of the alternative intervention system. A choice of this kind has implications both for courts and for social service systems.

Deinstitutionalization. The slogan "deinstitutionalization" was briefly useful for highlighting the evils of large, punitive, impersonal training schools for delinquents or horrible mass facilities for the retarded. However, campaigns often are carried away by their enthusiasms and create excesses. If children leave training schools only to spend time in local jails, or mental hospitals and prisons, or if they are dropped out of the statistics in one place because of out-of-state placement, the policy is questionable.

The balance and concern mobilized by the deinstitutionalization movement was constructive and we are not likely to revert to some very questionable practices. But the issues are such as to demand responses more subtle than those carried by an attack on excesses: what is needed is a balanced system of substitute care built into an integrated system of personal social services. The call to deinstitutionalize sounds only one of many needed cautions and offers very little of the needed overall guidance.

Program Dynamics. Available data suggest that some intervention strategies are defeated by questionable external constraints. Court-imposed commitment durations, court-dictated treatment approaches, outside administratively determined child groupings may completely undermine an educational program, a treatment system, a training curriculum. There is evidence that not everyone needs or can use a community program, at least a nonresidential one.[51] But residential arrangements should have constructive things to offer and be allowed to become more than costly warehouses. Any residential facility should be expected to offer a specific service, training, help; and research and practice could reasonably be expected to define the minimal conditions for implementing a mission. This would appear to be a starting point for administration, and a necessity for basic research testing. One begins, of course, with the accumulative evidence that smaller group homes are probably better than very large institutions, that—to quote Sarri and Vinter—justice, fairness, and humaneness are essential, and that local administration can be as oppressive and punitive as centralized state administration. Then, one asks, what place for whom, what program, how long, what program logic—and, based on research, does it work, for whom?

There is need to be careful about the word "treatment." Claudine McCreadie has pointed out that sometimes "treatment" means a very extensive personality restructuring and at other times only that the facility has a goal for the child or youth and a strategy for getting there.[52] No residential program should be undertaken without an individualized treatment plan in the latter sense. It is questionable whether resources, state of the art, and causal knowledge will sustain large-scale commitment to "treatment" in its other meaning for almost everyone.

Modest Expectations. Our problems are often beyond our understanding. At times they are understood but we see no likelihood of effectuating change unless we can intervene on the level of social policy. These facts, too, belong in the discussion and the debate, lest we adopt and then drop system organization and reorganization proposals, accept and then reject objectives and slogans as smokescreens for our real confusions and ambivalence. Policy makers and programers, too, are part of the society.

Juvenile Justice and Social Services

Whether or not status offenders belong in the courts, they do need help. Much of what is now in the juvenile justice system, plus the service systems dealing with dependent and neglected children, requires full integration into the personal social service systems discussed in Chapter 8. Only a broad service system can achieve the intervention range required and absorb the several semi-stigmatized groups under the somewhat more benign service umbrella. Only a comprehensive service system will achieve the needed range of own-family care, with community social service support; temporary or long-term substitute family care; group residential arrangements in the local community; specialized institutions and schools somewhat further from home. Clearly these are central, major tasks of the personal social services. They will not be well discharged if the system remains fragmented and uncertain of its future and direction. The United States has not settled whether it will attempt to restructure personal social services into an integrated system as it implements mandated planning under the new Title XX of the Social Security Act and other, related legislation. If it does not there will be an absence, a continual gap, in the case management–case integration–case accountability functions. Reforms in institutional care and the true integration of community-based and residential services should hardly be expected under such circumstances.

Nor can the personal social services remove themselves entirely from the juvenile justice system. As an adjunctive function, but a major one, the personal social services must help create and man the intake, community-treatment, and some of the group-residence and institutional facilities specific to that system. Education, psychiatry, rehabilitation, and related systems also have major roles and should be expected to carry the lead in some of the facilities. This too could occur given only local planning and service-integration provision at community and state levels which will consider the human services (the social welfare institutions) in their totality and introduce priority planning, operational coordination, needed definition of boundaries, and mutually supportive delivery systems.

Notes

1. Martin Wolins and Irving Piliavin, *Institution or Foster Home: A Century of Debate* (pamphlet; New York: Child Welfare League of America, 1964).
2. *Ibid.*, p. 26.
3. Joseph F. Meisels and Martin B. Loeb, "Unanswered Questions About Foster Care," *Social Service Review*, 30 (1956), 239. Cited in Wolins and Paliavin, *Institution or Foster Home*, p. 9.
4. A balanced view of what Massachusetts did and did not do appears in Lloyd E. Ohlin, Robert B. Coates, and Allen D. Miller, "Radical Correctional Reform: A Case Study of the Massachusetts Youth Correctional System," *Harvard Educational Review*, 44, No. 1 (Feb. 1974), 75–111. While positive, the authors note that they are basing themselves only on interviews and observation.
5. Alfred J. Kahn, "Agenda for Change," in Donnell M. Pappenfort, Dee Morgan Kilpatrick, and Robert W. Roberts, eds., *Child Caring: Social Policy and the Institution* (Chicago: Aldine, 1973), p. 312.
6. Martin Wolins, ed., *Successful Group Care* (Chicago: Aldine, 1974).

7. See, for example, Sanford J. Fox, "Juvenile Justice Reform: An Historical Perspective," *Stanford Law Review*, 22 (June 1970), 1187–1239; Anthony Platt, *The Child Savers: The Invention of Delinquency* (Chicago: University of Chicago Press, 1969); and Justine Wise Polier, "Myths and Realities in the Search for Juvenile Justice," *Harvard Educational Review*, 44, No. 1 (Feb. 1974), 112–24.

8. Mary Carpenter, "What Should Be Done for the Neglected and Criminal Children of the United States," in *Proceedings of the National Conference of Charities*, Vol. 70 (1875), cited in Fox, "Juvenile Justice Reform," p. 1193.

9. We have not done justice to the literature on labeling theory. In an intensive, costly overview with many participants, Hobbs reported to the Secretary of HEW that it is necessary to diminish "the harmful effects of classification and labeling while preserving their benefits in providing, obtaining and evaluating services." Nicholas Hobbs, *The Futures of Children: Categories, Labels and Their Consequences*. See also Nicholas Hobbs, gen. ed., *Issues in the Classification of Children* (2 vol.). The three volumes were published in 1975 by Jossey-Bass, San Francisco. Edwin Lenert has done much to develop the "secondary deviance" concept (delinquency as the product of labeling and experiencing its consequences). See Hobbs, ed., *Issues*, II, 147, for bibliography.

10. This assessment is documented in great detail by the National Assessment of Juvenile Corrections (University of Michigan), a major project funded by the Law Enforcement Assistance Administration of the U.S. Department of Justice. The codirectors are Dr. Robert Vinter and Dr. Rosemary C. Sarri. The national picture is gradually being filled in as a result of this effort—which will be cited at several points. Major interim reports from the Assessment project are cited in note 16, below.

11. Marvin Burt and Louis Blair, *Options for Improving the Care of Neglected and Dependent Children* (Washington, D.C.: Urban Institute, March 1971).

12. Alfred Kadushin, "Institutions for Dependent and Neglected Children," in Pappenfort et al., *Child Caring*, pp. 147–48.

13. Elaine Duxbury, *Youth Service Bureaus in California* (Youth Authority Progress Report No. 3; Sacramento, Cal.: California Youth Authority, 1972), p. 5, as quoted in Donald R. Cressey and Robert A. McDermott, *Diversion from the Juvenile Justice System* (Ann Arbor, Mich.: National Assessment of Juvenile Corrections, 1973).

14. Cressey and McDermott, *Diversion*, p. 7.

15. California Youth Authority, *National Study of Youth Bureaus* (DHEW-SRS Pub. No. 73-26025; Washington, D.C.: Youth Development and Delinquency Prevention Administration, 1973).

16. We have relied heavily on the following from the National Assessment of Juvenile Corrections, University of Michigan, Robert D. Vinter and Rosemary C. Sarri, codirectors. Several major reports, in process, will improve the available picture substantially: Mark M. Levin

and Rosemary C. Sarri, *Juvenile Delinquency: A Comparative Analysis of Legal Codes in the United States* (1974); Donald R. Cressey and Robert A. McDermott, *Diversion from the Juvenile Justice System* (1973); Vinter and Sarri, *Research Design Statement* (1972); Sarri, Vinter, and Rhea Kish, *Juvenile Injustice: Failure of a Nation* (processed, 1974); Vinter and George Downs, *State Juvenile Justice Systems* (processed, 1974); Sarri, *Under Lock and Key: Juveniles in Jails and Detention* (1974).

17. See Cressey and McDermott, *Diversion*, p. 32.

18. Craig A. McEwen, "Preliminary Analysis of Data from the 1973 Study of Subcultures in Selected Programs Serving Youth Committed and Referred to the Massachusetts Department of Youth Services" (Center for Criminal Justice, Harvard Law School, Jan. 1974), pp. 7–10.

19. Robert L. Smith, *A Quiet Revolution: Probation Subsidy* (DHEW-SRS Pub. No. 73-26011; Washington, D.C.: Youth Development and Delinquency Prevention Administration, 1973).

20. *Ibid.*

21. Ohlin, Coates, and Miller, "Radical Correctional Reform," p. 75.

22. Milton Luger in Hobbs, ed., *Issues*, I, 370.

23. Ohlin in Pappenfort et al., *Child Caring.*

24. Sarri et al., *Juvenile Injustice.* Emphasis in original.

25. CB, DHEW, *Children Served by Public Welfare Agencies and Voluntary Child Welfare Agencies and Institutions* (Washington, D.C.: GPO, 1971).

26. Robert D. Vinter, George Downs, and John Hall, *Juvenile Corrections in the States: Residential Programs and Deinstitutionalization* (prelim.; Ann Arbor: National Assessment of Juvenile Corrections, 1975).

27. Donnell M. Pappenfort and Dee Morgan Kilpatrick, *A Census of Children's Residential Institutions in the United States, Puerto Rico, and the Virgin Islands: 1966*, Vol. I: *Seven Types of Institutions* (Chicago: University of Chicago, Social Service Monographs, 1970).

28. LEAA, *Children in Custody: Advance Report on the Juvenile Detention and Correctional Facility Census of 1972–73* (processed; 1975).

29. Margaret Benjamin and Louise Murray, *Group Homes in New York City* (New York: Department of City Planning, 1973), p. 50.

30. *Ibid.*, pp. 53–54.

31. Sarri et al., *Juvenile Injustice*, pp. 15–16. Subject to correction as the research is completed.

32. Alfred Kadushin, "Institutions," p. 152.

33. President's Commission on Law Enforcement and Administration of Justice, *The Challenge of Crime in a Free Society* (Washington, D.C.: GPO, 1967), pp. 55–89, as cited in Lloyd Ohlin, "Institutions for Pre-Delinquent or Delinquent Children," in Pappenfort et al., *Child Caring*, p. 193.

34. Pappenfort and Kilpatrick, *Census*, Vol. I, table 17.

35. Henry Maas, ed., *Research in the Social Services: A Five-Year Review* (New York: National Association of Social Workers, 1971); Pappenfort et al., *Child Caring*; Wolins, *Successful Group Care*; *Review of Child Development Research*, Vols. I and II, ed. Martin L. Hoffman and Lois W. Hoffman (New York: Russell Sage Foundation, 1964, 1966), Vol. III (*Child Development and Social Policy*) ed. Bettye M. Caldwell and Henry N. Ricciuti (Chicago: University of Chicago Press, 1973). These sources are offered as a point of departure; a full listing would be very extensive.

36. Wolins, *Successful Group Care*, pp. 11, 31.

37. For a recent listing see Smith, *Quiet Revolution*, p. 18.

38. Irwin J. Goldman, *Multivariate Analysis of Characteristics Related to Post-Discharge Arrest, Post-Discharge Commitment and Non-graduation* (processed; Albany, N.Y. State Division for Youth, 1972).

39. New York State Social Services Law, Article 6, Sec. 371.4a.

40. New York State Family Court Act, Article 6, Part 1, Sec. 611.

41. New York State Social Services Law, Article 6, Secs. 371.5, 371.6.

42. Child Welfare League of America, *The Need for Foster Care* (New York: 1969), p. 24.

43. Office of Children's Services, Judicial Conference of the State of New York, *Juvenile Injustice* (New York: Oct. 1973), pp. 3–5.

44. "Audit Report on Rehabilitation of Adolescents at State Residential Facilities, Executive Department, Division for Youth," Report No. AL-ST-15-74, Office of the Comptroller, State of New York, p. 1.

45. "Agency Chiefs Appointed to Children's Commission," *Mental Hygiene News*, April 30, 1974, p. 1.

46. New York State Department of Social Services, *Foster Care of Children in New York State* (Program Analysis Report No. 54; Albany: DSS, Feb. 1974), pp. 8–9.

47. Blanche Bernstein, Donald A. Snider, William Meezan, *A Preliminary Report, Foster Care Needs and Alternatives to Placement* (New York: Center for New York City Affairs for the State Board of Social Welfare, 1975).

48. For example: New York State Board of Social Welfare, *Final Report and Recommendations* (May 1974); *Characteristics of Court Children Requiring Placement* (Nov. 1974).

49. Case material prepared by the Office of Children's Services, Judicial Conference of the State of New York.

50. Hobbs, *Futures of Children and Issues*, Vols. I–II.

51. Hobbs, *Futures of Children*, pp. 196–97.

52. Claudine McCreadie, United Kingdom, Report IV of Cross-National Studies: *Children's Institutions and Alternative Programs*, "Conclusions." (New York: Columbia University School of Social Work, 1976.)

Community Services for the Aged

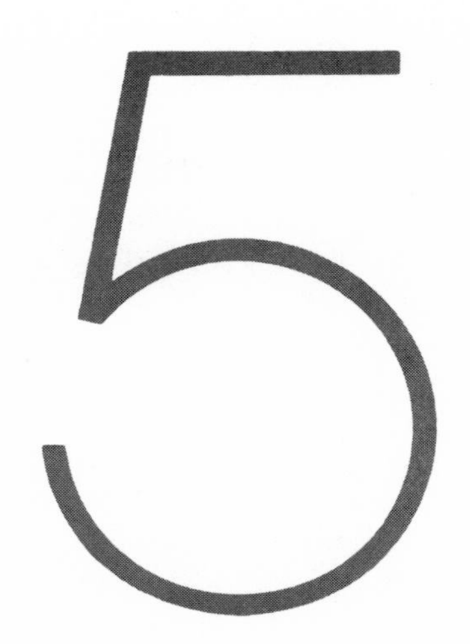

Context and Definition

Service provision for the aged differs from our other topics in that it covers a wide range of services directed at an entire population group. Community services for the aged must include both social utilities (services that should be available to all aged because they are old) and case services (special services that must be available on the basis of need, for the frail, impaired, isolated aged). The adequacy of these personal social services is predicated on the adequacy of the basic social services (e.g., income maintenance, health care, housing). Where the aged are concerned, the personal social services need to be particularly well integrated with housing and medical provision, a fact which introduces issues related to service delivery and delivery structures.

One of the most significant changes in twentieth-century American society has been the emergence of a sizable and increasingly influential population group—the aged, or according to the conventional chronological definition, people aged 65 and over. In 1900, there were 3.1 million people 65 and over, representing 4 percent of the total population. By 1940 the number had tripled to 9.0 million, almost 7 percent of the total population; and by 1970 it more than doubled again to 20 million. By mid-1975 there were 22 million aged, representing 10 percent of the total population. Current census projections anticipate an over-65 population of about 30.6

million in the year 2000, representing 11.6 percent of the overall population (assuming no change in the birth rate). Clearly, this development has important and varied implications: for the elderly themselves; for their relatives; for family structure and function; for the economic, political, and social institutions in our society; and for the planning, organization, and delivery of social welfare services. Yet regardless of the increased size of this population group, major interest in and urgent concern about the problems of the aged in this country has taken root only within the last two decades.

Historically, national concern as reflected in public policy emerged only in the 1930s, when, during a period of severe economic depression and high unemployment, the need to create more room in the labor market for younger workers led to the development of policies designed to ease the elderly out of the work force and to meet long-ignored needs. In reality, however, it was only in the 1960s that the aged emerged for the first time as a powerful political interest group. The first White House Conference on Aging was held in 1961, some forty years after the first similar national expression of concern regarding children. The Special Committee on Aging of the U.S. Senate, was established in 1961, also; successor to the Subcommittee on Problems of the Aged and the Aging, the Special Committee is one of the most influential advocacy organizations for the aged within the government. Most of the major national interest-group organizations representing an organized constituency of elderly and lobbying in their behalf were first established in the early sixties. A combination of increased numbers and the influence of the civil rights movement with its stress on minority rights combined to support the mobilization of an organized constituency of older Americans. At the same time, the availability of greater resources facilitated efforts at meeting these new and growing demands. As a consequence, the decade beginning in 1965 witnessed several important developments in U.S. public policy regarding the aged: major legislative enactments providing increased benefits for older people; greatly expanded federal expenditures; the establishment of a large number of facilities, programs, and services devoted to helping the aged.

Pronouncements of federal policy during these years reflect beneficence, concern, and commitment to the aged. For example, the Older Americans Act of 1965 specified the following ten national objectives: an adequate income; the best possible physical and mental health; suitable housing; full restorative services; opportunity for employment; retirement in health, honor, and dignity; pursuit of meaningful activity; efficient community services; immediate benefit from proven research; the free exercise of individual initiatives in planning and managing their own lives.

After the White House Conference on Aging, President Nixon announced a new national policy toward aging and the aged. He specified four major goals: "assuring an adequate income; assuring appropriate living arrangements; assuring independence and dignity; assuring institutional responsiveness and a new attitude towards aging."[1] In his address to the Conference, in December 1971, President Nixon specifically stated that "the greatest need is to help more older Americans to go on living in their own homes." Increasingly this theme has been stressed as a major national policy objective. Concern has been expressed about the need to "deinstitutionalize" the elderly, to develop "alternatives to institutions," and to expand community-based living and care facilities.

There is no question that the aged, representing 10 percent of the population in this country, are a powerful and articulate interest group. Since they are almost all eligible to vote and represent 17 percent of the eligible voters, even if only 51 percent do vote on average, they are a potentially significant political force. Evidence of their impact on public policy already exists.

Clearly, explicit national policy supports the aged in their general hopes and aspirations. However, the goals as they are expressed in legislative enactments or official statements are essentially rhetorical. The real question is whether or not these goals have been operationalized through legislative and administrative activities, and the extent to which they have been achieved as a result of public policy.

Before attempting any extensive review of social provision for the aged, some additional information must be provided as context for subsequent analysis. Among the questions to be answered first are: What do we mean when we talk of aging and the problems of the aged? Who are the aged in the United States today and where and how do they live? What are the generally agreed upon needs of the aged in this country? With this information in hand, we will turn to a description and analysis of social provision (policies and programs) for older Americans generally—in other words, to the question of what we are doing at present in this country to respond to the needs of older people and to achieve the goals we have so strongly supported. What legislation is there and how is it implemented, with what kinds of resources? What benefits and services exist?

What follows will include an overview of all social programs serving the aged. However, in order to focus more sharply on the issue of whether legislation and programs do in fact operationalize goals, we shall concentrate especially on one particular cluster of objectives, those that relate to "assuring appropriate living arrangements [and helping] more older Americans to go on living in their own homes." We shall review both the specific legislation and the programs, facilities, and services as well as the numbers and characteristics of the older people who use these programs. Finally, we shall try to identify those issues, questions, and problems that may impede desired goal attainment.

Definition of Aging

There is as yet no generally accepted theory of aging and only a limited coherent body of knowledge about it. Although the process of human aging involves physiological and psychological changes that are sequential, cumulative, and irreversible, it is generally agreed that the changes brought about through aging do not occur consistently in any one individual let alone in all people of the same chronological age. However irreversible the process of aging may be for all, its onset, its detriments, both felt and perceived, and its characteristics vary both within and among individuals. Even the onset of symptoms of old age may vary with the biological and psychological make-up of the individual and with his life history or socioeconomic class.

For present purposes we are focusing on the aged as a population group, not on aging as a process. We are employing the arbitrary chronological definition of "old age" or "aged" considered standard for much of the industrialized world; that is, that the chronological age of 65 or over represents old age. However, age 60 and over is used by the Older Americans Act as an eligibility criterion for certain programs and for allotment of federal funds among the states; age 55 is used by other sources (early retirement, etc.) to describe the older American; and the Anti-Discrimination Act uses 40 and over to describe older workers.

Thus, aging may be defined as a chronological category (65 and over) or as a physiological degenerative process. It may be defined operationally as that age at which functional limitations occur on physical mobility (e.g., the inability to climb stairs, to walk rapidly). In an economic context it may be defined as that age at which retraining for new skills does not pay the company (in terms of expected future employment) for the costs of retraining; or the age at which it is not cost-effective to hire an older worker because the expected length of future employment will not compensate adequately for the costs to the company of extending private pension benefits. Or it may be defined socially as that age when one exits permanently from the labor force, retires, and loses the status which comes from being gainfully occupied.

In viewing this whole group, it is essential that certain factors be kept in mind. First, the aged are not a single, homogeneous group. Chronologically they represent three distinct categories: the "young" elderly, those 74 and under; the "middle-aged" elderly, those between the ages of 75 and 84; and the "old" elderly, those 85 and over. In many ways those under 70 are more like the 55–65 group than those over 75. Second, and even more important, the primary differentiation of needs among the aged is a reflection of functional impairment more than anything else. Thus the aged may be categorized, or dichotomized, as those who are relatively active and those who are relatively inactive, a difficult distinction to make but one with obvious implications for service provision. (An alternative typology would categorize the aged into those who are active, those who are retired but well-functioning, and those who are retired and incapacitated.) Third, although as a group they are defined as a population at risk, for some the risk is greater than for others. Among the most vulnerable, regardless of whether the risk is poverty, physical or psychological impairment, or social isolation, or a combination of all three, are woman; minority group members, in particular blacks; the single and widowed; the very old.

Finally,

> the aging phase of life brings into sharp focus the interlocking of physical health, mental health, social, economic and environmental factors. For example, living arrangements are qualified by health, income, and family structure; mental and physical health are highly correlated; the capacity to function at a decent level of health and well-being depends on the availability of services, which in turn reflect broad social policies and legislative enactments. The interweaving of these factors and the difficulties in sorting them out have complicated the task. . . . It is clear, however, that the elderly are at higher risk than the younger populations. The nature and number of their dependencies are beyond voluntary and family resources, requiring public support.[2]

Characteristics of the Aged

In 1974, of the 22 million Americans aged 65 and over, most were under 75 (62 percent).[3] Half were under 73 and one-third under 70. The fastest-growing group among the elderly are those aged 75 and over. In 1900, the proportion over 75 was 29 percent, by 1970 this proportion had risen to 38 percent; and current estimates project 43 percent of the aged to be over 75 by the year 2000. More than 1.7 million Americans are 85 years of age or over.

Average life expectancy at birth (based on 1973 death rates) is 71.3 years for the total population, 67.6 for men and 75.3 for women. In 1900 the average life expectancy was 49 and in 1955 it was 69.5 years. In the past twenty years, average life expectancy at birth has barely changed. Although the chance of survival from birth to age 65 and the chance of survival from 65 to 80 are both much higher than in 1900, most of the increase in life expectation results from decreased infant and child mortality. Average life expectancy at age 65 has moved slowly from 12 years in 1900 to 15.3 years in 1973 (13.1 years for men and 17.2 for women). A medical breakthrough in the treatment or cure of the major causes of mortality at later ages (e.g., cardiovascular-renal disease) would expand longevity and increase the future size of the aged population in this country.

Most older people (12.8 million or 58 percent) are women. Forty years ago the proportion of men and women over 65 was about equal, while today there are 143 women for every 100 men. This proportion increases with age until in the 85 and older group there is a sex ratio of two women for every man.

Most older men are married (79 percent) and live with their wives; most older women are widows (52 percent) and live alone. There are four times as many widows as widowers. Among the several factors that explain this percentage, the principal ones are the higher mortality rates of men, the fact that men tend to be several years older than their wives, and the higher remarriage rates of widowers who may as readily take as wives women under 65 as over. As an illustration of this, 40 percent of married older men have wives under 65.

While the black population constitutes more than 11 percent of the total population, the black aged constitute only 7 percent of the total aged, a reflection of shorter life expectancy. Among older blacks, as among all the aged, women outnumber men.

In 1973, some 3.4 million or about 16.3 percent of the elderly were living in households with incomes below the official poverty threshold. In 1974, the median income for families with heads over 65 continued to be a little less than half the median income for younger families ($6,426 vs. $12,935).

The aged spend proportionally more on food, shelter, and medical care than other age groups, and they have the additional burden of living on reduced fixed incomes after retirement. The cost of medical care, the most expensive item for the aged, has risen sharply in recent years. Once the aged poor retire, they are likely to remain poor. Others who have adequate income prior to retirement may become progressively more impoverished as the cost of living increases, their expenses rise, and they are unable to obtain additional income. Although the percentage of aged poor in the United States increased for a substantial period of time (15.1 percent in 1959; 18.2 percent in 1968; 19.7 percent in 1969; 21.0 percent in 1971), in the past few years it has been decreasing as a result of increases in Social Security benefits.

Elderly women have always been the most economically vulnerable of the aged poor. The combined effects of job discrimination, lower social security benefits, and jobs with no pensions or minimal ones have exacerbated this condition. Nearly one half of all women aged 65 and over living alone or with nonrelatives subsist on incomes under $2,642 a year.

Similarly, aged blacks tend to be among the most impoverished. The likelihood that a nonwhite minority group member over 65 will be poor is twice as great as for the white aged and four times as great as for the total U.S. population. At a time when 16.3 percent of all aged live in poverty, 37.1 percent of the blacks are poor (as contrasted with 14.4 percent of the whites).

In general, older persons receive less than half the income and are twice as likely to live in poverty as their younger fellow-citizens. Clearly, the sex and race of a family head or individual are determining factors in the poverty status of families. Unattached or unrelated women over 65, black women more than white, and black-headed families, as well as all of those people over the age of 75, may be defined as the population at greatest risk of poverty.

Most elderly (82 percent) function well although as a group they constitute the most disabled and impaired segment of the population. Although illness, disability rates, hospital utilization (frequency and length of stay), and physicians' visits rise sharply with advancing age, only slightly under 5 percent are institutionalized (generally defined as chronic hospitals, psychiatric hospitals, chronic disease and nursing home units of general hospitals, homes for the aged, and nursing homes). Of those living in the community, about 8 percent are housebound and another 6 percent have limited mobility. It is the very old (those over 80), women, the single and widowed, and the poorest who suffer most from severe physical and psychological impairment.

Chronic illnesses are most characteristic of this age group as a whole and 80 percent of those over 65 have at least one chronic condition while one-half have two or more.

Medical costs have gone up twice as fast as the cost of living and hospital costs five times as fast. Out-of-pocket, per capita direct payments for medical treatment of the aged are higher now than they were before Medicare began (and this figure does not include the Part B premium charge).* The average health care expenditure for a person 65 or over in fiscal year 1974 was $1,218, 3.7 times the $330 spent for each person under 65. Of this amount, almost half went for hospital care. Older people represent 10 percent of the population but account for 30 percent of the health care expenditures. Of the health care costs for older persons, 60 percent came from public resources (a percentage that has been decreasing in recent years). Medicare covered 38 percent of the total costs per older person, reflecting a continuation of the decreasing role of Medicare also.

In 1974, about 22 percent of the elderly men and 8 percent of the women were in the labor force. Of these, most were classified in one of three low-earning categories, part time, agriculture, or self-employed. In general there is a declining trend in labor-force participation of men that begins at age 55 and accelerates after 65. While this is also true of women, overall labor-force participation for women aged 55–64 has risen over time from 27 percent in 1950 to 43 percent in 1971 and an anticipated 47 percent in 1980.

Elderly persons tend to be most numerous in the largest states. New York, California, Pennsylvania, Florida, Illinois, Texas, and Ohio each contains more than one million people over the age of 65; and together they account for one half of this population group.

*Nominal dollars only. This does not take into account inflation and the rapid increase in prices during these years; nor does it reflect the fact that in spite of this the aged are getting much more health care than before. Personal expenditures for medical care now serve a supplemental function.

One quarter lives in just three states (New York, California, and Pennsylvania). Arizona, Florida, Nevada, Hawaii, and New Mexico have had the most rapid rate of increase in the numbers of aged living in their states over the past decade. Those states having the highest percentage of elderly (over 12 percent) tend to be either those states with favorable climates to which the elderly migrate on retirement (e.g., Florida, with an estimated 15.8 percent 65 and over in 1974), or those midwestern states from which young people have migrated in large numbers leaving large concentrations of elderly behind. Of the 20.1 million people over 65 in 1970, over half (55 percent) lived in urban areas and most of these lived in central cities. Only about one quarter (27 percent) lived in rural areas.

Nearly 80 percent of the men and 60 percent of the women 65 and over were members of family units in 1974, and most men were family heads. Another 15 percent of the men and 36 percent of the women occupied their own houses or apartments alone or with nonrelatives. Thus, contrary to the popular view, about 95 percent of all elderly live in their own households and slightly less than 5 percent live in institutions—nursing facilities or long-term care facilities. However, rates of institutionalization do rise with age and for those over 75 the percentage in institutions rises to 6 percent for men and 8.1 percent for women (and an enormous 17.7 percent for those over the age of 85, 13.5 percent for men and 20.8 percent for women). Moreover, the 5 percent figure is deceptive, as one widely published report indicates; "While one in 20 seniors is in a nursing home or related facility on any given day, one out of five seniors will spend some time in a nursing home during a life time."[4]

Framework for Provision

It is generally accepted that although 5 percent of the aged currently reside in institutions some percentage of these might not if adequate provision existed in the community. Furthermore, 17 percent of those living in the community suffer from severe impairments and maintenance at home is dependent on a wide range of provisions including community facilities, services, programs, and so forth. Yet before looking at general social service benefits and programs that permit and facilitate the maintenance of the elderly in a community, we must examine the overall context of provision to meet essential needs. What exists in the basic areas of income maintenance, health services, housing, employment—those programs which provide the essential underpinnings of general social service provision? No services can possibly substitute for adequacy of provision in these areas, which are so critical in meeting the basic needs of all people.

Policy and Legislation

The two most important laws affecting the aged are the Social Security Act (1935) with its numerous amendments and, of much less significance thus far, the Older Americans Act (1965) and its amendments. The most important provisions of these laws are summarized below.

Although the first public provision by the states of old age pensions dates from 1915, these never provided adequate retirement coverage; they were means-tested and at best were enacted only by twenty-eight states. National concern for the aged was not a matter of public policy until 1935, when the *Social Security Act* was passed in the context of a severe depression. This landmark federal legislation defined the parameters of national policy and provision for the aged for almost three decades. It established a compulsory system of old age insurance for workers in commerce and industry, financed by a payroll tax paid equally by employers and employees, to pay benefits to retired workers only, at age 65, provided they were retired (as measured by earnings in covered employment). Among its specific provisions for the elderly the Social Security Act also authorized grants to state programs (the categorical program of Old Age Assistance) to share costs of financial aid, medical care, and social services to needy older people (those meeting specified standards of financial eligibility).

Amendments passed since then have modified and expanded the original bill. Thus, coverage is far more extensive today than initially (90 percent of those in paid employment are covered); benefits were expanded to include survivors and dependents; benefit levels have been increased; increased amounts of earnings are allowed before affecting benefits; a lower age is permitted for retirement at reduced benefits (62); benefits are assured for those covered who are aged 72 or more, regardless of level of earned income or participation in covered employment; benefits are adjusted in accordance with changes in the consumer price index; contributory taxes have increased.

Perhaps the most noteworthy amendments were the passage in 1962 of a program of medical assistance to the aged, in 1965 of Medicare, and in 1973 of Supplemental Security Income (SSI). The Social Security Amendments of 1965—Medicare—provided a national system of health insurance for the elderly. This legislation provided partial coverage of the costs of hospital and related care for Social Security beneficiaries aged 65 and over (and persons not so entitled who reached 65 before 1968) together with a voluntary contributory program to help meet the costs of physicians' services. The hospital insurance program is financed through a separate payroll tax and trust fund with a general revenue contribution for costs for uninsured individuals, while the voluntary medical program is financed half by the individual participant and half by the federal government out of general revenues. Also in 1965, the Congress passed Medicaid, a means-tested medical assistance program, which in effect has filled in some of the gaps for the low-income aged who do not have funds to supplement Medicare or are not covered.

The year 1973 saw the passage of the most recent landmark legislation as an amendment to the Social Security Act, effective January 1, 1974; this is a new program of income maintenance for aged, blind, and disabled persons with limited income and resources (SSI). This legislation covers all those elderly previously covered by the categorical program of public assistance, Old Age Assistance (OAA), as well as all those eligible for that program but not covered. The law also provides for state supplementation, assuring those who would receive less under SSI than previously under OAA that the state would provide the differential required to maintain that level. However, as SSI benefits increase, there is no requirement that states must continue this same differential rate; several states nevertheless have provided additional supplementation voluntarily. SSI is administered by the Social Security Administration and funds come from general tax revenues supplemented by state funds as indicated.

Title XX, an amendment to the Social Security Act, was passed in 1974. Replacing various social service titles, it includes provision for certain social services to the "needy" or poor elderly as defined within the states, within specified income limits.

Earlier, the year 1965 saw the passage of one other major legislative enactment affecting the elderly: the *Older Americans Act*. For the first time, there was created a central administrative office within the federal government concerned with the aged, the Administration on Aging (AoA) in DHEW. Its purpose was to make funds available to states to assist local governmental agencies and nonprofit organizations in implementing such activities as coordination of service planning and delivery; advocacy; development of information, referral, and counseling services; establishment of research and demonstration projects; and the training of personnel working in the field of the aging. Although it is a universal program, the primary focus was on funding demonstration projects; no real service coverage was authorized (or intended). Amendments passed in 1973 subsequently modified and expanded provisions of the Act, for the first time including provision for local level planning and for somewhat more extensive coverage by a specialized nutrition (feeding) program.

Other relevant legislation includes the Railroad Retirement Act of 1935, providing retirement payments similar in nature to provisions under the Social Security Act; Department of Defense and Federal Civil Service employee retirement; the National Housing Act, which includes special provisions for housing the elderly; legislation authorizing distribution of food stamps on a means-tested basis, by the Department of Agriculture; 1967 amendments to the Economic Opportunity Act, authorizing new programs of senior opportunities and services, emergency food, and medical services for the elderly poor; and provision of special tax relief for the aged (e.g., double exemptions on federal income tax for all years beginning at age 65).

Programs and Benefits

Cash Income Support Programs

Provision of income, directly or indirectly, is the dominant program strategy employed by the federal government with regard to the elderly. Well over 95 percent of federal expenditures for the aged are for Social Security, retirement, income supplement, and health programs. And the overwhelming proportion of these outlays are from the so-called trust funds—the payroll taxes contributed to equally by employer and employee (or self-employed) during working years. (At the rate of 11.7 percent on the first $14,100 in earned income, about 85 percent of all workers in covered employment have all earnings taxed;[5] and this percentage is by plan to be maintained as salaries rise.) It is these trust funds which finance the Social Security program, whose cash benefit program is by far the single most important federal program providing income for the aged (as well as survivors and disabled). In 1974, 91 percent of all the people 65 and over were protected under this form of social insurance and another 4 percent of the population was covered under other federal retirement systems (e.g., railroad pension, civil service); only 5 percent of the aged are without some form of protection from the federal government in retirement pensions.

Social Security is a universal social insurance program providing cash income to all eligible regardless of financial need and administered by the Social Security Administration, a separate government agency under DHEW. It constitutes the economic mainstay for the vast majority of older Americans. More than two-thirds of the retired single workers and one-half of all retired couples depend upon Social Security for more than 50 percent of their income. These benefits are almost the sole means of support (over 90 percent of total income) for 30 percent of the retired workers and 15 percent of elderly couples.[6] Between December 1969 and June 1974, Social Security benefits have been boosted by 68.5 percent, each increase eliminating some percentage of aged from the poverty rolls. As of June 1974, monthly benefits for beneficiaries ranged as follows: minimum, retired worker alone, $93.80; maximum, retired worker alone, $304.90; minimum, retired couple, $140.80; maximum, retired couple, $457.40. In addition, since 1975, Social Security benefits automatically reflect cost-of-living adjustments. Finally, the Social Security law ignores the first $2,400 of annual earnings from employment for beneficiaries under age 72 and, thereafter, deducts one dollar from benefits for each two dollars of earnings. This so-called retirement of earnings test is not applied for beneficiaries aged 72 or over.[7]

Regardless, in 1974 more than 3.3 million older Americans still had incomes below the poverty line ($2,352 for a single person; $2,958 for a couple).* Although this group is composed primarily

*This does not include an unknown amount of hidden poverty among the elderly. About one half of the million aged in institutions are estimated to be poor. Almost 2 million more aged persons are usually described as poor but not classified as such because they live in families with incomes above the poverty threshold. In addition to the over 5 million poor elderly, about another 6 million have incomes below the level of the Bureau of Labor Statistics intermediate budget.

of nonbeneficiaries of social insurance, it also includes almost 2 million people receiving minimum or low Social Security benefits. As of January 1, 1974, the federal program providing income maintenance for this group is Supplemental Security Income (SSI). This public assistance program, implemented as a result of a 1973 amendment to the Social Security Act, provides the first system for federally guaranteed incomes specifically for the aged, blind, and disabled and replaces the earlier categorical program of public assistance for the aged, Old Age Assistance, that had been in effect since 1935.

The number of people receiving Old Age Assistance (OAA) gradually decreased from 22 percent of the aged in 1950 to about 9 percent in 1973 (1.8 million), while the number on Social Security increased. SSI, effective January 1, 1974, is a selective or means-tested public assistance program, now providing a federal basic payment of $146 per month for individuals and $219 for couples to financially needy aged, blind, and disabled. It is financed from general revenues, administered by the Social Security Administration, and has an automatic cost-of-living adjustment built in. Asset and family responsibility rules and regulations are more flexible than those which prevailed under OAA.

Coupled with this federal program is a state supplemental program by which those states previously paying higher benefits to OAA recipients are required to continue to do so by the federal government and additional supplementation is encouraged by a federal guarantee that state expenditures for supplementation will not be higher than for 1972; the federal government picks up any additional cost incurred as a result of the anticipated increase in the numbers of SSI beneficiaries. It was projected that as a result of the absence of stigma attached to Social Security provision and the less restrictive provisions of SSI than those of many state OAA programs (no residence requirements, no relative responsibility, income and asset level of disallowance raised), approximately 3 million more aged would be covered by SSI than the 2 million previously receiving payments under OAA. Thus far take-up of this benefit has not reached the anticipated figures and totaled only 2.3 million aged recipients as of September 1975 (of the 4.2 million total SSI recipients).

Other Sources of Cash Income

Although no current figures are available with regard to the role played by earnings from employment, income from assets, and private pension payments to older persons, data from earlier years suggest that earnings represent the most important source, with private pensions and assets contributing comparatively minor sums. Although private pension plan payments are important supplements to such recipients, they cover only a very small percentage of the elderly. Adequacy of benefit levels, length of employment with a single employer, and limitations on categories of jobs covered continue to restrict the importance of private pensions as a source of income to many of the aged. About 35 million persons, only half the employees of private industry, work in jobs covered at present by some private employee benefit plan. Landmark private pension legislation was passed in 1974, designed to encourage the growth of private pension and welfare plans; ensure coverage and vesting rights within a reasonable period of time; provide greater equity in the tax treatment of private retirement savings among the taxpayer group involved; and guarantee against default through reinsurance.

Noncash Income Support Programs

Federal Nutrition and Food Programs. The need for a national food program for the elderly has been documented by the great number of aged who suffer from hunger and malnutrition. Those who are poor cannot afford a nutritionally balanced diet, even if they are knowledgeable about nutrition; many of those who are not poor lack knowledge and motivation for adequate nutrition. (A 1969 study commissioned by DHEW reported that one out of four elderly persons ate fewer than three meals per day and 88 percent of the diets were nutritionally inadequate.) Title VII (1973) of the Older Americans Act is explicitly designed to provide the elderly, especially the poor and minority, "with low cost, nutritionally sound meals." The states receive funds in proportion to the number of elderly residing in their state and, in turn, award grants to applicants within their priority geographic areas (those with high concentrations of low-income and minority elderly). Projects in these areas are supposed to establish congregate meal sites; a small number of home-delivered meals (e.g., meals on wheels) may also be provided in coordination with a congregate meal site, if it is deemed necessary to meet the needs of the bedridden and home bound. This is a universal program; individuals eligible are those 60 and over who may decide for themselves what they can pay for a meal, since no means test is required.

Appropriations for this program, administered by the Administration on Aging, were $99.6 million in 1974. The program was designed to serve a maximum of 250,000 meals daily to the elderly. Because of increased costs, it served only 220,000 in 1974.

The Food Stamps and Commodity Distribution Program, a USDA program, also provides income supplementation in the form of a food benefit to the elderly. Figures are not broken down to indicate the number of recipients who are elderly; however, the agency estimates that of the 15 million beneficiaries in 1973, about 10 percent were over 65, and about 14 percent were 60 and over. It is the Food Stamp Program which is by far the most important component. The dollar value of the food stamps is fixed, but eligibility as well as payment are directly related to income.*

Health. It is generally recognized that genuine retirement income security can never be achieved as long as heavy and unpredictable health costs threaten fixed incomes. Although Medicare is often described as the major federal program relieving most older Americans of the major burden of financial catastrophe resulting from acute illness, it is in reality a prepaid funding device, similar to the provision of social insurance, for the payment of part of hospital costs for the aged, financed by a payroll tax on earnings paid by employer and employee, and a supplementary, voluntary medical (e.g., physician's services) insurance program, paid for individually with matching contributions from the government out of general revenue.

However, even when these two parts of Medicare are put together, several important items that are part of the total health costs for people 65 and over are still left uncovered. This is what accounts for Medicare's reimbursing less than half the total health expenses of older persons. Among the items not covered are the following: out-of-hospital prescription drugs; long stays in nursing homes (or any stay except after hospitalization); dental care; eyeglasses; hearing aids. These exclusions, combined with the cost of deductibles and coinsurance, leave a large gap in the coverage of health care for the aged. Finally, Medicare is essentially insurance against acute

*In 1974, this 15 million total figure jumped to 20 million; however, there still are no precise figures regarding the aged. For more detail on this program see Kenneth Schlossberg, "Funny Money Is Serious," *The New York Times Magazine*, Sept. 28, 1975.

short-term illness, requiring hospitalization and/or institutionalization. It does not provide for preventive medical care, which remains the responsibility of the elderly themselves, nor does it provide for home care, except in very limited amounts under specialized circumstances (e.g., skilled nursing, less than 100 visits per year on referral by a physician after institutional care).

In addition, Medicaid, Title XIX of SSA, provides funding for certain types of health care for the financially needy not covered by Medicare. Funding for this program is provided by a matching mechanism from the general revenues of the federal government with a portion of the funding from state government revenues. (The federal government reimburses the states at a rate that ranges from 50 to 83 percent, depending on per capita state income.) Eligibility criteria and the extent of coverage under Medicaid vary from state to state but in general are at the public-assistance eligibility level or slightly above it. At best, both Medicare and Medicaid are limited programs; moreover, costs to participants in Medicare have continued to rise.

About half the people over 65 have private health insurance giving supplementary protection. Blue Cross and Blue Shield, the largest private insurance plan, provides coverage designed to fill in the gaps of Medicare for those over 65. Other commercial insurance exists also, some providing adequate coverage, some not.

As indicated above, Medicare tends to cover short-term stays in such facilities as hospitals and nursing homes fairly adequately, but not long-term stays. Long-term institutional care is available only for the financially needy under Medicaid. In each case, provision is for payment of care; direct provision of such care is through voluntary (nonprofit) and proprietary (profit-making) organizations. Since 1972, uniform standards are used for the purpose of defining what a "skilled nursing home" is (previously termed "extended care facility"). For other aged persons not needing around-the-clock nursing care and the other mandatory services provided by "skilled nursing homes" but unable to manage completely independently (in effect, needing more than room and board but less than skilled nursing), Intermediate Care Facilities (now termed "Health Related Facilities"), less expensive than nursing homes, have been developed; these are also covered by Medicaid.

One major problem for the elderly requiring such care is that in 1973 the average cost of nursing home care was $600 per month (and these costs have risen substantially since then), while the average social security income for retired individuals, even in 1974, was still under $200 per month. Long waiting lists exist for high-quality, voluntary, nonprofit, long-term institutions.

Finally, although national policy explicitly states that the health care needs of the elderly should be met first in one's home, with institutionalization offered only in extreme situations, home health agencies are declining in number and many others face serious financial problems; Medicare and Medicaid erect barriers to the development of home health services; less than one percent of Medicare expenditures go into home health care, and that figure has been declining.

Housing. In the past, federal programs designed to satisfy the housing needs of the elderly consisted primarily of efforts at increasing the supply of housing available. Thus, under the auspices of HUD were programs for the direct provision of low-rent public housing; and Farmers Home Administration (U.S. Department of Agriculture) provided low-interest loans for housing construction for rental purposes and improvement. To a much lesser extent, subsidies and supplements have also been provided. In 1972, 70,385 housing units for the elderly were authorized by HUD.

In 1973, however, a major curtailment in housing construction for the aged occurred. All federal programs providing housing for the aged were either terminated, or funds were frozen or impounded. In 1973 one HUD official estimated that between 400,000 and 500,000 nonsubsidized units could be sold to the elderly on a yearly basis, if they were specially designed for their needs (e.g., provide for physical safety from violence and accident, health care, availability of nursing and medical services, personal care, meals, and recreational services). If subsidies were included it was estimated that the demand might be for twice that amount.

The 1974 Housing Act provided a partial return to subsidized housing. It places primary stress on an expanded subsidized-leasing program in addition to including some provision for flexible "block grants" for conventional public housing (including congregate housing for the aged).

Specialized and innovative publicly funded demonstration housing projects do exist in limited numbers. Similarly, specialized housing for the aged and giant leisure villages for the aged complete with golf clubs, swimming pools, hobby shops, and the like are also available, designed and constructed by private commercial enterprises for the more affluent among the elderly. But little is available for the poor or working-class retirees.

Tax Benefits. Persons who arrive at age 65 are permitted double exemptions on their federal income tax for that year and each subsequent year. Some state income tax laws permit similar double exemptions. No federal property tax relief program exists at present; however, some states and communities do provide property tax relief for low-income elderly and some provide tax credits to eligible elderly renters. Unfortunately, such benefits are neither uniform nor adequate, and the income level for eligibility is very low. Since aged homeowners pay on the average more than 8 percent of their incomes for real estate taxes (almost three times that paid by the typical urban family of four), additional relief is essential.

Occupational Programs (Paid and Volunteer). As societal forces have undermined the role and status of the elderly, the federal government has stepped in with programs to compensate for the negative effect on the elderly population. The purpose of these programs is to increase the "supply" of societal roles available for the elderly. Two approaches are employed in these programs, all of which are very small in scale. First are means-tested programs providing reimbursement at minimum wage levels for socially purposeful activities by the elderly poor. (Most served in these programs are under 65, however.) Included among these are Foster Grandparents (part time, one-to-one care by the elderly of an institutionalized child), Green Thumb (employment of retired farmers three days a week to beautify public areas), and Senior Community Aides (elderly people working twenty hours a week in the areas of child care, homemaker services, etc.). Second, and the primary effort addressed to those over 65, are programs providing volunteer activities for the aged. Among these are SCORE (Service Corps of Retired Executives, offering the professional advice of retired businessmen), RSVP (Retired Senior Volunteer Program, encouraging the aged to use their many skills in community services), and VISTA (a program hiring the aged, among others, to work in poverty areas in the United States, as the Peace Corps does in foreign countries).

Most of these programs are directed to middle-class professionals and managerial retirees. Few (except for RSVP and VISTA) have outreach programs to publicize their activities. Funding for these programs is limited and the numbers served are small.

Considering the limited scale and coverage of federal programs providing occupational roles and services for the aged, it is worth noting that some present federal policy seems inadvertently to detract from meaningful social roles for the elderly. Employment for the purpose of earning income is probably the major source of role and need satisfaction for adults. Yet the liberalization of eligibility rules in social security provision encourages premature termination of the work role. Thus, more than 50 percent of all Social Security beneficiaries are receiving reduced benefits for early retirement (age 62). Although 22 percent of all males over 65 are in the labor force, this is a steadily decreasing number.

Social Services. Before a more extensive discussion of social service benefits, it is worth repeating that the federal government's major strategy with regard to the aged has been to provide income and/or income supplementation, either directly through cash programs or indirectly through payment of hospital and medical care (or tax benefits or other noncash benefits such as food or subsidized housing). Approximately $56 billion in federal expenditures went for the aged in fiscal year 1973. (This is generally considered an overestimate; however, the following proportions are the same even if the overall estimate is lower.) Of this, $54 billion went for income programs, while only $1.8 billion at most went for all other programs, less than 4 percent of the total of overall federal expenditures for the needs of the aged. By far the largest program in this category is the means-tested service program for needy aged, administered by SRS (DHEW) as authorized under the Social Security Act. Approximately $439 million was spent for social services to all adults under this program,[8] and of this about 60 percent ($260 million) was for services to the aged.

From 1962, Title XVI (grants to states for aid to the aged, blind, or disabled or for medical assistance to the needy aged) enabled states to operate a combined adult program. In January 1974, with the advent of SSI, Title XVI addressed the cash assistance program only, and Title VI covered the adult service program. Although about 40 percent of the states adopted Title XVI, the remainder continued to provide services to the aged through the other adult titles (I, IV, X, XIV). These services are provided by the states, funded out of general revenue through a combination of federal and state funds in a ratio of 75:25.

In January 1975, Title XX of the Social Security Act replaced all the earlier titles providing means-tested services (IV-A, VI) to adults and children. Where the elderly are concerned, Title XX requires that state services plans include at least three services for

SSI recipients (only one category of whom are elderly). More may be included if the state plan so indicates. Different services may be made available to the elderly in different areas of the state, if the plan so specifies. Moreover, the elderly population served may include those up to 115 percent of the national median income. Services may be provided free for people up to 80 percent of median income, but fees must be charged for those between 80 and 115 percent of national median income.

Of much less importance are the services provided under the Older Americans Act, primarily by project grants from AoA to the states (who in turn make grants to the localities, which then fund projects). Most of the direct service provision included here is to research and demonstration projects which are few in number, small in scale, and addressed to the "needy aged," the most vulnerable population group; these services are not means tested.

With regard to expenditures for services to the aged, as of the end of 1974, DHEW was unable to provide a categorical breakdown by state for expenditures by categories and amounts received by elderly recipients. Moreover, at present, there are no expenditure figures available from the states that would indicate the extent to which the states fund services for the aged.

There is also a wide range of social service programs provided by the voluntary sector. However, no figures indicate the numbers of programs that exist, the numbers of people served, or the dollar amount involved.

Agencies and Organizations

Governmental Agencies

The single department whose policies have the greatest impact on the elderly is DHEW. Included within it are the two agencies responsible for the major income-support programs: SSA, in charge of social insurance programs, Old Age, Survivors Disability and Health Insurance (OASDHI), and Supplemental Security Income (SSI); and SRS, responsible for administering Medicaid and AFDC programs and Title XX, the social services program. In addition, under OHD is AoA, the planning and policy-making body directed exclusively toward serving the aging, and the Federal Council on Aging, a special advisory committee established to influence policy-making within the executive and legislative branches of the federal government. There is also, within the National Institute on Health, a National Institute on Aging, specifically concerned with research and training related to the needs and problems of the aged.

Outside of the executive branch of government, the single most important organization influencing policy and program development for the aged is the U.S. Senate Special Committee on Aging. Established as a separate unit in 1961, this committee has been an increasingly powerful advocate for the elderly within Congress and the government generally. It publishes an annual report on developments in aging, as well as numerous special reports of hearings and studies.*

Apart from these major bodies, there continue to exist an incredible number and variety of agencies scattered within the federal government that directly affect the elderly American. In fact, approximately twenty agencies have statutory responsibility for programs and services for the aging and aged, and dozens of additional federal operations have considerable, if indirect, relevance. Of course, most programs funded by the federal government are in fact administered and operated by state and local governmental bodies. In the area of income maintenance alone, at least seven agencies, in addition to DHEW, have relevant programs: The Railroad Retirement Board is responsible for social insurance programs for railroad employees and their families. The Civil Service Commission administers a public retirement, disability, and health benefit system for federal retirees. Retired veterans, their families, and dependents receive cash payments from the Veterans Administration (some of these contingent on disability, not just age). The Department of Labor supervises the administration of the federal-state unemployment insurance program. The Department of the Treasury administers special tax provisions for aged citizens. And the Food Stamp and Surplus Commodities Programs of the Department of Agriculture serve many aging persons.

Many agencies have programs related to employment of the older worker. The Department of Labor provides counseling, training programs, placement services, and grant programs for supported employment; the Office of Economic Opportunity initially developed

*The Special Committee on Aging is not a legislative committee. There is a separate legislative committee on aging in the Senate that considers and reports out on bills. This is the Subcommittee on Aging of the Senate Committee on Labor and Public Welfare. The House of Representatives also has two similar committees, one a legislative committee and the other an advisory and advocacy committee that holds hearings, the Select Committee on Aging.

special programs employing older poor persons (Foster Grandparent Programs, Project Find, and Green Thumb), and subsequently many of these programs have been taken over by Action and other agencies. The Rehabilitation Services Administration provides rehabilitative services and sheltered workshops for older handicapped workers, and sponsors various research and demonstration projects on helping the older disabled worker return to employment. The Administration on Aging supports several demonstration projects relating to older workers, and the Office of Education supports others in the area of vocational education.

DHEW administers the major health programs, and of prime importance to older people are Medicare, Medicaid, research on health of the aging through the National Institute of Health and the National Institute of Mental Health, food and drug protection, and rehabilitation services for the chronically ill. The Department of Housing and Urban Development provides mortgage insurance for construction of both proprietary and nonprofit nursing homes. Loans to privately owned hospitals, nursing homes, and other health facilities are made by the Small Business Administration. The Veterans Administration operates many medical care facilities directly and is particularly concerned with long-term care programs for older and chronically ill veterans as well as being active in research on aging. The health program for retired military personnel is supported by the Department of Defense, and the Civil Service Commission is responsible for all retirees who are covered by the Federal Employees Health Benefit Act. The Department of Agriculture, the Office of Economic Opportunity, and the Administration on Aging give attention to the nutrition of older people.

Both the Department of Agriculture and the Department of Housing and Urban Development administer programs to help meet the housing needs of older persons. In addition to low-rent public housing units, Housing and Urban Development has several other programs, including supplements that help provide a broader range of housing.

Some training of professional, semiprofessional, and technical personnel in the field of aging is supported by grants from the National Institute of Mental Health, the Office of Education, and the Administration on Aging.

The challenge of coordinating diverse government programs into sustained and comprehensive policies and operations is always difficult. But the proliferation and distribution of activities and responsibilities within the federal government requiring coordinaton to meet the needs of aging seem exceptional.

Nongovernmental Organizations

The major nongovernmental bodies may be included under the following two major categories.

The first are national organizations such as the Gerontological Society, National Council on Aging, American Association of Retired Persons, National Council of Senior Citizens. These organizations tend to be advocacy, lobbying, and pressure groups, focused on research and/or policy impact.

The second are sectarian and nonsectarian voluntary organizations, focused on direct service provision. Although overall expenditures for the voluntary sector for services to the aged are not known (data are not broken down in such a fashion), these organizations do play a major role in program implementation at the local level. They operate programs in one of three ways: by contract with local government bodies in order to implement SRS means-tested programs; by contracts or grants directly from the federal government, in particular AoA, to implement, administer, and/or operate demonstration projects; by direct funding, administering and operating of programs out of their own funds.

Benefits and Services

What special efforts does our society make to help older people remain decently in their own homes as long as they wish? To live comfortably in one's own home implies, first, a sufficiency of the basic necessities of life—food, shelter, clothing—and this means adequacy of income, housing, and, in this day and age, health services. If the so-called "hidden poor" are included, over 5 million, or one out of every four older Americans, have an income below the poverty threshhold. More than 50 percent of the aged have incomes that equal less than half the median income. SSI, the federal program that provides a guaranteed income for the poor aged, maintains a standard that is well below the poverty level for both individuals and couples. Clearly we have not achieved our national objective of "assuring an adequate income" to the aged.

We do not have precise figures on the percentage of aged among the total number of people who use food stamps. We do know, however, that many more elderly are eligible than take up this benefit, and that where congregate and home-delivered meals are concerned, federally funded programs serve only about one percent of the aged. An additional number (relatively small) are estimated to be served in programs operated by various voluntary agencies.

The costs of medical care have increased sharply in recent years. At the same time, the extent to which public programs—in particular Medicare—cover such costs has decreased sharply. In effect only about 40 percent of the average medical expenses of an older person are covered by Medicare. Per capita out-of-pocket payments for medical care are now actually higher than they were before Medicare began. And despite the high costs of in-patient care in acute care facilities, the number of home health agencies have continued to decline because Medicare reimbursement policies inhibit the use of such services.

There is extraordinarily little that has been provided in the way of special housing for the elderly, and what little efforts there were in the past have decreased in recent years. Most estimates indicate that the current demand for such housing is very high, for both subsidized and unsubsidized specially designed living arrangements.

Clearly the necessities of life are not yet provided for the elderly, and insufficiencies in these areas have obvious consequences: inadequate income may lead to malnutrition and to health problems; inadequacies in health insurance coverage may lead to poverty; inadequacies in health services may result in institutionalization. And so forth. As we said earlier, no services can possibly substitute for adequacy of provision in the basic areas.

Yet 95 percent of the elderly still live in their own homes. Eighty percent of the men live in family settings, and 75 percent live with their wives. Sixty percent of the women live with their families, although only one-third live with their husbands. More than one-third of the women live completely alone or with nonrelatives. We know already that most of them are poor. Their homes are rarely designed for the special safety needs or comfort of old and frail people. Their Medicare insurance does not cover enough of their health care needs, and health services are inadequate. How then do they manage as well as they do? What do we provide that in some way alleviates these problems and provides support for older people living at home? What, if any, help, care, and services make this possible and how extensive is such aid? Who uses these services and how much do they cost?

Housing

Housing for the elderly includes a broad spectrum of living arrangements: single, detached, dispersed dwellings; apartments, condominiums, cooperatives; retirement hotels, boarding and personal service homes, and other similar congregate types of structures; multiservice homes for the aged; and specially planned retirement communities. Although chronic hospitals, long-term care wards of general hospitals, nursing homes, and health-related facilities provide shelter for the aged, their major purpose is to provide medical care; thus, they are better considered among the health facilities than with the community-based living arrangements serving the aged.

Yet meeting the housing needs of the elderly—and the availability of suitable housing for them—may determine whether they live independently or in an institution; whether they live in isolation or with friends and kin nearby; whether they live in safety or in danger. In addition to quantitative inadequacies in housing, there is also a problem of qualitative inadequacy. Poor housing may refer to inadequacy of the structure, lack of a congenial environment, isolation, inaccessibility to transportation and shopping. Much of the housing of the elderly has been described as substandard. Furthermore, the distribution of special housing for the elderly bears little or no relationship to the numbers of older people in the states; and the distribution among communities and localities within a state is equally haphazard. Finally, where such housing is located depends solely on the interest of the individual builder or organization. No overall planning for housing of the elderly by public, private nonprofit, and private profit sponsors exists. The total number of specially designed, multifamily public housing units for the elderly that were occupied, under construction, or approved as of 1973 was 452,414. Subsequently, funds were frozen for new housing construction and programs terminated. Although there has been some limited return to subsidized housing, little has been initiated since then and waiting lists for all such housing are very long.

There have been some innovative developments arising from demonstration projects funded by AoA. For example, the Gerontological Institute of the Philadelphia Geriatric Center built "intermediate housing" in Philadelphia that offers residence in nine small row houses in living arrangements between complete independence on the one hand and institutional care on the other. The houses, situated near the Center, were converted into small apartments to accommodate twenty-seven to thirty-six people. Three or four tenants live in each apartment. The rent, set within the context of social security and SSI benefits, includes building maintenance, janitor service, utilities, and heavy cleaning. Tenants bring their own furniture, and other services, as needed, can be made available from the Center.

In another experimental project, medium to large sized houses are used in a similar manner, establishing cooperative living arrangements known as "affiliated housing" containing groups of elderly unrelated people who agree to share household expenses, duties, and responsibilities in these houses.

To the extent that there is any "major model," considering the limited existence of public provision, it is the congregate housing concept which is currently defined as the most viable, providing a community resource for its own residents as well as other old people living in adjacent neighborhoods.[9] Such housing may be one of two types: congregate housing providing food and personal service; or housing for wholly independent living with recreational and activity programs. In neither type is medical care integrated into the housing, although proximity to such care and ready availability of medical and health services generally would be considered essential to both. (Even if such facilities are available, however, many people will continue to prefer to live in their own homes, either alone or with children or relatives.)

Whether in congregate housing or in ordinary living arrangements, in personal care facilities or in independent apartments, continuity and adequacy of such arrangements are often dependent on a panoply of services or care arrangements termed the personal social services. It is this group of services to which we now direct our attention.

Social Services

Federal provision of social services to the aged dates primarily from the 1962 Amendments to the Social Security Act. Not only did these amendments encourage provision of service to the aged, but they expanded eligibility criteria through regulations permitting former and potential welfare recipients as well as present recipients to receive services (and the categories of former and potential recipients were loosely defined). The primary purpose of the Act's social service program for adults was to reduce dependency and promote opportunity for independent living and self-support. (And this objective is still among those specified in the most recent amendments—Title XX.) In the case of the elderly, this means services specifically intended to support a variety of living arrangements as alternatives to institutional care. The states were required to provide certain services while others were optional. Overall, there has been a large area of discretion at the state level, with regard to the extent and kinds of services which might be offered.

Mandatory services for the aged (also the blind and disabled) effective to October 1975 have included the following: information and referral without regard to eligibility for assistance; protective services; services to enable persons to remain in or to return to their homes or communities; supportive services that would contribute to a "satisfactory and adequate social adjustment of the individual"; and services to meet health needs.

Optional services which the state might elect to include encompassed three broad categories: services to individuals to improve their living arrangements and enhance activities of daily living; services to individuals and groups to improve opportunities for social and community participation; and services to individuals to meet special needs.

In October 1975, Title XX of the SSA, the new Social Services title, was implemented. In effect, a special revenue-sharing plan with states to provide social services defined and developed by the state, Title XX is devoted to the achievement of five goals: self-support; self-sufficiency; protection; prevention of institutionalization; facilitating institutionalization if and when community care is not viable. At least one service must be provided for each of these goals and at least three services must be provided for SSI recipients. Other than this, no other services are mandated for the aged. It is assumed that those interested groups representing the aged will play an active role (along with all other interest groups) in planning for program development and allocating and deploying the limited resources available.

The other federal program providing services to the aged, the Older Americans program, defines social services similarly, listing its six types as follows: health, continuing education, welfare, informational, recreational, homemaker, counseling, or referral services; transportation services where necessary to facilitate access to social services; services designed to encourage and assist older persons to use the facilities and services available to them; services designed to assist older persons to obtain adequate housing; services designed to assist older persons in avoiding institutionalization, including preinstitutionalization evaluation and screening, and home health services; or any other services if such services are necessary for the general welfare of older persons.

The amount of federal expenditures, administrative auspices, criteria for eligibility of recipients, and extent and extensiveness of coverage is what distinguishes these two major programs. Although other programs may be under different auspices, the definition of social services and the types provided are all relatively similar.

Approximately $260 million dollars were spent under the SRS program of services to the aged for fiscal year 1973; about 30 percent of Old Age Assistance recipients were receiving services (these figures are notoriously soft and no precise data exist). Under the Older Americans program, for fiscal 1974, approximately $84 million was available for area planning, social services, and demonstration projects and just under $100 million for a nutrition program (to be described below). Neither program in fact was adequate for "coverage" in any comprehensive sense.

Eligibility and Utilization

The major distinction in public service provision for the elderly is that some services are universal and some are selective. Services provided by SRS under Title XVI of the Social Security Act (and subsequently under Title XX) are selective, means-tested services. Financial need and age (65 and over) are the basic criteria for eligibility for these services. At present, all recipients of SSI plus an additional percentage of those with incomes under 80 percent of median income may be eligible for services. (Under Title XX, eligibility criteria may vary with the service.) No really firm data (dollars, services, number of recipients) exist with regard to service utilization by older people.

In contrast, services provided by programs under the Older Americans Act are universal and not means tested, although a deliberate effort is made to direct provision to communities in which the percentage of elderly "at risk" is highest (minorities, women, single). As much can be said about programs provided for the aged by the voluntary sector, which also tend to be universal.

In general, funding and extent of coverage of social service is limited and nowhere near adequate for the number needing and wanting them. For example, appropriate housing is largely unavailable to rural elderly poor who may be most in need, and available in only very limited quantity even for the urban poor; the major congregate meals program is designed to serve about one percent of the elderly (granted all these may neither need nor want the service, but the target population the program addresses is equal to at least 16 percent of the elderly); it is generally agreed that senior centers are overcrowded and haphazardly placed; reduced fare programs are heavily utilized but they exist in only about a hundred cities. Often, even where services may be available in the market, costs are prohibitive for the poor, the working class, and some times even the middle class. In contrast, in a number of metropolitan areas, free or reduced fare (50 percent) transportation on public transport is available to the elderly; and delivered or congregate meals may be free, priced at what the recipient wishes to pay, or offered at very low, below-cost levels.

Program Models

Services for the elderly living in their own homes can be divided into two categories: in-home services and out-of-home services.

In-Home Services

Regardless of the names of specific public or voluntary programs, in-home services are generally held to include any or all of the following: homemaker services, home health aides, chore services, delivered meals, telephone reassurance.

The major program model in this category is the *Homemaker–Home Health Aide Service*, which provides a combination of the first three services listed above. Homemaker services originated in the United States during the 1920s, and although there has been some expansion over the years, primarily since the passage of Medicare, such services (on occasion combined with health aid services) are still not extensive. Yet they are generally defined as critical, both as a preventive service and as a treatment service, in helping the aged live comfortably in their own homes.

Homemaker services are provided by mature, specially trained women with skills both as homemakers and in personal care. The function of this service is to "help maintain and preserve a family environment that is threatened with disruption by illness, death, ignorance, social maladjustment and other problems."[10] Homemakers can assume full or partial responsibility for child or adult care and household management. Services are supposed to be performed under the general supervision of a nurse, social worker, or other appropriate health professional. But the homemaker is neither a substitute for such professional personnel, nor is she a maid.

Home Health Aide Services is a term referring to personal care services for a patient and may be used to include some of the services performed by a homemaker. The term itself was first used in the Medicare Regulations to describe the services eligible for reimbursement under that program.

Among the types of duties performed by homemaker–home health aides are light housekeeping, light laundry, preparation and serving of meals, shopping, simple errands, teaching of household routine and skills to well members of the family, general supervision of the children of the patient where young children are involved.

Homemaker-health services tend to be either hospital based (hospital extending services into the community) or community based, with connections if and when needed to other services and institutions. Services may be provided by many different kinds of private and public agencies. For example, visiting nurse associations (voluntary, nonprofit groups delivering nursing service to the home), public health services, community agencies, hospital-based programs. Within the community, they may be provided through a single service agency such as a Homemaker–Home Health Aide Services Program or a Meals on Wheels program; or a multiple-service agency that arranges for two or more types of services such as homemaker, nursing, physical therapy; or a coordinated program that arranges for a wide range of home services designed to meet the individual's needs through one centralized administration. In 1969, the National Council for Homemaker–Home Health Services, Inc., was named the national standard-setting body for those services provided under the program administered by SRS. A nonprofit, voluntary-membership organization whose purpose is the development of quality services as part of health and welfare services delivered in the home, this organization has become a primary standard-setting agency in the homemaker–home health field, stressing the development and expansion as well as implementation of such programs.

According to a report on home health services in the United States prepared for the U.S. Senate Special Committee on Aging, in January 1972 it was estimated that there were approximately 2,850 agencies providing homemaker–home health aide services in the United States: 1,300 serving families with children; 1,200 in health-related programs (both public and voluntary); 175 "single service" agencies (i.e., providing supervised homemaker–home health aide services to meet a variety of community needs); and 175 proprietary registries. By 1973, the total figure declined to 2,221, continuing a down trend that began over twenty years ago.

The estimated total number of homemaker–home health aides employed in these programs is 30,000 as against a total estimated need of 300,000. Furthermore, the report pointed out that, in addition to the decrease in the number of agencies providing such services, the ones that remain are curtailing service, narrowing coverage, and reducing the duration of care offered. Even considering the very limited number and extent of such services, distribution is poor and there are geographic areas of the country and large sections of the population having no services available. Hospital-based programs are in short supply, stress short-term intensive care, and do not have available community-based services to meet long-range needs. Community-based services are inadequate in number; all are substantially underfinanced.

Homemaker services are used by the aged in all groups, regardless of income or social status. Charges vary depending on whether the organization providing the service is public, voluntary, or proprietary, and depending on the particular auspice. Eligibility varies similarly, depending on the program auspices.

Total expenditures for home health services under Medicare remain at less than one percent of overall insurance expenditure and appear to be decreasing. Related expenditures under Medicaid are less than 0.5 percent of the dollar amounts paid out for all recipients, not just the aged. Average costs per patient served are difficult to determine since these relate in each case to the number of services provided, the quality of service (difficult to quantify), and the type of personnel providing service.

A second program model, in the category of in-home services, is *Meals on Wheels*. These are programs providing prepared hot meals, brought to older persons' homes, usually by volunteers, from a congregate kitchen. Such home-delivered meals provide a daily link for the homebound with the outside world. They give the recipient someone to greet each day, and sometimes the volunteer stays to visit during the meal. At the present time, the service continues to be a minor provision among federal programs for the aged. Title VII of the OAA Act provides the major federal nutrition program for the aged. Ninety percent of these funds are for congregate meals (described below), and up to 10 percent may be spent for home-delivered meals from congregate centers. Most Meals on Wheels programs are small scale and are funded and/or operated locally by voluntary organizations.

Eligibility for the program varies, depending on sponsorship and auspices. In some cases, need is defined as inability to market or prepare meals, or not having any regular help with such chores. In other programs, only financial need qualifies an otherwise needy person for this service. Charges for this home-delivery service vary according to the organization sponsoring the program (public, voluntary, proprietary) and according to the ability of the older person to pay. The program has limited funding, which has become a serious problem since the cost of food has risen sharply and the fuel shortage is affecting delivery, which is generally implemented by volunteers.

Many older people who live alone fear that they may have a fall or be taken suddenly ill and be unable to call for help. *Telephone Reassurance* programs provide a daily telephone contact for an older person who might otherwise have no outside contact for long periods of time. Recipients of this service are called at a predetermined time each day. If the person does not answer, help is immediately sent to the home. Usually in the event of no answer, a neighbor, relative, or nearby police or fire stations is asked to make a personal check. Such details are worked out when a person begins receiving this service. Telephone Reassurance generally costs little and can be provided by callers of any age, usually volunteers, teenagers, or older people themselves.

Friendly Visiting has been described as organized neighborliness because, in this kind of program, volunteers regularly visit isolated homebound older people once or more a week. They do such things as play chess and cards, write letters, provide an arm to lean on during a shopping trip, and just sit and chat. The essential element is to provide continuing companionship for an elderly person who has no one else to do it for him; older people themselves often prove most effective visitors.

Both Telephone Reasurance and Friendly Visiting are programs addressed to the need for lessening the social isolation of the aged. At best, they can provide a useful supplementary service to the homebound or isolated aged person only when all other in-home services are readily available.

Out-of-Home Services

Among the types of services included under the rubric out-of-home services are the following: information and referral, congregate meals, transportation, escort, socialization and participation, legal, and consumer services. Occupational and volunteer services also fall under this heading, but examples of these have been described earlier.

Perhaps the major program model in this category, providing a combination of several of the above services, is the *senior center.* The first publicly supported senior center was established in New York City about thirty years ago and the number expanded gradually until about ten years ago. The expansion of this type of program was accelerated by passage of the Older Americans Act, which provided funds through the AoA's state programs to communities to assist them in developing center programs (but not construction of facilities). During this same period, public housing for the elderly was designed to include space for center programs for residents of housing developments as well as other older people from the neighboring community.

Voluntary organizations, both sectarian and nonsectarian, have also been active in developing and operating such programs. A directory of senior centers in the United States published jointly by the AoA and the National Council on Aging listed 340 such centers in 1966; a recent directory published in 1970 listed 1,200, and the number keeps increasing. Centers vary greatly in the kinds of programs and services offered and in the elaborateness and adequacy of physical settings, but all do offer some contact with other elderly people and some links with needed services. Although, for the purpose of the directory, the definition of a senior center is merely "a program for older people provided in a designated facility open 3 or more days a week," the average center listed offered three or four recreational activities, and one or two types of counseling and community services. Among the typical services offered (and the best centers provide at least several of these) are the following: information, referral and brief direct services; casework assessment; casework counseling; service coordination; medical and psychosocial diagnosis; home health care; financial management; legal services and/or guardianship; transportation and/or escort services; cash for emergencies; volunteers' services; delivered meals.

One senior center in Washington, D.C., is described as follows:

> Columbia Center . . . opened on September 20, 1972 in order to enhance the mental and physical well being of the elderly . . . by providing them Social Services, Educational, and Recreational opportunities.
>
> These services include:
>
> Social Services: Crisis intervention and advocacy; Homemaker services; Housekeeping service; Private residential placement; Friendly visits; Food stamp and Social Security counseling.
>
> Education: Handicrafts; Sewing; Reading; Drama; Spanish; Creative writing; First Aid; Library; Afro-American history; Dance; Cooking; Group services for the blind; Physical fitness; Consumer education; Talks; Painting.
>
> Recreation: Trips; Parties; Bingo; Programs; Movies; TV; Pool; Musicals; Singing; Games; Ivakota Farm Retreat (year-round trips); Special monthly programs with local artists.
>
> Special Services: Legal service; Beauty service; Employment; Group shopping trips; Group check cashing.
>
> The Columbia Center is located in the basement and ground floor of a renovated church, office, and apartment building. The quarters have been completely renovated, with light, bright colors in the office and activity rooms. It is clean, inviting, and certainly a haven for the predominantly Black residents of the area. Some Spanish-speaking people are in the area, and the Center has made some effort to include them in activities. A Spanish-speaking secretary at the Center . . . has written letters and has translated for clients.
>
> Columbia is administered by the Family and Child Services of Washington, D.C. Local Model Cities (HUD) monies were used as the 25 percent match for the 75 percent Federal Title XVI funds.

The annual budget was $300,000, including start-up costs of $18,000 for the first year.[11]

Approximately one-third of these centers were funded under Title XVI of SSA; additional centers were funded under OEO and Model Cities programs. The average center reported about 280 members, comprising 32 percent of its community (usually 4,000 persons aged 65 and over). Based on estimates of space needed and average size of centers, the typical center is serving three to six times as many members as it should. These figures seem to indicate that older people are placing far more demands on centers for activities than there is available center space.

In recent years there has been substantial expansion in the establishment of *Information and Referral Services* for the elderly. The primary purpose of these specialized information and referral centers is to link older people in need of help with the services available in their communities. In addition, information and referral services have the potential for identifying recurrent needs and gaps in services for the elderly. For the most part, these services are provided by voluntary organizations, churches, labor unions. However, since the Older Americans Act includes provision of federal matching funds to state-approved information and referral projects, a growing number of special demonstration information and referral service projects have been funded.

Among the problems regarding this service is the lack of clear regulations covering the components of information and referral services. (Is it just information and referral? Does it also include follow-up? If so, how much and by whom?) Another is the tendency to assume that the service can in some way substitute for quantitative and qualitative service inadequacies. Information and referral services are of significant value only when they are defined as a way of ensuring access to other services, benefits, and rights—not as a substitute for them.

One program model that attempts to address two problems of the elderly—inadequate nutrition and social isolation—is the *congregate meal.* In the late 1960s, twenty-one pilot demonstration programs (many begun in 1968), administered under the auspices of AoA, clearly demonstrated the demand for nutritional aid for the elderly and firmly established the need for a federally supported nationwide program. As a consequence, in 1972 Congress enacted the Nutrition Program for the Elderly, which became Title VII of the amended Older Americans Act.

The purpose of this act is "to provide older Americans, particularly those with low incomes, with low cost, nutritionally sound meals served in strategically located centers, such as schools, churches, community centers, senior citizens centers, and other public or private facilities where they can obtain other social and rehabilitative services. Besides promoting better health among the older segment of the population through improved nutrition, such a program is aimed at reducing the isolation of old age, offering older Americans an opportunity to live their remaining years in dignity."

Congregate meal sites established under this program must serve at least 100 meals daily, five days a week. Individuals 60 and over residing in a project area are eligible for the service and decide for themselves the charge for a meal. No means test is required. For this program, the largest single congregate meal program in the country, Congress appropriated 99.6 million dollars. It serves about 220,000 people (meals daily).

Other congregate meal services are located in or affiliated with school cafeterias. Thus, school cafeterias may prepare food either for service to older persons after the students' lunch hour or to be delivered to other locations and served there. Some states (e.g., Massachusetts) have passed legislation reimbursing any school or nonprofit organization for the expense of serving a meal to the elderly, over a certain cost (50 cents as of 1973). In some programs the older people themselves help as custodians in the program.

Just as reduced fares for older persons are increasing ridership, some commercial restaurants and cafeterias are finding it profitable to serve well-balanced meals to older people at reduced prices.

After income, health, and housing, *transportation* is the most pressing problem for the aged. It usually accounts for between 7 and 11 percent of an elderly person's annual budget and generally the aged pay even more for transportation than for medical care. The effect of this on the aged poor is to disenfranchise them of the opportunity to utilize services and other facilities in the community.

Lack of means to move around a community can isolate a healthy and physically mobile person as completely as if he were bedridden. Most older people do not drive. Taxis are too expensive for many of them. Public transportation either does not exist or is extremely difficult for them to use. Moreover, it grows more expensive every day.

As a result, many older people do not use available free medical services or facilities because they cannot reach them. They cannot enjoy a free concert or visits to the park for the same reason. Small neighborhood shops, easy to reach on foot, have disappeared in many communities. Today, supermarkets are often located at distances too great for many older people to reach by walking, particularly with heavy packages to carry home, and so nutrition suffers. Financial problems may reach an unnecessary crisis when people have no way to get to a social security office. Some older people need an escort on trips either because of physical frailty or, in some areas, because they are afraid to venture out alone. Finally, part-time jobs and volunteer opportunities, which would keep many people active, are prohibitively expensive because of high transportation fares.

Four factors seem to be the primary cause of poor service for the aged by transportation systems: low incomes (about 9 cents of every dollar is spent on transportation); inconvenient location of their housing; a transportation network strongly oriented to the private automobile; and problems of orientation and maneuverability caused by the design and service features of the system.

A number of means for meeting these problems of mobility have developed in communities across the country. Among these programs are the following.[12]

Some community and voluntary organizations sponsor a special bus or van to take older people on needed trips. For example, one Administration on Aging demonstration project set up a senior citizens mobile service. This service provided transportation to more than 1,600 elderly people on a total of 30,000 trips. Forty-eight different agencies participated through referrals and requests for service and appointments for trips were scheduled a day ahead with two-way radios allowing last-minute changes when emergencies arose.

In nine Missouri counties a variety of U.S. Government surplus vehicles served the transportation needs of older people, and were operated under the auspices of a local OEO community action agency.

Some senior centers provide a bus that runs between the members' homes and the centers. For example, there are "dial-a-bus" systems by which center members may have standing reservations or may telephone in by noon of the day they wish to arrive. The twelve-passenger bus in one case is driven along three regular routes directed primarily at shopping areas and medical facilities. There is no charge for this particular bus service in the program described. A bus belonging to one of the senior centers takes members on tours or sightseeing trips away from the centers.

Over one hundred cities with public transportation systems have experimented with reduced-fare programs for older people during nonrush hours. For example, New York City and Chicago charge half fare; San Francisco charges 5 cents a ride; Seattle and Tacoma,

Washington, charge $2.00 for a monthly pass which can be used during nonrush hours. In several instances, reduced fares have not only made life happier for older people but have increased ridership to the point of increasing the transit company's total revenues.

One town in California provides free bus service to people of all ages within the city limits and to a major shopping center outside the city. Buses run every half hour and no one has more than one block to walk from any point in the eight-square-mile community to a bus stop.

Unfortunately, transportation, which has been described as "access to opportunity," continues to remain one of the more pressing concerns for the elderly. Despite the declared national policy that the elderly and handicapped should have access to mass transportation facilities, this has not been implemented. For one thing, implementation of this policy through the grant and loan provisions of the Urban Mass Transportation Act is discretionary for the Department of Transportation, though specific allotments have been made in the annual DOT budgets for funding of systems designed to meet special needs of the elderly and handicapped. There is also no specific legislative requirement that all grants and loans assure accessibility on the system to the elderly and handicapped before being approved for funding. Individual projects have been funded; model prototypes are being developed; but to date, no systematic implementation of the national policy on accessibility has been established.

Two Contrasting Models

The Jamaica Service Program for Older Adults (and L.I.F.E. Towers) is illustrative of the service model in which a community center facility is the fulcrum for comprehensive and coordinated service provision to the elderly living in the surrounding area. Operated under the auspices of Community Service Society, the largest voluntary, nonsectarian family service agency in the world, this program is located in a racially mixed but predominantly black, poor, and lower-working-class neighborhood. Approximately 30,000 people aged 60 and over live within a five-square-mile area that contains a major thoroughfare with several large department stores and supermarkets and excellent public transportation, all within two blocks of the main service facility. Funded for three years by a combination of public monies (federal funding via state and city offices on aging) and voluntary funds (Community Service Society plus a few very small local contributions), the program expects to be able to obtain permanent funding.

The original plan was for the center to be located in a nearby low-income housing project for the elderly but because of a delay in completing construction of the multiple-unit dwelling, the center began operations elsewhere, and subsequently decided that for maximum community contact, this separately located facility would be more effective. The theory is that it is more visible to the community at large, more accessible to them, and also provides a rationale for encouraging housing project residents to remain related to the overall community. In fact, two facilities exist now: the primary one occupies most of the first floor of a new five-story square-block building operated by the New York City Department of Social Services; a satellite facility is located on the ground floor of a nearby, just-completed public apartment house for the elderly (a building initially generated by the same local group that stimulated development of this whole program).

The major facility contains administrative offices; a small kitchen and lunch room where about two hundred people receive lunch five days a week (soup, a sandwich, and dessert), paying whatever they wish; space for a training program for graduate social work students; and meeting rooms of various sorts for classes (e.g., exercise, crafts, lectures), for committee meetings of professional representatives of local cooperating organizations (health, education, social services), or for senior citizen advisory council meetings (composed of members of local senior centers, as well as nonaffiliated older people from the community).

Approximately a thousand people are members of the center, one third of whom are men. In addition, about eight to ten thousand are reached by the center's program in some fashion. Most of the membership is aged 75 and over, although the most active volunteer workers in the program tend to be those between the ages of 65 and 75.

The program involves direct input from representatives of the whole spectrum of relevant services and programs in the community (hospitals, clinics, local community college, other senior centers, local business), from the elderly themselves (both those representing other senior centers as well as those who are completely unaffiliated), and from its own professional staff. It supplies direct services to the elderly in the main center and in the housing project, supplies indirect services via linkages with health and other facilities, and acts as a planning, coordinating, and service resource for all other senior centers (about twenty-six) in the community.

Both facilities are characterized by constant activity and casual intermingling of staff with older people, many of whom are also actively involved in volunteer activities around and in the center. The director's office and several other offices are open all day, easily accessible to members. The professionals who participate in the program are active as advocates, as service coordinators, and as resource people for the agency. For example, the Social Service Task Force, with about thirty people representing about twenty agencies (Catholic Charities, several hospitals, New York City Housing Authority, Social Security Administration, Health Insurance Program, Jewish Agency Services for the Aged, New York City Human Resources Administration, Visiting Nurse Service) met for one of its monthly meetings to discuss certain critical issues and problems regarding Supplemental Security Income and to make a concerted and unified effort at resolving problems in that program. At the same time, the Senior Citizens Advisory Council, composed of elderly members advocating on their own behalf, was meeting at another facility elsewhere in the community to discuss efforts at arranging for local banks to eliminate the service charge on checking accounts for the elderly. In addition, a staff group was discussing plans for beginning a new outreach program, whereby a mobile van with a doctor, nurse, and podiatrist would move through certain areas in the community where needed services were not readily available. This is a specific outreach effort, aimed at serving those still isolated elderly who are not yet participating in any other services available in the community.

Lunch is served daily at the center in a large, informally furnished room where people come both from the nearby housing project and from elsewhere in the community. During the day, various types of classes are held, contributing to the sense of activity and vitality that seems to pervade the center. For example, when we visited, a group of about twenty people were meeting for their first class in public speaking. The session began with an exercise in how to use the telephone as an effective instrument for communication. If some appeared contemptuous of such an elementary approach, several found their "assignment" in calling the Social Security Administration or a local health service quite helpful.

Near the center is a newly constructed public apartment house for the elderly and handicapped. This thirteen-story building, situated two blocks from the main center in a stable, working-class neighborhood with clean, attractively painted, and recently refurbished one- and two-family houses, is an unusually attractive example of such housing. Containing 212 studio and one-bedroom apartments for the elderly (average age 72) and the handicapped, it also has a health service unit, staffed by a local hospital and Community Service Society, with a full-time nurse on duty five days a week, a part-time physician on duty three half-days a week, and a podiatrist who comes once a week. Other facilities located in the building include a small communal kitchen and dining room on the first floor, several meeting rooms where classes are held (cooking, English as a second language, exercise), and an outdoor garden. Signs on the bulletin board in the central hall remind tenants that a beautician will come to their apartment and give them a hair wash and set for a modest fee. Signs also describe trips, both in and around the city, available for the tenants.

Eligibility criteria for residents in this housing project include a mandatory means test, and apartments are for the poor only. At the time of our visit, they paid an average of $50 per month for an apartment. The apartments themselves are all individually decorated and furnished. Most are occupied by women, but several couples as well as a few single men live there.

When the weather is sunny and pleasant, people sit on the benches outside. The several vacant spots in the open parking lot belonging to the house attest to the fact that many of the residents are away during the day, at work or visiting. Regardless, the communal rooms are well occupied with people participating in various classes. The tenants may either lunch in their own apartments, use the small communal kitchen, or go over to the center and eat with friends there. Most of the residents are totally independent; many use none of the available facilities other than the living arrangements themselves. Yet all expressed great satisfaction with the arrangement and several are active in the housing-based activities, as well as those of the neighboring center.

As in all similar housing we visited, the primary complaint is how long it took to obtain such an apartment and how few were available for others who needed and wanted such facilities—in particular, people who own their own homes nearby, but who can no longer afford to maintain them and have been unable to sell.

Our second illustration, the Jewish Home and Hospital for Aged, is an example of a multifunction living and care residential complex for the aged, including facilities for independent, sheltered, and institutional living. It is representative of the model that encompasses a continuum of living and care arrangements including in-home and out-of-home services, provided from a medical-facility base reaching out into the community. It is a large complex of residential and medical facilities, staffed by a combination of professionals (doctors, nurses, social workers, physiotherapists, occupational therapists), paraprofessionals, and lay volunteers. It is funded by a combination of private (voluntary) and public funding, under the sponsorship of the Federation of Jewish Philanthropies of New York City. The Kingsbridge Center is the newest component, located on 4.5 acres in a working-class community in the Bronx. Serving a population drawn from all over the city, it also provides direct services for the elderly living in the area immediately surrounding it. The center itself contains facilities and services encompassing the whole continuum of living and care arrangements for the elderly, from institutional to independent living. One building provides full medical and nursing services to 320 residents whose average age on entrance is 83 and whose average age while in residence is 87. A second building, opened in 1975, serves as a health-related facility (formerly termed intermediate care facility) for 500 residents requiring less than skilled nursing care. A day care center for the ambulatory elderly residing in their own homes in the nearby community opened in 1974. Here, the elderly requiring some care and attention during the day can find health services, various forms of therapies, and recreational activities. This day hospital is the first such program in New York City to be covered for reimbursement purposes by Medicaid.

Finally, there is a twelve-story apartment house illustrating some of the newer approaches to independent living for older men and women. The building contains 234 apartments occupied by 335 persons, who pay a monthly rental ranging from $450 for a studio apartment for one person to $760 for a one-bedroom apartment for a couple. The rental includes a "service package" (two meals a day and certain tenant services). The apartments are either one-bedroom or studios, and have a tiny kitchenette (two-burner range, small refrigerator, and sink) sufficient for preparing breakfast or a snack. The main meals of the day—lunch and dinner—are served to all residents in a spacious, attractively furnished dining room. In addition, off this room is a small wood-paneled bar where residents and their guests can serve themselves drinks. Nearby is a room used as a small movie theater or for guest speakers and other forms of entertainment. The building has a manager on the premises and other ancillary and supporting staff (e.g., housekeeping). No social services are available on the premises; however, medical care is available from a private physician who has an office in the building. Emergency night nursing is provided by staff of the Home. There is an attractive roof garden on the top of the building, with facilities for sitting as well as other activities, and a garden with wooden benches and chairs on the ground floor, in the courtyard between the house and the other buildings in the complex.

The average age of the tenants is mid-seventies. Although all were fully ambulatory when they first entered the building on its completion three years ago, some require much more care now than then. Interestingly enough, several seemed no less incapacitated than some in the nearby skilled nursing facility. Staff concurred with the impression and said as time passed often the only difference between the residents in the two facilities were that some continued to prefer the more independent facility.

The tenants interviewed were basically middle class and Jewish. A few receive SSI, but this is inadequate to cover their monthly living expenses, even at the lowest rate, and the administration is concerned as to what will happen subsequently to these tenants if there is no additional support. This facility is really for those who receive at least average social security benefits.

Tenants interviewed were highly enthusiastic about their accommodations and the facility generally. However, here too the same complaint and concern was expressed as in the housing facility. There is a three-year waiting list for an apartment and at present there is nowhere near adequate provision for specially designed, yet independent living arrangements for the elderly.

Research and Evaluation

Basic research and policy-oriented studies have some impact but are no more effective in the field of the aging than in most other arenas of domestic social policy.

Within recent years, individual research and demonstration projects funded by the federal government, and providing services to the aged, have been required to include provision for evaluating the program's effects and effectiveness. At best, however, these evaluations are project-specific, often with no generalizable findings. Furthermore, no real provision exists for the utilization of research findings. Legislation instituting a national nutrition program represents one of the few examples of program development occurring as a result of feedback from evaluation studies of completed demonstration projects.

Several surveys of the aged and "need studies" have been implemented. But few programs and little in the way of legislation have emerged in response to areas of identified need. Although the result of such studies may be used in support of—or to rationalize—a particular position, it is the emerging political power of the aged as an interest group that seems to have been most effective in achieving certain desired changes (e.g. increased social security benefits), not the result of research. In addition to the required evaluation studies of federally funded demonstration projects, such projects are regularly monitored by government officials also. What happens to these reports, as well as to the evaluation reports, is often difficult to determine. AoA has initiated several major studies, including one five-year impact study of the national nutrition program, a study to evaluate the impact of the area planning organizations, and a needs assessment study by each of the states. There is some attempt at developing social indicators for the aged also; major effort is being placed on developing a firm data base with regard to the aged, both nationally and on a state by state basis. At present, much data are not available or difficult to obtain; when available, they are not broken down into relevant categories nor are they kept consistently in each state (or even by each federal agency). Even data regarding federal expenditures for services to the aged are difficult to obtain and no systematic effort at analyzing and publishing data on federal outlays for the aged have been implemented since 1972. Official figures are never adequately justified and estimates of expenditures for the same program vary, depending on who—or what agency—is issuing the report. Similarly, identifying the total amount of—and programmatic authorization for—federal funds going into one particular community is equally difficult.

Commenting on the apparent lack of formal evaluations of federally funded programs for the aged, one high government official stated in 1974 that, "frankly, there are no good evaluation studies of services to the elderly. No valid, generalizable conclusions regarding national programs for the elderly exist." This statement and subsequent amplification of it is confirmed by other interviews with administrators as well as researchers working in the field. For example, although (as indicated above) some work is being done on the problem, there is no good national data base regarding the aged. Thus, baseline data are rarely available for use in evaluating the impact or long-term effects of a program. Furthermore, precise delineations of target populations are hard to come by, both because of the absence of data as well as problems regarding conceptual confusion and difficulty in defining eligibility criteria—e.g., What is the target population for the nutrition program? All elderly? All elderly poor? (and how is poor defined?) All "needy elderly"? (and how is need defined?); or, how is "target population" defined when eligibility criteria vary substantially among states?)

Objectives of programs are often diffuse (a problem for all social programs) and, even worse, unclear and potentially conflicting. For example, is the objective of the nutrition program to reduce secondary malnutrition or to increase socialization and reduce social isolation? If the former, among other things, consumers would need the option of either home-delivered meals or congregate meals, instead of the current overwhelming stress on congregate meals. If the latter, how is it measured?

In addition, even within one federal agency (AoA) there are no clear and consistent operational definitions of "service," "institution," a medical or non-medical facility, let alone what is meant by information and referral services (e.g., do they include follow-up or not?). Since similar discrepancies in the use of such terms are expressed in other federal agencies providing services for the elderly, it is no wonder that program people at the local level are confused. Inevitably, comparable evaluations of similarly labeled programs cannot be implemented.

Major problems continue to exist regarding efforts at costing out service programs for the purpose of cost benefit studies or cost effectiveness studies.

As pointed out by one well known researcher, should cost of care include governmental costs, or direct dollar costs, or should it also include total social costs (including costs of service provided by family members if the patient is maintained by them at home; costs of varying types of care, that is, differential quality of care or service;

and cost of service related to differential patient need, that is varying degrees of functional impairment)? "Thus home care may be very costly to society if it prevents employment of an employable spouse, or it will appear inexpensive if only government costs are counted because the major portion of the costs of care is absorbed by family. Similarly, day care may be a relatively economical alternative from a social cost perspective, but appears less desirable or more expensive because costs are borne by government and are visible."[13]

Related problems for evaluation research include the need to develop quantifiable measures for social costs (and for benefits), in particular, for quality of care or service, and for services provided by family members or neighbors. Basic to this is a need to develop a standardized classification of functional impairment.

Finally, as is mentioned repeatedly by experts, researchers, administrators and program people, criteria for evaluating programs or service impact are almost non-existent. In the area of community-based services for the aged there are almost no standards for well-being or service quality. The process of aging may be slowed temporarily but cannot be stopped; there is no "cure." What criteria can be utilized to evaluate effectiveness? Subjective response of consumers? Take-up or rate of service utilization? Can we compare "the quality of life" for different individuals and groups? Some beginning efforts at developing social indicators for the elderly have been initiated, but here, too, little has been accomplished.

However, it is worth noting that successful and generally acceptable evaluation studies of broad-aim service programs are few and far between. Little enough exists in other areas (e.g., service for children) where there has been concentrated and extensive effort for some years. The whole field of service to the aged is relatively new; evaluation studies are difficult to implement in all service realms and, inevitably, more difficult in a field in which data are so soft and criteria for evaluation so amorphous. The impact of research on policy development remains limited. Even a highly touted study of the need for home health services has had no noticeable impact on policies or programs.[14] Most decisions about expanded programs continue to be made on the basis of societal preference and influence, expressed in a political arena, not on the basis of conclusions from rational analysis.

It is generally agreed that all kinds of research are needed—basic and applied; interdisciplinary and single disciplines; biomedical and behavioral-social—if we are to make any substantial progress in understanding the processes and problems of aging, solving these problems, and in learning about the needs of the aged and how best to satisfy them. It is also agreed that expanded and improved research will not necessarily achieve its potential effects unless policy development and programing are so reorganized as to become increasingly sensitive to knowledge.

Programs in Action

Although often described as a "not atypical" American city, our sample city offers a wealth of services available to the elderly residents which tends to make it somewhat unusual in this respect. As in many other cities, 13 percent of its population is aged 65 and over (18 percent aged 60 and over), while the county as a whole is closer to the national average of about 10 percent aged 65 and over.

The city has an outstanding gerontological institute, whose existence and programs have directly and indirectly contributed to community interest in the field of aging. It supports and generates extensive basic and applied research, contributes to expanded innovative program development, and provides for the training and availability of different categories of professional personnel.

On a per capita basis, more public funds, especially federal funds, are available for services to the aged in this city than in almost any other community. One leading authority in the field of services to the aged, representing the voluntary sector, stated that if social services for the elderly were available in every community to the extent they were here, the cost to the federal government would be between $3.5 and $4 billion. Moreover, his prediction was that the city would soon be seeing a decrease in this funding.

Given this great interest and relatively high financial investment, what in fact is available for the elderly? To begin with, all major national programs for the aged, such as cash and noncash income support programs, Medicare, and so forth, are available here. In addition, and more specifically, there are the following: a planning and coordinating agency, under county auspices but with equal participation of both city and county; an advocacy organization, county-wide, under voluntary auspices; an access service, city and county-wide, under voluntary auspices; and public housing (multidwelling) for independent living arrangements, for city residents only. There are also a wide range of protected and congregate living and care arrangements, under voluntary and proprietary auspices, most located in or near the city. Among these are nursing homes, health-related facilities, congregate housing (or domiciliary or personal care facilities) with varying amounts of services provided, and day care services. In-home services, under public and voluntary auspices, primarily for city residents, include the following: home health services, chore services, telephone reassurance services, meals on wheels, friendly visiting, home repair services, counseling services. Out-of-home services, under public and voluntary auspices, primarily for city residents, include the following: reduced-cost transportation, escort services, employment and volunteer occupational services, congregate meals, legal services, recreation services.

For the most part, services are universal, rather than selective. In fact, only three services—public housing, the legal services program, and the county homemaker–home health services—are means tested, although almost all stress the low-income aged as the priority group for service. For several services (e.g., home repair, home health services under other than county auspices) there are graduated, income-related fees. In general, the target population for many programs is characterized as "isolated, vulnerable, aged 55 and over, of low income." (Clearly many of the programs are funded under the authorization of the Older Americans Act.)

Although there does appear to be stigma attached to several programs for the aged, such stigma is not correlated with means-tested programs, but rather with many of the programs for the aged generally. For example, of the means-tested services neither homemaker–home health services nor legal services are stigmatized, yet housing is. And of the non-means-tested services, transportation, home repair, and information and referral are not stigmatized while nursing homes, homes for the aged, and certain senior centers are. It appears that the stigma reflects the specific identification of "old and dependent" or "old and poor" rather than just "poor."

Service coverage seems extensive; however, this is only an impression because there is no precise definition of the target population, and obviously this varies with the specific service. The State Office on Aging has indicated that the target population includes about 3,000 elderly people. In fact, according to some of the programs visited, coverage is as follows: The advocacy organization claims a membership of 19,000. The access service agency, in 1973, processed over 4,000 requests (not including repeat requests from the same people) for information and referral from elderly people only, and each year the figure grows. The Model Project for the Aging (for all projects except the above access service) served over 4,000 elderly (also claimed to be an unduplicated count) and feel they could serve more, if they had the resources. Several of their projects have waiting lists for service (home repairs especially). Public housing contains 1,800 elderly tenants. At present there are 300 on a waiting list, and there is a two-month back-up to interview new applicants. And this is only for city residents; no public housing exists in the county. The eight-month-old legal service program has handled 200 cases during its existence. There is always a couple of weeks' delay in responding to requests for service. For home health services and transportation services, demand is substantially greater than available service, even in the city.

After income and health services, transportation, housing, and home health services are described as the priority services, those for which coverage remains critically inadequate. Needless to say, if this is true for the elderly in the city, it is far more true for rural residents, for whom almost none of these special services exist.

There is a special access service for the elderly located in the city with a satellite site in one of the semi-rural parts of the county. It is publicly funded, under the Older Americans Act, but operates under voluntary agency auspices. This service provides a telephone information and referral service including follow-up and some outreach services, and handled about 4,000 requests in 1974. It operates by preparing and distributing a directory or "Guide to Community Services for Older Citizens," a "Directory of Facilities Specializing in the Care of Elderly People," and a large number of leaflets and brochures. Yet even closely related agencies representing components of an integrated service system obtain half their clients through self-referrals or through other informal referral sources (friends, neighbors) rather than through this service; and more than three-fourths of those clients referred formally come from agencies other than this special service. It would appear that the service may be more important for providing information than for referrals. Most agencies do not appear to keep precise records regarding source of referral, but on an impressionistic basis, informal (self, neighbor, friend, relative) referrals appear to constitute the most frequent form of access. Formal referrals from related agencies (either administratively related such as from one Model Project unit to another, or functionally related, such as from the housing authority to legal services or to health services) appear to constitute the next major source of access. Last is the formal access system.

The services are about evenly divided between public and voluntary sponsorship, although in the field of aging these sectors are so intertwined as to make the distinction a difficult one. For example, housing is the only major publicly funded, administered, and operated program. The eight Model Project components are publicly funded but services are operated under voluntary auspices. The housing complexes with medical and other services, several health services, and even the various meal and nutrition programs are all administered and operated by voluntary agencies but largely with public funding. Most of these agencies are sectarian.

The facilities themselves vary widely depending on the service and program (see individual program descriptions). In general, most city programs serving the aged were established in the early 1970s and are in modern, attractive, and readily accessible locations. Yet here too, such services are neither available nor accessible, nor in attractive settings when they do exist, in the rural parts of the county.

In general, the medical programs are staffed with relevant medical personnel (doctors, nurses) and the programs providing nonmedical living and care arrangements are staffed with professional social workers (MSWs) as administrators and supervisors and B.A. workers and indigenous paraprofessionals as line workers and direct service providers. Most social service program staff are not professional.

The elderly appear to play a fairly active role in the planning, policy-making, and direct service provision parts of programs generally. The planning and coordination agency has an advisory board of lay elderly members. So do most other agencies serving the aged. Public housing has tenants' organizations which provide input from the elderly tenants, although often not sufficient to satisfy the tenants. Perhaps even more important is the advocacy–self-help organization, some of whose members are actively involved in task forces that analyze, assess, and monitor other programs having a distinct influence on priorities for further planning and programing. However, even though this organization is perceived as important and influential—and representative of the elderly themselves—and the community is concerned about the elderly and defines them as a priority group, there seems to be a paternalistic note in the operation of many of the programs, and the elderly continue to feel stigmatized by the very fact of their age. Physical impairment and dependency increase this. Experts in the field note that this is no more true in this community than in the country generally.

There is no one single pattern that describes the internal administrative structure of these programs. Most tend to follow conventional hierarchical patterns with a director, administrative and supervisory staff, and line staff providing direct service. Most have an advisory board and some have a policy-making board, too. However, there are important exceptions to this pattern that reflect efforts at innovation in both service organization and delivery. For example, the planning and coordinating agency includes administrative staff paid by the county and responsible to the county executive, yet policy is determined by a policy-making commission composed of an equal number of mayoral and county-executive appointees. There is also an advisory committee to the commission, composed entirely of potential service consumers. In addition, the directors of each program component of Model Project are part of an overall coordinating council. A similar structure includes directors of all nutrition programs. There appears to be some effort at developing new approaches to structuring organizations in order to make them more accountable to consumer needs and preferences and more effective with regard to delivering services generally.

Programs funded under the OAA are linked with the State Office on Aging, the Regional DHEW office, the federal AoA, and the city and county government. At times these multiple vertical linkages result in contradictory and conflicting directives. Since July 1974, the Area Agency on Aging has been responsible primarily to the state.

The voluntary programs are linked either to United Way (if nonsectarian and funded in part by this organization) or, if sectarian, to the relevant parent funding agency (in this community primarily Catholic Charities). For these agencies also, to the extent that they receive public funds, funding requests and new program developments will be subject to review by the area agency.

With regard to horizontal linkages and interagency relationships, at present, close connections exist only within the Model Project group. Linkages are only beginning to be developed by the area planning agency (the commission) with all other programs serving the aged. The assumption is that with its appointment as an area agency on aging for purposes of planning and coordination, all grants from the state or county that relate to services to the aged will be channeled through this one agency, thus providing some leverage and ensuring closer coordination and cooperation among the agencies in the community. Now only one program, structured as a component of both the planning agency and the advocacy organization, provides linkages with consumers and consumer groups generally.

Regardless of these efforts, linkages do not exist with autonomous agencies (e.g., DSS, Social Security) or with agencies outside the personal social service system generally (e.g., cash income maintenance programs, health, mental health).

This community is unusual in that the county legislature is concerned about and interested in social service needs and problems. Thus, general revenue-sharing funds have been channeled into certain programs (e.g., information and referral, a special emergency assistance fund for the elderly). In general, what is clear from any analysis of the funding resources of programs serving the aged is that public, especially federal, funds predominate, either directly by project grants from AoA or indirectly, by reimbursement under Medicare or Medicaid. In this context, it is interesting to note that there are no publicly provided social services for the aged under the auspices of the Department of Social Services except for a small number of homemaker services. Furthermore, the funding that was supporting the Model Project programs would not be available for long, and resources would have to be generated locally. Thus, the several component projects within Model Project will be competing against each other as well as with other service programs, in the field of the aging as well as in all other social service fields, for substantially reduced resources.

Although services for the aged appear to be more extensive than in most other communities, formal research and evaluation studies regarding service provision, alternative approaches to community care, programs generally, are no more prevalent here than elsewhere. In fact, there are no completed evaluation studies of programs or services, and no such studies in progress. A series of consumer monitoring and evaluation reports were planned by the Committee on Aged Alertness, part of the advocacy organization; however, this study was never completed.

Program Operations

Commission on Aging: A Planning and Coordination Agency

The Commission on Aging (COA) was created in 1971 by identical resolutions of city and county legislatures and became operational after a one-year planning period, in June 1972. It is composed of twenty appointed members—ten appointed by the mayor and ten by the county executive. Delegated by the mayor to be responsible for planning and administering a federal project grant for the establishment of an areawide model project on aging, the commission established seven functional committees (e.g., income maintenance, housing, health, personal social services, protective services) to identify gaps in community resources for the aged and to recommend programs to fill these gaps. Final recommendations were reviewed by an advisory committee composed entirely of potential service users. A combination of commission recommendations, advisory committee recommendations, and expert technical assistance resulted in the final development of eight new programs under the assorted sponsorships of existing local public and voluntary agencies.

Commission membership includes professionals, experts, and influential lay people, and is responsible for policy-making generally. An executive director and paid staff are responsible for day-to-day operations and overall administration of the major operating programs—Model Project and a nutrition program. Administrative authority for the component programs is in the hands of individual program directors (see below).

The duties and powers of the Commission on Aging are as follows: (1) to plan environmental and personal services to meet the needs of the elderly population through the evaluation of services and the identification of major problems affecting the elderly; (2) to stimulate and review needed programs and services for the elderly; (3) to conduct research on the needs of the elderly in this community and develop alternative means of meeting these needs; (4) to cooperate with elderly citizens and organizations servicing or representing them to meet the needs of the elderly population of the community; (5) to provide information about programs and services for the elderly in the community and sources of support for programs and services; (6) to encourage the cooperation of agencies servicing the elderly; (7) to recommend to and cooperate with federal, state, and local agencies in the development of public policy toward the elderly. But although the commission is defined as a planning and coordinating agency, according to its own staff "it does little planning or coordination because of lack of leverage and a morass of red tape. The only real coordination implemented is within Model Project." Most of what the commission is doing currently is administering Model Project and its component projects and the Title VII Nutrition grants. It has been active, also, in recruiting potential SSI recipients, in monitoring relevant legislation, and in representing the various interest groups concerned with the aged in Washington and the state capital.

In 1974, the commission was designated an Area Agency on Aging, an AoA-funded planning and coordination agency for the county, responsible to the State Office on Aging. Hereafter, all grants (federal, state, county) for services to the aged are supposed to be channeled through this organization. With this as leverage, and the need for its approval on funding requests, the commission hopes to have some impact on planning and program development. Unfortunately, the grant to the commission for 1974–75 was primarily for planning and coordination efforts and represented a substantial cutback in the overall funds available for direct service, as compared with the previous two years. Cutbacks for 1975–76 seem to indicate that there will be still less for the commission to plan, coordinate, and administer.

Finally, although its new status provides leverage with regard to service programs applying for funding, the commission has no authority vis à vis existing autonomous agencies in other systems (see above), nor is it clear what its role will be in the planning process mandated under Title XX.

Model Project for the Aging

Model Project is described as a "minisystem of comprehensive services for the aged, composed of 8 program components and an administrative division." Initial funding was received in February of 1972 for planning, and the Commission on Aging was delegated by the mayor to design the model. Originally funded under the old Title III of OAA, its first year's operating grant was over a quarter of a million dollars, and supplementary funding was provided by the county legislature out of general revenue sharing funds (for the information and referral project), and by various other organizations acting as administrative sponsors for individual projects. The second year's grant was larger. (Funding was projected initially on a five-year time frame; however, changes in the legislation at the federal level led to the withdrawal of funds by June 1975, two years earlier than originally intended.)

Seven of the projects are under the administrative auspices of voluntary organizations; one is under public agency auspices. Most address city residents' needs rather than rural residents', although five do serve both groups. Services are universal. Where fees are charged, as for the Home Handyman service, they are graduated and subsidized.

The target population addressed are those 55 and over who are "isolated, vulnerable and of low income." According to the State Office on Aging, 3,000 elderly are in this category. Yet the program claims to serve over 4,000 already and says it has not begun to tap potential demand for service—that existing resources limit the capacity to expand service provision.

The specific program components were designed to fill in gaps in service provision and were identified by professionals, experts, and consumers as representing priorities in service needs (see the section on the Commission on Aging, above). Social services integration, coordination with nonpersonal social services, the development of a service network, access, and accountability are all stressed both conceptually and operationally in this model. Each program has its own director and staff. The directors meet regularly in a coordinating council in order to ensure close cooperation and a sharing of relevant information. The background and training of individual project staffs vary enormously, from retired skilled workers (electricians, carpenters, plumbers) used by the Home Handyman project, to elderly indigenous counselors in Project CARE and paraprofessionals in the Coffee House program. Top administrative staff are professional social workers (MSWs).

The specific program components are as follows:

Project CARE is at the core of the Model Project service system, since its mandate is to locate and serve the hard-to-reach elderly. It is an outreach, access, case integration, and counseling program. It functions through the employment of three outreach teams (two are city-based, one is rural), each composed of a team coordinator and six part-time senior citizen outreach workers. Clients may be self-referred, referred by friends, neighbors, relations, or other agencies, or reached by the door-to-door contacts of the outreach workers. The service involves visiting the older person, identifying problems, counseling the elderly about such problems (if needed and desired), searching out solutions wherever possible. Where other services are needed, the workers make referrals, integrate multiple service provision, follow up on arrangements, and continue with the client until a satisfactory solution to the problem has been reached.

Call-a-Bus is a demand-activated door-to-door transportation service for low-income older city residents who have difficulty utilizing other transportation. The sponsoring organization has recently received a substantial federal grant from the Urban Mass Transportation Administration (DOT) to provide an expanded version of the service for the elderly and disabled residents of both city and county. Thus, Model Project's involvement is limited to policy-making and future program planning; it no longer operates the program.

Information and Referral is a special access service program for elderly people, operated by an organization that has been involved for some time in volunteer services and general information and referral. The program publishes a "Guide to County Services for Old People" and a "Directory of Long-Term Care Facilities for the Elderly." Staff include a director (social worker) and two full-time paraprofessionals. The office is open five days a week and arrangements are made for telephone and emergency coverage on a 24-hour seven-day-a-week basis. Telephone requests for information and assistance are accepted from all parts of the county and city. Where requests are for referral, callers may merely be steered to the appropriate resource (given the agency name, address, and telephone number) or a complete referral may be made with follow-up calls to assure satisfactory provision of service. Where callers have difficulty in explaining problems or requests, workers provide an outreach service by visiting them directly in their own homes. In the second year, more than 4,000 requests for information were received and over 3,000 referrals implemented.

Telephone Life Line is a telephone reassurance service provided under the same auspice as the Information and Referral service. The service involves older people who volunteer to telephone other, housebound elderly who need some reassurance, or just some company. Over two hundred people worked as volunteers during 1973 calling an equal number of isolated elderly and generating almost as many individual referrals to other services.

Home Services and Repairs (Home Handyman) Service provides low-cost minor home repairs for older people who cannot afford the full costs of such service. The consumer pays for labor and materials on a sliding scale ranging from nothing to full payment for labor at an hourly rate well under current market costs, plus materials. For 1973–74, supplementary funding for the program was provided by the Department of Labor. Almost from its inception, the demand for this program has been so heavy that adequate coverage is impossible, and an extensive waiting list is a constant problem.

Housing Services for the Elderly, under the auspices of the city's housing authority, provides information, advice, counseling, referral services, and placement for the elderly poor, Since only a limited amount of public housing is available for the elderly, and none outside the city limits, there are an enormous number of housing problems for low-income elderly. This program tries to identify possible housing and assist the elderly, especially those ineligible for public housing or unable to obtain it, in otherwise solving housing problems.

Coffee Houses are "drop-in" centers providing hot lunches three times weekly, and opportunity for socializing and recreation. The program is located in two public housing projects and is administered and staffed by the agency providing much of the homemaker–home health aide service in the community.

When we visited, a downtown *Multiservice Senior Center* for the elderly also provided a once-a-week hot lunch and various other recreational and educational activities. Within the context of the whole program, this seemed the weakest component. The physical facility was unattractive; few people seemed involved; little activity or social interaction was noted. Staff did not seem clear about the program, its function or goal. The program was closed, subsequently.

Aged Alertness is a program sponsored jointly by Model Project and the local advocacy organization (RWD) and functions as liaison between the planning agency, RWD (the largest organized group of service consumers in the community), and Model Project. Its role is to provide consumer feedback regarding service provision generally and facilitate consumer input into the planning and policy-making process, as well as into program evaluation.

Retire with Dignity

Retire with Dignity (RWD) is a local advocacy, self-help, and social action group composed entirely of senior citizens. Begun in 1969 with an initial grant from United Way, the program is funded now by both United Way (directly) and Model Project (indirectly, through the Aged Alertness program (described above). Its small annual budget covers three paid adminisrators (one of whom is part time) and supporting staff, office, and miscellaneous expenses (printing, postage, telephone, etc.). Almost all program activities are implemented via volunteer committees, such as a housing task force, a health task force, a minority concerns committee, an employment task force, and an Aged Alertness committee. In addition, there are legislative, research, and finance committees.

Among the program's activities are a consumer discount program; publication of a newsletter containing issues and items of interest to the elderly, going out to 20,000 persons monthly; compilation of a report covering 2,000 hours of home interviews to produce a computerized picture of the county's older population; a successful campaign for reduced fares on public transportation; establishment of an ongoing citizen monitoring group to inspect and assess nursing homes; development of an employment service for elderly people; and, finally, an attempt at a consumer evaluation of the Model Project program.

RWD's major objectives include identification of the major issues of concern to the aging, informing the community and relevant programs of the interests and needs of the aging, and involving the aged themselves in activities to bring about needed change.

The organization claims a current membership of 19,000 people aged 55 and over. Most are middle class, but efforts are now being made to increase the participation of low-income and minority people in the membership. Most of this membership is inactive. The director estimates that thirty-five to forty members, between the ages of 55 and 75, represent the active leadership core, working a forty-hour week in various volunteer capacities. In addition, efforts of this group are supplemented by an additional two hundred or more people who volunteer from a half day to four days a week. Membership is not dependent on anything other than interest; no fees are charged except for a once-in-a-lifetime $2.00 fee for the consumer discount program, for those who are interested and aged 62 or over.

The RWD office is centrally located in the downtown area in an attractive building. The facility itself is small, but several telephones are available as are meeting rooms, and there is a constant stream of members coming and going.

The organization is constantly receiving requests from other states concerning duplication of its program and is currently seeking funding to develop relevant training and organizational materials.

Special Living and Care Arrangements

A number of independent, sheltered, and congregate living and care arrangements are provided in the city, ranging from independent to institutional in type. One locating and referral service, Housing Services for the Elderly, a special program under the auspices of the city housing authority and a component of Model Project, has already been described above.

Public Housing for the Elderly serves approximately 1,800 elderly tenants, who live in 1,500 units located in all or part of ten different projects. This housing is for city residents only and is means tested. The current waiting list of 300 does not begin to reflect the real extent of demand or the inadequacy of coverage. These are apartments for independent living, located for the most part in high-rise buildings limited to elderly tenants only. Although housing is in great demand, these accommodations are stigmatized, described by some as the "end of the road"—just before placement in old age homes and nursing homes. Segregated and isolated, not very many tenants move here with any sense of pleasure. The few low-rise, centrally located houses are more desirable; however, high construction costs preclude such developments today. In theory, the so-called "family projects" with some units for the elderly are also more desirable. Yet in practice these too are described as "undesirable" because of lack of separate, safe, outdoor areas for the aged (and/or children and teenagers) and inadequate protective and safety measures for the aged in an environment full of active youngsters.

Tria Towers, a dramatically designed, world-famous example of public high-rise housing for the elderly, was completed in 1969 and planned to provide integrated housing for college youth and aged. Designed to include both dormitories for university students and a living facility for about 400 elderly capable of independent living, all interest groups (Housing Authority, Social Service Agencies, tenants, university administration) now agree that there is only limited contact between the university students and the senior citizen residents. When the Towers first opened, the university provided staff to facilitate interaction through special programs and services. However, this service was provided only for a very brief period of time, and once funds were withdrawn and the project discontinued, contact between the groups was minimal.

Furthermore, the building contains little in the way of special facilities or service for the elderly tenants. No communal eating facility exists, except for a cafeteria adjacent to the dormitory section. To reach this, the elderly must go outside, walk a short distance, go up and down several sets of stairs; in effect, frequent usage is precluded by this difficulty of access. Although there is a health clinic for the elderly in the building, staffing is limited and there are no physicians available there. A few communal rooms exist, but they are rarely used because there is no staff to develop programs, organize activities, or service the tenants. In general, there is no provision for supplementary in-home services of any sort (e.g., homemaker, home-health, chore) and no staff or system for linking tenants with needed services that might exist outside of the housing facility.

The *Werner Geriatric Center* is a multifacility living and care complex for elderly people aged 62 and over, providing a continuum from totally independent apartments (furnished by the residents as they wish) to a skilled nursing facility. It is projected to eventually serve 2,000 elderly persons, as follows: skilled nursing facility, 120 persons; health-related facility, 400; domiciliary facility (residence and personal care), 169; apartment complex, 240; ambulatory clinic, day care center, and home health services (numbers not decided as yet), for residents as well as those from the community. Only the nursing facility and the apartment complex were completed by 1974.

Opened in 1973, the apartment house contains 215 one-bedroom or studio units (240 persons) for middle-income individuals aged 62 or older who are in reasonably good health and able to function independently. Special safety and comfort measures are integrated into the design of the apartments and the building generally. When we visited, rentals ranged from $55 monthly to $269 (fair market rental), with the amount related to income. The minimum income allowed was $2,500 annually; the maximum was $13,000. In December 1974, there was a waiting list of 250 for an apartment (and, incidentally, a waiting list of 100 for space in the nursing home).

The range of services available is extensive (recreational services, physical therapy, occupational therapy, nursing, nutrition, counseling, transportation). Supportive nursing and medical services are provided through the nursing facility. Linkages with meals-on-wheels and transportation services are available from outside the complex; however, there is no formal linkage with the Commission on Aging, RWD, any of the other Model Project programs in the community, or any other health or medical resource. There is a shopping center, including a post office, in front of the apartment house. The only obvious limitation, in this unusually complete and comfortable facility, is that both the apartment house and the nursing home are situated on top of steep hills requiring automobile transportation between the two, although the actual distance is not great.

There is no concern about access to this center (in fact the facilities are largely unpublicized) because it is considered so desirable by residents, their friends, and relations that word of mouth is all that is needed. As indicated, extensive waiting lists exist for the already existing facilities as well as for those still in the process of construction.

Regardless of its obviously superior design and program, staff express concern about the following: extensive waiting lists for space in both facilities, but especially the apartment house; a tenant population that is largely middle class and white; criteria to be utilized for moving tenants from the apartment houses to the nursing facility when functioning deteriorates (a growing problem with each additional year tenants are in residence); absence of any communal eating facility in the apartment house, and the consequent difficulty in stimulating socialization among the tenants; assuring the availability of skilled, competent, dedicated staff, as the complex grows and need for such staff increases; and lack of tenant-resident-consumer input into policy and program.

Center for Legal Services to the Aging

Center for Legal Services to the Aging is a clinical law program under the auspices of the university law school providing legal experience for about fifteen second- and third-year law students, a related field experience for two graduate social work students, and legal and advocacy service to low-income elderly. The program was established in 1973 along the lines of an OEO neighborhood legal service program. Eligibility for service is dependent on a means test for those aged 55 and over (or disabled). Because it is a means-tested program, the director stated there is some stigma attached to use of the service. Ninety-five percent of the clients served during the first year were aged 65 and over. Approximately two hundred cases were handled and only about a two-week wait was necessary before clients could be seen.

Clients learn of the program through word of mouth or agency referrals. Seventy percent are self-referred; about 20 percent are referred from the social service staff of the housing authority; the remainder are referred from DSS and the County Mental Health Service. Few referrals come from the Information and Referral service. Most contacts are initiated by telephone, followed by an extensive in-person interview at the office of the program (60 percent of the clients) or in the client's home if preferred (40 percent). Usually only one or two personal contacts are required; however, one characteristic of serving the elderly is that they want far more personal attention than lawyers define as necessary. It is in this realm, therefore, that social workers play an increasingly active role, supplementing and supporting the work of the legal staff.

The project is located in a modern, attractive, one-story building in a residential area, near public transportation, with readily available parking space, and within walking distance of several buildings housing the elderly.

Open from 9 to 5, five days a week, the program combines direct legal services (70 percent of staff time), legal case advocacy, social action (a few class action suits), training and education for legal and social work students. This dual focus on service and training creates some tension around the number and type of cases served.

Included in the training component is a requirement that students be taught relevant substantive content about the aged and the problems of aging. Major categories of cases staff handle include landlord-tenant problems; problems related to SSI (e.g., not receiving checks, need for emergency funds); making out wills. An area of general concern for staff has been the disruption of normal access procedures for social service provision that has occurred as a consequence of the advent of SSI. According to staff, public social service provision for the elderly was negligible before SSI and nonexistent since.

Summary

In summarizing this review of an operating "system" of community services for the aged, we note that there appear to be three service systems involved, with only a superficial facade of integration among them: (1) a very small public, selective program addressed to the poor elderly; (2) a larger public universal program serving the poor and some of the middle class; (3) a voluntary universal program serving a middle-class, primarily white, population. In addition to a distinction between selective and universal services, eligibility criteria also reflect confusion regarding a definition of age (ranging from 55 plus to 65 plus) and conflict between city and county residence.

Coverage is difficult to assess because there is no clear, consistent definition of need and at present no figures which indicate who the service users are. Are they multiple service users predominantly? Individual service users? What are the priorities for service? These questions are important because of the ephemeral nature of most of the funding for social services for elderly in this community. Heavily dependent an AoA project grants and largely lacking in any other public service provision, the community may find itself facing a substantial curtailment in resources without any clear idea as to which services should receive priority.

A major program lack is the paucity of in-home homemaker–home health aide services. Acknowledging the need for this service, local personnel attribute its absence to the lack of federal support for it.

Finally, program integration, coordination, and linkages exist more in theory than in fact. In particular, there appear to be none between health, mental health, and social services. There is no indication that devices for case integration exist except in one project (Project CARE) nor does it appear that its absence is recognized as a problem in service delivery.

Trends and Issues

When we review the several existing, ad hoc, potentially conflicting, and often merely rhetorical policies regarding the aged in the United States, it is clear there is no coherent, overall national policy.

The dominant federal strategy for satisfying the basic needs of the aged is the provision of income (cash, voucher or other noncash income supplements). Yet there is general consensus that even this policy is inadequately supported. Even with the new SSI program and increased Social Security benefits, at least 15 percent of the aged are still poor and another 5 percent are described as the "hidden poor." But that figure is deceptive because the increase in Social Security benefits has tended to move a large group just over the poverty line but not much more, clustering under 125 percent of poverty income. The cash income of the elderly as a group is still clearly inadequate.

Furthermore, noncash income support programs continue to be in short supply. Even though the Congress has gone further with food stamps than either the USDA or the executive branch had intended, essential goods and services have come nowhere close to meeting existing quantitative demands; and rapidly expanding demand for the limited supply has led to sharply rising prices in several categories of goods and services, as well. Thus, for example:

U.S. health programs are essentially funding devices, not provision for service delivery, and the funding, by general agreement, has not produced adequate services for Medicare and Medicaid recipients. Medicare is supportive of acute, short-term care and treatment within institutions, not prevention, long-term, or home-based care. Funding for—or reimbursement of—this latter category of care remains largely nonexistent. In particular, it is the group just above the Medicaid eligibility line who are suffering the most.

A housing supply specially designed to meet the needs of the elderly has not emerged in response to normal market demands; in addition, public housing programs at the present time continue to be limited. There has been limited imagination and innovation in housing for the elderly, and community resistance and hostility to such facilities is increasing. Little is being done as a matter of public policy to offset or correct this. Housing conditions are at their worst in the suburbs and small towns because of zoning, land use, and access to transportation and services. Since in recent years, with the increase in Social Security benefits, more of the aged are moving from farms to nearby small towns, the paucity of appropriate housing in these areas is becoming even more of a problem.

What little exists in the way of social service provision can in no way substitute for these inadequacies. In fact, social services, too, are quantitatively and qualitatively inadequate, fragmented, and of dubious effectiveness. Data regarding the aged and their needs are imprecise, inconsistent, and not uniformly collected; nor are there firm figures regarding public (let alone private) expenditures for services for the aged. There are few standards or regulations regarding service quality and what little does exist is rarely enforced. Access to services remains limted; and a proliferation of miscellaneous small-scale service programs does little to provide comprehensive coverage.

Most people would agree that to examine income, health, and living and care arrangements in depth is to see the close interrelationship among them, yet U.S. policies treat these as separate and discrete categories of need. Moreover, only at extraordinarily high income levels can adequate health and residential care and services be purchased in the open market. By and large, the supply of these essential goods and services has not responded to demand at a price the overwhelming majority of the elderly can afford, nor do most older people have the information and knowledge to make good choices, given the limited resources available. Finally, there are problems such as loneliness, isolation, and the need for personal care—problems which may be inevitable with age—that cannot be satisfied with money alone.

Our position is, therefore, that regardless of the critical importance of income, neither cash nor noncash income support programs function at levels sufficient to meet the basic needs of the aged. Furthermore, even if basic provision were more adequate, certain kinds of social support services would continue to be needed. However, the types and extent of these services cannot be specified outside the context of basic provision. Social services cannot replace—or carry the burden of inadequacies in—cash income, health care, housing. Instead, what these services can do is supplement and complement existing provision.

Once there is a coherent national policy—and conflict over the nature and extent of basic provision is resolved—then we can be more precise about the quantity and quality of social support needed to implement a spectrum of living and care arrangements. Yet even this requires a perspective other than the traditional one followed in this country.

Historically, social services have been designed to meet emergency, crisis, and short-term needs. In contrast, aging, by definition a cumulative, degenerative, and inevitable process, requires extensive, ongoing, long-term help. To date, most programs are directed toward the already isolated aged, not toward preventing isolation. Although the family has been a major social care provider for the aged, we do little to support or enhance the family in this role. In fact, care and services are often provided only when family resources are severely strained or spouses pauperized, not when the aged are still able to be helped by family and friends. When service provision is related to medical care or built into private housing (e.g., "leisure home villages"), services are heavily utilized and the image is different. Since the historical approach to eligibility has been largely by means-test criteria, for many of the aged these services continue to be stigmatized, equated as they are with the poor and "welfare." Finally, existing patterns of take-up and service utilization continue to reflect confusion of social service provision and use with individual or personal inadequacy; and the value placed in our society on independence continues to inhibit service use by those who fear the image of dependence, as inevitable as it may be, when older.

Thus the major issues as currently debated include: the inadequacy of social insurance and social assistance benefits and the need to relate these to the cost of living; the inadequacy of health insurance and health services especially as they relate to preventive, long-term, and home-based care; the lack of specially designed and subsidized housing; the fragmentation, unresponsiveness, lack of coverage, and stigma attached to social services; and the failure to recognize the interrelationship of all policies affecting the aged especially income, health, housing, and social services. The very concept "living and care arrangements" implies an awareness of this interrelationship, yet in fact it is not implemented through legislation.

Living and Care Arrangements for the Aged: The Role of the Personal Social Services

The current national policy thrust reflects a distorted perspective and an inappropriate conceptualization of issues. The major rhetorical objective repeatedly stressed is to help older people live in their own homes as long as possible. The guiding "theme," "slogan," or organizing principle for relevant policy and program development is termed "deinstitutionalization"—or a search for "alternatives to institutions" or a stress on "community care." Because of this definition of the policy task our report has focused on this aspect of social provision. Our conclusions are as follows.

First, this is an inappropriate definition of task or focus because we have as yet no clear operational definition of "institution" or "community." The boundaries between institutions and noninstitutions, between community-based or non-community-based facilities, or between medical and nonmedical facilities, are unclear and inconsistent. Is the criterion for an institution merely size? Is a facility with space for 50 beds by definition "better" than a facility with 150 beds? When does a congregate care facility become an institution? Is the criterion geography? Is a nursing home in a centrally located part of a major city "better" than a facility in a suburban area (or vice versa)? Is a facility in a rural area outside of town community based? (Suppose friends and relatives live nearby?) How does one distinguish medical and nonmedical facilities? The current delineation relates to criteria for reimbursement under Medicare and/or Medicaid (numbers of beds, numbers and training of staff, hours of nursing and physician coverage, etc.). A multiple-housing dwelling for the elderly that contains a health service with a registered nurse on duty between 9:00 and 5:00, five days a week, a physician on duty three half-days a week, and a medical emergency service available by phone at all other times is still defined as a nonmedical facility. (And is this or is this not an institution?)

Current policy appears to be preoccupied with a search for cheaper forms of service. Without some firm criteria regarding the objectives of such services and comparable standards regarding quality of care, such a criterion seems both invalid and irrational. It seems fairly clear from the limited evidence that exists that, depending on the real needs of the elderly, protected, extensive, long-term medical and nursing care will continue to be necessary for some. The need for such care may even increase as more people live still longer with varying degrees of impairment. Clearly, one essential service need for older people will continue to be provision of high quality care in such facilities; and such care is cheaper when provided on a large scale than on an individual basis.

To formulate the problem as "deinstitutionalization" is to ignore the fact that aging is a degenerative and irreversible process, occurring over time and that the need is not for "no care" versus "intensive" or "extensive" care, but rather for a continuum of care—varying types and amounts of help, over time, including a selection from the range of in-home and out-of-home services mentioned earlier.

Second, the real issue would seem to be that given some criteria of need and preference, what kinds of service-facilities-programs best satisfy or are most appropriate for those needs? One major problem is the need to develop some standardized, consistent criteria for assessing individual needs and a standardized classification of functional impairment, and then to provide a continuum or spectrum of facilities and services as appropriate. One objective should be to permit people to remain in their own homes as long as they can and want to. When this is no longer possible, protected or congregate housing facilities with varying amounts of personal and medical care should be available in reasonably close proximity to relatives and friends.

The decision to live in one's own home, congregate housing, or a medical facility should be related to need and preference, not contingent on income as it often is today (e.g., a nursing home is fully reimbursable under Medicaid; SSI does not cover the rental of a sheltered housing unit).

The community in which the elderly live should be the real base of care and a continuum of all levels of care and service related to their individual needs should be available. Development of different models should be encouraged in response to consumer and community preferences, existing initiatives and facilities. (Illustrations of operating models have been provided earlier.) For example: hospital-based service systems with outreach to the community; systems based in community centers—or housing projects—with linkages to nearby hospitals; housing complexes with a complete package of supportive and supplementary services; housing with recreational facilities and other services available on request from agencies in the community. We do not know as yet whether there are different consequences of using different loci for service delivery or what the implications of this might be; therefore, we would urge experimentation and a pluralistic approach. When congregate housing arrangements are established, however, it must be recognized that tenant cohorts will continue to age and functional impairment will increase. If there is no anticipation of this (and of how to cope with the implications and consequences of it), such facilities will themselves become "institutions" in time.

What is lacking at present is real choice for the elderly when they need some care and help but do not need or want traditional institutionalization. They may want to remain in their own homes or to move to some specially designed dwellings where personal care and medical services are available if and when needed but where they can continue to be independent, mobile, and near friends and relatives. Thus far, such alternatives have been available only in limited amounts and only to the very wealthy in this country. Home-based help and care, with a full panoply of home health services, is not readily available under current social policy; nor are various types of specially designed subsidized housing; nor are the other social care services identified and described earlier; nor is any effort made at employing relatives, neighbors, friends to provide such care, as is done in other countries.* Only when such services exist and coverage is extensive will real options exist.

Once there is some consensus regarding national policy for the aged including programs directed toward providing a wide range of facilities and services supporting a continuum of living and care arrangements, two other important issues remain regarding the delivery of services: the need to integrate different service systems (health, income, housing, social services) as they affect the individual; and the need to clarify the structure of personal social services themselves.

Even if a coherent overall policy were to be developed regarding the aged, a major problem is how to integrate simultaneously needed services from different social sectors or from within the same social sector. Unless all programs for the aged were administered through one system or one system were to be assigned basic responsibility for integrating the others or one practitioner were to be given primary responsibility for ensuring provision, fragmentation would be inevitable. In particular, where the aged are concerned, needs are so interrelated that sanction for case integration must be specifically authorized.

Finally, exacerbating further the problem of fragmentation and stigma is the dual system of personal social services as it now exists in the United States. In effect we have two basic federal social welfare programs for the aged, and their respective state bureaucracies: the one means tested and administered by SRS and the other uni-

*Homemaker–home health services in the U.S. are startlingly inadequate when compared with other countries—a ratio of 1:7000 in the U.S., contrasted with 1:760 in Denmark, 1:670 in the U.K., 1:260 in Holland. Where the aged in particular are concerned, in Britain the ratio is 1 home help to every 182 elderly.

In the past, conventional arguments related to whether housing for the aged should be segregated (for the aged only) or integrated. When one talks with the elderly themselves, leaders of organizations representing them, or directors of programs serving the aged, this formulation of the issue seems completely inappropriate. The fact is that some elderly want to surround themselves with their age peers and others do not, and this is true regardless of income level. The issue continues to be one of providing options and choice, and responding to differences among the aged and their needs.

Sweden, for example, gives financial support to relatives who provide extensive care for elderly (or handicapped) family members. Such relatives compose close to a quarter of the pool of homemaker–home helps in Sweden. Supporting the family and subsidizing such forms of home care, instead of penalizing families now providing it as is our current policy, would be one way to expand community provision.

versal and administered by AoA. The primary system comprises all public provision and is means-tested; the secondary system includes a small public program as well as the whole voluntary service network and is universal, depending on user status and sometimes on diagnostic criteria. A single universal system, with combined status and diagnostic criteria (and these clearly and consistently defined and standardized) and all qualified by individual preference, might make for a far better system and also a more economical one with a simplified administrative base.

The Social Care Service

In reviewing community services for the aged, one is struck by the absence of a satisfactory, consistent organizing principle. Traditional formulations tend to utilize discrete, often dichotomous categories, such as institutional versus community-based provision, medical versus nonmedical care, long-term versus short-term care. Not only are the boundaries unclear but the distinction is often dysfunctional because this is not how needs are felt in the real world, where the needs of the aged are often cumulative and increase gradually over time. What is required in planning services for the aged is the development of a conceptual framework that encompasses a continuum or spectrum of needs. Moreover, we note: The major users of services other than socialization and recreational programs are those aged 75 and over. The most heavily used services are those involving a mix of health and social services. Regardless of whether they are provided in the home or outside the home, what characterizes these services is the element of practical personal care and help.

In searching for an accurate formulation to describe these services we employ a term used in Britain which we think is particularly appropriate: the social care services. More precisely, social care is a term describing a particular cluster of practical helping measures, including personal care and hygiene (assistance with bathing and dressing), home health services (light practical nursing, assistance in taking medication), homemaker services (meal preparation, light cleaning and laundry), shopping, chore, and escort services, and visiting and reassurance services.

Where the aged are concerned social care services can encompass both in-home and out-of-home services, delivered in ordinary or congregate housing, provided from either a medical or a social service facility. They do not represent all the personal social services. Clearly, other types of services are needed for the "young" aged adjusting to retirement, for those wanting leisure-time programs, and so forth. Yet it seems equally apparent that these services are essential in caring for the aged (and also for the handicapped).

In fact, it would seem that social care services could become the cornerstone of a personal social services system for the aged. Moreover, such a formulation of function and service could provide a new and important perspective on the personal social services generally and have major impact on how they are conceptualized. We will return again to this subject, in Chapter 8.

Toward the Immediate Future

U.S. policy toward providing social services for the aged is at a critical point now.[15] Historically, such provision has been limited in coverage, categorical in nature, and means tested. Certain services were mandated under the old age assistance titles of the Social Security Act, but coverage was poor because stress was on confirming eligibility and this is what most staff did. Little in the way of real service was provided to the aged. In fact, it was in response to the inadequacies of the program—and to its limitations to people on assistance—that the Older Americans Act was passed; but this legislation did not provide for extensive coverage either. Funding demonstration projects primarily, subsequent amendments have stressed support and separate administration of either specialized programs (e.g., nutrition) or planning and coordination efforts. Moreover, all funding support is time-limited and the matching formula is reduced over time. The coverage problem remains unsolved. Moreover, neither the national agency nor the local area agencies on aging have the authority to compel the coordination they identify as so important. The new SSA Amendment Title XX also mandates planning; in addition, it permits for more extensive coverage by expanding the possible eligibility base for services for both free and fee-paying clients. Although it mandates only one service for the aged, it does require at least one service for each of five goals, several of which clearly relate to the aged. Furthermore, the legislation includes no means test for information and referral services or for protective services to the aged. A state's planning process is required to be exposed to public scrutiny and review. Clearly, state plans will respond to public pressure—and inevitably there will be much pressure on the part of organized groups representing the aged. Finally, the regulations also have a clause mandating that the state plan provide for coordination with relevant programs. All this should make some difference in planning and providing social services for the elderly. With luck, some evidence of this should be seen soon.

Notes

1. Post-White House Conference on Aging Reports, *Toward a New Attitude on Aging, April 1973*, prepared for the Subcommittee on Aging of the Committee on Labor and Public Welfare and the Special Committee on Aging, U.S. Senate (Washington, D.C.: GPO, Sept. 1973), p. 8.

2. Elaine M. Brody, "Aging," *Encyclopedia of Social Work* (16th issue; New York: National Association of Social Workers, 1971), p. 51.

3. Unless otherwise indicated all data presented refer to 1973. The material covered in this section is derived from the following sources: Herman Brotman, "Every 10th American," prepared for inclusion in U.S. Senate, Special Committee on Aging, *Developments in Aging: 1974 and January-April 1975;* and *Developments in Aging: 1973 and January-March 1974.*

4. Quoted in Special Committee on Aging, U.S. Senate Subcommittee on Long Term Care, *Nursing Home Care in the United States: Failure in Public Policy* (Washington, D.C.: GPO, Nov. 1974).

5. According to Robert M. Ball, former Commissioner of Social Security Administration, in his testimony before the Special Committee on Aging, "Future Directions in Social Security," Hearing before the Special Committee on Aging, U.S. Senate, 94th Congress, 1st sess., Part 11, Washington, D.C., March 20, 1975, p. 948.

6. *Developments in Aging* (1974–75), p. 13.

7. As of January 1976 both maximum taxable income and benefit schedules were raised.

8. See the report of the Senate Subcommittee, *The Rise and Threatened Fall of Service Programs for the Elderly: A Report by the Subcommittee on Federal, State and Community Services of the Special Committee on Aging, United States Senate,* March 1973 (Washington, D.C.: GPO, 1973).

9. For an excellent review and analysis of the whole field of congregate housing for the elderly, see Marie McGuire Thompson, *Congregate*

Housing for Older Adults: A Working Paper Prepared for Use by the Special Committee on Aging, U.S. Senate (Washington, D.C.: GPO, Nov. 1975).

10. Brahna Trager, *Home Health Services in the United States: A Report for the Special Committee on Aging, U.S. Senate* (Washington, D.C.: GPO, 1972); *Home Health Services in the United States: A Working Paper on Current Status* (Washington, D.C.: GPO, 1973).

11. *The Rise and Threatened Fall of Service Programs for the Elderly.*

12. These and certain earlier program descriptions are derived from material made available by the Administration on Aging. See, for example, *Let's End Isolation* (Administration on Aging Publication No. 129, May 1973; Washington, D.C.: GPO, 1973).

13. William Pollak, *Costs of Alternative Care Settings for the Elderly* (Washington, D.C.: Urban Institute, 1973), p. 2.

14. Trager, *Home Health Services.*

15. In addition to items cited, the following readings are suggested: R. C. Atchley, *Social Forces in Later Life: An Introduction to Social Geronology* (Belmont, Calif.: Wadsworth, 1972); Zena Smith Blau, *Old Age in a Changing Society* (New York: Franklin Watts, 1973); Robert N. Butler, *Why Survive? Being Old in America* (New York: Harper & Row, 1975); Bernice L. Neugarten, ed., *Middle Age and Aging* (Chicago: University of Chicago Press, 1968); Matilda Riley et al., *Aging and Society* (3 vols.; New York: Russell Sage, 1968); Ethel Shanas et al., *Old People in Three Industrial Societies* (New York: Aldine, 1968); Bert Kruger Smith, *Aging in America* (Boston: Beacon, 1973); *The Political Consequences of Aging: The Annals,* vol. 415 (Sept. 1974); Eric Pfeiffer, M.D., *Alternatives to Institutional Care for Older Americans: Practice and Planning* (Raleigh, N.C.: Duke University Press, 1973).

Family Planning

Context and Definition

This chapter covers a field which is unique among those described thus far because the role of the personal social services in family planning is unabashedly ancillary. Regardless of how satisfactorily the service is provided, most people consider family planning to be part of the medical or health care system. Our particular focus, here, is on how people learn about and obtain this service. We are not concerned with the technology of contraception or with legislation regarding abortion per se. Instead, we are interested in such questions as: What is the role of the social worker in a medical program? What is the nature of the relationship between the medical and social service systems?

Broadly defined, population policy includes actions by government to influence mortality, fertility, and migration, usually to achieve explicit national demographic goals. Historically, the United States has never espoused an explicit national population policy. An implicit policy might be inferred from analysis of immigration policy and laws, the potential incentives and disincentives for controlling fertility inherent in various legislative enactments, and official pronouncements such as the recommendation of the Commission on Population Growth and the American Future that we should plan to stabilize our population. But any effort at inferring such a policy would only point up the major inconsistencies and lack of coherence that characterize this country's attitude toward controlling population.

Instead, policy and legislation in the United States have focused on one specific aspect of population control—namely, facilitating the regulation and control of individual fertility.* Regardless of the different and occasionally conflicting objectives of groups and individuals supporting this policy, it is this concern with family planning as fertility regulation policy that has characterized U.S. population policy over the last decade; and it is this that is the focus of the material presented here.

Historically, both primitive and civilized societies have sought to control reproduction through such means as abstinence, delayed age of marriage, infanticide, induced abortion, or crude forms of contraception. Until recently, however, control over family size and the timing and spacing of children in the United States was disproportionately the prerogative of those with access to private medical care. Then, in the late 1950s and 1960s, a number of forces met to create a new social and political climate that reduced the constraints on access to family planning services at the same time as the means of fertility control available to American citizens were modified and expanded. The assemblage of interdependent forces included mounting recognition of the dangers to humanity from accelerating population growth and the associated depletion of resources; the development of improved contraceptive technology; the emergence of new attitudes, norms, and structures regarding human sexuality, family forms, and life styles; the push for human rights and self-determination on the part of ethnic minorities, women, youth, consumer groups, and others. There was also growing concern about the social and individual consequences of illegitimacy, illegal abortion, and the health hazards associated with early and frequent childbearing. Finally, there was the rediscovery of poverty in the midst of American plenty, concern about its causes, and a desire to mitigate its effects.

Thus, implicit in current U.S. policy are several assumptions: First, unwanted pregnancy has undesirable social, health, and economic consequences for individuals and couples, and for their children. Second, unregulated population growth erodes the quality of life and contributes to economic, political, and social stress and tension in society generally. Third, facilitating individual fertility

*There are those who deny that facilitating voluntary and individual control of fertility can be considered as part of population policy. The relevant issues will be explored in the final section of this chapter.

control may lead to limiting population growth, thus improving the quality of life nationally as well as for individuals. Fourth, facilitation of fertility control requires both improved technology and expanded access to, and availability of, family planning services.

Family planning is a voluntary action by individuals to plan the number and spacing of their children—usually by preventing unwanted pregnancies but, in some instances, by enhancing the fertility of persons desiring children. Family planning services include those medical, social, and educational services deemed necessary to enable individuals to meet their family planning objectives.

Medical services include gynecological examinations, urinalysis, blood pressure tests, venereal disease screening, pap smears, pregnancy testing, sickle cell anemia testing, services to overcome infertility, and provision of a variety of fertility control methods including abortion and sterilization. *Social and educational services* comprise: outreach and follow-up (patient identification, location, contact, discussion, appointment, referral to other agencies for social services); facilitation services (transportation, babysitting, nonmedical counseling when necessary, in-clinic instruction and discussion); general community information and educational activities (through all media to all types of community institutions and individuals, including, for example, family life education, human sexuality and health, social and demographic rationales for family planning, in addition to information concerned with the specifics of contraceptive methods).[1] These three categories of service include those generally considered as comprising access.

Our purpose here—defined by the objectives of the work as a whole—is to review and analyze the role(s) played by social services in providing family planning services. Clearly, current U.S. policy underscores the importance of access in expanding the availability and provision of those services designed to facilitate individual, voluntary control of fertility. The personal social services are considered to have a broad access responsibility for the entire social sector.

What follows, therefore, will include a review of U.S. family planning policy, legislation, and programs—with particular stress on the extent to which expanded access has in fact been the dominant principle, how it has been implemented, and by whom, and what, as far as we know, have been the consequences. Our description of historical and contemporary features of family planning services in the United States will be limited to those aspects necessary for understanding the issues related to access.

Framework for Provision

Legislative and Administrative Issues

Until about sixty years ago, there were no organized family planning programs in the United States. The evolution of public support for family planning was slow due to legal, medical, and social constraints. Before the early 1960s the more effective family planning services were limited, generally, to those who had access to private medical care and provision; in effect, they were limited to those who could afford them. Only when general concern with achieving control and regulation of fertility began to grow, and when evidence from research suggested that the poor tended to have larger families because they had less access to family planning information and could not afford the services, did U.S. policy and laws begin to change.

Family Planning

The first major statutory changes occurred at the state level in 1965 and 1966, when five states repealed restrictions on the dissemination of contraceptive information. Soon after, twelve other states enacted legislation encouraging public health departments or welfare agencies to provide family planning services at public expense. By 1971, eighteen states had affirmative family planning laws, and the number of states with no laws restricting the distribution of contraceptives has been increasing. In 1965, the U.S. Supreme Court ruled that married couples have a constitutional right to practice contraception free of state interference. In 1972, two-thirds of the states permitted contraceptive services to be made available to women eighteen years of age and over on their own consent and one-third of these states included much younger females or specified no age limit.

The first federal involvement in family planning services occurred in 1942, when the surgeon general ruled that Maternal and Child Health funds (MCH) could be used for family planning services by states wishing to do so. Only a few states, all in the South, used federal funds to help finance these services in the forties and fifties; however, beginning in 1963, Maternity and Infant Care projects (MIC) gradually incorporated family planning services into comprehensive maternity care. Federal administrative policy in support of family planning services began to emerge only in the mid-sixties under pressure from Congress and President Johnson. The first federal efforts at implementing this policy was initiated in 1965, when the Office of Economic Opportunity began to make grants to finance voluntary family planning projects. DHEW issued its first policy statement on family planning in 1966. Subsequently, the objectives of U.S. policy were made explicit for the first time in a presidential message on health and education by President Lyndon Johnson: "We have a growing concern to foster the integrity of the family and the opportunity for each child. It is essential that all families have access to information and services that will allow freedom to choose the number and spacing of their children within the dictates of individual conscience."

Implementation of this policy by federal agencies continued to lag until they were prodded by additional legislation. In 1967 the Economic Opportunity Amendments designated family planning as a "special emphasis" component of the antipoverty programs under Title II. Family planning became one of eight national OEO programs—such as Head Start, legal services, and neighborhood health centers—funded directly by OEO to assist eligible low-income persons to control fertility and improve their economic status. These projects were transferred gradually to DHEW. (By the end of fiscal 1974 all family planning projects had been transferred to DHEW for continuing support or consolidation with DHEW family planning programs.)

Social Security Act amendments authorized federal funds for family planning services to be provided to eligible persons. Four titles of this legislation are relevant:

Title IV-A, known as the Aid to Families with Dependent Children programs, as amended in 1967, included a mandatory requirement for states to offer family planning services to present welfare recipients and, at the states' option, to certain former or potential welfare recipients. The Social Security amendments of 1972 included incentives for states to provide family planning services by increasing federal funding for these programs from a ratio of three dollars to every dollar contributed by the states, the general service reimbursement formula, to a ratio of 9:1. Moreover, any state failing to offer and provide services to current welfare recipients desiring them is subject to a one percent penalty reduction in its AFDC funds for the year. The regulations implementing these amendments include the following specifications:

Offer—An offer of family planning services occurs when a person is informed of the availability of these services and the means for obtaining them. The offer must be made to current recipients in writing. The requirement of a written offer may be met by a flyer, one to a family, with the assistance check. A record must be maintained of the offer. The offer must be made within 31 days of the first assistance payment, and once a year thereafter.

Beginning April 1, 1974, when an applicant is denied assistance or withdraws his or her application, or when a recipient's grant is discontinued, if the individual or family is eligible for family planning services under the State's IV-A plan, the agency, at that time, must inform the individual in writing that such services are available for three months from the time the individual was an applicant or former recipient. A record must be kept of the written notification.

Exception: The individual or appropriate family members have already requested and received family planning services or have requested same and the agency has initiated a plan for providing them which it expects to carry to completion.

When a written offer is not appropriate (e.g., illiteracy, language barrier) other arrangements for determining a recipient's desire for family planning services are required.

Request—A request for family planning service consists of a specific statement either orally or in writing, to the IV-A agency by an eligible individual requesting family planning services. Both written and oral requests must be documented.

Provide Promptly—Under the law, family planning services may be provided either directly by the IV-A agency staff or under arrangements with others, i.e., purchase under either IV-A or XIX or referral to some other resource such as MCH or family planning projects. The standard for promptness will be within 30 days of the date of request. This means that provision of those services furnished directly by the agency must have been initiated within 30 days. With respect to services provided under arrangements with others, the agency must have, within 30 days, made available the services of an appropriate family planning resource. This would include referral and any other facilitating arrangements, such as transportation, as needed.

Agency records must document the offer, the request for family planning services, and the disposition of each request, including the source from which services are to be provided and the method of payment.

In addition, in order to assure that Family Planning resources being used by the agency are adequately providing services as required, persons should be informed that they should notify the agency in an instance

when the person or agency to whom referred does not provide the services requested with reasonable promptness. A record of all such complaints should be kept to assure that satisfactory service is being provided.
The 1 percent penalty on Title IV-A funds will be applied in the ensuing fiscal year, when, during the previous year, less than 95 percent of the appropriate families were informed about family planning services and received family planning services as required.

Implementing regulations issued by DHEW extended coverage to all women married or single, childless or pregnant. Narrative reports were required of each state for fiscal 1973 due June 1, 1974, describing actions taken to meet the legal requirements during fiscal 1973. By April 1, 1974, states were to have installed statistical reporting and documenting systems to provide the means for annual reporting of their activities.

Title V, as amended in 1967, required that at least 6 percent of the funds appropriated for Maternal and Child Health services were to be allocated through formula and project grants to family planning services.* Authorization of these funds occurred as part of an overall program for promoting the health of mothers and children especially in rural areas and/or in areas having a concentration of low-income families. Individual persons served, however, did not have to meet specific eligibility requirements.

Title XIX, as initially passed in 1965, permitted family planning to be a reimbursable service depending on state administrative decisions, even though it was not a specific service identified within the program. However, little use of this source of funds was made by the states for several reasons (e.g., failure to develop a Medicaid program, paucity of funding or "federal matching," a state's failure to include family planning as a service within its Medicaid plan). But in 1972 federal statutes made family planning a mandatory element of state Medicaid plans and federal policy and created an incentive for state Medicaid plans to include family planning as a service by increasing the federal contribution to the financing of these services to a 9:1 ratio. Consequently, pressure was exerted on existing federally funded projects to seek third-party reimbursement, and this

*Formula grants are apportioned among the states and administered under a state plan approved by DHEW. Project grants are direct awards to public and nonprofit private organizations for family planning services exclusively or for a range of services, including family planning. Effective June 30, 1974, Title V Project Grants were folded into formula grants as provided by law.

legislation became an important factor in the growth and establishment of family planning services.

Title XX, effective October 1975, eliminated Title IV-A (among other titles). Under this title the individual states are required to develop their own plans regarding social service provision. (See Chapters 1 and 7 and the Appendix for a more extensive discussion of this amendment to the Social Security Act.) Family planning services are the only specifically mandated service. The one percent penalty remains for failure to offer and provide services to public assistance recipients. The range of potential service recipients is extensive. The legislation permits provision of free services to those whose income is under 80 percent of the national or state median income level (whichever is lower) and fee-paying services to those whose income is up to 115 percent of median income. However, since it is up to the states to define eligibility beyond public assistance levels it remains to be seen how extensive in fact this provision is and, even more important, whether the states elect to use the limited amount of Title XX funds for provision of family planning services or whether they opt instead for reimbursement under the open-ended Title XIX, a funding mechanism that is far more restrictive with regard to the eligible population.

Further affirmation of federal policy may be seen in a 1969 statement by President Richard M. Nixon emphasizing that no American woman should be denied access to family planning because of her economic condition.[2] He set as a national goal the provision of adequate family planning services within the following five years to all those who wanted but could not afford them.

Legislation creating the Commission on Population Growth and the American Future was enacted in 1970; and in 1972, in its final report, the Commission recommended a broad range of health, education, economic, and social programs to facilitate achievement of a stabilized population in the United States.

Also, in 1970, Congress passed the only major legislation specifically directed toward family planning, the Family Planning Services and Population Research Act, which established Title X of the Public Health Services Act. The Act established an Office of Population Affairs under the Secretary of DHEW to serve as the primary focus within the federal government for family planning services. It also required the Secretary to develop and to report annually to the Congress the results of a five-year plan for expanding family planning services.

Under the Act, grants and contracts are placed with public and nonprofit private organizations to provide comprehensive voluntary family planning services to all persons desiring them. Although no eligibility restrictions are specified, services are required to be given to low-income people; and regulations specify that programs must seek payment from third-party reimbursement sources whenever possible. (For purposes of this legislation, in 1972, "low income" was defined as an annual income of $5,000 or less for a family of four. This was equal at that time to 135 percent of the poverty level. This figure has not been changed since and in 1975 was slightly under the poverty level.)

Sterilization

Most states have no statutes referring to voluntary sterilization, in effect making the procedure legal for contraceptive or therapeutic reasons in all states. A few states require consent of the spouse; some states protect a hospital's or a physician's right to refuse to perform sterilization; all but one state prescribes a minimum age, usually 21, or that the individual be married or have parental consent.

Following the controversial sterilization of two young sisters in Alabama in 1973, DHEW proposed regulations relating to the sterilization of minors and mentally incompetent individuals, and placed a moratorium on the use of federal funds for such sterilizations. A federal court ruled that federal funds may not be used to sterilize minors and mentally incompetent individuals and ordered DHEW to revise the sterilization regulations to ensure that before informed consent for sterilization is given, competent adults are advised, both orally and on the consent form, that refusal to undergo a sterilization will not result in the loss of any federal benefits. Judge Gerhard Gesell noted that when Congress authorized family planning programs under Title X of the Public Health Services Act and Titles IV-A and XIX of the Social Security Act, it had insisted that all programs operate on a totally voluntary basis. He said there was "uncontroverted evidence" that poor people, particularly pregnant women whose deliveries would be paid for by Medicaid, have been coerced into accepting sterilization under the threat of losing welfare benefits and that the final regulations failed to ensure that federal funds were not used "to coerce indigent patients into submitting to sterilization."[3]

Abortion

This is a period of major change:

From a population exigency point of view, the past four years—1967 to 1971—have seen a revolution in the laws pertaining to abortion in the U.S. From the early 19th century until 1967, the entire trend in the country was in the direction of strict abortion laws—stricter indeed than the common law which freely countenances abortion at least prior to viability. Even the Catholic church had earlier had a more lenient position in connection with early abortion than did most states. However, the United States laws, by and large, made abortion a crime, even in the earlier stages of pregnancy, and most of them excepted from the prohibition only an abortion necessary to save the life of the mother. When the laws were passed, they may well have served a health purpose; abortion, in common with all other surgical procedures, was highly dangerous in the era before antisepsis, anesthesia, antibiotics, and so forth. Today, of course, abortion is not a hazardous procedure and, statistically, it is safer than childbirth. Notwithstanding that fact, however, until 1967, virtually all efforts to repeal or modify the laws failed. Then suddenly in 1967, the tide began to turn.[4]

There were a number of reasons for this, including the experience in Japan and Europe, where abortions in large numbers had been performed safely and were associated with spectacular drops in the birth rates. In 1967, the first laws liberalizing abortion were passed in California, Colorado, and North Carolina. By 1970, fifteen states had adopted such laws. On January 22, 1973, the United States Supreme Court ruled in a case involving a Texas woman that for the first trimester of pregnancy, the decision concerning abortion is a matter between a woman and her physician; during the second and third trimesters, states may regulate abortion in ways that are reasonably related to maternal health; for the last weeks of pregnancy, when the fetus is judged capable of surviving if born, any state may regulate or even prohibit abortion except where abortion is necessary to preserve the life or health of the mother.[5] Examples of permissible state regulation were cited: requirements regarding the qualifications and licensing of the person performing the abortion; and requirements regarding the facility where the procedure is to be performed, that is, whether it must be a hospital, or may be a clinic or some other place of less-than-hospital status, and its licensing. In a separate decision on the same day in a case involving the Georgia law, the Supreme Court ruled any residency requirement to be unconstitutional. Other aspects of the law that were invalidated were the requirements that abortions be performed in private accredited hospitals, that applicants be screened by hospital committees, and that there be certification by two independent doctors that continued pregnancy is potentially dangerous to the woman's health.[6] Following these decisions, thirty-one states adopted abortion laws which conform to the decisions. Some seventeen other states passed abortion laws in 1973, aspects of which have been challenged on constitutional grounds. There are a number of states where abortions are not yet available for any reason, so that women desiring the procedure must travel to another area. In addition, resolutions have been adopted in a number of states requesting Congress to propose constitutional amendments securing the right to life for the unborn, or giving to states the right to regulate abortion in ways that are reasonably related to maternal health; or to call for a constitutional convention to consider antiabortion amendments.

Summary

This brief overall review of major legislative enactments, judicial decisions, and administrative pronouncements and procedures pertaining to contraception, voluntary sterilization, and abortion reveals major differences, inconsistencies, and obstacles to access and provision. There are variations in eligibility requirements among different federally funded programs authorized under different laws. Moreover, eligibility varies among the states regarding programs funded under two sources of federal authorization (Titles IV-A and XIX—and, in 1975, XX), because some criteria for eligibility are set by the individual states, not by the federal government. Furthermore, the types of medical and social services that can be provided vary, depending on the federal authorization under which the program is established. Clearly, restrictive aspects of any of these laws or regulations limit access to family planning services insofar as they limit access to information, counseling, supplies, devices, and/or procedures.

Coverage and Utilization

Considering the restrictions that exist with regard to policy and legislation, how extensive are organized family planning services in the United States? What is the extent of federal funds supporting these programs? How many users are there, who are they, and who are the nonusers of organized family planning services?[7]

According to the Office of Population Affairs' *Fourth Progress Report to the Congress of the U.S. on Its Five Year Plan for Family Planning Services and Population Research,* the two major goals of organized family planning services programs are:

to make subsidized family planning services available throughout the country.

to make subsidized family planning services available to all who want but cannot afford them.[8]

To what extent have these objectives been achieved? In 1960 no more than 150 public and private health agencies, most of them affiliates of Planned Parenthood, operated organized family planning programs serving about 150,000 women. In fiscal 1969, 863,000 low-income women were served in 1,983 agencies. By 1974, 3,383 organized family planning programs in hospitals, health departments, and voluntary agencies served 3.4 million individuals living in 95 percent of all American counties. However, the annual rate at which the numbers of low-income women served has grown has decreased sharply within the last few years.

DHEW efforts to increase the number of states with Title IV-A contracts and Title XIX agreements to provide family planning services resulted in nineteen states having IV-A contracts by 1974 while negotiations were still in process in thirteen more states. Title XIX agreements existed in forty-two states, with negotiations continuing in five others. (A Title XIX agreement with a state is an agreement that the state will include family planning services as a covered service under the state Medicaid plan and such agreements specify which providers states will reimburse and the amount they will pay for services.)

Ninety-five percent of the counties in the United States are described as having some form of organized, subsidized family planning services (facilities or a physician-referral program) available to residents—two-thirds within their own boundaries and the remaining third within adjacent counties. Most counties without coverage are described as sparsely settled and have few low-income women.

Nearly all those using organized family planning service programs had low or marginal incomes.* About 54 percent of the 3.4 million women served were members of families with incomes equal to or

*In what follows, regarding the extent of coverage of family planning services in relation to income level, stress on the poverty level as a standard reflects the approach employed in the official government report to Congress. The relevant federal programs all are directed toward low-income individuals;

less than the poverty level, and 73 percent (2.5 million) were from families with incomes equal to or less than 150 percent of poverty. Eighty-six percent were from families with incomes equal to or less than 200 percent of poverty. About 1.5 million women from families with incomes below 150 percent of poverty were estimated to have received services from private physicians not associated with organized programs.

Nationwide, in 1974, over 69 percent of the 5.7 million women with incomes at or below 150 percent of poverty who were estimated to be at risk of unwanted pregnancy (e.g., between the ages of 15 and 44, not pregnant or trying to become pregnant, sexually active and fertile) received family planning services from either organized programs or private physicians. About 49 percent of the 3.5 million women with incomes between 150 and 200 percent of poverty received family planning services. Overall, 62 percent of all 9.2 million women with incomes at or below 200 percent of poverty were served.

Among women at risk with incomes at or below 150 percent of poverty, considerably higher proportions of women were served in organized programs than were served by private physicians in each region. Among women between 150 and 200 percent of poverty, a consistently higher proportion of women received services from private physicians.

Half of those served were 23 years of age or younger and almost 30 percent were still in their teens. Forty-five percent had never had any children and another 22 percent had had only one. Sixty-three percent of them were white. About 85 percent of the patients were using the most effective contraceptive methods (the pill, the IUD, and sterilization) at the time of their last clinic visit during 1974, while before enrolling in family planning programs more than half used no method or one of the less effective methods.

In fiscal 1974, federal appropriations for family planning were about $160 million; ten years earlier no public money was available for such services. Expenditures quoted in the GAO Report to Congress, *Improving Federally Assisted Family Planning Programs,* issued in April 1975, indicates a total of $217 million for fiscal 1974, with a note stating that "figures are estimates since exact amount applicable to family planning services was comingled with cost of other medical and social services."[9] According to the *Fourth Prog-*

---

the legislation is written this way; thus, data are analyzed in these terms without even indicating the relationship between, for example, 200 percent of poverty ($10,076 in March 1974) and median income ($13,801).

ress Report issued in May 1975, estimated expenditures for fiscal 1975 for family planning services were $186 million, and for fiscal 1976, $160 million.[10]

Over the past decade there has been an enormous increase in the number and distribution of programs providing family planning services. Yet limitations in attaining explicit and desired goals persist. For example, as mentioned in the *Fourth Progress Report,* the fact that a county is shown as having services available is not intended to imply that services are always accessible to all low-income people in the area. Many service providers have limited clinic capacity, and clinic locations are not always within easy reach of all women in the area; and many states still do not have IV-A contracts to provide family planning services.

Even more important than the increase in facilities and programs has been the increase in the numbers of individuals served. However, the growth rate for both program expansion and numbers served has decreased sharply, at a time when almost one-third of those women with incomes under 150 percent of poverty are still not receiving services (and almost 40 percent of those with incomes at or under 200 percent of poverty).

Unquestionably, federal expenditures supporting such programs have grown substantially, although precise figures regarding these expenditures are not available. Yet the expenditure trend is clearly downward. Moreover, although it is certain that these federal funds have been spent, it appears difficult to identify exactly where they have gone and what they have purchased.[11]

Although the extent of coverage by organized family planning programs is indicated in the data reported above, quantitative adequacy of such coverage—the relationship of supply to the demand for these services—is difficult to assess. (This issue of the adequacy of coverage is discussed again in the final section of this chapter.) We do not have complete data regarding individuals obtaining family planning services through sources other than organized service programs. Moreover, there are no precise data regarding how many women would want family planning services if they were informed about them, and if the services were available at low cost. We have some data that indicate many eligible women insist that family planning services were not offered them and that if such an offer were made, and subsidized services were readily available, they would use them. In addition, there are geographic areas (rural areas) and specific population groups, in particular teenagers, which remain inadequately served. Finally abortion services are still not available on an equal basis to women in different states, at different income levels, at similar costs or at costs related to ability to pay.

Part of the demand for organized family planning services is determined by eligibility requirements set by states for services subsidized by indirect funding programs (e.g., Social Services Title IV-A and Medicaid Title XIX) and part by services subsidized by the less restrictive direct-funding programs. Although low-income individuals are designated as a priority group in direct-funding programs, eligibility for services is not restricted to any income level. Since federal policy is decreasing direct funding and increasingly stressing development of fee schedules for service and obtaining third-party reimbursement wherever possible, the legally defined target population eligible for federally subsidized services must decrease because by definition that population becomes the "welfare poor" only.

To the extent unmet demand is assessed in terms of those defined as eligible, the likelihood is that those women served who come from families with low or marginal incomes, just below the poverty level, at the poverty level, and just above with incomes up to 150 or 200 percent of poverty, will decrease. In 1974, the maximum annual income level allowed by each state for AFDC eligibility ranged from a low of $2,208 in North Carolina to a high of $4,800 in Alaska. For a family of four, $5,038 was the poverty-level income figure for 1974. As of July 1973, the twenty-five states with family planning programs for the medically needy (as contrasted with public assistance recipients only) under Medicaid had maximum levels for eligibility which ranged from $2,800 in North Carolina to $5,000 in New York. Theoretically almost 6 million women could be provided subsidized family planning services through indirect funding programs; however, the real number is much less. Not all those eligible for public assistance or Medicaid have, in fact, applied. Not all states have included provisions for family planning services under Title IV-A, and where they are provided they may not be widely publicized or readily accessible.

It is also quite possible that given current expenditure levels and approach to provision, there will be no significant expansion in the numbers of very poor women served. Direct funding programs have also developed more restrictions with respect to how "low income" is defined. In 1972, "low income" was defined to mean $5,000 for a family of four, or 135 percent of the then poverty level. As of 1975 this figure had not changed, but it then covered less than 100 percent of the poverty level. Thus the number of women classified as "low income" is steadily decreasing, although in fact this is not true when holding constant the dollar income value. An upward revision of the income level was projected for 1976.

States' Narrative Reports

What follows is a review of thirty-three narrative reports from the states (for fiscal 1973 and the first six months of fiscal 1974) requested by SRS Regulations and Program Instructions for the implementation of the Title IV-A amendments mentioned earlier.* While the content of these reports is not consistent among the states, they do permit a kaleidoscopic impression of the offer and provision of organized family planning services reimbursed under IV-A. They reflect ambivalence, confusion, and variations and serve to remind us of the lack of any objective, quantitative or qualitative, systematic picture of what in fact is provided by the states through federal funds.

There is great unevenness in the quality of the programs and in the nature of the narrative reporting. Not all state reports discussed all areas pertinent to access services, or even the same areas; hence there is little basis for comparative analysis. Also, since there was striking variation in the level of detail it might be inaccurate to assume that those states not making reference to a specific area did not, in fact, cover the area. Moreover, for at least two states, brief reports obscured significant developments probably noted in earlier reporting periods.

All but six of the reports lack hard data concerning target population, numbers served, expenditures, and effectiveness. With new guidelines from SRS concerning documentation of offers, requests, provision, acceptance, and complaints in case records, this lack should be remedied in future statistical reports. Of the twenty-one states including funding data, eight states relied on Title XIX, four utilized Title IV-A funds to enter into contracts with service providers, and an additional nine reported the use of both authorizations, usually, but not always, utilizing XIX for current recipients and IV-A for former and/or potential recipients. Twelve reports did not specify funding data.

Of those including data on eligibility, two states offered family planning services to former and current public assistance recipients

*Not all states submitted reports.

and applicants and three other states to potential and current recipients. An additional eleven states offered services to all three groups. Bases of eligibility for potential recipients varied markedly —for example, "all those on general assistance or medical assistance," "$7,000 for a family of four," "$5,000 for a family of four," "those receiving protective children's services," "those who meet categorical requirements and the Department's standard of assistance," "all public assistance and youths receiving child welfare services," and "those under 200 percent of poverty." Several of these states specified that those not eligible for Medicaid will only be referred to free clinics. One such state added that if no free clinic exists, a special project utilizing IV-A funds should be developed as the responsibility of the district social service worker and supervisor in coordination with the regional program supervisor. Several states referred to the use of Title VI and XVI funds for the respective categorical groups having need of family planning services. Thirteen states restricted family planning services to current recipients.

With respect to the mandate for programs to prevent out-of-wedlock births, five states reported statutory difficulties. One state prohibited the sale of birth control devices to any unmarried person regardless of age (but the constitutionality of this law is being challenged). Two states served minors if a physician certified that withholding family planning services from them would constitute a hazard to their health. One of these two states, however, stipulated that such a minor will then be "counseled as to the deleterious effect of her activities. Every effort will be made to have parental consent and involvement in her care." In contrast, several states were actively committed to appropriate programmatic activity, including one program directed to teenage mothers.* One other state referred to counseling to acquaint putative fathers with the concept of family planning "where there is a continuing relationship." One state welfare department contracted with a local nonprofit agency to provide counseling services to teenagers already parents of out-of-wedlock children to help prevent future unwanted pregnancies. Still another state provided family planning services to the children in its child-

*Most authorities agree that programs should be directed to the nulliparous since the first out-of-wedlock pregnancy, especially in a teenager, already severely limits that mother's options in life (education, job, marriage, etc.). In the AFDC population, it is likely that the first illegitimate birth is the reason for the female head to be in need in the first place. Hence, preventive efforts would need to be directed to all sexually active minors in the caseload, both male and female.

welfare programs, including public wards and those in the custody of institutions. Another state indicated staff engagement in counseling, family life education, and teenage rap sessions in an effort to determine need for family planning services. Still another reported the participation of the welfare department in the state's School Age Parents Program through which it anticipated many more minors would become aware of the availability of family planning services.

With respect to access services, flyers submitted with the reports varied from mimeographed copies of the federal statute mandating services, which would probably be unintelligible to many readers, to well-designed brochures couched in easy-to-understand language. Three states mentioned bilingual flyers. Several states referred to the use of posters and displays in welfare offices and elsewhere. Some states also required eligibility workers to describe famliy planning services and, where there was interest or a request, to refer the client to a service worker who then would open a service record with continuing responsibility for referral, counseling, and follow-up. One report described an unusual access service contracted with Planned Parenthood: a skilled family planning counselor works full time at the major centralized intake office for Medicaid, food stamps, and public assistance, and "every AFDC applicant has the opportunity of an interview and information regarding family planning, and a record of the interview is filed in the case record." County welfare offices in some states assigned social workers to the provider agencies to verify eligibility and furnish support services, outreach, and follow-up. In one such state, with an outstanding program, county service workers were assigned to family planning clinics in 150 of 159 counties to certify eligibility and to offer ongoing support services to enable medical utilization; to assist with patient retention and follow up with dropouts; to provide counseling in office, home, clinic, and telephone contacts; and to assume an advocacy role (work with advisory committees, interagency meetings, identifying gaps, promoting community support, working on special projects, sex education, and family life education activities). They also supervise outreach workers and aides, and work with the media in disseminating information and education. These functions are apparently supported by an elaborate staff training program arranged through an interagency contract for joint teaching and learning by welfare and health personnel at the local and state levels. The report refers to the state's belief that the program has "assumed a comprehensiveness beyond equating family planning with birth control methods which is primarily a medical function." The added input of social services has "demonstrated the idea of the 'One Door' entry for a more complete range of services. These experiences were not measurable nor documented, but were related in positive ways by staff at both agencies at the local level."

Several other states referred to similar kinds of educational and social services, designed to help clients continue in family planning, and provided by the social work staff (although the reports may be more aspirational than operational in character).*

In a New York City health center (to be described later), eligibility is established by clinic staff, and once a year the Department of Social Services audits a sample. No certifications were overruled. In May 1974, DSS assigned one Bachelor's degree service worker full time to each clinic for social and educational services. The workers are supervised by three MSWs. (There is a central administrative staff of twenty-eight that includes a full-time professional social worker engaged in consultation and planning functions.) The director of the program, a public health nurse, reported that while the program does not need MSW workers at the service level, this new social work component will be an essential part of the program in helping patients with their questions and feelings, and making referrals for needed resources elsewhere. She also believes the presence of the social workers may increase the number of actual referrals from DSS since eligibility workers will take a more active interest and feel more comfortable in referrals made to colleagues. The assigned workers, all young, volunteered for the assignment, were carefully screened with respect to attitudes toward the poor and toward family planning, and then were trained as clinic team members. No data are available as to how many referrals are made by any of the personal social services, but the impression of staff is that the majority of patients are referred by other patients and by outreach efforts. Outreach workers (indigenous) no longer knock on doors; instead, outreach staff make formal and informal presentations to community groups such as welfare centers, day care centers, schools (hygiene classes), health fairs, PTAs, and Chinatown factories.

Although mandated in the regulations, only four of the thirty-three reports mentioned the provision of complaint machinery. One

*Only one state refers to a time study in which it was learned that their AFDC workers "devote just under 1% of their time to family planning services: information, assessment of needs, and referral."

utilized a family planning specialist in each region of the state who, in addition to liaison and staff-training functions, had the responsibility "to handle complaints." A second stated that appeal and complaint procedures included family planning services; the third referred to "procedures for complaints," without specifying time. The fourth included complaints among the processes of family planning services to be documented in the case records. Only three states referred to consumer participation, thereby possibly adding the advocacy function to access services. In one of these states a Sterilization Review Board ("for persons under 18 and other legally incompetent individuals") "has medical, legal, social and consumer participation." In a second state the governor's reorganization of the statewide Family Planning Council assures that 51 percent of the members are consumers, "and the same ratio is closely approximated in each Family Planning Project." The third state reported active consumer participation on a statewide committee which meets four times a year for program review. Several recommendations made by the consumer-members were reported to have been implemented.

Many states reported active staff development programs to prepare service staff for new responsibilities in initiating discussions of family planning with clients (beyond the initial mandated offer);[12] in providing education and information to the community through the media and through sex education and family life education activities; and in becoming knowledgeable concerning contraceptives. One such program was referred to above. Among the other programs, the more distinctive are characterized by their interdisciplinary nature in respect both to teachers and to learners; their use of faculty from schools of social work, schools of medicine, other university departments, and/or contractual arrangements with Planned Parenthood or other providers to furnish training to welfare staff; their utilization of state and regional consultants to train county supervisory staff in the planning and development of family planning seminars for agency personnel. A highly unique program involved the use of a visiting professor of population research to conduct interdisciplinary seminars, in community and personal attitudes toward family planning, for welfare and health staffs engaged in family planning services; lectures to other agencies having contact with potential clients including the departments of rehabilitation, mental health, public works, and education; and lectures to potential client groups in such places as university classes and dormitories, detention homes, and high school rap groups. He helped staff develop a reference library in family planning and trained them in techniques of research into support services for family planning.

One of the most significant findings in this cursory review of a limited number of state reports has to do with the linkages established with other systems. Early critics of the indirect funding mechanisms had declared that the only real contribution made by Title IV-A was to assist in the removal of state restrictions on referrals for family planning, especially for minors on their own consent.[13] However, now that states are beginning to understand and experience the usefulness of Title IV-A funds for the purchase of services, and spurred by the incentive and penalty provisions and the mandate to include family planning in Medicaid, their use of the indirect mechanisms has had at least one other felicitious consequence. This is the opportunity for new kinds of collaborative and contractual relationships between components of the social service system and components of the health system—public, voluntary and, to a lesser extent, proprietary (e.g., drugstores).

Exchange of staffs and functions and joint training of staffs for interdisciplinary practice were described above. Other kinds of system linkages reflected in the reports include extended contacts with all providers by two states in order to facilitate their cooperation regarding family planning for DSS clients. One state gave its providers estimates of the number of women of childbearing age who are "poor" (that is, former, current, and potential recipients) which they were asked to compare with their own estimates of poor women of childbearing age whom they presently serve, in order to determine the number not yet being reached.*

Another state reported a monthly dialogue between the welfare department and the staff of the Office of Family Planning within the state Department of Public Health in order to provide social service input into the unit's function of coordinating all family planning activities. Another state department reported serving on the Advisory Committee to the state Health Department along with representatives from county health departments, voluntary clinics, and private physicians in a cooperative effort to improve and expand services. Still another state reported membership on a statewide Family Planning Council, including participation on the Finance

*Only one state actually referred to any "test" of effectiveness in reaching the target population, with the following claim: "AFDC cases increased 17% from February 1973 to February 1974, but there was a corresponding increase in children under 21 in that period of only 11.5%, an indicator of effectiveness of family planning services."

Committee (budget review and program evaluation of family planning projects) through which more after-hours service, innovative programs for teenagers, and increased follow-up were achieved. Another state required all its IV-A providers to furnish orientation to all public welfare staff in their geographic areas to "strengthen coordination, facilitate referrals, and help case workers to provide information." In other states, welfare agencies cooperated with health departments in the joint formulation of policy and guidelines, production of materials for public information, and construction of model contracts and training packages. According to one report, "the contract to purchase family planning services from Planned Parenthood or other providers will require us to deal with our attitudes and practices as we cooperate with staff of another agency in providing a joint service to the community." A few states reported new arrangements with other systems—for example, work with extension offices and nutrition aides of the Department of Agriculture for outreach assistance; with the Department of Offender Rehabilitation for offering family planning services as persons become ready for discharge from institutions; with public housing to reach high-risk groups; and "with schools and other groups to make the county agency more visible and acceptable."

Several of the states reported taking an active stance in the community and with the public at large in an effort both to meliorate attitudes that prevent or interfere with the use of family planning services and to enhance the image of the agency as a nonstigmatized access to family planning services. One state uses the media and educational programs to "offer information and simplified referral to family planning services to anyone in the community requiring such services." Another state circulated to county offices a number of informational spot announcements for radio and TV and offered access and referral ("free if qualified") to men, to women, to the married, to the unmarried, and so on.[14] Perhaps the most innovative access mechanism of all is a trial program that was recommended in one state by its Governor's Special Council on Family Planning. This involved the distribution of nonmedical (nonprescriptive) contraceptive supplies by case workers in ten counties. "There was documented evidence of the value of this expanded casework role," and its adoption on a voluntary statewide basis was recommended as an additional option for clients.

And, finally, a state with one of the more impressive programs acknowledged concern about a separate access system for the poor: "The requirement to notify contributes to the resistance of those in need to come to a public agency. Singling out AFDC as the target group for special attention reinforces the feelings of those on AFDC that they are regarded as promiscuous and that our interest is to reduce the welfare rolls. . . . The county social service staff defend their clients against this implication and are concerned about their clients' feelings. We are attempting to word the notice so clients will welcome the service and not question why it was sent to them."

The overall impression gained from reviewing these thirty-three reports is that the states are in compliance with the law. Probably less than half of the fifty states, however, have exercised their option to provide access to free family planning services to persons other than current AFDC recipients, or at most the medically needy through Medicaid. Whether this is due to the lack of experience with a new kind of service, or competition with other social services under the ceiling imposed on Title IV-A, or fears of setting unwelcome precedents in serving "potentials" is not clear. Hence the usefulness of the indirect mechanisms in maximizing access to family planning services is not fully tested thus far. Current public assistance recipients, and the medically needy under Medicaid, are only a portion of the low-income population requiring subsidized family planning services. Concern with preventing dependency would address the needs of many others at marginal income levels as well.

Governmental and Nongovernmental Agencies

DHEW is the primary agency in the federal government responsible for supporting family planning services. Within DHEW four separate organizational units administer family planning programs under different legislative authorities, with different federal-state sharing arrangements, different eligibility requirements, and different degrees of direct administration of the various funds. The programs operate autonomously with little coordination among the organizational units.

The Office of Population Affairs under the Secretary of DHEW is the primary focus within DHEW and the federal government for family planning services. The Health Services Administration (HSA) administers and directly funds family planning programs authorized under Title X of the Public Health Service Act. The formula grant program authorized under Title V of the Social Security Act is administered by the states within broad federal guidelines.

The two other major family planning programs, authorized under Titles IV-A and XIX of the Social Security Act, are administered by the SRS, employ indirect funding mechanisms, and are considered part of a social welfare program, not a health program. These programs are considered by DHEW to be separate and distinct and to have been designed to meet different objectives.

Several other federally supported health programs also provide family planning services, but on a smaller scale. These programs involve DHEW's comprehensive health services programs and its Indian Health Services Program and the Department of Housing Urban Development Model Cities Program.

In general, federal policies and funding for family planning services are controlled by public law, executive branch decision, and congressional appropriations. Most publicly funded programs are supported by federal dollars (9:1 under Social Security Titles IV-A, XIX, and XX, 9:1 under Public Health Services Title X, and 1:1 under Social Security Title V formula grants).

Programs are operated at the state level and administered at that level by state departments of health, welfare, or human resources. At the local level, programs may be operated under public auspices (e.g., health departments, hospitals) or under voluntary auspices (e.g., free-standing family planning clinics, health maintenance organizations). In 1974, health departments comprised the majority of agencies providing family planning services, accounting for 52 percent of all provider agencies and serving 38 percent of all those using organized family planning programs. The second largest group of providers were hospitals, comprising 22 percent of the provider agencies and serving 18 percent of the user populations. Planned Parenthood and other voluntary agencies comprised 26 percent of the provider agencies and served 44 percent of the population of users. At the local level, programs may be funded directly, indirectly through third-party reimbursements, or indirectly through public agencies purchasing services from voluntary agency service providers, under federal authorization. Local providers frequently receive both direct and indirect funds.

The major voluntary agency for provision of family planning services is Planned Parenthood, many of whose local affiliates in addition to receiving philanthropic support and income from patient fees, now qualify for reimbursement under Title XIX for eligible patients. Some have entered into contractual arrangements with departments of welfare to serve AFDC recipients under Title IV-A provisions (now Title XX). Others may receive project funding under Title X. In addition to Planned Parenthood, other voluntary efforts include services provided by voluntary hospitals, neighborhood health centers, and other nonprofit groups, which may receive both public and private funds.

With regard to other than direct service provision, the Ford Foundation and the Population Council directly engage in or indirectly support biomedical and social research related to fertility control in the United States and abroad. Many private universities in the United States engage in research related to fertility trends and population matters and these activities may be supported by public and private funds. The Sex Information and Education Council of the United States (SIECUS) is a voluntary nonprofit organization based in New York City and engaged in the development and exchange of information and education related to human sexuality, including responsible parenthood and family planning. The National Alliance Concerned with School Age Parents (NACSAP), based in Washington, D.C., is engaged in designing a curriculum uniquely related to the needs of young persons facing early parenthood.

Program Models

Direct services at the local or consumer level show a variety of delivery patterns. Subsidized services are offered in health departments at specialty clinics or as part of maternal and child health (MIC and MCH) programs. They are provided by public and voluntary hospitals where family planning services may be offered in a separate clinic or integrated into other medical services. Such programs may have specialized staff or share the staff of another service. In the community, services are also provided in free-standing family planning clinics such as Planned Parenthood affiliates, in neighborhood health centers which may offer other health and/or social services, in mobile clinics, and in programs directed specifically toward youth. Some of these programs may provide abortions and vasectomies, and there are also specialty clinics providing these procedures on an out-patient basis. Female sterilizations and abortions are also performed in hospitals as in-patient procedures.

One example of family planning services provided under public auspices through neighborhood health centers is the *Family Planning*

Unit of the New York City Human Resources Administration.[15] The program began in 1967 as a few storefront family planning centers (clinics) funded under Title II of the Economic Opportunity Act. The unit now comprises eighteen centers in poverty areas. They offer a range of preventive health services (for example, well baby, pediatrics, VD, gynecology, sickle cell screening, nutrition guidance, prenatal) in addition to the usual medical and laboratory procedures of family planning clinics. Each center's staff reflects the ethnic groups of its community. A number of the centers have evening and Saturday hours. Each has a back-up hospital for medical problems and surgical procedures. Two centers have specialized services for male and female teenagers that were designed on the basis of teen-consumer recommendation and "demand." These two centers offer coed teen "rap sessions" on sexuality and other concerns, and feature free condom distribution as well as the full range of female methods.

The program is funded by a Title X (PHS) project grant, Title XIX (SSA) reimbursement for eligible patients (28 percent of the total patient load), and Title IV-A (SSA) on a contract with the State of New York. In fiscal 1973, the centers served 23,789 family planning patients for 44,938 visits, one third of whom were estimated to be current and potential AFDC recipients. The clinics are community sponsored and have community boards. Part of the director's task in her view has been to educate these boards to become advocates for improved services rather than merely dispensers of largesse in the form of clinic jobs.

A different kind of program that combines educational, developmental, and therapeutic functions in serving youth is The Door—An Alternative. This is a multiservice center operated under voluntary auspices, located in New York City and serving low-income inner-city youth, aged 15 to 21, referred by health agencies, the schools, child welfare agencies and institutions, housing facilities, and by word of mouth among teenagers themselves. The center, in operation since 1972 and funded by city, state, and federal drug programs and by a PHS Title X grant in family planning, has a professional staff of thirty-five, including psychiatrists, physicians, nurses, lawyers, social workers, psychologists, teachers, a vocational rehabilitation counselor, and three nutritionists. There is a volunteer staff of ninety professionals from the same disciplines, plus activities people, college students, and youth workers. Medical, nursing, and law students receive training at The Door and may soon be joined by social work students.

The Door accepts only multiproblem young people and utilizes a total approach through the following ten programs: general medical services, including prenatal; all forms of family planning services and procedures; sex education and sex counseling; drug counseling; psychiatric counseling; educational services (high school equivalency, tutoring, vocational counseling); nutrition guidance; social services (crisis intervention); legal services; activities workshops. About six hundred young people are actively engaged at any one period. Problems with sexuality, with drugs, and with families are the major preoccupations of the center's population. Both individual and group approaches are used in every program element and contact may be long or short term, limited or extensive. The focus of intervention is either developmental (identity tasks) or therapeutic (personal pathology). When successfully pursued, the latter becomes fused with the former.

Forty percent of the new clients enter the program through the general medical services, apparently finding it easier to define their problems in medical terms. The medical service sees about sixty new patients a month and roughly half of these are referred for family planning services in addition to those who come specifically for family planning. In a sense, The Door is its own access service, with each program element serving as access to every other. No matter which service is the entry point, however, many of the young people accept the offer of an "orientation group" experience, which, more often than not, then links them to other program elements. Eventually many have contact with the family planning, sex education service, either directly or because staff in that service bring program elements into other activities. The family planning program is structured as a social service, not a medical one, although there are the usual medical components. All new patients, unless emergencies, have three sequential interviews, psychosocial in nature, and, if ready, will be given the medical prescription for method on the third visit. The interviews cover sexual and personal and family history, perceptions of self and sexuality, and educational-psychological preparation for what is likely for some to be the first pelvic examination and hence potentially frightening. Patients are expected to come back monthly for a year, not only for medical supervision but for group sessions in sex education and for individual sex counseling where desired and indicated. Retention rates have been good.

Emphasis in sex education is on understanding one's own sexuality, on relationship needs, responsible sexual behavior, and legitimation of nonparenting roles. The center's philosophy is that young people can benefit from counseling because of misperceptions, ambivalence, guilt, estrangement from their own bodies, value conflicts, and the like.

Pregnant patients are helped to make their own decisions about continuing or terminating the pregnancy. Those deciding to continue are given prenatal care. Those desiring abortion may receive this service at other clinics. They then return to the center for contraceptive services and postabortion counseling. Hospitalization for any medical problem is available at a nearby municipal hospital.

Social workers serve as advocates vis-à-vis the community (jobs, housing, schools, peers, family, etc.). The Door maintains continuous personalized contacts with personnel of three hundred other agencies in attempting to connect young people back to the community in a nonfragmented and humanized way. Medical students serve as advocates vis-à-vis other medical settings where specialized or individualized medical needs are at stake. Law students serve as advocates in criminal and civil areas. Staff are all young, deeply committed, and have themselves designed the program, working on a voluntary basis for a year before funding was obtained. Observing this program, one senses that the potential for changing the environments which influence fertility decisions and behaviors is very great indeed.

At the proprietary level, family planning services are provided by private physicians to an estimated 26 percent of low-income women (150 percent of poverty and below) at risk of unwanted pregnancy. As with other medical services provided by the private practitioner, there are inadequate data concerning family planning services delivered by private doctors. Jaffe reviewed the available studies and found that most of them investigated physician attitudes toward aspects of family planning rather than the services actually provided. The studies are suggestive, however, in several areas of concern. Many doctors wait for patients to ask for advice, while many women think physicians should initiate the subject. Many physicians do not routinely offer services even at such appropriate times as the premarital, prenatal, and postpartum examinations. Restrictive or unclear statutes or the lack of affirmative laws, particularly in the area of services to unwed minors, results in hesitancy on the part of physicians.[16]

Also at the proprietary level, an unknown number of men and women are assumed to depend upon nonprescription methods obtained from vending machines and drugstores, despite the restrictive aspects of some state statutes. It has been established that nonprescription methods are less effective than the pill, IUD, or diaphragm; complaints about the safety and comfort of the condom, however, have lessened in other countries where more innovative design and technology is used, and instructions are enclosed. One authority states that the distribution of nonprescription methods has diminished.[17] Another expert estimates that condoms continue to be used by 9 percent of all couples in the United States, and still another reports that the condom is the second most widely used method in this country.[18]

Research and Evaluation

DHEW spent $51.4 million for research in the fields of fertility control and population growth in 1974.[19] Fertility research included evaluation of the medical effects of oral contraceptives and of vasectomy. The Center for Population Research, the major relevant research center, currently is exploring the social, psychological, and economic determinants of fertility. The Center supports both basic and applied research, studying alternative methods of safe and effective fertility control. One area of current study involves the search for new and effective chemical contraceptives for men and women that will not have undesirable side effects.

According to the GAO Report, *Improving Federally Assisted Family Planning Programs*, the National Center for Health Statistics (NCHS) is the federal agency responsible for developing and operating a coordinated reporting system for all federally funded and, to the extent possible, privately funded family planning programs in the United States. The purpose of the reporting system is to provide national and area statistics on the status of family planning and evaluation data for the efficient and effective development, operation, and evaluation of family planning programs.[20] The GAO Report concluded that reports generated by the present national system were of little value, describing them as "incomplete, inaccurate and tardy."

The technical assistance arm of Planned Parenthood also engages in research, in particular surveys of programs and program users, user characteristics, and patterns of utilization.

Programs in Action

Rather than provide a series of additional discrete descriptions of different types of family planning services programs, what follows is an overview of the whole range of organized family planning programs situated within our one city and county. The programs included in this overview are: the Planned Parenthood Family Planning Clinic; Birthright/Support (pregnancy counseling); the Neighborhood Health Center Family Planning Program; the County Family Planning Program; and the Medical Center Family Planning Program. Three services are public. One is sponsored by the federal government (DHEW); one by the state government; one by the county government. As we shall see, all three receive the major portion of their funds from the federal government. Two programs are sponsored by voluntary agencies, one sectarian and one nonsectarian.

Information and counseling regarding all devices and techniques relevant to family planning (including all forms of contraception and relevant procedures such as abortion, tubal ligation, laparoscopies, vasectomies), as well as the services themselves are available to both residents and nonresidents of the county. Services are provided on a countywide basis by one public agency, one public hospital, one voluntary hospital, and two voluntary service facilities. Services are provided on a citywide basis by one public neighborhood-based out-patient facility. Although one voluntary facility and the hospitals provide the whole range of services—access, family planning information, counseling, techniques, and surgical procedures—the other publicly administered family planning services do not provide surgical procedures. For clients of these services (primarily poor and minority), access involves referral to a second service.

Staff in all programs stressed that in practice services are universal, although there are graduated fees depending on income level. Staff emphasized that no person in need of service would be refused because of inability to pay; and inability may include a wide range of discretionary factors (e.g., a husband's refusal to pay for service provided to his wife).

Coverage seems extensive. However, several administrators stated that, based on existing data, low-income women are still not adequately served: many are not reached by the offer of service, and rural areas in particular are underserved. Defining the extent of coverage is difficult because there is no clear concept of the size of the target population and the extent of coverage by private physicians. In general, demand has increased as rapidly as services have become available and all existing facilities are now defined as at maximum capacity, given existing resources. At present, all programs either want to expand provision or are actually planning such expansion. The facility serving most middle-class women had doubled in size and coverage within the three years before our visit and was planning to expand again. This facility, which provides a comprehensive package of family planning services, has a two-week wait for abortions (and refers elsewhere for emergency needs), a one-month wait for vasectomies, and a two-month wait for laparoscopies. There is no wait at any facility for general counseling, information, or prescription of contraceptive drugs or devices.

There does not appear to be any stigma attached to using any of the available facilities. Although there is a means test for one service, it is not rigidly applied. Fees are standardized, but there are graduated fee scales. All public services stressed that no one requesting services is refused for financial reasons.

There are no specialized arrangements for ensuring access to family planning services. Few referrals are made through existing, formal access channels (e.g., information and referral services). Access may be by word of mouth, by announcements on radio and television, by lectures and talks given in a wide range of settings, by outreach services located at sites where potential users might congregate (e.g., laundromats, peoples' living rooms), by other physicians or other social service or medical agencies; or by advertisements, billboards, and leaflets.

In general, access seems readily available. However, it seems easier for middle-class users, who need negotiate only one facility to obtain any of a whole range of procedures, than for lower-class users, who are required, by the nature of the service system, to negotiate two facilities (and possibly two systems). For middle-class individuals using organized family planning services, free-standing medical clinics are available that provide a full complement of services—from counseling to contraceptive devices, sterilization, and/or abortion. In contrast, most lower-class users have access to family planning services through a social welfare program and a facility. For surgical procedures, a second, medical facility, must be negotiated.

There is also some self-selection in terms of which service is used by which population group. The major voluntary service is utilized primarily by middle-class people, although all other programs insist that the agency "bends over backward" in its efforts to extend the range of its clientele. On the other hand, because of its mandate, and its desire to avoid duplication of services, one public service handles only the poor.

All the facilities are clean, attractive, and readily accessible. The hospital has the disadvantage of being a large, complex bureaucracy and its family planning service is difficult to locate. A large medical facility such as this may be intimidating for some to negotiate alone. The facility that is most heavily used is a comprehensive free-standing service (Planned Parenthood). It is located in a converted private home on a main thoroughfare, near several new medical and legal services as well as near private residences. The waiting room is pleasant and informal. One other facility is neighborhood-based and another has several neighborhood satellites to ensure easy access to services. All facilities obtain reimbursement by Medicaid or private insurance companies, for the medical portion of their service, and are required to meet specified standards. They appear to do so.

Programs are either independent (e.g., Planned Parenthood, Neighborhood Health Service) or are components of a larger bureaucracy (e.g., the County Family Planning Service, under Maternal and Child Health Care, under the county Department of Health). Family planning services are staffed with both medical and nonmedical personnel. The latter include primarily social workers and indigenous paraprofessionals. Information and general counseling is usually provided by nonmedical staff, all of whom are women. The service itself (physical examination, provision of contraceptive devices, surgical procedures) is provided by medical staff, who are predominantly male. All outreach activities are conducted by nonmedical staff.

Regardless of whether the facility is free-standing or part of a larger institution, access is provided by nonmedical staff. The only variation is that in health or hospital settings greater use may be made of nurses in this role. In free-standing settings, social workers, both professional and paraprofessional, as well as specially trained lay counselors, predominate. Stress is placed on including staff who can relate to the population served. Therefore, staff include both young and older women, as well as those from a wide range of ethnic, social, and class backgrounds. Administrators also vary. In two they are physicians; in three, nonphysicians.

One of the major programs (Planned Parenthood) is part of a national voluntary network of specialized family planning programs; a second (the Neighborhood Health Center) is integral to the whole medical program, which is responsible to DHEW; a third (the county health department's Family Planning Program) is responsible to local, then regional, and federal government (DHEW).

There appears to be a close working relationship among all services within this network. They refer people to one another as needed, and there is consensus as to which services are used most by which groups. One public service uses family planning as an access service to other medical and social services, and workers there function as case integrators.

Costs are difficult to determine because there is no standard unit of service; there is some effort at delineating an "average" unit of service. The problems in comparative costing arise because, for example, the county service was required to hire staff that might otherwise not have been in the labor force and to institute an extensive in-service training program for this staff. In addition, it was also required to include a career development program, supporting further education for staff. This has added substantially to its overall costs (although the indirect benefits provided may be greater than those for other services).

Costs depend also on the range of services provided and the target population addressed—for example, the extensiveness of supportive services (counseling, etc.), the extensiveness of supplementary medical services, and the extensiveness of outreach services.

Programs obtain financing from the following sources: federal grants (DHEW-PHS Title V, SSA Title IV-A); Medicaid reimbursement (for medical service only); private insurance (for medical service only); private fees; local funds; private philanthropy (for Planned Parenthood and equal only to 12.5 percent of the annual budget).

Planned Parenthood

Planned Parenthood, a local affiliate of a national federation of programs, is the major single family planning resource in both the city and the county. It handles more than 50 percent of all individuals served in the city. Approximately 12,000–15,000 patients are seen annually, and 80 percent of these come just for contraceptive information, counseling, and devices. The program provides a "comprehensive fertility service" and includes five surgical clinics (three abortion clinics a week treating six or seven patients per clinic session; one vasectomy clinic weekly treating five patients per session; one laparoscopy clinic weekly treating four patients per session). The service is open five days and four evenings a week. The program provides on-site as well as off-site seminars on sex education and family planning. Staff are available without cost to give lectures to schools, clubs, and similar groups, and a regular newsletter is published by the program to disseminate information throughout the community.

The program is active in publicizing its services in schools, agencies, and clubs by means of leaflets, advertisements, and brochures, as well as the lectures and seminars mentioned above. Eighty percent of those using the service are self-referred; 10 percent come in response to radio and television spot announcements; 5 percent are referred by private physicians; 4 percent are referred by hospitals or health agencies; and only one percent of the cases are referred by social welfare agencies (Department of Social Services; Child and Family Service Agency).

The annual budget for this program was $500,000 in 1974. The funds were derived as follows: $250,000 from patient fees, $75,000 from private philanthropies and individual contributions, and $175,000 from Medicaid reimbursement and miscellaneous. Planned Parenthood is a universal program with a sliding-fee schedule depending on income. Because of its limited funds it is heavily dependent on patient fees (direct or third-party) and thus has difficulty in expanding its service to low-income patients who are not eligible for third-party reimbursement.

The service is essentially self-contained. Its own activities publicize the program and initiate access. It is the only program in which a full range of relevant surgical procedures are available in the same facility, and in the same program, as are general contraceptive information and counseling. Some follow-up counseling is also available; however, this is defined as one area of service limitation. Patients who need extensive ongoing counseling around family planning or related problems are referred elsewhere, either to a mental health clinic or to a private practitioner. Patients who need more extensive medical care are referred to local hospitals.

The Planned Parenthood facility is centrally located in a converted private house, at the corner of a main thoroughfare. A receptionist greets those who enter and obtains information about private insurance, Medicaid cards, and so forth. The waiting room itself is small, informal, and attractive with comfortable chairs, magazines, and brochures providing information about contraceptive methods and surgical procedures. Most of the patients are young—in their late teens or early twenties, and most are local residents.

Interviews are held in small, semi-enclosed cubicles at the rear of the waiting room. The counselor stressed that a direct and open approach is employed in asking questions and giving information. Privacy and confidentiality are provided for medical examinations and procedures, not for general information and counseling.

The counseling staff, who provide information and guidance concerning the various procedures, include professionals (social workers, guidance counselors, nurses) as well as paraprofessionals. Counseling staff range from young women in their twenties to middle-aged women, and are assigned to cases with an eye to "fitting" the personalities of the clients and the counselors. Qualified medical staff provide medical services and perform surgical procedures.

The demand for the service Planned Parenthood provides is clearly growing. The number of patients served had increased 200 percent during the five years prior to our visit and requests for service continue to grow. Although its clientele is primarily middle class, it is making efforts to expand its range. As mentioned earlier, a major problem in serving the poor is the problem of funding and reimbursement for service. Regardless, the program is highly regarded by other agencies and by lay people in the community.

Birthright/Support: Pregnancy Counseling Service

Established in 1971 as a volunteer pregnancy counseling, information, and referral service and funded jointly by the city diocese and Catholic Charities, Birthright/Support provides pregnancy testing, short-term counseling, and financial assistance, with the help of a small professional staff. Its primary objective is to serve young women concerned about pregnancy and needing information, counseling, and support. At the time we visited the program, it was located in the building occupied by Catholic Social Services, but was planning to move. The program describes itself as nonsectarian although it is reported that more than half the girls requesting services are Catholic.

The program provides the only free pregnancy testing service in the county. Staff follow up with each girl, interpreting test results. When the test is positive, the girl is acquainted with the services available to her during the duration of her pregnancy and afterward. In those cases where the tests are negative, the girl is counseled about her present sexual behavior and her responsibility to herself, her family, and the potential life within her.

The program receives an average of 225 telephone calls monthly, and many of the calls are from teenagers lacking in sex information who often panic and call after having an initial sexual experience the previous night. Therefore, much staff time goes into providing sex education, in addition to pregnancy counseling and contraceptive advice. (No direct services are provided regarding contraceptive methods.) More than three-quarters of the girls served are between the ages of 13 and 18; most are 15–16. About half the callers are seen more than once, and of those, half are involved in counseling. Medical, financial, and housing assistance are the services requested most. Although direct referrals to Planned Parenthood for contraceptive devices or for abortion are not made, the existence and availability of such services are made known, and the stance taken is that each person must decide for herself what procedures to follow. Counseling is also provided to young women after they have had an abortion, if they request it. Although the director is clearly opposed to abortion, she seems to provide an open and supportive attitude to the often confused teenagers who call on her program in search of help.

Neighborhood Health Center Family Planning Program

Originally funded by the Office of Economic Opportunity in 1968 as a neighborhood health service in a Model Cities catchment area, the Neighborhood Health Center is one of 150 remaining in the country. It is now funded by DHEW and serves the whole city, although primarily the lower-income areas. It has 27,000 registered patients, 18,000 of whom have visited within the past year. Its patient population is predominantly black (60 percent) and young. Fifty percent of all Medicaid patients in the city are registered at the center, a reflection of the fact that no primary care physician in town will accept Medicaid patients because of the problems of reimbursement. The center has a graduated fee schedule for patients above the poverty level; however, few fees are collected.

The facility is a modern two-story office building on a main thoroughfare. There appears to be a constant stream of patient activity in the center, which has recently expanded into an adjacent building.

At present, the center serves two hundred patients daily, the maximum case load the facility can handle. Since the demand for service continues to grow, the center plans to establish satellite health service centers at the outer edge of the community now served. Approximately six to seven hundred adult women under the age of 40 are seen monthly. About half of these come for prenatal visits and the other half for gynecological visits. The gynecological patients (over four thousand annually) are all seen automatically for family planning counseling and information and, upon request, are provided with contraceptive drugs or devices. Similarly, all adolescent girls are given family planning information and counseling. In effect, attendance at the clinic automatically ensures access to family planning services because it is integrated into the routine medical services provided. No abortion or surgical procedures are provided in the program; however, patients are referred from this clinic to the Family Life Program at the Medical Center, to the program at Memorial Hospital, or to Planned Parenthood.

County Family Planning Program

The Family Planning Program of the county Department of Health also serves approximately four thousand patients annually, but they are drawn from the county as a whole, not just from the city. It provides family planning information, counseling, and contraceptive supplies, in the context of a comprehensive health program. All patients are seen at least twice a year depending on the method of contraception used or on their medical condition. The program is one component of the Maternal and Child Health Program of the Department of Health. It is directed by a nonmedical administrative staff and provides services through four satellite centers located in readily accessible sites in low-income neighborhoods in the city and in rural parts of the county.

The program is unusual in this community in that it stresses access to the service through the use of thirteen paraprofessional outreach workers who try to facilitate access by making themselves readily available in places where potential patients tend to congregate. Thus, they are prepared to talk to women about the program in local laundromats, supermarkets, clubs, living rooms, and so on. In addition, they may be outposted in other clinics and facilities where potential users are likely to be. Transportation services are provided for women who do not have ready physical access to facilities, and special child care services are provided for women while they come for service. Administrators emphasize that "maximizing choice for women" is the only program objective.

The program was initially funded by a project grant and currently receives project grant funds through Title X of the Public Health Service Act as well as third-party reimbursements through Titles IV-A and XIX of the Social Security Act.

There are no rigid eligibility criteria for receipt of services; however, primary emphasis is upon provision of services to low-income individuals. When the program was originally established, it was agreed that its target population would be women not served by any existing family planning program. (Figures were obtained from a 1969 OEO study detailing numbers of women of low income and childbearing age in each county.) Sixty percent of those served at present are at or below the poverty level. In accordance with DHEW requirements, a graduated fee schedule is applied to patients who can afford to pay, but this criterion is applied flexibly. Fees depend on a weighted assessment based on income, number of children, and "ability of the woman to pay in her particular situation." Thus, if her husband objects to her obtaining service and she has no independent income, she is considered to be "needy." Ninety percent of those who pay fees pay no more than 25 percent of what the standard private patient fee would be. Until 1973, the service was both universal and free; since then, DHEW has increasingly stressed a fee-paying service for everyone over the poverty level.

The main administrative office of the program is located in the county health department in an old and unattractive building; however, this represents only one of five sites for service. The four satellite centers where most services are provided were deliberately selected and designed to be more accessible and attractive.

As mentioned earlier, access is seen as one of the most important parts of the program and is totally dependent on outreach activities. The program provides access to family health services generally and draws on its own staff as well as health department social workers and nurses, as needed, to implement the service. Therefore, the outreach workers are often involved as case integrators, responsible for linking patients with other needed services—both medical and nonmedical—and for ensuring provision of such services once referrals are made.

An advisory board, composed of representatives of the major agencies likely to be utilized by service recipients, facilitates close cooperation between the services. Membership includes representatives of the Neighborhood Legal Service Program, Planned Parenthood, the Medical Center, the Neighborhood Health Center, the State Medical Society, and several consumer groups. Close linkage with other agencies providing family planning services—and cooperation from them—is essential, since by law federal funds provided under Title X may not be used to pay for abortion. The problem of payment for abortion is most acute for patients who are just above the Medicaid eligibility level.

The program is currently serving as many users as it can, given current resources. The demand for service continues to grow, and there is concern regarding funding levels, eligibility criteria, and changing administrative guidelines generally.

Medical Center Family Planning Program

The Family Planning Program at the Medical Center includes two subsidiary programs. One is an information and counseling service where nurses and social workers see patients on intake and provide counseling concerning contraceptive methods and techniques, and physicians provide medical services (e.g., gynecological examinations, tubal ligations). The second, the Family Life Program, provides abortion services. The two programs provide services to approximately a thousand patients annually, 50 percent of whom are on Medicaid. Most patients are from the city or the surrounding county, although a few are from outside the county limits.

More than half the patients are self-referred. Twenty percent are referred by private physicians, 15 percent from the Neighborhood Health Center, and the remainder from the County Family Planning Service or from Planned Parenthood.

The facility, although modern and clean, is large and impersonal. The clinic is difficult to locate. However, the service itself has an attractive waiting room, and the nursing staff are supportive, warm, and informal.

The Family Life Program operates two clinics a week, one for intake and one for abortions and checkups. The Family Planning Clinic operates one afternoon a week. All intake and counseling are done by nurses or social workers.

Trends and Issues

Family planning and the programs designed to implement it raise three types of issues: those related to family planning policies and service programs generally; those related to the achievement of U.S. policy objectives; those related to the role of the personal social services in providing family planning services.

Family Planning Policies and Service Programs

In summarizing the debate in the United States regarding the nature and function of fertility control policy, Frederick Jaffe identifies three major positions (and also describes the analogous positions espoused in the current international debate regarding population policy in developing countries).[21]

The first position, a holistic approach, is that only with the elimination of poverty can the poor be expected to take advantage of modern contraceptive methods. Supporters of this approach argue that funding family planning services and providing services to the poor is a waste of money unless massive resources are directed toward the redistribution of wealth and power (and such services are unnecessary if poverty is eliminated). This argument is analogous to the institutional change versus social services debate of the 1960s, wherein social services were often described as "band-aids" that could have no impact without major institutional change (e.g., the elimination of poverty; redistribution of income) and would be unnecessary if such change were effected. The current perspective seems to have reduced, if not eliminated, the dichotomy between these strategies. They are no longer assumed to be mutually contradictory and, increasingly, one can point to countries with planned economies and full employment and see emerging many of the traditional social services (family counseling, home helps for the aged, residential treatment for delinquents, etc.). The same is true regarding "elimination of poverty versus fertility control": not even in China was a thrust for economic and social development considered to negate the need for family planning services (and other policies aimed at regulating individual fertility).

The second position, in effect the direct opposite of the first, is that the "culture of poverty" fosters sexual looseness and a desire to have large families; that the poor are not motivated to use modern birth control methods; that if they were so motivated, modern contraceptive methods are readily available; that welfare payments and other social benefits provide incentives for the poor to have more children; and that only by coercion will the poor control or regulate fertility. This position surfaced in congressional debate in the late 1960s and early 1970s around pending legislation and can be seen in administrative practice in family planning service programs in several states. It is all too evident when one reviews some of the bills introduced (but not passed, thus far) as recently as 1973 in the state legislatures of Illinois, New Hampshire, Indiana, Ohio, and Tennessee which would have put pressure on poor people to be sterilized. As a consequence of these and other similar actions, many who would have supported expanding access and availability of family planning services feared possible misuse of this policy and the stigmatizing of family planning services "for the poor alone." A small group raised the possibility of genocide, further frightening potential supporters and confusing the issues.

The third position, which has dominated U.S. policy and legislation for the past decade, is directed at helping individuals achieve their own fertility goals by expanding access, availability, and provision of family planning services including the most modern and effective methods and techniques available. This position, and the programs established as a consequence, have been supported by law and policy that changed over the past decade from actively deterring effective voluntary regulation of fertility to facilitating it through the use of public resources to expand access. As a consequence, over the past decade a growing number of low- and marginal-income individuals have begun to use effective (or more effective) methods of fertility control. Jaffe remarks, "fertility rates (and the incidence of unwanted births) have declined more rapidly in recent years among poor and near-poor women than among women above the poverty level (although significant differentials remain)."[22]

This policy has not been implemented as a substitute program for economic and social development; instead direct efforts at controlling individual fertility are viewed as valuable by themselves to individuals and society, complementing, interacting, and supplementing other policies and programs designed to improve the quality of life generally.

Although all three positions continue to be debated, current indications seem to be that the third position will continue to prevail in the United States.

The Achievement of American Policy Objectives

In a speech delivered in June 1974, Secretary of DHEW Caspar Weinberger stated that "the goal of making family planning services available to all who need but cannot afford them is approaching fruition." The question raised here is to what extent that statement is accurate. Unquestionably, enormous advances have been made in expanding the numbers of facilities or the number of physician referral services providing family planning services to poor and near poor women; and an equally large increase has occurred in the numbers of women using such services, and as a consequence using effective contraceptive methods. But it is equally clear that the objective of reaching all who need and want services but cannot afford them has not been attained, and this is confirmed by official government reports. Even though it is impossible to estimate precisely the extent of unmet need for organized family planning services, surveys and reports indicate that coverage is still not adequate to meet existing, known demand. Many programs indicate maximum capacity for service has been reached. Trends in federal policy and expenditure would indicate decreasing support for this objective in the mid-1970s and a potential for decline in the numbers served. The rate of expansion for new programs and facilities has become negligible and the rate of increase in numbers of women served has decreased sharply.

Since 1972, budgetary constraints have limited the expansion of family planning programs at a time when almost all knowledgeable people would concede that services are still inadequate in rural areas and that the growing numbers of sexually active teenagers remain largely unserved.

Furthermore, since 1972, growing stress on setting fee schedules and obtaining third-party payments conflicts with the expressed objective of expanding access and availability of services. Here, too, where teenagers are concerned the need is for creative and innovative programing—possible only with direct funding, which is now less and less available. Verifying eligibility for teenagers while maintaining confidentiality may also present problems. Moreover, the obstacles to obtaining reimbursement under Medicaid generally may in fact be impossible to overcome, or even be cost ineffective, from the statements made in the GAO Report.

Legal and administrative restrictions limiting access continue to exist as a consequence of different laws, different federal authorizations, and different eligibility criteria, especially where such criteria are set by the individual states. One result here may be inequities in access, based on place of residence.

Direct funding of service programs is decreasing and indirect funding is growing slowly. The overall trend in federal expenditures supporting family planning programs seems significantly downward. Considering the ceiling on expenditures under Title XX, it seems highly unlikely that states which are spending the maximum amount allowable for social services will allocate some of these scarce resources to providing family planning services, especially when an alternative, if more restrictive, open-ended funding source is available (Title XIX). Eight states have not included family planning as a covered service in their Medicaid plans, and in late 1974 only half the states had designated a "medically needy" category to cover individuals with incomes beyond the maximum income permitted in the state to be eligible for public assistance. Furthermore, eligibility criteria varied so among the states that the maximum income permitted for eligibility as "medically needy" in one state could be lower than the income criterion for eligibility in another. Finally, states' failure to include abortion as a covered service impeded access to what many defined as an essential back-up family planning service. However, as of late 1975 all states were described as being "in compliance" with regulations requiring minimal coverage under one or another program.

As a consequence of all these developments, the target population of poor and near-poor women is now being defined far more restrictively to mean not just poor women but welfare recipients only, at a time when 31 percent of those women from families with incomes at or under 150 percent of poverty are still not served. Instead of expanding to provide service, efforts will apparently need to contract, and the population served may decrease rather than increase.

Since access implies, at the very onset, quantitative adequacy of service, availability and proximity of service, and eligibility for service, without these basics information, counseling and education, and referral can have little impact. Any policy that decreases support of existing family planning service programs implies limitations of access. In addition, any policy that restricts the population eligible for services restricts access. Policy stressing the use of Medicaid as a funding mechanism could impede access for the near poor—and even some of the poor—and is increasingly limiting access to welfare recipients only. As serious as such restrictions may be for the marginally poor woman now closed off from obtaining service, there are several other equally serious consequences.

By limiting subsidization of services to welfare recipients only, the whole issue of a stigmatized service with nefarious and coercive objectives could be raised again. Considering the broad range of support for provision, the explicit aim of reaching all who cannot afford such service, the proven percentage of near poor who would use subsidized services if available, and the potential negative consequences of a stigmatized service or one seen as coercive, it seems hard to rationalize the policy shift.

Moreover, if one objective of family planning policy is "to prevent dependency"—to prevent unwanted pregnancies that may force women to leave the labor force and "go on welfare"—it seems totally irrational not to make subsidized family planning services accessible and available to those with marginal incomes.

To take another perspective, the question of access is complicated by the issue of "intent." In other words, too little access is an obstacle to obtaining service, and an open door is essential to reach the service. But access only facilitates. If no services exist there is frustration; if pressure is exerted to use services there is coercion.

As a consequence many "gatekeepers" fail to ensure access out of confusion, discomfort, or ignorance. (To avoid the Scylla and Charybdis of coercion on the one hand and impeding or barring on the other, one approach might be to develop a massive publicity and advertising campaign and provide free or heavily subsidized family planning services to all—which is what many countries with national health programs do.)

The Role of the Personal Social Services

Family planning services in the United States reflect a basic confusion inherent in federal legislation authorizing these programs. The services are perceived in part as health services and in part as social welfare services. This confusion is increased by the conflicting objectives of legislation, program administrators, and staff. And the cleavage that exists between the health and welfare systems in all areas can only add to this.

Any review of program operations reveals that the overwhelming majority of service recipients are self-referred or referred by relatives, friends, or neighbors. The only nonpersonal referral source that channels large numbers of people to family planning services is the mass media. People learn of the availability of family planning services through radio and television spot announcements—and occasionally through direct mail advertising, flyers, or newspaper ads. They may be referred from one hospital clinic to another. But relatively few referrals come from social agencies, be they public or private.

It may be an indicator of limited contacts, or ineptness, of social workers—or of the gap in communication between social and medical agencies—but social work in fact plays a minor role as a gatekeeper for family planning services. However, like many other services, success may create its own increased demand for services, and the need for a specialized access system may decrease, as long as service capacity continues to meet demand. In particular, once family planning services are considered generally acceptable and are available to all, the need for a specialized doorway might disappear. In effect, it may be because family planning services in the United States are means tested—perhaps the only means-tested family planning service program that exists—that a specialized access system is required. If family planning were a subsidized medical service, available to all free or at low cost, the only social services needed would be the same as those needed by patients served in any medical facility, for any medical or surgical procedure.

On the other hand, where a specialized access service may be needed, and where social workers may have an important role to play, is in relation to teenagers. Teenage pregnancy rates have increased in recent years, as has the rate of illegitimate births among teenage girls. All organized family planning programs indicate a downward trend in the age of those requesting service, in particular those requesting service for the first time. Two of the programs described earlier stress the ignorance, confusion, and anxiety of teenagers who may be as much—or more—in need of sex education, information, and counseling as they are of family planning services. Clearly, it is important to reach these young people and provide information, counseling, and help in ways that are acceptable and accessible to them. This would seem to constitute an important role for social workers working with adolescents, and raises other questions about the need for specialized programs for these young people generally. Increasingly, adolescent medicine is emerging as a medical specialty. Another question might be the extent to which any program, social, educational, or medical, should be taking greater account of this category of young people's needs. We recognize that issues of confidentiality and children's versus parental rights, as well as the problem of eligibility for service of a minor where criteria specify parental income levels, may require further consideration; however, the problem is an important one and the need for service and program development is clear.

Finally, to be clear about access, intent, availability, and provision it is essential to know exactly what is or is not provided in the individual states, in programs funded with federal dollars. In theory, all states are "in compliance" with the requirement to offer and provide family planning services to welfare recipients. Yet exactly what is or is not being done is not at all clear. Our cursory review of the 1974 states' narrative reports, as we have seen, reveals inconsistencies, confusion, and haphazard provision, at best. An enormous range in eligibility requirements, the nature of services provided, and attitudes toward recipients is evident. Even more important, no real effort has been or is being made to inspect and/or confirm exactly what is provided and how. In effect, just as for social services, the federal funds are spent, but what is in fact provided for that money, what service recipients obtain, is impossible to assess. Any real concern with access implies some assurance regarding what one has access to, and this no one really knows, as yet.[23]

Notes

1. Taken from "A Family Planning Glossary," *Family Planning Perspectives*, 4, No. 3 (1972), 345. Note the inclusion of "demographic rationales for family planning."

2. Richard M. Nixon, *Presidential Message to Congress on Population*, July 18, 1969: "It is my view that no American woman should be denied access to family planning assistance because of her economic condition. I believe, therefore, that we should establish as a national goal the provision of adequate family planning services within the next five years to all those who want them but cannot afford them. This we have the capacity to do."

3. *Family Planning/Population Reporter: A Review of State Laws and Policies*, 3, No. 2 (April 1974), 25–26.

4. Harriet F. Pilpel and Peter Ames, "Legal Obstacles to Freedom of Choice in Areas of Contraception, Abortion and Voluntary Sterilization in the United States," *Population and the American Future: The Report of the Commission on Population Growth and the American Future* (Washington, D.C.: GPO, 1972), pp. 59–84.

5. "Pregnancy Termination," Dept. of Medical and Public Affairs, The George Washington University Medical Center, in *Population Report*, Ser. F, No. 1 (April 1973).

6. *Ibid.*

7. Much of the data which follow are derived from the Office of Population Affairs, *Fourth Progress Report to the Congress of the U.S. on Its Five Year Plan for Family Planning Services and Population Research*, May 1975 (processed).

8. *Ibid.*, p. 3.

9. GAO, Report to the Congress, *Improving Federally Assisted Family Planning Programs* (Washington, D.C.: DHEW, April 15, 1975), p. 9.

10. Office of Population Affairs, *Fourth Progress Report*, pp. 32–33. Elsewhere in the same report (p. 58) the figure for fiscal 1975 is given as $167.4 million.

11. See State Narrative Reports summarized below and GAO Report, pp. 53–64.

12. This is an important feature in access since studies have shown reluctance among women to bring up the subject even with their physicians and a corresponding hesitancy on the part of physicians to initiate discussion. See, for example, R. C. Hulbert and R. H. Settlage, "Birth Control and the Private Physician: The View from Los Angeles," *Family Planning Perspectives,* 6, No. 1 (1974), 50–55. This finding also suggests the desirability of specialty clinics.

13. See, for example, Jeanie Rosoff, "How States Are Using Title IVA," *Family Planning Perspectives,* 4, No. 4 (1972), 31–43.

14. For an enlightening debate on the merits of media use in increasing access, see J. R. Udry, L. T. Clark, C. L. Chase, M. Levy, "Can Mass Medical Advertising Increase Contraceptive Use?" *Family Planning Perspectives,* 4, No. 3 (1972), 37–44, and "Letter from Readers," *ibid.,* 4, No. 4 (1972), 2.

15. Information developed in personal interview with the Director, Ella MacDonald, July 29, 1974.

16. Frederick S. Jaffe, "Family Planning Services in the United States," in *Aspects of Population Growth Policy,* p. 242.

17. *Ibid.*

18. Charles F. Westoff, "The Modernization of United States Contraceptive Practice," *Family Planning Perspectives,* 4, No. 3 (1972), 9.

19. Caspar W. Weinberger, "Population and Family Planning," *Family Planning Perspectives,* 6, No. 3 (1974), 171.

20. GAO Report, p. 53.

21. Frederick Jaffe, "Fertility Control Policy, Social Policy and Population Policy in an Industrialized Country," *Family Planning Perspectives,* 6, No. 3 (1974), 164–67.

22. *Ibid.,* p. 167.

23. As we go to press, Charles F. Westoff reports, in "The Decline of Unplanned Births in the United States" (*Science*, Jan. 9, 1976), that married American women are close to control of their pregnancies. This is not true of unwed mothers and of some of the most deprived of the married women.

7

The Delivery of Social Services

Context and Definition

The earlier chapters have supplied extensive illustration of the range of social provision nationally and locally with regard to five different topics or problem areas. But how do people learn about, reach, obtain the services, benefits, and rights that do exist, and what formal arrangements are there for dealing with these matters? Where there is need for more than one service (at one time or over time; within one service system or in several systems, if "systems" they are; for an individual or a family), what devices exist, if any, for facilitating or ensuring that individuals obtain those services? At what level of government or at what point in the continuum between the enactment of provision and the receipt of service are these devices implemented? This chapter will attempt to view service provision from another perspective, namely that of the structure and organization of services generally and the arrangements under which services are delivered to the consumer.

First, however, we shall set up a vocabulary for our discussion. In describing arrangements for organizing and delivering services, certain concepts and terms recur in official statements of policy, in legislation, in descriptions of programs, and in the literature. The most important of these are *access, integration* (program, services, case integration, coordination), and *accountability.* To provide an appropriate context and framework for subsequent material, then, we should define each of these and describe the general structure and function of the relevant category of service-program-measure-device.

Access. Access services include all arrangements which inform people about the availability of rights, benefits, or services; clarify eligibility (connect the rights, benefits, and services to people's particular situations); help them establish eligibility; refer them to appropriate offices and services; get them physically to appropriate offices and facilities; help assure responsiveness on the part of benefit providers or service providers to the needs of applicants. Some access services are universal (any problem, any client); some are selective (only the poor); some are categorical (only specified groups or problems, such as drug addicts, old people, housing); some are particularistic (only members of specified unions, or churches, or racial-ethnic groups, or religious groups). Some access services are free-standing (not part of any other organization, like the British Citizen's Advice Bureaus) and some are connected with other services (like the information services connected to settlement houses or hospitals or social security offices).

An access service has a number of identifiable tasks: (1) to provide simple information, such as where a service is located or how to get there. (2) To provide information about more complex matters, such as social insurance benefits, or the provisions of a law, or the program of an institution. (3) To clarify the relevance of a statute or a provision or a program for one specific person or family (potential eligibility, etc.). (4) To give a person or persons advice about how to proceed. This involves both clarifying what is possible and suggesting a course of action. (5) To steer a person to an agency or service able to help. The inquirer is told what and where the service is but nothing is done to help him get the benefit or service. (6) To refer a person to the right agency. Arrangements are made for an introduction or an appointment. The client's situation may be clarified through a phone call or a letter or a referral summary. (7) To get clients physically to appropriate offices and facilities. This may involve transportation or escort services when needed. It may include child-minding to permit a mother to get to clinics or agencies. (8) To provide a supporting, friendly relationship. Some clients drop in periodically for a friendly chat, often supplemented by information and advice, even though their main help must come from another agency or they do not need any other specific ongoing help. (9) To help the inquirer with the contact or to make it for him. This goes beyond a mere referral. The social worker or someone else may accompany the client to the agency and may interpret his need, or may go with him before the court, for example. (10) To diagnose the "underlying" or basic problem of people who come for information and advice. Not taking the request literally, this service interprets its understanding of underlying needs to the client or to those to whom referrals are made. (11) To carry out formal diagnostic study (social and/or psychological and/or psychiatric and/or physical). Some access services are diagnostic services or centers; some include formal diagnostic studies among their functions. (12) To carry on continued counseling or treatment. This is not the core access task but it can be a service of a unit that also offers access service. (13) To carry on advocacy activities—to intervene in a variety of ways through legal or lay means to make an agency or system more responsive to the needs of a case than it is initially or so as to modify the law-system-agency-regulations on behalf of a category of people or cases. (14) To conduct general community education about services and problems. (15) To recruit potential clients, when new programs begin, when new laws are passed, when new problems arise. (16) To carry out case integration and case accountability activities (see elsewhere in this chapter). As in the instance of counseling or treatment, this is not the access activity, but it may be included in a unit which also offers an access service.

Integration. Integration arrangements (measures, devices, services) include all provision for assuring the effective meshing of the services offered by different units, bureaus, departments, agencies, programs, service systems with regard to the needs of consumers. The purpose of these arrangements is to eliminate fragmentation, gaps, and occasional unnecessary duplication in service provisions, to enhance access to services generally, and to improve the delivery of services to the client or consumer.

Integration may occur at various levels, ranging from the initial authorization of service or benefit to receipt by the consumer. Services can be integrated at the level of authorization by legislation or administrative guidelines, as in the Veterans' Centers set up after World War II or the Delinquency Prevention Projects of the 1960s. They can be integrated at the administrative level by deliberate comingling of funding resources, as has been done by some recently established umbrella agencies at the state level. They can be integrated at the delivery level through centralized access and intake services or through the colocation of different services. They can also be integrated at the case level by the use of special workers whose function it is to mesh services offered by different programs or agencies around the needs of a specific individual or family.

At each of these levels, different devices or mechanisms may be employed to facilitate such integration. Thus, services may be integrated by a number of means. The client himself, as a consumer of multiple services, may integrate his own individual package. A special practitioner may oversee integration, whether this practitioner is a generalist worker who assumes overall responsibility for services needed, a specialist worker providing the primary service who also coordinates other supplementary services, or a multiservice or multidiscipline team including representatives of several different service systems. Integration may be provided by a special facility, such as a multipurpose, multiservice neighborhood service center. Or it may be provided by a special coordinating service, such as a centralized access and linkage system or a centralized intake system, or a special administrative structure such as a planning and coordination superagency.

The tasks involved may cluster around the provision of services (coordinating and interrelating administrative or programmatic activities from different units or bureaus or agencies or service systems) or around the receipt of services (meshing of those different services as needed by an individual case—person, group, or family).

In this context there are two major approaches to integration. Case integration is provision for assuring the effective meshing of services around the needs of a specific person, group, or family. "Meshing" here means interrelating and assuring harmonious cooperation and mutual reinforcement. Case integration includes meshing of simultaneous services and interventions of different units, bureaus, agencies, programs, as they affect one person, a family, or a group at one period of time or over time. Program integration (sometimes termed coordination) deals with the meshing of planning-administrative and/or programing activity in contrast with the meshing of activity around the individual case as in case integration.

Accountability. Finally, accountability involves arrangements to assure delivery of needed services, keeping a client in view for his own or for community protection, following through on a case-group-community problem unless or until there is a deliberate decision that the matter should be dropped, or meeting standards as specified by law or administrative guidelines. Accountability may be upward, to a higher administrative or legislative authority. Questions addressed may include: Is the policy being carried out as explicitly stated? Is the program being implemented as initially planned? Or accountability may be downward, with regard to ensuring responsiveness to the needs and wants of the consumer, client, or community. Arrangements and devices for provision may include: regulatory and standard-setting activities and procedures; assigning specific responsibility to a particular person or unit; monitoring activities by regulatory agencies or officials, by lay citizen groups, or by consumer groups; program evaluations—professionally implemented research studies or consumer assessments. Concern for accountability may focus on the program-service-benefit or on the consumer-client-case, on efficiency or on effectiveness, or on both.

Focus of Presentation. In the United States today, there is no existing national network of locally (or otherwise) based access services. Similarly, there is no national integrated social service system and no nationally instituted, locally based structure for providing general (personal) social services. The U.S. failure to develop such a coherent network or system stems from a variety of factors.

First, and most important, the whole history of social service development in the United States is a story of state—not federal—priority in general social services and of categorical programs established in response to discrete problems (e.g., blindness, orphanhood, old age). This latter is the pattern followed by most countries until the problems presented by such fragmentation stimulate public concern until enough pressure builds for restructuring and reorganizing the system and/or developing measures for improving service delivery. Until that time no system can or will emerge. Even then categorical interests may remain dominant.

Second, the one existing structure which might have developed into such a system—the service arm of the public welfare system, a system expected both to certify eligibility for child assistance and to deliver services—almost collapsed when services and income-maintenance programs were separated early in the 1970s and service staff were either switched to eligibility tasks or were left with limited support and no clear sense of role or function except for continuing tasks in child welfare. The states were unable effectively to develop new, coherent service delivery systems for social services under the Social Security Act in the course of a two-year White House–Congress stalemate over social service regulations. This stalemate was resolved when President Ford signed P.L. 93-647 on January 4, 1975. The implementation date was October 1, 1975, but it is too early to predict consequences (see below).

Third, for the past six years, U.S. policy has stressed implementation of an income strategy as the means for helping people in need. Even though income-support programs (both cash and noncash) have continued to be inadequate to meet existing needs because of disagreement over reform of income-maintenance programs for families, the explicit preference for this strategy resulted for some time in a relative lack of interest in program developments which might be perceived as more relevant to a service strategy.

Fourth, growing federal stress during the late sixties and early seventies on decentralization of policy and programing through general and special revenue sharing, block grants, and administrative measures decreased the likelihood of any "standard" approach. In fact, the general national tendency to favor programing—and to some degree policy—decentralization is antithetical to such a development, which implies a somewhat centralized approach to both.

Fifth, the voluntary sector, sectarian and nonsectarian, has always been significant and autonomous in several U.S. regions in the social services field. Since 1967, Social Security Act social service funds have been expended either through public departments or by purchased care (proprietary or nonprofit agencies). In fiscal 1972, of $2.771 billion social services funds from this source, $1.731 actually went to purchased services. For a variety of historical and political reasons related to suspicion of government and protection of voluntarism, the fact of public funding has not been converted into an opportunity to construct a coherent system.

In lieu of any real development of a service network or system, what does exist is recognition of and concern with certain problems: limited provision for access; fragmentation of service provision; duplication of services; discontinuities in service and care; inequities, inadequacies, and unresponsiveness in service provision and delivery. Evidence of this concern is extensive in the literature of the last decade.[1] The problems are identified as integral to legislative enactments (funding categorical programs), to planning (discontinuities in designing programs), to policy (contradictory and conflicting eligibility criteria), to programing (discrete activities covering one geographic area but not an adjacent one, or one population group but not related groups), to administration (differing and/or discretionary guidelines and instructions to staff). Additional evidence of concern is reflected in the multiple but fragmented initiatives at the national level—piecemeal and ad hoc policies and programs expressed in legislation, congressional testimony, official statements, administrative guidelines and regulations, expenditures, and occasional research and demonstration projects.

Perhaps the most comprehensive statement of the problem was provided by Elliot Richardson, as Secretary of DHEW, in January 1973:

> Since 1961, the number of different HEW programs has tripled, and now exceeds 300. Fifty-four of these programs overlap each other; 36 overlap programs of other departments. This almost random proliferation has fostered the development of a ridiculous labyrinth of bureaucracies, regulations and guidelines.
>
> The average State now has between 80–100 separate service administrations and the average middle-sized city has between 400 and 500 human service providers—each of which is more typically organized in relation to a Federal program than in relation to a set of human problems. In spite of our efforts at administrative simplification, there are 1,200 pages of regulations devoted to the administration of these programs with an average of 10 pages of interpretive guidelines for each page of regulations. The regulations typically prescribe accounting requirements that necessitate separate sets of books for each grant; they require reports in different formats for reporting periods that do not mesh; eligibility is determined program by program without reference to the possible relationship of one program to another; prescribed geographic boundaries for service areas lack congruity. In general, confusion and contradiction are maximized.
>
> Although studies indicate that more than 85 percent of all HEW clients have multiple problems, that single services provided independently of one another are unlikely to result in changes in clients' dependency status, and that chances are less than 1 in 5 that a client referred from one service to another will ever get there, the present maze encourages fragmentation.[2]

What follows is an overview of these national initiatives, as reflected in legislation, major program models, and relevant research. With this national backdrop, we will turn to a description of service delivery in one city for a look at operating programs. Here the focus will be on how services are in fact organized and delivered at the local level, in order to identify and analyze relevant issues and problems.

Responses to Fragmentation

Legislation

In effect, until the passage of the Social Service Amendments of 1974 containing a new and separate Title XX for social services, there was no legislation pointed specifically at access, integration of services, or the development of a cohesive social service structure or system. And the effects of Title XX are as yet uncertain. Of course, many laws have implications for these issues—in particular the myriad laws establishing those categorical programs providing obstacles to developing an integrated service network. For our purposes, however, only those aspects of legislation reflecting efforts at eliminating these obstacles—or initiating such a system—will be described here.

The original *Social Security Act* (1935) introduced the concept of "statewideness" and contained a requirement for developing a state plan. Although this requirement was never implemented, the legislation provided a base and a potential structure for the subsequent development of a statewide social service system. Amendments encouraged states to expand social service provision by increasing the rate at which expenditures for services were reimbursed (1962). In 1967, regulations permitted information and referral services (access services) to be defined as an optional social service, and thus subject to reimbursement. No further effort was made to influence the service structure or the delivery system under this legislation, however, until the initiatives to separate service and eligibility programs (1970–74) and the passage of Title XX of the Social Security Act (see below).

Although the 1960s saw increased legislative activity aimed at developing a more comprehensive approach to coordinated planning and/or service delivery, most of these initiatives were in categorical or specialized areas. In 1963, passage of the *Community Mental Health Act* introduced the concept of the community mental health center, an integrated complex of facilities and services. It was to be a function, not necessarily a place, and the range of services included in such a center were to be preventive, diagnostic, in- and outpatient treatment, consultation, education, and training—in effect an integrated service network under the amorphous umbrella of community mental health. (The mental health–social service relationship is a subject to which we shall return later in the chapter.) To qualify for funds to construct facilities, a state was to submit an overall state mental health plan designating a single agency to administer the plan. Individual project applications were subject to the state agency's approval before submission to Washington. Although the major objective of this legislation was to stimulate development of comprehensive mental health planning at the state level, no operating funds were provided. To overcome this lack, construction grants were provided to achieve policy and program objectives. As a consequence, the program ended up stressing facilities rather than planning a coordinated, comprehensive service system. (Although some centers did in fact provide a wide range of services.)

In 1966, legislation aimed at implementing comprehensive health planning was passed (*Comprehensive Health Planning and Public Health Service Act*). Addressing again the issues of a "compartmentalized" approach to provision—multiple programs with conflicting or unrelated objectives and guidelines—this legislation aimed at encouraging development of a state planning process and planning structure and provided federal support for provision of basic public health services.[3] The community mental health program, hospital planning efforts, and certain specialized regional medical planning were to be permitted to continue, but were to be integrated into the whole program in each state. In the context of what became known as "Partnership-for-Health Planning," federal guidelines were to be focused on planning structure and process and on generalized goals; program content and operations were to emerge from state plans. This legislation enacted an intergovernmental approach to planning not required by any earlier legislation.

While the health and community health legislation described above addressed issues of planning a coordinated service system within one system, or a portion of the system, other legislation reflects concern with affecting the delivery of services at the local level.

Title II-A of the *Economic Opportunity Act* (1964) invented the concept of a "community-action agency" as the means for planning and implementing the whole range of antipoverty programs. In part because it soon became clear that intervention at the level of service delivery alone could not implement change without support at higher administrative levels, many of these agencies began to operate more of their own service programs. In short order, these programs emerged as a third delivery system (public, voluntary, antipoverty) rather than operating as an integrative force. In addition, the need to coordinate services as well as to plan, initiate, help, and advocate, coupled with the inadequacy of available resources and miscellaneous political pressures, hampered the extent to which any one role could be developed. Over time the direct service function became predominant and, as a neighborhood service center, has come to represent a major form of service delivery at the local level (see below).

The *Demonstration Cities and Metropolitan Development Act* of 1966 (Model Cities Act) authorized grants through the Department of Housing and Urban Development to enable cities to plan, develop, and carry out comprehensive city demonstration programs. The specific problem this legislation was designed to solve included the discreteness of federal programs in education, manpower, housing, health, mental health, social security, public assistance, and poverty; the consequent fragmentation of service provision at the local delivery level; discontinuities and conflicts in program goals; gaps in services. By providing federal funds for planning and implementing programs designed by local initiators at the local level to coordinate federal programs, the Act created an incentive in limited city areas for local governments to develop some devices that would lead to greater integration of services. (Here, too, the major device developed was the neighborhood service center.) At best, however, the geographic focus of the Act was small. In addition, the potential effect of the legislation was further diluted by reducing funding for the program as a whole at the same time as the number of "demonstration sites" were expanded.

On a much less important level, another federal approach was the development of a "concerted services program," which for a brief period of time sought the development of a coordinated social service program to be integrated into all public housing. (Whether such a program is appropriate, or may become completely stigmatized, is a separate issue.) Only a few programs ever were fully implemented.

Legislation in the seventies has demonstrated a return to a concern with planning and administration, in one instance just for a categorical group. Title III of the amended *Older Americans Act* (1973) has as its purpose encouraging state and local agencies to develop comprehensive and coordinated service systems for older people. It provides for the establishment of area agencies on aging to plan and implement such a system. Leaving aside the issue of whether or not establishing a separate service system for older people is advisable, one concern is that present appropriations stress this planning and coordinating function without providing resources for adequate service provision. Furthermore, no sanction exists, as yet, for coordinating the Older Americans Program services with those outside it.

In short, there is a legislative heritage of categorical initiatives for integration—mental health, health, housing—each seeing itself as the integrating nucleus and none achieving personal social service integration. States could create public welfare networks of services under the Social Security Act, but in fact stressed eligibility determination as a major function and left social services underdeveloped. The large statewide child welfare system, categorical, stressed child placement and adoption, not a general social service role. The antipoverty centers were multifunction and often generalist, but income-selective in clientele.

Title XX, mentioned in several of the earlier sections, does constitute a potentially new framework. It was enacted in late 1974 as a partial "block grant" or "special revenue sharing" approach to those social services previously financed under the public assistance provisions of the Social Security Act. In contrast to earlier requirements that specific federally mandated services be available to recipients in each of the public assistance categories, the new title simply requires one service directed to each of five goals and at least three services for recipients of Supplementary Security Income, the federalized adult assistance category. (These could, presumably, be the same as those addressed to the goals.) States are penalized financially if they do not offer and provide family planning services to interested public assistance recipients. The service goals are broad and flexible, retaining some of the "instrumental" orientation of the previous decade, but allowing more range and accepting the notion that some services can and must sustain dependency, since not all persons in need of help can become self-sustaining. The goals are stated as follows: (1) achieving or maintaining economic self-support to prevent, reduce, or eliminate dependency; (2) achieving or maintaining self-sufficiency, including reduction or prevention of dependency; (3) preventing or remedying neglect, abuse, or exploitation of children and adults unable to protect their own interests, or preserving, rehabilitating, or reuniting families; (4) preventing or reducing inappropriate institutional care by providing for community-based care, home-based care, or other forms of less intensive care; or (5) securing referral or admission for institutional care when other forms of care are not appropriate, or providing services to individuals in institutions. States are assigned a specified share of a ceiling ($2.5 billion), based on population, and they qualify for reimbursement (75 percent for most services and for administration, evaluation, and planning) on the basis of having carved out a creditable planning process including opportunity for public participation. Reimbursement is higher for family planning (90 percent). Eligibility is broadened well beyond actual, or former, or potential, cash assistance recipients, the earlier constraint. Half the expenditures must be reserved for those at the public assistance level. Between that level and 80 percent of the state median income (but not above the full national median) the state may offer free or fee service (as it may to public assistance recipients). Fees must be charged those between 80 and 115 percent of the state median. Income limits may vary by service category and by user category. Information and referral services and services to prevent abuse, neglect, or exploitation of children or adults unable to protect themselves are not to be means tested at all.

Especially relevant to the present discussion is the specification in Title XX, Sec. 2004, of the required components of the state's proposed comprehensive service plan, as quoted below. While it is not yet known just what will occur in the course of implementation, paragraph H offers leverage for coordination. The plan must indicate:

(A) the objectives to be achieved under the program,

(B) the services to be provided under the program . . . together with a definition of those services and a description of their relationship to the objectives to be achieved under the program and the goals described. . . .

(C) the categories of individuals to whom those services are to be provided, including any categories based on the income of individuals or their families,

(D) the geographic areas in which those services are to be provided, and the nature and amount of the services to be provided in each area,

(E) a description of the planning, evaluation, and reporting activities to be carried out under the program,

(F) the sources of the resources to be used to carry out the program,

(G) a description of the organizational structure through which the program will be administered, including the extent to which public and private agencies and volunteers will be utilized in the provision of services,

(H) a description of how the provision of services under the program will be coordinated with the plan of the State approved under part A of title IV, the plan of the State developed under part B of that title, the supplemental security income program established by title XVI, the plan of the State approved under title XIX, and other programs for the provision of related human services within the State, including the steps taken to assure maximum feasible utilization of services under these programs to meet the needs of the low income population,

(I) the estimated expenditures under the program, including estimated expenditures with respect to each of the services to be provided, each of the categories of individuals to whom those services are to be provided, and each of the geographic areas in which those services are to be provided, and a comparison between estimated non-Federal expenditures under the program and non-Federal expenditures for the provision of the services described in section 2002(a)(1) in the State during the preceding services program year, and

(J) a description of the steps taken, or to be taken, to assure that the needs of all residents of, and all geographic areas in, the State were taken into account in the development of the plan.

In short, within constraints states must plan, engage citizens in planning, subject their plans to evaluation in the political process, provide for program coordination. It is too early to tell whether they will grasp the opportunity inherent in Title XX to rethink service delivery and create new coherence. Title XX could become another battleground of the categories, a contest among powerful service groups "to divide up the pie."

The 93rd Congress also passed P.L. 93-383, the *Housing and Community Development Act* of 1974, which combines ten community development programs into special revenue-sharing block grants, as well as revising and/or continuing major housing programs for families of low and moderate income. Especially relevant in the present context is the stated goal of "continuing efforts on all levels of government to streamline programs and improve the functioning of agencies responsible for planning, implementing, and evaluating community development efforts." Moving away from narrow selectivity, the Act calls for service eligibility consistent with the stance of Title XX and supports programs toward "the expansion and improvement of the quantity and quality of community services, principally for persons of low and moderate income, which are essential for sound community development and for the development of viable urban communities."

Also immediately relevant is the 1973 *Community Employment and Training Act* (P.L. 93-203) in its call for supportive services to enable people to obtain and retain jobs and in its requirement that the government unit serving as prime sponsor establish a planning council which includes consumer participation.

Thus, there are legislative initiatives, not yet widely implemented or visible, which could provide leverage for improved social service planning and coordination. What will be built upon this potential base is yet to be determined.

Government Agencies

During the 1960s, the Office of Economic Opportunity, the Department of Housing and Urban Development, and DHEW were the agencies taking major responsibility for initiating and implementing changes in social service delivery—with relevant measures also supported by the National Institute for Mental Health (NIMH) multiservice centers, localized and involving paraprofessional staff, were featured. Despite several initiatives, there was little comprehensive coordination or service integration. OEO is now a free-standing Community Services Administration with a more limited role, expected eventually to join DHEW. At present, it is primarily DHEW, in particular the Office of the Secretary, that is spearheading the service integration thrust. At the initiation of this office an interagency task force, composed of representatives from Social and Rehabilitation Services, the Office of Education, the Office of Human Development, the Administration on Aging and regional DHEW offices, has been operating a services integration research and demonstration program with funds set aside from agency research budgets. Within this group, it is the Office of the Secretary and SRS who have been most active.

In addition, two federal agencies have been established specifically for the purpose of coordinating planning and policy with regard to two major population groups. One is the Office of Child Development, established in 1969, and the other is the Administration on Aging, established in 1965. Neither agency has any real authority to coordinate or integrate programs authorized under any other department or agency. (Both of these agencies are subunits of a broader coordinating administrative entity, the Office of Human Development.)

The other major governmental bodies involved in planning and/or policy-making in this area are two independent agencies, the Office of Management and Budget and the Advisory Commission on Intergovernmental Relations. OMB has assisted in efforts at implementing more coordinated planning through procedural directives regarding the process by which certain local programs are funded. ACIR, an independent body established in 1953 by act of Congress and responsible both to the President and to Congress, is currently addressing the issue of the impact of federal aid on state and local governments and its consequences for program development.

Finally, at the nonfederal level, twenty-six states have established departments of human resources to coordinate planning and programing in related areas, and some multistate regional organizations (e.g., Appalachia), substate regions, counties, and cities (e.g., New York) have done similarly.

Nongovernmental Groups

Simply because of their status, nongovernmental organizations can have no major role in integrating services, or in developing a coherent delivery system. In fact, they often merely add to the already existing fragmentation and serve as special interest groups in opposing federal initiatives for integration. (For example, in 1973–74 a strongly backed proposal to combine two major national voluntary organizations, Family Service Association of America and Child Welfare League of America, was defeated.) Where they can and do play a role is in the development of new devices for implementing access or case integration. Although experimentation with new models of service delivery may be of interest to some voluntary organizations, the lack of sanction and authority as well as the enormous gaps in philosophy, style, staffing, and so on precludes the transferability of such models into an overall system. While publicly supported demonstration projects under voluntary agency sponsorship have attempted pioneering efforts, in fact there are few illustrations in recent years of new service models being developed by the private sector and adopted subsequently by the public sector.

The major achievement of these organizations has been in refining and expanding provision of access services, in particular information and referral services (although, in fact, the neighborhood service centers first established in the 1960s also stressed this function). The National Center for Voluntary Action and the United Way, a federation of voluntary, nonsectarian service organizations, have been active in developing such programs. In addition, United Way has stressed development of common concepts and definitions of services and program components, and like all other voluntary federations, it has emphasized coordinated approaches to fund raising, planning, and program expenditures. Similarly, in specialized problem areas (e.g., physical handicap, mental health) categorical agencies have developed specialized access services (e.g., Easter Seal, National Association of Mental Health). A review of programs and services provided by national or local federations seems to indicate that categorical programing predominates, although occasional efforts are being made to develop mechanisms for integration of service at the individual case level.

Program Models

Just as there is no national legislation specifically focused on coordination, integration, access, service delivery, there is no national pattern of program development. What follows, therefore, will include identification of: (1) programs which emerged as a consequence of the federal legislation described above; (2) programs which emerged as a result of federal administrative initiatives; (3) programs which emerged in response to federal research and demonstration efforts; (4) programs which emerged in response to state initiatives; (5) programs which emerged from miscellaneous local initiatives, both public and voluntary. In each category, only one or two major program models will be described.

Programs Resulting from Federal Legislation

The neighborhood service center—or the multiservice center—was an outgrowth of the juvenile delinquency program of the early 1960s and the community action program of the mid-1960s; its development was expanded still further under the Model Cities program of the mid-1960s.[4] Designed as a structural response to the problems of service fragmentation, inaccessibility, and unresponsiveness, it was intended to demonstrate a new approach to service delivery at the local level by providing integrated, relevant, comprehensive, and coordinated services in a physically accessible setting by responsible and competent staff. Regardless of the variations among the more than fifteen hundred centers which developed during the last decade, most shared certain general purposes and features, namely: access services (information, advice, referral, brokerage, follow up, advocacy); a melange of concrete services to individuals and families in addition to access, including several or all of the following—counseling, day care for children, employment counseling, training and job placement, recreation and group work, help with housing problems, legal services, homemakers, health aides, meals-on-wheels, congregate meals; originally, social action and class advocacy efforts at making public agencies, service bureaucracies and local governments more responsive to neighborhood needs. (This third function has gradually disappeared for a number of reasons ranging from the political pressures on the centers to refrain from adversarial activities and the intransigence of the established bureaucracies they were trying to change, to the real need for direct service provision in the communities served and the concommitant pressure to expand such provision.)

For the most part none of these centers developed a really integrated system of service provision, and few were anything like comprehensive in their range of provision. Most have tended to contain the core services of the host agency (and all are established by one or another host agency) and a few others besides. Essentially, they provide a series of contiguous services in one structure, thereby facilitating access. Certain major service providers are often unrepresented in such a facility, yet provision may be expedited within the context of those available through the case advocacy–case integration roles workers developed.

It is primarily through facilitating access and developing case integration devices that this model has been effective; neither integration nor coordination of services has been implemented successfully. (See below for a review of the research relevant to this conclusion.) With minor changes, this model continues to exist today, representing a major form of local or neighborhood-based service delivery—colocation of multiple services in the guise of an integrated delivery system.

Another federally motivated response to fragmentation is the neighborhood legal service center, which was developed out of the OEO antipoverty program in an effort to provide access and advocacy to the poor and minority groups. It has continued as an effective approach to direct provision of legal services generally, as well as in its role of case and class advocacy, although the latter has recently become somewhat truncated by the elimination of the legal "back-up" centers from the program and the limitations placed on class action law suits under recent Supreme Court decisions. Its continued viability is illustrated by efforts at expanding this model into other functional areas, such as neighborhood legal service programs for the aged (see Chapter 5).

Programs Resulting from Federal Administrative Initiatives

The 4-C program—Community Coordinated Child Care—was developed at the initiation of OCD to facilitate the decategorization of certain programs serving children. In effect, this was an attempt at community-coordinated planning for day care through grass roots participation. It failed because of the absence of any clear relationship of the local program to existing higher administrative structures or to other programs affecting children. (See Chapter 2.)

Among the more important devices aimed at facilitating development of more integrated programs are various grant coordinating mechanisms, such as consolidated funding, integrated grant administration program, review and comment processes, and, most important, the procedure announced by OMB in a memorandum generally referred to as "Circular A-95." This procedure aims at coordinating planning and programing activities by a notification, review, and comment system. In effect, local governments submit an official "notification of intent" to a multicounty or regional clearinghouse (there are about 470 in the country at present) which clears it with regard to other related agency's interests (e.g., there are about eighteen hundred relevant single-purpose agencies—for example, manpower, air quality control, health) and channels it upward to the appropriate federal agency. Most applications are approved. Although no real sanction exists to restrict further action for the few receiving negative recommendations, such a response has effectively inhibited further development. Another portion of this directive, requiring relevant planning to utilize existing geographical districts, has not been implemented; thus, planning with multiple and conflicting geographical boundaries persists (e.g., health planning districts, area planning for the aging, law enforcement agency districts).

Finally, current DHEW policies supporting "Services Integration" projects, "Partnerships to Improve Delivery of Services" projects, and "Capacity Building" projects, represent DHEW efforts at encouraging, supporting, assisting state and local governments in their efforts at developing a comprehensive, integrated service system. Although concrete support is limited (no legislative mandate exists, as yet, and little funding is available), this explicit statement of policy implemented through the expenditure of discretionary funds in the form of research and demonstration grants (see below) does represent official sanction, and therefore provides some leverage for states to implement relevant policies, stimulating program development at the state level.

Programs Resulting from Federal Research and Demonstration Efforts

In the context of the proposed Allied Services Act, since fiscal 1971 DHEW has been operating Services Integration Target Organizations, an interagency services integration research and demonstration program intended to identify effective approaches to achieving service integration. Funds for this effort have been set aside from individual agency research budgets, with project funding decisions made by a SITO Task Force composed of OS, agency, and regional DHEW representatives. As of fiscal 1974 there were thirty-one active SITO projects, of which twenty-six were operating projects at state, substate regional, county, municipal, or neighborhood levels. The projects are described in a DHEW memorandum as varying widely in terms of focus, design, quality, and the likelihood of producing data of national significance. These programs employ different approaches to achieve the goal of service integration without making any clear distinction as to what is being integrated, the nature of the integration process, or where—at what governmental level—the process occurs. Among the approaches employed are the following seven.

One is a state-level superagency, department of human resources, or office of human development, in which one agency is assigned administrative responsibility for coordinating the planning and programing activities of several others (e.g., health, corrections, mental health). Such an agency may also be developed at a city level (in New York, Seattle, Chattanooga, Minneapolis, among others.) However, unless the service system is restructured within this new entity, this approach appears to involve imposing a new administrative superstructure on top of an existing—if fragmented and categorical—system. In some states efforts are being made to restructure and reorganize the service delivery system generally, but obstacles to achieving this continue to exist.

A second is the use of centralized information services or management information services (MIS). This approach is discussed later in the chapter.

Another is the use of neighborhood service centers or multiservice centers similar to those described earlier.

Fourth are centralized access and intake services. These appear to be similar to the MIS, but provide access and intake only, with no ongoing service provision at the same site, although workers refer clients for appropriate service elsewhere and provide follow-up to ensure provision. These workers function, therefore, as case integrators, keeping responsibility for a case until services are provided elsewhere, then relinquishing responsibility. Where multiple services are required simultaneously, it is not clear whether responsibility for coordinating provision continues with this service or not.

Still another approach is the "case manager." This alternative (or supplementary) approach names a worker in either a multiservice center, an access and intake service, or another program as the "person in responsibility" for a case. The manager stays with it through multiple simultaneous referrals (to the client or other members of his family) or referrals over time until all needed services have been provided.

An unknown additional number of demonstration projects are designed to provide models of "services integration." These cannot be clearly identified because no precise, agreed-upon definition of "services integration" exists at DHEW, and no clear criteria for separating out such programs has been developed.[5]

Finally, there are Child Advocacy projects funded by OCD, NIMH, OE. These are aimed at developing and structuring an integrated approach to advocacy, access, and service integration for children.

Programs Resulting from State Initiatives

The state Department of Human Resources or Human Development is the major model to emerge in response to state initiative (see above for a brief description). As of 1974, some twenty-six states had developed such agencies. There is no consistent pattern as to which, or how many, of the human services are included under this umbrella. There are also county and city efforts along such lines.[6] There are also state Offices of Child Development, like the federal OCD, aimed at coordinating planning and programing for children, and state Offices on Aging, with a similar function for the aged.

Although no really good statewide information system is yet in place, several states are moving toward Management Information

Systems, or centralized, computerized data banks containing consistent information regarding service users, resources, and the like. Major efforts are under way in Georgia, Florida, Maine, Kentucky, North Carolina, Michigan, and Oregon. However, here too there is no consistency between states as to the type of information to be collected or the nature of the classification scheme to be employed.

Programs Resulting from Miscellaneous Local Initiatives

In addition to the neighborhood service centers, neighborhood legal services, centralized access and intake services, and case integration services described above, other programs that have been developed as a result of local public and voluntary initiatives include: local access services (both general and categorical information and referral services); complaint services; telephone services (visiting, reassurance, counseling); transportation and escort services; outreach services. Since illustrations of these exist in our local community (and in fact represent the predominant pattern for program development in most localities), they will be described extensively as individual operating programs below.

Summary

We can gain a rough idea of the quantitative scale of these programs by glancing at a few figures on their numbers and distribution. In most cases we regard these figures as quite soft, representing vague estimates and approximations, and they should not be construed to represent anything firmer. For example, as of 1970 more than 3,300 neighborhood service centers were identified, and 2,500 sampled, in a national survey.[7] However, 38 percent of these had existed before 1964, and would thus represent settlement houses and similar types of agencies rather than any new concept of multiservice centers. If we keep these qualifications in mind, however, the following figures may be illuminating: Approximately 1,000 neighborhood legal services existed as of 1974. Twenty-six states have departments of human resources or some similar agency representing a combination of health, education, and welfare functions. Twenty-six operating SITO projects exist, ranging from state level to neighborhood level. Most are at the county level. There are 100 information and referral services under the auspices of local United Way agencies; 50 Call-for-Action radio complaint services, with 2,500 volunteers staffing emergency and referral "switchboards" in forty states; 300 "Hot Lines." But there are no hard data regarding information and referral programs nationally with a clear definition as to the type of program included: Must it be free standing? If part of an existing program, how much staff time must be directed toward this service? What kind of staff is needed—telephone operator? special worker? What is the nature of the service?

Research and Evaluation

As we have seen earlier in this chapter, policies and programs are fragmented. As much can be said about research. There is no existing research specifically directed toward answering such questions as: Are integrated services better, or more effective, than nonintegrated services? Which devices, mechanisms, or structures facilitate the integration of services more than others? What variables enhance, or impede, integration of services? Which of these can be controlled? By whom? How do the costs of integrated service provision compare with the costs of non-integrated services? And perhaps underlying all of this, what exactly is meant by integration of services, and which services specifically are to be integrated.*

Extensive research has been done on multiservice centers, although it is composed primarily of surveys or exploratory-descriptive studies. Some efforts have been made to evaluate the effectiveness of these centers, but as yet no clear measures of effective service delivery have been developed, precluding any rigorous evaluation. However, even in this limited context, certain important conclusions can be noted.

Most multiservice centers represent the colocation of multiple services, not one integrated or comprehensive service. There is little evidence of center capacity to coordinate services of independent

*New research initiatives on these issues are being launched out of OS, DHEW, as we go to press.

agencies. Center directors have difficulty controlling staff, who often retain primary loyalty to the parent or host agency and its goals, policies, procedures. Even when the administrator has direct authority over staff, coordination and integration may not occur.[8]

There are no research findings regarding the impact of establishing umbrella agencies at the state level on service delivery (costs, benefits).

One major study was commissioned "to understand more clearly the nature and progress of ongoing effort in services integration and to identify among possible Federal actions, those most conducive to support of this effort." This study attempted to clarify the concept of "services integration," define it, identify critical variables which inhibit or facilitate integration of services, and evaluate or assess the impact of integration of services on accessibility, continuity of service, effectiveness, and efficiency of service delivery.[9] A sample of thirty-three projects was selected from an unknown universe, a universe that remains unknown because there is no consensus in DHEW about what constitutes a "services integration" project let alone what constitutes a successful one.

The study findings revealed the following: Integration of services in these projects was not extensive even in projects described as successful. The process of integration takes time and requires substantial external support. Administrative and community support for the objective of integrating services is essential to achieve it. Strong program leadership is critical for success. Single-point funding can have a major impact on ensuring integration. Access and continuity of services appear to be enhanced by service integration (but whether this is due to greater service availability or service integration only could not be discerned). There is no indication of any reduction of costs as a consequence of integrating services. Neighborhood service centers acted as a shelter for service providers rather than as a single coherent delivery system. The effect on local service delivery systems of reorganizing services into statewide departments of human resources will require several years before any valid assessment can be made.

Major conclusions indicate that there is little support for a unified, integrated service system from service providers or categorical interest groups, or from consumer groups, but that such an approach appears to improve access and service delivery. If it is to be implemented on a broader scale, more DHEW support is necessary both directly in the form of technical assistance and indirectly by urging this policy against state and local government opposition. Finally, implementation of this policy requires specific DHEW requirements and guidelines for program development. Nothing in the findings indicated any differential outcome related to the model of "services integration" or device or mechanism employed.

Twenty-two SITO projects, identified as the research and demonstration expression of DHEW's "services integration" and "capacity building" strategy, are described within a framework of human service systems, in another research study.[10] These Services Integration Target Organization projects were intended as a pre-test of the Allied Services Act, to develop and test out new techniques for coordinating, managing, and evaluating human services programs at different levels of government from state to neighborhood. Funded under the umbrella of "services integration," in reality these projects were never designed as a coherent research and demonstration effort. The projects were planned and funded haphazardly without any clear concept of what was meant by "services integration," with no specific goals, nor any consistent (and therefore comparable) design. Some projects are state-based, some multicounty, some county, some municipal, some neighborhood, some a combination. Designs are not comparable; there is no identification of variables to be studied, no specificity of outcome or outcome measures. Individual evaluations exist for many of these projects but generalizable conclusions inevitably are limited.

Current research efforts are focused on demonstration projects aimed at "capacity building," "Partnerships to Improve Delivery of Services" grants, and related activities; they reflect problems similar to those in the research described above. In reviewing those demonstration projects funded under the umbrellas of "service integration," "capacity building," and so on, it seems clear that random innovation, not systematic experimentation, is the approach taken.[11] At present a major evaluation study is projected to review all completed evaluation studies of "services integration" projects as well as to assess directly the new "capacity building" and "partnership" projects described earlier. DHEW is also planning to support a series of demonstrations aimed at identifying effective patterns of policy planning, programing, and service integration in local government.[12] It also is funding at Aspen Systems, Rockville, Maryland, a new clearinghouse on service integration.

Programs in Action

Thus far in this chapter we have reviewed the national scene with regard to legislation, policies, and programs relevant to the organization and delivery of social services—both those services described in detail in the earlier chapters as well as all other services delivered at the local level. We have indicated that there is no standard, guaranteed, nationally instituted, locally based structure for providing access to services generally or for delivering either particular categorical or general social services. Some of the categorical programs do follow nationally guided patterns and we have looked at major "models" in earlier reports, especially in Chapters 2–5. However, there is neither a standard delivery system for general social services as such nor a standard pattern for planning, coordination, or service integration—despite national efforts of late to encourage integration at the case and program level and to facilitate access.

Now, in order to understand how existing legislation and policy actually are implemented at the local level, and how services are organized and delivered in real life under these circumstances, we turn to the more detailed picture of service delivery in our northeastern community. Our objective here is not evaluation, but further clarification of the issues facing those who would argue that more system and coherence should be introduced—or that the present pattern should be preserved.

Overview of the Community

Our city contains a wide variety of manufacturing and service industries, which contribute to the relatively stable economy in the city generally. Although no city is completely representative of all others, this one has many characteristics that make it more representative than most. It has experienced many changes and problems since World War II. Its overall population (about 200,000) has declined while that of the surrounding county has increased (470,000 in 1973). The number and types of minority groups have increased and its racial composition today is the same as that of the nation generally. The percentage of young people and elderly in the population has grown beyond the national average. And family income, educational levels, and labor force participation generally (both employment and unemployment rates) continue to linger behind the country as a whole. Only in its religious composition is the city clearly atypical: it is more heavily Catholic than most.

The government consists of a mayor, a nine-member council with a president at its head, and a judicial branch. In addition, there is a city auditor and a board of education responsible for the city school district. The mayor is the single most powerful of all the elected city officials, having control of the city budget and administration as well as veto power over the school budget. The mayor's appointive power extends over two different types of agencies: agencies with joint city and county responsibilities (e.g., aging, the local museum, the Drug Abuse Commission) and those operating under the city's jurisdiction only (e.g., fire, police, transportation, housing).

The county has a similar tripartite form of government with a strong county executive (who has powers similar to the mayor's, with the exception of the schools, which run independently), a county legislature, and a judicial branch. The major difference in responsibility between city and county is that the city controls all urban renewal and housing activity (and none of this activity occurs in the towns outside the city) and the county government controls all the social welfare services. These latter are provided primarily by county departments of health, mental health, and social services.

The county legislature is composed of twenty-four legislators: ten with constituents entirely from the city; ten with constituents entirely from the towns and villages; and four with mixed city-county constituencies. Also within the boundaries of the county are 19 towns, 15 villages, 18 school districts, and 438 special districts for sewer, drainage, water, and refuse facilities and services. The towns and villages provide such basic services to their residents as fire, police, and public works, while the county government supplements these with health, social, and other special services.

Both federal and state governments have various liaison offices in the city, which also is the site of several federal agency offices because of its central location.

Various types of jurisdictional arbitrariness and overlap exist between city and county and these have been increased as the population in the county has grown. Thus, sometimes the city and county offer the same services, each with its own program planning and administrative staff (e.g., the public employment program, criminal justice planning, youth programs). At other times, especially when required to do so by state or federal law, a program will be jointly planned, administered, and operated.

In addition to social provision under public auspices (county and city), a large number of services are also provided by private nonprofit (voluntary) agencies, generally with a combination of private and public funding. Here, too, there are often overlaps and boundary uncertainties between the public city and county agencies on the one hand and the voluntary agencies on the other. Operating largely autonomous programs, these voluntary agencies have various types of administrative linkages, both horizontally, at the local level, and vertically, with national parent or affiliate organizations. Thus, the major agencies do some of their fund-raising jointly through one local organization, using it, also, as a vehicle for leadership and coordination. This organization, the United Way, is a local unit of a national, nonsectarian funding and planning organization serving local service agencies and organizations. Among the major voluntary agencies are Catholic Charities, a multifunction agency related to its national body; Family and Child Service Agency, an amalgam of traditional family and child welfare services affiliated with Family Service Association of America and Child Welfare League of America; and a local branch of the Salvation Army. In recent years these voluntary agencies have received significant public funds through purchase-of-care project grants and subsidy programs for some of their activities. Each of these supports a number of general as well as specialized programs.

Finally, there are quasi-public agencies also, like CHANGE and Model Cities, which are administratively autonomous (that is, they are not directly responsible to the county or city government) but are publicly funded. Their boards are partially selected by and partially accountable to publicly elected officials. Some of the programs operated by these agencies are administered jointly with certain of the local voluntary agencies. In effect, they represent a third category of social programs.

Social Programs: The Backdrop

Even this very sketchy overview reveals some potential for gaps or difficulties in service delivery in this city as a consequence of separate jurisdictional areas within the social sector at all levels, between public and voluntary sectors, and between city and county as well as federal, state, and local governments and programs. Further detail will sharpen the picture.

We have already described and illustrated in other chapters this city's programs in the fields highlighted in the volume. Measured against comparable programs elsewhere in the nation, the city's programs providing day care, away-from-home care, and family planning services are fairly representative, its handling of the problem of abuse and neglect has led to some new and innovative developments, and, finally, its programs for the aged are far more extensive quantitatively and qualitatively than is characteristic of most other U.S. communities.

In addition to provision in these areas, the city has numerous other social programs, many of which tend to cluster in defined social fields: health, education, income maintenance, housing, justice, manpower. Thus, for example, in 1973, before the federalization of the adult public assistance categories, the public assistance caseload was 9,921 cases (or 25,281 persons). Of these, Old Age Assistance was supplied to 1,354 persons; Aid to the Disabled to 1,954; Aid to the Blind to 43; Aid to Families with Dependent Children to 20,572 (14,844 children and 5,728 adults, or 5,682 cases); and Home Relief to 1,153 persons (947 cases). The average financial grant per case per month was $179.49 and the per person average was $70.44. (The statewide figures were $196.87 and $81.52 respectively.) In addition, 8,243 individuals received medical assistance but not cash assistance. Almost 1,000 children were in foster care (141 in institutions, 852 in foster family homes). The assistance programs were administered by the County Department of Social Services, foster care by a complex public-voluntary mix.

The local health system includes several hospitals, clinics, a neighborhood health center, the county departments of health and mental health, private physician and nursing services, skilled nursing homes and other chronic care facilities, substance abuse and treatment programs. In the education system are the public schools, the independent schools, several colleges and universities, and special educational programs such as the "T Schools." The income maintenance (cash) programs include benefits provided through the local social security agency as well as the Department of Social Services (public assistance). Housing includes benefits and services provided by the city housing authority and the various public housing projects. The police and the local judiciary are included in the justice system; and most of the employment services, job training, and career counseling programs fall within the manpower system (although here the boundaries are less clear).

Finally, there are a large number of miscellaneous services that remain, services that are variously called "human services" (as are those listed above) or "other social services." Some of these services are partially in one of the above systems, yet are also characterized by something else. For example, some we have already identified and studied intensively are child care (partly education, partly early child development, and partly "something else"); services to abused and neglected children (partly health–mental health, partly justice, partly education, partly "something else"); care for delinquent and dependent children (justice, health, education, and the "something else"); community care of the aged (all sectors, yet having an additional not-yet-specified component). Among other services which seem to cut across several systems are probation (justice, education, and ?) and services for the mentally retarded (mental health, education, and ?). Furthermore, there still remain some services that are clearly not in any of the above systems: general information and advice services; services that stress help for personal problems (marital conflict, parent-child conflict, personal crises or stress); help with child care and child rearing (foster care, adoptions, child guidance); help, socialization, recreation for youth and for the handicapped.

It is these services—those which do not fall within existing defined fields or which cut across several fields and include some characteristics integral to no others—which are the focus of our report on service delivery: What are these services? What do they do? How do they relate to one another? Can they be classified and labeled?

Our discussion of the national picture of service delivery and view of current trends in policy and program development indicates clearly that the country is at a transition point. Recognition of the pervasiveness of certain problems—quantitative and qualitative inadequacies of services, fragmentation of provision, unresponsiveness of services to consumer needs and preferences—as well as the failures or limitations of previously attempted solutions, has stimulated a search for new approaches.

We began, therefore, by attempting to obtain the answers to certain basic questions:[13] What services exist? How do people learn about and obtain services? If more than one service is needed, how do people obtain them? How do they proceed—or how are they channeled—from one service or program to another? Is there some special person or function or device that assures the client-consumer of obtaining the several services that may be needed? Are there certain services or agencies that seem to be related, connected, or linked particularly closely? (Since we were not surveying clients or client needs directly, our focus here was on how the services and programs relate to one another and what the major sources for referrals to and from each agency are.) Are there certain agencies which seem to stress more generalized provision than others? If so, how do they differ from other more specialized agencies or programs and how do they relate to them? Are there any devices for ensuring that consumer responses to provision—consumer needs and preferences—are integrated into the planning and development of new programs or change in existing ones?

The rationale for these questions derives from our initial section, where the case is made for access, integration, and continuity of care. It is recognized that those operating the individual programs may not have mandate or sanction to create the coverage or interrelationships posited. Yet these would seem to be legitimate questions from the consumers' point of view.

What Services Exist?

About nine hundred separate social programs exist in this city and the surrounding county; most are in the city itself. Three hundred fifty participated recently in a survey of social programs instituted by a joint city-county Task Force (see below for more detail). Several dozen of these were visited personally by our project staff; some were described in earlier chapters and others will be described subsequently. Close to a hundred officials, administrators, practitioners, and interested laymen were interviewed regarding these services and programs and the issues and problems relevant to them. Our objective was to obtain material sufficient to illustrate how services are organized and delivered in actual practice. The picture which has been developed is not a complete one, by any means, nor is there any effort on our part to assess quality or evaluate impact or effectiveness. A picture is what we tried to obtain, and a description of what we saw is what we will try to convey.

How Do People Learn About and Obtain Services?

Among those agencies providing general access services—information, referral, brokerage, follow-up, advocacy, and advice—are the Community Volunteer Center, Inc., the city, CHANGE (the local community action agency), Model Cities, Catholic Social Services, Call-for-Action (a radio complaint service incorporating a strong advocacy component), and the Salvation Army. One expert stated that at one time every major agency in the community had such a service, and advertised it. Although the Community Volunteer Center, a United Way agency, is the largest access service agency in the city (and in the county), both it and the city publish separate directories of community services; and so do several other agencies.

In addition to the above, there are various specialized or categorical access services, many of which publish their own directories. Among these are the Health Information and Referral Service (based at the County Department of Health), the Information Center for Women, Guide to Community Services for Mothers Alone, and Pregnancy Information Service. With regard to access to legal rights and entitlements and advocacy, at least three additional programs exist: the Neighborhood Legal Service; the Legal Center for the Aged; Retire with Dignity (RWD).

Thirteen hundred social programs are listed in the five most comprehensive, general directories. Needless to say many programs are listed in several directories, but the largest single directory (Community Services Directory published by the Community Volunteer Center), lists about nine hundred separate programs.

Other forms of provision designed to facilitate access to other services and benefits include various outreach programs. Among these are telephone services (visiting and reassurance, information and advice), outreach services (counseling, etc.), and transportation, especially for the elderly and handicapped.

A final note regarding all these services is that most are under voluntary auspices, and are supported largely by voluntary funds.

A quite detailed description of the major access service agency follows—both to clarify the contents of such service and to introduce some questions about this function which must be considered in the last part of the chapter.

The Volunteer Center, Inc. is a combined information and referral service and an organization for the promotion of volunteerism in the community. Established in 1939, the agency was originally intended to provide a formal structure for recruiting volunteers and channeling them to appropriate institutions, organizations, and agencies needing help. In the early 1960s, after making a survey of community needs, the local United Way agency recommended the establishment of an information and referral service. Beginning in 1966, it provided funding support for the Center to take on this supplemental function. From then until 1972 the program was essentially a one-person service stressing provision of resource and service information to agency and professional personnel. In 1972, COA (the local Council on Aging) recommended the establishment of a consumer-oriented information and referral service for the elderly as one component of a proposed County Model Program on Aging (MPA) and approached the Center as the natural institutional base to house and administer such a program. Enthusiastic community support for this program indicated a potential demand and support for a more broadly based consumer service and this was reflected subsequently when the county legislature decided to assign some revenue-sharing funds to this service.

At present, this agency is operated under the auspices of the United Way, the "community chest" and central services agency in the volunteer sector. The major program components include a general information and referral service, a special information and referral service for the elderly, and a recruitment and placement service for volunteers. Minor programs include a Christmas Program (collection and distribution of in-kind gifts for the needy), a telephone lifeline–reassurance and visiting program, and a volunteer program for the elderly. The agency is funded by the Administration on Aging for its information and referral service for the elderly; by the federal volunteer program, ACTION; and by the United Way and the county legislature for its remaining operations.

The program is centrally located in a recently remodeled downtown office building. The office is attractive and modern, with several meeting rooms and communal rooms where clients and volunteers can be accommodated. The atmosphere is relaxed and informal. Regardless, 90 percent of the clients continue to use the telephone for service requests rather than come to the office personally, although the other program components (volunteer services, etc.) do make active use of the facility. In addition, the agency has two satellite information and referral programs: one is located at the local university and the other in an expanding suburban community, currently growing rapidly in response to the establishment of new industries in the area.

People learn about the information and referral program through various means. The service is advertised on radio and television through spot announcements. Direct mail advertising includes all sorts of brochures and leaflets describing the program. Other access services such as Call-for-Action and the various categorical programs (e.g., Health Information Service) refer to this service, as do professionals in other agencies. Finally, as is true for all other resources, word of mouth referrals from previous users satisfied with the service bring in many new requests.

No fee is charged and anyone and everyone can and does use the service. However, the elderly (those 55 and over) account for 60 percent of the clientele. In general, the target population includes all residents of the county, but in fact it is city residents who utilize the services most.

About forty calls are received daily, and most involve just providing information and/or "steering" people to the right resource. Active involvement in making referrals, follow-up, and advocacy are required only in a small percentage of the requests. Where the elderly are concerned, requests may reveal problems in coping generally, or need for more extensive service. In such cases, and when requested to do so, the staff may visit callers in their own homes, exploring needs and helping delineate priorities for help. However, the vast majority of calls involve only one contact, and almost all are limited to a very few contacts. Continuity of service is not a function of this agency. Overall, about half the requests received at any given time are repeats, although data supporting this estimate are weak.

The case flow during the last few years has been as follows: in 1972, approximately 3,500 people were served (not number of requests), with a staff of 1.5; in 1973, approximately 6,000 served with a staff of 3; in 1974 (6-month period), almost 6,000 people with a staff of 4.

The service operates twenty-four hours a day, seven days a week. Outside of regular working hours, a staff of sixteen volunteers (mostly professionals either from the program itself or from other agencies) rotate in offering a week's coverage for emergency purposes. A telephone answering service covers the phone and the person on duty carries a "beeper" for a week at a time, calling in to the service when a "beep" is received. There are about six to eight emergency calls each week, most of which are not true emergencies but rather requests for service that can wait, or indirect expression of some need for reassurance. The volunteers serve one week every three months. Agency policy is that this type of coverage is important for the agency's image and to ensure coverage in the case of the occasional real emergency.

In addition to this information and referral service, the Center publishes the major single directory of community services, another dirctory listing community services to the elderly, and other specialized directories as well. All are updated annually.

The major areas in which services are requested are: financial assistance, especially for emergency needs (this has increased enormously since passage of SSI); health assistance and service (emergency health service requests are processed directly; nonemergency health-related requests are referred to the Health Information Center); counseling, especially for parent-child problems, marital problems, individual or other interpersonal problems; legal services, information and advice.

The major service requests for which no resources are available—indicating needs for which help is either nonexistent or inadequate—include the following: child care for nights (when mothers work at night) and after-school programs when mothers are working a regular day; emergency shelters for isolated homeless women; drying-out places for women alcoholics; group homes for single women of all ages; a more extensive emergency financial assistance fund; halfway houses for the mentally ill or mentally fragile; housekeeping services for older people (yard work, window cleaning, grass cutting, heavy cleaning), which should be universal with a graduated fee scale; transportation services, in particular for the elderly (the existing special services all involve two-day notice; what is needed here is an emergency service); small-scale congregate homes for the elderly encompassing the range of care required by individuals who can cope with independent living most of the time but have occasional episodes during which they need more supervision (something almost like an old-fashioned boarding house).

Staff of the Center include eleven in the main office plus another three in the satellite centers (excluding clerical staff). There is an overall director of the program and a policy-making advisory board composed of locally prominent lay people and professionals. The information and referral service (the major program component of the agency) is directed by a professional social worker. Three paraprofessionals who have had extensive experience working in community agencies and are familiar with community resources complete the staff. Two speak Spanish fluently and the third is equally fluent in Italian; thus the various ethnic groups in the community can be appropriately served. In addition, a researcher was hired to improve data collection and begin to develop a system whereby accurate data can be collected regarding requests made (needs identified) and satisfied as well as those which can not be satisfied (unmet needs), illustrating priorities for future planning. Other information and referral services are now beginning to coordinate efforts toward this objective; they are feeding data in regarding their requests, both met and unmet, in order to help develop a centralized data collection system.

The Center is the largest of the existing information and referral services in the community; it serves the most people and answers the largest number of requests. Its relationship to the County Department of Social Services (DSS), the social security agency, resources related to serving the aging, and day care programs is extremely close. It works cooperatively with the existing categorical access services (e.g., Health Information, Information Center for Women). At present, limited data are kept about people served—the nature of their requests, the characteristics of those requesting each category of service, action taken, and so on. However, there is emerging concern about this. There is recognition that a large number of people still do not use the service, and there is concern about expanding use, but little knowledge about how to do so. There is awareness of the fact that only a small proportion of those availing themselves of community services are channeled through any of the formal access services, but no information as to whether this is good, bad, normal, or what. Apart from the self-evaluation study now in process, no other evaluation studies exist or have even been implemented.

It is worth repeating here something mentioned in earlier chapters. For the services studied most extensively and for those others for which we have data, it seems clear that by far the most people using services in this community reach these services without the use of formal access channels even though such channels are particularly extensive. Most clients are self-referred or referred by word of mouth of friends or relatives; some are referred by other agencies. For certain programs (e.g., services for the aged) formal channels are heavily utilized; for others (e.g., family planning) they play a very minor role; and for still other services, the decision to use the service is not a voluntary one (e.g., institutions for delinquents).

When one looks at access services directly, there is no doubt that they are being utilized heavily, and increasingly so. Yet there still seem to be large numbers of people who are eligible for services and need them, but do not use them out of ignorance or dissatisfaction with what is available, or for other, unknown reasons. What the numbers of these people are, is, at best, an estimate. The reasons for their failure to utilize these services remains unknown; and how to reach them continues to be a problem.

Dealing with Multiple Service Needs

Multiple service situations are common in this field. What occurs when more than one service is needed in this city? Data regarding the numbers of people requesting multiple services, or indicating the existence of several problems requiring multiple services, are at best soft. No precise figure is available regarding the numbers of cases characterized by multiple service needs, or the average number of services that are requested. Our conclusions are, therefore, impressionistic.

In reviewing case records from three of the largest agencies serving families, records selected by the agencies as representative of typical operations, we found that most gave evidence of multiple problems and multiple service needs. However, there does not appear to be any consistent pattern regarding referrals. Thus, in one instance, a mother came for counseling around family problems. The record discloses that she had health problems requiring medical care, that her alcoholic husband frequently abused her, that their son was truanting from school, and that their housing was inadequate. The worker concentrated on counseling around the family and marital conflict problems, referred the woman to a local hospital for care, and contacted the school for information about the child. After a number of contacts, the whole case was referred to the Department of Social Services, Children's Services.

In another case, records describe a case conference involving the Department of Social Services, the Department of Health, the landlord's attorney, a representative from the Department of Sanitation, the County Sheriff, and Children's Services. There is no reason given for calling the conference; nor is there any indication of the outcome. Regardless, several disparate services and institutions apparently were involved with this family, indicating at the very least the existence of several problems.

A third case involved a mother and her two children, one of whom was in foster care. It was noted that one agency was working with the foster family and child, and a second agency with the natural mother and her second child.

A fourth case involved a family of five in which the mother complained about being overwhelmed with household tasks and child rearing, about the loss of public assistance payments, and about her inability to get to the clinic to keep appointments, although physical symptoms continued to disturb her.

In all these cases, the records reveal multiple client problems and needs and multiple service needs. But there is no consistent pattern or system by which consumers obtain these services. Some consumers go themselves to several different agencies for services. Sometimes this means overlapping and conflicting interventions to solve problems; sometimes they may be mutually supportive and reinforcing. Some clients announce multiple problems and needs and find the solutions identified by workers in the context of the function specific to the agency providing the original service. Thus, family counseling or marital counseling may be defined as solving many different types of problems. In some instances, when problems become too complex, the whole case is referred to another agency, and the process begins again. Of course, sometimes referrals are implemented and clients do obtain other, needed services. But there is no service system which assures consensus in dealing with situations involving multiple problems—or which specifies how such clients are to be served, and how such problems are to be solved.

Continuity of Care and Accountability

In reading case records, we also found that failure to obtain service for clients, inability to assure provision of service from other agencies, ignorance about which other agencies are involved in a case and why, and limited knowledge about available resources seem more characteristic of most cases than evidence that a worker assumes or is assigned responsibility for following through on services requested for a client or integrating others being provided. Fragmentation of provision—and fragmentation of client—is a common theme. With rare exceptions, neither programmatic devices nor worker roles exist to facilitate or implement continuity of care.

Only one program is specifically structured and explicitly designed to implement such a function. This program is the Child Abuse Coordinator Program described earlier (Chapter 3). Its major objective is to eliminate the fragmentation typical of such cases. Appropriate intervention may involve a minimum of medical care for the child, counseling services for the parents, day care for the child, home aides for the family, and legal services. Organizing this panoply of services, ensuring provision, avoiding interdisciplinary and interagency conflict, and acting generally to assure the best care for child and family require special expertise by a special worker whose major function is not to provide service directly but to ensure the meshing or integration of services needed by each case.

No other program illustrates this function or role; nor is there any that appears to be designed to do so. There are, however, some illustrations of individual workers in a number of different agencies whose function is somewhat akin to this, out of individual inclination, professional ethics, or particular orientation to practice, rather than by deliberate administrative or programmatic design. We must conclude that the fact that others do not do so reflects current division of responsibility and role definitions within and between agencies.

Illustrative of how an individual worker may function in this role is one case described earlier. Intervention was initiated by the worker at a day care center, who contacted a public health nurse out of concern for a child's health. Subsequently, the worker arranged for help for the mother around nutrition, budgeting, housekeeping tasks. Through her efforts, a home aide was involved when the mother had a stroke. When it seemed as if the family might lose its public assistance support for day care, the worker alerted the family and helped them take the necessary steps to avert this. At the conclusion of a letter sent to the mother regarding an application for a summer program for another child, the worker assured the mother that she would continue to help the family as needed, if other problems arose. Such willingness to assume responsibility for continuity of care and skill at initiating requests for service and obtaining it as needed is not representative of most cases we reviewed but would appear to be an essential function which should be guaranteed by the system to specific categories of cases.

Service Integration

Unfortunately, data regarding agency relationships are also soft; and the complexities of the picture are overwhelming. In general, few agencies keep records regarding referral sources, and even when they do, these are usually incomplete or inaccurate. For many agencies a telephone call rather than a formal letter with a copy kept on file is the usual approach;* and no indication is made as to why one resource (a particular hospital, a certain day care center) is

*One factor affecting the formality or informality of referrals may be the requirement for supervisory signatures on referral letters, in some agencies. The easier alternative is a telephone call.

chosen over another. Agencies are unable to describe and document, quantitatively, their referral patterns; the limited and, for the most part, descriptive data they have available do not permit any real analysis. At best, therefore, the conclusions which follow are impressionistic and tentative, although we are convinced that the picture we obtained is at the least a vague representation of reality and more probably quite close to accuracy.

In support of our conclusions, public officials and agency administrators express great concern about problems of service fragmentation. Newspaper articles and discussions with community leaders reflect this concern also. Indeed, the concern was great enough to lead to the establishment, through city, county, and United Way collaboration, of a Task Force on Human Services Integration to deal specifically with this problem. As part of this effort, three task force committees were established for the fields of health, education, and social services, with membership concentrated on executives of the major funders and providers of services in the community. Subsequently, these initiatives received DHEW encouragement, as evidenced in receipt of a grant as a "capacity building" project. In fact, this is one of the few illustrations of local programs designed to integrate services that have emerged in response to current federal policies and initiatives in this area. Its first undertaking will be in programing for a multipurpose neighborhood service facility built under housing legislation.

It is worth noting here that very few examples of programs directed at solving problems of service fragmentation have emerged as a consequence of the federal initiatives in this area described earlier. This seems indicative of how limited federal efforts have been. For example, except for the recently constructed building, planned years ago, there are currently no multiservice centers in the city, although there were currently several under antipoverty and community action programs earlier. Only one federally funded Neighborhood Legal Service program exists in the community today. The capacity building program described above is the only illustration of programs resulting from federal administrative initiatives, while the County Agency on Aging and the earlier MPA program (both described in Chapter 5) illustrate federal research and demonstration programing efforts as well as programs emerging in response to federal legislative initiatives.

Other than in the field of mental health, no integrative programs have begun as a result of any state initiatives. As yet no other special initiatives have emerged in this state.

On an operating basis there are some programs which reflect partial efforts at service integration, generally around a particular population group or problem category. Thus, there are efforts at integrated planning for services for the aged (COA) and for day care (Day Care Coalition). There is one multiservice program focused on serving the aging, but its services are provided at different sites and the component parts are under different auspices. (These three programs mentioned above have already been described in detail in Chapters 2 and 5). There are two multiservice voluntary agencies (Catholic Charities and Salvation Army) with component, categorical services provided at different sites. Also, CHANGE, the county community action agency, operates, funds, carries out advocacy, and offers access (see below). There is no single multiservice center in which different services are provided at one site, or through one centralized access system.

Most of what does exist in this community has emerged from specific, focused local initiatives. Although some reflect emerging developments around the country (the specialized programs described earlier for the aged, for intervention in problems of abuse and neglect), most are traditional public and voluntary agencies attempting as best they can to meet the needs of children and families.

To illuminate the problem, a brief description of all five largest agencies providing the relevant services follows. Our objective is to illustrate the core of what exists and the foundation on which building must take place. Even more important, our purpose is to make the case for new initiatives. The agencies to be described are the Family and Child Service Agency, Catholic Social Services, the County Department of Social Services (DSS), Salvation Army, and CHANGE.

We note first that only one of these agencies is completely under public auspices, and one is semipublic, although funding for all is substantially public. Obviously, where funding is concerned, only public monies support the Department of Social Services and CHANGE. However, the other voluntary agencies are also heavily subsidized by public funds; directly, through contracts for purchase of services and other per capita and subsidy arrangements and revenue-sharing contribution; less directly, through third-party payments; and indirectly (with an interpretation subject to debate), through the tax-deductible status of private philanthropic contributions.

All these programs are administratively structured in hierarchical fashion, with directors, supervisors, and line staff. The voluntary agencies all have advisory boards and policy-making boards. None of the agencies are completely autonomous; all are responsible or responsive to higher administrative authorities, but to different degrees: DSS to the county executive and legislature; Catholic Social Services to Catholic Charities; Family and Child Service as well as Catholic Charities, in part, to United Way. The CHANGE board is composed of nine city-county government representatives, seven from county agencies and organizations, nine from its own advisory councils, and two from its youth council.

Physically, in terms of geographic location and the actual site, office, and facilities of each agency, there is a dichotomy between public and voluntary agencies. All the major voluntary services are located in one central downtown area, near one another. Office space and waiting rooms are attractive and spacious, and rarely crowded. In fact, in one agency one had a distinct sense of facilities that are underused. In contrast, the public services are located across the town, in old and crowded and noisy facilities. Little privacy is available for clients to talk with staff, who are seated in rows of desks, one next to the other, and operate out of a crowded waiting room as well. Telephones ring constantly; the noise is constant and overwhelming. CHANGE uses store fronts close to its clientele.

All programs service the entire county, in theory; but in actual practice most clients come from the city and its immediate environs. Patterns of service use still reflect earlier habits—the poor are more predominant in the caseloads of DSS and the working class in the caseloads of the voluntary agencies. However, there have been some changes. Thus, a poor family may use a day care center operated by the Family and Child Service Agency. DSS can reimburse the agency for day care services to clients whose income makes them eligible for this means-tested benefit. Similarly, eligible clients may use home health services through DSS, Family and Child Services, or Catholic Social Services. In general, DSS services are selective (means tested) except for protective services for children and family planning services. The voluntary agency services are universal, with fees charged on a graduated basis.

Major differences among the agencies are revealed, however, in the composition of their programs, the kinds of problems brought by clients, and the nature of the worker response in handling problems.

The Department of Social Services, the county public welfare agency, handles the largest number of general social service cases, most of them multiproblem in nature. Many seem to be reopenings of earlier cases. Most involve children; few cases here or in any of the other family agencies involve the elderly. (One wonders how many more elderly were served before passage of SSI, or whether this pattern has existed for some time.) For the most part, except where it takes primary responsibility in foster care or adoption, this agency acts as a conduit or channel—or perhaps an access service—connecting, or rather trying to connect, clients with other needed services. The case records reveal numerous efforts at reaching for other resources and limited success in doing so. One has a sense of the frustration and impotence of the worker in dealing with complex and overwhelming problems, limited resources, and no sanction for obtaining help or cooperation from other services, public or private.

Lacking resources for a coverage program, the Department covers what it must (child welfare and protective services), contracts for service wherever possible, cooperates with community initiatives (the child abuse program), and responds to new need. At the time our review was being completed, the Department was preparing to create a special unit for service to those returning to the community from psychiatric facilities and eligible for public assistance and/or Medicaid.

Family and Child Services seems to be an agency in transition. Half the program is quite traditional: family counseling (marital conflicts, parent-child conflicts) and child welfare services (foster care, adoptions). Here the agency functions as a self-contained, somewhat isolated unit. Client problems are defined in the context of the service provided. Few other resources are ever employed. Little effort is made to define problems in broader perspective or to intervene in different ways. In contrast, services provided families participating in the agency's day care center program reflect a sense of community involvement, a vitality, perspective, sense of commitment, and level of worker responsibility that is very different. Whether because the clients are different, the workers are different, or the site for providing service is different, case records reveal a complex picture of client problems, worker roles, and interventions employed. Multiple resources are contacted and services obtained; continuity of care is stressed and case advocacy and case integration often implemented; workers actively intervene in complex situations, are alert to new or related problems, and stay with the case as long as help is needed.

Catholic Social Services, as part of Catholic Charities, is the nearest thing to an integrated service system under one administrative auspice. It provides services to families, to children, to youths, and to the elderly. Specific services include long-term counseling, adoptions, foster care, services to unmarried mothers, group residences for neglected and delinquent youth; related resources such as long-term care facilities for the elderly, medical services, day care programs, are also available.

In general, the atmosphere is warm and supportive. Here, as at Family and Child Services, professional staff are predominant but paraprofessionals are also utilized in certain programs. Bureaucratic routines are kept to a minimum and staff seem less harassed, have higher morale, and seem to display a genuine concern for people served. There are close linkages to leading national thinking about institutions for children and programs for the aged.

Continuity of care is stressed far more here than in either of the other services described, perhaps in part because it is easier to implement. Many more related services and resources are available directly through Catholic Charities, facilitating a broader perspective on intervention and provision. This agency illustrates the advantages of integrating various services with related functions within one structure, advantages that are available to none of the other programs.

Salvation Army, another voluntary, multifunction agency, gets substantially more than half its funds from public sources and operates both highly professional and more traditional "charity" programs. It includes an all-day day care unit, an after-school day care program, several "drop in" after-school centers, an emergency shelter for women and children (the only one in the community), a men's shelter for skid-row alcoholics, a group home for adolescent girls, a large Golden Age Center program, and a Family Service Department. The latter is a "hard service" unit which responds to cases, mostly self-referrals, with food, shelter, clothing. It also offers referral and a lot of "advocacy" for people needing public assistance, SSI, emergency relief. There is only occasionally long-term counseling on an adult or adolescent family problem or what we call ongoing case integration.

CHANGE is an acronym for the county community action agency, a semipublic corporation of the sort which developed in many communities during the antipoverty war and continues as a public structure housing, sometimes coordinating, occasionally planning, those services to the poor not assigned to county or city welfare, health, or education agencies. In a rational plan the services would have been located in public welfare, but the separate structures were created a decade ago in a search for access to services by minority people, a desire for "maximum feasible participation" in planning, control, and staffing by disadvantaged consumers, interest in unorthodox programing and staffing, and a need to remove some programs from the imagery of and user attitudes toward public welfare. CHANGE assembles its budget of roughly $5.4 million from all levels of government. Its basic operation of almost $1 million is supported by the Office of Economic Opportunity, and it also receives over $300,000 for Head Start. The city and county provide other funds for work with the aged, a learning center, youth services, youth employment, summer camps, day care. DHEW provides other funds for child health screening and services for the aged. CHANGE both receives money from other local units and the Department of Social Services and passes money to others. It works through delegate agencies, funding a literacy program and two neighborhood centers. It contracts for services with units which, in turn, have other funding sources: Spanish Language Alliance (in turn, multiservice); a Girls' Service League; a dramatic arts program. It also directly administers services to the aging (five programs) and services in youth centers, a summer day camp, a remedial learning center, an alternative school, a consumer information center, a summer lunch program, youth employment programs, and emergency food and medical service. Its core access, advocacy, and community action activities are based in eight neighborhood centers. Local assessment is that the emphasis is on access, not case integration or expert ongoing help, in these latter units. The program as a whole, serving the poor, is significant, if small, and parallels much that exists in other public and private bodies.

Consumers and Program Development

In the area of ascertaining and responding to consumer preferences, too, initiatives are limited and fragmented. No formal effort is made as yet to obtain data from access services that might indicate such things as the size and nature of demand for existing services or for nonexistent services; or that would reveal changing patterns of demand or preference; or that would reveal consumer response to certain types of service. Informal use of such data are reported widely and some more formal efforts are reported to be under way.

There is little effort made to involve consumers directly or indirectly in policy making and program development. Some consumer participation exists in day care programs, and some in services for the aging, through RWD, but little beyond this. And except for RWD, no use is made of consumer evaluations of services and no attempt has been made to institutionalize consumer review or monitoring of services on an ongoing basis.

Very little exists in the way of formal, or informal but consistent, interrelationships between and among social agencies. Furthermore, there is little in the way of shared definitions of agency function. Each defines how the other should meet the needs of the person referred but the perceptions of function vary between the sender agency and the receiving agency. Thus, what one agency refers out to another is often defined as an inappropriate referral by the receiving agency, and vice versa. For all the reasons already given, this situation is not satisfactory.

Mental Health–Social Service Linkages

Our local study is not yet rounded out, since we have not dealt as yet with mental health programs in their relationship to the personal-general social services. It has been clear throughout this volume that at certain points these systems are or should be mutually supportive. This type of formulation does not, however, deal with the obvious tendency over the last several decades for community health programs to overlap substantially with the general social services. Nor have we as yet explored possible optimal patterns, should the social services become more systematically organized. The local social services study described in the previous section focused particularly on these questions.

The community's mental health resources are in many ways outstanding—as are its professionals. Its service volume is high. Other communities would be delighted at the variety and quality of mental health services.

Like other American cities, this one did not have private psychiatric care, even for the affluent, until the 1920s. Before that it relied on the state hospital system. By the early 1930s there was a "psychopathic hospital" for the more hopeful cases. Clinics and out-patient services developed in the 1940s and 1950s and in the mid-1950s voluntary agencies also offered out-patient and consultation service to children and adults. State reimbursement gave this activity a boost, as did the federal mental health center expansion of the mid-1960s.

Most recently, as drugs and new attitudes shifted the emphasis to community care and hospital populations declined markedly, the state began to think more about relationships between state psychiatric hospitals (state operated) and local out-patient and preventive efforts (county operations with state financial aid which, in turn, often subcontract to the voluntary sector).

Specific 1973 legislation mandated "joint and continuous planning" by the county mental health facility commissioner and the commissioner of the state mental health facility covering each region or county. The county commissioner was assigned responsibility to initiate and coordinate the planning. Since the County Mental Health Department is the contracting agency, as well, for all other voluntary and public psychiatric and mental health programs in the county, the mandate would appear to involve all the components of the current nonprofit mental health system. As is also true elsewhere private psychiatry is largely outside this system.

At the time of our field study, mental health was page one news in the local press, and there was a major county-state controversy under way. The content of the debate dealt with programing issues and state-local roles and was real. One backdrop was political jockeying and the presence of different parties in the majority on each side.

The substance of the controversy, which led to the appointment of a county legislative commission to investigate the mental health services of the county, was a series of allegations that the locally based State Psychiatric Center—a new program, partially opened in 1972 in the context of a strategy of hospital decentralization and increased community care—did not accept enough referrals, especially involuntary admissions, that patients were discharged prematurely or would simply leave (run away) because of insufficient security, that the criminal justice system was not adequately served by the Psychiatric Center and that clinical policies or practice of the Center were weak or unsound, as documented in specific cases. In the background there also was a complaint heard statewide: neither county nor state psychiatric services provide for the very disturbed delinquent and "out of control" children and youth—who often are shot back and forth like ping-pong balls between the two and commit outrages in the interims when no one takes responsibility. Many charges were levied back and forth and case stories of abuse were reported in the local press, with some concern expressed about privacy and confidentiality.

It is not within our scope to assess the controversy except to note that by most standards current in its field the Psychiatric Center is a high-quality facility—and is as yet still being built. What is here relevant is that the debate and investigation sharpened the questions and created a strategic moment in our own search for understanding of a limited, yet central, issue: the definition of system boundaries between mental health and social services and the creation of linkages.

Backdrop: Systems and Tasks

This locality is in the midst of a process being seen in many places: the shift from long-term, often lifelong, custodial care in distant, inaccessible state hospitals to treatment in the local community. The in-patient census is down and the action has moved from the "distant" state hospital, over fifty miles away, to the Center, a new facility under the state. When the controversy broke, the Center had been active for two years, and the statistics had been "turned around": this was a "hospital," most of whose patients were receiving community care. Under the administrative system, "teams" cover specified geographic areas. In-patient units for each team are located on the main campus. Day treatment and out-patient services are located at eleven different locations.

A 1973 overview is revealing—935 in-patient admissions of which 65 percent were voluntary and 35 percent involuntary. The average patient among the 1973 admissions remained on in-patient status for 23.1 days. There also were 408 admissions to day hospitals, followed by an average stay of 5.5 months, the identical duration of out-patient service (970 admissions). By 1973 the Center was coping with half the county's in-patient admissions, the others being divided among six other agencies. In short, a picture fully consistent with the most forward-looking philosophy of mental health administration being promulgated by leading professional groups and NIMH.

One need not take sides to find evidence in available data and hearings disclosures of a number of conflicts. One is very major *debates about philosophy*: Did the community really want community care and the inevitable risks? Did families really want their mentally ill close by? Another is *role confusion*: Would county or state set the community care pace and pattern and create the resources? Should, or could, a state facility move more quickly than the county? Was state policy *the* policy? Another is *value conflicts*: How would there be reconciliation of police responsibility for protection and the psychiatric concern with sound professional practice? How is community crisis balanced against personal crisis? A fourth is *personality conflicts*: Which professionals would set the community tone and direction? Then there are *planning problems*: How could programs evolve naturally and effectively while subject to crisis budget policy on the two governmental tiers affected? (Some of the missing resources would have been in place had there not been a state budget freeze the year before). *Coordination problems*: Could a county governmental unit take the planning and coordination lead and expect to shape the role and operations of a state service unit? Could two units (county department and state hospital) achieve integration and coherence while channeling their accountability through two subunits at the regional and state level which, while in one department and perhaps sharing goals, have somewhat different missions? And *priority problems*: How would the community rate the hospital's concern for the very ill, the difficult cases, as contrasted with a private psychiatry emphasis on "existential" problems, not mental disorder, a tendency in some psychiatric agencies to "de-medicalize" entirely? Whom does the community want most to help if it can't serve everyone? And if people needed counseling and personal, practical help, would the community support this through psychiatric programs or general social service programs? What banner is best? Finally, added to all these, are *agency role problems*: While psychiatry was often practicing counseling, some of the voluntary family agencies—as already noted—had consultation services supported by county mental health and thought of themselves as giving either intensive psychotherapy or a preventive mental health service. What is psychiatry; what is general social service?

As we have noted, we explored daily social service operations, analyzing the questionnaire produced by the social services task force, then pursuing the agencies by phone follow-up and interview with the questions: Where do you get most of your cases from? To whom do you refer most often? What occurs? What is your core case role? We compared the emerging picture with the system and role perspectives of the county mental health staff and the Psychiatric Center professionals. An interesting pattern emerged: the mental health program was almost invisible from the personal social services perspective. One unit, since disbanded, offered diagnostic evaluation and referrals on a crisis basis, serving law enforcement agencies. A few clinics appeared as places to get diagnostic guidance. That was about it. And some cases were known as having been in hospitals. Occasionally some were referred to hospitals. Thus there was no correspondence at all between the community health center literature about the preventive role of the system and what one saw here in a community known for its well-trained psychiatric professionals. As indicated, three family agencies were granted funding by the County Mental Health Department for consultation and saw themselves as both general social service agencies and as mental health centers. Or at least one certainly saw itself as straddling.

The data gathering and analysis confirmed that the problems are fundamental. When asked about the relationship of the mental health services to the personal social services in terms of hierarchy or teamwork or sharing of role and function, a social planner in the voluntary sector said, "It's just one more system." In short, personal social services, mental health, employment, medical care, are systems with tasks. They overlap and compete. Their interrelationships are not patterned as the result of any systematic coordination or planning process. This is not an impression; it is a conclusion from the questionnaires of the task force to all general-personal social services in the city, from the telephone follow-ups, and from the case record reviews.

Moreover, something else was also going on which emphasized that patterning is essential. The Center leadership, from the perspective of the state facility, estimated that some 30 percent of the cases in their service system were there not primarily out of psychiatric need but because of "social deficits or problems"—housing needs, financial problems, difficulties in access to health services, and the like. Here we rely on their estimate. We did not read records.

Not that the hospital was without benefit of any cooperation at all. The bulk of its load was on community care service, and about half the service was handled in one way or another by the health department, especially public health nurses, or by social welfare agencies, particularly the county welfare department. However, arrangements were ad hoc and chance; there was and is no clear policy framework because these several elements are not part of any overall operative, effective planning system. Some of the arrangements are set by statute and resources: if a person needs cash assistance, there are several places to go for an emergency and one for the ongoing help for which he is eligible. In general medical care, too, there are defined options and possibilities. The Health Department visitors, in theory, take the lead in community care cases "where the problems are primarily physical, even if there are secondary psychological problems." But there are no operative criteria as to which cases, in fact, "are primarily psychological and have secondary physical problems." Dedicated practitioners solve role questions on a day-to-day basis and, of late, health visitors have managed to get mental health assessments of their patients as needed, but at the administrative level there is uncertainty. There are major unresolved issues of role, function, coordination mechanisms, responsibility for taking the lead. Beyond this, there is disorganization. It is not clear who gets what service, why, with what priority—and through what cooperative pattern.

The same generalization follows if the vantage point of observation is county mental health. If people come to the County Mental Health Office to ask for aid, a newly structured county evaluation team assesses cases and refers them to contract agencies. Many of the situations do not call for psychiatric service or medical care. If a need is understood, the team does what it can. Within its own field, it has no clear plan as to what it will or should do and what is the province of the state facility. Where the county mental health team encounters a need for what we here call personal social services—and this often occurs—its own judgment and ability to locate someone who will help is the determinant of what follows. There are no systems, boundaries, agreements, mechanisms to coordinate and integrate. Very disturbed people or complex multiproblem situations demand a "case management" or case integration function. Such function is not structured into any local service system.

At the time of our review, the County Mental Health Department was building its planning capacity and moving away from direct operations. It had closed its adult clinic and was considering closing the child guidance clinic too. Its future function would be to plan and coordinate, thus avoiding conflicts about operational roles, but the evaluation team was needed because of the absence of any clear access system for psychiatric care. The county department would also continue to plan for mental health, a field with unclear parameters which cannot itself resolve interfaces with related systems.

Out of the county-state confrontation, when the community exploded, came an increased county commitment to develop planning capacity, with agreement that the initiative belongs to the county in shaping federal and state investment, plus local public and voluntary contributions, into a mental health system stressing deinstitutionalization and continuity of care. Noting that much of the tension had arisen when state facilities discharged people into communities which could not offer them residential arrangements, the two state facilities—the Psychiatric Center and the School for the Retarded—joined with the county department to launch a new voluntary agency, Community Living Services, Inc., which was gearing up for service. This agency would offer housing and rehabilitative services to those "mentally disabled" who were likely to achieve independence within two years.

On a related issue involving tension between systems and public complaint, it was agreed that the Center would develop facilities for those patients who are both emotionally disturbed and retarded. The School for the Retarded would staff these facilities.

For the moment, this ended the crisis, although it hardly represented full, operationally effective agreement about what service should come out of a hospital and what out of a county mental health office, what is best purchased from the voluntary sector, and what should be public direct service. County systems and state systems basically set their own parameters. Even when voluntary agencies with contracts perform poorly, the county department finds it politically impossible to end funding. Although the Center is a direct operation, the County Mental Health Department assumes that it is better to contract for service if possible. The validity of that assumption, at present, is a matter of faith. Its price in administration duplication is unknown.

None of the discussion or planning under way confronts the question of which people should be served out of a mental health system and who should be sent elsewhere. The Center's formal policy is that it should deal with the moderately or severely mentally ill—or, at least, some part of the mental health system should deal with them. Our case explorations and interviews disclose what the Center confirms: they will not take the case if there are other "support" systems in the county, and if it represents a "simple human service problem." Since this is hardly a fixed and uniformly applied criterion, it may have been behind some of the difficulties which led to the public debate. The county's readiness to take on cases derives not from any sharply delineated criteria but from a desire to help where possible. Many clients are served just because they come in and seek help—

even if the need is not for psychiatric intervention. If we sum up state and county definitions, this can hardly be said to be a mental health "system" or a coherent policy. And the voluntary family agencies are not any more clear: they will "refer out" if clients have "very serious" problems demanding medication and intensive daily care. Otherwise, they carry on.

The legislative committee assigned to report on the conflict debated at meetings and in the press. Under the spotlight, state-county cooperation improved. The situation became somewhat more calm. The fiscal committee report urged that the primacy of county responsibility for overall mental health planning be made clear by state legislative and administrative action—and that the recommended deputy county executive to be in charge of human services work on the problem of better relationships among health, mental health, and "other county human service agencies." Much else was proposed relating to consumer and community involvement, to a review board and ombudsman process, to community-based living alternatives and supportive services, and to the filling in of service gaps, especially for those who are shuttled back and forth among training schools and other correctional facilities, state hospitals, state schools for the retarded. No initiatives were taken on the fundamental questions about system boundaries and linkages involving medicine, psychiatry, education, housing, and general social services —or about the case-integration function.

One sign of "system" is the presence of case integration—assurance of case accountability and initiative to assure meshing of and consistency among simultaneous or sequential services affecting a case. The Center's personnel, when pressed, see themselves as taking on this role where they feel the need because, otherwise, patients fail in the community. However, they prefer "direct practice" and have a very limited concept of the role of case integration. The County does less. The evaluation team refers people to service and pays for it, but does not follow up. The exception is in county crisis intervention, where responsibility is carried as far as necessary, but even that is defined as something rather brief. This city, for all its investment of money, time, and commitment does not have more than episodic provisions for this role whether in the county or state units in mental health or among the personal social service agencies.

If all of this reads like free enterprise, publicly subsidized, it is. The city's ethic emphasizes local home rule and voluntarism. It is suspicious of central power. This is hardly a foundation for system building. State legislation allows the possibility of more system but does not mandate it. National conceptualizations about mental health outline essential functions but do not assure their assignment and implementation locally. In short, while there is ad hoc coordination of some provision of service and some programs, none of this gets at basic issues: an overview which supersedes subsystems, service which defines itself as continuing work with very disturbed or dependent people whatever the specific agency in which they may need service, "coverage" service rather than busy agencies, a division of roles and tasks which is geared to effectiveness, efficiency, and economy.

We have seen that the personal social services are not per se organized as system. The mental health programs clearly are not either even though definitions of function and concepts essential to role assignment obviously exist. Small wonder, then, that several hundred questionnaires about agency case flow—and related follow-up interviews—reveal no clarity on the boundaries between mental health and personal social service, or anything approaching consensus about a desirable pattern of case flow. The state-county mental health "blow up" occurred largely because the state released into the community patients for whom there was no adequate provision—and no one asked whether the problem should be solved within the mental health system alone. (Many people see the solution in better county planning, closer state coordination, and the resource to be created by Community Living Services, Inc.) When the Psychiatric Center staff and county staff met, they assumed that the public health and social services programs in the county would continue to do what they had been doing, but no one proposed a more basic reorientation in which social services or public health might have a larger part. No one proposed talking to the housing authority, despite legislation which calls upon housing authorities to help with residential arrangements for those needing community care. The human services theory books may affirm that a community care system should or must involve health, mental health, social services—but in our city this is not an operative idea.

Possible Roles and Linkages

It is not possible to clarify the function of the personal social services and the optimal ways of organizing their delivery without a perspective on mental health system boundaries and ways of implementing sound linkages between these fields. First, however, we briefly review relevant observations from several earlier chapters.

The child care report deals with provisions for a public social utility: family day care, center care, preschools, and before-and-after school arrangements which contribute to the socialization and development of normal, average children. The philosophy calls for integrating handicapped children into regular programs as much as possible, but developing special therapeutic and treatment units for those with major handicaps and deficits. In short, child care facilities as institutions for the "normal" require psychiatric case-finding capacity. The specialized child care treatment resources may need consultation. Staff, then, need some appropriate exposure in their training and also require consultation arrangements. Children in need of psychiatric case supervision belong in psychiatrically run day treatment programs, part of another system—case services.

One could substitute the phrase "community living and care arrangements for the aged" for "child care" in the above paragraph and, again, the generalizations would hold. Homemakers, special apartments, centers, congregate meal arrangements, are public social utilities for average people. But because they serve high-risk groups they should be organized and staffed for early case finding. As disabilities and problems develop, the elderly need case services, which include medical treatment, social care, protection. Here psychiatric consultation or even guidance may be needed and should be part of the agency operations plan. Then, a small minority may require ongoing treatment and care of such intensity as to demand living arrangements under medical (including psychiatric) auspices.

By contrast, programs to serve abused, battered and severely neglected children are, by definition, case services. Our findings document the need for multidisciplinary interventions. The core case-finding, reporting, and accountability mechanisms are part of public child welfare (general social services), but treatment may be located in one of several systems—including the psychiatric—depending on the case situation. Often an interdisciplinary team will need to work closely on those situations to be dealt with in the community, and the team could be based in one of several systems (health, psychiatry, personal social services, law enforcement). Adults treated on an out-patient basis or as committed offenders also might be served under any of these auspices.

The conceptualization of institutions and community-based facilities for delinquent and neglected children could be even more clear-cut. At one end of the continuum, where the family does not exist or cannot play its role, these are substitute living arrangements. At the other, these are milieus for intensive treatment. The auspice is—or should be—personal social service, education, general medicine and psychiatry, depending on which discipline is required to take the lead and orchestrate the program to achieve the assigned emphasis. Many of the facilities will need to be multidisciplinary, but current confusions will not be erased until each has a clear character, and thus a sense of where the leadership should come from. The problem today derives from the attempt to implement conflicting objectives through programs torn by value conflicts.

Family planning and abortion services are in transition. The technology requires medical administration and supervision. The personal social services have a role in education and access. The education system and the general medical field, including public health nursing, have major educational roles. Where individuals confront emotional problems and personal crises around family planning or abortion they will require personal social service help, which may be based in a medical facility (hospital) or free-standing social service agency and may need to call upon psychiatric consultation. Occasionally referral for psychiatric intervention will be necessary.

To sum up and generalize: The community human service system needs some treatment resources under psychiatric auspices, needs access to psychiatrists for consultation, and depends upon some psychiatric contribution to the education of professionals from a number of disciplines. These are not new or startling notions, but we do underscore our need to say "psychiatric" because the phrase "mental health" does not serve to delineate for everyone what social institution and what series of concepts is intended. The expertise involves prevention of, identification of, and intervention with moderate and severe mental disorder. While not completely operationalized (since behavior is defined as "mental disorder," not in terms of fully externalized criteria but only when the psychiatric profession expresses readiness to take responsibility for the domain), the concept of a psychiatric intervention system as a speciality within medicine facilitates social planning, since it also permits delineation of education, religion, personal social services, law enforcement, and other related human service systems or institutions in their own separatenesses. "Mental health," which is sometimes goal, sometimes service, and sometimes evaluation, is too diffuse for planning purposes requiring role differentiation and it belongs to a period of excessive expectations. A viable service system should be able to identify its core cases so as to create relatively viable boundaries with other systems and to achieve community consensus about them. The mental health conceptualization lends itself to the opposite effect.[14]

Our international explorations and our U.S. study suggest that semiautonomous service fields, all within the social sector, must have relatively clearly conceptualized functions—and identifiable boundaries—before linkage systems which are fully effective can come into play. Our summary, above, places psychiatry (we shall substitute that term for "mental health") vis-à-vis personal social services in a variety of settings. Now we turn to the strategic question: What is suggested about the role of personal social services in implementing the current psychiatric (community mental health) emphasis on community-based treatment and community care?

This exploration has identified the personal social services as having three types of primary functions: information and access for the total social sector; socialization and development; treatment and rehabilitation. The special domain is the social adjustment and functioning of individuals and family units. The preoccupation is with a person or group within a situation. The service loci are home, substitute home, community-based residence, residential institutions under social service auspices, and other social institutions where the general social service staffs are adjuncts (school, court, clinic, hospital, factory, residential institution for the handicapped, prison, social security office).

This perspective explains why the development and servicing of community support systems is so central as a role of the personal social services everywhere and why its frequent absence in American communities creates so great a gap in what is now called community mental health. Robert Morris has recently called attention to the importance of "social care" as a general social service mission in the United Kingdom and its potential in the United States.[15] In the United Kingdom each neighborhood has its assigned local authority social work department, on duty constantly for response to psychiatric emergencies, clearly charged with after-care for the physically and mentally ill and for the frail aged, thus incorporating what was previously "mental welfare." In such a system, there is no question but that social care and accountability for cases on a community care status belongs in the local social services office. There is a clearly defined, cooperative mechanism for movement into and out of psychiatric facilities. Where ongoing psychiatric treatment and surveillance are essential, there is no problem with defining the domains of day hospitals, psychiatric rehabilitation programs, and psychiatrically operated transitional community residences. Nor are there problems in delineating the spheres of out-patient psychiatric clinics (all of which may require psychologists, social workers, nurses, educators, and others on adjunctive staff). There are obvious and real operational problems but a system to work with and improve is in place.

The deficit in our illustrative city (and, insofar as this city is a good illustration, the U.S. deficit) is more nearly defined. During the latter weeks of our field work, the county public social services department established a special unit to cope with the processing of emergency financial assistance applications from those going into or leaving psychiatric facilities, nursing homes, or other community care arrangements. Too much suffering had occurred because policies and practices had not meshed. All this was much needed but, as noted, no one raised in a major way any larger question about the role of county social services vis-à-vis the Psychiatric Center and County Mental Health in the after-care controversy; nor was there clarity, when Community Living Services, Inc., was set up, about just which part of its work was psychiatry and which part personal social services. The personal social services agencies were not involved in a significant sense, yet the planned facilities—hotels, halfway houses, transitional apartments, respite (temporary) care—covered both domains.

The "solution" to this city's crisis, in short, like the "solution" to similar crises elsewhere, dealt with immediate resource deficits and role conflicts and led to some agreement for improved operations between the hospital and county mental health and to the creation of useful facilities. However, the planning frame was inadequate. Much of the public debate dealt with entry points, information, and community protection—important matters, but not a full agenda. There was no comprehensive exploration of how a modern urban community might organize social care, a community support system, for the mentally ill—or for the frail aged, the retarded, the handicapped, and those in after-care status from institutions of other kinds. The failure to cope on this level is understandable: the personal-general social services are in transition and it is far from certain that they will evolve satisfactorily (but why not begin somewhere?). The response to the crisis did not involve a planning system with a mandate broad enough to generate all options.

Options for Community (Social) Care

As indicated earlier, federal legislation and administrative initiatives call for a more comprehensive, a larger, view of the social planning domain. Title XX urges it. The device of appointing one state unit as a single state agency under several categorical funding programs is available to all state governments. A state agency in such a role might consider at least three approaches to more basic reform of community (social) care for the mentally ill.

Approach A. One possibility is to create a free-standing personal social service system in every locality, using resources under Title XX, Medicaid, community mental health, and special medical projects and housing funding. The personal social service system could be assigned four functions: (*a*) social (community) care for the mentally ill and for other dependent categories (as described above); (*b*) counseling and direct case services and helping, as appropriate for the general social services (family and child welfare, services for the aged, adolescent social services, etc.); (*c*) administration of specified public social utilities (homemakers–home health aides, congregate meals, food programs, community centers, vacation programs, etc.); (*d*) information, advice, referral and advocacy services, available to all residents and addressing all service systems.

Approach B. A second approach would be to limit the personal social service system to *b*, *c*, and *d* above and to develop the social care system out of the public health department, under the leadership of public health nursing, and place social workers in that program as adjuncts.

Approach C. A third approach is to launch an empirical process of task analysis and experimentation with alternatives, working in the medical, psychiatric, and general social service systems—until there is evidence as to what works best.

Along similar lines, there are three major strategies for handling local social-psychiatric emergencies: a general emergency system, based in the personal social services, involving duty "rotation" of the staff covering, *a, b,* and *d*; one emergency system for personal social service purposes (child abuse, protection of the aged, etc.) and a parallel system for psychiatric emergencies and suicides, based on community mental health centers and psychiatric out-patient services; a police-fire emergency service which calls upon either of the above two systems, as appropriate, while carrying on its indispensable activities.

There are other issues of role, function, and organization as well. This listing only suggests the approach. There is a case to be argued for each and experience to be distilled. What needs to be understood from the outset is that just as a neighborhood multiservice center or any other local service delivery innovation cannot conquer the problem of fragmentation and competition (or noncommunication) among program personnel at the federal level, so negotiations between county and state personnel (mandated) or cooperation between them and public welfare and education authorities (encouraged) cannot achieve lasting results unless there is a planning system with adequate sanction. The sanction can develop in two ways: a human resource administrative authority at the state level with legal authority and fiscal power which is real; devolution of real decision power to the locality and the creation there of a comprehensive planning instrument. Thus far, in the evolution of American federalism, the states with comprehensive human resource authorities either have not found it desirable to give them sufficient power or have not found it possible because of continuing federal categorical constraints. When there is devolution to localities, it seldom breaks out of categorical or parochial perspectives and thus far has not generated a broader authority which plans in the public interest.

Thus, to summarize, while work continues on specific and daily problems of operation, more basic solutions require clear assignment of functions and role (our vantage point stresses clarity for the general social services) and the creation of social planning and administrative implementation authority. This approach may seem a long way around, but it may be the most effective and efficient route to improved patient care.

Summing Up a Nonsystem

The issues and problems, as we have seen, are graphically illustrated in our sample city. This is a city containing a wide range and number of social agencies. Political, civic, and professional social welfare leadership is conscientious and committed and deserves respect for continuing efforts to solve difficult and in some cases insurmountable problems. Some of these problems clearly cannot be solved at the local level. The city's social services reflect problems that characterize local social services throughout the country: the consequences of categorical federal funding; a dichotomy between public and private (voluntary) sectors in which roles are in transition; the preoccupation of the local taxpayer not with total costs but only with local tax shares; the lack of any consistent delivery structure or system, as among or between jurisdictions; and the absence of any clear consensus about function or purpose which would locate generalist, specialist, and integrating tasks. Agencies do not object to cooperating with one another, but they are not designed to achieve such an objective, and since they compete for project grants, they do not share information fully. Fragmented themselves, they cannot undo the problems and consequences of fragmentation, without help. Competing for scarce resources, they cannot cooperate fully. Officials, lay and professional leaders, practitioners, all express concern about the inadequacy of service coverage and take-up, gaps in provision, problems in identifying the nature and magnitude of social needs, and the fragmentation of provision generally. The review has validated the reality of their concerns.

Our descriptive overview of service delivery in this community indicates clearly that there is no unified, comprehensive, or coherent group or cluster of services that are readily identifiable as a personal or general social service network. The "something else" which we saw and monitored earlier, and which the British identify as "personal social services," has not been organized in the United States as a "system" or "network" to parallel health or education, for example. There is no single delivery structure which channels services from funder through provider to consumer. There is no consensus about whether many of these services belong in one of the other existing social service systems (health, education, housing, income security, etc.) or in another, unnamed system which would weld them together. While individual agencies and service providers may have their own goals, there is no community clarity regarding the function of many of these services. Thus, there are no clear boundaries delineating these areas of provision; nor are the boundaries clear at the interface between the defined social sectors and this other, amorphous, unnamed cluster. When we attempt to locate operationally the components of a delivery system, we discover there is no unified approach to ensuring access to services generally, although access services as such abound; the range of interventions are disparate and services are haphazard and fragmented; provision for feedback and reporting is limited at best.

If the objective is to help people, there must be some way to facilitate their obtaining that help. A nonsystem does not take complexity and make it coherent, effective, and efficient. To sum up and illustrate the difficulties encountered, we list some of our observations about service delivery in our city, stressing that they are typical of such difficulties in almost all other communities and that none of this is a comment on this locality per se:

There is a large group of disparate services that fall into none of the existing defined service systems; and another equally large group that encompasses several systems yet has additional components that are more characteristic of the above group than any other sector. These components seem to involve such functions as liaison, personal help, and socialization.

Public policy is premised on agencies which are interrelated and should be integrated. Yet in this community and probably in the United States generally, many of them relate to very few other agencies, and others (e.g., the county Department of Social Services) act only as conduits between agencies, never really performing any continuing function of their own, and often not even effectively performing the liaison function.

Clients come to these services with multiple needs. Case records, program visits, and interviews seem to indicate that large areas of unmet needs—and gaps in service provision—continue to exist, yet adequate documentation for this as well as data regarding service utilization generally and client needs and preferences are still unavailable. (We do recognize the potential dangers of a good, centralized data collection system as well as the potential benefits.)

Rarely are the multiple needs of clients satisfied by one agency. And almost as infrequently is service sought for a client elsewhere, and successfully obtained. Most people who really want several services, and are able to manage themselves, go to more than one agency to obtain needed help. We do not know what happens to the others; but clearly, according to case records, they exist.

The interrelationship of the health service and social service needs of clients are repeatedly stressed in social service agency case records, program visits, and interviews. Yet there is frequent evidence of conflict between these two "systems." Referrals to health services are not implemented, service is not forthcoming, or complaints are registered about the inadequate coordination of efforts. Here are two types of help that seem to be closely related as far as client needs are concerned where gaps and fragmentation in provision seem overwhelming (and it is the client who suffers).

Family agencies perceive themselves as filling a mental health service function although mental health services define them as outside their boundaries.

Mental health services surface as a diagnostic tool but rarely as treatment or other related intervention. They are largely invisible in the cases we have studied.

Services provided under one auspice or administrative structure may be integrated but they set their own narrow boundaries and do not relate much to agencies outside these. (For example, COA and MPA have little to do with other agencies serving the aged. And Catholic Charities services to the aging clearly have no relation to the former program.)

Fragmentation of services is a constant complaint recognized by all. Some aspects of this, especially in relation to the individual client or family, can be rectified at the delivery level. Yet we see no real efforts by planners, providers, or practitioners to develop new devices or new roles to minimize fragmentation.

Many of the service systems, especially the large bureaucratic services, are defined as unresponsive to consumer needs. Practitioners in these services acknowledge this criticism but little is done at any level to remedy the problem.

Because boundaries and function are confused, there is no evidence of any cohesive system emerging; agencies define themselves as being part of a system that does not want them, or as being part of no system because there is none to which they can relate; turf problems preclude individual agency efforts at integration except where implemented through specific funding guidelines (or on an informal personal basis). What exists is a nonsystem of several hundred disparate programs, services, agencies, which do not identify with one another and see little in common with each other, although clients often confuse one for the other or lump them together in one amorphous entity, as represented by "the social worker."

In a larger frame, we note, for example, that in the midst of a large public controversy about community care as a transition from or alternative to the mental hospital, the social services which are universally expected to be the nucleus of "living and care arrangements" were not seen as having either a carefully defined role or relevant linkage arrangements. They enter some cases in relation to income, housing, and Medicaid eligibility, and the county social services department is now beginning to make service provision against a backdrop of confusing state social service procedures and of other partial and fragmented efforts by a state hospital and a county mental health department as well. No one knows which cases are whose core responsibility—who, in short, guarantees ongoing support.

Or we note that the major multifunction voluntary agencies, as well as CHANGE, have no internal program coherence or community role. The initiatives depend on internal agency need assessment, crossed with grantsmanship, information, and political influence. One develops a new program for the aged, another takes the lead in after-school day care, a third is the only family agency in a new voluntary center, several operate community group homes for children. No one agency covers an area or a population group, or assumes full responsibility for a public task. All are heavily subsidized by the taxpayer. All doubt that a coverage service based in the public sector will be effective or of high quality. Many elected public officials and administrators agree; hence the pattern. Social welfare traditions and the public ethic about the role of government are deeply entrenched, or at least appear to be.

Some of the leadership, public and private, would like to have a better ongoing system to "divide up the turf," and one concept of planning. Others meet to deal with shared problems when the going gets tough (Why are community group homes not full and what is now needed? How can the family service agencies find more money?). The United Way planning staff, with a broad view of the status of services, has only limited sanction vis-à-vis the voluntary sector: in unserved areas it tries to create integrated service focused on small neighborhoods, based in centers which are a cross between the settlement house and a multiservice center. Several of these operate; two or three are models of their kind. But there is no sanction. The new city multiservice model neighborhood facility, a large operation soon to open, will cover much of the same territory yet not encompass some of the basic services needed by large population groups.

Thus there are three systems—or four—and therefore none: the coverage by the county Department of Social Services; the network of CHANGE multifunction, largely access, centers; the model neighborhood large multiservice facility; the United Way–initiated small centers—and, of course, where they exist, Catholic Charities, Salvation Army, Family and Child Service—or the decentralized adult services, the centralized child guidance services, and the many contract services of County Mental Health, often overlapping in functions or separated by vague boundaries.

In reviewing what we found in our city and in identifying what we perceive as the major issues and questions to be addressed, we have employed some of the concepts identified earlier relating to the construction of a service delivery system and their implicit evaluative criteria, namely: *access*—how people learn about and obtain services; *channeling*—how people move or are moved from one service to another, as they need additional services; *case integration*—the meshing of multiple services as needed by a client at one time or over time; *program or service integration*—the interrelationship of different programs or services; *accountability*—assuring the responsiveness of services to consumer needs and preferences. Of course, employing the concept of a delivery system as a standard for analysis and assessment represents a perspective on what is essential for service delivery. It is certainly *not* what has been mandated nationally by government, urged by the professions, attempted or even envisioned in this city. In fact, there is no agency, organization, or individual with the authority or sanction to implement such a system or structure. Yet it seems clear to us that it is this lack of coherence that is at the core of service delivery problems.

The observations are not adequately reported unless we stress that, in fact, this is not a negative evaluation of service delivery in this particular city or county. Many individual programs are excellent; they would be rated highly anywhere and the very existence of community concern and interest in problems related to service delivery has positive implications. Nor should this be read as criticism of one community for its failure to develop a social service system or network. It makes no pretense of having such a system or of being able to develop one. It could not itself overcome federal categorization, fragmentation, reporting requirements, and definition of voluntary agency prerogatives.[16]

What we are doing is acknowledging what exists and describing it, in full knowledge of the fact that our city is probably typical of most communities in the United States—better in some areas of provision and worse in others—and suffering with the same or similar problems in service delivery as all others. The questions remain: How can the perennially identified problems of service delivery—inaccessibility, fragmentation, quantitative and qualitative inadequacies in provision, unresponsiveness to consumer needs and preferences—be solved unless intervention occurs at all governmental levels from national to local? If such initiatives are to be forthcoming, what specifically is needed? Who can do it? Is there a case for establishing a personal or general social service system that would represent a cohesive, unified network of social provision? Are the issues raised valid? Are the components we have identified correct? Is this the direction of solution? If not, what are the alternatives? The final chapter proposes that there are signs of the emergence of a personal social service system—and that the development needs a boost at federal, state, and local levels.

Notes

1. Peter Marris and Martin Rein, *Dilemmas of Social Reform: Poverty and Community Action in the United States* (New York: Atherton, 1967); Rein, "The Social Service Crisis" and "Coordination of Social Services" in Rein, *Social Policy: Issues of Choice and Change* (New York: Random House, 1970), pp. 47–69, 103–37; Alfred J. Kahn, *Theory and Practice of Social Planning* and *Studies in Social Policy and Planning* (New York: Russell Sage Foundation, 1969); Kahn et al., *Neighborhood Information Centers* (New York: Columbia University School of Social Work, 1966); Kahn, "Perspectives on Access to Social Services," *Social Work,* 15, No. 3, (April 1970), 95–101; Robert Perlman and David Jones, *Neighborhood Service Centers* (Washington, D.C.: GPO, 1967); Edward J. O'Donnell, "An Organizational Twiggy: A Review of Neighborhood Service Centers," *Welfare in Review,* 5, No. 8 (1967), 6–11; O'Donnell, "The Neighborhood Service Center: A Place to Go and a Place to Be From," *Welfare in Review,* 6, No. 1 (1968), 11–21; O'Donnell and Otto M. Reid, "The Multi-Service Neighborhood Center: Preliminary Findings from a National Survey," *Welfare in Review,* 9, No. 3 (May-June 1971), 1–8; O'Donnell and Marilyn M. Sullivan, "Service Delivery and Social Action through the Neighborhood Center: A Review of Research," *Welfare in Review,* 8, No. 9 (Nov.-Dec. 1969), 1–12; Alfred J. Kahn, "Service at the Neighborhood Level: Experience, Theory, and Fads," *Social Service Review,* Vol. 50, No. 1 (March 1976).

2. Elliot L. Richardson, *Responsibility and Responsiveness (II)* (Washington, D.C.: DHEW, Jan. 18, 1973), p. 19. See the Social Services Research and Demonstration work plan for fiscal years 1974 and 1975, prepared for the Office of the Secretary as background for a report on services integration for indication of continuing concern with fragmentation. See also testimony supporting the proposed and apparently moribund Allied Services Act.

3. Lyndon Johnson, Special Message, March 1966, as quoted in Kahn, *Studies in Social Policy,* pp. 234–35.

4. See Perlman and Jones, *Neighborhood Service Centers*; Melvin B. Mogulof, "Neighborhood Service Centers," *Encyclopedia of Social Work* (16th issue; New York: National Association of Social Workers, 1971), pp. 857–65; O'Donnell, "Neighborhood Service Center"; Kahn, "Service at the Neighborhood Level."

5. Marshall Kaplan, Gans, and Kahn, *Integration of Human Services in HEW: An Evaluation of Services Integration Projects,* Vol. I (Washington, D.C.: DHEW, 1973).

6. An interesting conceptual analysis is contained in Human Services Institute for Children and Families, Inc., *Alternative Approaches to Human Services Planning* (Arlington, Va.: The Institute, 1974). Also see The Research Group, Inc. and Marshall Kaplan, Gans, and Kahn, *Human Resource Services in the States,* 1972, for a group of case studies and an effort to conceptualize options.

7. O'Donnell, "An Organizational Twiggy."

8. Perlman and Jones, *Neighborhood Service Centers,* pp. 34–37; Kirschner Associates, *A Description and Evaluation of Neighborhood Centers* (Washington, D.C.: OEO, 1966), p. 45; Abt Associates, "Findings and Conclusions of Neighborhood Center Study," *Comprehensive Neighborhood Program* (Washington, D.C.: OEO, Oct. 1970); O'Donnell, references cited earlier, as well as O'Donnell and Reid, *The National Inventory of Multi-Service Neighborhood Centers* (Washington, D.C.: DHEW, SRS, 1971).

9. See Marshall Kaplan, Gans, and Kahn, *Integration of Human Services,* I, intro., 1.

10. Stephen D. Mittenthal et al., *Twenty-Two Allied Services (SITO) Projects Described as Human Service Systems* (Wellesley, Mass.: The Human Ecology Institute, 1974).

11. For clarification of this distinction, see Alice Rivlin, *Systematic Thinking for Social Action* (Washington, D.C.: The Brookings Institution, 1971), ch. 5.

12. Dr. Gary Massel, "Comprehensive Human Services Planning and Delivery" (processed; Social and Rehabilitation Service, Department of Health, Education, and Welfare, Dec. 1974).

13. What follows is based on data obtained from a recently completed, joint, city-county sponsored questionnaire survey of all social programs in the county (not just individual agencies or organizations) other than those specifically defined as health or education. In addition, these data are supplemented by information obtained through telephone interviews and in-person interviews with directors and staff regarding certain aspects of the survey, as well as interviews and program visits relevant to our specific topics. Finally, case record reading in three of the major agencies in the community provided still another source and

category of data for observations and conclusions regarding service delivery.

14. See "Community Psychiatry: Boundaries and Intergovernmental Relations in Planning," in Alfred J. Kahn, *Studies in Social Policy and Planning* (New York: Russell Sage Foundation, 1968), pp. 194–242. Also, David A. Musto, "Whatever Happened to 'Community Mental Health'?" *The Public Interest*, No. 39 (Spring 1975), pp. 53–79.

15. Robert Morris, rapporteur, *Toward a Caring Society* (New York: Columbia University School of Social Work, 1974), and Robert Morris and Delwin Anderson, "Personal Care Services: An Identity for Social Work," *Social Service Review*, 49, No. 2 (June 1975), pp. 157–74.

16. Were New York City not always defined as atypical we would have cited it. The conclusions are similar if one looks at the social services report of the Scott Commission, a New York City review completed in March 1973: State Study Commission for New York City, Task Force on Social Services, *Social Services in New York City* (Albany, N.Y.: 1973). A Community Council of Greater New York Committee updated the situation as of June 1975 and found no significant changes; see "Report of the Subcommittee to Follow-up Scott Commission Recommendations" (processed; New York: Community Council of Greater New York, 1975).

The Emergence of the Personal Social Service System

The Conceptual Base

Clearly we have been too long satisfied with anachronism, ambiguity, half-measures, and mediocrity in social service policy and practice. Despite short-run policy failure, our society has recognized, come to value, and institutionalized education, income security, and health systems. It has more or less begun to face employment-manpower and housing as essential public institutions. But these five systems (to which most countries apply the generic term "social services" and for which Americans seem to prefer "human services" or "social welfare programs") do not among them cover all of the nonmarket service provisions obviously essential to human welfare in an urban industrial world. Systematic review suggests that the time has arrived to face the emergence of the sixth human service system: what the British have called the "personal social services,"[1] an identifiable domain of growing importance which clearly would benefit by conceptualization, assessment, and organization.

After the five established and accepted systems have been covered, there remains a long and significant list of social sector programs. That "something else" includes service activities and fields variously identified with names such as the following: child welfare, family services, community programs for the aged, community centers and settlements, homemakers, day care, congregate meals and meals-on-wheels, self-help and mutual aid activities among the handicapped, institutional care and residential treatment of adjudicated delinquents and children in need of supervision, advice services for adolescents, protected residential arrangements for young people living away from their families.

These and similar programs, as we noted in the earlier chapters, are in many ways interdependent. They respond to needs and demands which, in turn, grow out of the conditions of modern living. They contribute to primary group life and relationships, to individual functioning, to a person's capacity to grow and to respond to others. They deal with individuals vis-à-vis institutions, groups, individuals, relatives. They focus on persons-in-situations, in relation to one another and to themselves. These programs in their totality, and if organized to facilitate their interrelationships, may be conceptualized as the sixth social service.[2] They should be defined and organized, because only the deliberate reshaping of what has grown by accretion into a working system will provide a way to maximize the responsiveness and effectiveness of what is offered. The alternative is program competition, "lost cases," gaps in provision, public confusion, and a failure to mesh what should be mutually reinforcing efforts.

Our conviction that the personal social services constitute an emerging system grows out of our international comparative work, as it does out of our U.S. review.[3] It is clearly possible to identify a group of activities, functions, tasks, service models which do not necessarily or in fact belong to the other major systems and are often, but not always, thought of in relation to one another. They are sometimes coordinated or even integrated in policy and action by consumers, public officials, voluntary agencies, or practitioners. However, in the rigorous sense of the term, there is a lack of system in most places for formally and effectively identifying elements which belong among the personal social services and organizing them as such. The personal social services clearly are identifiable and could be systematized but need the supports of policy and administrative action.

The conceptual base for system may be specified. We conclude from analysis of what now exists that *the personal social services* are services available by nonmarketplace criteria. Need, demographic category, or status is the determinant, not ability or inability to pay, even though there may be fees, partial fees, or no fees. The services are addressed to one or more among the following tasks: *contributing to socialization and development*; that is, offering daily living and growth supports for ordinary, average people (not just problem groups), a role shared with other nonmarket services but involving unique programs; *facilitating* individual or family *information* about *and access* to services and entitlements anywhere in the social sector (all six social service fields); *assuring* for the frail aged, the handicapped, the retarded, the incapacitated, a basic level of *social care* and aid necessary to support functioning in the community or in substitute living arrangements (the social care concept is elaborated below); *providing help, counseling, guidance,* which will assist individuals and families facing problems, crises, pathology to reestablish functional capacity and/or overcome their difficulties; *supporting mutual aid,* self-help, and participation activities aimed at prevention, overcoming problems in community living, and contributing to the planning of relevant services; *integrating* the variety of different programs or services in different systems or within the personal social services as they affect individuals and families, to assure service meshing for maximum effectiveness.

These personal social services include both public social utilities and case services. The utilities are programs available at consumer initiative for which entitlement is a matter of citizenship or age or related status. They are largely programs which buttress daily living and contribute to socialization and development, functioning under present social circumstances as the family, primary group, or village once did. The case services, by contrast, are entered after a diagnostic or assessment process, agreement by a "gatekeeper" (diagnostician, evaluator, etc.) that there is need or eligibility. The process may be a court adjudication, a medical review, a social study, a psychiatric assessment, a psychological test.

Many of the personal social services are or should be utilities (preschool programs, senior citizens' centers, community centers, residential schools, family planning services). Many are case services (programs for abused and neglected children, institutions for delinquents, nursing homes for the disabled). A personal social service network clearly requires both. A single program model (day care, for example) may be a utility (for all eligible children whose parents choose to use the service) or a case service (for children in disorganized homes who need supportive help).

Utilities, by their nature, are universal, not limited to those who pass a means test. Case services may be selective, for the poor alone, or universal. Universal services may impose differentiated fees, determined by income, as long as the right to the service is not reserved for those below a specified income level. Universal services may serve average people facing ordinary circumstances; case services involve illness, problems, maladjustment, difficulty.

The personal social services, because they include both utilities and case services, are significant for average people, as they are for those with occasional or constant personal problems and those whose disadvantage or disorganization is pervasive. Selectivity—organizing services for the poor alone—would close them out unnecessarily and unwisely to many users. Universalism is the general strategy cross-nationally—services available to and good enough for any citizen (though some instances of restored selectivity under financial constraint have occurred). The organizational task under universalism is to assure access and to allocate priorities, if rationing is needed, so as to guarantee that the poor are not closed out by others who recognize a good thing when they see it.

Any effort to organize personal social services into an effective and efficient system faces difficult boundary problems. One begins with a partially developed series of case services and utilities, fragmented by eligibility rules and administrative structures, some of them currently selective and some universal. These services variously overlap with or may be considered to be part of health, education, corrections, housing, manpower efforts. The boundaries may be quite vague, but they are nonetheless important to and defended by practitioners in each system. Even where the mood favors collaboration, it may be difficult to formulate decision rules which grow out of solid knowledge as to what works best. To illustrate we may note the need to define medical and social work roles in the obviously needed collaborative efforts in programs for abused and battered children or services to the frail elderly.

We found, internationally, convergence toward common elements in the delivery system for personal social services, even though some trends are not yet resolved. In general, there is a tendency toward a free-standing system, with some personal social services outposted as adjuncts to other systems. That is, personal social services are being organized as network, but some of the staff do their daily work in other agencies and institutions—schools, hospitals, social security offices, and so on. A possible and far less frequent alternative, which creates enormous problems of program coordination and case integration, attaches personal social services to other systems without creating a free-standing delivery system as a "home base" at all.

We read the American picture as favoring a core free-standing personal social service system which, in turn, could outpost staff to other institutions (courts, schools, hospitals) much as health departments currently outpost doctors to schools to serve school health programs. The elements out of which system could develop—we noted in Chapter 7—are the structures for public welfare services and child welfare in most counties, antipoverty and housing service programs, those components of community mental health which really are personal social services, and a variety of categorically based social services in such fields as health, education, and rehabilitation (school social work, medical social work, and so on).

An understanding of the validity of universalism in the personal social services confirms the trend of the past several years toward operational separation of means-tested income maintenance programs from service programs—a separation developed both to objectify and to protect the right to money (since acceptance of service must not be conceived of as a valid test of financial need) and to avoid program stigma, an inevitable consequence if services are reserved or required for relief recipients alone. Although separation makes it easier for clients to satisfy discrete needs, it leaves open the problem of identifying the high-risk, vulnerable client who comes only for financial assistance and does not request what may be badly needed help. The separation of income maintenance and service programs, therefore, requires special provision for identifying such cases and channeling them for appropriate aid.

Public-voluntary separateness is everywhere a constraint upon the creation of system. Voluntary programs tend to be age-categorical (for the aged, for children, for youth) or they are problem-pathology specific (delinquency, mental health, the handicapped). This orientation has a long and understandable history but it becomes an obstacle to program coordination and to case integration at the operational level. It is a major roadblock to accountability as well.

Not that one cannot imagine a personal social service system which integrates the public and voluntary effectively and joins them in a true system. Our cross-national studies show this to be the case in a number of countries. However, creation of a coverage system, enforcement of standards, and assurance of provision for case accountability, all apparently require both legal mandate and public-sector commitment. These are found in some U.S. jurisdictions but are not general. Nor are they the expectation in recent social service legislation in the United States. The most common way to talk about public-voluntary relationships here is to formulate the issue as creation of a "partnership." Because this term is ambiguous, such formulation really dodges the basic issue. The personal social services do show signs of maturing as a system; but a system—which implies integration and accountability—cannot be achieved without a much clearer and more substantially assertive public role or at least formal public-voluntary compacts, publicly sanctioned. Differences among states in this country as far back as a decade ago document the fact that the public role is the crucial variable in determining whether there is or is not an integrated delivery system. If public authority will guarantee standards, system, and accountability, the voluntary sector resources can be extremely well deployed—well deployed, that is, not merely as expert separate services (which they could be even on an isolated island) but as components of a responsible network of coverage governed by public priorities.

Affirmation of the significance and validity of a personal social service system does not require exaggerated claims or a lack of balance. Our studies of care for the aged, abused children, children's institutions, to cite only a few, certainly make it clear that a social policy which does not base itself on availability of suitable employment and adequate income maintenance, health, housing, and educational programs will be continually frustrating and incapable of progress. The personal social services are a needed component of social policy, not a substitute for it. They are a complement of cash, in-kind, housing, health provision, not a cheaper alternative or a diversion. They require only modest funding (perhaps one percent of GNP now), as contrasted with income transfer, education, or health programs, but this modest cost does not signify unimportance. (For cost comparisons, see the Appendix.)

The personal social services merit recognition and stability because they clearly have their own validity. Our specific field reviews and international studies document that even cash, adequate cash, must be supplemented by in-kind benefits and services; cash is no substitute for all services. Public education, parks, public transportation, a water supply, are offered as utilities because sometimes public and private priorities do not coincide, and it is public policy to assure goods and services even if people will not use their money to purchase them. As much may be said of some social services (child welfare? information and referral? family counseling?). Services also are offered outside the market at times as a way to protect consumers from professional provider monopolies (adoption? child guidance? nursing homes? homemakers–home healths?). Or the motive in offering a service in the social sector may be to take advantage of economy of scale or to guarantee the availability of a program which no market could produce at a guaranteed profit and keep its price reasonable (family counseling? specialized residential treatment? rehabilitation of several categories of the handicapped?).

Finally, it is apparent, as we think of abused and neglected children, of children in need of supervision and delinquents, of the frail aged and disturbed adults, that some social welfare programs involve an element of control, stigma, sanction, and protection. Many people in need will not turn to such programs, nor should they be expected to; yet the society cannot therefore ignore need. Many potential clients will not pay for the help, whatever their resources, but something must be done (protective services? friendly visitors? probation? residential treatment? abuse–battered child detection? secure detention? family support litigation?).

Society organizes some services because the market will not function to assure them or to assure access. It tends toward a universal comprehensive system because drug abuse, alcoholism, marital problems, parent-child difficulties, child abuse, emotional disturbance, and physical handicap do not spare even people with enough money, good housing, advanced education, or jobs. Old age, adolescent separation from families, developmental and socialization needs of children are normal, nonproblem statuses which cross income and class lines. The personal social services are needed as part of the total societal response to modern living. They are not a substitute for other valid responses, but other responses are not interchangeable with them either. Personal social services have developed in recent decades, and they are everywhere identifiable and significant. They are striving toward coherence. Perhaps the time has come for recognizing and promoting the institutional maturity of the "sixth social service" to use the British term, or what in the United States might be the sixth "human service program."

To go beyond the haphazard, fragmented, and transient arrangements of the past is to move toward administrative autonomy and relative stability. This is the fundamental premise here. One cannot speak of child care, or programs for the aged, and see them as transitory social arrangements. Women are in the labor force. Families want their children to have group experiences. The aged population grows and seeks out the services which make noninstitutional living possible. What modern hospital imagines itself without a medical social work department? What church federation or court sees itself without professional marital counseling? We did not cover programs for drug addicts or alcoholics in our research, and we touched only peripherally on marital counseling and on programs which deal with parent-child problems. But who will consider these, or school social services, or social work supports for medical programs for handicapped children, and define them as transitory, temporary, emergency-only for the society—even though any individual may not need the service at all or may need it on only a very temporary basis?

In short, the so-called "residual" perspective is wrong: these are not temporary measures to meet needs that will fade away from our communities. The responses to these needs are not less valid morally as exercises of community responsibility than are education programs or health facilities. These are not marginal arrangements. Along with the other five human services the personal social services, the sixth, are institutional arrangements which are natural, inevitable, morally respectable, in modern urban industrial society.

The personal social services, then, not only strive for recognition and coherence, but they should be expected to. They are part of the new service society, the consumer society of the industrial urban world. They are worldwide, cover all social and economic systems, under one name or another—and are growing.

Organizational and Administrative Requirements

Public social utilities follow general principles of public administration. It has been noted in Chapter 7 that a free-standing personal social service delivery system may organize its case services around the following processes: information, referral and other access activities; case assessment and evaluation; delivery of direct benefits and social care services; counseling; program and service coordination and case integration; accountability; reporting, evaluation, and feedback. Such organziation is not easy to implement since it requires the settling of boundary issues, reassignment of tasks, agreements on case flow and procedures, definitions of agency rights and sanctions, assignment of personnel and resources, and public interpretations of roles and relationships—all after the universalism-selectivity balance has been determined.

Once the political decisions are taken and the resources allocated, successful translation of current beginnings into a fully operational and effective personal social service enterprise thus will require specific policy choices, as well as legislative, administrative, and organizational measures at the several levels of government.

The effort will need to be deliberate. The United States has been given to fits of periodic empathy for and concern with individuals or families whose problems fit into spotlighted categories: delinquency or neglect, retardation or abuse, the poverty of old age. The spotlighting follows upsetting incidents, dramatic case stories, or new research findings; but it may be short lived. The legislation and funding follow the public arousal or new fad. It is not knowledge of effective intervention but concern, or sentiment, or organizational dynamics, which take over. Each special institution or program meets real needs but is not in balance or in a position to work in relation to other programs or institutions. Thus, basic family welfare efforts or core child care and child welfare services which must be a point of reference may be ignored and neglected while case finding for abused children or residential services for delinquents receive large investments and cannot succeed in any basic sense. The process is understandable and even to be predicted. But, as a result, popular categorical programs achieve only a fraction of their potential success and large populations needing basic service are deprived.

Categorical approaches, whatever their appeal, do not by their nature make adequate provision for service coherence or service integration. The problem has been illustrated in earlier chapters. Those who would serve families in a preventive or therapeutic sense cannot assure them the cash maintenance, housing, health service, special education, and personal social services they require to fit their specific circumstances because that is not how social institutions are organized. Most people will not suffer because of this; they do their own coordinating, whether in the marketplace or in the bureaucratic systems. However, complex, long-developing problems respond only to multifaceted, coordinated interventions. For people with such problems and disability, the delivery system must be concerned with case continuity, case integration, accountability, and with balanced social provision.

Thus, if the personal social services are to discharge their potential, they must be helped to emerge as system vis-à-vis categorical personal social service programs which have specific mandates and over which the federal administrators who guide the social service development may have limited formal prerogatives.

At the federal level this will require further clarification within the Congress and DHEW as to whether the service programs which have gradually emerged out of the social service titles of the Social Security Act (especially, at this writing, Titles IV-B and XX) are or are not to serve as the foundation upon which states and localities will be permitted, even encouraged, to build a personal social service system out of the many categorical elements now operating. Law and regulations now offer the opportunity: a flexible "revenue sharing" approach to federal funding in this field. There is a mandate for popular response to and participation in planning and enough flexibility to permit states to define and develop services which reflect their own demographic and cultural uniqueness and needs (how many aged, poor, cultural minorities, unattached youth, etc.). In addition, congressional refusal to include in the legislation a constraining definition of social services permits the evolution of a personal social service system containing a blend of components appropriate to a state: social care; access, referral, and advocacy; developmental and socialization "utilities"; case services involving social treatment in the community as well as institutional and residential care; rehabilitation. What is more, the permeable boundaries allow unique state experimentation with multidisciplinary mixes and with placing or not placing various components in the personal social service network, on the one hand, or in health, education, justice, mental health, on the other.

Also of help are the fact that under federal social service regulations information and referral services (the access system) must be universal, as must the protective service program. Also the eligibility and fee rules are so formulated as to move the rest of the system far along toward universalism and away from a "poor law" tradition of services designed for the poor alone.

On the side of constraint are state long-range fiscal problems and expenditure ceilings which could inhibit growth; fund-matching requirements difficult for the poor states; some "invasions" upon planning flexibility in the form of specified allocation of resources, specified goals to be addressed, and groups to be assured service. On the one hand such requirements (too changeable for summarization here[4]) do protect especially needy and vulnerable groups. On the other, they constrain local planning and may discourage creation of a general social service delivery system able to meet all needs, staffed as required with specialists, and using whatever outposting and outreach is essential to serve groups at risk.

Favoring one system for all is the fact that since late 1975 regulations to implement services funded under the Social Security Act do permit a universal system to be constructed. One delivery system could serve those for whom there are to be no fees at all, because of their poverty or public assistance status, those who are to pay fees, but cannot pay economic cost, and those able to carry their weight. This permits, but does not mandate or guarantee, a comprehensive universal system for people of all income groups, a prerequisite for system. A state might (*a*) assign free services to those who are poor, (*b*) use graduated fees for those whose incomes reach the maximum specified in the legislation (currently 115 percent of the state median income), sharing what is the deficit with the voluntary sector, and (*c*) charge fees at the level of economic costs with those able to pay. Even categories (*a*) and (*b*) would bring into one service system most service users and would require it to become a system good enough for any citizen, not a stigmatized poor-law service.

Also favoring one system are the service integration initiatives outlined in the previous chapter and the encouragement cited there for social sector coordination in 1975 Social Security Act amendments. However, there are contradictions, especially in the form of conflicting mandates to coordinate which appear in other legislation, also affecting local social service programs and service delivery in mental health, manpower, health, education, community development. Thus far, the legislation has not created a hierarchy among related programs nor does such hierarchy exist within the administrative structure. In effect, each major service system, each institution, sees itself in the generalist coordination or lead role and rejects others who would take the lead. This is not supportive of a personal social service development, nor is it helpful to the other systems. The contradictions will continue in Washington and will create problems for the states until clear policy emerges.

In short, the entire initiative toward a personal social service system, the policy, the planning, the resolution, are partial. As yet, there is no lead agency with mandate and resources to create an integrated personal social service system in the United States—and to develop the necessary pattern of relationships with agencies and systems at its boundaries.

To summarize: The United States has major legislation and substantial program development, out of which could come a new social institution, a new element in the domestic social sector—the personal social services. There is need, effective demand, some knowledge, a technology, structure, personnel—and there is growth. Also, there is a partial and potential legislative and administrative framework. But there also is controversy, ambivalence, and uncertainty. There are contradictory categorical, voluntary, and other-system initiatives. Those who could grasp the opportunity are often branded with the long-standing public attitudes to public welfare, to "poor law"; they are the unpopular messengers in a society tired of pathology, problems, and taxes. Others, in more or less parallel fields, have their own thrusts and objectives.

For a decade or more social service in the United States coped with problems of federal fragmentation and indecision by raising the slogan of decentralization. Where federal programs were fragmented, unrelated, even inconsistent, legislation or regulation sometimes gave program initiative in the social sector to cities or counties, often even bypassing state irresolution, saying: "We don't seem to be able to work it out in Washington. Why don't you try." And when local government could not overcome barriers, it adopted multiservice centers and community control as integrating devices and often implied: "We don't know how, but certainly you service providers must." These devices seldom achieved desired objectives.[5] They could not even assure the qualitatively improved or even expanded services justified by the larger investment. They could not ordinarily end fragmentation and achieve service integration, case integration, accountability in service delivery.

The federal role in shaping personal social services cannot be bypassed. Federal categorical programs carry regulations, procedures, reporting requirements, standards, and staffing patterns which often supersede the announced solutions through local initiative. No multiservice center can satisfy the needs of a group of independent administrative systems at higher levels. It is not possible to create an integrated operation without coping with elements of professional culture and the characteristic delivery patterns associated with specialized bureaucratic systems. Nor is it feasible to devise an integrated local system while reporting to four or five or seven different administrational structures at the state level.

Thus, it is essential to begin at the federal level, to do even more at the middle tier, the state, and at the intermediate tier, the city.

For there cannot be an integrated, operating personal social service system locally unless there is attention to the conditions for its realization.

Progress in creating a personal social service system will depend in part on further sorting out at the federal level. Perhaps this requires some expansion of the several administrative devices discussed in Chapter 7, which free local jurisdictions from legislative and regulatory mandates and reports and do permit services integration. Perhaps there is need for amalgamation and coherence among the several forms of social sector special revenue sharing through new legislation. Whether through administrative action or legislation and budgetary practice, the initiatives will need to be reflected in federal guidelines and regulations not merely mutually consistent among themselves but also mutually supportive.

The technical assistance and monitoring bureaus and agencies at DHEW should also evolve in time from a structure which reflects current fragmentation and mutually unrelated initiatives into one which supports system and integration. At present there is the Social and Rehabilitation Service, administering some programs directly derived from the old public welfare statutes and others that contain new opportunities and mandates. But there is also an Office of Human Development, concerned with problems and age-status groups, and not limited to the poor alone. With service delivery now separated from administration of the income-maintenance eligibility investigation, there is no case for an SRS and an OHD at the service end (or there would be no case if concern for means-tested Medicaid and Aid to Families with Dependent Children had a more suitable administrative locus and were fully separated from personal social services).

The evolution of a personal social service delivery system would be enhanced if Older Americans Act services, and services for the aged under the public assistance titles, and if Child Welfare Services, as well as services to children under the public assistance titles, became the concern of the same administration. It is more than a matter of merging of the two streams of services to the aged or the two streams of services to the children, means tested and non-means tested. It is also a question of providing to a responsible administrative agency a mandate to be concerned with children, the aged, the youth, families, as well as a variety of problem groups and need categories in one system. Because a personal social service system must be not only universal but also to a degree comprehensive, it needs organizational representation consistent with its mission.

Only such a development would make it reasonable to deal with services belonging to the personal social services but now otherwise located, as well as with boundary problems demanding effective co-operative work—personal social services in relation to employment, education, health, mental health, housing. In any case these are difficult issues which will need to be approached experimentally. Unless at the personal social service end there is some degree of unity and coherence, there is no possible approach to colleague professionals on the other side of the fence.

Some states have probably moved further than the federal government in providing necessary conditions for an integrated personal social service system. There are several types of human resource and public welfare agencies at the state level which are experimenting with integrated management or integrated delivery systems under their own auspices, through direct operation, or by encouragement and support of local activities. Federal backing and reorganization would enhance the prospect. Exchange of experience and cooperation would help substantially. Development of planning capacity would be useful if the interest were in results, not in compliance with required ritual.

Not all states have taken this pathway. A minority have chosen to create the single state social service agency which the Social Security Act requires as a condition for federal funding, but then use it only to channel service funds to other systems: corrections, mental health, education, housing, manpower. If this pattern persists or expands, the initiatives toward a free-standing personal social service system will die out and the United States will need to pursue the alternative option: personal social services as adjuncts to other institutions. Evidence thus far reported in our earlier chapters and in the cross-national study[6] suggests that the problems of fragmentation, unclear roles, and ineffective service are likely to remain unsolved under such a regime.

The eventual testing ground will be the locality. Not a locality working in isolation, not one trying to solve alone (by operating multiservice centers or encouraging citizen involvement) complex legislatively and organizationally induced and long-standing problems of structure, regulation, mission, repertoire, all of which have been left unresolved in the state capital or at DHEW. Only a locality allowed to "take off" because the foundation is right and because issues have been faced in Washington and in the state capital could move toward needed structures and determine just what type of system will meet its needs. Obviously, there is required a range of experimentation and testing and the ultimate adoption of diverse solutions in a country which could not manage without pluralism. Those who would do this work at the local level need guidance, models, training supports, and encouragement. The planned variations within and between localities are the way to shape the system.

The local pattern will need to provide for both general and specialized information, referral, advocacy, and case assessment services, able to appeal to all potential users of utilities and case services, whatever the individual's capacity to seek services out. There will be need for a front-line unit, whether an outposted "team" or an individual practitioner, able to authorize many direct services and benefits, as well as to provide basic counseling, referral to specialists, and case continuity in complex situations—along the lines of what is described in Chapter 7. The core activity of the unit would be general social work practice, a social work counterpart of general medical practice. Whether in the same system, by referral to other public systems, through purchase of care in the voluntary sector, there will also need to be many types of specialist help. And the local personal social service unit will require provision for case integration, accountability, and feedback to the planners and programmers. There is experience and expertise in these activities, but practice and structures are not yet standardized.

For the United States the new element in the local system, part of the core of the general practice, and the component which will dramatize the need that all people have for this system is what might be called "social care." Ignored or undervalued by some as a function of the personal social services in the past because it was not intensive therapy, delegated by others as an adjunct to the medical system, because it quite often deals with the handicapped and ill people, social care has been placed under the spotlight recently by Robert Morris as a core element for the personal social services in the future.[7]

For the purpose of the cross-national study we have found the following definition helpful: Social care is a term describing a cluster of practical helping measures, including (*a*) personal care and hygiene for old and handicapped people (assistance with bathing and dressing); (*b*) home-health services, including light practical nursing and assistance in taking medication; (*c*) homemaker or home-help services, such as meal preparation, light cleaning, personal laundry; (*d*) chore, shopping, and escort services; (*e*) friendly visiting and telephone reassurance services.

Social care programs require medical and social work elements. They could be located in medical or personal social service systems or operate out of a neutral base and serve both. But the personal social service unit must offer access to and work in close relation to social care services, whatever the operating base. The aged, handicapped, retarded, emotionally disturbed, or victims of personal and family emergencies have great need for such services. Not as status-conferring as intensive personal counseling, perhaps, they are absolutely vital components of community care and support systems. The personal social services are central to the social care access system, their sound rationing and their effective use. The personal social service delivery system could be organized to offer, in its several components, social care, substitute care, intensive counseling, in-kind benefits, access services.

The commitment to system coherence and coverage, as noted, will require some resolution of public-voluntary roles, with the leadership taken on the state or federal level, since the burden of resolution will be too great for any locality. Clearly responsibility for policy and coverage (as for finance) is public. The base-line access and case integration system, too, probably requires public operation. But, if preferred, the remainder of the system could be constructed out of a mix. The public system could integrate voluntary resources, as specialized programs or as front-line "contract" services, if there were a mandate and will for strong public auditing and enforcement of standards.

To translate the beginnings of a U.S. personal social service system into a fully operating reality thus would require: federal legislative, administrative, and budgetary mandates to cope with categorization and fragmented programs; reorganization and new support structures at DHEW; encouragement of state human service reorganization, already under way, to be made effective and committed to creating a service delivery structure; local experimentation with alternative models for personal social service systems. These models will need to combine access provision, one of several forms of general practice, provision for case integration, accountability arangements, as well as a strong core of social care services, an essential element in the new personal social service system. We see little likelihood that a strong system can evolve except on the basis of public operation of front-line services and accountability for whatever is supplied through the private sector.

Social work education has major responsibility for staffing the personal social services with practitioners, administrators, and planners, and there is need to go further in conceptualizing general practice and its relation to specialty, a subject on which there has been recent stalemate. For the social work profession is called upon to find ways to assure front-line competence while providing substantive field expertise in diverse categorical and technical arenas. Its practitioners will need to be geared for interdisciplinary work at all levels, since whatever the system boundaries, people are complex wholes. To be adequately responsive, social work will need to cope with the internal value systems of its profession: the tendency to undervalue skill in administering social care and in-kind benefits while favoring intensive counseling, even though the personal social service system needs many types of practitioners as well as the managers, administrators, researchers, and planners essential for the successful development of this increasingly large and important program of government.

We have proceeded in each part of this volume from description and analysis to a formulation of possibilities and a projection of futures. We have concluded program and policy analysis in this final chapter with both projection and advocacy. For we see the stirrings of the sixth social service and we recognize its potential. We observe widespread need, but are aware of obstacles. The development is worldwide and there is knowledge and experience, so there is a basis for hope. Yet the legislative, organizational, professional, and cultural obstacles are substantial. There are still many Americans who think that only the poor, the handicapped, and the disturbed need social services. So there is uncertainty.

The personal social services have come too far to disappear. They are too useful, and sought by to many elements in our society, to be wiped out. But they could grow slowly, serve the well-to-do one way and the poor in another, and remain more fragmented and less effective than they could be. That would be too bad. The personal social services as comprehensive, universal system could gain in effectiveness and thus in their service to the society. They could be integrating elements, forces for social cohesion and even for some resource redistribution. The need is all around, and effective response is within grasp. We are quite close. What are essential now are wisdom, commitment, and serious work.

Notes

1. An earlier proposal that Americans use the name "general social services" apparently has not taken hold. See Alfred J. Kahn, *Social Policy and Social Services* (New York: Random House, 1973).

2. See Peter Townsend et al., *The Fifth Social Service* (London: The Fabian Society, 1970). Townsend's original list did not include employment-manpower. However, see Beatrice G. Reubens, *The Hard to Employ: European Programs* (New York: Columbia University Press, 1970).

3. The cross-national report on services and service delivery contains extensive documentation. See Alfred J. Kahn and Sheila B. Kamerman, *Social Services in International Perspective* (pub. pending, 1976). Related material on the aged, day care, youth programs, school meals, etc. appears in Alfred J. Kahn and Sheila B. Kamerman, *Not for the Poor Alone: European Social Services* (Philadelphia: Temple University Press, 1975).

4. See the latest social service regulations under the Social Security Act.

5. Alfred J. Kahn, "Service Delivery at the Neighborhood Level: Experience, Theory and Fads," *Social Service Review*, Vol. 50, No. 1 (March 1976). Also see Chapter 7.

6. Kahn and Kamerman, *Social Services in International Perspective.*

7. Robert Morris and Delwin Anderson, "Personal Care Services: An Identity for Social Work," *Social Service Review*, 49, No. 2 (June 1975), 157–74.

Appendix

Social Welfare in the American Community

This book began as a U.S. report in a cross-national research effort.[1] To avoid the ambiguity of high-level generalization and the uncertainty of meaning of abstract technical concepts—which would have invalidated international comparisons—we undertook concrete description and "pointing." We sought operational definitions. We asked everywhere: What are the laws, the formal policies, the funding arrangements, the administrative prerogatives, the staffing patterns, the measures of need, the coverage rates, and the utilization patterns? How does each service look and operate in the locality or "on the ground" where client meets practitioner and facility? What is believed known about the results and effects, and how it this known? How does the cluster of agencies and services in one field, or addressing one problem, relate to other agencies and fields both in the formal sense and during specific service activities? What, then, is the implicit policy, the institutional goal; is there an ongoing debate and a thrust toward reform or change?

Because we were working in different kinds of countries and were interested in the interplay between social services and society we asked for material about societal context. Such material was intended, also, to orient readers who did not have a full picture of social welfare measures in other than the personal social services. We prepared similar material for the United States and present some of it in this appendix, for the use of students.

What follows is a brief attempt to cover a vast territory: the demographic, governmental, economic, and societal context of the U.S. social services scene. Here the term is used broadly, in its worldwide meaning, to cover all of social welfare: the nonmarket social sector. Special attention is given to the five great service and benefit fields, the backdrop for the emerging sixth field, the personal social services.

Background

The United States is a heavily industrialized and urbanized country. Only 4–4.5 percent of the civilian labor force is employed in agriculture. Urban and suburban residents constitute 74 percent of the total population. Approximately one family in five changes its place of residence each year, but almost two-thirds of the moves take place within the county and fewer than 4 percent are between states. In 1970, over one-quarter of the population resided in a state other than the place of birth.

In mid-1973, 7.9 percent of the population were under 5 years old, 16.5 percent were 5–13, 8.0 percent were 14–17, 12.5 percent were 18–24, 13.6 percent were 25–34, 10.8 percent were 35–44, 11.3 percent were 45–54, 9.2 percent were 55–64, and 10.1 percent were over 65. The median age was 28.4. There were 95.5 males per 100 females, the men outnumbering women slightly to about age 25, after which ratios decline until they reach 89.5 per 100 in the 55–64 age cohort and 70.3 per 100 at ages 65 and over.

The population grew by 13.5 percent between 1960 and 1970 and by 3.0 percent between 1970 and 1973. The 1973 net growth per 1,000 persons was 7.1, made up of a birth rate of 14.9, a death rate of 9.4, and a net civilian immigration rate of 1.6. In 1973 the marriage rate per 1,000 was 10.9, representing very little change for four years; the divorce rate of 4.4 had jumped from 3.5 in 1970. Infant mortality was 17.7 per 1,000 live births in 1973, the lowest rate ever for this country; the estimated 1974 rate of 16.5 is even lower.

In 1973, blacks constituted 11.3 percent of the total population (but over 14 percent of those under age 15); other racial and ethnic strains constituted 1.4 percent. Two-thirds of the population is Protestant, one-fourth Roman Catholic, 3 percent Jewish. The remainder have other or no religious affiliations.

In fiscal 1973 the gross national product was $1,294.9 billion, the total personal consumption expenditure $805.2 billion, the per capita personal disposable income $4,295. The corresponding 1974 totals (provisional data) were: gross national product, $1,396.7 billion; personal consumptive expenditure, $877 billion; per capita disposable personal income, $4,623.

The gross average weekly salary in private sector production in 1973 was $144.32 for 37 hours of work. Salaries have grown with recent inflation. Unemployment in 1973 averaged 4.9 percent, rising to 5.6 percent in 1974. By January 1975 the unemployment rate was 8.2 percent: 5.2 percent for family heads, 20.8 percent for teenagers, 13.4 percent for non-whites. Median family income in 1973 was $12,050; median income for individuals was $4,134. Median white family income was $12,600 and median black family income $7,270. Table A-1 indicates income distribution. The percentage of aggregate income by each fifth of families in 1973 was as follows: lowest fifth, 5.5 percent; second fifth, 11.9 percent; third fifth, 17.5 percent; fourth fifth, 24.0 percent; highest fifth, 41.1 percent; top twentieth, 15.5 percent; all below median ($12,050), 25.5 percent.[2]

Table A-1. Families and Unrelated Individuals by Total Money Income (1973)

Income interval	Families	Unrelated individuals
	% of total population	
(Under $1,500)		(14.0)
Under $3,000	6.0	38.1
$3,000–$4,999	8.6	20.0
$5,000–$6,999	9.4	12.8
$7,000–$9,999	14.9	13.5
$10,000–$11,999	10.7	
($10,000 and over)		(15.7)
$12,000–$14,999	14.8	
$15,000 and over	35.5	

Source: U.S. Bureau of the Census, *Current Population Reports*, ser. P-60, No. 97: *Money Income 1973 of Families and Persons in the United States* (Washington, D.C.: GPO, 1975), tables 10, 21, 22, 29.

Poverty data are reported in the United States with reference to a "line" which adjusts to family size, region, farm or nonfarm residence. The line is updated every few years. Its key element is the cost of a standard food budget and the relationship of that to other fixed living costs. The low-income (poverty) line for a family of four was $5,038 in 1974, $4,540 in 1973, $4,137 in 1972, $3,968 in 1970, and $2,973 in 1959.

Poverty totals and percentages declined dramatically from the mid-1960s, when the antipoverty programs began, until the inflation and recession of the past several years. The following poverty totals are representative: 1962, 38,265,000 (21 percent of the population); 1972, 29,900,000 (15.6 percent); 1973, 22,973,000 (11.1 percent); 1975 (estimated), 27,100,000 (12.7 percent).[3] The declines of the 1960s were probably more the result of economic growth than of targeted efforts. Poverty affects far larger proportions of minority populations. Thus, while black rates declined too, from 49.6 to 32.5 to 31.2 percent from the midsixties to the midseventies, the black rate remained almost three times that of whites.

The highest probability for poverty occurs among black female-headed households with children, among farm laborer families, and for black urban widows. The next highly vulnerable groups—but with far lower probability—are (in descending order) white urban widows, college students, street corner youth, rural widows and their families, inner-city families, unskilled workers and their families.[4] In 1974, 15.5 percent of all U.S. children, a total of 10.2 million, lived in poverty families.

Government

The federal system in the United States involves a constantly shifting balance among the powers, resources, and roles of local, state, and national governments. There is also an observable series of historical shifts within each level among executive, judicial, and legislative branches.

The government spends 21.4 percent of the country's total product of goods and services, its GNP, of which 19.0 percent is direct federal expenditure and 2.4 percent goes to state and local governments. States, in turn, spend 8.5 percent of the GNP, of which 5.4 percent is direct state expenditure and 3.0 percent goes to local government. These units of government obtain their revenues, in turn, from the individual income tax (33 percent), corporate income tax (12 percent), social security tax (15 percent), excise and sales taxes (15 percent), property tax (11 percent), other taxes (13 percent).[5] A variety of nonuniform and separately negotiated regional structures and special district arrangements between and within states provide vehicles for local jurisdictions to cooperate and share resources for such purposes as water supply, waste disposal, law enforcement, institutional care.

In the social services, broadly defined, the national government operates directly programs for veterans, federal personnel, Indians, and violators of federal law, and also carries out certain research efforts in health as well as administering the major standardized income maintenance programs (Old Age, Survivors, Disability, and Hospital Insurance; Supplementary Security Income for the aged and disabled). States administer unemployment insurance (apart from special federal programs for veterans, railroad workers, and government employees) and workmen's compensation (here, too, there are three federal programs). Other programs of income maintenance, medical care for the needy, education, child care, direct delivery of goods and services, housing, personal social services, correctional programs, food stamps, and surplus foods are delivered by either state or local governments (often with partial or complete federal funding), or by the voluntary sector acting for them—depending upon the governmental structure within a given state and the relevant federal requirements.

Traditionally, social services have been state or local concerns but federal funding patterns, research and demonstration grants, and efforts to help cities directly led to increased federal action and initiative on the one hand or federal bypassing of states on the other, especially between 1964 and 1970. State prerogatives were reestablished somewhat over the past several years, but federal involvement remains large and federal influence considerable as a result of the substantial federal part in overall funding, the advance approval of "plans" (as required by legislation in many fields), and the continuation of project and research-demonstration funding (usually involving a direct application to Washington and continued project surveillance by federal officials—and sometimes including direct city or county application and operation).

The federal government grants-in-aid to states and localities have increased rapidly over the past decade. The $43.1 billion total for 1973 was distributed in the following categories: general revenue sharing (only a small part to social services), 15.3 percent; public assistance, 27.6 percent; health, 2.5 percent; education, 10.1 percent; economic opportunity and manpower, 8.4 percent; miscellaneous social welfare, 13.1 percent. Other categories were highways, urban affairs, agriculture, miscellaneous.[6]

The administration of President Richard Nixon advocated a rearrangement of prerogatives, on the premise that Washington is better at collecting taxes than at direct administration of programs. Under the title New Federalism, it proposed that federal revenues be shared with the states on both an "open-ended" basis ("general revenue sharing") and in several specific fields ("special revenue sharing"). A general revenue-sharing bill passed in 1972 allocated $30.2 billion for a five-year period to state and local governments.

Variations on special revenue sharing were enacted in the fields of manpower, housing, health resources planning, and the general social services (see Title XX, below). The administration of President Gerald Ford has followed a similar policy.

As the Congress has attempted to deal with this approach through hearings and legislative action, and as the executive branch has sought to specify its own proposals in the form of legislative drafts or administrative regulations, difficult issues have arisen with reference to: (1) the guarding of national responsibility and commitment, on the one hand while permitting diversity and flexibility in accord with the state and local preferences and priorities, on the other (How does general or special revenue sharing assure policy direction?); (2) the implementation of standard-setting and accountability if grants are to be general purpose (What form of auditing is reasonable?); (3) the assurance of certain essential programs in each jurisdiction (Should states or localities deny citizens, even if they are locally in the minority, certain programs deemed essential by the Congress?); and (4) the encouragement of planning, coordination, efficiency, coherence of programs (Is the New Federalism consistent with the parallel recognition of the price of fragmentation, lack of system-network, etc.?)

The debate is ongoing and shifting. Interest groups on the national and state levels, even powerful interest groups, fear "too much" revenue sharing since they believe that categorical legislative enactments at the national level and the related requirements that states operate specific programs at the state or local levels protect their own interests. Public officials, too, even local officials, do not necessarily favor "decategorization," since they must deal with local employee groups and consumer-client interest groups, which see their own security as tied to categorical requirements. It is also alleged that when the moment comes for the translation of the principles of New Federalism into specific statutes and regulations, both the executive branch and federal agencies find it difficult fully to give up some of their own high-priority policy interests and program objectives. The policy reports and program analyses on individual topics reflect this unresolved, ongoing debate.

In recent years, overall appropriation legislation for major departments and programs in the social sector have often been delayed well beyond the start of the fiscal year because of differences between Congress and President about specific policy and general fiscal-monetary matters. Also, the Congress has enacted ("authorized") major new social initiatives and then delayed appropriation. Finally, determined to keep overall expenditures within defined limits as part of his economic policy, or to block specific program expenditures as part of his social policy, President Nixon, during his term, refused to release ("impounded") certain funds appropriated by the Congress.

As this volume reveals throughout, the effects of such developments have been considerable at the local level: programming instability and uncertainty; last-minute funding, which results in wastefulness and poor implementation; an inhibition to long-range local and state planning; opportunistic shifting of staffs and program foci.

A number of developments may promise improvement of this situation. The courts have begun to constrain the impounding of funds and the executive branch is releasing appropriated monies, if gradually. More basically, while the United States has no formal planning machinery corresponding to planning ministries or departments in some countries, the Congress has enacted major legislation to strengthen its money-authorization and allocation processes. In general, a budgetary planning capability has been created in the Congress to match that in the executive ("Congressional Budget Office"). A mechanism now exists to develop and to enact a congressional budget ceiling and to keep the authorizations-appropriations within such ceilings, reconciling differences between the houses and among various committees in competition for resources. The ceilings define congressional response to the executive budget. Changes are made in deliberate, systematic fashion as the year proceeds. While major differences about fiscal or monetary policy, or about sound federal-state relationships, could continue to create budgetary stalemates, the new structures and procedures may permit better use of the budgetary process for overall planning purposes, both by the executive and by the legislative branches.

At several points in recent decades, the Council of Economic Advisors has played a significant, if partial, planning role, but its scope is once again narrow. Planning in most fields of domestic and foreign policy by congressional committees, regulatory boards, and departments, in their programing and budgetary efforts, is considerable, if often disjointed, uncoordinated, and somewhat spasmodic. Special commissions, task forces, and committees, official and semi-official, are constantly at work, with similar results. A demand for management effectiveness has created an incentive for some departmental and executive branch planning over the past decade.

The Department of Health, Education, and Welfare, for example, has added substantially to its staffs for policy development, programing, and fiscal planning, and has experimented with a planning system related to budgeting and emphasizing cost-benefit studies (PPBS) and with another system known as "management by objective." It also has been utilizing a variety of operations-research and systems-analysis techniques. The Office of the Secretary of the Department has a program evaluation and development staff, as have the large subunits (education, social security, and the rest) and the major bureaus and agencies under them. Indeed, some problems of coordinating evaluation and planning have developed.

Since the late 1960s, much emphasis has been placed upon program and project evaluation, as well, and congressional mandates often require the funding of evaluation contracts in relation to major program initiatives. (A specified percentage of the research-demonstration budget is being reserved for evaluation.) Private consulting organizations or university centers have taken on such proposals with mixed results. There has also been major, large-scale, controlled social experimentation in connection with proposals for new income-maintenance programs, new approaches to organizing schools, initiatives in health delivery, and so on. Several have paid off well for planning, even though much of the research and reporting has been unfocused and the outside evaluations from management consultation firms often have been of little use.

Whether they request funds for special projects or research-demonstration or apply for grants-in-aid on an ongoing basis, states are in constant contact with Washington bureaus and departments. Some states and a few cities maintain ongoing liaison and lobbying staffs in the capital. Normally, however, the appropriate department or division personnel in the state confer with their federal counterparts, submit applications to them, and respond to their auditing and inspection requirements. Over the past decade, the federal government has created a regional structure, and many of the negotiation, review, and auditing functions are decentralized to that structure. However, the role of the regions (ten in number for most purposes) varies by department or bureau and changes over time with the cabinet officers and top department personnel. In general, true decentralization to the region is rare, and local jurisdictions often find it possible and profitable to deal directly with Washington and to consider regional clearance a ritual, though there are important exceptions.

In the human services, serious efforts at coordination on the regional level among DHEW subunits and between them and Labor, Housing and Urban Development, and antipoverty program personnel have been frequent and sometimes profitable. Formal clearance procedures, designed in Washington, have at times encouraged the effort. But none of this has dealt basically with program fragmentation and lack of coordination at the planning, administration, and service delivery levels—despite considerable official concern (see Chapter 7).

Thus far administrative devices, regional structures, revenue sharing, and planning incentives which permit a measure of program "decategorization" (as in the health field) have not overcome the fact that social programs have developed incrementally over a long period of time, are generally limited to categories of people or problems or needs and are seldom reintegrated or consolidated in a basic way. DHEW is said to have three hundred major programs. See Chapter 7 for a statement by a previous DHEW secretary concerning fragmentation.

In general, government programs are formally organized and highly structured. To assure the quality of personnel and avoid politicization, the original Social Security Act required that employees be selected through merit systems ("civil service"). Similar legislative requirements at state and local levels in other fields, including most "social sector" programs, means that most permanent personnel are appointed after written and/or oral examinations, formal evaluation of education, relevant experience or a combination of these. (Special "credits" may be given to veterans and others at certain times.) Temporarily funded programs and all programs in their start-up periods may appoint provisional personnel under a looser system.

The Social Services

An Overview

Although most of the social service programs we discuss here (or "social welfare," or "social sector," or "social" programs—depending on usage) are within the domain of DHEW, there is no cabinet department without some social service impact or responsibility, and several have major roles. For example, Agriculture is involved with food stamps and commodities, Commerce with local economic development and job creation, Defense with social services for military personnel, HUD with public housing and with community development, Interior with major recreation resources, Justice with correctional programs and prevention, Labor with manpower programs, State with international cooperation and exchanges, Transportation with the impact of highway construction on community life, Treasury with the family impact of tax policy, including tax deductions for child care. There is a separate Veterans Administration with responsibilities in income maintenance, health, education, and social service generally.

A measure of coordination is achieved periodically at the White House level by a Domestic Council (whose role has shifted with the White House staffing situation) and a currently powerful Office of Management and Budget, which combines budget-making and control with administrative oversight and policy planning. In some senses it is an instrument for considerable domestic sector planning, the degree varying by administration and personnel.

Some planning initiative and policy coherence in the social sector is also achieved (or an ongoing struggle with the Office of the President is carried out) through the activities of major, powerful standing committees and subcommittees of the Congress which concern themselves with social security, income maintenance, health, education, manpower, and related matters. Especially important in the House, from this perspective, are two committees: Education and Labor, and Ways and Means, and their major subcommittees. In the Senate there is the Committee on Labor and Public Welfare. Each chamber also has powerful committees on Appropriations and Rules.

DHEW, truly a superagency, has five major units, large enough to be designated as cabinet-level departments in some countries (see Figure A-1). The *Social Security Administration* is responsible for social insurance and medical-hospital insurance (Medicare) and Supplementary Security Income. *The Public Health Service* covers the Center for Disease Control; the Food and Drug Administration, Health Resources Administration; the Health Services Administration; the National Institutes of Health; the Alcohol, Drug Abuse, and Mental Health Administration; and the President's Council on Physical Fitness. The *Social and Rehabilitation Service* is responsible for a variety of personal-general social services, for Aid to Families with Dependent Children, and for Medicaid, a means-tested medical program.* The *Education Division* includes the Office of Education and National Institute of Education. And the *Office of Human Development*, in the Office of the Secretary, is responsible for social services for several special groups (children, the aged, the physically handicapped, Indians, youth).

*The "social" and "rehabilitation" aspects recently were split by legislation, the latter moving to the Office of Human Development.

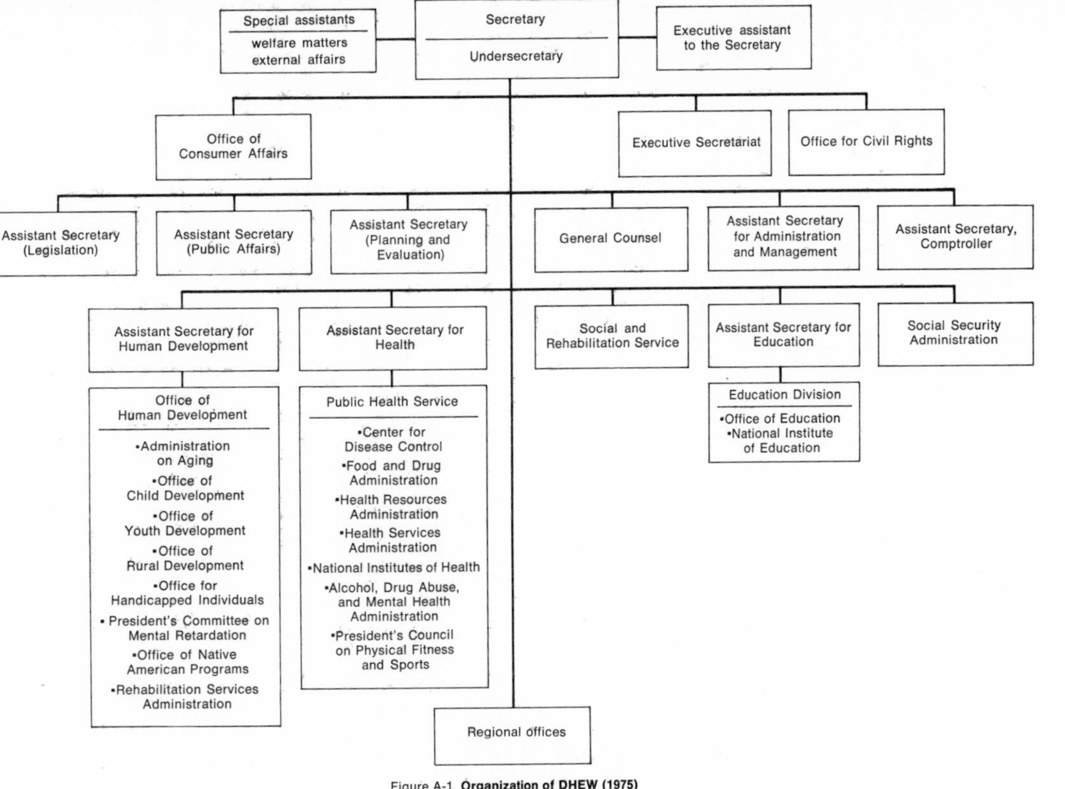

Figure A-1. **Organization of DHEW (1975)**

We may summarize the scale of the U.S. social service commitment, clarify classifications used at the federal level, describe the relative roles of the public and voluntary sectors, and review the roles of federal, state, and local government by summarizing expenditure data as assembled by the research staff of the Social Security Administration.

In 1973 the United States spent over two thousand million dollars ($214.2 billion) on governmental social welfare programs, or the equivalent of $1,002 per person.[7] The 1974 total was $242.4 billion, or $1,126 per capita. This expenditure amounted to 18 percent of the gross national product in 1974, and 17.5 percent in 1973, compared with 17.5 percent in 1972 and 11.8 percent in 1965. If private expenditures are included, the total for 1973 was $299 billion, or 24.5 percent of the GNP, and for 1974 the overall total was $336.3 billion, or 25 percent of GNP.*

Over half of the federal budget (52 percent) is now assigned to social welfare. The proportion grew from 47 percent in 1972.† Overall government spending for social welfare during the same period went from 53 to 55 percent of the total expenditures for all levels of government.

The role of the federal government in this field continues to grow since it commands the bulk of the revenue sources. In 1974, 58 percent of all government social spending came from federal revenue and special trust funds and 42 percent from local government. The federal share varies by field: social insurance, 83.8 percent; public aid, 63.2 percent; health and medical programs, 57.0 percent; veteran's programs, 99.7 percent; education, 11.1 percent; housing, 82.6 percent; "other social welfare" (general social services), 54.4 percent. The proportion of all federal, state, and local budgets assigned to social welfare totaled 56 percent in 1973, having grown steadily from 42 percent in 1965. The expenditures on the federal level were 52.1 percent of all federal expenditures. On the lower tiers, social welfare commanded 62.6 percent of the expenditures of state and local government. Of the 1974 expenditures, 38 percent were from trust funds accumulated through earmarked funds or contributions. However, "discretionary" expenditures for social welfare shared the rise, from

*While we here also report increases for fiscal 1974, much of the increase represented inflation. The 1973–74 increase was actually the smallest real increase since 1960.

†Even if trust fund expenditures are left out, the social welfare rise has been from 38 to 45 percent between 1970 and 1972 of all governmental expenditures or from 24 to 35 of federal expenditures.

34 percent of such government resources in 1965 to 45 percent in 1974.

Given the public expansion, private expenditure declined proportionately (from 36 percent of all social welfare in 1965 to 29 percent in 1974). Private sources dominated only the field of health expenditures.

U.S. social welfare expenditure patterns are not unlike those of other major industrial countries. Social security expenditures as a portion of gross national product lag, however, since we alone do not have a children's allowance and since most countries have elaborate cash sickness benefits for short-term illness for wage and salary workers, as well as general health insurance.[8]

Public social welfare expenditures, 71 percent of the total, dominate income maintenance, education, and the general social services (in the sense of this study, even though often called "welfare" in official reports), and federal funds cover 58 percent of these public expenditures. Private expenditures include direct consumer payments in health and education, expenditures of private employee-benefit plans (especially group health and life insurance), private health insurance, all expenditures through private philanthropy in the general social services and related fields, and in-plant health services in industry.

The authors of the historical expenditures series from which the above data derive offer the following by way of explanation:

> Social welfare, as defined for this series, is intended to embrace those public programs that directly contribute to or are concerned with the well-being of individuals and families with respect to basic human needs in the areas of income maintenance, health, welfare, education, and housing. In the health area, because of their direct importance for personal health care, the definition also includes public health control activities, consumer protection, and other programs that affect or are designed to improve health conditions in general.
>
> . . . The economic status of the individual or family receiving benefits is not a criterion under the definition. . . . Furthermore, the public program does not necessarily have to involve a government subsidy. . . . An included program may be financed either through general revenues, earmarked taxes, or voluntary contributions.[9]

There are a number of major program categories, the exact total depending on how detailed the breakdown, which have their counterparts in most countries and which are generally recognizable as defining the social welfare domain (or what might be called "the social sector," "social program," or—in the British sense—"social services"). They are social insurance, public aid (public assistance or social assistance), health and medical programs, veterans' programs, education, housing, manpower-employment, and "other social welfare" (close to the personal social services, in the British sense).*

We have assembled Table A-2 from the Skolnik-Dales analysis for 1973 and the framework of the Merriam-Skolnik monograph already cited. Several observations are of special interest—in the sense of providing a backdrop for our examination of the personal social services. First, and central, is the large and growing United States commitment to programs and benefits similar to those in most other major industrialized countries. Whatever the continued rhetoric about the "dangers" of welfare-state social welfare aid by government, the United States has found it no less necessary than have other urbanized, industrialized, complex societies to offer protection against predictable risks, assure an underpinning of personal security under all occupational and social statuses, offer a "floor" of socialization-education-health-housing-food-income to all residents, open opportunity to its deprived and its handicapped, enact and implement certain concepts of social justice and fairness, and protect itself against—or control—dangerous and unacceptable deviance. There is a debate as to how important these several different motives are or should be, and the facts suggest that different institutions and programs are defined and regarded in different ways. In any case, the programs extend into the entire population and very few are limited to the poor or the deviant. The expenditures for DHEW at the federal level have for several years exceeded those for defense and related activities, as already noted (see Table A-3).

Moreover, although a given president or party will be more or less enthusiastic about specific programs, their rate of growth, and the details of their character and philosophy, the long-term trend is toward growth, expansion, greater coverage, and a larger public role. Growth has been exceptionally rapid since 1965. In the 1965–74 period, public expenditures for this purpose have tripled, showing an annual growth rate of 13.6 percent, outdistancing the inflation very considerably—until 1974.[10] The largest rise was in public aid, social insurance, health expenditures—when one includes Medicaid and Medicare (see below). General social services showed a slightly better-than-average growth.

*Employment-manpower is not included in the social welfare expenditures services.

Table A-2. Social Welfare Expenditures in the United States (fiscal years 1973–74)

Type of expenditure	Total public expenditures (mill. of $)	From federal funds (mill. of $)	From state or local funds (mill. of $)	Per capita (public only) (mill. of $)	Public (% of GNP)	Federal (% of total)	Public (% of total)	All expenditures*: Percent of GNP	All expenditures*: Millions of dollars
Total	214,178.9 242,386.3	122,533.6 139,579.9	91,645.3 102,806.4	1,001.65 1,125.59	17.5 18.0	57.2 57.6	70.2 71.1	24.5 24.9	300,687 336,266
Social insurance	86,117.8 98,502.0	72,232.4 82,508.0	13,885.4 15,994.0	401.83 456.41	7.0	83.9	85.4†	9.1†	112,050†
Public aid	28,697.0 33,628.1	18,066.7 21,237.3	10,630.3 12,390.8	134.58 156.58	2.3 2.5	63.0 63.2	85.4	9.3	126,035
Health and medical programs	12,639.5 14,054.4	6,697.7 8,005.0	5,941.8 6,049.4	59.28 65.44	1.0 1.0	53.0 57.0	38.0 39.6	7.7 7.8	94,234 104,240
Veterans' programs	12,951.5 13,922.7	12,903.3 13,877.7	48.3 45.0	60.13 64.19	1.1 1.0	99.6 99.7			
Education	65,257.6 72,763.1	7,389.1 8,045.8	57,868.5 64,717.3	305.91 338.66	5.3 5.4	11.3 11.1	83.6 83.9	6.6 6.7	81,237 90,525
Housing	2,180.3 2,581.7	1,750.4 2,131.7	429.9 450.0	9.01	0.2	80.3 82.6			
Other social welfare	6,335.2 6,934.2	3,494.0 3,774.2	2,841.2 3,160.0	29.71 32.29	0.5 0.5	55.2 54.4	85.1 86.2	1.4 1.5	17,394 20,265
GNP (bill. of $)	1,294.9 1,397.3								

Source: Office of Research and Statistics Social Security Administration, *Social Security Bulletin*, Jan. 1974 and Jan. 1975. Top figure for each type is for 1973; bottom figure is for 1974.

*NET-adjusted to omit duplication from use of public and private social welfare funds for medical care and education service.

†All income maintenance.

Table A-3. Major Categories of Federal Expenditure

Category	Expenditures (% of total)					
	1950	1960	1970	1973	1974	1975 (est.)
Social Welfare						
Cash income maintenance	15.2	22.3	23.3	29.7	30.3	32.2
Helping people buy essentials*	6.3	1.2	3.4	9.3	10.1	10.9
Social program grants†	0.7	1.4	4.5	6.0	5.3	6.0
Defense, space, and foreign affairs	41.8	53.7	44.6	33.5	33.0	31.6

Source: The Budget of the U.S. Government as compiled in The Brookings Institution, *Setting National Priorities: The 1974 Budget* (Washington, D.C.: The Institution, 1974), p. 5, and *1975* (1974), p. 6.

*Housing grants, Medicare, food stamps, tax benefits for homeowners, etc.

†Vocational education, manpower training, health services, urban renewal, aid to specific elementary and secondary education projects, grants to states for social services, etc.

The following listing, prepared for a congressional committee report, will serve as orientation to the "cash" and "in kind" income transfer programs in the United States.[11]

Cash Transfer Programs

Non-income-tested social insurance and related programs
- Old-age, survivors, and disability insurance (OASDI)
- Railroad retirement benefits—retirement, disability, and survivor's insurance
- Federal-state unemployment compensation system
- Railroad unemployment insurance
- Trade readjustment allowances (TRA)
- Compensation to veterans with a service-connected disability
- Death compensation and dependency and indemnity compensation to survivors of veterans for service-connected deaths
- Special benefits for disabled coal miners

Income-tested cash transfer programs
- Supplemental security income for the aged, blind, and disabled (SSI)
  - federal SSI Program
  - state supplementation of the federal SSI benefit
- Aid to families with dependent children (AFDC)
- Pensions for veterans with non-service-connected disabilities
- Pensions for widows and children of veterans
- General assistance to Indians
- Assistance to Cuban refugees

In-Kind Programs

Health care: Non-income-tested
- Medicare—hospital insurance (HI)

Medicare—supplementary medical insurance (SMI)
Indian health services

Health care: Income-tested
Health assistance for veterans with non-service connected health needs
Medicaid (MA)
Public health services to individuals

Housing: Income-tested
U.S. Department of Housing and Urban Development Programs:
Low-rent public housing
Section 235 homeownership assistance for low-income families
Section 101 rent supplement program (Housing and Urban Development Act of 1965)
Section 236 interest reduction payments—Rental and cooperative housing for lower income families
Section 8 lower income housing assistance
U.S. Department of Agriculture Programs
Section 502 USDA low- to moderate-income housing loans (Housing Act of 1949)
Section 515 rural rental housing loans
Farm labor housing loans and grants
U.S. Department of the Interior Programs
Indian housing improvement program

Housing: Non-income tested
Housing assistance for veterans
Other housing programs

Food programs
Food stamp program
National school lunch program

Other Programs

Programs for federal employees
Income maintenance provisions for federal civilian employees
Military retirement

State and local programs
State and local government employee retirement programs
State workmen's compensation programs and temporary disability programs
General assistance (GA)

Cash Transfers

Of the total of $126,035 million, the income maintenance item in Table A-2, largest expenditure is federal. Virtually the entire labor force is covered and eligible for cash benefits under *social insurance* for retirement, death, survivorship, disability. (Nine of ten people in paid employment and self-employment are currently covered; of recent retirees, only 7 percent were not eligible for some benefits.) The program is federally administered. The bulk of the population is covered by the basic Social Security system, but there are specially designated programs for railroad workers and some public employees. The program is financed by a payroll tax involving employer and employee contributions, and a relatively small amount of general tax revenue. In 1972 the Congress added an automatic cost-of-living clause to the legislation. Also among the insurances are state-administered unemployment insurance, workmen's compensation (invalidity insurance), and state temporary disability insurance.

In 1972–73, when the social insurances paid out some $86 billion, *public assistance* expended $28.7 billion. Well over one-third of the public assistance costs were carried by state and locality. Effective January 1, 1974, however, several major categorical programs—previously run by state and local governments with the help of federal grants-in-aid—were transferred to federal operation, with optional state supplementation, including what had been public assistance programs for the aged, disabled, blind. Under a new title, Supplementary Security Income (SSI), this supplementary benefit, a means-tested program, will only gradually be fully defined in a legal sense. It partakes of both guaranteed income (grant levels are specified by law) and social assistance (means test, asset review, etc.) and is administered within the Social Security Administration. The remaining major public assistance program is Aid to Families with Dependent Children, administered on the state and local level with federal grants-in-aid based on a complex formula favoring poor states. States and localities may also operate a residual "general assistance" with no federal matching (for adults or families in need who do not fit any categories) and a state supplement to SSI. The benefit picture is summarized in Table A-4.

Variations in benefit levels among states for the categories not federalized are considerable, reflecting state cost levels, fiscal capacity, and attitudes toward public assistance recipients.

Another perspective on coverage is provided by figures summarizing fringe benefit coverage and financial and health service arising out of employment status. These fringe benefits are separate from OASDHI, the Social Security systems. Public and private employees are included. In 1970, of the workers taking part in employee benefit plans, 69.4 percent were covered for life insurance and death benefits, 52.1 percent for accidental death and dismemberment, 80.2 percent for hospitalization, 79.2 percent for surgical fees, 71.1 percent for

Table A-4. Current Income Maintenance (1974)

Type of beneficiary	Benefits in current-payment status	
	Number	Average amount ($)
OASDHI cash benefits in current-payment status*		
Total monthly beneficiaries	30,853,979	
Retired workers and dependents	19,409.560	
Retired workers	15,958,492	188.21
Wives and husbands	2,826,022	95.76
Children	625,046	70.01
Disabled workers and dependents	3,911,951	
Disabled workers	2,236,928	205.69
Wives and husbands	411,795	61.89
Children	1,263,228	56.37
Survivors of deceased workers	7,254.228	
Widowed mothers	573,557	134.23
Children	2,888,046	126.51
Widows and widowers	3,677,477	177.29
Disabled widows and widowers	92,126	125.87
Parents	23,022	157.52
Special age-72 beneficiaries	278,240	
Primary	273,336	64.12
Wives	4,904	32.18
Lump-sum death payments	1,269,829	253.86
Other cash benefits		
Unemployment insurance		
Av. weekly insured unemployment†	1,989,242	62.93 weekly
Supplementary Security Income†		
Aged	2,115,358	146.00 indiv.‡
Blind	73,951	219.00 couple
Disabled	1,464,157	
Aid to Families with Dependent Children†		
Families	3,190,046	240.70
Children	7,731,295	60.80 per capita
Total recipients	10,740,609	
General assistance (state and local)†		
Cases	517,764	132.24
Recipients	750,336	91.25 per capita
Emergency assistance§		
Families	26,697	116.34

Source: Date from reports of the Social Security Administration.

*Calendar year 1974.

†July 1974.

‡The SSI guarantee set nationally in the original law was $130 for individuals and $195 for couples. It was raised to $140–$210 as of Jan. 1, 1974, as Congress responded to the inflation and raised social insurance benefits. On July 1, 1974, the rate became $146–$219. There is state supplementation federally administered or state administered, as well, adding close to ⅓ to expenditures, operative in 33 states, covering 41 percent of all SSI recipients and averaging $72.15 monthly in the period covered.

§22 states-territories, mid-1974.

regular medical expenses, 35.8 percent for major medical expenses, 50.7 percent for temporary disability (including formal sick leave), and 48.3 percent for retirement.[12] All except the last two categories include public and private employment; the figures for temporary disability and retirement are only for private employment.

Unemployment insurance loads vary with the unemployment rate and depend on whether individuals have exhausted their coverage and whether coverage is extended because unemployment rates are high and, thus, no jobs are believed available. About three-quarters of the work force is variously covered, with rules and coverage length and amount varying by state. Also administered on a state basis is workmen's compensation (invalidity insurance), covering about 85 percent of the work force.

In 1928–29, before the Great Depression, social insurance was limited largely to workmen's compensation and public employee retirement, while public assistance was a state responsibility. The present system was essentially created in the mid-1930s, with several major coverage increases occurring over time in the insurance categories and more generous and broader coverage in the assistances, the latter depending upon state take-up and matching of federal grants-in-aid. Social insurance expenditure totals for as recently as 1949–50 were under $5 billion, and that was double the public assistance costs. By 1964–65 social insurances paid out $28 billion and public assistance over $6 billion. By 1968–69 the social insurance expenditure total had reached $48.7 billion and public assistance $13.4 billion. Although the insurance growth has been greater than that for assistance, insurance is seen as part of an acceptable, popular approach to meeting need related to predictable and socially accepted risks. The public assistance rise ($16.5 billion in 1969–70, $21.3 billion in 1970–71, $26 billion in 1971–72), was largely concentrated in the unpopular AFDC category (three-fourths of the assistance cases), which covered many unmarried, deserted, separated mothers and their children; the public and the political leadership responded with concern, anger, and determination to put a stop to the process. Nonetheless, despite a variety of work-incentive reforms, job training requirements, and stringent audit rules—and a consequent end to the growth in the rolls (causation is here quite unclear)—the program remains essentially intact and more basic social assistance reform for mothers, families, and/or children is still under debate. In the meantime the adult categories of assistance have been taken over for federal operation.[13]

Thus, each county or smaller jurisdiction has a federal Social Security office, which is also the entry point for SSI, the adult assistances; it has a state-operated employment office, the contact point for unemployment insurance; and it has a state or local public welfore or public assistance office (depending on whether the system is state-operated or delegates operation to the locality), for general assistance and AFDC, and perhaps for supplementary aid to the aged, blind, disabled. (As we have seen, the state public assistance office or its locally delegated public welfare office was in the past also the center of various public social services. In the past several years, money and service have been administratively separated to some extent, but not completely, and that separation has been done differently in different jurisdictions.) In administrative arrangements or grant levels, no two state programs are the same, since the states do their own "needs" computation for assistance, take more or less advantage of matching funds, and meet either all of the "need" as thus computed, or only a portion, if state treasuries lack resources or are not given state legislative assent.

According to Levitan's analysis, "cash transfers account for approximately 45 percent of all income received by the poor and about 5 percent of that of the nonpoor." OASDHI benefits alone reached one family in four in 1973 (or one in eight Americans on all levels). The program redistributes income from higher-paid to lower-paid retirees and from the current working generation to previously working generations. Despite the label it is not an insurance program in the true sense.[14]

In 1970 about 4.7 million people were collecting some benefits, at various levels, from private pension plans. Half of all those receiving wages and salaries are covered by pension or profit-sharing plans and one-third of new retirees will be receiving benefits soon. In general, coverage has been low and, until recent legislation, there was very limited vesting of rights for employees who changed jobs or had limited tenure. Private pensions do represent significant income guarantees upon retirement for middle- and upper-income workers.

For several decades after the 1930s, public officials and social work professionals stressed cash and opposed food benefits in kind. Nonetheless, especially in low-grant states, a commodity program (tied to agriculture policy and disposition of surplus) remained important. During the decade beginning in the mid-sixties, as poverty facts were disseminated and the nutritional problems of the aged and of children underscored, there was an enormous increase in school-meal programs for children and congregate eating for retired adults and, especially, in the distribution of food stamps. The latter program involves the right for low-income and public-assistance recipients to purchase stamps worth considerably more than cost for food purchases. The latter program in particular has become a significant supplement to income-maintenance programs, and in some senses an alternative to more basic income-maintenance reform.

Fifteen million Americans were using food stamps at an annual cost of $2.9 billion in fiscal 1974. As the 1975 recession and unemployment deepened, there were 19 million participants and an expenditure rate approaching $6 billion, an enormous rise in a few years. This growth is explained, in part, by congressional support of in-kind benefits while refusing any social assistance reform to help families and, in part, by a new readiness by the low-income work force to draw upon this benefit during the 1974–75 recession. As the totals grew, Congress discussed cutbacks; it had not intended such widespread enrollment.

Health and Medical Programs

In the past, the major public commitment to provision of health care in the United States has been through Veterans Administration hospitals and the Public Health Service (prevention and research). The modern era in public health and medical programs began with legislation in 1965 creating the Medicare and Medicaid programs. Substantial implementation began on July 1, 1966. Two other federal initiatives, the Regional Medical Program and Comprehensive Health Planning, enacted in 1966, have had some limited impact on state and local health planning, project initiation, and coordination, being more visible and effective in some parts of the country than in others. In addition, the antipoverty program of the mid-1960s generated a limited number of neighborhood health centers, which provided comprehensive coverage in a few areas, but were mainly designed to demonstrate an approach to service. These centers were sponsored by OEO and other federal agencies. DHEW has sponsored a variety of other local family and child health programs.[15]

The overall distribution of the health cost burden in 1972 is summarized by Mueller:

> Total national expenditures for personal health care (excluding expenditures for insurance premiums and administrative expenses of public programs, as well as for research, construction, and government public health activities and fund-raising expenses of philanthropic organizations) amounted to $76.5 billion in 1972. Private health insurance met 25.5

percent of this amount (compared with 25.9 percent in 1971); 35.6 percent came from direct out-of-pocket payments by consumers, 37.5 percent was met by public funds, and 1.4 percent came from philanthropy and industry. Thus, in 1972, *private payments by consumers—out-of-pocket and through private health insurance—made up approximately 61 percent of the total national expenditures for personal health care.*[16]

The situation is regarded as unsatisfactory because most private insurance covers hospitalization and, perhaps, physician services within the hospital, but leaves great gaps in coverage for physician service through home and office visits and because its delivery and financial structure offers no incentives to preventive work (see Table A-5). Only half the population has coverage for "major medical" needs (especially catastrophic illness), and most private policies have liability ceilings which limit coverage. Private insurance premium costs, private physician and hospital bills, for all but the briefest episodes of service are major financial burdens to people of average income. Serious illness often becomes a financial catastrophe as well for those above the "medical indigency" means-test level.

Table A-5. Private Health Insurance Coverage (1973)

Service	Percent of population covered	
	All ages	65 and over
Hospital care	75.8	57.4
Physician services		
Surgical	75.1	53.6
In-hospital visits	73.4	41.1
X-ray and lab	73.1	40.8
Office and home	33.5	19.3
Dental care	10.4	1.1
Prescribed drugs (out of hospital)	59.8	18.5
Private duty nursing	56.9	16.8
Visiting nurse	58.7	22.3
Nursing home care	33.1	30.3

Source: This chart and much of the relevant text relies on Nancy L. Worthington, Office of Research and Statistics, Social Security Administration, "National Health Expenditures," as reported in *Social Security Bulletin*, Feb. 1975. The Health Insurance Association of America reports estimates several percentage points higher than those here shown.

Beyond all this, about 20 percent of those over sixty-five have no private health insurance; disproportionate numbers of southerners and poor people are unserved. In fact, 60 percent of older poor people and 40 percent of older blacks are uncovered. For them, the strengthening of public programs is the only hope.

In this context, a major new reform involving some pattern of more general health insurance and incentives to assign more of the personal care delivery to "health maintenance organizations" is being encouraged, explored, debated, and experimented with. Medicare and Medicaid, while they have helped a good deal, are not regarded as meeting the problem, as we have seen.

Medicare constitutes Title XVIII of the Social Security Act and offers health insurance to individuals sixty-five and over covered by social security (now abbreviated as OASDHI, to signify old aged, survivors, disability, and health titles). One part of Medicare, the mandatory part, deals with hospital coverage and related benefits (covering the bulk of costs for up to 90 days of hospitalization, home health services, and extended care in the post-hospitalization period). This section is financed out of matched employer-employee contributions through the payroll tax, as is all of social security. The "voluntary" part, financed by enrollees and the federal government out of general revenues, pays part of the fees of doctors and surgeons, prescription drugs, diagnostic work-ups, and medical supplies. There is a system of deductibles and enrollee payments for each part. Medicaid (see below) pays for all of this for those aged persons who are on public assistance. The "medically needy" above the public assistance level are treated differently in the several states.

As of 1973 there were 20.9 million people aged sixty-five and over covered under Medicare for hospital protection—almost the entire elderly population; similarly, 96 percent of the eligible aged (20.6 million) were covered by the supplementary medical insurance. In 1973, 10.6 million enrollees used one or both reimbursed services one or more times. There were 4.7 million monthly users of hospital benefits and 10.5 monthly beneficiaries of supplementary medical insurance in 1973.

Medicaid, also enacted in 1967, is medical assistance for the poor, and covers some of those above the assistance level, to a point specified in each state. (Early enactments were relatively generous in some states but cutbacks were mandated by the Congress and the states in the face of exploding costs in the late 1960s.) Medicaid is paid for out of federal grants-in-aid, much like public assistance, and there is a variable state matching requirement, 17 to 50 percent (which the state may share with its localities). Medicaid covers all standard medical services. Eligible are those receiving or eligible for public assistance in a state and—depending on state policy— other poor persons at a somewhat higher level who do not receive public assistance. There were 23.5 million beneficiaries in 1973 at a cost of $8.7 billion and a federal share of $4.78 billion.

These programs, supplementing widespread private hospital and health insurance programs, have protected the very poor from the financial consequences of catastrophic illness and have probably assured a much improved base of health coverage for the aged, generally, and for all individuals at the public assistance level or just above it (but this varies by state). Private philanthropy and local government have received a degree of financial relief in many places where previously they offered the only available medical coverage for the poor. However, since Medicare offers no protection against prolonged hospitalization or extremely serious illness, many of the aged have high costs—until their funds are exhausted and they are eligible for Medicaid. Moreover, the programs have been accompanied by a catastrophic inflation of hospital and doctor costs; patients allegedly are often required to supplement coverage to the level of pre-Medicare fees; many population elements—particularly those just above the Medicaid eligibility level—still carry excessive and at times disastrous personal cost burdens; major rises in costs have not been accompanied by increased health coverage or improved care. The cost inflation has been terribly hard on the uncovered. These developments explain the current search for new service delivery mechanisms (health maintenance organizations), the institution of an elaborate peer review structure (to assure that only essential service is given and that it is given well), and a search for an auditing and payment system which will create economy incentives in the hospitals and extended care facilities. They also are behind proposals for more comprehensive health insurance.

By way of summary, then, we may note the growth of the investment in health (see Table A-6). The 1949–50 total was $12 billion. By 1972–73 it was $94 billion, and it was over $100 billion in 1973–74. The 1974 public to private ratio was 55:45. Of the public expenditure in 1972–73, the federal to state-local ratio was 2:1; the federal share was almost 70 percent in 1974. Private health insurance covers about one-fourth the cost of personal health care, while philanthropy and industrial in-plant service covers 1 percent. The governmental share (since Medicare-Medicaid) has leaped from 21 percent in 1965 to 38 percent in 1974. Direct consumer payments, declining to 35 percent in 1974, remain exceedingly heavy by international standards.[17]

The following picture of public medical provision is based on what is known from federal financial payment records: *Medicare* (July 1973) covered 23.5 million aged, disabled, and chronically ill people at an annual expenditure of $9.5 billion, including hospital care involving service to 10.6 million in 1973 and covering some 34 million bills for other-than-hospital care during 1973. *Medicaid* covered 19.1 million poor people (overlapping with Medicare where the individual cannot meet deductibles or where benefits are exhausted), at an expenditure of $4.6 billion.

Table A-6. Health Expenditures

Year	Total (% of GNP)	Public (% of total)	Personal health care (% of total): Private (direct payment)	Personal health care (% of total): Private (insurance)	Personal health care (% of total): Public	Per capita (average) (in $)
1949–50	4.6	25.5	68.3	8.5	20.2	78.35
1959–60	5.2	24.7	55.3	20.7	21.7	141.63
1969–70	7.2	36.5	40.4	24.0	34.2	333.57
1972–73	7.7	38.0	39.6	25.1	36.6	441.94
1973–74	7.7 or 7.8	39.6	35.4	25.6	37.6	485.36

Source: Office of Research and Statistics, Social Security Administration, *Social Security Bulletin*, Jan. 1975, p. 15, and Feb. 1975, p. 5. Percentages do not add up to 100 because of several small omissions.

From the consumers point of view, this constitutes a mixed and complex system. Most individuals use (and pay) their own private physicians, whether general practitioners or specialists. Medicaid and Medicare eligibles have some or all of their bills paid for them. Medicaid adequacy varies by region and state. Individuals in prepaid group systems have most of their hospital bills paid, but little of their home and office medical service is covered. Some have their bills paid by private insurance. Many have a significant part of their bills —usually for surgical and diagnostic procedures—paid by nonprofit group insurance coverage such as Blue Cross–Blue Shield. In some neighborhoods the poor use neighborhood health centers for more or less comprehensive coverage, and may have better care than full-time low-pay workers. When hospitalization is needed, the same complexity is found, but coverage rates for some insurance are larger: Medicare-Medicaid for the poor and those over sixty-five; nonprofit group plans or union fringe plans for many others.

Education

Education has traditionally been a charge upon local government. However, the federal government became involved early in helping in the construction of facilities for vocational education and, then, higher education. It also assisted areas which had special burdens because of the presence of federal facilities, such as army installations. A much broader series of grants and direct federal aid to education was launched in legislation passed in 1965 in response to the challenge of "Sputnik," and, later, to help schools in disadvantaged neighborhoods which were under pressure to desegregate.

The increased investment in education from all sources and from public funds in particular, is recorded in Table A-7.

Table A-7. Public Expenditures for Education

Year	All education expenditures (% of GNP)	All public education expenditures (% of GNP)	Federal funds (% of public expenditure)
1949–50	4.1	2.5	2.3
1954–55	3.7	2.9	4.3
1959–60	4.4	3.6	4.9
1964–65	5.2	4.3	8.8
1968–69	6.0	4.9	11.3
1969–70	6.5	5.3	11.5
1970–71	6.9	5.6	11.6
1971–72	6.8	5.5	11.1
1972–73	6.6	5.3	11.3
1973–74	6.7	5.4	11.1

Source: Alfred M. Skolnik and Sophie R. Dales, "Social Welfare Expenditures, 1972–73," *Social Security Bulletin*, Jan. 1974, and "Social Welfare Expenditures, Fiscal Year 1974," *ibid.*, Jan. 1975.

In general, elementary and secondary education are carried out by boards or departments under local government, largely through local and state financing and—as noted—modest federal aid for specific program purposes. In addition, many students attend private elementary and secondary schools, often under sectarian auspices. In fact, this tendency has grown in the past two decades because of the efforts at desegregation of public education, the large black and Puerto Rican migration to the cities, and an alleged decline in the quality of public education in many cities. Constitutional constraint on public funding of religious education has blocked state or federal financial aid to sectarian schools and state policy has often prohibited aid to nonsectarian private schools, thus forcing them to rely largely upon tuition—despite some grants for materials, equipment, and special programs. A small number of young people also attend elite and expensive boarding schools at the middle and postsecondary levels.

Standards, requirements, and curricula are locally controlled, but within constraints set by state financing and public boards, by the rules of accrediting bodies, by the requirements for admission set by higher institutions, and by court orders related to desegregation, equal opportunity, and rights to education.

Higher education, including technical schools, two-year (community) colleges, and four-year colleges and universities are operated both by local and state government (and financed by tax dollars plus generally modest tuition) and by private bodies. Federal aid at various times has assisted dormitory and building construction, research, and library services in both the public and the private universities. State and federal governments have developed an expanding program of direct student aid, student loans, direct grants related to enrollment—as the percentage of students completing college has reached over 30 percent of secondary school graduates. Nonetheless, the decline in new endowments for private higher education, the great inflation in operating and building costs, and the inability to add further to tuition (which meets 30 to 40 percent of operating costs) has placed many of the leading private universities in financial danger.

Housing

Most U.S. housing is a marketplace activity, not classifiable under social welfare. Nonetheless, especially since World War II, a system of mortgage guarantees, publicly funded, has had a major impact on housing and suburban growth generally. Other initiatives followed as market imperfections and failures have been acknowledged.

In 1969 a major, if vague, federal commitment was undertaken to build or rehabilitate 26 million housing units over the decade. Of these units, 6 million were to be constructed or rehabilitated with federal assistance. Some 20 million units were to be constructed without direct federal assistance but, if necessary, the federal government would intervene to assure a sufficient flow of credit. The direct assistance has been concentrated in five programs: low-rent public housing, rent supplements directed to low-income families, mortgage assistance for low-income families, rental assistance for low-income families, and subsidized loans for rural and small-town borrowers.

The entire effort has lagged. Since the initiative is largely public, the current system of federal program review and the shift to a mix of specialized revenue sharing and more mandated programs are likely to result in considerable change. In addition, while it is not known whether proposals to increase direct housing supplements or mortgage-payment supplements to low-income persons (as contrasted with subsidy and incentives to builders or to local government) will actually materialize, interest has been aroused; implementation would substantially change the United States housing effort.

For the present, an analysis made at the Brookings Institution in the early 1970s serves to sum up the public program.[18]

Favorable tax treatment of homeowners—especially personal income tax deductions related to local real estate taxes and interest payments on mortgages—is most valuable for those with the highest personal incomes. Overall annual federal cost is some $7 billion. Similar benefits accrue to owners of rental property through depreciation in excess of true economic depreciation. This is a very much smaller sum than the tax deductions for taxes and interest.

Federal Housing Administration (FHA) mortgage insurance and Veterans Administration loan guarantees protect lenders and have had major impact on the housing market through relaxation of home financing terms. They have encouraged detached-home suburban expansion, and not multiple-dwelling construction, thereby shaping the character of the housing market, and have favored the middle class over the poor. FHA loans have helped over 8,620,000 families achieve home ownership in the period up to 1970. VA has aided over 7,000,000 families.

Establishment of federal credit institutions has increased the flow of credit to housing (Federal National Mortgage Association, Government National Mortgage Association, Federal Home Loan Mortgage Corporation, Federal Home Loan Bank). Only the second of these "gives explicit subsidies," whereas the others, according to Aaron, "created to improve the operations of the home mortgage market, have since 1966 sought to insulate housing from the full effects of monetary policy and thus to alter income distribution as well as resource allocation."[19]

Low-rent public housing, created through state and local efforts with federal subsidy (except in a few instances), is the major housing program for low-income families. Some 800,000 federally supported units housed 2.5 million people in mid-1970. (Almost half of those in public housing are not receiving public assistance. Not all public housing residents are poor, as formally defined, but the total in the early seventies represented about one-tenth of the poverty population. Public housing in 1970 was 70 percent nonwhite, even though half the entering tenants were white; nonwhites do not move out as rapidly.) Some public housing has a very bad public image, some has created racial-ethnic ghettos, and some has been so badly vandalized as to require abandonment. But Aaron reports that "most projects have extremely low vacancy rates and long waiting lists for admission," since, apparently, the "actual and prospective tenants seem to regard public housing as a better buy than any housing available to them on the free market."[20]

The aids from the federal government are actually diverse, and subject to shifting policies and strategies and differing evaluations: direct loans; annual contributions (the major item); exemption from federal income taxes on bonds; special payments for the elderly, disabled, handicapped and for those displaced under urban renewal, as well as for very large and poor families. Aaron has estimated that, taken together, these measures have given each public-housing household, a small fraction of all low-income households, an average subsidy of $800.

A variety of efforts have been made over the years to help low- or middle-income households buy or rent adequate homes. These several *housing assistance programs*, to use Aaron's term, have relied most heavily on private builders and developers, have deferred the public costs for several decades, have related aid to economic conditions of households, and for the most part have attempted to assist economic and social integration. The two programs longest in operation are (*a*) below-market interest-rate loans on housing for lower middle-income families and (*b*) rent supplements. The newer programs promote (*c*) home ownership and (*d*) rental and cooperative housing for low-income families. The latter three programs tie assistance to income in that personal expenditure of 20 or 25 percent of income is set as a ceiling. However, administrative complexities and alleged abuses have led to the apparent abandonment of program *a* and promise likely ends to *c* and *d*, while *b* may become a large strategy but will focus on the tenant, not the builder. As of 1970, below-market interest-rate loans had resulted in the building of 6,250 units; rent supplements had produced 90,800 units; home-ownership assistance, 106,071 units; and rental assistance, 97,724 units.

Rural home loans, a self-evident category, constitute a large if often unnoticed program of assistance and subsidy to relatively low-income (but not poor) small-town dwellers.

The enactment of a bloc grant program (Housing and Community Development Act of 1974) allows states considerable leeway in repackaging federal funding to meet their own housing program and urban development needs.

Manpower and Employment Programs

Normally assigned to the Department of Labor, but with overlaps with DHEW, especially the Social and Rehabilitation Service and the Office of Education, and often integrated with income maintenance and child care efforts, manpower programs can hardly be claimed organizationally by social service advocates. Nonetheless, some such programs are part of, others coordinate with, and some include general social service components. All this is apart from, if increasingly related to, the state-operated placement and unemployment insurance offices connected with the U.S. Employment Service.

The lead agency is the Manpower Administration of the U.S. Department of Labor. Current programs for the "hard to employ," various training and protected work efforts, and the job creation programs now spend some $4–5 billion in a constantly developing strategy. A Manpower Advisory Committee offers policy guidance and monitors the overall program. (Certain, but not all, of these costs appear in Table A-2 under "other social welfare.")

Levitan's summary of the effort provides a convenient overview. He notes that manpower programs

> included efforts directed to specific categories of clients as well as comprehensive programs with broad eligibility criteria. In varying combinations, the following labor market services are offered:
>
> 1. outreach to identify the untrained and undermotivated as well as intake and assessment to evaluate their needs and abilities;
> 2. adult basic education to remedy the absence or obsolescence of earlier schooling;
> 3. prevocational orientation to expose those of limited experience to alternative occupational choices;
> 4. training persons lacking a rudimentary education for entry-level skills;
> 5. residential facilities for those who live in sparsely populated areas or who have a home environment that would adversely affect attempts to overcome their disadvantages;
> 6. work experience for those unaccustomed to the discipline of the work place;
> 7. creation of public-service jobs to upgrade the skills of the disadvantaged until they can compete for permanent public careers;
> 8. countercyclical creation of public employment opportunities to absorb jobless workers in a high unemployment economy;
> 9. subsidized private employment for the disadvantaged;
> 10. job placement and labor market information services;
> 11. job coaching to work out supervisor-worker relationships once a job is found;

12. job development efforts to solicit job opportunities suited to the abilities of the disadvantaged job seeker;

13. training allowances to provide support and incentives for those undergoing training; and

14. supportive services—such as medical aid and day care centers for mothers with small children—for those who need assistance to facilitate entry or resumption of work.

Despite the large price tag and the wide variety of available labor market services, manpower programs are adequate only to help a small proportion of the people who need such services. . . . Few projects, if any, offer all the listed services, and participants rarely receive the precise package they need. Complementary programs are insufficiently coordinated, and the individual may be ineligible or unaware of needed programs because of their diversity.[21]

The major manpower legislation in the field has included: a frequently amended Vocational Educational and Rehabilitation Act, largely implemented by local school districts to which federal and state funds are channeled; an Adult Basic Education program, which originated in the antipoverty program; a major, comprehensive Manpower Development and Training Act (1962), amended and updated in a number of ways to include retraining and on-the-job training; a largely residential Job Corps offering basic education and vocational training to severely deprived youth; special training programs in the armed forces to help educationally disadvantaged servicemen attain high school equivalency and to assist others in the transition to civilian jobs; a Work Incentive (WIN) program for welfare recipients to offer some initial incentive and support for job training and, later, to emphasize on-the-job training and placement; The Neighborhood Youth Corps (NYC), offering after-school and summer work experience for youth, originally part of the antipoverty program; Public Service Careers and Public Employment Program legislation, which in 1966 added New Career components, to place disadvantaged and poorly educated enrollees in paraprofessional jobs in both public and private health, welfare, housing, and educational programs; a large and growing Public Employment Program (PEP), launched in 1971, which reflects current unemployment and inflation and has countercyclical economic goals, and may serve over 900,000 people in 1975; a joint governmental-business effort to help "hard core unemployed" through on-the-job training in the JOBS program ("Job Opportunities in the Business Sector"), launched in 1968 and recognized as effective, if too small; the Comprehensive Employment and Training Act (CETA), enacted in 1973, a form of special revenue sharing, allowing more integrated planning at the state level.

The proliferation of programs and their different success rates have led to much experimentation over the past decade with access devices, delivery structures, coordination within and among manpower programs, and linkages with other systems. To describe these efforts would take us beyond the objectives of this section.[22] Recent special revenue-sharing legislation in manpower and related fields passed in 1973 and 1974 will permit considerable state decategorization and planning initiative. Of some interest is an earlier Concentrated Employment Program (CEP), under which local community action agencies, most of them creations of the antipoverty program, offered intensive individualized manpower services to local residents. The evolution of these centers was one of many developments underscoring the manpower–general social service boundary question.

These, then, are the other-than-personal social services, five major institutionalized fields of service, most of them well established in public acceptance.

Notes

1. Sheila B. Kamerman, *Child Care in Nine Countries* (Washington, D.C.: OCD-DHEW, 1975); Alfred J. Kahn and Sheila B. Kamerman, *Social Services in International Perspective* (pub. pending, 1976).

2. U.S. Bureau of the Census, *Current Population Reports*, ser. P-60, No. 97: *Money Income in 1973 of Families and Persons in the United States* (Washington, D.C.: GPO, 1975), tables 10, 21, 22, 29.

3. Robert D. Plotnick and Felicity Skidmore, *Progress against Poverty* (New York: Academic Press, 1975).

4. *Ibid.*, ch. 5.

5. For an introduction to U.S. budgets as policy instruments see the annual volumes *Setting National Priorities*, published by the Brookings Institution, Washington, D.C., and with a series of different authors, for fiscal years 1971–75.

6. Sophie Dales, "Federal Grants to State and Local Governments," *Social Security Bulletin*, Oct. 1974, pp. 26–27.

7. The expenditure analysis is documented and elaborated in Alfred M. Skolnik and Sophie R. Dales, "Social Welfare Expenditures, 1972–73," *Social Security Bulletin*, Jan. 1974, and "Social Welfare Expenditures, Fiscal Year 1974," *ibid.*, Jan. 1975.

8. Max Herlick, "National Expenditures on Social Security in Selected Countries, 1968 and 1971," *Research and Statistics Notes, 29-1974*, Office of Research and Statistics, Social Security Administration, DHEW, Oct. 18, 1974.

9. For detailed definitions, conceptual problems, historical statistics, and detail, see Ida C. Merriam and Alfred M. Skolnik, *Social Welfare Expenditures under Public Programs in the United States, 1926–66* (Social Security Administration Research Report No. 25; Washington, D.C.: DHEW, 1968). The quotation is from p. 11.

10. Skolnik and Dales, "Social Welfare Expenditures, 1974," pp. 10–12.

11. *Handbook of Public Income Transfer Programs, 1975*, Subcommittee on Fiscal Policy, Joint Economic Committee, *Studies in Public Welfare*, Report No. 20 (Washington, D.C.: GPO, 1974), pp. v-vi.

12. *Social Security Bulletin*, April 1972.

13. The failed effort to enact a negative income tax, abolishing all traditional public assistance, is described in Daniel P. Moynihan, *The Politics of a Guaranteed Income* (New York: Random House, 1973).

14. Sar Levitan, *Programs in Aid of the Poor for the 1970's* (rev. ed.; Baltimore: Johns Hopkins University Press, 1973), ch. 2, quotation on p. 21.

15. The data are from the Social Security Administration. A descriptive overview is offered in Levitan, *Programs*, ch. 3. Issues and assessment are covered by Herbert E. Klarmon, "Major Public Initiatives in Health Care," *The Public Interest*, No. 34 (Winter 1974), pp. 106–123.

16. Marjorie Smith Mueller, "Private Health Insurance in 1972: Health Care Services, Enrollment, and Finances," *Social Security Bulletin*, 37, No. 2 (Feb. 1974), 39. Emphasis added.

17. Nancy L. Worthington, Office of Research and Statistics, Social Security Administration, "National Health Expenditures," as reported in *Social Security Bulletin*, Feb. 1975.

18. Summarized briefly from Henry J. Aaron, *Shelter and Subsidies* (Washington, D.C.: The Brookings Institution, 1972), Apps. A and B.

19. *Ibid.*, p. 91.

20. *Ibid.*, p. 108.

21. Levitan, *Programs*, pp. 102, 104.

22. Levitan, *Programs*, our major source, offers an accessible summary as do his more detailed studies, some with collaborators, such as Sar A. Levitan and Robert Taggart, eds., *The Emergency Employment Act* (Salt Lake City: Olympia, 1974); Sar A. Levitan and Garth L. Mangun, *Federal Training and Work Programs in the Sixties* (Ann Arbor, Mich.: Institute of Labor and Industrial Relations, 1969).

Index